Choices

A Basic Writing Guide with Readings

Choices

A Basic Writing Guide with Readings

FOURTH EDITION

Kate Mangelsdorf
Evelyn Posey
The University of Texas at El Paso

BEDFORD/ST. MARTIN'S
Boston ◆ New York

For Bedford/St. Martin's

Developmental Editor: Gregory S. Johnson
Senior Production Editor: Harold Chester
Senior Production Supervisor: Nancy Myers
Executive Marketing Manager: Rachel Falk
Art Director: Lucy Krikorian
Text Design: Lisa Delgado/Delgado and Company
Copy Editor: Rosemary Winfield
Photo Research: Linda Finigan
Cover Design: Elizabeth Tardiff
Cover Photo: ©iStockphoto.com/Viktor Johannsson
Composition: Stratford/TexTech
Printing and Binding: R.R. Donnelley & Sons Company

President: Joan E. Feinberg
Editorial Director: Denise B. Wydra
Editor in Chief: Karen S. Henry
Director of Development: Erica T. Appel
Director of Marketing: Karen Melton Soeltz
Director of Editing, Design, and Production: Marcia Cohen
Managing Editor: Shuli Traub

Library of Congress Control Number: 2007920788

Manufactured in the United States of America.

2 1
l k j i h

For information, write: Bedford/St. Martin's, 75 Arlington Street,
Boston, MA 02116   (617-399-4000)
ISBN-10: 0-312-44780-9 (Student Edition)
ISBN-13: 978-0-312-44780-9 (Student Edition)

ISBN-10: 0-312-44791-4 (Instructor's Annotated Edition)
ISBN-13: 978-0-312-44791-5 (Instructor's Annotated Edition)

Acknowledgments
Acknowledgments and copyrights appear at the back of the book on pages
640–42, which constitute an extension of the copyright page.
It is a violation of the law to reproduce these selections by any means
whatsoever without the written permission of the copyright holder.

Three, "Writing for Different Situations"; and Part Four, a grammar handbook with exercises.

Part One presents three introductory chapters that help students view writing as a purposeful, creative endeavor. Chapter 1 presents the stages of the writing process and follows one student through each stage. Chapter 2 focuses on the elements of good paragraphs, giving students the opportunity to learn and practice the essential building blocks of the essay. Chapter 3 explains common patterns of development with examples to demonstrate each one.

Each of the six chapters in Part Two, "Writing to Share Ideas," presents reading selections, a writing assignment, and a guide to writing an expressive, an informative, or a persuasive essay on a particular theme using an appropriate pattern of development. Instructors can select the chapters that best fit their goals and students' interests. Each chapter includes five writing steps and shows how one student carried out the assignment:

Step One: Explore Your Choices. Students read and respond to three essays by professional writers on the chapter's theme.

Students then gather ideas about the three topics in the chapter's readings, thus gaining a rich source of materials for their own essays through activities such as prewriting, consulting with others, questioning, and reflecting.

Step Two: Write Your Discovery Draft. Referring to the ideas they have gathered in Step One, students choose a topic and write a discovery draft. The chapter includes an example of how one student writer moved from gathering ideas to drafting.

Step Three: Revise Your Draft. This step includes the core of the rhetorical instruction. Explanations are concise and are supported by numerous activities and models from both student and professional writers. Students use peer review to critique each other's drafts, guided by assignment-specific questions that reinforce the chapter's instruction. Students revise their drafts, using instructions in the chapter and their own classmates' suggestions. The chapter also presents a revised version of the student draft as a model.

Step Four: Edit Your Sentences. Students complete sentence combining activities to expand their repertoire of sentence patterns. Students learn and practice elements of grammar, spelling, and punctuation and by referring to the handbook in Part Four. Again, an edited version of the student essay that appeared in draft and revised form models the editing process.

Step Five: Share Your Essay. Students share their final essays with an audience. Depending on the chapter's assignment, students might

Preface

In our early years of teaching developmental writing, we searched for a textbook that would actively lead students through each step of writing an essay. Our ideal text would be complete, offering a rhetoric, a reader, and a handbook. It would also let students choose their own topics and enable them at the outset of the course to write whole essays. It would offer many models of the writing process, allow students to read and write about their own cultural contexts, and help them use computer technology to enhance their writing. This book would also teach critical thinking, engage students in collaborative learning activities, and help students apply what they learn in class to other classes and the workplace. Above all, it would respect the wealth of knowledge and experience that developmental students bring into their writing classroom.

Because we were never able to find such a book, we decided to write *Choices: A Basic Writing Guide with Readings*. Now in its fourth edition, *Choices* offers developmental students comprehensive step-by-step instruction for writing expressive, informative, and persuasive essays. It showcases the writing process, presents a wide variety of engaging assignments, and maintains a respectful tone. It strengthens students' reading, thinking, and writing skills; validates their diverse and unique cultural experiences; and helps them use computers and the Internet for communication and learning. Most important, it builds students' confidence by encouraging them to think of themselves as writers with important ideas to communicate in college and in the workplace. This approach works because, rather than simply talking about how to write, it gets students actively involved in writing.

How *Choices* Works

Choices is divided into four sections: Part One, "Composing Ourselves, Writing for Others"; Part Two, "Writing to Share Ideas"; Part

share their essays with friends or family, submit them to their school or local newspaper, post them on blogs for readers around the world to access and respond to, or send them as letters to a public official.

Chapter Checklist. Each chapter includes a chapter checklist, providing an opportunity for students to check off what they have learned in that chapter.

Reflecting on Your Writing. Finally, students reflect on their writing experience and are encouraged to go to the *Choices* Web site to download and complete a Writing Process Report.

Additional Readings. Each chapter concludes with three additional professional models, on the same topics as the earlier chapter readings, to provide students with more ideas for their writing.

The five chapters in Part Three, "Writing for Different Situations," provide instruction in and support for the writing assigned in Part Two as well as in various academic situations. This part covers journals (Chapter 10), summaries (Chapter 11), research (Chapter 12), timed writing tests (Chapter 13), and résumés and cover letters (Chapter 14).

As students work on assignments in Parts One, Two, and Three, they can easily refer to Part Four, a concise handbook of grammar, usage, punctuation, spelling, and mechanics. The handbook is meant to be a practical resource, showing students how to identify and correct problems rather than explaining grammatical concepts and terms at length. Numerous activities provide practice in correcting common errors, and boxed material as well as two separate sections highlight guidelines and grammar for multilingual students.

The Features

Step-by-step guidance through the writing process, illustrated with student models. At the heart of *Choices* are the six writing assignment chapters in Part Two, which guide students through the steps of the writing process: exploring choices, drafting, revising, editing, and sharing their work with others. Each chapter's abundant writing activities and examples of student writing in process give students the support they need where they need it. The emphasis throughout is on helping students communicate effectively to a specific audience rather than simply practicing a particular mode of writing.

A dual thematic/rhetorical structure. Each of the writing assignment chapters in Part Two focuses on a particular theme *and* the rhetorical patterns of development for writing on that theme. The chapters move students from personal matters to broader cultural and social issues; from expressive to informative to persuasive writing. In addition, Chapter 3, "The Patterns of Development," illustrates each of the rhetorical patterns with example paragraphs.

Three engaging topic choices for each assignment. Each assignment chapter in Part Two offers three potential topics, illustrated with professional readings, for students to choose from. This unique approach (which inspired the title of the text, *Choices)* encourages students to write about what interests them and gives flexibility to the classroom instructor.

A progressive skill-building approach. As students progress through the chapters in Part Two, the assignments and questions following each reading become more advanced, and students learn how to include sources in their writing, distinguish fact from opinion, and recognize logical fallacies.

Help with writing paragraphs and improving sentences. Chapter 2, "Crafting Paragraphs," helps students develop and organize paragraphs, introductions, and conclusions. In addition, each assignment chapter in Part Two features sentence-combining and editing activities for the grammar problems students are likely to encounter with that type of writing.

Preparation for writing for different academic situations. Part Three gives students advice on dealing with writing situations they will encounter in other college courses and on the job. Separate chapters focus on conducting research, taking essay exams, and keeping journals. The fourth edition now includes coverage of writing summaries and writing résumés and cover letters.

Comprehensive handbook with extensive ESL coverage. The handbook in Part Four covers sentence grammar, word choice, spelling, punctuation, and mechanics, with more than 150 exercises that give students abundant opportunities to practice correcting sentences, editing paragraphs, and combining sentences. The handbook also includes "Tips for Multilingual Writers" boxes throughout that address ESL concerns as well as a thorough discussion of ESL issues in Chapter 23, "Guide for Multilingual Writers."

New to This Edition

A greater emphasis on the patterns of development. The fourth edition features enhanced coverage of the rhetorical patterns throughout, including a new chapter — "The Patterns of Development" — in Part

One, with paragraphs from professional writers that exemplify each of the patterns. In addition, each of the assignment chapters in Part Two encourages students to write using the patterns that best suit the themes and audiences students will be addressing.

Improved organization and design. Each of the six assignment chapters in Part Two has been streamlined and reorganized to better guide students step by step through the writing process. The fourth edition of *Choices* also features an all new design that improves the navigability and clarity of the text.

Two new writing assignment chapters. Two of the six writing assignment chapters in Part Two are new: Chapter 8, "Considering the Media," and Chapter 9, "Making a Difference." Each of these new chapters focuses on a theme developmental students will relate to and want to write about.

New readings, new springboards to writing. Two-thirds of the reading selections in the fourth edition are new. These engaging, diverse readings provide students with accessible models for each of the assignment topics and serve as springboards for their own writing: for example, Samuel L. Jackson on the representations of minorities in film, Donald Trump on succeeding in the workplace, Nora Okja Keller on the role food plays in her cultural identity, and Anthony Beal on New Orleans' first post-Hurricane Katrina Mardi Gras.

New coverage of writing summaries and writing résumés and cover letters. Part Three now includes coverage of essential skills students will need in school and beyond: writing summaries and writing résumés and cover letters.

An expanded handbook with more exercises. The handbook in Part Four has been expanded to cover such key editing and grammar concerns as expanding and combining sentences and improving word choice and now includes 157 exercises, 54 percent more than the previous edition. In addition, the *Choices* Web site provides access to thousands of online and print grammar exercises.

Ancillaries

Print

The Instructor's Annotated Edition offers marginal teaching and resource tips that include discussion prompts, strategies for teaching ESL students, ideas for collaborative learning, and more. It also contains answers to all exercises and suggestions for using other ancillaries.

Additional Resources for Instructors Using **Choices,** prepared by Sandra Blystone and Bruce Thaler, provides new and seasoned instructors alike with the support they need for teaching developmental writing. Part One includes information and advice on working with basic writers, facilitating collaborative learning, teaching ESL students and speakers of nonstandard dialects, and assessing student progress. Part Two includes grammar diagnostic, mastery, and exit tests.

Readings for **Discoveries,** a supplement to Kate Mangelsdorf and Evelyn Posey's *Discoveries: A Step-by-Step Guide to Writing Paragraphs and Essays,* provides eighteen additional essays written by professional writers, two illustrating each of the nine rhetorical patterns of development.

The Bedford/St. Martin's ESL Workbook, by Sapna Gandhi-Rao, Maria McCormack, and Elizabeth Trelenberg, provides a broad range of exercises covering grammar issues for multilingual students of varying language skills and backgrounds.

From Practice to Mastery, by Barbara D. Sussman, Maria C. Villar-Smith, and Carolyn Lengel, provides the instruction, examples, and resources students need to practice for — and pass — the Florida College Basic Skills Exit Tests on reading and writing.

Teaching Developmental Writing: Background Readings, **Third Edition,** edited by Susan Naomi Bernstein, offers more than two dozen professional articles on topics of interest to developmental writing instructors, accompanied by suggestions for practical applications in the classroom.

Electronic

The **Choices** *Web site, bedfordstmartins.com/choices,* offers a variety of resources for instructors and students, including: *Exercise Central,* an online database of more than 7,000 self-scoring grammar exercises with feedback; comprehension quizzes for each reading selection and chapter in the book; student and instructor FAQs for each chapter; additional writing assignments; *Supplemental Exercises,* a downloadable collection of grammar exercises; and PowerPoints of each chapter's key concepts.

Re:Writing Basics, bedfordstmartins.com/rewritingbasics, is a new collection of free online resources for the developmental writing class. This easy-to-navigate Web site allows students to connect directly to the largest collection of grammar and writing exercises, tutorials, diagnostic tests, and guides to help them master essential college writing skills and learning strategies.

Exercise Central to Go: Writing and Grammar Practices for Basic Writers is a CD-ROM with hundreds of practice items for writing and editing skills. Drawn from the popular *Exercise Central* collection, the practices provide instant feedback and have been extensively class-tested. No Internet connection is necessary.

The Testing Tool Kit CD-ROM is a comprehensive and easy-to-use test bank with nearly 2,000 questions that instructors can use to create tests and quizzes. Ideal for assessment, it can be used to generate exercises that are tailored to course goals.

Acknowledgments

Choices reflects years of collaboration with students, teachers, and editors, and we are especially grateful to the many people who have helped us improve this fourth edition, especially the students at The University of Texas at El Paso who helped us pilot new materials for this edition. Our special thanks go to Jesus Ramirez, Sandra Cordero, Leslie Lozano, and Melissa Ruiz, who allowed us to use their writing. Michael Merritt and Yolanda Ochoa helped us find new readings. Ceci Rhymes and Lluvia Rodarte helped with the details of copying and mailing manuscript copy.

We also thank the following reviewers for many suggestions that we incorporated into the text: Deborah Anderson, Bristol Community College; Amy Beaudry, Quinsigamond Community College; Andrea Berta, The University of Texas at El Paso; Emily Blair, Solano Community College; Kenneth Brewer, Santa Barbara City College; Jessica Bryant, Eastern Kentucky University; Paul Bush, Bowling Green Community College; Gabriella Derusha, University of Wisconsin–Marinette; Henry Ellis, Broward Community College; Ann George, Northwestern Michigan College; Lauri Humberson, St. Philip's College; Lisa Kekaha, Butte Community College; Janet Kirchner, Southeast Community College; Tamara Kuzmenkov, Tacoma Community College; Renee La Rue, Montgomery College; Ann Modzelewski, University of California–Riverside; Luis Nazario, Pueblo Community College; Jo Pantaleo, Queensborough Community College; Joanna N. Paull, Clarion University; Carolee Ritter, Southeast Community College; Marlisa Santos, Nova Southeastern University; Sharon K. Schakel, Mesa State College; Beverly Schellhaass, Lakeshore Technical College; Nancy Thompson, Clark College; Luke Vassiliou, Abraham Baldwin College; Monalinda Verlingia, College of the Desert; Gledy Wariebi, Prince George's Community College; William V. Wheeler, Portland Community College.

For the many improvements to this edition, we thank our editor Gregory Johnson, who provided exceptional guidance, constant encouragement, and a large number of excellent readings from which to choose. A very special thank you goes to our development editor Ellen Kuhl who was the creative force behind many of the improvements. She carefully revised and edited each chapter, bringing insight and extensive knowledge to the project. We also thank Harold Chester for ably guiding the text through the editing process and Rachel Falk for her unflagging enthusiasm for our work. Finally, we thank Nancy Perry, Erica Appel, Denise Wydra, and Joan Feinberg — no words can adequately describe our respect for their abilities and appreciation for their continued support.

Kate Mangelsdorf
Evelyn Posey

Brief Contents

PART ONE   COMPOSING OURSELVES, WRITING FOR OTHERS   1

1   The Writing Process   3

2   Crafting Paragraphs   37

3   The Patterns of Development   61

PART TWO   WRITING TO SHARE IDEAS   77

4   Explaining a Personal Change: *Using Description and Narration*   79

5   Examining a Culture: *Using Examples and Process Explanation*   127

6   Investigating a Workplace: *Using Classification and Definition*   181

7   Evaluating a Subject: *Using Comparison and Contrast*   233

8   Considering the Media: *Using Cause and Effect*   287

9   Making a Difference: *Using Argument*   337

PART THREE   WRITING FOR DIFFERENT SITUATIONS   385

10   Keeping Journals   387

11   Writing Summaries   399

12   Conducting Primary, Library, and Internet Research   407

13   Taking Timed Writing Tests   445

14   Writing Résumés and Cover Letters   469

PART FOUR   HANDBOOK WITH EXERCISES   479

15   Writing Sentences   481

16   Expanding Sentences   505

17   Combining Sentences   522

18   Improving Sentences   542

19   Improving Word Choice   565

20   Improving Spelling   571

21   Improving Punctuation   581

22   Improving Mechanics   606

23   Guide for Multilingual Writers   614

Contents

Preface   v

PART ONE
COMPOSING OURSELVES, WRITING FOR OTHERS   1

Chapter 1   The Writing Process   3

Writing Assignment   4

Reading to Improve Writing   5

A Writer's Composing Process   7

Step 1. Explore Your Choices   8
Analyzing Your Audience and Purpose   8
    A Writer's Audience   8
    A Writer's Purpose   9
Gathering Ideas   12
    Brainstorming   12
    Freewriting   13
    Clustering   14
    Asking Questions   15
    Reading   15
    Consulting with Others   15
    Relating Aloud   16

Step 2. Write Your Discovery Draft   16
Choosing a Topic   17
Sharing Your Ideas   19
    Write a Preliminary Thesis Statement   19
    Get Organized   20

Step 3. Revise Your Draft   21
Developing Your Ideas   21
Building Your Essay   22

Step 4. Edit Your Sentences   23
Using Standard Written English   23
Correcting Errors   25

Step 5. Share Your Essay   25

One Student's Writing Process   27
Kwan's Ideas   27
Kwan's Drafting   27
Kwan's Revising   29
Kwan's Editing   32
  Kwan Lu, "Mediation, Not Lawsuits"   *32*
Kwan's Sharing   34
CHAPTER CHECKLIST   34

Reflecting on Your Writing   35

Chapter 2   **Crafting Paragraphs**   37

WRITING ASSIGNMENT   38

Topic Sentences   38

Unity   42

Organization   43
General-to-Specific Order   43
Topic-Illustration-Explanation Order   44
Progressive Order   44
Directional Order   45
Question-and-Answer Order   45
Specific-to-General Order   46

Special Kinds of Paragraphs   48
Introductions   48
  Pose a Question   *48*
  Provide an Interesting or Surprising Fact   *49*
  Tell a Story   *49*
  Describe a Vivid Image   *49*
  Define a Term   *50*
  Break Your Topic into Categories   *50*

Narrow the Topic   *50*
State the Thesis   *51*
Conclusions   52
Restate the Thesis   *52*
Summarize Your Points   *53*
Broaden the Focus   *53*

One Student's Paragraph   55
Melissa's Choices   55
Melissa's Drafting   56
Melissa's Revising   57
Melissa Ruiz, "After Katrina"   *57*
Melissa's Editing   57
Melissa's Sharing   58
CHAPTER CHECKLIST   59

Reflecting on Your Writing   59

Chapter 3   **The Patterns of Development**   **61**
WRITING ASSIGNMENT   62

Description   63

Narration   64
Chronological Order   64
Flashback   65
Dialogue   65

Examples   66
Facts   66
Expert Testimony   67

Process Explanation   68

Classification   68

Definition   69

Comparison and Contrast   70

Cause and Effect   72

Argument   72
CHAPTER CHECKLIST   **74**

Reflecting on Your Writing   74

PART TWO
WRITING TO SHARE IDEAS   77

Chapter 4   **Explaining A Personal Change:** *Using Description and Narration*   79

Reading Essays about Personal Changes   80
A Significant Person   81
  Joshua Bell, "My Maestro"   81
A Memorable Event   83
  James Dillard, "A Doctor's Dilemma"   83
An Important Period   86
  Malcolm X, "Prison Studies"   86
Writing Assignment   90

Step 1. Explore Your Choices   90
Analyzing Your Audience and Purpose   91
Gathering Ideas   91
  Brainstorming about a Significant Person   92
  Relating a Memorable Event   93
  Clustering about an Important Period   95

Step 2. Write Your Discovery Draft   96
Choosing a Topic   97
Sharing Your Ideas   97

Step 3. Revise Your Draft   99
Developing Your Ideas   100
  Description   100
  Narration   101
Building Your Essay   102
  Revise Your Thesis Statement   102
  Add Topic Sentences   103
  Strengthen Your Focus   105
A Student's Revised Draft   106
  Jesus Ramirez, "Baseball Memories"   107

Step 4. Edit Your Sentences   109
Combining Sentences Using Coordinating Conjunctions   110
Correcting Run-on Sentences   112
A Student's Edited Essay   114
  Jesus Ramirez, "Baseball Memories"   114

Step 5. Share Your Essay   115
Chapter Checklist   116

Reflecting on Your Writing 116

Additional Readings 117
A Significant Person 117
  Thomas L. Friedman, "My Favorite Teacher" 117
A Memorable Event 119
  Cheryl Peck, "Fat Girls and Lawn Chairs" 119
An Important Period 122
  Brent Staples, "Black Men and Public Space" 122

Chapter 5   Examining a Culture: *Using Examples and Process Explanation* 127

Reading Essays about Cultures 128
A Cultural Symbol 129
  Nora Okja Keller, "My Mother's Food" 129
A Cultural Tradition 133
  Kevin Kling, "Hook, Line, and Television" 133
A Cultural Hero 136
  John Culhane, "Oprah Winfrey: How Truth Changed Her Life" 136
WRITING ASSIGNMENT 141

Step 1. Explore Your Choices 141
Analyzing Your Audience and Purpose 142
Gathering Ideas 143
  Clustering about a Cultural Symbol 143
  Asking Questions about a Cultural Tradition 144
  Freewriting about a Cultural Hero 146

Step 2. Write Your Discovery Draft 147
Choosing a Topic 147
Sharing Your Ideas 148

Step 3. Revise Your Draft 149
Developing Your Ideas 150
  Examples 150
  Process Explanation 151
Building Your Essay 153
  Write an Effective Introduction 153
  Write a Powerful Conclusion 156
  Connect Ideas 157
A Student's Revised Draft 161
  Sandra Cordero, "El Grito de Dolores" 161

Step 4. Edit Your Sentences   163
Combining Sentences Using Conjunctive Adverbs   163
Correcting Sentence Fragments   166
A Student's Edited Essay   168
   Sandra Cordero, "El Grito de Dolores"   168

Step 5. Share Your Essay   169
Chapter Checklist   170

Reflecting on Your Writing   170

Additional Readings   171
A Cultural Symbol   171
   Gerald Hausman, "Feather"   171
A Cultural Tradition   173
   Anastacia Marx de Salcedo, "Pass the Pernil, Save Room for the Tarta"   173
A Cultural Hero   176
   Jeremy Dorn, "A Hero's Last Ride"   176

Chapter 6   Investigating a Workplace: *Using Classification and Definition*   181

Reading Essays about Work   182
An Occupation   183
   The Editors of WetFeet.com, "Career Profile: Science"   183
Workplace Communication   185
   Perri Klass, "She's Your Basic L.O.L. in N.A.D."   185
A Job-Related Problem   189
   Donald Trump, "You're Hired!"   189
Writing Assignment   193

Step 1. Explore Your Choices   193
Analyzing Your Audience and Purpose   194
Gathering Ideas   195
   Freewriting about an Occupation   195
   Brainstorming about Workplace Communication   196
   Consulting Others about a Job-Related Problem   197

Step 2. Write Your Discovery Draft   198
Choosing a Topic   198
Sharing Your Ideas   199

Step 3. Revise Your Draft   201
Developing Your Ideas   201
   Classification   201

Definition   203
Building Your Essay   204
   Find Information to Strengthen Your Support   204
   Outline Your Plan   205
   Correctly Use Research Material   206
A Student's Revised Draft   210
   Kathy Chu, "Helping Children Heal"   210

Step 4. Edit Your Sentences   213
Combining Sentences Using Subordinating Conjunctions   213
Correcting Pronoun Reference and Agreement   215
   Pronoun Reference   216
   Pronoun Agreement   216
A Student's Edited Essay   218
   Kathy Chu, "Helping Children Heal"   219

Step 5. Share Your Essay   221
CHAPTER CHECKLIST   221

Reflecting on Your Writing   221

Additional Readings   223
An Occupation   223
   Tamera Helms, "Lessons in Shrimping"   223
Workplace Communication   226
   Rita Warren Hess, "American Workplace Slang and Jargon"   226
A Job-Related Problem   229
   Ellen Goodman, "The Company Man"   229

Chapter 7   Evaluating a Subject: *Using Comparison and Contrast*   233

Reading Essays That Evaluate   234
Evaluation of a Product   235
   Leander Kahney, "The Joy of iPod: iCandy for the Ears"   235
Evaluation of a Performance   237
   Diane Heiman and Phyllis Bookspan, "Sesame Street: Brought to You by the Letters M-A-L-E"   237
Evaluation of a Place   240
   John Garvey, "Christo's Gates: An Unexpected Pleasure"   240
WRITING ASSIGNMENT   242

Step 1. Explore Your Choices   243
Analyzing Your Audience and Purpose   243
Gathering Ideas   244

Brainstorming about a Product   245
Asking Questions about a Performance   246
Freewriting about a Place   248

Step 2. Write Your Discovery Draft   249
Choosing a Topic   249
Sharing Your Ideas   250

Step 3. Revise Your Draft   252
Developing Your Ideas with Comparison and Contrast   253
Building Your Essay   254
Express Your Judgment   255
Give Criteria   257
Provide Evidence   260
Keep a Balanced Perspective   262
A Student's Revised Draft   263
Jody Albert, "Avoid Dryden Hall"   263

Step 4. Edit Your Sentences   266
Combining Sentences Using Relative Clauses   267
Correcting Comma Splices   269
A Student's Edited Essay   271
Jody Albert, "Avoid Dryden Hall"   272

Step 5. Share Your Essay   274
CHAPTER CHECKLIST   275

Reflecting on Your Writing   275

Additional Readings   276
Evaluation of a Product   276
Ann Hodgman, "No Wonder They Call Me a Bitch"   276
Evaluation of a Performance   280
Anthony Beal, "Let the Good Times Roll"   280
Evaluation of a Place   282
Nicholas Jennings, "A Palace of Rock"   282

Chapter 8   Considering the Media: *Using Cause and Effect*   287

Reading Essays about the Media   289
A Censorship Issue   289
Michael Crowley, "Let's Shut Them Down"   289
A Representation Issue   292
Samuel L. Jackson, "In Character"   292

A Lifestyle Issue   295
   Brent Staples, "What Adolescents Miss When We Let Them Grow Up in Cyberspace"   295
WRITING ASSIGNMENT   298

Step 1. Explore Your Choices   298
Analyzing Your Audience and Purpose   299
Gathering Ideas   299
   Freewriting about a Censorship Issue   300
   Brainstorming about a Representation Issue   301
   Consulting Others about a Lifestyle Issue   302

Step 2. Write Your Discovery Draft   303
Choosing a Topic   303
Sharing Your Ideas   304

Step 3. Revise Your Draft   306
Developing Your Ideas with Cause-and-Effect Analysis   306
Building Your Essay   307
   Make a Claim   308
   Provide Pro Points   309
   Respond to Con Points   312
   Organize Pro and Con Points   314
A Student's Revised Draft   316
   Reginald Jones, "Newspaper Ad Sparks Controversy"   316

Step 4. Edit Your Sentences   319
Combining Sentences Using Introductory Phrases   320
Correcting Subject-Verb Agreement Problems   321
A Student's Edited Essay   323
   Reginald Jones, "Newspaper Ad Sparks Controversy"   323

Step 5. Share Your Essay   325
CHAPTER CHECKLIST   326

Reflecting on Your Writing   326

Additional Readings   328
A Censorship Issue   328
   Judy Blume, "Is Harry Potter Evil?"   328
A Representation Issue   330
   Mark Andrejevic, " 'Reality' Camera Goes from Candid to Cruel"   330
A Lifestyle Issue   332
   Janna Malamud Smith, "Online but Not Antisocial"   332

Chapter 9　**Making a Difference:** *Using Argument*　337

Reading Essays about Problems and Solutions　339
A Health Problem　339
　Greg Critser, *"Don't Eat the Flan"*　339
An Education Problem　341
　Laura D'Andrea Tyson, *"Needed: Affirmative Action for the Poor"*　341
An Environmental Problem　344
　Patrick Moore, *"Going Nuclear: A Green Makes the Case"*　344
WRITING ASSIGNMENT　348

Step 1. Explore Your Choices　349
Analyzing Your Audience and Purpose　349
Gathering Ideas　350
　Relating Aloud about a Health Problem　350
　Freewriting about an Education Problem　351
　Reading about an Environmental Problem　353

Step 2. Write Your Discovery Draft　354
Choosing a Topic　354
Sharing Your Ideas　355

Step 3. Revise Your Draft　356
Developing Your Ideas with Argument　357
　State the Problem　357
　Provide Evidence　358
　Propose a Solution　360
Building Your Essay　361
　Avoid Faulty Logic　361
　Persuade Your Readers　362
　Use a Reasonable Tone　364
A Student's Revised Draft　365
　Li Chiang, *"Tollroad on the Information Superhighway"*　365

Step 4. Edit Your Sentences　367
Combining Sentences Using Appositives　368
Correcting Shifts in Person　369
A Student's Edited Essay　371
　Li Chiang, *"Tollroad on the Information Superhighway"*　371

Step 5. Share Your Essay　373
CHAPTER CHECKLIST　374

Reflecting on Your Writing　374

Additional Readings   375
A Health Problem   375
   Elizabeth M. Whelan, "Perils of Prohibition"   *375*
An Education Problem   378
   Mary Sherry, "In Praise of the F Word"   *378*
An Environmental Problem   380
   Mark Hertsgaard, "A Global Green Deal"   *380*

PART THREE
WRITING FOR DIFFERENT SITUATIONS   385

Chapter 10   Keeping Journals   387

WRITING ASSIGNMENT   388

Why Writers Keep Journals   389
   Lucy Calkins, from The Art of Teaching Writing   *389*

Personal Journals   390

Dialogue Journals   392

Learning Logs   394
CHAPTER CHECKLIST   397

Reflecting on Your Writing   397

Chapter 11   Writing Summaries   399

WRITING ASSIGNMENT   400

Writing a Summary   400
Reread the Original Text   401
Write the Summary   401
   Main Idea   *401*
   Important Supporting Points   *402*
   Conclusion   *402*
CHAPTER CHECKLIST   404

Reflecting on Your Writing   404

Chapter 12   Conducting Primary, Library, and Internet Research   407

WRITING ASSIGNMENT   408

Preparing to Conduct Research   408
Narrow Your Topic   408
Write Research Questions   409

Primary Research   409
Making Observations   410
Surveying Others   410
Conducting Interviews   411

Secondary Research   413
Locating Sources of Information   413
  Print Sources   413
  Electronic Sources   414
  Other Sources of Information   416
Evaluating Sources of Information   417
Avoiding Plagiarism   418
Taking Notes   420
  Philip Zimbardo and Anne Weber, "Cross-Cultural Perspective: Culture Shock"   423
Quoting Information   425
Paraphrasing Information   427
Summarizing Information   428
Documenting Sources   430
  In-Text Documentation   430
  Works Cited Page   432

Sample Research Paper   436
  Leslie Lozano, "Culture Shock"   437
CHAPTER CHECKLIST   442

Reflecting on Your Writing   442

Chapter 13 Taking Timed Writing Tests   445
WRITING ASSIGNMENT   446

The Essay Exam   446
Preparing for an Essay Exam   447
  Learn about the Test   447
  Anticipate the Questions   447
  Develop a Study Routine   447
Taking the Essay Exam   448
  Analyze the Questions   448
  Gather Ideas   450
  Write Your Response   451
  Revise and Edit Your Response   451
Sample Essay Question and Student Response   452

In-Class Timed Writing about a Reading   453

Preparing for In-Class Timed Writing about a Reading   454
Develop a Reading Routine   454
Keep a Reading Journal   454
Keep a Vocabulary List   454

Performing In-Class Timed Writing about a Reading   455
Read Carefully   455
Write Your Response   456

Sample In-Class Writing Question and Student Response   456
Brian A. Courtney, "Freedom from Choice"   457

Multiple-Choice Writing Tests   460

Preparing for a Multiple-Choice Writing Test   461
Learn about the Test   461
Anticipate the Questions   461
Develop a Study Routine   461

Taking a Multiple-Choice Writing Test   462
Analyze the Questions   462
Choose Your Responses   462

CHAPTER CHECKLIST   466

Reflecting on Your Writing   466

Chapter 14   Writing Résumés and Cover Letters   469

WRITING ASSIGNMENT   470

The Résumé   470

Required Information   470
Contact Information   471
Education   471
Work Experience   471

Optional Sections   472
Career Objective   472
Skills   472
Honors and Awards   472
References   472

Format and Grammar   473

Sample Résumé   473

Cover Letter   475

Sample Cover Letter   475

CHAPTER CHECKLIST   477

Reflecting on Your Writing   477

PART FOUR
HANDBOOK WITH EXERCISES   479

Chapter 15   Writing Sentences   481

A. Subjects   481
Compound Subjects   481
Subject Pretenders   482
  Prepositions   482
  Prepositional Phrases   485

B. Verbs   487
Action and Linking Verbs   487
  Action Verbs   487
  Linking Verbs   488
  Helping Verbs   488
  Compound Verbs   488
Verb Pretenders   489
  Verb + -ing   489
  To + Verb   491
Verb Tense   493
  Regular Verbs   495
  Irregular Verbs   495

C. Subject-Verb Agreement   497
Singular and Plural Forms   497
Indefinite Pronouns   500

Chapter 16   Expanding Sentences   505

A. Phrases   505

B. Clauses   508
Independent or Main Clauses   508
Dependent or Subordinate Clauses   509
Relative Clauses   511

C. Pronouns   514
Pronoun Reference   515
Pronoun Agreement   516

D. Adjectives   518

E. Adverbs   520

Chapter 17 Combining Sentences 522

A. Coordination 522
Coordinating Conjunctions and Commas 522
Conjunctive Adverbs and Semicolons 524

B. Subordination 526
Subordinating Conjunctions 526
Relative Pronouns 528

C. Sentence-Combining Exercises 531
Specific Methods of Combining Sentences 531
Various Methods of Combining Sentences 537

Chapter 18 Improving Sentences 542

A. Sentence Fragments 542

B. Run-on Sentences 546

C. Comma Splices 551

D. Misplaced Modifiers 556

E. Dangling Modifiers 558

F. Active and Passive Voice 560

G. Parallelism 562

Chapter 19 Improving Word Choice 565

A. Vocabulary 565
Meaning from Context 566
Learn Roots, Prefixes, and Suffixes 567

B. Unnecessary Repetition 568

C. Wordiness 569

Chapter 20 Improving Spelling 571

A. Spelling Rules 571

B. Commonly Misspelled Words 576

C. Commonly Confused Words 578

Chapter 21 Improving Punctuation 581

A. Commas 581

B. Semicolons 592

C. Colons   594

D. End Punctuation   595

E. Apostrophes   597

F. Quotation Marks   602

Chapter 22   Improving Mechanics   606

A. Capital Letters   606

B. Italics   610

C. Abbreviations   611

D. Numbers   612

Chapter 23   Guide for Multilingual Writers   614

A. Articles   614

B. Count and Noncount Nouns   616

C. Prepositions   618

D. Omitted or Repeated Subjects   621
Omitted Subjects   622
Repeated Subjects   623

E. Word Order   624
Adjective Placement   624
Adverb Placement   626

F. Verbs   627
Verb Tense   627
Helping Verbs   630
Verbs Followed by Gerunds or Infinitives   634
Two-Part Verbs   636
Participles Used as Adjectives   638

Index   643

PART ONE

Composing Ourselves, Writing for Others

1. The Writing Process

2. Crafting Paragraphs

3. The Patterns of Development

Writing is an important way to communicate — in class, in the workplace, and for personal enjoyment. Many of us are writing more than ever by text messaging on our cell phones or communicating via e-mail. As a result, good writing skills are a must.

In Part One, you'll discover why writers write and how they go about getting their ideas down on paper. You'll discover your own writing process and begin to use it to communicate the important ideas you have to share. As you learn how to write effective paragraphs, an important step when putting your ideas in writing, you'll also discover patterns you can use to develop your writing.

The Writing Process

In this chapter, you will write a brief essay about your attitude toward writing. As you work on your essay, you will

- Learn how to read to improve your writing.

- Learn how to analyze your audience.

- Examine different purposes for writing.

- Explore the steps of the writing process.

- Discover several strategies for gathering ideas.

- Learn the importance of standard written English.

- Follow one student through the writing process.

What comes to mind when you think of a writer? You might picture a writer you like to read, such as Maya Angelou, Stephen King, or Dave Barry. Or you might think of the stereotypes we have of writers, such as the newspaper reporter who pounds out a late-breaking story minutes before a deadline or the tortured poet who wears a beret, lives in a cold attic, composes brilliant sonnets on scraps of paper, and dies before receiving any recognition.

Writers are more common than you might imagine. A consumer who writes a letter to the electric company is a writer. So is a student who completes a report for a course, a child who writes her name for the first time, a father who records the birth of his baby in a journal, and an engineer who writes a proposal to build a bridge. A lover who sends a valentine is a writer, and so is an angry voter who composes a letter to the city council. A writer is anyone who uses written language to communicate a feeling, a fact, or an opinion.

If the idea of writing frightens you, you are not alone. Even the most experienced writers get anxious when faced with a new project. But understanding how writers find ideas, organize them, and complete a writing assignment can help you to relieve any fears that you might associate with writing. How do writers transform their ideas into a polished piece of writing to be shared with readers and turned in for a grade? What do they do first, next, and last? As you'll learn in this chapter and throughout this book, polished writing is best completed over a period of time in distinct steps. Good writing takes effort, but with practice, you'll discover that it's not nearly as frightening or mysterious as it may seem.

Writing Assignment

Your first assignment is to "compose yourself" as a writer. Think back over your life to discover how you feel about writing. Does writing excite you, or does writing make you anxious? Does writing come easy to you, or do you struggle to find the right words?

You might want to get your ideas flowing by writing for a few minutes nonstop in response to the following questions:

- What have been some of the most important writing events in your life? Consider not only formal writing assignments for school or work but also letters, journals, and e-mail messages.

- What languages have you used for writing? Do you enjoy writing in one language more than another? Why?

- Who was most influential in your development as a writer? How did this person influence you?

- Can you recall any times when you felt inadequate as a writer? What was the event? Why did you feel this way? What changes did you make as a result?

- What three words best describe you as a writer? Discuss these three words.

   Use your best ideas to write a brief essay for your classmates and instructor that explains how you feel about yourself as a writer.

READING TO IMPROVE WRITING

Throughout this book, you'll have the opportunity to read sample essays written by both professional and student writers. Before every writing assignment in Part Two, for example, you will find three essays on the topics you will be asked to write about. You will also follow the progress of a college student as he or she completes the same assignment that you are working on.

As a college student, you're already familiar with at least some of the benefits of reading. You know that textbooks and other assigned readings can teach you new skills or give you information about a subject. You might read a newspaper to keep up with what's going on around you, or you might enjoy reading a novel and comparing it with the movie version of the same story. Some people read as they commute to and from work to make the ride pass more quickly.

The advantages of reading multiply when you read as writers read — to learn how to improve their writing. When you examine a piece of writing to learn how the author communicates a certain idea, you're like an athlete who watches a game to observe the moves of the players. Examining the writing strategies of a particular author helps you use these strategies in your own writing. If you read like a writer, you can learn ways to organize, develop, and express your ideas in your own writing.

Suppose you can't decide how to begin a paper on whales for your biology course. Around the same time, you read an article on hallucinogenic drugs in *Outside* magazine called "One Toad over the Line," written by Kevin Krajick. Here is its beginning:

   It's big, it looks like a cowpie with eyes, and many people believe it can bring them face to face with God. It's the Colorado River toad, a once obscure amphibian whose fame has spread in recent years thanks to the venom secreted by its skin. When dried and smoked, the venom releases bufotenine, a substance that one California drug agent calls "the most potent, instantaneously acting hallucinogen we know."

From this paragraph, you learn two strategies for beginning an essay. First, a startling comparison ("a cowpie with eyes") can get your audience's attention. Second, stating the topic of an essay (in this case, the hallucinogen bufotenine) at the beginning helps your audience understand right away what your piece is about.

HOW TO Be an Active Reader

- Preview the text.
  - Think about the title and what it means to you.
  - Think about whether you recognize the author's name.
  - Read any headings, captions, charts, and lists.
- Read the text.
  - Read carefully, underlining the most important points.
  - Circle and look up the meanings of words you don't know.
  - Briefly list the main points in the margin.
- Write to comprehend and remember.
  - List or outline the most important points.
  - Write your personal reactions to what you have read.
  - Review these notes before class.

Reading can also improve your vocabulary. Suppose that one of your favorite authors is the suspense novelist Mary Higgins Clark. Here's an excerpt from Clark's *While My Pretty One Sleeps*, a book about a fashion designer named Neeve:

> To Neeve's dismay, as she crossed Thirty-Seventh Street she came face to face with Gordon Steuber. Meticulously dressed in a tan cashmere jacket over a brown-and-beige Scottish pullover, dark-brown slacks and Gucci loafers, with his blaze of curly brown hair, slender, even-featured face, powerful shoulders and narrow waist, Gordon Steuber could easily have had a successful career as a model. Instead, in his early forties, he was a shrewd businessman with an uncanny knack of hiring unknown young designers and exploiting them until they could afford to leave him.

The word *meticulously* might not be familiar to you, but from the context of this passage you can guess that it means "carefully" or "precisely." From this passage, you can also guess that *uncanny* means "unusual" or "remarkable" and that *exploit* means "to use." Verify your guesses by looking up unfamiliar words in a dictionary, and keep a list of new words and their meanings so you can refer to them when you read and write.

A WRITER'S COMPOSING PROCESS

Although it's easy to think of writing as simply putting words on paper, writers use a particular *writing process*, or method, to turn ideas into finished essays. Generally, here is the writing process that many writers follow:

Step 1. Explore your choices.
Step 2. Write a draft to discover your ideas.
Step 3. Revise the draft to make your ideas clearer for readers.
Step 4. Edit the draft for standard written English, grammar, spelling, and punctuation.
Step 5. Share the final draft with an audience.

You'll probably find that your writing process does not exactly follow the steps in the order outlined here but that you prefer to move back and forth among the various steps. For example, while revising an essay you may discover you need more information. To get that information, you have to return to exploring your choices. You may discover, too, that you prefer to revise for quite a while, producing perhaps three or four revised drafts. Figure 1.1 illustrates the recursive nature of the writing process.

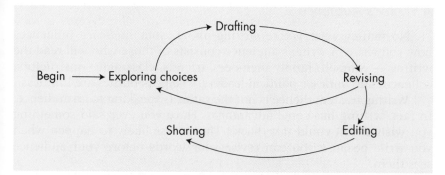

FIGURE 1.1.   The Recursive Nature of the Writing Process

Use Your Computer Wisely
As you learn more about your writing process, keep in mind that your best writing tool is between your ears. The computer has no ideas, no imagination, and no feeling. You bring these qualities to your writing.

To discover your own writing process, experiment with the various ways of exploring choices, drafting, revising, editing, and sharing explained in this chapter and throughout Part Two of this book. The methods that work best for you will lead you to discover your preferred writing process. Let's get started.

STEP 1. EXPLORE YOUR CHOICES

The first step of the writing process, often called *prewriting*, includes all that you do before you actually begin to write a draft. This step involves activities such as writing, talking, reading, and thinking. But first, you must think about who will read your essay and why you're writing it.

Analyzing Your Audience and Purpose

As you begin to work on an assignment, you want to keep your reader in mind. After all, you're writing to communicate something of interest, so you want to be sure the reader gets your message. It's also important to understand the kind of message you want to communicate. The more you know about your audience and your purpose, the easier it will be for you to write.

A Writer's Audience

No matter what you're writing about, your *audience* influences how you write. A writer's audience consists of those who will read the writing — yourself, family members, friends, classmates, instructors, colleagues at work, or political leaders. The possibilities are limitless.

Writing to an audience is not the same as speaking to an audience. In fact, writing has some advantages. Have you ever said something you wished you could take back? This is less likely to happen when you write because you can revise your words before your audience sees them.

Writing is also different from speaking because your audience isn't actually in front of you. When you speak, your audience can smile, frown, or ask you questions. When you write, however, you must envision, or picture in your mind, how your readers will respond to your words. To envision your audience, ask yourself these questions:

- *Who are my readers?* Sometimes your reader is someone specific, such as the sociology professor who will read your term paper or the fellow students who will see your flier about an upcoming event at the student union. At other times, your readers will be the general public, such as subscribers to the local newspaper who read your letter to the editor.

- *What do my readers know about my topic?* Your readers' knowledge of the topic is important because you don't want to bore people by telling them what they already know. Instead, you want to tell them something new — where they might go for career counseling, how to fix their VCR, whom they should vote for in the next election.

- *What do my readers need to know about my topic?* Answering this question can help you decide how much information you need to give your readers. For instance, if you're explaining how to change a tire, will your readers know what a tire jack is? Or must you describe it and explain how to use it?

- *How do my readers feel about my topic?* If your readers know nothing about your topic or might even find it dull, you'll want to find a way to get their interest. Or your readers may be opposed to your message. If you're writing a letter asking your supervisor for a raise, don't assume that he or she will automatically agree with you. Instead, try to anticipate your supervisor's reasons for not giving you a raise and take them into account when you make your case.

A Writer's Purpose

Whenever you write, whether for yourself or others, you have a *purpose*. Most writing is primarily expressive, informative, or persuasive.

Expressive Writing. In *expressive writing*, writers communicate their thoughts, feelings, and personal history. When you keep a diary, write an e-mail to a friend, or tell about something that happened to you, you're writing expressively.

In the following example of expressive writing, student Scott Weckerly describes the morning he left home for college:

The impact of saying good-bye and actually leaving did not hit me until the day of my departure. Its strength woke me an hour before my alarm clock would, as for the last time Missy, my golden retriever, greeted me with a big, sloppy lick. I hated it when she did that, but that day I welcomed

```
her with open arms. I petted her with long, slow strokes,
and her sad eyes gazed into mine. Her coat felt more silky
than usual. Of course, I did not notice any of these
qualities until that day, which made me all the sadder
about leaving her.
```

This sample paragraph is expressive because it describes Weckerly's thoughts and feelings at an important time in his life. When he tells us that the reality of his departure didn't sink in until that morning, we understand what he was thinking. By describing his reactions to his dog, we know he was sad about leaving home. In re-creating an important incident in his life, Weckerly's writing is expressive.

Informative Writing. Sometimes we write not to express ourselves but to convey information. *Informative writing* explains: it tells how something works, how you can do something, what something looks like, how two things are alike or different, or what the cause or outcome of an event is. Informative writing typically uses facts, examples, or statistics. Most writing we encounter is informative. Nutritional labels on food containers are informative, as are directions for how to set up a computer or administer CPR. Textbooks, including the one you're reading now, are also in this category. Most sections of the newspaper are informative.

The following example of informative writing is from the *Los Angeles Times*:

> An average of 35.5 million viewers tuned in to the two-hour *Idol* premiere, according to preliminary figures from Nielsen Media Research. It was the most-watched season opener yet for the series and the No. 1 entertainment program on television so far this season; the only program of any kind to draw more viewers was this month's Rose Bowl, with 35.6 million.
>
> — SCOTT COLLINS, "*Idol's* Fifth-Season Opener Its Biggest Yet"

This piece of writing is informative because the author uses facts and statistics to compare the number of viewers of *American Idol* to other television programs.

Persuasive Writing. *Persuasive writing* differs from expressive and informative writing because it attempts to change a reader's opinion or convince a reader to take a particular action. Newspaper editorials and advertisements are two types of persuasive writing. The *Times Picayune* wants you to support the school bond issue, and Ben and Jerry's wants you to buy its brand of ice cream. Some of the world's most memorable writing is persuasive, such as these words from

President John F. Kennedy's 1961 inaugural address: "Ask not what your country can do for you; ask what you can do for your country."

Martin Luther King Jr.'s famous "I Have a Dream" speech is another example of persuasive writing. His purpose was to motivate civil rights workers to continue striving for racial equality. Here's an excerpt:

> Go back to Mississippi, go back to Alabama, go back to South Carolina, go back to Georgia, go back to Louisiana, go back to the slums and ghettos of our northern cities, knowing that somehow this situation can and will be changed. Let us not wallow in the valley of despair.

As with many persuasive pieces, King's audience is urged to believe something — in this case, that the battle for civil rights will be won. At the same time, the audience is told to do something: King wants the marchers to return home to continue the fight.

HOW TO Know Your Purpose for Writing

- *Expressive:* You write to communicate your thoughts, feelings, and personal history.

- *Informative:* You write to explain something that you learned — how it works, what it looks like, what the cause or outcome of an event is.

- *Persuasive:* You write to convince others to accept your opinion.

While most writing is primarily expressive, informative, or persuasive, rarely is a piece of writing entirely one type. Much of the time, all three types occur in a single piece. The *primary purpose* is the one that you consider the most important reason for writing that piece.

GROUP ACTIVITY 1: Identify Purposes

Working in groups of two or three, identify the following paragraphs as primarily expressive, informative, or persuasive.

1. From the *Comtrad Industries Catalog*:

> We are so confident that the 900 MHz cordless phone is the best phone on the market that we challenge you to compare it to any other. For a limited time, you can buy the 900 MHz phone at the factory-direct introductory price of $399. Try it for 30 days. If

you don't agree that this phone gives you incredible clarity and convenience, return it for a full refund.

Purpose: _____

2. From Frommer's *Australia* by Elizabeth Hansen:

Is Paul Hogan in *Crocodile Dundee* a typical Aussie? Some Australians might like you to think so, but facts show that less than 15% of the population lives in rural areas. Instead, the average Australian lives in one of eight capital cities and has never seen native fauna anywhere but in a zoo or wildlife park.

Purpose: _____

3. From the *American Association of Retired Persons Bulletin*:

We must create a more positive and accurate image of aging and help people recognize that people are living longer, more productive lives. As a nation, we must let go of our obsession with the number of years in life and focus instead on the life in those years.

Purpose: _____

4. From *One Writer's Beginnings* by Eudora Welty:

Of course it's easy to see why they both overprotected me, why my father, before I could wear a new pair of shoes for the first time, made me wait while he took out his thin silver pocket knife and with the point of the blade scored the polished soles all over, carefully, in a diamond pattern, to prevent me from sliding on the polished floor when I ran.

Purpose: _____

❀ Gathering Ideas

Once you know your audience and purpose, you can begin to gather ideas for any topic that you might want to write about.

Imagine, for example, that you are taking a course in criminal justice and your instructor gives you the following essay assignment: "Write a two- to three-page essay in which you explain a problem in the criminal justice system. Suggest a solution for the problem." Any of the following methods could help you explore possibilities for your essay.

✳ Brainstorming

When you brainstorm, you list all the thoughts that come into your head on a topic. You don't consider whether your ideas are good or bad;

you just write them down. For the criminal justice assignment, you could brainstorm a list of problems in the criminal justice system, such as prisons that are overcrowded or innocent people who are jailed.

Here is student writer Jerry's list on problems in the criminal justice system:

Some problems
should kids be tried as adults?
does it make them more responsible?

Another problem
racial profiling
can it be prevented?
prisoners being released and doing more crimes
no schools in prison
you just get out of prison and do more crimes
how to stop this?

In addition to brainstorming by yourself, you can brainstorm in a group with other people. In this case, you would name a topic and then ask each group member to call out ideas on it. Asking others to brainstorm with you greatly increases the number of ideas you have to choose from for your essay.

Freewriting

Freewriting means writing for a specific period of time without pausing or until reaching a certain page limit. You don't stop, go back, or correct freewriting. You can focus on one topic or go on to new ones as they pop into your mind. Freewriting helps you develop fluency as a writer.

Here is student writer Crystal's freewriting about the use of DNA evidence in the court system:

Heard on the news that they released another prisoner because DNA evidence showed he was innocent. He'd been in jail for eleven years! How sad. DNA evidence is so much better than any other way of seeing if someone is guilty. They gather DNA evidence from a tiny piece of skin. It's like fingerprints. Everyone has their own DNA. I hope more innocent prisoners can be released. They should be given money for the time they had to spend in jail.

Use Your Computer to Brainstorm or Freewrite
If you can't resist correcting your writing, try using invisible writing. Simply turn down the brightness on your monitor so that you can't see what you're writing. This forces you to stay in touch with your thoughts instead of worrying about what you have already written. As with all the writing you do on a computer, remember to save your work.

Clustering

Clustering is similar to brainstorming, but instead of listing your ideas, you draw a cluster of those ideas. To begin clustering, you write your subject in the center of a blank page, and draw a small circle around those words. Then, as ideas about the topic come to mind, you write them down, put circles around them, and draw lines from them to the center circle. As you think of additional details, you circle and join them to their main ideas. Clustering can thus help you organize your ideas as well as generate ideas.

Figure 1.2 shows how student writer Lee used clustering to gather ideas about problems in the criminal justice system.

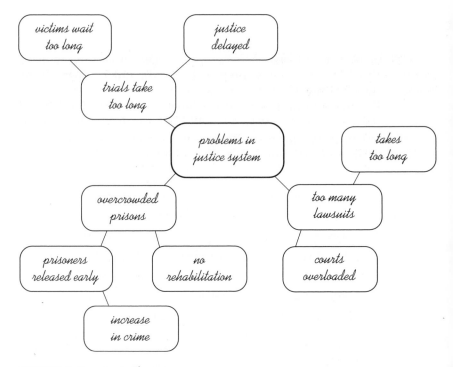

FIGURE 1.2. Lee's Clustering

Asking Questions

The six questions that journalists use to gather details about the news can also help you discover ideas about your topic:

- Who?
- What?
- When?
- Where?
- Why?
- How?

Reading

When you gather ideas for an essay, you may discover that you need to learn more about your topic. The more books, articles, and Web pages you read, the more supporting details you'll find. Regular reading will also help spark your own ideas for writing.

When you use outside reading to gather ideas, keep in mind that some sources are better than others. You want to find information that is reliable. Whenever you look at an article, a book, or a Web page, find out who wrote it, and try to figure out the writer's point of view and purpose. Knowing these things will help you decide whether the information is something you should use.

Consulting with Others

Consulting with people who know about your topic is an excellent way to gather information and interesting details for your paper. Also, you can enliven your writing by using quotations from the discussion.

The first step is finding someone to consult with. For the criminal justice assignment, for instance, you could talk to a family member or friend involved in the criminal justice system, such as a police officer or an attorney. You could also consult with someone who has been a victim of a crime or has been accused of committing a crime.

HOW TO Consult with Others

- Prepare questions to ask. You might begin with the journalists' questions: Who? What? When? Where? Why? How? Avoid yes-no questions.

- Listen carefully, and take notes.

- Ask questions when you don't understand something.

- Go over your notes with the person to fill in any gaps in your understanding.

Relating Aloud

Relating aloud simply means talking about your topic with others. Tell friends or classmates about what you plan to write, and get their feedback. Do you need more details? Do they ask questions that indicate you need to supply background information? Talking through what you plan to write is also a good way to realize that you have more to say than you think.

HOW TO Gather Ideas

Use one or more of these strategies:

- *Brainstorming:* List all thoughts that come to mind about a topic.

- *Freewriting:* Write without stopping for a certain period of time (five to ten minutes) or a certain page length.

- *Clustering:* Write down your topic in the middle of a page, and circle it. Write down more specific ideas, circle them, and draw lines to connect them to the larger idea.

- *Asking questions:* Ask a series of questions about the topic, such as, "Who? What? When? Where? Why? How?"

- *Reading:* Read and take notes on your topic.

- *Consulting with others:* Ask a knowledgeable person about your topic.

- *Relating aloud:* Talk about your topic with others.

After you have tried some of these ways to gather ideas, be sure to reflect on your topic possibilities for a few hours or days, letting your ideas percolate before you begin to write.

STEP 2. WRITE YOUR DISCOVERY DRAFT

A *discovery draft* is a first attempt at getting your ideas down on paper. When you write a discovery draft, concentrate on writing down your ideas without being too concerned about things like sentence structure, word choice, grammar, spelling, or punctuation.

Drafting styles vary widely. Some writers draft quickly and spend considerable time revising; others draft more slowly and write fewer drafts. You may write out your discovery draft by hand, type it, or use a word processor. The more you practice and experiment with writing, the better you'll know what works for you.

Choosing a Topic

Sometimes a topic will be given to you. For instance, your psychology instructor might ask you to write a definition of neurosis, or your supervisor at work might ask for a brief report on your visit to a local manufacturing plant. In such cases, you'll know what to write about, although you may not always be interested in the topic.

Often you'll have more choice. All of the writing assignments in Part Two of this book, for instance, ask you to gather ideas on three broad topics before you select one to write about. In such cases, your job is to select a topic that will interest you and your readers. In the criminal justice assignment, for example, you would need to select a problem in the criminal justice system to write about and then think of a solution to that problem.

HOW TO Select a Topic

Make a list of possible topics. Then answer the following questions:

- How much does this topic interest me?

- How much do I know about this topic?

- If I select this topic, how much, if any, research will I have to do? Is this research available to me? Can I complete the research in time to write the paper?

- Is the topic narrow enough to be explained in detail, given the word or page limit?

- How well does this topic satisfy the audience? For instance, if the reader wants an informative essay, will this topic lead to an informative essay?

Use your responses to these questions to decide on a good topic.

Once you have identified a general topic, you need to make sure that it is narrow enough to be sufficiently developed in the space you have. For instance, suppose that you want to write about how advertising on television has changed. As you start to write, you realize you could probably write a book on that topic. To narrow the topic, ask yourself questions such as "What kind of advertising? What time period should I cover? What particular change do I want to focus on?" Questions like these help you narrow a broad topic so you can go into more depth.

HOW TO Narrow a Topic

Break the topic into parts by asking these questions:

- What particular thing happened?
- Who is involved?
- What is the time period?
- What type is it?
- Where does it happen?
- Why does it happen?
- How does it happen?
- What is the result of it?

GROUP ACTIVITY 2: Narrow Topics

Working with two or three other students in your writing class, assume that a sociology instructor has asked you to write a three-page essay about how technology has changed American life. Using the questions in "How to Narrow a Topic" above, rewrite the following topics to make them narrow enough for a three-page essay.

EXAMPLE: BROAD TOPIC: How transportation has changed American life

NARROWED TOPIC: The influence of cars on the creation of

suburbs in the 1950s

1. How computers have changed our lives
2. Recent changes in telephone technology
3. How technology has changed the home
4. Negative effects of technology
5. How travel has changed in recent years

Sharing Your Ideas

Once you have selected and narrowed your topic, the next step is to write a discovery draft that puts your ideas together. Most of the time, this first draft will be very rough. Paragraphs might be skimpy; the organization might not make any sense; sentences will probably have mistakes in them. That's fine. The purpose of a discovery draft is just to see what you have to say. Nobody writes a perfect, finished essay in one try.

Write a Preliminary Thesis Statement.   As you begin a draft, first think about your *thesis statement*, the sentence (or sentences) that explains the main point of the essay. This thesis statement will probably change as you refine your ideas when revising, but it's a good place to start.

From a reader's point of view, a good thesis statement makes an essay easier to understand. From a writer's point of view, an effective thesis statement gives you a lot more to say than an ineffective one.

A good thesis statement does three things:

- It announces the topic of your essay.
- It shows, explains, or argues a particular point about the topic.
- It gives the reader a sense of what the essay will be about.

Compare the following ineffective and effective thesis statements.

INEFFECTIVE	My daughter was arrested last week for shoplifting.
EFFECTIVE	After my daughter was arrested for shoplifting, I made several important changes in how I raise my children.
INEFFECTIVE	Some people think that having more female police officers is good.
EFFECTIVE	Increasing the number of female police officers has helped the police department handle domestic violence and child abuse cases more effectively.

In the first example, we learn the topic, but a particular point isn't being made. In the second example, the point being made is too vague for the reader to predict what the essay will be about.

Where should your thesis statement appear in your essay? Usually, the thesis is given in the first or second paragraph. Knowing the main idea from the start gives your reader a road map for reading the whole essay.

HOW TO Write a Thesis Statement

Ask yourself these questions about your topic:

- What point do I want to make about my topic?

- How can I show, explain, or argue this point?

- How can I break this point down so that I can develop one idea about it in each section of my essay?

GROUP ACTIVITY 3: Evaluate Thesis Statements

Working in small groups, identify the following thesis statements as either effective or ineffective. Then rewrite the thesis statements that need improvement.

1. Soap operas are some of the best shows on television.
2. A successful marriage requires patience, good communication, and a sense of humor.
3. There have been too many budget cuts at this university.
4. If you have time on your hands, do community volunteer work.
5. Even though I didn't make the Olympic ski team, my years of training taught me important skills such as discipline, time management, focus, and persistence.

Get Organized.   Once you have a topic and a working thesis statement in hand, look back at the ideas you gathered during prewriting. Decide which ones appear most promising, and use the techniques you have learned to gather as many more ideas as you think you might need. Some writers prefer to organize their ideas before they begin to write. Others prefer to discover what they have to say while writing the discovery draft.

As you draft, use your thesis statement as a guide. (Keep in mind that you are free to change your thesis statement later.) After all, your discovery draft is for exploring your ideas. The most important thing is to write.

HOW TO Organize an Essay

- *Introduction:* Hook the reader, give background information, and state the thesis.

- *Body Paragraphs:* Give the main point of each paragraph in a topic sentence. Use details, facts, and examples to support each topic sentence.

- *Conclusion:* Refer back to the thesis. Explain the importance of the subject.

 Draft Your Essay
Using your word-processing program, try to write an entire draft of your paper in one sitting, using any freewriting or brainstorming that you already saved in a file. If you reach a place where you need additional information, write "Add information here" in bold or colored type to remind yourself to add material to this part of your paper.

STEP 3. REVISE YOUR DRAFT

When you revise, you improve your discovery draft. You want your reader to understand what you have to say and to be interested in reading your essay.

While you may write only one discovery draft, you may revise it many times. The more you revise, the better your essay will be.

Developing Your Ideas

The more you read, the more you'll notice that writers make their essays more interesting and convincing by developing them in detail. Supporting details increase interest, help readers understand a writer's thoughts, and support the writer's main ideas.

Writers use specific methods, or patterns, to develop the details in their paragraphs and essays. The most common of these patterns are description, narration, exemplification, process explanation, classification, definition, comparison and contrast, cause and effect, and argumentation. Chapter 3 explains in detail how each of these patterns works, and the Developing Your Ideas section in each chapter in Part Two shows you how to use them in your own writing.

Use the Cut-and-Paste Function to Revise
As you revise, use the Cut-and-Paste function of your word processor to move sentences or blocks of text. The easiest way to do this is to highlight the text you want to move and drag it to the new location. Print different versions to compare which is more effective.

Building Your Essay

When you build your essay, you look for ways to clarify your ideas for your readers, such as adding topic sentences to your paragraphs, giving more supporting details, or rearranging your points. The questions in How to Revise an Essay, below, will help you find ways to improve the content and organization of your draft.

HOW TO Revise an Essay

Ask yourself these questions as you revise:

- Have I followed all the instructions for this assignment?
- Do I begin the essay in a way that encourages my reader to continue reading?
- Do I need to revise my thesis statement?
- Do I include enough main ideas to support my thesis statement?
- Do I support each main idea with details?
- Do I vary my sentences and use the appropriate words?
- Do I end the essay clearly?

One way to revise is to set your paper aside for a day or two, reread it, and then rewrite it as you see fit. A better way to revise is to enlist the help of others, a strategy that is often called *peer review*. Ask a friend or classmate to read your paper and suggest ways it could be improved.

HOW TO Give and Receive Feedback on Your Writing

When you're giving someone suggestions for revision, follow these guidelines:

- Always say something positive about the piece.

- Be specific. Don't say, "You need to improve the organization." Say, "Why don't you combine your second and third paragraphs?"

- Don't make the feedback personal. Focus on the writing, not the writer. Don't say, "I can't believe you really believe that!" Say, "I was confused by your claim. Do you mean the death penalty should be used for all convicted drug felons?"

When you're receiving feedback on your paper, follow these guidelines:

- Write down the suggestions you receive.

- Ask questions to clarify what the readers are suggesting.

- Don't take the suggestions personally. Remind yourself that your classmates are discussing your writing, not you. The more suggestions you receive, the better your essay will be.

STEP 4. EDIT YOUR SENTENCES

When you edit, you revise your sentences and words so that they communicate clearly. Since you have already devoted a great deal of time and effort to communicating your ideas, you don't want to spoil the essay with awkward sentences or distracting errors.

Using Standard Written English

You may identify yourself as an English-speaking person, but actually you speak a dialect of English. A *dialect* is a variety of a language, and every language has many dialects. Dialects are characterized by pronunciation, word choice, and sentence structure. People speak different dialects based on where they live and their ethnic backgrounds. Here are some examples of dialects:

1. From *The Quilters: Women and Domestic Art*. Rosie Fischer is talking in 1974 about her life on a farm in Rowlett, Texas:

   Well, anyway, I was dreaming on havin' all kinds of pretty things in my home after I married. Well, I found out right quick that livin' out on a farm, what with all the chores that had to be done, a person didn't have a whole lot of time for makin' pretty things.

2. From Robert Kimmel Smith's *Sadie Shapiro's Knitting Book*, a novel about a Jewish widow from Queens, New York:

"Listen, darling," Sadie said patiently, "we all have our ways and that's it. . . . I lived with my son Stuart and his wife for three years after my Reuben died, he should find eternal peace. And what happened? My daughter-in-law and I drove each other crazy. I'm a neat person, I think you can tell that, but she. . . . Well, I wouldn't exactly call her a slob, but the best housekeeper in the world she isn't. Not that I want to talk badly about her, mind you. But by me you don't wash a floor with a mop. That's not what I call clean."

3. From "Black Children, Black Speech," an essay by Dorothy Z. Seymour:

"C'mon, man, les git goin'!" called the boy to his companion. "Dat bell ringin'. It say, 'Git in rat now!'" He dashed into the school yard.
"Aw, f'get you," replied the other. "Whe' Richuh? Whe' da muvvuh? He be goin' to schoo'."
"He in de' now, man!" was the answer as they went through the door.

Northern, southern, and midwestern dialects have developed from the languages spoken by European immigrants. The structure of African American spoken English is similar to several West African languages. In the Southwest and California, dialects such as Chicano English have developed as a result of Mexican immigration.

All these dialects are different from standard English, which is taught in American schools and used in business, government, and the media. The written version of standard English is standard written English (or SWE).

The following examples show the differences between standard written English and three dialects:

AFRICAN AMERICAN SPOKEN ENGLISH	He always be walkin' dere.
SWE	He always walks there.
CHICANO ENGLISH	They put his broken arm a cast.
SWE	They put his broken arm in a cast.
CREOLE ENGLISH	In Main Street have plenty shop.
SWE	Main Street has plenty of shops.

Because standard written English is generally considered the appropriate language to use in school and business, every chapter in Part Two of this book shows you how to use it in your writing. However, no language is better than another; languages are just different. Standard written English is a tool that will help you advance in college and in your workplace. It doesn't replace the other regional or ethnic dialects you might speak; it adds to them.

Correcting Errors

Before you can consider an essay finished, you must check your revised draft for any errors in grammar, spelling, and punctuation. It's perfectly acceptable to make mistakes when you're drafting and revising. Most writers do. But if your readers are distracted by errors in your writing, they'll pay less attention to what you have to say. You'll have several opportunities throughout this book to learn what the most common errors are and how you can fix them. You should also refer to the Handbook in Part Four whenever you have a question about the correct way to structure a sentence. Remember: Editing is not a punishment; it is your final chance to make a good impression on your readers.

Use the Spell-Check and Grammar-Check to Edit
Be careful when you use the spell-check and grammar-check features of your word-processing program. While spell-check helps you to spot typos and words that you have misspelled, it won't spot all errors. For instance, it won't notice if you use *their* when you're supposed to use *there* or *to* when you meant *too*. Grammar-check also has limitations. For example, it tends to label all long sentences as incorrect, when in fact the length of a sentence has nothing to do with its grammatical correctness.

STEP 5. SHARE YOUR ESSAY

In the final step of the writing process, you share your revised and edited essay with your audience. You may just submit your essay to your instructor for a grade. But if you're proud of what you have written, you may wish to share it with your classmates as well.

At times, you may share your writing in a more public way. For example, you may submit it to your local or campus newspaper for possible publication. Many magazines are also interested in sharing essays and articles submitted by their readers. If your essay proposes a change of some kind, you might want to use it as the basis of a letter that you send to a public official who can take action.

HOW TO Use the Writing Process

Exploring Your Choices

- Analyze your audience.
- Discover a purpose for writing.
- Brainstorm, freewrite, cluster, ask questions, read, consult with others, relate aloud, or reflect.

Drafting

- Select and narrow a topic.
- Write a tentative thesis statement.
- Get your ideas down on paper.
- Don't be concerned about sentence structure, word choice, grammar, spelling, and punctuation.

Revising

- Focus on helping your audience understand your essay.
- Improve your organization and supporting details.
- Strengthen the introduction, thesis statement, and conclusion.
- Polish sentence structure and word choice.
- Use peer review.

Editing

- Correct errors in grammar, spelling, and punctuation.
- Use a dictionary and the Handbook in Part Four.
- Don't rely on spell-check and grammar-check to catch all errors.

Sharing

- Share your final draft with your audience.

ONE STUDENT'S WRITING PROCESS

On the following pages, you'll follow Kwan Lu, a student writer, as he writes an essay for his criminal justice class. As you follow Kwan through the writing process, think about your own writing process and the ways that it resembles or differs from his. Here is the assignment Kwan was given:

> Write a two- to three-page essay for your instructor in which you explain a problem in the criminal justice system. Suggest a solution for the problem.

Kwan's Ideas

After receiving the assignment, Kwan thought first about his audience and his purpose. Although he planned to show his final draft to the attorneys he worked for, he knew his primary audience was his criminal justice instructor. Because the purpose of the essay was informative, he knew he would have to include a great deal of information to show the instructor he was knowledgeable about the topic.

In his journal, Kwan explained how he chose a topic and started to gather ideas for his paper:

If you would like to start a journal, turn to Chapter 10 for more information.

Feb. 9

A couple of weeks ago, I started working as a clerk in a law firm. When I got the essay assignment in my criminal justice class, I remembered that I had overheard one of the attorneys talking about a couple getting a divorce who were seeing a mediator. I asked the attorney to explain what a mediator was. She gave me a lot of information. I took notes on what she said. When I got home, I decided to do some clustering before I lost interest in the topic.

Kwan's Drafting

Using his notes from the interview with the attorney and his clustering (Figure 1.3), Kwan wrote the following discovery draft. (Note that the draft includes the types of errors that typically appear in a first draft.)

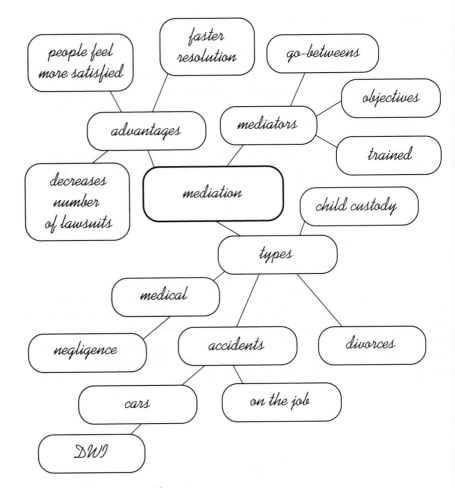

FIGURE 1.3. Kwan's Clustering

Mediation, Not Lawsuits

There are many lawsuits in our court system that are
unnecessary. People just want revenge or money no
matter what. One way to get rid of so many lawsuits
is to have people who are fighting go to a mediator. A
mediator tries to get people to agree on a solution
before the case ends up in court. For instance, a
wife is angry at her husband because he's been
unfaithful. He wants to share custody of the kids,
she decides she wants full custody so he'll never see

his kids again. She knows he's an OK father, she just
wants to get back at him. If they go to a mediator,
the mediator might be able to make the wife see that
she isn't think of what's right for the kids. She
might agree to share custody of the kids. A mediator
can help with other kinds of disagreements such as
a family that is fighting with another family or a
person injured in a car accident who wants money from
the person who hit her car. Mediation can keep cases
that are unnecessary from filling up the courts and
keeping other important cases from being heard.

Kwan's Revising

After finishing his discovery draft, Kwan reflected again on his
audience and purpose. He decided that his instructor would want an
essay that would be easier to follow; after all, she had over a hundred
students who would be turning in essays. This meant that his essay
had to be better organized and more fully developed, with a good thesis statement. Kwan asked several students in the criminal justice
class to read his discovery draft and give him suggestions for revision.

In his journal, Kwan explained how he revised his essay:

Feb. 13

Before I revised my essay, I wrote a new thesis
statement: "Unnecessary lawsuits could be prevented
if more people would use the services of a mediator."
I based the rest of the essay on this thesis
statement. I used a standard essay format--
introduction, body paragraphs, and a conclusion.
I decided that I needed to show my readers that
unnecessary lawsuits do exist, so I gave several
examples of them. Then, to show my audience (mainly
the instructor) that I know all about mediation,
I decided to explain how a mediator works. I also
worked hard on my introduction because sometimes
people form their opinion of the essay based on the
introduction. The conclusion and the title gave me
problems. I'm still not happy with them.

Here is Kwan's revised draft. (You may spot errors that Kwan will
correct when he edits his draft.)

Mediation, Not Lawsuits

Introduction is developed.

Thesis is clearer.

Problem is described.

Examples support main idea of the paragraph.

Examples clarify the writer's main point.

Topic sentences are used in all body paragraphs.

Evolution and change are everyday occurences. In the past, our legal system was simple. Trials happened quickly, and the guilty were punished. In the past few years however the legal system has become more complicated. Consider the cases of O.J. Simpson and Scott Peterson. It can take months or years for important cases like these to come to trial because the courts have too many other cases to settle. One of the biggest problems the legal system faces is unnecessary lawsuits. Unnecessary lawsuits could be prevented if more people would use the services of a mediator.

Currently, our court system is clogged with lawsuits that are a result of people being injured, disabled, or even killed because of other people's neglagence. If people are seriously hurt or killed because of this behavior, the victims and their families often consider a lawsuit. At this time, the victims are angry, sad, and hurt. You often hear them say, "I just want revenge," or "I want them to suffer like we have." They don't consider the time, energy, and money that go into a lawsuit. When they are overwhelmed by their emotions. They also don't realize that they will have to relive the crime over and over when they testify. While they may deserve some money, a lawsuit probably isn't the best way to get it.

Sometimes people file a lawsuit simply to get money, even when their injury is small. Perhaps this was the case when a woman sued McDonald's because she burned herself spilling coffee. Divorces often result in unnecessary court hearings. For instance, a wife might sue her husband for sole custody of the children, she claims that her husband is a bad father, but the real reason she wants custody is that she's hurt because he had an affair. She might say, "He won't get away with this." In a case like this, the children suffer because of the anger and imaturity of their parents.

There's a solution for the problem of unnecessary lawsuits: a mediator. This is a person who is trained to help people solve disagreements; often they have a background in both counseling and law. Judges sometimes send people to a mediator to see if their conflict can be resolved before they end up in a costly court battle. A local judge tells people in his courtroom, "If I have to render a decision, one of you is going to lose and be very unhappy. If you can reach a compromise, both of you will win." Mediators, who have no prior opinion or knowledge about the dispute, try to calm down both sides so that they can discuss the issues and come to a resolution agreeable to both. Usually, the mediator and the people involved in the disagreement will meet in the same room if the two sides get too emotional, the mediator will separate them and act as a go-between. The resolution might include the agreement that one person will pay another a certain amount of money. A couple getting a divorce might agree to share custody of their children. Two fighting families might agree to stop insulting each other in public.

Solution is described in detail.

Mediation won't stop all lawsuits. Not all people will come to an agreement, and some lawsuits involve injuries too great to be settled out of court. However, mediation works well in many cases. Because some attorneys believe they make more money through court cases, they don't always send their clients to a mediator. I believe this is a mistake. Many people should try to resolve their differences through mediation before they end up in a long, expensive, and painful court case.

More examples make the writer's ideas clearer.

Conclusion refers to the topic of the essay.

GROUP ACTIVITY 4: Analyze Kwan's Essay

Discuss the following questions with your classmates.

1. How effective is the title of Kwan's essay? What title would you suggest instead?
2. Does Kwan's introduction make you want to read the essay? Why or why not?
3. How effective is Kwan's thesis statement?
4. What details did Kwan add to the revised draft to improve his essay?

5. Give an example of a sentence that Kwan revised so that it was easier to understand.

6. How effective is Kwan's conclusion? What more would you suggest he add?

7. What else could Kwan do to improve his essay?

Kwan's Editing

Kwan described editing his essay in his journal:

```
Feb. 15

    I used my spell-checker to catch a lot of misspelled
words. I used the grammar-checker a few times. I showed the
draft to a friend who's really good in English, and he caught
some problems with sentence structure. Then I proofread my
paper by reading it from the end to the beginning.
```

Here is Kwan's edited essay. (The underlining indicates where he corrected errors during the editing stage.)

Correct essay format used.

```
Kwan Lu
Professor Heath
Criminal Justice 100
12 November 2006
```

```
                    Mediation, Not Lawsuits
```

Spelling error corrected.

Missing commas inserted.

```
    Evolution and change are everyday occurrences.
In the past, our legal system was simple. Trials
happened quickly, and the guilty were punished. In
the past few years, however, the legal system has
become more complicated. Consider the cases of O.J.
Simpson and Scott Peterson. It can take months or
years for important cases like these to come to trial
because the courts have too many other cases to
settle. One of the biggest problems the legal system
faces is unnecessary lawsuits. Unnecessary lawsuits
could be prevented if more people would use the
services of a mediator.
    Currently, our court system is clogged with
lawsuits that are a result of people being injured,
```

disabled, or even killed because of other people's
<u>negligence</u>. If people are seriously hurt or killed
because of this behavior, the victims and their
families often consider a lawsuit. At this time, the
victims are angry, sad, and hurt. You often hear them
say, "I just want revenge," or "I want them to suffer
like we have." <u>They don't consider the time, energy,
and money that go into a lawsuit when they are
overwhelmed by their emotions</u>. They also don't
realize that they will have to relive the crime over
and over when they testify. While they may deserve
some money, a lawsuit probably isn't the best way to
get it.

    Sometimes people file a lawsuit simply to get
money, even when their injury is small. Perhaps this
was the case when a woman sued McDonald's because she
burned herself spilling coffee. Divorces often result
in unnecessary court hearings. <u>For instance, a wife
might sue her husband for sole custody of the
children; she claims that her husband is a bad
father, but the real reason she wants custody is that
she's hurt because he had an affair</u>. She might say,
"He won't get away with this." In a case like this,
the children suffer because of the anger and
<u>immaturity</u> of their parents.

    There's a solution for the problem of unnecessary
lawsuits: a mediator. <u>A mediator is a person who is
trained to help people solve disagreements; often he
or she has a background in both counseling and law</u>.
Some judges send people to a mediator to see if their
conflict can be resolved before they end up in a
costly court battle. A local judge tells people in
his courtroom, "If I have to render a decision, one
of you is going to lose and be very unhappy. If you
can reach a compromise, both of you will win."
Mediators, who have no prior opinion or knowledge
about the dispute, try to calm down both sides so
that they can discuss the issues and come to a
resolution agreeable to both sides. <u>Usually, the
mediator and the people involved in the disagreement
will meet in the same room. If the two sides get too
emotional, the mediator will separate them and act as
a go-between</u>. The resolution might include the

Spelling error corrected.

Sentence fragment corrected.

Comma splice corrected.

Spelling error corrected.

*Vague pronoun reference
improved and pronoun-
antecedent agreement fixed.*

Run-on sentence corrected.

agreement that one person will pay another a certain
amount of money. A couple getting a divorce might
agree to share custody of their children.

Mediation won't stop all lawsuits. Not all people
will come to an agreement, and some lawsuits involve
injuries too great to be settled out of court.
However, mediation works well in many cases. Because
some attorneys believe they make more money through
court cases, they don't always send their clients to
a mediator. I believe this is a mistake. Many people
should try to resolve their differences through
mediation before they end up in a long, expensive,
and painful court case.

Kwan's Sharing

Writing in his journal, Kwan summed up his feelings about the
final draft of his assignment:

Mar. 1

I had no idea what grade this essay would get. I was
hoping for a B. I was shocked when I got an A! All that
revising really paid off. That gave me the guts to show it
to the attorney I had interviewed. She said she was impressed
by it. My confidence in my writing has improved a lot. I
almost look forward to my next writing assignment.

CHAPTER CHECKLIST

- ❑ There are five steps in the writing process: exploring choices, drafting, revising, editing, and sharing.
- ❑ The writing process is recursive; that is, you often need to go back and forth among the steps.
- ❑ Your audience affects what you write. Identify your audience — your readers — and take into account what they know about your topic, what they don't know about your topic, and how they feel toward your topic.
- ❑ You may have three purposes for writing:
  - ❑ Expressive writing communicates thoughts, feelings, or personal history.

❏   Informative writing conveys information.

❏   Persuasive writing seeks to change the reader's opinion or to convince the reader to take a particular action.

❏ The techniques for gathering ideas include brainstorming, free-writing, clustering, questioning, reading, consulting with others, relating aloud, and reflecting.

❏ When you draft, focus on getting your ideas down on paper. Use a tentative thesis statement as a guide.

❏ When you revise, aim to improve your writing and to communicate your ideas effectively and clearly.

❏ Skilled writers usually revise a draft several times.

❏ Standard written English (SWE) is taught in American schools and used in business, government, and the media. It is important to learn SWE for writing in college and in the workplace.

❏ When you edit your writing, eliminate errors in grammar, spelling, and punctuation, which if left uncorrected may prevent your reader from focusing on your message.

❏ Share your finished writing with others.

REFLECTING ON YOUR WRITING

To help you reflect on the writing you did in this chapter, answer the following questions:

1. What did you learn from writing this essay?

2. How will your audience benefit from reading your essay?

3. If you had more time, what more would you do to improve your essay before sharing it with your readers?

4. How will learning about the writing process help you?

Using your answers to these questions, complete a Writing Process Report for this chapter (you can download a report form at **bedford stmartins.com/choices**). Once you complete this report, freewrite about what you learned about the writing process and about yourself as a writer.

Crafting Paragraphs

In this chapter, you will write a paragraph about a meaningful photograph. As you work on your paragraph, you will

- **Compose topic sentences.**

- **Learn about paragraph unity and organization.**

- **Practice writing special kinds of paragraphs.**

Just as a football game is divided into quarters, an essay is divided into paragraphs. The quarters of a football game divide the game into shorter time periods so that athletes won't get overtired and spectators won't get bored or confused. Similarly, paragraphs divide information into chunks so readers can more easily follow your ideas. Paragraphs separate the main ideas of an essay into easily understood sections. They tell your readers where one main idea ends and another begins. They also help your readers make connections between these ideas. This chapter focuses on important elements of good paragraphs: topic sentences, unity, development, and organization. You'll also learn to write special types of paragraphs, such as introductions and conclusions.

Writing Assignment

Imagine you are applying for a job as an after-school tutor for children. You are required to submit an application form and letters of recommendation. Because your potential employer is interested in knowing something about your character, you also have to submit a writing sample in which you describe a photograph that is meaningful to you in some way. The photograph can show an important family occasion, such as a wedding or birthday, or it can depict a special place or a gathering of friends. Alternatively, you can select a photograph either of a historical event that captures your attention or of a person who interests you. Write a paragraph in which you describe the photograph and explain what it reveals. Assume that your readers do not have a copy of the photograph.

Use the writing process when you compose your paragraph. As you read in Chapter 1, the steps in the writing process are

- Exploring your choices.
- Drafting.
- Revising.
- Editing.
- Sharing.

TOPIC SENTENCES

When it comes to paragraphs, the phrase "one thing at a time" is useful to remember. The "one thing" that you explain in a paragraph is stated in a topic sentence. To write an effective topic sentence for each paragraph in your essay, follow these guidelines:

- Break up your thesis statement into several specific supporting ideas.
- Write a complete thought for each of these specific ideas.

A topic sentence functions as a mini-thesis for each paragraph. Here are some examples of thesis statements and the topic sentences that might follow from them:

THESIS STATEMENT Hiking is excellent exercise because it strengthens muscles, offers a chance to enjoy nature, and relieves stress.

To review the characteristics of a strong thesis statement, turn to p. 19.

Topic Sentences

- Hiking provides a strenuous workout for many parts of the body, especially leg and back muscles.
- Whether in the desert or in the woods, hikers enjoy beautiful scenery and clear air.
- A hike in a beautiful area takes people completely away from the daily grind of school, family, and work.

These are effective topic sentences because they support the thesis statement that hiking is excellent exercise.

Here is another set of topic sentences that supports the thesis statement:

THESIS STATEMENT If this university continues to increase tuition year after year, it will no longer be an asset to our community.

Topic Sentences

- As a result of tuition increases, families on limited incomes will not be able to send their children to college.
- Students who have already spent several years in college — and who have invested thousands of dollars in their education — will be forced to drop out.
- High school students will lack the motivation to study because they'll feel that college costs too much.
- Companies will decide not to locate here because they won't be able to find well-educated workers.

These topic sentences are effective because they explain the effect that tuition increases will have on the community. Consider one more set of examples:

THESIS STATEMENT Before I moved to the United States, I lived in Japan, a very different country and culture.

TOPIC SENTENCES

- Housing is much more spacious in the United States than it is in Japan. Even small apartments in this country are large by Japanese standards.
- Americans are informal, and even strangers use first names, whereas people in Japan are reserved and formal.
- People in the United States emphasize individuality, whereas people in Japan emphasize conformity to a group.

HOW TO Write a Topic Sentence

- Write several complete thoughts that make a point about your thesis statement. These are your topic sentences.
- Check that these topic sentences tell something informative and interesting about your thesis statement.
- Check that you can add details to show or explain these topic sentences.
- Check that you are writing on the topic assigned.

GROUP ACTIVITY 1: Write Topic Sentences

With your classmates, write several topic sentences for each of the following thesis statements.

1. No two people could be more different than Matt and Jerry, but they are my two closest friends.
2. Living with your parents when you're an adult has its disadvantages, but so does living on your own.
3. Personal management skills are important for students holding a full-time job while working toward a college degree.
4. Today's communications technology — from cellular telephones to e-mail — makes life more stressful, not more efficient.
5. Because anyone can use it, the Internet can be a dangerous place for children and adults alike.

Should your topic sentence appear at the beginning, middle, or end of the paragraph? A topic sentence can fall anywhere in the paragraph. Most often, however, it comes first. Just as placing the thesis statement at the beginning of an essay helps guide the reader through the paper, putting the topic sentence at the beginning of the paragraph helps guide the reader through the paragraph. To put it another way, giving the main idea at the beginning is like giving the reader a hook on which to hang the details that follow.

In the following paragraph, the topic sentence (italicized) comes first. The author, Garrison Keillor, states in the topic sentence that when he was a child, denim pants represented freedom to him. In the rest of the paragraph, he gives facts and examples to support this idea.

> *Thus denim came to symbolize freedom to me.* My first suit was a dark brown wool pinstripe bought on the occasion of my Aunt Ruby's funeral, and I wore it to church every Sunday. It felt solemn and mournful to me. You couldn't run in a suit, you could only lumber like an old man. When church was over, and you put on denim trousers, you walked out the door into the wide green world and your cousin threw you the ball and suddenly your body was restored, you could make moves.
>
> — GARRISON KEILLOR, "Blue Magic"

Sometimes, however, you may need to provide background information or explain the connection between two paragraphs before the topic sentence can be presented. In either case, the topic sentence may fall in the middle of the paragraph. In the following paragraph, the topic sentence (italicized) is given after the first sentence, which explains the connection between this paragraph and the previous one:

> I don't mean that some people are born clearheaded and are therefore natural writers, whereas others are naturally fuzzy and will never write well. *Thinking clearly is a conscious act that writers must force upon themselves, as if they were working on any other project that requires logic: adding up a laundry list or doing an algebra problem.* Good writing doesn't come naturally, though most people obviously think it does. Professional writers are constantly being bearded by strangers who say that they'd like to "try a little writing sometime" — meaning when they retire from their real profession, which is difficult, like insurance or real estate. Or they say, "I could write a book about that." I doubt it.
>
> — WILLIAM ZINSSER, "Simplicity"

Occasionally, placing a topic sentence at the end of a paragraph can dramatize the main idea. In the following example, the topic sentence (italicized) appears at the end. By giving several specific examples before stating the generalization, the writer emphasizes the main point of the paragraph:

> Most black Americans are not poor. Most black teenagers are not crack addicts. Most black mothers are not on welfare. Indeed,

in sheer numbers, more white Americans are poor and on welfare than are black. *Yet one never would deduce that by watching television or reading American newspapers and magazines.*

— Patricia Rayborn, "A Case of 'Severe Bias'"

GROUP ACTIVITY 2: Write Topic Sentences

With your classmates, brainstorm for several minutes about a photograph. In addition to describing the photograph, jot down ideas about what the photograph means to you. Then as a group, write topic sentences that summarize each group member's thoughts about the photograph.

UNITY

Once you have an effective topic sentence, you need to make sure that all other sentences within the paragraph relate to the topic sentence. This is called *paragraph unity*. Paragraphs that lack unity contain sentences that distract and confuse readers because they aren't on the topic. These are called *irrelevant sentences*. In the following paragraph, several irrelevant sentences have been added (in italics); notice how these irrelevancies distract you from the topic of the paragraph.

I went to high school in the Fifties, when blue denim had gained unsavory cultural associations — it was biker and beatnik clothing, outlaw garb, a cousin to the ducktail, a symbol of Elvis, and as such, it was banned at our school. *Elvis Presley was my favorite singer at the time.* Every September, we were read the dress code by our homeroom teacher: you could wear brown denim, or grey, or green, but not blue. *Blue is my favorite color.* Why? "Because," she explained. *She lived a block away from me.* There have to be rules, and blue denim was a statement of rebellion, and we were in school to learn and not to flaunt our individuality. So there.

— Garrison Keillor, "Blue Magic"

During the drafting stage, you may include irrelevant sentences as you focus on getting your thoughts on paper. When you revise, however, you need to eliminate them to achieve paragraph unity. Reread your paragraphs and topic sentences, and delete any statements that are off the topic.

GROUP ACTIVITY 3: Improve Paragraph Unity

With your classmates, read the following sentences. Place a check-mark next to the sentences that do not relate to this topic sentence: *I had defied a direct order, but I didn't expect my dad to do anything about it.*

_____ My dad looked like he was trying to recover from a gunshot wound.

_____ Gun control is a topic I would like to write about some day.

_____ His eyes fluttered and his mouth gaped. "You're saying no to me?" was all he could say.

_____ "Yea, I'm saying no to you."

_____ I felt like a newborn colt, prancing around, kicking, testing my limits.

_____ Riding horses is one of my favorite hobbies.

_____ "Well, pack your bags and leave," he shouted.

_____ Uh-oh, I hadn't expected that.

_____ My Samsonite bag is stored on the top shelf of my closet.

_____ "Okay, I will."

ORGANIZATION

You must organize the ideas in your paragraphs. If you don't, your readers won't be able to follow what you're saying, they'll become frustrated, and they'll stop reading. You can use general-to-specific order, topic-illustration-explanation order, progressive order, directional order, question-and-answer order, and specific-to-general order to organize your ideas.

General-to-Specific Order

General-to-specific order is one way to organize ideas in a paragraph. Whereas general statements are broad, specific statements are more focused. For example, the statement "I love dogs" is general because it refers to all dogs. But the statement "I love my dog Rupert because he's smart, funny, and affectionate" is specific because it cites a particular dog and several details.

In general-to-specific order, the most general idea is given at the beginning of the paragraph in the topic sentence. The more specific ideas that follow help support and explain the general statement.

The *quinceañera*, or coming-out party, is a tradition for many young Latinas. In this ritual, parents proudly present their fifteen-year-old daughter to their community. The ceremony consists of a Mass followed by a dinner and dance. Fourteen young couples serve as the girl's court. Long formal dresses, tuxedos, live music, and video cameras are all part of the spectacle.

Topic-Illustration-Explanation Order

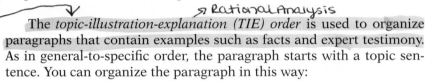

Rational Analysis

Topic Idea.

The *topic-illustration-explanation (TIE) order* is used to organize paragraphs that contain examples such as facts and expert testimony. As in general-to-specific order, the paragraph starts with a topic sentence. You can organize the paragraph in this way:

Top to bottom

- State the topic. *Evidence*   one paragraph
- Give an illustration (such as a fact or expert testimony).
- Explain the significance of the illustration.

The topic-illustration-explanation method of organization is used in the following paragraph about an American cultural symbol — the T-shirt. Notice that the writer states the topic, gives an illustration, and then explains why the illustration is important.

T-shirts with political or controversial statements can require the viewer to think about the message. A few years ago the slogan "A woman's place is in the House" was seen on many T-shirts. To understand this slogan, the viewer had to know the original saying, "A woman's place is in the home," and then realize that the word *House* on the shirt referred to the House of Representatives. The House of Representatives, a part of Congress, has always had fewer female than male members. A person wearing this T-shirt, then, advocated electing more women to political office.

In this paragraph, the topic is stated in the first sentence: T-shirts with political statements may require some thought. To illustrate, the writer uses a slogan — "A woman's place is in the House" — and then explains the significance of the slogan.

Progressive Order

least to most important.

Another way of organizing the ideas in your paragraphs is to use *progressive order*, in which ideas are arranged from least to most important. Since the final idea in a paragraph (or in an essay, for that matter) is the one that readers tend to remember most readily, ending with the most important idea is usually very effective. Thus, rather than presenting your examples randomly, you can arrange them progressively to emphasize the most important one.

Here's another paragraph from the essay about the American T-shirt. Notice that the writer uses progressive order to illustrate the various functions that the T-shirt serves in our culture.

> The common, ordinary T-shirt tells us much about the American culture. The T-shirt is a product of our casual lifestyle. People have been known to wear T-shirts under blazers at work and under evening dresses at the Academy Awards. The T-shirt is also associated with sexuality — think of the Calvin Klein ads in magazines and on buses. Most important, the T-shirt gives us a way to express ourselves. It tells others about our favorite schools, sports teams, or cartoon figures. It can also let others know our political views — whether or not they care to know.

In this paragraph, the most important function of T-shirts is stated at the end. The writer emphasizes this function with the introductory words *most important*.

Directional Order

When you use *directional order*, you describe something from one location to another, such as left to right, down to up, or near to far.

For example, suppose you want to describe a photograph of your brother taken while he was in the Air Force. To organize your description, you might use top-to-bottom directional order, as in the following example:

> This is my brother Antonio in his Air Force uniform. His face is clean-shaven, and his haircut is regulation-style. He's smiling his big lopsided smile. He has an athletic build, like a bodybuilder's. He wears his uniform proudly. It is perfectly pressed, and every brass button is perfectly shined. The crease in his pants is as sharp as a blade. His shoes are like black mirrors.

Question-and-Answer Order

Question-and-answer order is another method for organizing ideas in a paragraph. It involves asking a question at the beginning of the paragraph and then answering that question in the rest of the paragraph. In the following paragraph, the writer uses the question-and-answer method when discussing the causes of homelessness:

> What's the root of the homeless problem? Everyone seems to have a scapegoat: Advocates of the homeless blame government

policy; politicians blame the legal system; the courts blame the bureaucratic infrastructure; the Democrats blame the Republicans; the Republicans, the Democrats. The public blames the economy, drugs, the "poverty cycle," and the "breakdown of society." With all this finger-pointing, the group most responsible for the homeless being the way they are receives the least blame. That group is the homeless themselves.

— L. Christopher Awalt, "Brother, Don't Spare a Dime"

Specific-to-General Order

In *specific-to-general order*, the most specific ideas are stated first, and the general idea appears at the end of the paragraph. Use this type of organization when you want to position a topic sentence at the end of a paragraph.

In the example that follows, the writer organizes ideas from the most specific to the most general:

> The audience gasps as colors explode in the night sky — red, blue, yellow, green. The explosions grow bigger and bigger until they cover the night sky, and then they slowly disintegrate like silvery rain. Although everyone enjoys a fireworks spectacle on the Fourth of July, few understand the origin of this ritual celebration. The Fourth of July commemorates America's fight for independence, and the fireworks are to remind us of the historic battles that ended the Revolutionary War.

HOW TO   Organize a Paragraph

The **topic sentence** states the main point of the paragraph. **Support sentences** include details that support your topic sentence arranged using one of these methods: general-to-specific, topic-illustration-explanation, progressive, directional, question-and-answer, specific-to-general order. The **concluding sentence** restates the main point of the paragraph.

- Indent the first line of each paragraph five spaces.

- Use margins of one inch on each side of the page.

- Check that each sentence is a complete thought and ends with a period (.), question mark (?), or exclamation mark (!).

GROUP ACTIVITY 4: Identify Types of Paragraph Organization

With your classmates, identify the type of organization in each of the following paragraphs as general-to-specific, topic-illustration-explanation (TIE), progressive, directional, question-and-answer, or specific-to-general. Some types of organization may overlap.

1. With about a half-billion passengers a year boarding scheduled U.S. flights, air travel has become so routine that it's easy for people to forget what's outside their cabin cocoon. The atmosphere at 35,000 feet won't sustain human life. It's about 60 degrees below zero, and so thin that an inactive person breathing it would become confused and lethargic in less than a minute.

   — *Consumer Reports*, "Breathing on a Jet Plane"

   Organization: _____

2. When you need a new car, do you go to the nearest auto dealer and buy the first car you see? Most of us don't. We shop and compare features, quality, and price. We look for the best value for our money.

   — O. M. NICELY, "Using Technology to Serve You Better"

   Organization: _____

3. When you go on a hike in the desert, the least of your worries is snakes and scorpions. If you stay away from them, they'll stay away from you. Instead of worrying about reptiles and bugs, worry about the sun. To avoid a serious burn, apply sunscreen to exposed skin and wear a hat. Most important, bring plenty of water — at least a gallon per person.

   Organization: _____

4. When many dogs hear the words "Let's go on a hike!" they can't contain their excitement. They wag their tails, jump up and down, and even bring their leashes to their owners. Most dogs love to hike, and their owners love to take them. Just as with humans, though, dogs need to be prepared for a rigorous day on the trail.

   Organization: _____

5. Almost everyone knows that smoking is bad for one's health, yet more and more young people are smoking every day. According to the National Cancer Institute, one million Americans begin to smoke each year, and most of them are teenagers. Experts believe

that many young people are taking up smoking because they think smoking will make them look "cool."

Organization: _____

SPECIAL KINDS OF PARAGRAPHS

In addition to focusing on topic sentences and paragraph unity, development, and organization, you need to keep in mind the special requirements of two different but important types of paragraphs: introductions and conclusions.

Introductions

First impressions are important. In a job interview, employers prefer someone who is well spoken and neatly dressed over someone who mutters and is dressed to go to the gym. Similarly, the introduction to an essay provides the readers with a good first impression of your ideas.

In a short essay (two to three pages), the introduction usually consists of only the first paragraph; longer essays often have introductions that are several paragraphs in length. A good introduction has three characteristics: it gets the readers' attention, narrows the topic, and states the thesis.

The technique of getting your readers' attention is often called the *hook*. You want your introduction to grab your readers and pull them into your essay, just as a hook lures a fish to bite on the line. In addition to getting the readers' attention, the hook contains information relevant to the topic of your essay. A hook can consist of a question, an interesting fact, a brief story, or a vivid image, or it can be a definition or classification of key terms to help the reader begin to understand the topic.

Pose a Question.   Posing one or more *questions* at the start of an essay can arouse readers' curiosity about your topic, making them want to read on to find the answers. In the following introduction, the author uses a question to begin her essay about her father's heroism during World War II.

> "Who is your hero and why do you admire him?" is the question my son, Andy, had to answer on his application to a private school. The school's headmaster made an eloquent speech linking the growing incidence of drug abuse, suicide, and violence among teenagers to the absence of heroes in contemporary life.
>
> — Irina Hremia Bragin, "What Heroes Teach Us"

Provide an Interesting or Surprising Fact.   Introducing a topic with *facts* — statements that can be verified as true — has two important effects on readers. It signals them that you know your topic well, and it encourages them to read further to see what you have to say. An interesting or surprising fact can also get the readers' attention, as in this essay on how to drive safely:

> The first automobile crash in the United States occurred in New York City in 1896, when a car collided with a bicyclist. We've had 100 years since then to learn how to share the road, but with increasingly crowded and complex traffic conditions, we're still making mistakes, mostly because we assume that other drivers — and their vehicles — will behave the way we do.
>
> — CAROLYN GRIFFITH, "Sharing the Road"

Most readers would be intrigued by the date of the first car accident and would want to read more about this topic.

Tell a Story.   Beginning with a *brief story* or an *anecdote* related to a topic can help draw readers into your essay because most readers like to read about other people's lives:

> The Hollywood blockbuster had been playing for about 20 minutes when one of the characters took a gunshot in the face, the camera lingering on the gory close-up. Fifteen rows from the big screen, a little girl — no more than six years old — began shrieking. Her mother hissed, "Shut up," and gave her a stinging slap.
>
> — ALVIN POUSSAINT, "Let's Enforce Our Movie Ratings"

In addition to getting readers' attention, this story illustrates the writer's point that movie ratings need to be enforced.

Describe a Vivid Image.   An introduction that contains vivid *description* sets the scene and draws readers into your essay. Because readers like to imagine scenes, a vivid image is another effective way to hook readers:

> A woman in a left-turning Dodge zooms through two pedestrians like a football running back. A man in a Mitsubishi flosses his teeth — at 30 m.p.h. — grabbing the steering wheel between string tugs. An ambulance, siren screaming, races through traffic, with a man in a Jaguar sneaking behind it all the way.
>
> — WILLIAM ECENBARGER, "America's Worst Drivers"

This lively description of out-of-control drivers introduces the topic of bad driving.

Define a Term. Defining the meaning of a word works well in an introduction when you need to explain an unfamiliar topic for your readers. In the following introductory paragraph, the writer uses definition to ensure her readers' understanding of her topic and thesis statement. Notice also that she uses humor in the definition to further engage her readers. Her thesis sentence is the last one in the paragraph.

> As a lifelong crabber (that is, one who catches crabs, not a chronic complainer), I can tell you that anyone who has the patience and a great love for the river is qualified to join the ranks of crabbers. However, if you want your first crabbing experience to be a successful one, you must come prepared.
>
> — Mary Zeigler, "How to Catch Crabs"

Break Your Topic into Categories. You may wish to use *classification* in an introduction when categorizing by types can help narrow your topic and focus your readers' attention on the one type discussed in your essay. For example, in the following introduction, the writer classifies various types of musicians before focusing attention on the essay's topic: the two types of musicians who play percussion instruments, "drummers" and "percussionists." The writer's thesis statement comes last in the introduction.

> Quick — what do you call a person who plays a trumpet? A trumpeter, of course. A person who plays the flute is referred to as a flutist, or flautist, if you prefer. Someone who plays a piano is usually known as a pianist, unless of course he plays the player piano, in which case he is known as a player piano player rather than a player piano pianist. Got the hang of this yet? Okay, then, what do you call someone who plays that set of instruments belonging to the percussion family? Why, you call him a percussionist, don't you? Wrong! It's not quite as easy as all that. There are two types of musicians who play percussion instruments, "drummers" and "percussionists," and they are as different as the Sex Pistols and the New York Philharmonic.
>
> — Karen Kramer, "The Little Drummer Boys"

Narrow the Topic. An introduction announces the general topic of the essay and then narrows the subject to the more specific point stated in the thesis. Just as a photographer focuses the lens on a specific object for greater clarity, a writer narrows the scope of the essay.

In the following example, the writer introduces the general topic of ethnic diversity (in the first paragraph) before focusing on his main point of ethnic conflict:

> The history of the world has been in great part the history of the mixing of peoples. Modern communication and transport

accelerate mass migrations from one continent to another. Ethnic and racial diversity is more than ever a salient fact of the age.

But what happens when people of different origins, speaking different languages and professing different religions, inhabit the same locality and live under the same political sovereignty? Ethnic and racial conflict — far more than ideological conflict — is the explosive problem of our times.

> — Arthur Schlesinger Jr., "The Cult of Ethnicity, Good and Bad"

By gradually narrowing his topic to ethnic and racial conflict, Schlesinger prepares his readers for his thesis that "ethnic and racial conflict . . . is the explosive problem of our times."

State the Thesis.

After getting the reader's attention and narrowing the topic, you're ready to state your thesis. Generally, the thesis appears at the end of the introduction; depending on the length and complexity of the essay, it can range from one sentence to several sentences long. As you read in Chapter 2, the thesis of an essay states the topic; shows, explains, or argues a particular point about the topic; and gives the reader a sense of what the essay will be about.

For more information about thesis statements, turn to p. 19.

In the following introduction, notice how the writer attracts the reader's attention, narrows her topic, and then states her thesis (italicized):

"Welcome to Rio Bravo Grill! Can I get y'all a margarita?" With those words I began my stint as a full-time waitress, apartment renter, and bill payer in downtown Atlanta. It was the first time I had ever truly been on my own, with no help from my parents except for the occasional sardonic words of advice or chastisement. At that time I had no idea what I wanted to do with my life. I had recently been forced to leave the United States Air Force Academy, and I didn't know what to do next. My life had always been planned around a career in the Air Force, and I had never pictured myself as anything else. *My leaving and subsequent return to the academy, as well as my experiences during the time I was out, taught me a lot about myself, the world around me, and where I want to go from here.*

> — Andrea L. Houk, "The Honor Principle"

HOW TO Write an Introduction

- Use a hook such as a question, an interesting fact, a brief story, a vivid image or description, a definition, or classification to get readers' attention.

- Narrow the topic to one main point.

- Write a thesis statement.

GROUP ACTIVITY 5: Unscramble an Introduction

The following sentences are from the introduction of an essay about a young college student's reaction to the birth of his child. The sentences are out of order. With several other classmates, put the paragraph into the correct order.

———— I thought I would have to give up my dream of graduating from college in four years.

———— When I discovered I was going to be a father at age nineteen, I thought my life was over.

———— Now, however, I can't imagine my life without my daughter.

———— Instead, I would need to find a full-time job to support my new family.

———— She has taught me that despite the responsibilities of parenthood, the joy and love make it worthwhile.

———— In fact, I thought I would have to give up going to college altogether.

Conclusions

Often the last thing people read is what they remember the best. Therefore, your conclusion needs to be well written and memorable. The standard way to end an essay is to restate your thesis, summarize your major points, and broaden your focus.

Restate the Thesis.   By restating your thesis, you ensure that your readers remember your main point. However, don't use the same words you used in your introduction. Instead, vary your word choice so that your main point isn't unnecessarily repetitive. The restated thesis can appear at either the beginning or end of the conclusion.

STATEMENT OF THESIS INTRODUCTION	If we make it a point to be considerate of all the occupants of our roadways, from cars and trucks to motorcycles and pedestrians, we can make our streets much safer places to be.
RESTATEMENT OF THESIS (ITALICIZED) IN CONCLUSION	But no matter how much time elapses, the basic principles of sharing the road safely won't change much. Just watch out for *the big guys, cut the little guys some slack, pay attention to "vehicular diversity,"* and above all, enjoy the ride.

— CAROLYN GRIFFITH, "Sharing the Road"

By varying her word choice, Griffith restates her thesis in an interesting way.

Often, an *effective quotation* can restate your thesis in an interesting, attention-getting way that emphasizes your main point. In the conclusion to an essay on the benefits of exercise, the writer ends with a quotation from a working mother who recently ran a marathon, thus emphasizing the success of a woman who found time to exercise.

> When working moms make an effort to exercise and put sweat and tears into getting into shape, they're showered with benefits both immediate and long term. Right from the start they feel exhilarated and energized; and over time they gain self-confidence and a sense of accomplishment. "Think about it," says Irene Sang, an optometrist in South Pasadena, California, and a single mother of two who went from being overweight and at risk for diabetes to running her first marathon this fall. "Exercise is guaranteed to make you feel more relaxed, more confident, and healthier. How can you pass up such an opportunity?"

Summarize Your Points.   For a lengthy and complex essay, a *summary* can pull ideas together and reinforce main points in the conclusion. The author of an essay on the New England clambake summarizes her important points about the clambake in her conclusion:

> A clambake may remind you of Boston and Paul Revere's ride, but to ensure a successful meal, remember these important points: start early, dig a pit that is at least two feet deep, feed the charcoal fire with hardwood, and use seaweed-soaked canvas. While your clams are cooking, get out the iced tea and beer and enjoy playing volleyball or strolling along the beach while taking part in this cherished New England tradition.

Broaden the Focus.   In your introduction, you state the general topic and then narrow your focus until you give the thesis statement. In the conclusion, however, you want to broaden your focus — widen the lens of the camera — to tell your readers how your main point connects to other important ideas.

In his introduction to "The Cult of Ethnicity, Good and Bad," Arthur Schlesinger Jr. writes that "ethnic and racial conflict . . . is the explosive problem of our times." Notice that in his conclusion, Schlesinger broadens his focus by suggesting a solution to this conflict (italicized):

> The growing diversity of the American population makes the quest for unifying ideals and a common culture all the more urgent. *In a world savagely rent by ethnic and racial antagonisms,*

*the United States must continue as an example of how a highly dif-
ferentiated society holds itself together.*

— ARTHUR SCHLESINGER JR., "The Cult
of Ethnicity, Good and Bad"

By ending his essay with the suggestion that the United States should
serve as a model of unity, Schlesinger leaves his readers with a sense
that action must be taken.

In the following example from an article about the popularity of
collecting baseball cards, the writer concludes with a call for action by
asking readers to consider joining a baseball card club:

After collecting baseball cards for several years, our greatest
desire is to start a baseball card club in Los Angeles. If you would
be interested in joining such a club, write to the above address
with a note, "Count me in!"

HOW TO Write a Conclusion

- Restate the thesis to remind readers of your main point.

- Sum up what has been said in the essay.

- Broaden the focus or make an additional observation about your
  main point.

GROUP ACTIVITY 6: Unscramble a Conclusion

The following sentences are from the essay about a young college student's reaction to the birth of his child. The sentences are out of order.
With a group of your classmates, put the sentences in the correct order.

_____ Because of her, I get angry when I hear people talk about
how bad it is when young people have children.

_____ In fact, for some people it's the best thing that can ever happen to them.

_____ It's not always bad.

_____ My daughter has improved my life in many ways, from making
me more responsible to teaching me what love really means.

Online Writing Labs (OWLs)
Share your introduction, thesis statement, and conclusion
with a tutor in an online writing lab. Go to **bedfordstmartins
.com/choices** and click on "Annotated Web Links."

ONE STUDENT'S PARAGRAPH

As you recall, the writing assignment for this chapter is to write a paragraph for part of a job application in which you describe a photograph and explain what it reveals about your life. On the following pages, you'll follow Melissa Ruiz, a student writer, as she writes her paragraph for this assignment. Use Melissa's writing process as a guide to writing your own paragraph.

Melissa's Choices

In her journal, Melissa freewrote about the assignment after she had looked through several photographs:

> I thought it would be easy to pick a photo. I guess I didn't realize a big part of this application is finding a good photo I'd really want to write about. I looked through my photo albums but couldn't decide. Should I write about my trip to Mexico? How my family celebrates Christmas? My younger sister? Then I saw it. On the floor was a stack of newspapers, and on the front page of one of them, there was a picture of a Red Cross worker helping victims of Hurricane Katrina. They look so sad, and I knew this was a better picture to write about, since it's so emotional, and Hurricane Katrina is something that everyone has feelings about.

After selecting the following photograph, Melissa brainstormed about it in her journal:

The young woman is wearing a white t-shirt with the big Red
Cross logo on back.
Her back is to the camera, can't see her face
Her hair is up in a bun.
The older woman's dark, sad eyes look through rose-tinted
glasses.
She looks away, probably has been crying
She looks old and sad, short hair
The older man has white hair that is balding.
He looks down, his tiny eyes peek out, big bags under his eyes
They both look lost.
What does this photo mean to me?
I appreciate what I have — a home, food, my family and
friends.
Anything can happen; you just never know.

Melissa's Drafting

After studying the photograph again and referring to her brainstorming, Melissa wrote the following discovery draft. (Note that the
example includes the types of errors that typically appear in a first
draft.)

After Katrina

As soon as I look at this photograph, I get sad. I
mean, I don't know this couple, I've never met them, but I
know they're suffering because of what Hurricane Katrina did
to their home. They look so sad, as if their about to cry,
and they probably have been already. The wife's dark eyes
look through her rose-tinted glasses and out into nothing.
She folds her hands tightly and rests them under her chin.
The husband's sad eyes barely peek through big bags. It's
as if neither one of them are really there--they're lost
in sadness. This photo makes me realize how fortunate I am
to have a home and that my family and friends are safe,
because you never know what can happen to you unexpectedly.
My heart goes out to this couple, who are probably hundreds
of miles away from their home, just wishing for the
nightmare to be over.

Melissa's Revising

Melissa read her paragraph aloud to several classmates, so they could give her suggestions for revision. Because her classmates were confused about her main point, Melissa decided to begin her paragraph with a topic sentence that would be supported by the rest of the paragraph. Her classmates also suggested that Melissa organize the sentences in the paragraph and include more description.

Here is Melissa's revised draft. (Because she focused on getting down her ideas, you may spot editing errors she still needed to correct.)

After Katrina

A photograph I found in the newspaper reminds me to appreciate what I have in life. In the photo, a young woman who is wearing a big red cross on the back of her white T-shirt facing a couple who were victims of Hurricane Katrina. The couple is older, the husband's white hair is balding, and the woman's face is wrinkled. The wife folds her hands tightly and rests them under her chin. Her dark eyes look through rose-tinted glasses and out into nothing. She looks like she wants to cry, and she probably has already. The husband's sad eyes barely peek through large puffy bags. His fist holds up his downturned face. He's probably thinking about how their lives and home has been torn apart and he just wishes for the nightmare to be over. They both look as though they're not really there: they're lost in sadness. The misfortune they are suffering is a reminder that there's no telling what can come along to effect your life and change it forever. Seeing this photo makes me cherish the very simple and basic things in life, like a roof over my head, food to eat, and the safety of my family and friends. Its sad but true: we usually don't appreciate what we have until we have already lost it.

Topic sentence added.

Details added.

Conclusion added.

Repetition of topic sentence.

Melissa's Editing

To help her edit her paragraph, Melissa sought help from a tutor at her college's writing center. She also used the spell-check on her word-processing program.

Here is Melissa's edited paragraph. (The underlining indicates where she corrected errors during the editing stage.)

After Katrina

Verb tense fixed.

Comma splice fixed.

Subject-verb agreement fixed.

Spelling error corrected.

Apostrophe added.

This photograph I found in the newspaper reminds me to appreciate what I have in life. <u>In the photo, a young woman who is wearing a big red cross on the back of her white T-shirt faces a couple who were victims of Hurricane Katrina. The couple is older; the husband's white hair is balding, and the woman's face is wrinkled.</u> The wife folds her hands tightly and rests them under her chin. Her dark eyes look through rose-tinted glasses and out into nothing. She looks like she wants to cry, and she probably has already. The husband's sad eyes barely peek through large puffy bags. His fist holds up his downturned face. <u>He's probably thinking about how their lives and home have been torn apart</u> and he just wishes for the nightmare to be over. They both look as though they're not really there: they're lost in sadness. The misfortune they are suffering is a reminder that there's no telling what can come along to <u>affect</u> your life and change it forever. Seeing this photo makes me cherish the very simple and basic things in life, like a roof over my head, food to eat, and the safety of my family and friends. <u>It's</u> sad but true: we usually don't appreciate what we have until we have already lost it.

Melissa's Sharing

In a journal entry, Melissa explained how she shared her paragraph:

After I revised my paragraph, I read it aloud to my group and then showed them the photograph. They told me that I really captured the details and emotion in the photo. They too could see how sad the couple looked. Then I turned the paragraph in to my teacher for a grade.

CHAPTER CHECKLIST

❑ Remember the phrase "one thing at a time" when you write paragraphs. The "one thing" you explain in each paragraph is stated in the topic sentence.

❑ Write effective topic sentences by breaking down your thesis statement into several specific supporting ideas. Then write a complete thought for each specific idea.

❑ Maintain paragraph unity by sticking to the topic introduced in your topic sentence.

❑ Organize the ideas in your paragraphs by using
  ❑ General-to-specific order.
  ❑ Topic-illustration-explanation (TIE) order.
  ❑ Progressive order.
  ❑ Directional order.
  ❑ Question-and-answer order.
  ❑ Specific-to-general order.

❑ In an introduction, get the readers' attention, narrow your topic, and state your thesis.

❑ In your conclusion, restate your thesis and broaden your focus.

REFLECTING ON YOUR WRITING

To help you reflect on the writing you did in this chapter, answer the following questions.

1. In your description of a photograph, which step of the writing process (exploring choices, drafting, revising, editing, and sharing) did you find the easiest to do? Which was most difficult? Why?

2. What pleases you most about your paragraph?

3. If you had more time, what parts of your paragraph would you continue to revise? Why?

Using your answers to these questions, complete a Writing Process Report for this chapter (you can download a report form at **bedford stmartins.com/choices**). Once you complete this report, freewrite about what you learned in this chapter about crafting paragraphs and what you still hope to learn.

The Patterns of Development

In this chapter, you will write a brief essay about how you manage your time. As you work on your essay, you will

- Learn about description, narration, exemplification, process explanation, classification, definition, comparison and contrast, cause and effect, and argument.

- Practice using the nine patterns of development.

Suppose you visit one of your favorite Web sites and find words scattered randomly over the screen. Photos and artwork are upside down or obscured by blotches of color. Incomprehensible music blares out from your speakers. The Web site has no order. You don't know what to look at first, and you can't understand what message is being conveyed. Similarly, a paragraph that lacks order will confuse and frustrate readers, who won't be able to understand the connection between your ideas or the main point you're trying to make.

When you write a paragraph, you use a topic sentence that focuses on only one idea, and you organize, in a logical order, the sentences that support that topic sentence. You also follow a particular pattern of development that helps you expand and structure your thoughts. While some paragraphs might contain several patterns, most of the time only one pattern will be dominant. Following the patterns of development enables writers to

- Increase readers' interest.
- Communicate their thoughts clearly to their readers.
- Support their main ideas.

Nine common patterns for developing paragraphs are description, narration, exemplification, process explanation, classification, definition, comparison and contrast, cause and effect, and argument.

Writing Assignment

The director of the first-year orientation program at your college has asked students to write an essay in which they explain how they structure their time as college students. Some of these essays will be published in an orientation booklet distributed to new students to help them balance the pressures of college, work, family, and friends.

Write an essay in which you explain how you manage your time. For instance, do you schedule study time each day to prepare for your classes? Do you take classes only in the evening because of your job? Do you study for tests while waiting for the bus? Do you bring your lunch with you to avoid the long lines in the food court? Use the steps in the writing process — exploring your choices, drafting, revising, editing, and sharing — when you compose your essay.

DESCRIPTION

When you use description in your writing, you allow your readers to become more involved. The key is to go beyond describing experiences in general ways ("We had a great time; that day really changed me") to describing them in enough detail that your readers relive those moments with you.

Notice how one writer, Benjamin Alíre Saenz, improves the following sentences from his short story "Ceballeros" by adding description in the revised version:

ORIGINAL

He was getting good grades in everything except chemistry. And the teacher hated him. His brother wrote to him and told him to calm down, told him everything would be all right.

REVISED

He was getting good grades in everything except chemistry. If he didn't pass, he'd have to go to summer school because it was a required course. All those good grades, and it had come down to this. He was a borderline student in that class and he knew it, but there wasn't any time. There wasn't any time.

And the teacher hated him. He could feel the teacher's hatred, the blue-eyed wrestling coach who favored athletes and nice-looking girls.

His brother wrote to him and told him to calm down, told him everything would be all right. "Just graduate and go to college. Do whatever it takes, just don't join the Army."

To use description, start with a general statement, and add details to make it more specific. Use these questions:

- Who is involved?
- What happens?
- When and where does it happen?
- Why does it happen?
- How does it happen?

Here's an example of a general statement to which detailed observations have been added:

ORIGINAL

My cousin's wedding was really beautiful.

REVISED

My cousin Veronica's wedding took place in the flower garden of Haven Park on a sunny June day. Veronica and Samuel took their vows surrounded by red, pink, and yellow roses. In addition to the three bridesmaids and the best man, my four-year-old son, Jason, was the ring bearer. I've never seen Jason smile so much. Other family members were both smiling and crying. My aunt Liz had tears streaming down her face as she watched Veronica and Sam walk through the garden arm in arm. Even my uncle Albert, usually so stern, had tears in his eyes.

GROUP ACTIVITY 1: Use Description

With several classmates, add description to make the following paragraphs more interesting and vivid. Use the journalist's questions: Who? What? When? Where? Why? How?

1. The first time I baby-sat for my brother's children was a disaster. One of them kept throwing things around. The other one wouldn't stop crying. I was relieved when my brother and his wife returned home.

2. I was so happy when the Little League team I coach won the city tournament. The final play was very suspenseful. The score was tied. The parents were probably more nervous than the players. But no one could have been happier than the kids when they won.

3. One of my favorite pastimes is backpacking in the mountains. I love the fresh air and the scenery. At night, my friends and I lie awake and look up at the stars. One night, we even saw a shooting star.

NARRATION

Narration is writing that tells a story that is based on either fact or fiction. You use narration when you want to develop ideas by relating a series of events. In most cases, you will organize events in chronological order. Occasionally, however, you might use a flashback. You might also use dialogue to make a narrative more immediate and real.

Chronological Order

Generally, stories are told in the order in which they actually happened, called *chronological order*. Imagine that you want to narrate a story about your family's tradition of taking a family photograph at the start of every new year. Here's how you might organize a narrative paragraph in chronological order:

> On picture-taking day, we all rush around trying to get ourselves to look as good as possible for the camera. In the bathroom, my mother puts makeup on my stepfather's nose to hide the redness caused by a cold. I hear my stepsister tell my parents she refuses to be in the picture because her hair is too puffy. My brother rushes into the kitchen to clean up the grape juice he spilled on his shirt, while I look through the cupboards in the utility room for shoelaces. Finally, we're ready to make our trip to the photographer's studio.

Notice how the sentences in the paragraph are arranged in the order in which the events of the story occurred.

Flashback

An alternative way to organize a narrative is to use a *flashback*: you begin the story in the middle, flash back to the beginning, and then resume telling the story in the middle again. You often see this technique used in movies: the picture becomes fuzzy, and a scene from an earlier time appears. The flashback technique is useful when you want to contrast then and now or highlight a key scene. Here's how the paragraph about the picture-taking ritual might be organized using the flashback technique:

> In the photograph, my family appears calm and relaxed. Our hair is perfectly combed, and our clothes are neatly pressed. The expressions on our faces seem calm and happy. But as I stare at the photograph, I recall the chaos that preceded the snap of the camera. My stepfather had such a terrible cold that my mother had to put makeup on his nose to cover the redness. My stepsister didn't want to be in the picture because her hair was too puffy. My brother had spilled grape juice on his shirt, and I had broken my shoelace. To make matters worse, we had a flat tire going to the studio. But when I look at this photograph, I know it was all worthwhile.

Dialogue

In a narration, *dialogue* consists of the actual words that people say, indicated by quotation marks. Use dialogue when you want to highlight an important scene or portray a certain person through his or her own words.

Dialogue can make a narration more interesting and fast paced. Consider this narrative paragraph:

> I couldn't have survived my first semester in college without my roommate, Lisa. She encouraged me to study harder, helped me find a job, and introduced me to new friends. One night, while I was studying for my calculus exam, I became so frustrated I yelled and threw the calculus book across the room. Lisa comforted me. That's the kind of roommate she was.

Here's the same paragraph, expanded to five paragraphs to include dialogue. Notice that the dialogue makes the scene more vivid.

> I couldn't have survived my first semester in college without my roommate, Lisa. She encouraged me to study harder, helped me find a job, and introduced me to new friends. One night, while I was studying for my calculus exam, I became so frustrated that I yelled as loud as I could, "I can't take it anymore!" Then I threw the calculus book across the room.
>
> Lisa, who was studying for her psychology exam, looked up at me from across the room. "What's wrong with you?"
>
> "I can't do this! I know I'm going to flunk!"
>
> "Calm down," she said, putting her book down. "Let me see if I can help." She spent the next hour explaining the problems to me.
>
> That's the kind of roommate she was.

EXAMPLES

In writing, examples are used to clarify, explain, and support ideas. Two of the most common types of examples are facts and expert testimony.

Facts

Facts provide support for your ideas. Unlike opinions or guesses, facts are statements that can be objectively verified as true. For example, the statement "Golden retrievers are beautiful" represents the opinion of the writer. In contrast, the statement "A golden retriever is a breed of dog" is a fact that can be verified in an encyclopedia or other reliable source. Facts may include names, dates, numbers, statistics, and other data relevant to your topic or idea. Notice in the following paragraph that facts are used to support the idea that Asian Americans are a diverse group:

Asian Americans are an especially diverse group, comprised of Chinese, Filipino, Japanese, Vietnamese, Cambodians, Hmong, and other groups. The largest Asian American groups are Chinese Americans (24 percent), Filipino Americans (20 percent), and Japanese Americans (12 percent). Other groups, such as Vietnamese, Cambodians, Laotians, and Hmong, are more recent arrivals, first coming to this country in the 1970s as refugees from the upheavals resulting from the Vietnam War. In the 1980s, Koreans and Filipinos began immigrating in larger numbers. The majority of Asian Americans live in the West.

> — Bryan Strong and Christine DeVault,
> *The Marriage and Family Experience*

Expert Testimony

Statements made by knowledgeable people are considered *expert testimony*. Examples supported by expert testimony make your writing more convincing. For example, citing the surgeon general's warning that cigarette smoking greatly increases your risk of lung cancer is more convincing than offering the statement without support or citing someone with no medical background or authority to advise American citizens on health matters.

In the following paragraph, the author uses expert testimony to convince her readers that eating meals together as a family is a vitally important activity:

> In fact, it's the experts in adolescent development who wax most emphatic about the value of family meals, for it's in the teenage years that this daily investment pays some of its biggest dividends. Studies show that the more often families eat together, the less likely kids are to smoke, drink, do drugs, get depressed, develop eating disorders, and consider suicide, and the more likely they are to do well in school, delay having sex, eat their vegetables, learn big words, and know which fork to use. "If it were just about food, we would squirt it into their mouths with a tube," says Robin Fox, an anthropologist who teaches at Rutgers University in New Jersey, about the mysterious way that family dinner engraves our souls. "A meal is about civilizing children. It's about teaching them to be a member of their culture."

> — Nancy Gibbs, "The Magic of the Family Meal"

PROCESS EXPLANATION

Writers use a technique called *process* to explain how something works or how to do something. Cookbooks and repair manuals come to mind when we think of process writing, but bookstore shelves are filled with all sorts of other "how to" books explaining processes — from how to use a computer to how to arrange your closet.

In a paragraph about your favorite hiking trail, for instance, you might explain the process of preparing to hike the trail and locating the trailhead, as Laurence Parent does in the following paragraphs about hiking to Wheeler Peak in New Mexico:

> Be sure to get a very early start on this hike. To minimize problems with storms, you ideally want to be on the summit before noon. Snow flurries are possible even in mid-summer. Be sure to take rain gear and extra-warm clothing. Lightning and hypothermia are real threats on Wheeler Peak and the exposed summit ridge.
>
> At just short of one mile you will pass marked Trail 63, the Long Canyon Trail to Gold Hill, coming in from the left. Ignore it and continue climbing up the northeast valley. Just past the trail junction, the trail hits an old road. Turn left onto the road and follow it the rest of the way up the valley.
>
> — LAURENCE PARENT, *The Hiker's Guide to New Mexico*

In process writing, it is important to use transitions and to present each step in the process clearly so that your readers can follow along with you.

CLASSIFICATION

Writers use *classification* to organize their ideas and thereby to aid their readers' understanding of those ideas. When you classify, you categorize something into types on some particular basis. For example, you might classify cars on the basis of their type or size (sports car, SUV, compact, midsize, and full-size) or on the basis of their country of origin (Volvos and Saabs from Sweden, Hyundais and Kias from Korea). You might also classify cars on the basis of their resale value, safety record, popularity as indicated by sales, or some other basis you deem important.

In the following paragraph about the camera collection of Cheng Jianguo, a student from China, the writer classifies cameras first by type and then by name:

Cheng mainly collects China-made cameras. The brands of Chenguang, Tiantan, Changhong, Huashan, Changle, Yuejin, Haiou, and others vividly show the development of China's camera industry. In addition, he has also gathered many different types of foreign cameras, some produced early in this century. They include the Leica and Roland from Germany, Minolta and Fuji models from Japan, and Kodak and Browning cameras from the United States as well as models from the former Soviet Union and Czechoslovakia.

— Beijing Review, "Camera Collector Cheng Jianguo"

GROUP ACTIVITY 2: Use Narration, Examples, Process Explanation, and Classification

Following are several topic sentences. For each one, decide with your group whether you will use narration, examples, process explanation, or classification as the primary method of development. Then use that method to develop the topic sentence into a brief paragraph.

1. With the right tools, it's easy to change a flat tire.

   Primary method of development: _____

2. Rock music can be divided into various categories.

   Primary method of development: _____

3. I'll never forget the first time I tried to drive a car.

   Primary method of development: _____

4. The music on my iPod illustrates the different parts of my personality.

   Primary method of development: _____

DEFINITION

Writers use *definition* to explain and clarify. Thus, when you define something, you tell your reader what it means. A good definition has two parts: first the term being defined is placed in a general category, and then an explanation of how it fits within that category (a discussion of its distinguishing features) follows. For example, to define the term *skydiving*, you might first define it generally as a risky sport and then explain what distinguishes skydiving from other risky sports, such as rock climbing and hang gliding.

In the following paragraph, the writer first defines the Sierra Club's Inner City Outings (ICO) program and then goes on to describe its activities. He thus categorizes the topic generally as a type of community-outreach program before pointing out its distinguishing feature: it takes disadvantaged young people out of the city and into the "natural world" for a time.

> Now in its 23rd year of operation, ICO is one of the Sierra Club's longest-running and most successful community-outreach programs. Its dedicated corps of volunteer leaders works year-round to get disadvantaged young people of diverse ethnic and cultural backgrounds out of their concrete-and-asphalt environs and into the natural world.
>
> — MARK MARDON, "City Kids Go Wild"

COMPARISON AND CONTRAST

When you *compare*, you identify the similarities between two or more things; when you *contrast*, you identify the differences between things. Sometimes the focus is on one or the other, but at other times both similarities and differences are included.

Writers use comparison and contrast to clarify relationships. How are people, places, or ideas alike? How are they different? For example, in the following paragraph, the author writes about the voluntary separation between black and white students at his high school. He contrasts the distance he now feels from his black friend with the closeness he felt when they were younger:

> Ten years ago, we played catch in our backyards, went bike riding, and slept over at one another's houses. By the fifth grade, we went to movies and amusement parks, and bunked together at the same summer camps. We met while playing on the same Little League team, though we attended different grade schools. We're both juniors now at the same high school. We usually don't say anything when we see each other, except maybe a polite "Hi" or "Hey." I can't remember the last time we talked on the phone, much less got together outside of school.
>
> — BRIAN JARVIS, "Against the Great Divide"

When you write a comparison, you can order your ideas point by point or subject by subject. Point-by-point organization means that you explain two topics according to points of comparison. For instance, you can compare two coworkers by examining their work habits, personalities, and professionalism. Each section in the body of the essay focuses on one of the points.

First section: work habits
 Explain work habits of coworker 1
 Explain work habits of coworker 2
Second section: personalities
 Explain personality of coworker 1
 Explain personality of coworker 2
Third section: professionalism
 Explain professionalism of coworker 1
 Explain professionalism of coworker 2

Alternatively, you can organize your ideas subject by subject; each coworker is discussed only once in the body of the essay.

First section: coworker 1
 Work habits, personality, professionalism
Second section: coworker 2
 Work habits, personality, professionalism

GROUP ACTIVITY 3: Find Similar Subjects for Comparison

Work with your classmates on the following list of subjects. For each main subject, identify three similar subjects that could be used to make a comparison.

EXAMPLE: SUBJECT: Ford Explorer

SIMILAR SUBJECTS: Cadillac Escalade, Lincoln Navigator, Hummer H2 _____

1. Subject: The movie *X-Men*

 Similar subjects: _____

2. Subject: McDonald's

 Similar subjects: _____

3. Subject: Buffalo wings

 Similar subjects: _____

4. Subject: Wal-Mart

 Similar subjects: _____

CAUSE AND EFFECT

When you use *cause and effect*, you explain why something happened (the cause) and what the result of it was (the effect). Writers use cause and effect to show a necessary or logical connection between two things. It is not enough to say that two things happened at the same time. For example, if a freeze ruins the orange crop and orange prices go up, that's cause and effect. If there also happens to be a full moon on the night of the freeze, that's a coincidence. It is the freeze, not the full moon, that ruins the crop.

In the following paragraph, the author explains the problems that arise when people unfairly stereotype each other. He shows a clear and logical connection between the cause (stereotyping) and the effect (a loss of individuality).

> Hence, quite aside from the injustice which stereotypes do to others, they impoverish ourselves. A person who lumps the world into simple categories, who typecasts all labor leaders as "racketeers," all businessmen as "reactionaries," all Harvard men as "snobs," and all Frenchmen as "sexy," is in danger of becoming a stereotype himself. He loses his capacity to be himself — which is to say, to see the world in his own absolutely unique, inimitable, and independent fashion.
>
> — ROBERT L. HEILBRONER, "Don't Let Stereotypes Warp Your Judgments"

ARGUMENT

When you make an *argument*, you try to persuade readers to change their perspectives or alter their behavior in some way. In a paragraph that uses the argument pattern, the topic sentence contains the *claim*, or your argumentative point. The rest of the paragraph contains *reasons* and *evidence* that justify the claim.

In the following paragraph, the writer uses reasons and evidence to support his claim that a disproportionate number of poor people are given the death penalty:

> The death penalty is not only racist but inegalitarian. Most prisoners on death row come from the poorest classes, those excluded from American society. They're criminals, we are told. Without a doubt. But has the society that puts them to death really given them the same chance as those more fortunate? Moreover, capital punishment strikes mainly those who don't

have the money to hire competent, motivated and well-paid lawyers. Financial inequality before the law can lead to the worst possible consequences. Do Americans know that during a period of almost 20 years after the U.S. reinstated the death penalty, the overall rate of prejudicial error in the capital punishment system was 68%? Worse still, many innocent people have been condemned to death. Some have been saved in extremis, but how many others have been executed without anyone asking for a reconsideration of the trial? If a crime that goes unpunished is a challenge to society, the execution of an innocent person is the worst act that any community of free men can commit. It is the complete negation of justice. What kind of justice is it that, in order to avenge victims, becomes criminal itself by executing innocent people?

— ROBERT BADINTER, "Death Be Not Proud"

HOW TO Use the Patterns of Development

- Write a topic sentence that supports your thesis statement.

- Support each topic sentence with details that increase interest and help the readers understand your main point.

- Use patterns of development such as description, narration, examples, process explanation, classification, definition, comparison and contrast, cause and effect, and argument.

- Add or delete sentences to improve your paragraph.

- Write a concluding sentence.

GROUP ACTIVITY 4: Develop Ideas Using Definition, Comparison and Contrast, Cause and Effect, or Argument

Following are several topic sentences. For each one, decide with your group whether you will use definition, comparison and contrast, cause and effect, or argument as the primary method of development. Then use that method to develop the topic sentence into a brief paragraph.

1. The meaning of *love* differs from person to person.

    Primary method of development: _____

2. Since the implementation of the TV show rating system, violence in children's programming has decreased.

   Primary method of development: _____

3. Cheerleading is a sport in its own right, not just a peppy sideshow for the football game.

   Primary method of development: _____

4. Both my boss and my best friend are total introverts.

   Primary method of development: _____

CHAPTER CHECKLIST

❑ The patterns of development help readers make sense of your thoughts.

❑ Description helps readers picture your ideas.

❑ Narration allows you to tell a story.

❑ Examples let you clarify, explain, and support ideas.

❑ Process explanation helps you to explain how something works or how to do something.

❑ Classification leads you to categorize something into types.

❑ Definition allows you to tell the reader what something means.

❑ Comparison and contrast lets you explain similarities and differences.

❑ Cause and effect helps you to explain why something happened and its result.

❑ Argument lets you persuade readers to change their perspective or perform an action.

REFLECTING ON YOUR WRITING

To help you reflect on the writing you did in this chapter, answer the following questions:

1. Which patterns of development did you use in your essay about managing your time and balancing work, school, family, and friends? Why?

2. Which pattern do you think is the easiest to use? The hardest to use? Why?

3. How will learning about the patterns of development help you as a writer?

Using your answers to these questions, complete a Writing Process Report for this chapter (you can download a report form at **bedford stmartins.com/choices**). Once you complete this report, freewrite about what you learned in this chapter about the patterns of development and what you still hope to learn.

PART TWO

Writing to Share Ideas

4. Explaining a Personal Change: *Using Description and Narration*

5. Examining a Culture: *Using Examples and Process Explanation*

6. Investigating a Workplace: *Using Classification and Definition*

7. Evaluating a Subject: *Using Comparison and Contrast*

8. Considering the Media: *Using Cause and Effect*

9. Making a Difference: *Using Argument*

Writing provides a permanent record of our ideas. Writing also allows us to communicate with others and to share what we know in ways that entertain, inform, and persuade.

In Part Two, you'll learn how to improve your writing as you write to share your ideas. You'll experiment with different methods of gathering ideas and practice writing discovery drafts. You'll learn how to revise and how to use the patterns of development to expand and organize your thoughts. You'll improve your sentences and learn how to choose just the right word to communicate what you want to say. You'll edit your writing to ensure that you communicate your ideas clearly. Finally, you'll share your writing with an audience.

4

Explaining a Personal Change

Using Description and Narration

In this chapter, you will write about a significant person, event, or period in your life. As you follow the steps of the writing process, you will

- **Gather ideas by brainstorming, relating aloud, and clustering.**

- **Develop your ideas using description and narration.**

- **Practice writing effective thesis statements, topic sentences, and unified paragraphs.**

- **Combine sentences with coordinating conjunctions.**

- **Learn how to correct run-on sentences.**

- **Share your essay with your classmates.**

We all have memories of the important people and events in our lives. Some of these memories are happy: a supportive mentor, the birth of a child, a special vacation. Others are less pleasant: a cruel coworker, a serious traffic accident, or a long-term illness.

Although memories may be pleasant or unpleasant, they change who we are and how we see ourselves. To a great extent, we are all defined by the important people, events, and times in our lives. In this chapter, you will learn how to write an essay that shows how someone or something in your past has changed you. Exploring your own memories in writing will help you better understand who you are and what is meaningful to you.

Once you have written about your personal history, you can share your written memories with the people who are close to you. This is what good writing is about — communicating something important to readers so that they are better informed.

GROUP ACTIVITY 1: Think about Personal Changes

The family in the photograph on page 78 represents three generations: grandmother, father, and children. What does the photograph tell you about this family? What can you tell about the family members from the expressions on their faces as they look at a photo album? What memories might they be sharing? Share with your classmates some of your own memories of significant people, events, and periods of your life.

READING ESSAYS ABOUT PERSONAL CHANGES

Reading is an excellent way to start thinking about a topic. Learning other people's stories may spark some memories from your own past. At the same time, examining what others have written will help you discover new strategies for sharing your ideas. Before you start work on your own essay, read the following short essays about how a significant person, a memorable event, or an important period changed someone. As you read, pay close attention to how the writers use description and narration to explain their thoughts to their readers.

A Significant Person

JOSHUA BELL

My Maestro

Joshua Bell became interested in music at an early age. His parents, eager to encourage their son's interests, gave him his first violin when he was four years old. Even though he liked to play computer games, basketball, and tennis, by the age of twelve he was committed to play-ing the violin. When he was fourteen, he made his professional debut with the Philadelphia Orchestra and later toured with major orches-tras in the United States, Europe, Australia, and Asia. He has recorded numerous classical works and played with musical legends such as the cellist Yo-Yo Ma. In this essay, Bell credits his maestro, or master teacher, Josef Gingold, for showing him that music could be "more than a hobby."

1   As a boy, I played the violin surrounded by ghosts. My teacher, Josef Gingold, plastered his Bloomington, Ind., studio walls with autographed photos of musical greats he admired or had met on his travels. Their faces watched our music-making, and inspired my small fingers to coax songs from the strings.

2   When I became Gingold's pupil at age 12, he was already a legend at Indiana University, a gregarious Old World exile who had played under Arturo Toscanini and George Szell.

3   We almost didn't meet. The day before my first solo recital — which someone had convinced him to attend — I was tossing a boomerang at my parents' farm. My mother fretted whether this was wise. Sure enough, the boomerang whirled back and sliced my chin open. The ER doctor stitched me up. Two inches to the left and I couldn't have held my violin. But I played, wounded.

4   Gingold liked what he heard. I enrolled in a chamber music program he taught that summer in upstate New York. There, I realized I had never met anyone who found music so fun. He would play two parts of a string quartet at once. He laughed and laughed, and I left those lessons buzzing. My parents saw my excitement, and asked Gingold to continue to teach me back at home. He was wary. Too many children had been pushed on the violin, Gingold thought, and were living others' dreams. But he let me try.

5   So I went to his studio with the ghosts on the walls, to enter the long tradition of one musician's hands guiding another's. My teacher taught me that music could be more than a hobby. It could be a life.

6   Born in Russia in 1909, he came to America in 1920 and studied violin with Vladimir Graffman. In 1937 he won a spot in

the NBC Symphony Orchestra, and later was the Cleveland Orchestra's concertmaster.

But Gingold found his true calling as a teacher. He was a   7
musical inspiration for kids, who brought him joy. Unlike many maestros, he refused to scold his students, a decision that stemmed from a childhood horror. As a boy, he had once played his violin at a school assembly. His fellow students loved it, and applauded for so long the principal had to order them to stop. Later, Gingold's art teacher pulled him aside. "Let me see your hands," she said. "Are those the hands that made that beautiful music?" He beamed, so proud to be recognized for what he could do. Then she took a wooden pointer, smacking his palm so hard it damaged a nerve. Years later, he still felt pain. The teacher had decided he shouldn't feel so good about himself. That stuck with him. He went the opposite way with his students.

Sometimes I wish he had been more strict. I was a kid, I   8
goofed off. He wanted me to have a normal childhood and was secretly pleased when my mother told him I'd spent all day playing video games instead of music. During my afternoon lessons, we'd take breaks and listen to records. He let me play his Stradivarius. I was amazed by the depth of sound, the colors floating from that instrument. He helped me create a very personal relationship with music, but he did not teach me how to play every note. Many teachers have students copy all their fingerings. Gingold gave me the tools to teach myself — chamber music, solos, anything.

I studied with him for nine years, and he became the grand-   9
father I didn't have. In my family, everyone played an instrument. During holidays, we gathered for informal concerts we called musicales. One year, Gingold joined us. He invited some of his international students to come play too. He led our little orchestra most of the night in this multicultural circle of warmth and music, tucked away from the Indiana cold. He couldn't stop smiling. With Toscanini or in a crowded living room, he was happy if he had a violin in hand.

Gingold didn't pull strings to further my career, but I pushed   10
myself. Soon the spotlight found me. I made my professional debut at 14, playing Mozart's Third Violin Concerto with the Philadelphia Orchestra. He flew to see me. At 17, I played at Carnegie Hall, and he saw me there, too, smiling like a proud grandpa.

When I moved to New York at 21, I couldn't see Gingold as   11
much as I'd have liked. His health was failing, and I dreaded the day he would leave me. On New Year's, 1995, I paid him a visit, bringing a photo of him I wanted autographed, to hang on my wall like the ghosts on his. I walked into his house, and in his hand he had one last gift for me — a rare picture of Niccolò Paganini, the crown jewel of his studio collection. He signed his own photo. I played. We talked through that last wonderful

afternoon. The next day he had a stroke. He died two weeks later.

Early success can be dangerous for a musician. You hear of prodigies who rise fast and flame out. Sometimes that's because teachers spoon-feed these young people every musical idea. At some point they feel they don't need teaching anymore, so they stop learning. Gingold was always learning. So am I. 12

Someday I want to teach too. Gingold's ghost — the autographed photo on my wall hung next to Paganini — will be watching. 13

READING ACTIVITY 1: Build Your Vocabulary

Determine the meanings of the following words from the context of Joshua Bell's essay. Then check their meanings by looking up the words in a dictionary: gregarious (2), fretted (3), wary (4), maestros (7), Stradivarius (8), fingerings (8), prodigies (12).

READING ACTIVITY 2: Read to Improve Your Writing

Discuss the following questions about "My Maestro" with your classmates.

1. Why is Josef Gingold a significant person in Bell's life? Where does Bell express this main point?
2. Reread the paragraph about Gingold's childhood experience at a school assembly (7). How does this story help explain why Gingold is special to Bell?
3. What do you want to know about Josef Gingold that the writer doesn't tell you?
4. What details does Bell use to show how his violin teacher influenced his life?

A Memorable Event

JAMES DILLARD

A Doctor's Dilemma

James Dillard is a professor at Columbia University College of Physicians and Surgeons and is clinical director of Columbia's Rosenthal Center for Complementary and Alternative Medicine. Dillard is recognized as one of America's leading authorities on pain and pain management, a topic on which he has written several books, including Alternative Medicine for Dummies *(1998) and* The Chronic Pain Solution *(2002). In this essay, Dillard describes how and why — as a doctor in training — he helped an accident victim in spite of the risks that a potential malpractice lawsuit could pose to his career in medicine.*

1   It was a bright, clear February afternoon in Gettysburg. A strong sun and layers of down did little to ease the biting cold. Our climb to the crest of Little Roundtop wound past somber monuments, barren trees and polished cannon. From the top, we peered down on the wheat field where men had fallen so close together that one could not see the ground. Rifle balls had whined as thick as bee swarms through the trees, and cannon shots had torn limbs from the young men fighting there. A frozen wind whipped tears from our eyes. My friend Amy huddled close, using me as a wind breaker. Despite the cold, it was hard to leave this place.

2   Driving east out of Gettysburg on a country blacktop, the gray Bronco ahead of us passed through a rural crossroad just as a small pickup truck tried to take a left turn. The Bronco swerved, but slammed into the pickup on the passenger side. We immediately slowed to a crawl as we passed the scene. The Bronco's driver looked fine, but we couldn't see the driver of the pickup. I pulled over on the shoulder and got out to investigate.

3   The right side of the truck was smashed in, and the side window was shattered. The driver was partly out of the truck. His head hung forward over the edge of the passenger-side window, the front of his neck crushed on the shattered windowsill. He was unconscious and starting to turn a dusky blue. His chest slowly heaved against a blocked windpipe.

4   A young man ran out of a house at the crossroad. "Get an ambulance out here," I shouted against the wind. "Tell them a man is dying."

5   I looked down again at the driver hanging from the windowsill. There were six empty beer bottles on the floor of the truck. I could smell the beer through the window. I knew I had to move him, to open his airway. I had no idea what neck injuries he had sustained. He could easily end up a quadriplegic. But I thought: he'll be dead by the time the ambulance gets here if I don't move him and try to do something to help him.

6   An image flashed before my mind. I could see the courtroom and the driver of the truck sitting in a wheelchair. I could see his attorney pointing at me and thundering at the jury: "This young doctor, with still a year left in his residency training, took it upon himself to play God. He took it upon himself to move this gravely injured man, condemning him forever to this wheelchair. . . ." I imagined the millions of dollars in award money. And all the years of hard work lost. I'd be paying him off for the rest of my life. Amy touched my shoulder. "What are you going to do?"

The automatic response from long hours in the emergency 7
room kicked in. I pulled off my overcoat and rolled up my
sleeves. The trick would be to keep enough traction straight up
on his head while I moved his torso, so that his probable broken
neck and spinal-cord injury wouldn't be made worse. Amy came
around the driver's side, climbed half in and grabbed his belt
and shirt collar. Together we lifted him off the windowsill.

He was still out cold, limp as a rag doll. His throat was 8
crushed and blood from the jugular vein was running down my
arms. He still couldn't breathe. He was deep blue-magenta now,
his pulse was rapid and thready. The stench of alcohol turned
my stomach, but I positioned his jaw and tried to blow air down
into his lungs. It wouldn't go.

Amy had brought some supplies from my car. I opened an 9
oversize intravenous needle and groped on the man's neck. My
hands were numb, covered with freezing blood and bits of broken glass. Hyoid bone — God, I can't even feel the thyroid carti-
lage, it's gone. . . . OK, the thyroid gland is about there, cricoid
rings are here. . . . we'll go in right here. . . .

It was a lucky first shot. Pink air sprayed through the IV 10
needle. I placed a second needle next to the first. The air began
whistling through it. Almost immediately, the driver's face
turned bright red. After a minute, his pulse slowed down and
his eyes moved slightly. I stood up, took a step back and looked
down. He was going to make it. He was going to live. A siren
wailed in the distance. I turned and saw Amy holding my overcoat. I was shivering and my arms were turning white with cold.

The ambulance captain looked around and bellowed, "What 11
the hell . . . who did this?" as his team scurried over to the man
lying in the truck.

"I did," I replied. He took down my name and address for 12
his reports. I had just destroyed my career. I would never be
able to finish my residency with a massive lawsuit pending. My
life was over.

The truckdriver was strapped onto a backboard, his neck in 13
a stiff collar. The ambulance crew had controlled the bleeding
and started intravenous fluid. He was slowly waking up. As they
loaded him into the ambulance, I saw him move his feet. Maybe
my future wasn't lost.

A police sergeant called me from Pennsylvania three weeks 14
later. Six days after successful throat-reconstruction surgery,
the driver had signed out, against medical advice, from the hospital because he couldn't get a drink on the ward. He was being
arraigned on drunk-driving charges.

A few days later, I went into the office of one of my senior 15
professors, to tell the story. He peered over his half glasses and
his eyes narrowed. "Well, you did the right thing medically of
course. But, James, do you know what you put at risk by doing
that?" he said sternly. "What was I supposed to do?" I asked.

"Drive on," he replied. "There is an army of lawyers out 16

there who would stand in line to get a case like that. If that driver had turned out to be a quadriplegic, you might never have practiced medicine again. You were a very lucky young man."

The day I graduated from medical school, I took an oath to   17
serve the sick and the injured. I remember truly believing I would be able to do just that. But I have found out it isn't so simple. I understand now what a foolish thing I did that day. Despite my oath, I know what I would do on that cold roadside near Gettysburg today. I would drive on.

READING ACTIVITY 3: Build Your Vocabulary

Determine the meanings of the following words from the context of James Dillard's essay. Then check their meanings by looking up the words in a dictionary: somber (1), dusky (3), heaved (3), sustained (5), quadriplegic (5), thundering (6), gravely (6), condemning (6), traction (7), magenta (8), thready (8), intravenous (9), arraigned (14).

READING ACTIVITY 4: Read to Improve Your Writing

Discuss the following questions about "A Doctor's Dilemma" with your classmates.

1. What is Dillard's thesis? Does he regret helping the victim of a car accident? Why or why not?

2. Examine how the author orders the events in his story. Why does he include details about things that happened before and after he helped the truck driver?

3. Compare how Dillard feels about this event now — as a licensed medical doctor — with how he felt about it as a medical student.

4. Reread paragraph 8, in which Dillard describes the truck driver's body. How does the author's use of description help explain why he was willing to risk his medical career?

An Important Period

MALCOLM X

Prison Studies

Malcolm X (1925–1965) rose from a world of street crime in the Harlem section of New York City to become one of the most powerful African American leaders of the civil rights movement in the 1960s. On February 21, 1965, at the age of thirty-nine, he was shot and killed. Malcolm X told his life story in The Autobiography of

Malcolm X (1964), written with the assistance of Alex Haley (1921–1992), author of the slave saga Roots *(1976). The following selection from* The Autobiography *refers to a period that Malcolm X spent in federal prison. In the selection, Malcolm X explains how his inability to express himself led him to learn how to read and write.*

Many who today hear me somewhere in person, or on television, or those who read something I've said, will think I went to school far beyond the eighth grade. This impression is due entirely to my prison studies. 1

It had really begun back in the Charlestown Prison, when Bimbi first made me feel envy of his stock of knowledge. Bimbi had always taken charge of any conversation he was in, and I had tried to emulate him. But every book I picked up had few sentences which didn't contain anywhere from one to nearly all of the words that might as well have been in Chinese. When I just skipped those words, of course, I really ended up with little idea of what the book said. So I had come to the Norfolk Prison Colony still going through only book-reading motions. Pretty soon, I would have quit even these motions, unless I had received the motivation that I did. 2

I saw that the best thing I could do was get hold of a dictionary — to study, to learn some words. I was lucky enough to reason also that I should try to improve my penmanship. It was sad. I couldn't even write in a straight line. It was both ideas together that moved me to request a dictionary along with some tablets and pencils from the Norfolk Prison Colony school. I spent two days just riffling uncertainly through the dictionary's pages. I'd never realized so many words existed! I didn't know which words I needed to learn. Finally, to start some kind of action, I began copying. 3

In my slow, painstaking, ragged handwriting, I copied into my tablet everything printed on that first page, down to the punctuation marks. 4

I believe it took me a day. Then, aloud, I read back, to myself, everything I'd written on the tablet. Over and over, aloud, to myself, I read my own handwriting. 5

I woke up the next morning, thinking about those words — immensely proud to realize that not only had I written so much at one time, but I'd written words that I never knew were in the world. Moreover, with a little effort, I also could remember what many of these words meant. I reviewed the words whose meanings I didn't remember. Funny thing, from the dictionary first page right now, that *aardvark* springs to my mind. The dictionary had a picture of it, a long-tailed, long-eared, burrowing African mammal, which lives off termites caught by sticking out its tongue as an anteater does for ants. 6

I was so fascinated that I went on — I copied the dictionary's next page. And the same experience came when I studied 7 that. With every succeeding page, I also learned of people and places and events from history. Actually the dictionary is like a miniature encyclopedia. Finally the dictionary's A section had filled a whole tablet — and I went on into the B's. That was the way I started copying what eventually became the entire dictionary. It went a lot faster after so much practice helped me to pick up handwriting speed. Between what I wrote in my tablet, and writing letters, during the rest of my time in prison I would guess I wrote a million words.

I suppose it was inevitable that as my word-base broadened, 8 I could for the first time pick up a book and read and now begin to understand what the book was saying. Anyone who has read a great deal can imagine the new world that opened. Let me tell you something: from then until I left that prison, in every free moment I had, if I was not reading in the library, I was reading on my bunk. You couldn't have gotten me out of books with a wedge. Between Mr. Muhammad's teachings, my correspondence, my visitors — usually Ella and Reginald — and my reading of books, months passed without my even thinking about being imprisoned. In fact, up to then, I never had been so truly free in my life. . . .

As you can imagine, especially in a prison where there was 9 heavy emphasis on rehabilitation, an inmate was smiled upon if he demonstrated an unusually intense interest in books. There was a sizable number of well-read inmates, especially the popular debaters. Some were said by many to be practically walking encyclopedias. They were almost celebrities. No university would ask any student to devour literature as I did when this new world opened to me, of being able to read and understand.

I read more in my room than in the library itself. An inmate 10 who was known to read a lot could check out more than the permitted maximum number of books. I preferred reading in the total isolation of my own room.

When I had progressed to really serious reading, every night 11 at about ten P.M. I would be outraged with the "lights out." It always seemed to catch me right in the middle of something engrossing.

Fortunately, right outside my door was a corridor light that 12 cast a glow into my room. The glow was enough to read by, once my eyes adjusted to it. So when "lights out" came, I would sit on the floor where I could continue reading in that glow.

At one-hour intervals the night guards paced past every 13 room. Each time I heard the approaching footsteps, I jumped into bed and feigned sleep. And as soon as the guard passed, I got back out of bed onto the floor area of that light-glow, where I would read for another fifty-eight minutes — until the guard approached again. That went on until three or four every morning. Three or four hours of sleep a night was enough for me. Often in the years in the streets I had slept less than that.

I have often reflected upon the new vistas that reading   14
opened to me. I knew right there in prison that reading had
changed forever the course of my life. As I see it today, the ability to read awoke inside me some long dormant craving to be
mentally alive. I certainly wasn't seeking any degree, the way a
college confers a status symbol upon its students. My home-
made education gave me, with every additional book that I read,
a little bit more sensitivity to the deafness, dumbness, and
blindness that was afflicting the black race in America. Not long
ago, an English writer telephoned me from London, asking
questions. One was, "What's your alma mater?" I told him,
"Books." You will never catch me with a free fifteen minutes in
which I'm not studying something I feel might be able to help
the black man. . . .

Every time I catch a plane, I have with me a book that I   15
want to read — and that's a lot of books these days. If I weren't
out here every day battling the white man, I could spend the
rest of my life reading, just satisfying my curiosity — because
you can hardly mention anything I'm not curious about. I don't
think anybody ever got more out of going to prison than I did.
In fact, prison enabled me to study far more intensively than
I would have if my life had gone differently and I had attended some college. I imagine that one of the biggest troubles
with colleges is there are too many distractions, too much
panty-raiding, fraternities, and boola-boola and all of that.
Where else but in prison could I have attacked my ignorance by
being able to study intensely sometimes as much as fifteen
hours a day?

READING ACTIVITY 5: Build Your Vocabulary

Determine the meanings of the following words from the context of
Malcolm X's essay. Then check their meanings by looking up the
words in a dictionary: emulate (2), painstaking (4), inevitable (8),
engrossing (11), intervals (13), feigned (13), vistas (14), dormant (14).

READING ACTIVITY 6: Read to Improve Your Writing

Discuss the following questions about "Prison Studies" with your
classmates.

1. In what ways is the period of time spent reading significant in
   Malcolm X's life?

2. How do you think this period in the author's life affected him after
   his release from prison?

3. Which details about Malcolm X's prison life do you find especially
   interesting? Why?

4. Go through Malcolm X's essay, and underline his topic sentences. Does the author include any details that don't directly support these points? If so, how do these details affect your response to his essay? Would "Prison Studies" be better or worse without them?

Writing Assignment

What made you the person you are today? Introduce yourself to your classmates and your instructor by writing a brief essay that explains how something in your past changed your sense of who you are and what's important to you. You (or your instructor) may decide to approach this assignment in one of several ways:

■ Write about a person who has had an impact on you.

OR

■ Write about an event that was memorable for you.

OR

■ Write about an important period in your life.

Follow the guidance and activities in this chapter to discover, develop, and polish your ideas into a finished essay that readers will find interesting and expressive.

STEP 1. EXPLORE YOUR CHOICES

If you're like most people, choosing something to write about is a challenge. Of all the people you have known and things you have experienced, how can you possibly pick one to help explain who you are? Before you choose a topic to write about, you first will think about who your readers are and what you want them to know about you. Then you will learn some techniques for gathering ideas and use those techniques to explore the three major topic possibilities (people, events, or time periods) presented in this chapter. Experimenting with your options will help you to identify the most promising topic to write about and to find good details to support your ideas.

Analyzing Your Audience and Purpose

You are writing an essay about a significant person, a memorable event, or an important period in your life because you want the other students in your class to know you better. Your classmates are your readers. Before you write for this audience, consider what you know about them as well as what they already know about you. What do you want your classmates to learn about you?

For more on audience and purpose, see pp. 8–12.

Consider also the kind of essay that will help you explain something in your life that changed you. You may want to express your thoughts and feelings about someone important, as Joshua Bell does in "My Maestro," or like James Dillard you might inform your readers of something you learned. You might even want to persuade your classmates to think differently about something that matters to you, as Malcolm X does in "Prison Studies." Understanding what your purpose is will help you write an essay that accomplishes that goal.

WRITING ACTIVITY 1: Analyze Your Audience and Purpose

Your responses to the following questions will help you decide how to approach this chapter's assignment.

1. Does the assignment call for primarily expressive, informative, or persuasive writing?
2. What is the average age of your audience?
3. How many readers are female? How many are male?
4. What parts of the country or world are they from?
5. How many have had experiences like yours?
6. In what ways are your readers similar to or different from you?
7. How will these similarities and differences with your readers affect the way you write your essay?

Gathering Ideas

When you gather ideas, or *prewrite*, you explore your thoughts about a topic without worrying about where those thoughts will lead you. Many different methods can help you discover ideas before you write. In this chapter, you will review three of these methods (brainstorming, relating aloud, and clustering) and use each method to explore one of the three possible topics: a significant person, a memorable event, or an important period in your life. As you practice these

For more on ways of gathering ideas, see pp. 12–16.

techniques, you may decide to apply the ones that work best for you to your other topic choices as well.

Brainstorming about a Significant Person

One of the most productive techniques for gathering ideas is *brainstorming*. When you brainstorm, you write down everything that comes to mind without judging which ideas are better than others or how they might connect. Instead, you express as many thoughts as possible so that you can go back and select the ones that are most helpful.

Think about the significant people in your life. Who would you name? You might name your parents, a partner, a teacher, or a friend. You might even remember an acquaintance or a stranger you met only once but who nevertheless gave you a new perspective at a critical time in your life. Whomever you choose, the person should be someone who has influenced your sense of who you are and who you strive to be.

If you have trouble thinking of things to write about someone who is important to you, answering the following questions can help you get started:

- How would you describe this person to someone who has never met him or her?
- How would you describe some of the places you have visited with this person?
- What special objects do you associate with this person? Why?
- What song, book, or movie do you associate with this person? Why?
- What holidays or other special occasions are memorable because of this person? Why?
- How do you feel when you think of this person? Describe these feelings.
- Why is this person important to you?

Here's how one student writer, Jesus Ramirez, brainstormed about his father. He started by answering a few of the questions listed above, and wrote down other ideas as they occurred to him.

My father
short (5' 6"), green eyes, brown hair, lots of hair
in good shape
kind
understanding
always tries to be helpful

soft-spoken, but firm!
doesn't talk much, but when he does everyone listens!
we've been so many places together that it's hard to name only a few:
    grandparents' house
    Uncle Jim's
    church
    the mall
    auto-parts store
    Disneyland
    fishing
    baseball games
rents movies for us to watch together
Field of Dreams — dad loves baseball so much that if he had a
cornfield he'd turn it into a baseball field, too
anything about baseball
Cardinals' cap
remote control
favorite chair
newspaper
coffee mug

Brainstorm on Computer

To gather ideas through brainstorming, create a word-processing file, and type the questions about a significant person that are listed on page 92. Once you have entered the questions, brainstorm the answers, and save your file.

WRITING ACTIVITY 2: Brainstorm about a Significant Person

Think of someone who has meant a lot to you, and write or type that person's name at the top of a page. Then brainstorm whatever comes to mind. You may use the questions on page 92 to get started, but follow whatever direction your mind takes you.

Relating a Memorable Event

In addition to the people in your life, events have changed you in some way. Whether you did something to make these events happen (such as earning a scholarship or running a marathon) or saw them change your life unexpectedly (such as discovering a talent or learning you need surgery), such moments have influenced who you are.

One good way to explore ideas about an important event is to *relate* it — to talk about it with other people. By simply sharing a story or a thought orally without the pressure of having to write it down, you will usually discover that you have quite a bit to say about it. At the same time, you have the advantage of an audience that can provide immediate feedback — giving you a sense of what will interest your readers and how you can best explain your ideas.

After thinking about some of the important events in her life, student writer Karla Jaramillo decided that her classmates might be interested in the time her mother almost died. Karla told them about that event as another student took notes. This is her story:

> It all began on my first day in fifth grade. I wanted to go shopping for school supplies. My mom didn't really want to take me, but I just had to get some things. My older sister Ana offered to drive since my mom has heart trouble, and my mom decided she wanted to go with us after all. We spotted another one of my sisters, Mary, driving my Dad's truck. We knew she could only be going to her boyfriend's house. My mom had forbidden Mary to see him because he was separated but not divorced. "Do you want me to follow her?" Ana asked. My mother said yes.
>
> At last the truck stopped and Mary went to the front door of the house. Her boyfriend came out and hugged her. My mother was hysterical! She leaped out of the car and ran toward the house, yelling at Mary to get in the car. Mary kept screaming, "I hate you! I hate you!" Then mom sank to the ground. She began to gasp for breath.
>
> Mary's boyfriend called 911, and Mom was taken to the hospital. I was really scared. I thought my mother was going to die. I prayed hard, and we all cried a lot. After a while, things turned out all right. She had had a heart attack, but she was going to live.

Karla's story prompted many questions from her peer response group. For example, one student asked, "Did your mom and sister make up?" Others asked, "Can you remember anything else that was said?" and "How did you feel during all of this?" Finally, someone asked Karla why this event was significant to her.

Relating the event aloud and reading over her classmate's notes from the discussion helped Karla focus on the details and understand what the story meant to her. Answering the group's questions also helped Karla identify her main idea: although it was a terrible crisis, her mother's heart attack brought the family closer together.

WRITING ACTIVITY 3: Relate a Memorable Event

Working with a small group, relate a memorable event out loud. The moment may be happy or sad, but it should have markedly affected who you are. Ask someone to take notes on your story, or use a recording device. When you finish relating aloud, respond to the group's questions about your topic. Then read over your classmate's notes from the discussion (or listen to the recording) to gather additional ideas.

Clustering about an Important Period

Unlike an *event,* which occurs at a specific time or on a particular day, a *period* includes events that take place over a long time. For example, you could write about a summer that you spent away from home, your first six months of marriage, or the year that you shed a significant amount of weight.

Clustering is another useful technique that can help you gather and organize your thoughts. Especially if you're a visual thinker, drawing connections can open your eyes to fresh ways of looking at something.

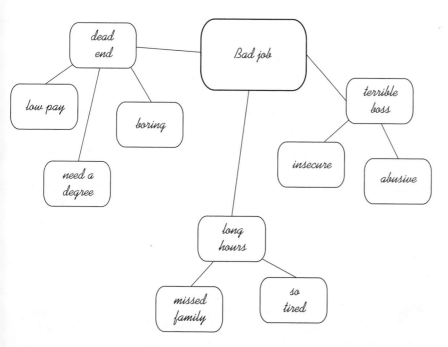

FIGURE 4.1.   Maria's Clustering

To begin clustering about an important time in your life, write a word or phrase that describes that time in the center of a blank page, and draw a circle around the word. As ideas about the topic come to mind, write them down, put circles around them, and draw lines from them to the center circle. As you think of ways to describe your ideas, write down the descriptions, circle them, and join these circles to the ideas they describe.

Student writer Maria Talberg clustered her ideas about an important period in her life — the three years she worked at a job that made her so unhappy that she decided to return to college. (See Fig 4.1, p. 95.)

WRITING ACTIVITY 4: Cluster about an Important Period in Your Life

Spend a few minutes thinking about a time in your life that was very happy or very unhappy and that had a profound effect on who you are today. In the center of a blank page, write a word (or phrase) that describes that time, and draw a circle around the word. Then write down any words or phrases about the period that occur to you, and draw lines to connect related ideas. For each word or phrase you write, try to think of additional words and phrases related to them.

STEP 2. WRITE YOUR DISCOVERY DRAFT

For more on drafting, see pp. 16–21.

It's time to move to the stage of the writing process where you put your ideas together so that you can see what you have to work with.

When you write a discovery draft, you aim to explore possibilities rather than follow a map that's already been drawn. You might find that your thoughts take you in an unexpected direction: follow the path that seems most interesting to you. You'll have time later on to revise and edit your discovery draft.

Draft on Computer

If possible, use a word-processing program to write your discovery draft. Having a draft on computer will make revising your essay much quicker and easier.

Choosing a Topic

You have gathered ideas on three possible topics — a significant person, a memorable event, and an important period in your life — that changed you in a meaningful way. Before you can begin drafting, you must choose one topic to write about.

Review all of the material you compiled as you gathered ideas, and look for a promising topic that you can develop into an essay that explains how something changed you. You might discover that one option — a person, an event, or a period — gave you the best ideas. On the other hand, if you find that one theme emerged as you explored different topics, consider creating a topic that combines two or three ideas. For example, you might connect your significant person with a significant event or period in your life. Whatever you decide to do, be sure to choose a topic that you have many ideas about and that will interest both you and your readers.

Student writer Jesus decided to write about a significant person — his father — but he was also drawn to write about what attending baseball games with his father meant to their relationship. This combined topic allowed Jesus to provide supporting details and thereby develop his ideas more fully in his discovery draft.

WRITING ACTIVITY 5: Choose Your Topic

Review your brainstorming, notes made by your classmates when you related aloud to other students, and your clustering. Based on the ideas you have gathered, decide which topic will be most interesting for you and your readers (and make sure you have something to say about it). To ensure that you have generated enough details to support a draft, you may want to do more brainstorming, relating aloud, and clustering on the topic of your choice.

Sharing Your Ideas

When you begin drafting, try to write a preliminary thesis statement that indicates the main point of your essay. You then can use this statement as a guide while you write. As you draft, feel free to use ideas that you have already gathered and to add new ones as they come to you. Remember that your main goal at the drafting stage is to get your ideas down on paper. You'll revise and edit your essay later.

Use E-mail or Networked Discussion
E-mail your discovery draft to your fellow students for feedback. Alternatively, if you have access to a networked computer lab, discuss your draft online with other students in the

class, on your campus, or even at different colleges. Whether you e-mail or discuss the draft online, ask your readers (1) what interested them the most about your draft and (2) what they want to know more about. Use their responses to help you decide where to add supporting details.

Student writer Jesus, whose brainstorming you saw earlier in the chapter, wrote the following preliminary thesis statement and discovery draft about going to baseball games with his father. (Note that Jesus's draft includes the types of errors that typically appear in a first draft.)

<u>Preliminary thesis statement</u>: My father taught me valuable lessons.

I love this sport because of my father. My father is the reason I love baseball. He cares for his family. He's always putting them above everything else. He works hard at his job so that we have all of the necessities of life. He loves to rent videos for us to watch, too. Ever since I was two years old, my father has taken me to baseball games. My father taught me valuable lessons.

On one occasion, a player struck out two times. He threw his bat out on the baseball field. My father told me that the next time, he would strike out again. I didn't believe him when the player was at bat again, I was ready to disprove my dad. But he was right. I asked him how he knew that the batter was going to strike out. He told me that it is very hard to get things accomplished though anger or frustration. Anger gets in the way of performance.

My father also used baseball to show me the importance of not giving up. During one ball game, a pinch hitter struck out three times. The American League has allowed designated hitters since 1973. As he stepped up to the plate for the fourth time, the crowd was booing and cursing him. I played little league baseball and nobody ever shouted bad things at us no matter how many times we struck out. The people in the stands always encouraged us. I asked my dad, "Why are all these people being rude to this player?"

He said that it was because he was not doing well. He was having a bad night, but that did not make him a bad player. He said the important thing was that the player kept trying no matter how many times he struck out.

But of all the times I went with my father to the ball games, this one stands out. It was a warm afternoon when my father asked me to go with him. I love warm days in September. When we got there, it was very cold. The wind was blowing. I remember that I was just wearing shorts my legs were freezing. My father had to put his arms around my bare legs to protect me. My memories of my father at the ballpark will always be special to me. He used baseball games to teach me about life.

WRITING ACTIVITY 6: Write Your Discovery Draft

First, write a preliminary thesis statement that identifies your topic and explains why the person, event, or period you are writing about is important to you. Then write a discovery draft that explores your ideas. Don't worry about the details. For now, focus on getting all of your ideas in writing. If you wish, you may write drafts on two or three topics to see which one you prefer to continue working on.

✳ STEP 3. REVISE YOUR DRAFT

When you revise a discovery draft, you focus not only on what you want to communicate to your audience but also on how you communicate it. In this stage, you concentrate on supporting your ideas and making your points easy to follow. Writers often move back and forth among the stages of the writing process. Thus, it's possible that as you revise you might need to return to the gathering-ideas stage. After you've gathered enough ideas, you can go back to revising.

As you revise, always think about what your reader needs to know to understand the significance of that special person, event, or period in your life.

For more on revising, see pp. 21–23.

✳ Developing Your Ideas

For more on description and narration, see pp. 63–64 and 64–66.

When you wrote your discovery draft, you probably wrote the story quickly, as Jesus did. While you revise, you want to add details that make your piece interesting and memorable. You need to go beyond describing experiences in vague, general ways to describing them with details that help your readers feel that they were there with you.

For this chapter's writing assignment, you will develop your ideas and support your thesis statement by using description and narration. These strategies serve several important functions in an essay:

- They increase the reader's interest in your topic.
- They help the reader understand your main ideas.
- They help to convince the reader to accept your viewpoint.

✳ Description

Although you have firsthand experience of the person, event, or period you're writing about, your readers don't. Consider adding description to make your essay more colorful and interesting. As you learned in Chapter 3, using description creates vivid images that explain how something looks, sounds, smells, tastes, or feels. For example, James Dillard, in "A Doctor's Dilemma," draws on sight, touch, and smell to describe the injured truck driver. This description of the accident victim helps readers feel like they were at the scene themselves.

> He was still out cold, limp as a rag doll. His throat was crushed and blood from the jugular vein was running down my arms. He still couldn't breathe. He was deep blue-magenta now, his pulse was rapid and thready. The stench of alcohol turned my stomach, but I positioned his jaw and tried to blow air down into his lungs. It wouldn't go.

HOW TO Use Description

- Draw on as many senses — sight, sound, smell, taste, and touch — as you can.
- Be specific. Instead of "The apartment smelled bad," write "The apartment smelled of stale cigarettes and boiled cabbage."
- Make comparisons, such as "The baby's eyes are like gray marbles."
- Avoid common phrases, such as "as pretty as a picture" or "as cute as can be."

WRITING ACTIVITY 7: Use Description to Develop Your Ideas

Use the following questions to brainstorm for descriptive details about a person, thing, or place: How does it smell? Taste? Sound? What does it feel like? Look like? Review your answers, and select details to add interest to your essay.

Narration

Whether you're writing about a person, an event, or a period in your life, you probably have at least one story to tell. As you learned in Chapter 3, you can use *narration* to describe an event or a series of events as they happened in time. Good narration includes specific details, and it often contains dialogue in which people's actual words are quoted.

In the following example from "My Maestro," Joshua Bell explains in narrative form why his violin teacher never punished his students:

> As a boy, he had once played his violin at a school assembly. His fellow students loved it, and applauded for so long the principal had to order them to stop. Later, Gingold's art teacher pulled him aside. "Let me see your hands," she said. "Are those the hands that made that beautiful music?" He beamed, so proud to be recognized for what he could do. Then she took a wooden pointer, smacking his palm so hard it damaged a nerve. Years later, he still felt pain. The teacher had decided he shouldn't feel so good about himself. That stuck with him. He went the opposite way with his students.

HOW TO Use Narration

- To support your thesis, tell a series of events in the order in which they occurred.

- Narrate only the most important events.

- Use descriptive details and dialogue to illustrate important points.

Student writer Jesus reviewed his discovery draft and decided that he could use narration to explain the time his father kept him warm at a game. He drafted this narrative for his revision:

```
I told my father that I was cold, but I didn't want to
leave. He then suggested that we move to another place where
the wind didn't blow as hard. But when we moved to the new
```

place, it was still cold, so my father sat in back of me and said "bend your knees toward your chest and lean back." Then he put his warm hands on my legs, like a duck protecting his duckling from bad weather or a predator that might hurt him.

WRITING ACTIVITY 8: Use Narration to Develop Your Ideas

Review your discovery draft, looking for ideas that you could expand with a story. Draft at least one narrative paragraph that supports the main idea of your essay (you may or may not decide to use it in your revised draft). Include descriptive details, and if possible, quote some dialogue.

Building Your Essay

Once you have developed your ideas, you want to make sure that your essay communicates those ideas as clearly as possible. In this chapter, you will focus on organizing your thoughts so that your readers can understand your message.

To organize, first review your thesis statement to ensure that it is effective. Next, make sure that each of your paragraphs has a topic sentence so that readers can follow your train of thought. Then check that the details in each paragraph support their topic sentences.

Revise Your Thesis Statement

When you started your discovery draft, you prepared a preliminary thesis statement to help guide your writing. When you revise, you need to make sure that your thesis statement reflects what you actually wrote and helps prepare readers to understand your ideas.

As you learned in Chapter 2, an effective thesis statement

- Announces the topic of the essay.
- Shows, explains, or argues a point about your topic.
- Gives a sense of what the essay will be about.

For more on writing a thesis statement, see pp. 19–20.

A thesis statement may be one or two sentences, and normally it appears at the beginning of an essay. In the introduction to "Prison Studies," for example, Malcolm X provides the following thesis statement about a significant period in his life:

Many who today hear me somewhere in person, or on television, or those who read something I've said, will think I went to school far beyond the eighth grade. This impression is due entirely to my prison studies.

In addition to indicating the topic of the essay (education), this thesis statement shows a point (the author is well educated even though he finished only the eighth grade) and gives a sense of what the essay will be about (how Malcolm X used his time in prison to educate himself).

For his discovery draft, student writer Jesus wrote the following preliminary thesis statement: "My father taught me valuable lessons." This early thesis statement was a good start because it announces a topic (Jesus's father) and shows a point about the topic (his father taught him valuable lessons). As he reviewed his draft, however, Jesus realized that what he wrote about was how his father used the sport of baseball to teach him about life. He revised his thesis statement to reflect the focus of his essay: "My father used baseball to teach me valuable lessons about life."

WRITING ACTIVITY 9: Revise Your Thesis Statement

Reread the preliminary thesis statement you wrote for your discovery draft. Does it announce the topic, show a point about the topic, and give a sense of what the essay will be about? Because your discovery draft may have gone in a different direction than you expected, revise your thesis statement as necessary to make it more effective.

Add Topic Sentences

Once you have a revised thesis statement, you need to show how the different parts of your essay develop your main idea. The best way to guide your readers is to provide topic sentences that explain how the details in each paragraph support the thesis statement. As you revise, make sure that every paragraph includes a topic sentence.

For more on topic sentences, see pp. 38–42.

As you learned in Chapter 3, effective topic sentences break up a thesis statement into several supporting ideas and express a complete thought for each of those specific ideas. For example, here are some of the topic sentences Malcolm X provides in "Prison Studies." Notice how each of these topic sentences identifies a specific supporting idea that develops the essay.

THESIS STATEMENT

Many who today hear me somewhere in person, or on television, or those who read something I've said, will think I went to school far beyond the eighth grade. This impression is due entirely to my prison studies.

TOPIC SENTENCES

It had really begun back in the Charlestown Prison, when Bimbi first made me feel envy of his stock of knowledge.

I saw that the best thing I could do was get hold of a dictionary — to study, to learn some words.

I suppose it was inevitable that as my word-base broadened, I could for the first time pick up a book and read and now begin to understand what the book was saying.

I have often reflected upon the new vistas that reading opened to me.

A topic sentence may fall anywhere in the paragraph. Most often, however, it comes first. For example, in the following paragraph from "A Doctor's Dilemma," the topic sentence (italicized) comes first, and the rest of the paragraph tells us what Dillard imagined:

> *An image flashed before my mind.* I could see the courtroom and the driver of the truck sitting in a wheelchair. I could see his attorney pointing at me and thundering at the jury: "This young doctor, with still a year left in residency training, took it upon himself to move this gravely injured man, condemning him forever to this wheelchair. . . ." I imagined the millions of dollars in award money. And all the years of hard work lost. I'd be paying him off the rest of my life. Amy touched my shoulder. "What are you going to do?"

Revise with Color

To help you examine particular aspects of your draft, use the color feature on your word-processing program. For instance, you can write your topic sentences in green. This technique makes it easier for you to focus on one aspect of your text at a time. Remember to return the sentences to black when you're preparing your final draft.

WRITING ACTIVITY 10: Revise and Add Topic Sentences

Reread your discovery draft, and underline your thesis statement and the topic sentence in each paragraph. Where necessary, revise the topic sentences to show how each paragraph supports your thesis statement. If any paragraphs are missing their topic sentences, add them.

Strengthen Your Focus

As you learned in Chapter 3, once you have effective topic sentences for each paragraph, you need to make sure that all other sentences within a paragraph relate to its topic sentence. If a paragraph includes any sentences that do not support the topic sentence, you can revise them to make them clearly relate to your point, move them to another paragraph, or remove them from your essay.

For more on paragraph unity, see pp. 42–43.

The following paragraph from Jesus's discovery draft includes several sentences that do not support the topic sentence. Notice how these irrelevant sentences (underlined) detract from the topic sentence (in italics):

My father also used baseball to show me the importance of not giving up. During one ball game, a pinch hitter struck out three times. The American League has allowed designated hitters since 1973. As he stepped up to the plate for the fourth time, the crowd was booing and cursing him. I played little league baseball and nobody ever shouted bad things at us no matter how many times we struck out. The people in the stands always encouraged us. I asked my dad, "Why are all these people being rude to this player?" He said that it was because he was not doing well. He was having a bad night, but that did not make him a bad player. He said the important thing was that the player kept trying no matter how many times he struck out.

Here is the same paragraph from Jesus's draft with the irrelevant sentences removed:

My father also used baseball to show me the importance of not giving up. During one ball game, a pinch hitter struck out three times. As he stepped up to the plate for the fourth time, the crowd was booing and cursing him. I asked my dad, "Why are all these people being rude to this player?" He said that it was because he was not doing well. He was having a bad night, but that did not make him a bad player. He said the important thing was that the player kept trying no matter how many times he struck out.

Save Your Drafts

As you revise, save copies of your drafts. You can do this by printing out copies, or you can save the drafts in separate files. Number or date the drafts to avoid confusion. These drafts can be included in a portfolio of your work to show your writing improvement. Also, many instructors like to examine students' drafts to evaluate their writing processes. Be sure to keep backup copies of your files.

GROUP ACTIVITY 2: Strengthen Focus

With the other members of your peer group, read the following paragraph, and underline the topic sentence. Cross out any irrelevant sentences that don't support the topic sentence.

The results of the election for student body president would be revealed at the meeting that day. My stomach was in knots anticipating the outcome. I knew that being president would be trying, but it was a risk worth taking. Once I took a risk when I rode the Shock Wave roller coaster at Six Flags. "You can breathe," a classmate said, but I didn't want to miss a word of the announcement. I took a CPR course when I was thirteen and learned a lot about how to get someone breathing again. Slowly but surely, the Dean of Students announced the name of the next president. The Dean of Students is a really nice woman who just moved here from California. Holding my breath hadn't helped because I still didn't hear what she said. My friends gave a little cheer and the rest of the group applauded and chanted, "Speech, speech, speech." I was an awful public speaker, but as the newly elected student body president, I gave it my best.

WRITING ACTIVITY 11: Strengthen Your Focus

Examine your current draft, checking each paragraph for sentences that don't support the topic sentence. Make your paragraphs more unified by deleting, relocating, or revising any irrelevant sentences that you find.

A Student's Revised Draft

Before you read Jesus's revised draft, reread his discovery draft on page 98. Notice how in the revision he has used description and narration to develop his ideas, improved his thesis statement and topic sentences, and strengthened his focus. (You will notice a few errors in the revised draft; these will be corrected when Jesus edits his essay later on.)

Baseball Memories

To some, baseball is just a sport where someone tries to reach base before getting thrown out. To others, it is "America's pastime," a baseball stadium filled with people cheering, eating hot roasted peanuts, and when the seventh inning approaches, singing "Take Me Out to the Ball Game." To me, though, baseball will always be more than just a game because my father used baseball to teach me valuable lessons about life.

1

The introduction is more interesting.

From the time I was two years old, my father took me to baseball games. On one occasion when we were at a game, a player struck out two times and threw his bat out on the baseball field. My father told me that the next time, the player would strike out again. I didn't believe him when the player was at bat again, I was ready to disprove my dad. But he was right. I asked him how he knew the batter would strike out again. He told me that it is very hard to get things accomplished through anger or frustration. Anger gets in the way of performance. He added that I should not throw things when I get mad because this could hurt someone else or myself. Instead, he suggested that I take the time to think things over before I do something that I will regret later on.

2

The main point of the paragraph is clearer.

He also used baseball to show me the importance of not giving up. During one ball game, a player struck out three times. As he stepped up to the plate for the fourth time, the crowd booed and cursed him. I asked my dad, "Why are all these people being rude to this player?" He replied, "He is one of the best players the team has, but he is not doing too well. There are days when we are not ourselves we are humans and make mistakes. Just because he struck out three times does not make him a bad person. You should learn from his experience: life is made of strikeouts, but it doesn't matter how many strikeouts you have. What matters is that you get another chance to hit the ball. If you are confident, you will succeed, but if you are not confident and do not believe in yourself, you will fail."

3

Dialogue makes the father's advice easier to understand.

But of all the times I went with my father to the ball games, one stands out. It was a warm afternoon

4

This description makes the essay more interesting and the point clearer.

when my father asked me to go with him. When we got there, it was very cold. The wind was blowing. I remember that I was just wearing shorts my legs were freezing. I told my father that I was cold, but I didn't want to leave. He suggested that we move to another place where the wind didn't blow as hard. When we moved to the new place, it was still cold my father sat in back of me and said, "Bend your knees toward your chest and lean back." Then he put his warm hands on my legs, like a duck protecting his duckling from bad weather or a predator that might hurt him. Not only did I feel warmed by my father, but I felt protected as well.

The conclusion is more extended and doesn't leave the reader hanging.

5   My memories of my father at the ballpark will always be special to me. He used baseball to teach me the importance of controlling my temper. He taught me not to throw or hit things when I become upset. He also used baseball to teach me to work toward goals without giving up. Like a batter facing that next pitch, he taught me to face life head-on.

GROUP ACTIVITY 3: Analyze Jesus's Revised Draft

Use the following questions to analyze how Jesus has improved his draft through revision.

1. What is Jesus's thesis statement? How did he improve it from his preliminary thesis statement?
2. How well does Jesus use topic sentences? After examining all of his topic sentences, focus on one paragraph. Identify the topic sentence, and explain how the idea in the topic sentence is developed in the paragraph.
3. What details has Jesus included to improve his essay?
4. Look back at paragraph 1 of Jesus's discovery draft (p. 98). He omitted two sentences in his revision. Why do you think he decided to omit these? Was it a good decision?
5. Does Jesus convince you — his reader — that his father used baseball to teach him about life? Explain.
6. What other revisions could Jesus make to improve his draft?

WRITING ACTIVITY 12: Peer Review

Now that you have made some revisions to your discovery draft, form a group with two or three other students, and exchange copies of your drafts. Read your draft aloud while your classmates follow along. Then ask your group members the following questions about your paper. Write down your classmates' responses. If you don't understand what a classmate is suggesting, ask for clarification before you write it down. You will want to read these notes later for suggestions on how to improve your draft.

1. What do you like best about my essay?

2. What is my thesis statement? Do I need to make the thesis clearer?

3. Examine my topic sentences. How well do they connect to my thesis and indicate the main idea of each paragraph?

4. Where in the draft could I better develop my ideas by using description or narration?

5. Is each paragraph in my draft unified? Or do some paragraphs contain irrelevant sentences that need to be omitted or revised?

6. Where in my draft did my writing confuse you? How can I clarify my ideas?

7. Have I followed all the instructions for this assignment?

Use Online Peer Review

If you have access to a networked computer lab, you may do peer review online. Send your suggestions for revision to the author's e-mail box.

WRITING ACTIVITY 13: Revise Your Essay

You have already developed your ideas, revised your thesis statement, added topic sentences, and strengthened your focus. But your classmates probably have given you additional suggestions for improving your essay. Taking your classmates' peer review responses into consideration, revise your draft as a whole so that readers will understand how a significant person, event, or period in your life changed you.

STEP 4. EDIT YOUR SENTENCES

When you wrote and revised your discovery draft, you were busy getting your thoughts on paper. Your sentences may not have come out as clearly as you would like, and you probably made some mistakes. You're now ready to edit your draft for readability and correctness.

Read your revised essay carefully, looking at each word for errors in grammar, spelling, and punctuation and for awkward sentences. Consult the Handbook in Part Four of this book and a dictionary. As you edit your essay for this chapter's assignment, you will focus on combining sentences with coordinating conjunctions and on eliminating run-on sentences.

Combining Sentences Using Coordinating Conjunctions

One way to ensure that your ideas are well received is to consider sentence variety. Readers get bored easily when they read many sentences that are short and sound alike. You may have noticed, for example, that Jesus's drafts contained many short sentences. To improve his writing, Jesus decided to use a technique known as *sentence coordination.*

Like Jesus, you can combine short, closely related sentences with *coordinating conjunctions.* Here are seven coordinating conjunctions and their meanings:

for	because
and	in addition
nor	neither
but	opposite
or	alternatively
yet	opposite
so	as a result

One way to remember these words is to think of the word *FANBOYS,* which is spelled with the first letter of each of the seven coordinating conjunctions.

For more on sentence combining and coordination, see pp. 522–24.

Use an appropriate coordinating conjunction to combine short, closely related sentences. Put a comma before the conjunction.

SHORT SENTENCES

```
    Last Saturday, I went to an outlet store to buy a
business suit. I saw a movie with my best friend.
```

COMBINED SENTENCE WITH *AND*

```
    Last Saturday, I went to an outlet store to buy a
business suit, and I saw a movie with my best friend.
```

SHORT SENTENCES

```
    The plane was an hour late getting to Cleveland. I
missed my connecting flight.
```

COMBINED SENTENCE WITH *SO*

The plane was an hour late getting to Cleveland, so I
missed my connecting flight.

SHORT SENTENCES

I gave my girlfriend another chance to show her
commitment to me. She started dating my best friend.

COMBINED SENTENCE WITH *BUT*

I gave my girlfriend another chance to show her
commitment to me, but she started dating my best friend.

HOW TO Combine Sentences Using Coordinating Conjunctions

- To be sure that two closely related sentences are complete, check that each one has a subject and a verb and that each conveys a complete thought.
- Select an appropriate coordinating conjunction (*for, and, nor, but, or, yet, so*).
- Use a comma before the coordinating conjunction.

EDITING ACTIVITY 1: Combine Sentences Using Coordinating Conjunctions

Combine the following sentences with an appropriate coordinating conjunction.

EXAMPLE   I played baseball when I was young. I lost interest in the sport.
                                              , but I

1. Baseball is a multimillion dollar business. It is also one of America's oldest organized sports.

2. Baseball is still popular. Newer sports, such as basketball and football, have become more popular.

3. Hundreds of Major League Baseball players earn more than a million dollars a year. Many athletes are attracted to the sport.

4. Women's softball has increased in popularity. This game is played at many colleges and at the Olympics.

5. At this time, a softball player can't earn a living playing softball. Not many athletes are interested in the sport professionally.

WRITING ACTIVITY 14: Combine Your Sentences

Examine your revised draft for short, closely related sentences. Where it makes sense to do so, combine them with coordinating conjunctions.

Exercise Central
For additional practice with using coordinating conjunctions to combine sentences, go to **bedfordstmartins.com/choices** and click on "Exercise Central."

Correcting Run-on Sentences

For more on run-on sentences, see pp. 546–51.

Remember, the more your readers pay attention to errors in your writing, the less attention they pay to what you have to say. Run-on sentences are an especially common mistake.

A *run-on sentence* occurs when two complete sentences, or *independent clauses*, are written together without any punctuation between them as if they were one sentence. Here are some examples of run-on sentences:

RUN-ON Arizona has some of the hottest spots in the country don't visit it in August.

RUN-ON Going to college while working full time has been hard I never get enough sleep.

RUN-ON Student athletes often experience great pressures to do well they might need extra support from their schools.

RUN-ON I bought a minivan after I had my third child we needed the room.

Correct run-on sentences in one of three ways:

- Use a period.

    CORRECT Arizona has some of the hottest spots in the country. Don't visit it in August.

- Use a semicolon. You may follow the semicolon with a conjunctive adverb (such as *however, in addition, also, therefore, furthermore*) and a comma if you like.

CORRECT Going to college while working full time has been hard; I never get enough sleep.

CORRECT Student athletes often experience great pressure to do well; therefore, they might need extra support from their schools.

- Use a comma and a coordinating conjunction.

CORRECT I bought a minivan after I had my third child, for we needed the room.

EDITING ACTIVITY 2: Correct Run-on Sentences

Correct each of the following run-on sentences by adding a period, a semicolon, or a comma and coordinating conjunction.

EXAMPLE Everybody has at least one whacky relative ~~mine~~ . Mine is my

uncle.

1. My uncle has a plastic spider he likes to take it out of his pocket to frighten young children.

2. When there's a full moon, our cat gets crazy he climbs the curtains and howls when we try to get him down.

3. My youngest daughter is only three she can already write her name.

4. My father was treated for cancer he's doing well now.

5. I'm returning to school to enter one of the health-care professions I plan to be a physical therapist.

Exercise Central
For additional practice with correcting run-on sentences, go to **bedfordstmartins.com/choices** and click on "Exercise Central."

WRITING ACTIVITY 15: Edit Your Sentences

Read your essay carefully, looking at each word for errors in grammar, spelling, and punctuation. Focus on run-on sentences. Use a dictionary and the Handbook in Part Four of this book to help you find and correct any mistakes.

A Student's Edited Essay

Using the Handbook in Part Four, Jesus corrected the errors in his essay. His corrections are underlined.

```
Jesus Ramirez
Professor Posey
English 0311
16 April 2006
```

Baseball Memories

To some, baseball is just a sport where someone tries to reach base before getting thrown out. To others, it is "America's pastime," a baseball stadium filled with people cheering, eating hot roasted peanuts, and when the seventh inning approaches, singing "Take Me Out to the Ball Game." To me, though, baseball will always be more than just a game because my father used baseball to teach me valuable lessons about life.

From the time I was two years old, my father took me to baseball games. On one occasion when we were at a game, a player struck out two times and threw his bat out on the baseball field. My father told me that the next time, the player would strike out again. I didn't believe him. When the player was at bat again, I was ready to disprove my dad. But he was right. I asked him how he knew the batter would strike out again. He told me that it is very hard to get things accomplished through anger or frustration, for anger gets in the way of performance. He added that I should not throw things when I get mad because this could hurt someone else or myself. Instead, he suggested that I take the time to think things over before I do something that I will regret later on.

He also used baseball to show me the importance of not giving up. During one ball game, a player struck out three times. As he stepped up to the plate for the fourth time, the crowd booed and cursed him. I asked my dad, "Why are all these people being rude to this player?" He replied, "He is one of the best players the team has, but he is not doing too well.

A run-on sentence is corrected.

Sentences are combined.

1

2

3

There are days when we are not ourselves; we are humans and make mistakes. Just because he struck out three times does not make him a bad person. You should learn from his experience: life is made of strikeouts, but it doesn't matter how many strikeouts you have. What matters is that you get another chance to hit the ball. If you are confident, you will succeed, but if you are not confident and do not believe in yourself, you will fail."

A run-on sentence is corrected.

But of all the times I went with my father to the ball games, one stands out. It was a warm afternoon when my father asked me to go with him. When we got there it was very cold, and the wind was blowing. I remember that I was just wearing shorts, so my legs were freezing. I told my father that I was cold, but I didn't want to leave. He suggested that we move to another place where the wind didn't blow as hard. When we moved to the new place, it was still cold, so my father sat in back of me and said, "Bend your knees toward your chest and lean back." Then he put his warm hands on my legs, like a duck protecting his duckling from bad weather or a predator that might hurt him. Not only did I feel warmed by my father, but I felt protected as well.

4

Sentences are combined.

A run-on sentence is corrected.

My memories of my father at the ballpark will always be special to me. He used baseball to teach me the importance of controlling my temper, and he showed me not to throw or hit things when I become upset. He also used baseball to teach me to work toward goals without giving up. Like a batter facing that next pitch, he taught me to face life head-on.

5

Sentences are combined.

✳ STEP 5. SHARE YOUR ESSAY

Share your final essay with your instructor and classmates, either by distributing printed or e-mailed copies or posting it to a class Web site. Ask your peer reviewers to comment on the improvements you made after their review of your draft. Don't be surprised if someone says, "I can't believe this is the same essay. It's so much better!"

CHAPTER CHECKLIST

❑ I analyzed my audience and purpose.

❑ I gathered ideas on my topic by brainstorming, relating aloud, and clustering.

❑ I wrote a discovery draft.

❑ I revised my draft by

    ❑ Using description and narration to develop ideas.

    ❑ Revising my thesis statement.

    ❑ Adding topic sentences.

    ❑ Improving paragraph unity.

❑ I combined short, closely related sentences with coordinating conjunctions.

❑ I edited my draft to correct errors, including run-on sentences.

❑ I shared my draft with my instructor and classmates.

REFLECTING ON YOUR WRITING

To help you continue to improve as a writer, answer the following questions about this assignment:

1. Did you enjoy writing an expressive piece in which you shared your thoughts and feelings?

2. Which method of gathering ideas worked best for you?

3. Which details most improved your essay?

4. If you had more time, what parts of your essay would you want to improve before sharing it with readers? Why?

Using your answers to these questions, complete a Writing Process Report for this chapter (you can download a report form at **bedford stmartins.com/choices**). Once you complete this report, freewrite about what you learned in this chapter.

A Significant Person

THOMAS L. FRIEDMAN

My Favorite Teacher

Thomas L. Friedman has been a foreign affairs columnist for the New York Times *since 1981. He holds a master's degree in modern Middle East studies from Oxford University in England, and he has won three Pulitzer Prizes for journalism. Friedman has written several best-selling books, including* From Beirut to Jerusalem *(1989), which won the National Book Award;* The Lexis and the Olive Tree: Understanding Globalization *(2000); and* The World Is Flat: A Brief History of the Twenty-First Century *(2005). If we're lucky, we find someone in our lives who teaches us what is truly important. In "My Favorite Teacher," which first appeared in the* New York Times *on January 9, 2001, Friedman tells of such a person.*

Last Sunday's *New York Times Magazine* published its annual   1
review of people who died last year who left a particular mark on the world. I am sure all readers have their own such list. I certainly do. Indeed, someone who made the most important difference in my life died last year — my high school journalism teacher, Hattie M. Steinberg.

I grew up in a small suburb of Minneapolis, and Hattie was   2
the legendary journalism teacher at St. Louis Park High School, Room 313. I took her Intro to Journalism course in 10th grade, back in 1969, and have never needed, or taken, another course in journalism since. She was that good.

Hattie was a woman who believed that the secret for suc-   3
cess in life was getting the fundamentals right. And boy, she pounded the fundamentals of journalism into her students — not simply how to write a lead or accurately transcribe a quote, but, more important, how to comport yourself in a professional way and to always do quality work. To this day, when I forget to wear a tie on assignment, I think of Hattie scolding me. I once interviewed an ad exec for our high school paper who used a four-letter word. We debated whether to run it. Hattie ruled yes. That ad man almost lost his job when it appeared. She wanted to teach us about consequences.

Hattie was the toughest teacher I ever had. After you took   4
her journalism course in 10th grade, you tried out for the paper, *The Echo*, which she supervised. Competition was fierce. In

11th grade, I didn't quite come up to her writing standards, so she made me business manager, selling ads to the local pizza parlors. That year, though, she let me write one story. It was about an Israeli general who had been a hero in the Six-Day War, who was giving a lecture at the University of Minnesota. I covered his lecture and interviewed him briefly. His name was Ariel Sharon. First story I ever got published.

Those of us on the paper, and the yearbook that she also supervised, lived in Hattie's classroom. We hung out there before and after school. Now, you have to understand, Hattie was a single woman, nearing 60 at the time, and this was the 1960's. She was the polar opposite of "cool," but we hung around her classroom like it was a malt shop and she was Wolfman Jack. None of us could have articulated it then, but it was because we enjoyed being harangued by her, disciplined by her and taught by her. She was a woman of clarity in an age of uncertainty. 5

We remained friends for 30 years, and she followed, bragged about and critiqued every twist in my career. After she died, her friends sent me a pile of my stories that she had saved over the years. Indeed, her students were her family — only closer. Judy Harrington, one of Hattie's former students, remarked about other friends who were on Hattie's newspapers and yearbooks: "We all graduated 41 years ago; and yet nearly each day in our lives something comes up — some mental image, some admonition that makes us think of Hattie." 6

Judy also told the story of one of Hattie's last birthday parties, when one man said he had to leave early to take his daughter somewhere. "Sit down," said Hattie. "You're not leaving yet. She can just be a little late." 7

That was my teacher! I sit up straight just thinkin' about her. 8

Among the fundamentals Hattie introduced me to was the *New York Times*. Every morning it was delivered to Room 313. I had never seen it before then. Real journalists, she taught us, start their day by reading the *Times* and columnists like Anthony Lewis and James Reston. 9

I have been thinking about Hattie a lot this year, not just because she died on July 31, but because the lessons she imparted seem so relevant now. We've just gone through this huge dotcom-Internet-globalization bubble — during which a lot of smart people got carried away and forgot the fundamentals of how you build a profitable company, a lasting portfolio, a nation state or a thriving student. It turns out that the real secret of success in the information age is what it always was: fundamentals — reading, writing and arithmetic, church, synagogue and mosque, the rule of law and good governance. 10

The Internet can make you smarter, but it can't make you smart. It can extend your reach, but it will never tell you what to say at a P.T.A. meeting. These fundamentals cannot be downloaded. You can only upload them, the old-fashioned way, one by one, in places like Room 313 at St. Louis Park High. I only 11 regret that I didn't write this column when the woman who taught me all that was still alive.

READING ACTIVITY 7: Build Your Vocabulary

Determine the meanings of the following words from the context of Thomas L. Friedman's essay. Then check their meanings by looking up the words in a dictionary: annual (1), lead (3), transcribe (3), comport (3), harangued (5), admonition (6), imparted (10), portfolio (10).

READING ACTIVITY 8: Read to Improve Your Writing

Discuss the following questions about "My Favorite Teacher" with your classmates.

1. Select the one sentence in Friedman's essay that you think best captures the essence of Hattie M. Steinberg. Then explain why this sentence describes her well.

2. Explain the significance of this sentence in your own words: "She [Hattie] was a woman of clarity in an age of uncertainty" (5).

3. Why does the author believe that Hattie's lessons are still important in the Internet age?

4. Friedman writes at the end of his essay, "I only regret that I didn't write this column when the woman who taught me all that was still alive." If you could write a letter to someone who has influenced you, who would that person be?

A Memorable Event

CHERYL PECK

Fat Girls and Lawn Chairs

Cheryl Peck, a resident of Three Rivers, Michigan, for years had written for her own and her friends' pleasure. In 2002, with the help of a friend, she self-published Fat Girls and Lawn Chairs, *a collection of her humorous essays. The book was then republished in 2004 by Warner Books, a major publisher. Her second book,* Revenge of the Paste Eaters: Memoirs of a Misfit, *was published in 2005. In the following essay, which is an excerpt from* Fat Girls and Lawn Chairs, *Peck describes why fat girls never trust lawn chairs.*

Due to the wear and tear of aging, I have lost half an inch in height. I have mourned that half an inch because — in my mind — it was the half inch that kept me from being as wide as

I am tall. Back when I still had this half an inch and thought of myself as tall and lithe, I happened into a mall bathroom where, as I emerged from the stall, a teenaged girl was scowling critically at her reflection in the mirror. Disgusted with herself, she grasped the roll of fat that was hanging disgracefully over the belt of her size four jeans and she wailed to her friends, "I am SUCH a cow. . . ." And then she saw me. That a size four child is distressed because her babyfat won't stay inside her jeans is probably not all that funny: but the stunned panic on her face when she saw me warned me that I was either going to have to laugh at her or kill her. I walked out of the restroom chuckling about a herd of tiny size four cows.

I have a friend who is smaller than I am. Several, actually; but I know this particular friend is smaller than I am because she gave me all of her "fat" clothes. Not all of them fit. She had been biking, hiking, golfing and starving herself into a thinner, more athletic image, and like many of us who are zaftig, she was in a "thin" period. This was, admittedly, a few years ago. The passion that kept her moving and hungry apparently burned out, and like me, she has been eating her Wheaties. She still probably is smaller than I am. This might matter to me or to her, but it is probably splitting some very fine hairs as far as our thinner friends can tell. But after a weekend outing, I now have the reputation for being the thinner of the two of us by the grace of a lawn chair.

I was once small enough to fit comfortably in the lap of a lawn chair. I think smaller people probably take lawn chairs for granted, but that is because they have never been hugged in the butt by The Thing That Won't Let Go. And they have never had the experience that scarred my friend.

We'll call her Kristen. It's a pretty name and it's not hers. Kristen brought a lawn chair to a gathering of our friends. It was a weekend outing, a long holiday in which we conspired to gather at someone's cottage, float around the lake on rafts, eat massive quantities of food and describe this adventure by some obscure athletic event that at least half of us participated in. We call it "The Canoe Trip." This distinguishes it from "The Cross Country Ski Trip" where we gather at the lodge, float around in the Jacuzzi, eat massive quantities of food and some of us even go outside.

My friend Kristen was quite proud of her lawn chair. It was new. It was cute. It was a steal. Kristen is a woman who enjoys her toys, and it was a lawn chair to inspire the envy of all of her friends. She set up her lawn chair on the deck, arranged her towel, her drink, and the direction she was facing, and then she sat down. And the lawn chair, which was inexpensive and probably made by Chinese — none of whom are notably large people — began to spread out on the deck, spraddle-legged like a giraffe on ice, and slowly — excruciatingly slowly — it lowered her utterly without escape or grace until she was flat on her butt on the deck, the wounded chair parts welded around her and refusing to let go.

My friends prepare themselves for their athletic events by emptying a rather impressive number of beer cans, and they fortify their resolve, while performing these athletic feats, by emptying even more beer cans, and when they return to the deck to think back on the amazing athletic feats they have just performed, they empty more beer cans — so by the time Kristen's butt connected with the deck, our friends had thrown themselves into the spirit of her adventure. They awarded her Olympic scores for the fall and its execution. One or two of the more nimble attempted to mimic the stages of her descent. There was a great outpouring of merriment and glee, not all of which was tempered with the sensitivity befitting the occasion.

If you took a poll of fat girls, you would knock on a lot of unfriendly doors before you would find the jolly, fun-loving sport who would answer, "Heck, yes, I love to sit down in a lawn chair that breaks, dumps me on my ass in front of all of my friends, and leaves me there to wonder, *how am I ever going to get back up?*" Kristen would not be one of those women.

She was embarrassed. She was humiliated. She was furious. She managed to roll back onto her feet and then she grabbed the offending corpse and pointed to the faulty welds that had betrayed her. She declared the chair "defective." She planned to go directly to the store where she bought it on the way home and demand her money back. She stood there shaking mutilated sticks of aluminum and plastic weave as if expecting them to reassemble themselves and mumble an apology. For every faltering giggle she heard the rest of the weekend, be it chair-related or not, she asserted that it was not her fault the chair broke, that it was a bad chair, a weak chair, a poorly made and overpriced, cheap chair, and that she would, come hell or high water, exact her revenge on the seller.

Of course this only antagonized the situation. Sometimes good sportsmanship makes you look good and sometimes it just keeps you from looking worse. The urge to imagine this conversation between Kristen and the chair seller inspired friends who had never engaged in imaginary conversations before. The moment she walked out of a room someone would turn to someone else, mug a look of stunned outrage and mutter, "I just sat down in it ONCE and the darned thing BROKE. . . ." And everyone would burst out laughing all over again. And because she would not give, not even break a single rueful little grin, the incident has never truly died.

When she bought her house, for her housewarming one of our friends bought her a matched set of oversized lawn chairs. They are very nice chairs. I believe I've even had occasion to sit in one of them.

I did track down the chair-giver and make him sit in it first. 11
Kind of a trial sit. No self-respecting fat girl ever really trusts a
lawn chair.

READING ACTIVITY 9: Build Your Vocabulary

Determine the meanings of the following words from the context of
Cheryl Peck's essay. Then check their meanings by looking up the
words in a dictionary: lithe (1), scowling (1), zaftig (2), conspired (4),
spraddle-legged (5), fortify (6), resolve (6), tempered (6), faltering (8),
antagonized (9), mug (9), rueful (9).

READING ACTIVITY 10: Read to Improve Your Writing

Discuss the following questions about "Fat Girls and Lawn Chairs"
with your classmates.

1. In your own words, what is the main point of Peck's essay?
2. What effect did the lawn chair incident have on Kristen? On her
   friends? How was the author changed by it?
3. List five words that describe how Kristen's friends reacted to the
   broken lawn chair.
4. Focus on a paragraph that contains many descriptive details.
   Explain how these details help the author make her point.

An Important Period

BRENT STAPLES

Black Men and Public Space

*Have you ever noticed you were making someone else uncomfortable
not because of anything you were doing but because of what you
are — male or female, black or white, young or old, skinny or heavy,
rich or poor? Perhaps you've even felt such discomfort about someone yourself. Some kinds of prejudice can be relatively harmless (an
American who avoids French fries because France was against the
war in Iraq hurts no one). Other kinds can be deeply damaging. In
"Black Men and Public Space," African American journalist Brent
Staples uses examples from his own life to show how hurtful prejudice can be. This essay originally appeared in* Harper's *magazine.*

My first victim was a woman — white, well dressed, proba- 1
bly in her early twenties. I came upon her late one evening on a
deserted street in Hyde Park, a relatively affluent neighborhood

in an otherwise mean, impoverished section of Chicago. As I swung onto the avenue behind her, there seemed to be a discreet, uninflammatory distance between us. Not so. She cast back a worried glance. To her, the youngish black man — a broad six feet two inches with a beard and billowing hair, both hands shoved into the pockets of a bulky military jacket — seemed menacingly close. After a few more quick glimpses, she picked up her pace and was soon running in earnest. Within seconds she disappeared into a cross street.

That was more than a decade ago. I was twenty-two years old, a graduate student newly arrived at the University of Chicago. It was in the echo of that terrified woman's footfalls that I first began to know the unwieldy inheritance I'd come into — the ability to alter public space in ugly ways. It was clear that she thought herself the quarry of a mugger, a rapist, or worse. Suffering a bout of insomnia, however, I was stalking sleep, not defenseless wayfarers. As a softy who is scarcely able to take a knife to a raw chicken — let alone hold one to a person's throat — I was surprised, embarrassed, and dismayed all at once. Her flight made me feel like an accomplice in tyranny. It also made it clear that I was indistinguishable from the muggers who occasionally seeped into the area from the surrounding ghetto. That first encounter, and those that followed, signified that a vast, unnerving gulf lay between nighttime pedestrians — particularly women — and me. And I soon gathered that being perceived as dangerous is a hazard in itself. I only needed to turn a corner into a dicey situation, or crowd some frightened, armed person in a foyer somewhere, or make an errant move after being pulled over by a policeman. Where fear and weapons meet — and they often do in urban America — there is always the possibility of death.

In that first year, my first away from my hometown, I was to become thoroughly familiar with the language of fear. At dark, shadowy intersections, I could cross in front of a car stopped at a traffic light and elicit the *thunk, thunk, thunk, thunk* of the driver — black, white, male, or female — hammering down the door locks. On less traveled streets after dark, I grew accustomed to but never comfortable with people crossing to the other side of the street rather than pass me. Then there were the standard unpleasantries with policemen, doormen, bouncers, cabdrivers, and others whose business it is to screen out troublesome individuals *before* there is any nastiness.

I moved to New York nearly two years ago and I have remained an avid night walker. In central Manhattan, the near-constant crowd cover minimizes tense one-on-one street encounters. Elsewhere — in SoHo, for example, where sidewalks are narrow and tightly spaced buildings shut out the sky — things can get very taut indeed.

After dark, on the warrenlike streets of Brooklyn where I live, I often see women who fear the worst from me. They seem to have set their faces on neutral, and with their purse straps strung across their chests bandolier-style, they forge ahead as though bracing themselves against being tackled. I understand, of course, that the danger they perceive is not a hallucination. Women are particularly vulnerable to street violence, and young black males are drastically overrepresented among the perpetrators of that violence. Yet these truths are no solace against the kind of alienation that comes of being ever the suspect, a fearsome entity with whom pedestrians avoid making eye contact.

It is not altogether clear to me how I reached the ripe old age   6
of twenty-two without being conscious of the lethality nighttime pedestrians attributed to me. Perhaps it was because in Chester, Pennsylvania, the small, angry industrial town where I came of age in the 1960s, I was scarcely noticeable against a backdrop of gang warfare, street knifings, and murders. I grew up one of the good boys, had perhaps a half-dozen fistfights. In retrospect, my shyness of combat has clear sources.

As a boy, I saw countless tough guys locked away; I have   7
since buried several, too. They were babies, really — a teenage cousin, a brother of twenty-two, a childhood friend in his mid-twenties — all gone down in episodes of bravado played out in the streets. I came to doubt the virtues of intimidation early on. I chose, perhaps unconsciously, to remain a shadow — timid, but a survivor.

The fearsomeness mistakenly attributed to me in public   8
places often has a perilous flavor. The most frightening of these confusions occurred in the late 1970s and early 1980s, when I worked as a journalist in Chicago. One day, rushing into the office of a magazine I was writing for with a deadline story in hand, I was mistaken for a burglar. The office manager called security and, with an ad hoc posse, pursued me through the labyrinthine halls, nearly to my editor's door. I had no way of proving who I was. I could only move briskly toward the company of someone who knew me.

Another time I was on assignment for a local paper and   9
killing time before an interview. I entered a jewelry store on the city's affluent Near North Side. The proprietor excused herself and returned with an enormous red Doberman pinscher straining at the end of a leash. She stood, the dog extended toward me, silent to my questions, her eyes bulging nearly out of her head. I took a cursory look around, nodded, and bade her good night.

Relatively speaking, however, I never fared as badly as   10
another black male journalist. He went to nearby Waukegan, Illinois, a couple of summers ago to work on a story about a murderer who was born there. Mistaking the reporter for the killer, police officers hauled him from his car at gunpoint and but for his press credentials would probably have tried to book him. Such episodes are not uncommon. Black men trade tales like this all the time.

Over the years, I learned to smother the rage I felt at so often   11
being taken for a criminal. Not to do so would surely have led to
madness. I now take precautions to make myself less threatening. I move about with care, particularly late in the evening. I
give a wide berth to nervous people on subway platforms during
the wee hours, particularly when I have exchanged business
clothes for jeans. If I happen to be entering a building behind
some people who appear skittish, I may walk by, letting them
clear the lobby before I return, so as not to seem to be following
them. I have been calm and extremely congenial on those rare
occasions when I've been pulled over by the police.

And on late-evening constitutionals I employ what has   12
proved to be an excellent tension-reducing measure: I whistle
melodies from Beethoven and Vivaldi and the more popular
classical composers. Even steely New Yorkers hunching toward
nighttime destinations seem to relax, and occasionally they
even join in the tune. Virtually everybody seems to sense that a
mugger wouldn't be warbling bright, sunny selections from
Vivaldi's *Four Seasons*. It is my equivalent of the cowbell that
hikers wear when they know they are in bear country.

READING ACTIVITY 11: Build Your Vocabulary

Determine the meanings of the following words from the context of
Brent Staples's essay. Then check their meanings by looking up the
words in a dictionary: uninflammatory (1), quarry (2), wayfarers (2),
errant (2), elicit (3), warrenlike (5), bandolier (5), bravado (7), ad hoc
(8), labyrinthine (8), give a wide berth (11), constitutionals (12).

READING ACTIVITY 12: Read to Improve Your Writing

Discuss the following questions about "Black Men and Public Space"
with your classmates.

1. What main point is Staples making about how black men in public
   spaces are perceived?

2. What examples does the author provide to support his main point?

3. Why do you think Staples ends his essay by describing the precautions he takes to avoid being mistaken for a criminal?

4. Have you ever felt that your presence was causing a stranger discomfort? Describe one or two of these moments and the feelings
   they evoked in you.

5

Examining a Culture

Using Examples and Process Explanation

In this chapter, you will write about a cultural symbol, tradition, or hero special to you. As you follow the steps of the writing process, you will

- Gather ideas by clustering, asking questions, and freewriting.

- Develop your ideas using examples and process explanation.

- Practice writing introductions and conclusions and making connections with transitions and keywords.

- Combine sentences with conjunctive adverbs.

- Learn to identify and correct sentence fragments.

- Share your finished essay by posting it to a Web log.

Have you ever traveled to another country? Were you surprised by what you saw and heard? Did people drive on the left or right side of the road? How did they entertain themselves? Were shopping practices different than what you are accustomed to? Were you introduced to new foods or styles of dress? Although unsettling at times, such encounters enable us not only to learn about other cultures but also to better understand our own.

The term *culture* refers to the customs, beliefs, values, objects, and languages shared by members of a particular group. Although many people grow up as part of a single culture — Vietnamese, Brazilian, or German, for instance — more and more people are recognizing themselves as *multicultural,* or as having roots in more than one culture. In addition to identifying ethnic heritage or national origin, *culture* can also refer to the beliefs and customs of a particular group. (The hippie culture of the 1960s, for example, favored social and personal rebellion, encouraged a distinctive lifestyle, and came to use the peace sign as its symbol.) Although members of a given culture might take its unique characteristics for granted, outsiders are sometimes fascinated, puzzled, or even frightened by things they don't understand.

By examining a specific aspect of a culture to which you belong, you can gain a stronger understanding of your own beliefs and values and will probably want to share your knowledge with others. As you work through the readings and activities in this chapter, you will practice transforming a personal experience into an essay that teaches your readers about something important to you.

GROUP ACTIVITY 1: Think about Cultures

The photo on page 126 shows members of a family making tamales, a common Latin American cultural tradition. A Christmas tree stands in the background, and paper decorations hang in the windows. With several classmates, brainstorm a list of foods, decorations, activities, or historical figures that are a part of how you celebrate a particular holiday. Why are these things important to your understanding of this holiday and your own culture?

READING ESSAYS ABOUT CULTURES

Most of us are fascinated by how other people live, think, and behave. In fact, learning about unfamiliar cultures is one of the major reasons that people travel. But not everybody has the chance to visit new places or people. For those who can't travel (and even for those who can), reading about other cultures is a popular way to learn something about them. Before you start considering possibilities for your own writing, read the following professional essays about a cultural symbol (the Korean delicacy kim chee), a cultural tradition (ice fishing in Minnesota), and a cultural hero (media guru Oprah Winfrey). Notice how the writers provide examples and explain processes to help readers understand what their subjects mean to them.

A Cultural Symbol

NORA OKJA KELLER

My Mother's Food

Nora Okja Keller is a freelance writer and journalist who often writes about the intersection of Korean and American cultures. Her articles have appeared in Newsweek, Time, *and the* New York Times. *She has also written several books, including the novels* Comfort Woman *(1998), which won the American Book Award, and* Fox Girl *(2003). Keller was born in Seoul, Korea, but her family immigrated to the United States, settling in Hawaii, when she was a young child. As a teenager, she rebelled against her mother's Korean culture in an effort to be seen as "American." In "My Mother's Food," Keller writes about the role food played in her rebellion.*

I was weaned on kim chee. A good baby, I was "able to eat anything," my mother told me. But what I especially loved was the fermenting, garlicky Chinese cabbage my mother pickled in our kitchen. Not waiting for her to lick the red peppers off the won bok, I would grab and gobble the bits of leaves as soon as she tore them into baby-size pieces. She said that even if my eyes watered, I would still ask for more.

Propping me in a baby carrier next to the sink, my mother would rinse the cabbage she had soaked in salted water the night before. After patting the leaves dry, she would slather on the thick red-pepper sauce, rubbing the cloves of garlic and green onion into the underarms of the cabbage, bathing it as she would one of her own children. Then, grabbing them by their dangling leafy legs, she would push the wilting heads into five-gallon jars. She had to rise up on tiptoe, submerging her arm up to the elbow, to punch the kim chee to the bottom of the jar, squishing them into their own juices.

Throughout elementary school, our next-door neighbor Frankie, whose mother was the only other Korean in our neighborhood, would come over to eat kim chee with my sisters and me every day after school. We would gather in our garage, sitting cross-legged around a kim-chee jar as though at a campfire. Daring each other on, we would pull out long strips that we would eat straight, without rice or water to dilute the taste. Our eyes would tear and our noses start to run because it was so hot, but we could not stop. "It burns, it burns, but it tastes so good!" we would cry.

Afterward when we went to play the jukebox in Frankie's garage, we had to be careful not to touch our eyes with our wrinkled, pepperstained hands. It seemed as if the hot, red juice soaked through our skin and into our bones; even after we bathed, we could still feel our fingers tingling, still taste the kim chee on them when we licked them. And as my sisters and I curled into our bed at night, nestling together like sleeping doves, I remember the smell lingered on our hands, the faint whiff of kim chee scenting our dreams. 4

We went crazy for the smell of kim chee — a perfume that lured us to the kitchen table. When my mother hefted the jar of kim chee out of the refrigerator and opened the lid to extract the almost fluorescent strips of cabbage, she didn't have to call out to us, although she always did. "Girls, come join me," she would sing; even if we weren't hungry we couldn't resist. We all lingered over snacks that lasted two or three hours. 5

But I didn't realize that I smelled like kim chee, that the smell followed me to school. One day, walking across Middle Field toward the girls' locker room, a girl I recognized from the gym class before mine stepped in front of me. 6

"You Korean?" she asked. She narrowed eyes as brown as mine, shaped like mine, like mock-orange leaves pinched up at the corners. 7

Thinking she could be my sister, another part-Korean, part-Caucasian *hapa* girl, I nodded and welcomed her kinship with a smile. 8

"I thought so," she said, sneering. Her lips scrunched upward, almost folding over her nostrils. "You smell like one." 9

I held my smile, frozen, as she flitted away from me. She had punched me in the stomach with her words. Days later, having replayed this confrontation endlessly in my mind (in one fantasy version, this girl mutated into a hairy Neanderthal that I karate-chopped into submission), I thought of the perfect comeback: "Oh yeah? Well, you smell like a chimpanzee." At the very least, I should have said *something* that day. Anything — a curse, a joke, a grunt — anything at all would have been better than a smile. 10

I smiled. And I sniffed. I smiled and sniffed as I walked to the locker room and dressed for P.E. I smiled and sniffed as I jogged around the field, trying to avoid the hall and other girls wielding field hockey sticks. I smiled and sniffed as I showered and followed my schedule of classes. 11

I became obsessed with sniffing. When no one was looking, I lifted my arms and, quick, sniffed. I held my palm up to my face and exhaled. Perhaps, every now and then, I would catch the odor of garlic in sweat and breath. I couldn't tell: the smell of kim chee was too much a part of me. 12

I didn't want to smell like a Korean. I wanted to be an 13
American, which meant having no smell. Americans, I learned
from TV and magazines, erased the scent of their bodies with
cologne and deodorant, breath mints and mouthwash.

So I erased my stink by eliminating kim chee. Though I 14
liked the sharp taste of garlic and pepper biting my tongue, I
stopped eating my mother's food.

I became shamed by the kim chee that peeked out from 15
between the loaf of white bread and the carton of milk, by the
odor that, I grew to realize, permeated the entire house. When
friends pointed at the kim-chee jars lined up on the refrigerator
shelves and squealed, "Gross! What's that?" I would mumble, "I
don't know, something my mom eats."

I also stopped eating the only three dishes my mother could 16
cook: *kalbi ribs, bi bim kooksoo,* and Spam fried with eggs. (The
first "American" food my mother ever ate was a Spam and egg
sandwich; even now she considers it one of her favorite foods
and never tires eating it.)

I told my mother I was a vegetarian. One of my sisters ate 17
only McDonald's Happy Meal cheeseburgers (no pickle); the
other survived for two years on a diet of processed-cheese sandwiches on white bread (no crust), Hostess DingDongs, and rice
dunked in ketchup.

"How can you do this to me?" my mother wailed at her 18
American-born children. "You are wasting away! Eat, eat!" She
plopped heaps of kim chee and *kalbi* onto mounds of steaming
rice. My sisters and I would grimace, poke at the food, and
announce: "Too fattening."

My mother had always encouraged us to behave like proper 19
Korean girls: quiet, respectful, hardworking. She said we gave
her "heartaches" the way we fought as children. "Worse than
boys," she'd say. "Why do you want to do things like soccer,
scuba, swimming? How about piano?"

But worse than our tomboy activities were our various ado- 20
lescent diets. My mother grieved over the food rejected. "I don't
understand you," she'd say. "When I was growing up, my family
was so poor, we could only dream of eating this kind of food.
Now I can give my children meat every night and you don't want
it." "Yeah, yeah," we said, as we pushed away the kim chee, the
Koreanness.

As I grew up, I eventually returned to eating kim chee, but 21
only sporadically. I could go for months without it, then be hit
with a craving so strong I would run to Sack-n-Save for a
generic, watery brand that only hinted at the taste of home. Kim
chee, I realized, was my comfort food.

When I became pregnant, the craving for my own mother 22
accentuated my craving for kim chee. During the nights of my
final trimester, my body foreign and heavy, restless with longing, I hungered for the food I had eaten in the womb, my first
mother-memory.

The baby I carried in my own womb, in turn, does not look   23
like me. Except for the slight tilt of her eyes, she does not look
Korean. As a mother totally in love with her daughter, I do not
care what she looks like; she is perfect as herself. Yet I worry
that — partially because of what she looks like — she will not
be able to identify with the Korean in me, and in herself. I recognize that identifying herself as Korean will be a choice for
her — in a way it wasn't for someone like me, who looks pure
Asian. It hit me then, what my own mother must have felt looking at each of her own mixed-race daughters; how strongly I do
identify as a Korean American woman, how strongly I want my
child to identify with me.

When my daughter was fifteen months old, she took her   24
first bite of kim chee. I had taken a small bite into my own
mouth, sucking the hot juice from its leaves, giving it "mother-
taste" as my own mother had done for me. Still, my daughter's
eyes watered. "Hot, hot," she said to her grandmother and me.
But the taste must have been in some way familiar; instead of
spitting up and crying for water, she pushed my hand to the
open jar for another bite.

"She likes it!" my mother said proudly. "She is Korean!"   25

I realized that for my mother, too, the food we ate growing   26
up had always been an indication of how Korean her children
were — or weren't. I remember how intently she watched us
eat, as if to catch a glimpse of herself as we chewed.

Now my mother watches the next generation. When she vis-   27
its, my daughter clings to her, follows her from room to room.
They run off together to play the games that only the two of
them know how to play. I can hear them in my daughter's room,
chattering and laughing. Sneaking to the doorway, I see them
"cooking" in the Playskool kitchen.

"Look," my mother says, offering her grandchild a plate of   28
plastic spaghetti, "noodles is *kooksoo*." She picks up a steak.
"This *kalbi*." My mother is teaching her Korean, presenting
words my daughter knows the taste of.

My girl picks up a head of cabbage. "Let's make kim chee,   29
Halmoni," she says, using the Korean word for *grandmother*
like a name.

"Okay," my mother answers. "First, salt." My daughter   30
shakes invisible salt over the cabbage.

"Then mix garlic and red-pepper sauce." My mother stirs a   31
pot over the stove and passes the mixture to my daughter, who
pours it on the cabbage.

My daughter brings her fingers to her mouth. "Hot!" she   32
says. Then she holds the cabbage to my mother's lips, and gives
her *halmoni* a taste.

"Mmmmm!" My mother grins as she chews the air.   33
"Delicious! This is the best kim chee I ever ate." My mother sees
me peeking around the door.

"Come join us!" she calls out to me and tells my daughter,   34
who's gnawing at the fake food. "Let your mommy have a bite."

READING ACTIVITY 1: Build Your Vocabulary

Determine the meanings of the following words from the context of
Nora Okja Keller's essay. Then check their meanings by looking up the
words in a dictionary: won bok (1), slather (2), nestling (4), extract
(5), flitted (10), Neanderthal (10), wielding (11), permeated (15), sporadically (21), accentuated (22).

READING ACTIVITY 2: Read to Improve Your Writing

Discuss the following questions about "My Mother's Food" with your
classmates.

1. What did kim chee symbolize for Keller when she was a child?
   Why did she stop eating it?

2. How did Keller's mother react when her children refused to eat
   Korean food? What does her reaction suggest about what the
   dishes symbolized in her mind?

3. How did the meaning of kim chee change for the author after she
   had a child?

4. Why do you think the author wants her daughter to think of herself as Korean?

5. How does Keller use examples and process explanation to explain
   what kim chee is and what it means to her?

A Cultural Tradition

KEVIN KLING

Hook, Line, and Television

*Playwright and commentator Kevin Kling writes about the beauty
and peculiarities of Minnesota, his home state, which is known for
its frigid temperatures and adaptable citizens. Rather than stay
indoors during the cold weather, Minnesotans have developed a tradition of winter sports, one of which is ice fishing. In "Hook, Line,
and Television," Kling explains the tradition of ice fishing, which
involves unique social interactions as much as it does fishing.*

Every year the call goes out: the ice is safe. Open water has   1
turned into prime real estate, and villages of tiny shacks pop up

overnight. Thus ice-fishing season opens in Minnesota, home of the nation's icebox, where carpaccio is still made with carp and especially frigid winters are referred to by their year, like fine wine. Although months of subzero temperatures test the heartiest souls, some people actually live in this state on purpose. As I overheard one Northern gentleman say, "When you freeze paradise, it's bound to last a little longer."

Mille Lacs Lake is one of the most popular spots for ice fishing in the Land of 10,000 Lakes. It covers more than 200 square miles in the middle of Minnesota and is known for its walleye, arguably the best-tasting fish you can pull from fresh water. Once the ice sets — late November or early December, depending — local resort owners start renting out ice-fishing houses and hauling them out onto the lake, where bars, churches and the random bowling alley follow. By January, there will be around 5,000 angling abodes on the ice, which qualifies as a small city in Minnesota. (And at Gull Lake, more than 9,000 folks competed in last year's annual Brainerd Jaycees Ice Fishing Extravaganza, but that's a one-day affair involving less housing.) 2

To most people below the 48th parallel, ice fishing must seem like pounding your head against the wall, in that it's not doing it in the first place that makes the most sense. While it's true that it's not for everyone, it sure beats staying cooped up inside your house for six months. Here are some basics to get you started: 3

First, find a spot on the lake where the ice is thick enough to support your car without its dropping through. If you're unsure, watch someone else drive out first. Next, auger a fishing hole in the ice. An ice auger is like a posthole digger with a large screwlike cutting blade rotated by hand or motor. In the fun department, the powered ice auger sits just behind the chain saw and way ahead of the power leaf blower. 4

Most people opt for an ice-fishing house, a 10- by 16-foot shack with a propane stove and holes in the floor. The holes are usually covered by hinged plywood that can be flipped up for fishing. Some fishing houses are rudimentary, but others come with stereos, TVs, kitchens, bunk beds, couches, or even hot tubs and saunas parked next door. Ice anglers tend to have a lot invested in their fish houses. The shacks are usually painted to reflect the owner's personality, hobby, favorite sports franchise or cause. On the lake, brilliant colors are an advantage. An all-white house probably wouldn't be found until spring. 5

You'll need an ice-fishing pole with a reel, monofilament line and bobber. An ice-fishing pole looks pretty much like any other fishing pole but shorter, since casting isn't an option. You'll need a skimmer, or slotted ladle, for clearing out the ice that will form on the hole, and a five-gallon plastic bucket to haul your gear and your catch, or "tonnage." For bait, use a minnow or wax worm on a hook with a brightly colored weight. The best fishing is usually just off the bottom of the lake, which 6 is only about 40 feet deep at most. A slight tug, or "jigging," on the line every few seconds draws attention to the bait.

There are other ways to increase your luck, such as using feeding-time charts and depth finders and topographic maps of the lake bottom that show ridges and shoals. Every fisher man or woman has a secret weapon, a lure that will make a fish react against its better judgment, whether by seduction, rage or appetite. Some folks spray their lures with fish oil to take away the human scent. (A word of caution: keep the fish oil away from the beer.)   7

The fun of ice fishing is that you never know what you might catch: perch, trout, northern pike, muskie, crappie — even the coveted walleye. Or you can drop a line down deep and try to snag something prehistoric with a lantern on its head. You just don't know what's going to come out of that hole. Maybe a trophy fish — something to take to the taxidermist, maybe a reason to fix up the basement, put a piece of shag carpet over the oil stain, make wise investments with confidence gained and spend more time with the family. A whole world of new possibilities opens. I heard about one guy who felt a tug on his line and pulled up sharply to set the hook. There was a tremendous fight until finally up through the hole came a license plate. He threw the plate in the corner and was rebaiting his line when he had a fearsome epiphany. He ran outside to see the hole in the ice where his truck had been. (That one may be apocryphal.)   8

We used to call ice fishing "sitting around practicing for when we got old," but now we just call it "sitting around." Many fisherpeople use a "tip-up," a device that sends up a flag when a fish bites. This frees one to multitask — that is, fish and play cards, fish and watch TV, fish and learn Spanish, and so on. Other warning systems include buzzers, bells, whistles, car alarms and voice-activated computers ("I believe you have a fish, Dave"). I knew a high-school band teacher who rigged cymbals to crash when a fish took the bait.   9

Northern Minnesota is known for its stoic Nordic types, but to ice fish I think you also have to have a sense of humor. The people, like the weather, seem cold at first, but then you get used to them. Just remember: when a guy sitting next to you doesn't talk to you for hours, it doesn't mean he doesn't like you. If he then asks, "Cold enough for you?" take it as a sign of affection. Answer with, "I'd wear a coat," and you'll be fine.   10

READING ACTIVITY 3: Build Your Vocabulary

Determine the meanings of the following words from the context of Kevin Kling's essay. Then check their meanings by looking up the words in a dictionary: carpaccio (1), angling (2), abodes (2), rudimentary (5), casting (6), taxidermist (8), epiphany (8), apocryphal (8), stoic (10), Nordic (10).

READING ACTIVITY 4: Read to Improve Your Writing

Discuss the following questions about "Hook, Line, and Television" with your classmates.

1. What did you learn about ice fishing from reading Kling's essay?
2. A culture consists of the behaviors and beliefs that are characteristic of a certain group of people. In what ways are people who fish in the Minnesota winters part of a culture?
3. In your own words, describe one of the processes that ice fishers use — for example, to set up their huts or to increase their luck.
4. Explain the significance of the title of the piece, "Hook, Line, and Television."
5. What other sporting events are similar to ice fishing in the way that people behave?

A Cultural Hero

JOHN CULHANE

Oprah Winfrey: How Truth Changed Her Life

John Culhane is a journalist who writes about American culture and entertainment. His articles have appeared in the New York Times Magazine, *the* Los Angeles Times, *the* Chicago Tribune, American Film, Reader's Digest, *and* Newsweek. *Many Americans consider Oprah Winfrey a contemporary cultural hero because of the way she triumphed over personal hardships and has encouraged others to do the same. In the following essay, Culhane describes one of Winfrey's most precious values: telling the truth.*

In January 1984 a phenomenon hit the airwaves. Chicago's WLS-TV needed someone to take over its floundering morning program, which ranked third in local competition for the 9 a.m. slot. So it brought in a little-known news anchor from Baltimore. Her name was Oprah Winfrey.

Earthy, articulate and spontaneous, Oprah seemed to have a knack for connecting emotionally with her guests, her studio audience and her viewers. In a single season, she brought the show to the number one spot in its time period. In 1985 the program was retitled *The Oprah Winfrey Show,* and in 1986 it was syndicated nationally. Oprah won an Emmy for the 1986–87 year, and her approximately 20 million loyal viewers have made her program television's most popular daytime show.

But hers is not the typical celebrity success story, by any   3
means. Oprah actually calls her program "a kind of ministry."
And there is something more, something intensely personal and
powerful in the advice she often gives nervous guests before air
time. "Just tell the truth," she says quietly, gazing directly into
their eyes. "It'll save you every time."

It is a lesson Oprah learned against great odds. Signifi-   4
cantly, this woman noted for the unflinching honesty of her
interviews learned the value of truth only after she tried — and
failed — to lie her way to happiness.

As Oprah explains: She was born January 29, 1954, in   5
Kosciusko, Mississippi, to an unmarried 18-year-old farm girl.
Vernon Winfrey, a soldier at Fort Rucker, didn't even know until
much later that Vernita Lee had become pregnant with his child.

The infant was named after Orpah, the sister-in-law of Ruth   6
in the Bible. (The midwife misspelled the name "Oprah" on the
birth certificate.) Shortly after, Vernita Lee left Oprah in the
care of the child's grandmother and headed for Milwaukee,
where unskilled black women could find jobs as maids.

On the farm where she was reared, little Oprah began her   7
broadcasting career declaiming to the pigs in the barnyard. At
three, she was reciting in church. By the time her grandmother
enrolled her in kindergarten, Oprah could already read and
write well enough to send a note to her teacher: "Dear Miss New.
I do not think I belong here." Agreeing, Miss New advanced her
to the first grade, where envious classmates soon nicknamed her
The Preacher.

"From the time I was eight years old," says Oprah, "I was a   8
champion speaker. I spoke for every women's group, banquet,
church function — I did the circuit. Anybody needed anybody
to speak anything, they'd call me." Oprah begins to recite, in the
commanding voice she's had since childhood, from the famous
old poem "Invictus" by William Ernest Henley:

> *Out of the night that covers me,*
> *Black as the Pit from pole to pole,*
> *I thank whatever gods may be,*
> *For my unconquerable soul.*

Oprah grins. "Very impressive, especially when you're eight."   9

Between ages six and nine, Oprah lived part-time with her   10
mother in Milwaukee, part-time with her father in Nashville.
But then she moved in full-time with her mother. Perhaps her
precociousness was one reason the relationship was difficult. In
Oprah's words, "My mama really wasn't prepared to take on this
child — me."

Oprah's childhood innocence came to a traumatic end when,   11
at nine, she was raped by a teen-age cousin. "Three people
abused me from the time I was nine until I was fourteen," she

says. The horror of this sexual abuse would come out years later on one of Oprah's famous talk shows, but at the time she kept it secret, and it fed an enormous sense of shame and insecurity.

When Oprah was thirteen, she decided new, octagon-shaped glasses would make her beautiful and popular. Her mother refused, telling Oprah they couldn't afford such an extravagance. The next day, after her mother had gone to work, Oprah smashed her old glasses on the floor. She pulled down the curtains, knocked over a table and threw things around the room. Then she called the police. 12

"I decided to be unconscious when they came in and to have amnesia." 13

At the hospital, the doctor brought her mother to her bed, but Oprah pretended not to recognize her. "All we know is that someone broke into the apartment, hit her over the head and broke her glasses," explained the doctor. 14

"Broke her *glasses*?" asked Vernita Lee. "Do you mind if I'm alone with the child for a few minutes?" 15

The mother glared at her daughter and counted to three. As Oprah tells it: "She got to two, and I knew she was going to kill me. And so I said, 'It's coming back to me now . . . you're my mother!' She dragged me from the bed and we went home. Yes, I got the octagons." 16

But Oprah wasn't any happier. She ran away from home, only to be brought back. 17

She tells these stories on herself with her usual candor and humor, but it seems clear that the teen-age Oprah was using theatrical lies to win acceptance and love, just as she had won admiration in the past through her dramatic speaking roles. 18

Finally, Vernita Lee had had enough. "And that's how I ended up with my father." 19

Vernon Winfrey had married and grown into a responsible member of the community, a barber and pillar of the Baptist church. He and his wife, Zelma, were unsettled by the heavily made-up teen-ager with the tight skirt and belligerent expression. "You will not live in this house unless you abide by my rules," he told her. Those rules, and, more important, Vernon Winfrey's air of confidence and certainty, would change Oprah's life. 20

His first rule was that she had to be home by 11 p.m. Another was that she read a book a week and submit a written report on it. When she came home with C's on her report card, he told her: "If you were a child who could only get C's, then that is all I would expect of you. But you are not. So in this house, C's are not acceptable." 21

Oprah found herself getting home by ten minutes before eleven. And she became an honor student and president of the student council. But the most significant turn-around was her newfound honesty. 22

"I never told another lie. I wouldn't dream of making up a   23
story to my Dad. Let me tell you, there is something about
people who believe in discipline — they exude a kind of assur-
ance and realism."

Five feet, seven inches tall, about 135 pounds, with the   24
same dramatic eyes and magnetic presence we see today, Oprah
entered a Nashville beauty pageant in high school. She figured
she would be asked what she planned to do with her life, and
calculated the best answer would be: "I want to be a fourth-
grade schoolteacher."

But on the morning of the interview, she happened to watch   25
the *Today* show, then featuring Barbara Walters. And when the
judges asked her about her life's ambitions, she found herself
stating firmly: "I believe in truth, and I want to perpetuate truth.
So I want to be a journalist."

She won the contest and was offered a part-time news posi-   26
tion at a local radio station. In an oratorical contest, sponsored
by the Elks, she won a four-year scholarship that she used to
attend Tennessee State University in Nashville.

Once she was in college, the management of the CBS affili-   27
ate in Nashville offered her a job on television.

In 1976, the year she should have graduated, Oprah still had   28
to make curfew — which her father had now extended to midnight. Later that year, she moved to Baltimore to join WJZ-TV;
"her primary motive," according to her official biography, "was
to escape her father's curfew." And in Baltimore, destiny — in
the form of a Chicago TV station searching for a talk-show
host — found her.

The topics on her nationally syndicated show have ranged   29
from overcoming weight problems (a longtime concern for
Oprah, who recently shed more than 60 pounds) to racism. For
her most famous show, in February 1987, she went to an all-
white county in Georgia and asked an audience composed
entirely of white residents some simple questions: "Why has
Forsyth County not allowed black people to live here in 75
years? What is it you're afraid black people are going to do?"
Though there were some dissenters, Oprah found many in her
audience who believed in co-existence with blacks. The show
made newspaper stories across America.

Through her show, Oprah won a substantial victory over   30
herself. Her lawyer had advised her against ever disclosing that
she had been sexually abused as a child, arguing that many
people still blame the victims of abuse. He didn't want his client
to suffer from that stigma. Oprah agreed. Nevertheless, during a
program in which victims of sexual abuse spoke of their experiences, Oprah suddenly decided to tell her story. She put her
arms around another victim and wept with her. It was an honest, moving moment. . . .

Now there was just one more old fence to mend. Every time   31
she visited, her father warned her that she would not amount to
anything without a college degree. Oprah had left Tennessee
State without a diploma: she had finished all her course work,
but not her senior project.

Through a friend, Oprah made discreet inquiries: Would   32
Tennessee State University waive the senior-project requirement if Oprah did independent work or study? TSU would not.

Oprah had to re-enroll and then put together a project to   33
fulfill her requirement in the media course. So she did it. TSU
informed her that she would receive her diploma at the 1987
commencement ceremonies and invited her to address the
graduating class.

Vernon Winfrey was in the audience that packed Howard C.   34
Gentry complex on TSU's North Nashville campus. "Even though
I've done a few things in life, every time I've come home, my
father has said, 'You need that degree,'" she told the crowd. "So
this is a special day for my dad." With that, she announced she
was establishing scholarships at the school in his name.

She was her father's daughter, too, in the advice she gave to   35
fellow graduates: "Don't complain about what you don't have.
Use what you've got. To do less than your best is a sin. Every
single one of us has the power for greatness, because greatness
is determined by service — to yourself and to others."

She was Oprah the graduating senior, and she was also   36
Oprah the famous and wealthy entertainer. But she was still the
Oprah they used to call The Preacher, who had herself learned
the most valuable lesson of all: *Just tell the truth. It will save you
every time.*

READING ACTIVITY 5: Build Your Vocabulary

Determine the meanings of the following words from the context of
John Culhane's essay. Then check their meanings by looking up the
words in a dictionary: floundering (1), earthy (2), articulate (2), unflinching (4), precociousness (10), octagon (12), candor (18), belligerent (20), abide (20), dissenters (29).

READING ACTIVITY 6: Read to Improve Your Writing

Discuss the following questions about "Oprah Winfrey: How Truth
Changed Her Life" with your classmates.

1. What did you learn about Oprah Winfrey from this reading that
   you didn't already know?
2. Of the events that are described by Culhane, which one do you
   think had the most effect on Winfrey? Why?

3. According to the author, why is telling the truth so important to Winfrey?

4. Do you admire Winfrey? Why or why not?

5. How does Culhane keep his audience interested in his topic?

Writing Assignment

What cultures do you belong to? Consider your ethnic heritage, religion, age group, schools, workplaces, interests, social activities, and pastimes. Have you ever noticed that people who are unfamiliar with one of these cultures don't always understand it? No matter what your background is, your experience has given you specialized knowledge and a unique perspective. For this chapter's assignment, your goal is to teach Web log visitors something about a culture you know well. You (or your instructor) may decide to approach this assignment in one of several ways.

- Write about a cultural symbol you are familiar with.

  OR

- Write about a tradition that has special meaning for you.

  OR

- Write about a person who is a hero to members of a particular group.

Follow the guidance and activities in this chapter to discover, develop, and polish your knowledge into a finished essay that readers will find interesting and informative.

STEP 1. EXPLORE YOUR CHOICES

After a little thought, you should be able to identify several different cultures that have influenced who you are and how you look at the world. Your family heritage and the region where you grew up, for example, probably hold special meaning for you. You might belong to an activity club or a sports team, you may identify with fans of a particular kind of music, or you could participate in an online community. In addition to having multiple cultures to consider, you will explore three topic possibilities — a cultural symbol, a cultural tradition, and a cultural hero — before you choose one topic to develop.

As you begin to search for essay ideas, think about who might read your essay and what they may already know (or not know) about a culture you belong to. For now, you will keep your options open by working with all three of the topics suggested in the assignment. Once you have tried out these possibilities, you will have a better idea of what topic — or topics — will be most productive.

Analyzing Your Audience and Purpose

For more on audience and purpose, see pp. 8–12.

Because you will post your finished essay to a Web log, anybody with Internet access will be able to read it. In addition to your instructor and classmates, your audience may consist of family members, friends, and even complete strangers. Because your readers will come from different cultures, you need to figure out how much they might already know about your topic and what their attitude toward it may be. You will also need to provide plenty of context and detail so that a person who is unfamiliar with your culture will be able to understand what you have to say about it.

Consider, also, what you want to accomplish with your essay. Remember that the assignment is to teach blog readers something about a culture they might not fully understand. Although you may also be interested in expressing your feelings or persuading your readers to do something or think a certain way, always keep in mind that your goal is informative — to give them new information.

WRITING ACTIVITY 1: Analyze Your Audience
                    and Purpose

Your responses to the following questions will help you decide how to approach your topic.

1. How will readers find your blog? What interests or search terms might lead a person to it?
2. What is your reader's average age?
3. What percentage of your readers are likely to be female? Male?
4. What parts of the country or world could they be from?
5. What might your readers already know about your topic? If you asked them to list five words about your topic, which five might they list?
6. What do your readers need to know about your topic? What terms and concepts will you need to define? What objects or events would you need to describe in detail?
7. How might your readers feel about your topic? Will they find it interesting, or will you have to work to get their attention?

Gathering Ideas

Before you begin writing, it's always a good idea to explore a few topics by using different techniques. Trying out several possibilities often leads to unexpected ideas, and you might be surprised to discover which topic you have the most to say about. In the previous chapter, you gathered ideas by brainstorming, relating aloud, and clustering. In this chapter, you will again use clustering, but you will also add two more tools for gathering ideas about a cultural symbol, tradition, and hero — questioning and freewriting. Although the activities prompt you to use one technique for each topic possibility, don't hesitate to use additional approaches that work for you.

For more on gathering ideas, see pp. 12–16.

Clustering about a Cultural Symbol

A *symbol* is something that stands for or represents something else. For example, the American flag symbolizes the United States and also stands for freedom and democracy. The Star of David stands for Judaism, and a pink triangle symbolizes gay pride.

For more on clustering, see p. 14.

Some symbols are formal and permanent representations, such as the flag of the United States or the Statue of Liberty. As you discovered reading "My Mother's Food," however, symbols can be quite ordinary and represent any number of things for different people. Cultural symbols can take almost any form and often tell us what the people of the culture consider important.

To gather ideas about a cultural symbol that you might want to write about, try *clustering*, a technique that works especially well for visual topics. As you learned in the previous chapter, you start a cluster by putting a word or phrase in the center of a blank page and drawing a small circle around it. Write down other words or phrases that your topic brings to mind, draw small circles around them, and use lines to connect related ideas. If you need a starting point or if you get stuck, the following questions can help jump-start your thinking:

- Describe the object to someone who has not seen it before.
- When was the last time you encountered or used the object?
- What ideas, events, or other objects do you associate with the object?
- How does the object symbolize the culture's lifestyle or beliefs?

Here's how one student, Clara, used some of these questions to create a cluster about a cultural symbol that interested her — an artificial Christmas tree.

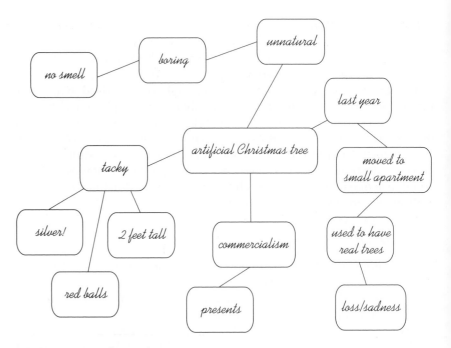

FIGURE 5.1. Clara's Clustering

WRITING ACTIVITY 2: Cluster about a Cultural Symbol

Select an object or image that symbolizes contemporary American culture or another culture that has influenced you. Then create a cluster that connects the words and phrases that you associate with this symbol. You may use the questions on page 143 to get started, but don't limit yourself to them.

 Cluster on the Computer
Use the drawing or picture option of your word-processing program to create your cluster.

Asking Questions about a Cultural Tradition

Put your clustering about a cultural symbol aside for now. Next, you want to gather ideas about another possible topic for your essay — cultural traditions.

A *tradition* is an event or activity repeatedly performed in the same way, usually to celebrate a culture's heritage and to bring people closer together. Many families develop traditions, such as annual reunions, that bring them together. A *cultural tradition,* however, extends beyond a family's rituals because it reflects the values of a whole culture.

Thanksgiving and the Fourth of July are cultural traditions unique to the United States. Some American cultural traditions have been adapted from other parts of the world and changed to suit American lifestyles and values. In Ireland, for example, St. Patrick's Day is a solemn Roman Catholic religious holiday, whereas in America the day has lost most of its religious overtones and has become a public festival that celebrates Irish heritage. New cultural traditions develop all the time. Kwanzaa, for instance, was started in 1966 by African Americans who adapted the customs and beliefs of several African tribes to celebrate their heritage and to foster a sense of community among Americans of African descent.

A good way to gather ideas for an essay about a cultural tradition is to use the six questions reporters often ask to ensure that they get every detail of a news story:

- *Who* participates in this tradition?
- *What* happens during the tradition?
- *Where* is this tradition practiced?
- *When* does this tradition take place?
- *How* is this tradition celebrated? (For example, do special clothes, food, music, or dance accompany it?)
- *Why* is the tradition important to the participants?

Here is how one student, Sandra Cordero, answered the reporter's questions about a Mexican tradition, the holiday El Grito de Dolores:

Who? This tradition is celebrated by people in Mexico. The governor of each city pretends to be Miguel Hidalgo. The people of the city attend a parade.

What? This tradition has people reenact the time when Miguel Hidalgo persuaded the people of Dolores to fight for freedom from Spain.

Where? This tradition is celebrated in every town and city in Mexico.

When? El Grito de Dolores takes place on the evening of September 15 and the morning of September 16.

How? Fireworks are set off, a parade is held, and some people dress in traditional costumes.

Why? The Mexican people use this tradition to celebrate their freedom from Spain.

WRITING ACTIVITY 3: Ask Questions about a Cultural Tradition

Select a tradition that you know well. Then use the journalist's questions — who, what, where, when, how, why — to generate ideas for an essay that could explain it to readers who aren't familiar with the tradition.

Make a Chart

Make a chart of questions about a cultural tradition and your responses to them by using a spreadsheet or the Tables tool in your word-processing program. If your ideas encompass more than one tradition, the chart can also help you compare and contrast your responses.

Freewriting about a Cultural Hero

Put your writing about a cultural tradition aside for now. It's time to explore a third possible topic before you select one topic for your essay.

We all have personal heroes — family members, friends, teachers, or coaches — whom we admire because of their courage, dedication, or hard work and who serve as role models. *Cultural heroes* are known by many people within a culture and inspire an entire culture. Some cultural heroes are a part of a group's heritage, others come from contemporary life, and still others are fictional characters. Sacagawea, the Dalai Lama, Mother Theresa, Martin Luther King Jr., Nelson Mandela, César Chávez, and Luke Skywalker are just a few examples of cultural heroes.

Who are some of your heroes? Although you may be able to list several people who have inspired you, you may not be certain that they are cultural heroes or that you know enough about them to fill a whole essay. You can find out if a person is a good subject for an essay by freewriting.

To freewrite, write without stopping for a certain period of time or until you reach a given page limit. Don't pause, go back, or make corrections; don't try to put your thoughts in order; above all, don't worry about whether your ideas are good or not. Just keep writing, and see what you have to say. You can start by answering these questions:

- What facts do you know about this person (age, accomplishments, and so on)?
- Which five words best describe this person?
- What do you most admire about this person?
- What makes this person a cultural hero?

Here's how one student, Mark, gathered ideas about the reggae musician Bob Marley by freewriting:

> Bob Marley was a great musician. I love his music. Most people only know one or two of his songs, like Buffalo Soldier and No Woman, No Cry. But he wrote a lot of songs that celebrated Jamaican culture. Political too. Marley was a Rastafarian. People think it's all about marijuana, but it's a serious religion. Bob Marley is a famous and respected musician. His reggae popularized Jamaican music for the rest of the world. He also celebrated his Jamaican heritage by reminding people of the beauty and strength of Jamaican culture. My dream is to visit Jamaica someday. Bob Marley died tragically at age thirty-six, but his spirit lives on in his music. His son Ziggy is a reggae artist too.

WRITING ACTIVITY 4: Freewrite about a Cultural Hero

On your own or with a group of classmates, brainstorm a list of cultural heroes. Consider musicians, athletes, public officials, religious leaders, actors, entrepreneurs, celebrities, and ordinary people who are widely known because of their extraordinary talent, dedication, or achievements. Then select a hero who interests you, and freewrite about that person for at least ten minutes.

STEP 2. WRITE YOUR DISCOVERY DRAFT

Now that you have experimented with at least three different topics that you might want to explore in an essay, you should be ready to begin a discovery draft. Remember that nobody creates a perfect essay in one try. Writing a discovery draft is a lot like the freewriting you did earlier in this chapter: experiment, let yourself wander, and feel free to make mistakes. You can focus on the details later when you revise and edit.

Choosing a Topic

You have gathered ideas on three aspects of culture — a symbol, a tradition, and a hero — and now have a rich source of material for writing. But you need to decide how to proceed.

Start by looking over the materials you wrote during your clustering, questioning, and freewriting. Which topic generated the most useful ideas? Which topic (or topics) are you most interested in pursuing? Which one will your readers want to learn about?

As you consider options for your discovery draft, you may stick with one of the three topics listed in the assignment (a cultural symbol, tradition, or hero), or you might decide to combine related topics. For instance, you could describe a cultural symbol that is part of a cultural tradition, or you might discuss a tradition that honors a cultural hero, as student writer Sandra Cordero does in the draft below.

Whatever you decide, the topic you choose should be one that interests you and that you are already fairly well informed about.

WRITING ACTIVITY 5: Choose Your Topic

Review your clustering, questioning, and freewriting, and identify or create a topic that you will enjoy writing about and that your audience will enjoy reading. If you wish, you may do more clustering, questioning, and freewriting (or whatever prewriting techniques work best for you) to gather additional ideas on one or more topics before you move forward.

Sharing Your Ideas

For more on thesis statements, see pp. 19–20.

Once you have settled on a topic, write a preliminary thesis statement to help focus your thoughts. As you draft and new ideas emerge, you can revise your thesis as many times as you need to.

If necessary, you might want to collect some basic information — such as dates and names — to get started. Most of the material for your discovery draft, however, should come from your own knowledge and experience. Keep your audience and purpose in mind as you decide what to include. Above all, remember that your main goal right now is to get your ideas down on paper. You'll have time later on to expand, fine-tune, and edit your draft.

Student writer Sandra Cordero used the reporter's questions to gather ideas about a Mexican holiday called El Grito de Dolores. She then wrote the following discovery draft about this cultural tradition that is meaningful to her but unfamiliar to most people outside of Mexico and the American Southwest. Her preliminary thesis statement is underlined. After reading the draft, discuss with your classmates what Sandra might do to revise it. (Note that the example includes the types of errors that typically appear in a discovery draft.)

El Grito de Dolores

I am proud to be part of the Mexican culture. The Mexican culture honors events important to its history. To celebrate Mexico's independence, Mexicans have El Grito de Dolores. El Grito de Dolores tells about what happened the day when the fight for our

independence was over. <u>Every Mexican participates in
this event because it's the way we thank our heroes
and ancestors for giving us freedom.</u>

*The preliminary thesis
statement*

   Our celebration begins the night of the 15th of
September. The main event is celebrated in Mexico's
capital, which is El Distrito Federal. The holiday is
celebrated everywhere in Mexico. Even the most little
towns have their own celebration. People get together
in the Main Plaza to celebrate the fiesta. Exactly at
midnight, the governor of each city goes on top of
the municipal building. "¡Viva Don Miguel Hidalgo!"
he yells to honor the person who made our
independence possible. The words "¡Viva México, Viva
México, Viva México!" give honor to our country.

   On the morning of the 16th of September, people
get together on the main street to see the parade.
The parade includes children, business leaders,
government leaders, clubs, police officers, and
firefighters. Everyone under the sun. On this day,
everyone feels the freedom that this day brought.
Every town in Mexico has a street called "16 de
Septiembre" where it begins and ends.

   We give honor to the men who made us free. Mexicans
believe in traditions. By giving honor to the men who
made us free, we thank them our ancestors for the
freedom that they have given us.

WRITING ACTIVITY 6: Write Your Discovery Draft

Prepare a preliminary thesis statement, and build on the ideas you
gathered during Step 1 to write a discovery draft. Remember that
your audience is visitors to a Web log and that your purpose is to
teach them something about a cultural symbol, tradition, or hero
important to you. For now, focus simply on getting your ideas in
writing. If you have any trouble, consider writing drafts on one or
more topics before you decide which one to continue working on.

STEP 3. REVISE YOUR DRAFT

   When you revise a discovery draft, you concentrate on clarifying
and supporting your ideas. Resist the urge to correct errors when
revising; you will do that during the editing stage.

The revision skills you learned in the previous chapter will also help you improve your essay about a cultural symbol, tradition, or hero. Check that (1) your thesis statement identifies your topic and expresses your main idea, (2) each paragraph has a topic sentence, and (3) your essay is well focused. In this chapter, you will learn how to use examples and process explanation to develop your ideas. You will also learn strategies for writing an effective introduction and conclusion, and you will practice connecting ideas with keywords and transitions.

Developing Your Ideas

An essay must be well developed to be convincing. In other words, you need to support your points with information. Detailed information helps the reader understand your subject and makes your essay more interesting. Two methods of development — examples and process explanation — are especially appropriate for an essay on a cultural symbol, tradition, or hero.

Examples

For more on using examples, see pp. 66–67.

Examples provide specific details that make a main point vivid and concrete. The most common type of examples are *facts*, or statements that can be verified to be true. Examples may also be specific *instances or events* that illustrate your main point, relevant *personal experiences*, or other people's *opinions*.

In his essay "Hook, Line, and Television," writer Kevin Kling uses examples to support his point that ice fishing is enjoyable because of the surprises it offers. Notice that he starts his paragraph with a topic sentence (underlined) and then provides several examples of surprises — verifiable facts, imagined possibilities, and specific instances — to support his idea:

> The fun of ice fishing is that you never know what you might catch: perch, trout, northern pike, muskie, crappie — even the coveted walleye. Or you can drop a line down deep and try to snag something prehistoric with a lantern on its head. You just don't know what's going to come out of that hole. Maybe a trophy fish — something to take to the taxidermist, maybe a reason to fix up the basement, put a piece of shag carpet over the oil stain, make wise investments with confidence gained and spend more time with the family. A whole world of new possibilities opens. I heard about one guy who felt a tug on his line and pulled up sharply to set the hook. There was a tremendous fight until finally up through the hole came a license plate. He threw the plate in the

corner and was rebaiting his line when he had a fearsome epiphany. He ran outside to see the hole in the ice where his truck had been. (That one may be apocryphal.)

Like Kling's, a paragraph that provides examples should include a topic sentence that explains what point the examples are meant to illustrate. It should provide enough examples and details to help your readers understand your main point. In addition, the examples should be clear, believable, and interesting for your audience.

HOW TO Use Examples

- Express a main idea in a topic sentence.

- Support the main idea with facts, specific instances or events, personal experiences, or expert opinions.

- Be sure that every example is clear, believable, and interesting.

- Check that you have provided enough examples to help readers understand your main point.

- Add details that develop your examples.

WRITING ACTIVITY 7: Use Examples to Develop Your Ideas

Review your discovery draft, looking for ideas that could be made clearer with examples. Add examples to at least one paragraph by expressing your point in a topic sentence and supporting that point with several facts, instances, experiences, or opinions. Be sure that you provide enough examples to support your idea and that you include details that help your readers understand your point.

Process Explanation

Writers use a technique called *process explanation* to show readers the series of steps needed to do something or to make something work. You may have read a recipe that explains how to cook something, a newspaper article that explains how wastewater is recycled or how a new law is passed, or a magazine article that describes how to repair a motorcycle or organize your desk. Each of these is an example of using a process explanation to develop a main idea.

Consider, for example, how Nora Okja Keller uses process explanation in "My Mother's Food" to explain how her mother made kim chee:

For more on using process explanation, see p. 68.

Propping me in a baby carrier next to the sink, my mother would rinse the cabbage she had soaked in salted water the night before. After patting the leaves dry, she would slather on the thick red-pepper sauce, rubbing the cloves of garlic and green onion into the underarms of the cabbage, bathing it as she would one of her own children. Then, grabbing them by their dangling leafy legs, she would push the wilting heads into five-gallon jars. She had to rise up on tiptoe, submerging her arm up to the elbow, to punch the kim chee to the bottom of the jar, squishing them into their own juices.

HOW TO Use Process Explanation

- Introduce the process you will describe.

- Provide the steps in the process in the order that they occur.

- Include details so that your reader can follow the process easily.

- Use keywords and transitions to move your reader from step to step.

After reviewing her discovery draft, student writer Sandra Cordero decided that she could use process explanation to give her readers a better sense of how the celebration of El Grito de Dolores begins. She drafted this paragraph for her revision (note that it includes the kinds of errors typical in the drafting and revision stages):

```
The celebration begins in the main plaza exactly
at midnight the governor of each city goes on top of
the municipal building. "¡Viva Don Miguel Hidalgo!"
he yells to give honor to the person who began the
movement for independence. ("Viva" means "long
live.") The people shout, "¡Viva México! Viva
México! Viva México!" Fireworks light up the night
sky. Everyone celebrates the country's independence.
```

WRITING ACTIVITY 8: Use Process Explanation to Develop Your Ideas

Exchange discovery drafts with a classmate. Read your partner's draft, and circle any sections that suggest a possibility for process explanation. (For example, in a draft about a cultural tradition, one paragraph might tell what participants do.) In the margins, say what you don't understand about a process, and ask for more information.

Your classmate should do the same for your paper. Using your partner's comments, add process explanation to your draft where it will
make your topic easier to understand.

Use the Comment Feature When Peer Reviewing
Consider exchanging electronic copies of drafts with a
classmate (on disk or by e-mail). You can use the Comment
feature of a word-processing program to insert notes, questions, and suggestions for revision into each other's drafts.
Before you print, you can keep, hide, or remove the
comments.

Building Your Essay

Now that you have added details to your essay, you'll want to make
sure that readers understand how those details work together to explain
a cultural symbol, tradition, or hero. As you learned in Chapter 4, a
strong thesis statement, clear topic sentences, and unified paragraphs
will help you communicate your thoughts clearly. Readers also expect
an essay to have an interesting introduction and a forceful conclusion,
and keywords and transitions can help readers connect your points
throughout an essay. Let's look first at introductions.

Write an Effective Introduction

The *introduction* to an essay serves three purposes: it gets your
readers' attention, it narrows the topic, and it provides your thesis
statement. By using the opening sentences of your essay to hook your
readers' interest, you persuade them to continue reading. By narrowing
your topic and presenting your thesis statement up front, you give your
readers a road map of sorts. Although introductions are often only one
paragraph with the thesis statement at the end of the paragraph, in
longer essays introductions may be two, three, or more paragraphs.

As you learned in Chapter 2, several techniques can help you hook
your reader's attention, narrow your topic, and lead to your thesis
statement. For an essay about a cultural symbol, tradition, or hero,
consider opening with description, interesting or surprising facts, a
brief story or anecdote, or a question — as the authors of the readings
in this chapter do.

Give a Description. An introduction that contains vivid *description*
sets the scene and draws readers into your essay. Kevin Kling, in
"Hook, Line, and Television" uses this technique to help readers imagine just how cold Minnesota is in the winter:

Every year the call goes out: the ice is safe. Open water has turned into prime real estate, and villages of tiny shacks pop up overnight. Thus ice-fishing season opens in Minnesota, home of the nation's icebox, where carpaccio is still made with carp and especially frigid winters are referred to by their year, like fine wine. Although months of subzero temperatures test the heartiest souls, some people actually live in this state on purpose. As I overheard one Northern gentleman say, "When you freeze paradise, it's bound to last a little longer."

Relate Facts. Introducing a topic with *facts* — statements that can be verified as true — has two important effects on readers. It signals to them that you know your topic well enough to teach them something, and it encourages them to read further to see what you have to say. The second paragraph of Kevin Kling's introduction to his essay on ice fishing, for example, is filled with surprising facts that grab a reader's attention:

Mille Lacs lake is one of the most popular fishing spots for ice fishing in the Land of 10,000 Lakes. It covers more than 200 square miles in the middle of Minnesota and is known for its walleye, arguably the best-tasting fish you can pull from fresh water. Once the ice sets — late November or early December, depending — local resort owners start renting out ice-fishing houses and hauling them out onto the lake, where bars, churches and the random bowling alley follow. By January, there will be around 5,000 angling abodes on the ice, which qualifies as a small city in Minnesota.

Tell a Story or Anecdote. Beginning with a brief *story* or *anecdote* can help draw readers into your essay because most readers like to read about other people's lives. Nora Okja Keller, for example, opens her essay about the cultural symbolism of kim chee with a personal anecdote about her love for the spicy pickled cabbage:

I was weaned on kim chee. A good baby, I was "able to eat anything," my mother told me. But what I especially loved was the fermenting, garlicky Chinese cabbage my mother pickled in our kitchen. Not waiting for her to lick the red peppers off the won bok, I would grab and gobble the bits of leaves as soon as she tore them into baby-size pieces. She said that even if my eyes watered, I would still ask for more.

John Culhane tells a longer, more detailed story to introduce a cultural hero in "Oprah Winfrey: How Truth Changed Her Life":

In January 1984 a phenomenon hit the airwaves. Chicago's WLS-TV needed someone to take over its floundering morning program, which ranked third in local competition for the 9 a.m. slot. So it brought in a little-known news anchor from Baltimore. Her name was Oprah Winfrey.

Culhane continues the story of Oprah's early career success, narrows his focus to her reputation for telling the truth, and then provides his thesis statement in the fourth and final paragraph of his introduction:

> Significantly, this woman noted for the unflinching honesty of her interviews learned the value of truth only after she tried — and failed — to lie her way to happiness.

Ask a Question. Posing one or more questions early in an essay can rouse readers' curiosity about your topic and encourage them to keep reading to find the answers to those questions. To improve her discovery draft (p. 148) about El Grito de Dolores, for example, student writer Sandra Cordero started her revised draft (p. 161) with a vivid description of the celebration and added a simple question to engage her readers:

    What is "El Grito de Dolores"?

Cordero uses the remainder of her essay to answer this question for her readers.

HOW TO Write an Effective Introduction

- Grab your readers' attention — perhaps with description, a surprising fact, a brief story or anecdote, or a question.

- Narrow your topic.

- Conclude with a thesis statement.

WRITING ACTIVITY 9: Revise Your Introduction

Reread the introductory paragraph of your essay. Then rate your introduction on a scale of 1 to 4 according to the following list:

1. Effective (forceful, attention-getting hook; clearly stated thesis statement)
2. Adequate (satisfactory hook; clearly stated thesis statement)
3. So-so (uninteresting hook; vague thesis statement)
4. Ineffective (no hook; no thesis statement)

Discuss your rating with your classmates. Then revise the introduction to your essay using one of the techniques discussed in this chapter. Also look at your thesis statement to see how you can make it more effective. It should announce your topic clearly and reveal its significance.

Write a Powerful Conclusion

The *conclusion* serves two major functions in an essay: it makes clear that you have made the point you introduced at the start of the essay, and it draws the essay to a satisfactory close. Thus, in the conclusion you do not include new material or end abruptly; instead, you wrap up what you have already said. Try to leave your readers with a lasting impression about your topic and its significance. For most short essays, the most effective way to conclude is to restate your thesis and broaden your focus.

Restate the Thesis. By *restating the thesis* with different wording in your conclusion, you remind readers of the significance of your topic and reinforce your main point or idea. For example, John Culhane provides versions of his thesis statement in both the introduction and conclusion to "Oprah Winfrey: How Truth Changed Her Life":

STATEMENT OF THESIS IN INTRODUCTION	This woman noted for the unflinching honesty of her interviews learned the value of truth only after she tried — and failed — to lie her way to happiness.
RESTATEMENT OF THESIS (ITALICIZED) IN CONCLUSION	She was Oprah the graduating senior, and she was also Oprah the famous and wealthy entertainer. But she was still the Oprah they used to call The Preacher, who had herself learned the most valuable lesson of all: *Just tell the truth: It will save you every time.*

Broaden the Focus. By *broadening the focus* of an essay in the conclusion, you connect your topic to something larger to show readers why it is important to them.

Because you have special knowledge of the topic, you can inform others about how to put the information you have provided to good use. A good way to broaden the focus of a personal essay about a cultural symbol, tradition, or hero is to conclude with a suggestion that your readers do something or that they continue thinking about how the topic affects them. In his conclusion to "Hook, Line, and Television," for example, Kevin Kling offers some tips for readers who might want to give ice fishing a try:

Northern Minnesota is known for its stoic Nordic types, but to ice fish I think you also have to have a sense of humor. The people, just like the weather, seem cold at first, but then you get used to them. Just remember: when a guy sitting next to you doesn't talk for hours, it doesn't mean he doesn't like you. If he then asks, "Cold enough for you?" take it as a sign of affection. Answer with "I'd wear a coat," and you'll be fine.

WRITING ACTIVITY 10: Revise Your Conclusion

Ask several members of your peer group to rate the concluding paragraph of your draft on a scale of 1 to 4 according to the following list:

1. Powerful (memorable closure; main point reinforced)
2. Adequate (interesting closure; main point reinforced)
3. So-so (uninteresting closure; main point reinforced)
4. Ineffective (no sense of closure; main point not reinforced)

Ask your group members to suggest how you could make your concluding paragraph more interesting and forceful. Use their suggestions and your own ideas to revise your conclusion, making sure that you restate your thesis and broaden your focus.

Connect Ideas

In addition to improving your introduction and conclusion when you revise your essay, be sure you show how your main idea and your supporting points are connected. You can do this by strengthening your thesis statement, by including topic sentences for each paragraph, and by using keywords and transitions.

Use Keywords. One way to connect your ideas is to repeat *keywords* — words that relate to the topic being discussed. By repeating a keyword, you keep your reader focused on the topic. In the following paragraph from "Hook, Line, and Television," for example, notice how the repetition of a keyword (underlined) contributes to the flow of ideas and reminds readers that the topic is ice fishing:

> First, find a spot on the lake where the <u>ice</u> is thick enough to support your car without its dropping through. If you're unsure, watch someone else drive out first. Next, auger a fishing hole in the <u>ice</u>. An <u>ice</u> auger is like a posthole digger with a large screw-like cutting blade rotated by hand or motor. In the fun department, the powered <u>ice</u> auger sits just behind the chain saw and way ahead of the power leaf blower.

In addition to repetition of the same keyword, you can use pronouns and synonyms as keywords. A *pronoun,* such as *it* or *them,* takes the place of the original word; a *synonym* is another word or phrase that refers to the same thing as the original keyword. In the following paragraph, notice how Nora Okja Keller's use of synonyms (underlined) for the keyword *kim chee* helps connect her ideas:

> We went crazy for the smell of <u>kim chee</u> — a perfume that lured us to the kitchen table. When my mother hefted the jar of

kim chee out of the refrigerator and opened the lid to extract the almost fluorescent strips of cabbage, she didn't have to call out to us, although she always did. "Girls, come join me," she would sing; even if we weren't hungry we couldn't resist. We all lingered over snacks that lasted two or three hours.

Add Transitions.   Another way to connect your ideas is to use *transitions*. Transitions show your readers how one idea relates to the next, making your writing easy to follow.

Most commonly, transitions are words or phrases that connect sentences within a paragraph. Here is a list of the relationships expressed by some of the most common transitions:

- *to add information:* additionally, and, also, as well, furthermore, in addition, too
- *to show differences:* but, in contrast, on the other hand, whereas
- *to show similarities:* as, in comparison, in the same way, similarly
- *to show time:* after, at that time, before, by then, during, meanwhile, now, since, sometimes, soon, then, until then, when, while
- *to show cause and effect:* as a result, because, consequently, hence, thereby, therefore, thus
- *to contradict or contrast:* although, but, however, in contrast, nevertheless, or
- *to add emphasis:* actually, furthermore, indeed, in fact, in truth, moreover, most important
- *to give an example:* for example, for instance, specifically, such as
- *to show sequence:* finally, first, last, next

When you use a transition, be sure it expresses the correct relationship between ideas. Notice how effectively Nora Okja Keller uses transitions (underlined) to connect ideas about her daughter's reaction to her first taste of kim chee:

When my daughter was fifteen months old, she took her first bite of kim chee. I had taken a small bite into my own mouth, sucking the hot juice from its leaves, giving it "mother taste" as my own mother had done for me. Still, my daughter's eyes watered. "Hot, hot," she said to her grandmother and me. But the taste must have been in some way familiar; instead of spitting up and crying for water, she pushed my hand to the open jar for another bite.

In longer essays, writers sometimes use *transitional paragraphs* to make ideas flow smoothly. A transitional paragraph connects the main idea in one section of an essay to the main idea of a section that follows it. This type of paragraph is usually from one to three sentences in length and, unlike most paragraphs, does not need a topic sentence.

John Culhane, for example, uses a transitional paragraph in "Oprah Winfrey: How Truth Changed Her Life":

> She tells these stories on herself with her usual candor and humor, but it seems clear that the teen-age Oprah was using theatrical lies to win acceptance and love, just as she had won admiration in the past through her dramatic speaking roles.

In this transitional paragraph, the author concludes his discussion of Oprah's lies and begins relating how Oprah started telling the truth.

Improve the Flow of Ideas

Use the **bold** function of your word processor to highlight the keywords in each paragraph. Check that your keywords pertain directly to the topic of the paragraph. Add, delete, or revise keywords as needed. Then use the *italic* function to highlight the transitions in each paragraph. Add transitions where the flow of thought seems disconnected or where there are no transitions in a long section. (Remember to remove the highlighting of keywords and transitions before printing your essay.)

HOW TO   Use Keywords and Transitions

Keywords and transitions provide a road map that can help readers connect your ideas.

■ To help readers follow your main idea, repeat keywords, and use pronouns and synonyms.

■ To move your readers to a new idea, use transitional words and phrases.

■ To move your readers from one major part of your essay to another, write a brief transitional paragraph.

GROUP ACTIVITY 2:   Add Keywords and Transitions

In the following paragraphs from *And the Beat Goes On: A Survey of Pop Music in America* by Charles Boeckman, keywords and transitions have been deleted. Work with your classmates to make the paragraphs more coherent by adding keywords and transitions.

In the 1950s, a revolution began in America. There was nothing quiet about it. It had happened before most people woke up to what was going on. It has been one of the most curious things in our history. The young people banded together, splintered off into a compartment totally their own. They formed their own culture, economy and morals. A generation of young people was totally immersed in its own music. It symbolized, reflected, dictated the very nature of its revolution.

The stage was set. Out of the wings stepped a young Memphis truck driver with a ducktail hair style and a sullen, brooding expression — Elvis Presley with his rock 'n' roll guitar. In 1954, a black group, the Chords, had played the rock 'n' roll style. In 1955, Bill Haley and a white group, the Comets, recorded the hit "Rock around the Clock." They lacked Elvis's charisma. They lacked his sex appeal. Elvis did more than sing. He went through a whole series of gyrations filled with sexual implications. It was just the thing for the mood of the hour. His voice trembled and cried out. His guitar thundered. His torso did bumps and grinds and shimmies. A whole generation of young people blew its cool.

WRITING ACTIVITY 11: Add Keywords and Transitions to Your Essay

Working in a group of three or four students, distribute copies of each group member's draft, and evaluate how well ideas are connected. On each draft, circle the keywords, synonyms, and pronouns, and underline the transitions. Your peers should do the same for your draft. Discuss with your classmates how each of you can improve the use of transitions. Then revise your draft, using your group's suggestions to add keywords and transitions.

A Student's Revised Draft

Throughout this chapter, you have been following Sandra Cordero as she gathered ideas and drafted an essay about El Grito de Dolores, a Mexican tradition that she thought others would be interested in learning more about. Before you read Sandra's revised draft, review her discovery draft on pages 148–49. Notice how Sandra revised by adding examples and process explanation to help her readers imagine themselves at the celebration. She inserted transitions to make her ideas flow more smoothly, and she added information about the cultural tradition that her readers may be unfamiliar with. (You may notice some errors in her revised draft; Sandra will correct these errors when she edits her essay.)

El Grito de Dolores

"¡Viva México! Viva México! Viva México!" hundreds of people cry out at the same time. Gathered in the town plaza at midnight on September 16, they are celebrating one of Mexico's most important holidays, El Grito de Dolores. The holiday honors the men and women who fought for Mexico's independence. On this day, Mexicans feel united as they celebrate their history.

The keyword holiday *is introduced.*

What is El Grito de Dolores? This expression means "the cry from Dolores," and it refers to an important event that happened early in the morning on September 16, 1810. At this time, Mexico was ruled by the Spanish king. But a priest named Miguel Hidalgo called together his parishioners at his church in Dolores, Guanajuato, Mexico. In a speech that was later called "El Grito de Dolores," Hidalgo urged his people to fight for freedom. This was the beginning of the Mexican revolution against Spain. Since then, the holiday is celebrated everywhere in Mexico. Even the smallest towns have their own celebrations.

Background information is added.

The transition at this time *is added.*

The transition since then *is added.*

The celebration begins in the main plaza exactly at midnight the governor of each city goes on top of the municipal building. "¡Viva Don Miguel Hidalgo!" he yells to honor the person who began the movement for independence. ("Viva" means "long live.") The people shout, "¡Viva México! Viva México! Viva México!" Fireworks light up the night sky. Everyone celebrates the country's independence.

The keyword celebration *is repeated.*

The keyword celebrates *is repeated.*

The next part of the celebration is a parade held on the morning of September 16. On the street called

Examples are added.

"16 de Septiembre." Every town in Mexico has a street with this name. The parade includes children, business leaders, government leaders, members of clubs, police officers, and firefighters. Green, red, and white streamers float through the air. People waving little Mexican flags to show their pride in their country.

The keyword celebration *is repeated.*

Mexico is sometimes divided because of politics. The 16th of September is a day of unity. El Grito de Dolores brings the Mexican people together in a celebration of their ancestors who fought for freedom.

GROUP ACTIVITY 3: Analyze Sandra's Revised Draft

Use the following questions to discuss with your classmates how Sandra improved her draft.

1. Is the purpose of Sandra's revised draft clear? What is her purpose?
2. What is Sandra's thesis statement? Could it be improved?
3. Does Sandra tell her readers enough to understand the cultural tradition? Explain.
4. How effective is Sandra's introduction? Conclusion?
5. Are the paragraphs in Sandra's revised draft better developed than those in her discovery draft? Do the ideas flow together better? Explain, and give examples.
6. How could Sandra's revised draft benefit from further revision?

WRITING ACTIVITY 12: Peer Review

Form a group with two or three other students, and exchange copies of your drafts. Read your draft aloud while your classmates follow along. Take notes on your classmates' responses to the following questions about your draft.

1. What did you like best about my essay?
2. How interesting is my introduction? Did you want to continue reading the paper? Why or why not?
3. What is my thesis statement? Do I need to make my essay's thesis clearer?
4. Where in the essay could I add examples and process explanation to help deliver my message?
5. How can I use keywords and transitions to make my ideas flow better?
6. Where can I combine sentences to improve the writing?

7. Where in the draft did my writing confuse you? How can I clarify my thoughts?

8. How effective is my conclusion? Do I end in a way that lets you know it's the end?

Use Online Peer Review
If your class has a Web site, see whether the peer review questions listed in Writing Activity 12 are available on the site. If they are, you may be able to respond to your classmates' drafts electronically.

WRITING ACTIVITY 13: Revise Your Draft

Finish revising your discovery draft by using the work you completed for Writing Activities 7 to 12 and your classmates' suggestions for revision. Make your introduction and conclusion as strong as they can be. In addition, develop your ideas with examples and process explanation, and use keywords and transitions to connect ideas. If you have time, look for irrelevant or unnecessary material that can be omitted, and experiment with moving sections of your draft to achieve the best presentation.

STEP 4. EDIT YOUR SENTENCES

So far in revising your paper, you have focused on improving your introduction and conclusion and on helping your ideas flow by using keywords and transitions. Now you're ready to make your sentences more readable and to edit your finished essay for correctness. Remember, errors distract your readers from what you have to say. In this chapter, you will learn how to combine sentences with conjunctive adverbs and how to identify and correct sentence fragments.

Combining Sentences Using Conjunctive Adverbs

By combining short, closely related sentences, you can clarify the relationship between ideas and make them easier to understand. Sentence combining also eliminates unnecessary words and keeps readers' interest by varying the types of sentences in an essay.

For more on sentence combining, see Ch. 17.

If your draft has short, complete sentences that are closely related, consider combining some of them with *conjunctive adverbs,* words and phrases that help readers understand how two ideas are related to each other. The following conjunctive adverbs are often used to combine sentences. Remember, a complete sentence has a subject and a verb.

CONJUNCTIVE ADVERBS

also	meanwhile	specifically
besides	moreover	subsequently
consequently	nevertheless	then
finally	next	therefore
furthermore	otherwise	thus
however	similarly	

To combine sentences with a conjunctive adverb, place a semicolon before the adverb and a comma after it. Notice how the sentences in the examples below make more sense when they are combined this way.

DISCONNECTED   My neighbor brings me flan whenever she makes a batch for her children. My pants are getting tight.

COMBINED   My neighbor brings me flan whenever she makes a batch for her children; consequently, my pants are getting tight.

DISCONNECTED   Hurricane Katrina devastated New Orleans. The first Mardi Gras after the disaster was a success.

COMBINED   Hurricane Katrina devastated New Orleans; nevertheless, the first Mardi Gras after the disaster was a success.

The conjunctive adverb can also appear in the middle of the second sentence, as in this example from Sandra Cordero's draft:

DISCONNECTED   Mexico is sometimes divided because of politics. The 16th of September is a day of unity.

COMBINED   Mexico is sometimes divided because of politics; the 16th of September, however, is a day of unity.

As you can see from this example, commas are placed both before and after the conjunctive adverb when it is in the middle of the sentence.

HOW TO Combine Sentences Using Conjunctive Adverbs

- Check that each of the two sentences you plan to combine has a subject and a verb and expresses a complete thought.

- Select a conjunctive adverb that shows how the sentences are related.

- Combine the two sentences with a semicolon, the conjunctive adverb, and a comma.

- If a conjunctive adverb appears in the middle of the second sentence, put commas before and after it.

EDITING ACTIVITY 1: Combine Sentences Using Conjunctive Adverbs

Combine the following pairs of sentences with conjunctive adverbs. Be sure you punctuate the combined sentences correctly.

EXAMPLE   In the United States, we play ~~"soccer." The~~ rest of the
$\overset{\text{"soccer"; however, the}}{\wedge}$
world calls the sport "football."

1. Sports competitions are some of the most important cultural traditions throughout the world. International sports competitions increase national pride.

2. In many countries, soccer is the most popular sport. The World Cup tournament draws huge crowds of fans.

3. Many fans watch the games with friends at neighborhood bars. Celebrations often spill into the streets.

4. Some fans drink too much. Others take the competition very seriously.

5. Violent behavior and riots have caused problems at past tournaments. Most countries vie for the honor of hosting the World Cup.

WRITING ACTIVITY 14: Combine Your Sentences

Examine your revised draft for short, closely related sentences. Where it makes sense to do so, combine them with conjunctive adverbs.

Exercise Central

For additional practice with using conjunctive adverbs to combine sentences, go to **bedfordstmartins.com/choices** and click on "Exercise Central."

Correcting Sentence Fragments

For more on sentence fragments, see pp. 542–46.

A *sentence fragment* is an incomplete sentence: it looks like a sentence, but something is missing.

A *complete sentence* contains a subject and a verb and expresses a complete thought. The subject tells who or what is doing the action. The verb explains the action or links the subject to the rest of the sentence.

The following are complete sentences. In each, the subject is italicized, and the verb is underlined.

SENTENCES

My *sister* attended graduation.

Jerry enjoys holidays.

I left class early.

He is my closest friend.

Unlike a sentence, a *sentence fragment* does not express a complete thought. A sentence fragment may be a *phrase,* a group of words that lacks a subject or a verb.

PHRASES

Attended graduation. (missing subject)

Cinco de Mayo. Jerry's favorite holiday. (missing verb)

Left class early. (missing subject)

My closest friend. (missing subject and verb)

To correct a sentence fragment that is a phrase, add the missing subject, verb, or both.

SENTENCES

My drill sergeant attended graduation.

Cinco de Mayo *is* Jerry's favorite holiday.

Abrian left class early.

Liza is my closest friend.

A sentence fragment may also be a *dependent clause,* a group of words that contains a subject and a verb but doesn't express a complete thought.

DEPENDENT CLAUSES

When my drill sergeant attended graduation.

Because it is Jerry's favorite holiday.

After Abrian left class early.

Since Liza is my closest friend.

There are three ways to correct a sentence fragment that is a dependent clause:

- Combine it with another sentence.
- Add information to make it a complete thought.
- Delete the conjunction or pronoun that starts it.

SENTENCES

I was proud when my drill sergeant attended graduation.

We went out for Cinco de Mayo because it is Jerry's favorite holiday.

Abrian left class early.

Liza is my closest friend.

HOW TO Correct Sentence Fragments

To identify a sentence fragment, ask yourself the following questions about each sentence in your essay:

- Does the sentence have a subject?

- Does the sentence have a verb?

- Does the sentence express a complete thought?

If you answer "No" to any of these questions, you have a sentence fragment. To correct the sentence fragment,

- Add the missing subject or verb or both.

  OR

- Combine the fragment with the sentence before or after it.

  OR

- Delete any words (such as conjunctions or pronouns) that make the clause dependent.

EDITING ACTIVITY 2: Correct Sentence Fragments

Correct each of the following sentence fragments by adding a missing subject or verb, by connecting a fragment to the sentence before or after it, or by adding information to form a complete thought.

1. My favorite custom is hiding Easter eggs. Because it's fun for everyone.

2. Since I left home. My mother calls me every other day.

3. Approaching my home.

4. Never a dull moment.

5. Forgot to celebrate my birthday!

Exercise Central
For additional practice with eliminating sentence fragments, go to **bedfordstmartins.com/choices** and click on "Exercise Central."

WRITING ACTIVITY 15: Edit Your Sentences

Read your essay word for word, looking for errors in sentence structure, grammar, spelling, and punctuation. Focus on finding and correcting sentence fragments. Also ask a friend or classmate to help you spot errors you might have overlooked. Then correct the errors you find, using a dictionary and the Handbook in Part Four of this book to help you.

A Student's Edited Essay

You probably noticed that Sandra's revised draft contained errors in sentence structure and punctuation. Sandra corrected these errors in her edited essay. Her corrections are underlined.

El Grito de Dolores
Sandra Cordero

"¡Viva México! Viva México! Viva México!" hundreds of people cry out at the same time. Gathered in the town plaza at midnight on September 16, they are celebrating one of Mexico's most important holidays, El Grito de Dolores. The holiday honors the men and women who fought for Mexico's independence. On this day, Mexicans feel united as they celebrate their history.

What is El Grito de Dolores? This expression means "the cry from Dolores," and it refers to an important event that happened early in the morning on September 16, 1810. At this time, Mexico was ruled by the Spanish king. A priest named Miguel Hidalgo called together his parishioners at his church in Dolores, Guanajuato, Mexico. In a speech that was later called "El Grito de Dolores," Hidalgo urged his people to fight for freedom. This was the beginning of the

A sentence fragment is corrected.

Mexican revolution against Spain. Since then, the holiday is celebrated everywhere in Mexico. Even the smallest towns have their own celebrations.

The celebration begins in the main plaza. Exactly at midnight, the governor of each city goes on top of the municipal building. "¡Viva Don Miguel Hidalgo!" he yells to honor the person who began the movement for independence. ("Viva" means "long live.") The people shout, "¡Viva México! Viva México! Viva México!" Fireworks light up the night sky; meanwhile, everyone celebrates the country's independence.

Sentences are combined.

The next part of the celebration is a parade held on the morning of September 16 on the street called "16 de Septiembre." Every town in Mexico has a street with this name. The parade includes children, business leaders, government leaders, members of clubs, police officers, and firefighters. Green, red, and white streamers float through the air. People wave little Mexican flags to show their pride in their country.

A sentence fragment is corrected.

A sentence fragment is corrected.

Mexico is sometimes divided because of politics; the 16th of September, however, is a day of unity. El Grito de Dolores brings the Mexican people together in a celebration of their ancestors who fought for freedom.

Sentences are combined.

STEP 5. SHARE YOUR ESSAY

Blogs, a term for diaries that are posted on Web sites, are rapidly growing in popularity — for those who write and read them. Many colleges and universities provide blog space for their students. Some even recruit volunteers to write blogs that help potential students prepare for the college experience.

Share your essay with a wide range of readers by posting it to a campus Web log portal or to one of your own blogs. (If you don't have a blog, ask a staff member at the campus computer center to show you how to set up one.) E-mail the URL for the site to your instructor, your family and friends, and your classmates (especially students who come from cultures other than your own, including members of a campus organization for international students). Be sure to include a Comments or Feedback option so that readers can share their responses with you. You'll be surprised by how many people read and learn from your essay. (Don't forget to visit your classmate's blogs and to share your responses with them.)

Free Blogging Services
Many Web sites make it easy to create and maintain your own blog. To find a free blog hosting service, go to **bedford stmartins.com/choices** and click on "Annotated Web Links."

CHAPTER CHECKLIST

❏ I gathered ideas on a cultural symbol, tradition, or hero by clustering, asking questions, and freewriting.

❏ I developed the ideas in my paragraphs with examples and process explanation.

❏ I strengthened my introduction by hooking readers, narrowing my focus, and providing a thesis statement.

❏ I wrote a strong conclusion that restates my thesis and broadens the topic.

❏ I made my ideas easier to understand by connecting them with keywords and transitions.

❏ I combined closely related sentences by using conjunctive adverbs.

❏ I eliminated sentence fragments.

❏ I posted my finished essay to a Web log.

REFLECTING ON YOUR WRITING

To help you continue to improve as a writer, answer the following questions:

1. Did you enjoy writing about an aspect of your culture? Why or why not?

2. Which topic did you choose — a cultural symbol, tradition, or hero? Why?

3. What types of changes did you make to your essay when you revised?

4. If you had more time, what further revisions would you make to improve your essay? Why?

Using your answers to these questions, complete a Writing Process Report for this chapter (you can download a report form at **bedford stmartins.com/choices**). Once you complete this report, freewrite about what you learned in this chapter.

A Cultural Symbol

GERALD HAUSMAN

Feather

Gerald Hausman is a poet, writer, and teacher. He is also a student of Native American mythology and folklore and has published dozens of books on these subjects. In "Feather," which is an excerpt from Turtle Island Alphabet: A Lexicon of Native American Symbols and Culture *(1992), Hausman writes about the symbolic importance of the feather in Native American life.*

For decorations of war, worship, and as an expression of flight, the feather is the universal Native American symbol. In Arctic regions, the Indian sought water birds. On the North Pacific coast, they captured or killed ravens and flickers. In California, the tribes hunted woodpeckers, meadowlarks, crested quail, mallard ducks, blue jays, blackbirds, and orioles. Around the southwestern pueblos, hunters went after eagles, hawks, turkeys, and parrots. Using the feathers and skins and even bodies of birds, the tribes made clothes, masks, hats, blankets, and robes.   1

Parkas in the Arctic were made of water-bird skins sewn together, the feathers acting as insulation and waterproofing. Tribes to the south used the skins of young waterfowl, while still downy, and sewed them into robes. Eastern tribes cut bird skins into strips and wove them into blankets in the same way that western tribes used rabbit skins.   2

Captain John Smith and other early European settlers observed that the Indians of the East fashioned turkey robes: feathers tied in knots to form a network out of which beautiful patterned cloaks were wrought.   3

Fans and other accessories of dress were made of wings or feathers by the Iroquois. The western Eskimo sewed little sprays of down into the seams of garments. California tribes decorated their basketry with feathers; quills of small birds were incorporated into basketry in much the same way as porcupine quills. Of course, one of the most common uses of the feather was in arrow making. For giving directness in flight, arrow feathers were split so that halves could be glued to the shaft of the arrow in twos and threes.   4

An unusual use of bird scalps was practiced by certain California tribes, who used them as money, being both a standard of value and a medium of exchange.   5

The down feathers of birds have a special value to Native 6
Americans. Light and airy, fluffy and snowy, these feathers can
be seen as a bridge between the spirit world and Mother Earth,
or simply as messenger and prayer feathers. *Pahos*, as they are
called among the Hopi, are used to mark sacred sites and to
summon the deities as well as to ask their blessing.

The symbolism of the feather is a compression, so to speak, 7
of the bird. Humankind, seeing that birds can fly, has always
been desirous of flight. The mythology of angels, airborne deities
residing in heaven or heavens, is common to the collective
human tribe. The wish to fly, understood on its primary level, is
merely the desire to have something one does not or cannot
have. On a deeper philosophical level, however, flight is the
dreamlike movement of the unconscious, the freedom of will,
the connection between the spiritual and the material. In flight,
man releases his earthbound nature and is reborn in spirit. . . .

READING ACTIVITY 7: Build Your Vocabulary

Determine the meanings of the following words from the context of
Gerald Hausman's essay. Then check their meanings by looking up
the words in a dictionary: insulation (2), wrought (3), incorporated
(4), medium (5), summon (6), deities (6), compression (7), unconscious (7).

READING ACTIVITY 8: Read to Improve Your Writing

Discuss the following questions about "Feather" with your classmates.

1. What are some examples of the different ways that Native
   Americans have used feathers?
2. Why did down feathers have special value?
3. Why has the feather become the "universal Native American symbol" (1)?
4. Explain the author's meaning in this sentence: "In flight, man
   releases his earthbound nature and is reborn in spirit" (7).
5. How does Hausman use description to support his points about
   the feather in Native American culture?

A Cultural Tradition

ANASTACIA MARX DE SALCEDO

Pass the Pernil,
Save Room for the Tarta

Many immigrants find that their children often forget or don't ever even learn the language and culture of their ancestors. In "Pass the Pernil, Save Room for the Tarta," Anastacia Marx de Salcedo, a correspondent for the Boston Globe, *describes how a parents' group uses food to ensure that their children feel connected to their heritage.*

It's 11:30 a.m. on a Sunday before Easter and Fátima Serra, 1
Douglas Massidda, and their two children are the first arrivals —
and only 30 minutes late. Fátima balances a large, flat copper
pan with steam escaping from under its foil cover, which is keeping warm a Spanish omelet. Douglas carries a tureen of bean
and littleneck stew, a shopping bag filled with assorted Spanish
liqueurs, and a box of Dominican cigars.

Their children, Marina, 10, and Enrique, 6, and our three 2
daughters, Amalia, 10, Dalila, 3, and Eloisa, 2, disappear into
the living room. We know we won't see them again until the
egg hunt. Grown-up shoulders relax. With a nod to parental responsibility, someone shouts after them, "¡Español, por favor!"
("Spanish, please!") Then we follow the scent of hot fat into the
kitchen, where my husband, Jorge Antonio, who is from Cuba,
is working intensely making *tostones,* double-fried green plantain slices.

Our group of Spanish-speaking families, which has been 3
meeting for almost 10 years, was formed so that our children
would hear our native language spoken outside the home. From
the beginning, we've had two simple rules: No English, and families must take turns organizing the monthly gathering. This
month, Jorge and I are hosting an Easter potluck at our house in
Cambridge.[1] There are 30 people (slightly more than half of them
under the age of 10) representing professions as diverse as music,
advertising, academia, and finance, and places as far-flung as
Argentina, Cuba, Chile, Panama, Puerto Rico, and Spain, as well
as some who, like me, were born in the United States.

The food will be as varied as the company — a happy mix of 4
traditional Spanish fare, itself a cocktail of southern European
and Islamic cultures, and of Latin American cooking, a result of
recent encounters among Spanish, African, and indigenous

---

[1] A suburb of Boston, Massachusetts.

American traditions. None of the dishes is especially linked with the Easter holiday, although the buffet will include a famous almond cake made for over 500 years by the Order of Saint James of Compostela in Spain.

The kitchen is getting too busy for conversation, but that's OK. We have a pitcher of frosty mojitos — rum, lime, sugar, and spearmint — to console us while we're entertained by Jorge's plantain production line. It's a complicated procedure. Peel the thick-skinned vegetable under running water. Cut into chunks. Submerge in simmering oil. Fish out. Smash. Fry again. Fish out. The last stage is the most difficult; the crispy disks require round-the-clock protection. Survivors will be piled on a plate with a sprinkle of lime juice and kosher salt.   5

The doorbell rings again. A small phalanx of Tapiero children rushes the doorway at heights varying from knee (Lukas, 2) and waist (Nicolas, 6) to chest (Christina, 10). Their mother, Lisa, staggers in under the weight of three bulging Shaw's[2] bags; then her husband, Eddie, enters holding something in a big roasting pan.   6

"Is the oven hot?" he shouts, wrenching open its door and shoving in a half-cooked piece of meat. This was supposed to have been a pernil, or roast leg of fresh pork. But at 8:00 the night before, Eddie had called, sounding somber. "I'm at the Brazilian butcher's in Somerville,"[3] he said. "Guess what? They sold my pernil to someone else." Pernil is traditionally eaten during the holidays in Latin America; it is not carried regularly at supermarkets or specialty butchers here, so Eddie had special-ordered his earlier in the week.   7

Even at that late hour, we tried to find one. Jorge headed out to cruise the meat cases of nearby grocery stores. I hit the phones, trying to sweet-talk local barbecue joints into selling me a spare hog haunch on a busy Saturday night. Eddie, meanwhile, began negotiations with the shop owner, and they solved the crisis. Two pork shoulders will take the place of the hind leg.   8

As the pernil bronzes in its garlic, soy sauce, and orange juice marinade, Eddie turns his attention to the preparation of *lagarto*, or alligator. This isn't real alligator meat, but rather a flank steak slit down the middle and stuffed with bacon and the spicy sausages, *chorizo*. The graphic name comes from the resemblance to an alligator's stomach after a good meal. After he assigns Douglas garlic duty, a responsibility not to be taken lightly in Latin cooking, Eddie tenderizes the meat by pounding along to a CD by Ruben Blades, his Panamanian compatriot.   9

Other families straggle in, herding children and bearing their culinary contributions. The Fernándezes, both language   10

---

[2] A New England supermarket chain.
[3] A suburb of Boston, Massachusetts.

professors, with 5-year-old Mariel and baby Lukas, carry a trio of Spanish desserts. The Amadors, musicians, and their twin 9-year-old girls, Sonia and Alisa, offer red chili enchiladas from Brian's native New Mexico. The Wheeler-Lópezes, financiers with 10-year-old Alejandro and 8-year-old Sarita, arrived with that old Cuban standby, black beans and rice. The last to ring the bell is saxophonist Pati Zarate with toddler Daniela, baby Carolina, and her Chilean cousin Felix Díaz, who is at Boston University studying law. Their offering: four hearty appetites.

But first, the egg hunt. Before we can count "uno, dos, tres," 11 the children have descended on the muddy yard and are combing every square inch of ground, bush, and tree for foil-wrapped chocolate eggs and *cascarones,* confetti-filled egg shells, a tradition borrowed from Mexico. Smash! Sonia cracks an egg on Marina's head. Smash! Marina cracks one on her mother's. A cascaron hunt combines two kid-pleasing activities: finding stuff and breaking stuff. In no time at all, the yard is strewn with colorful bits of paper and eggshell and everyone is laughing.

When we open the back door again, a garlic-infused cloud 12 escapes. The pernil is done. Cooks cram into the kitchen to primp their dishes. Fátima ladles creamy stew into cups, topping each with a few mahogany littlenecks; she slices the omelet and drapes it with melting strips of roasted peppers. Brian broils the cheesy top of his enchilada casserole. Alba López stirs the black beans and samples white rice from the pot. The tostones (what's left of them) are escorted to the dining room.

Pernil and lagarto, both dripping with cooking juices, are 13 carved. On the sideboard, Marisol Fernández fiddles with the placement of a cross-emblazoned *tarta de Santiago,* coffee flan, and lemon yogurt cake. Wines from Spain, Argentina, and Chile are uncorked, fruit juice is sloshed into paper cups. People spring into position around the buffet.

All our parties end the same way: out in the yard, huddled 14 around a table littered with sticky glasses, watching the darkness descend. Douglas is master of ceremonies, distributing cigars and pouring brandies and liqueurs into his traveling snifters. After seven hours of fiesta we still don't want to stop. At this point, we indulge in a recurring collective fantasy — a trip together. Where we would go isn't important. Italy? Panama? Mexico?

"Let's advertise," suggests Eddie, "for a Latino with a yacht. 15 But seriously, this year, let's make it happen."

"Let's go to Martha's Vineyard," says Rosi Amador, our resi- 16 dent realist. Nacho Fernández pulls out a dollar to start the vacation fund.

"Got your guitar?" Eddie asks Brian. Brian shakes his head. 17 A lack of instruments is no impediment. With Rosi leading us off, we launch into an original rendition of "El Cuarto de Tula" (Tula's Room), the Cuban classic recently revived by the Buena Vista Social Club.

"And she didn't put out the candle," we wail happily. The   18
singing drifts up into the quiet Cambridge night.

READING ACTIVITY 9: Build Your Vocabulary

Determine the meanings of the following words from the context of
Anastacia Marx de Salcedo's essay. Then check their meanings by looking up the words in a dictionary: tureen (1), littleneck (1), plantain
(2), indigenous (4), phalanx (6), wrenching (7), somber (7), haunch
(8), compatriot (9), culinary (10), infused (12), emblazoned (13), impediment (17).

READING ACTIVITY 10: Read to Improve Your Writing

Discuss the following questions about "Pass the Pernil, Save Room
for the Tarta" with your classmates.

1. Why have the author and several of her Spanish-speaking friends
   established a tradition of gathering once a month?
2. What are some examples of cultural traditions that the guests use
   at the party?
3. Reread paragraph 6. Why does Marx de Salcedo describe the
   process of making *tostones*?
4. Identify at least three keywords that the author repeats throughout the essay to help readers follow her point.
5. Underline the transitional words and phrases used in this essay. How
   do they help you follow the events that Marx de Salcedo describes?

A Cultural Hero

JEREMY DORN

A Hero's Last Ride

*Jeremy Dorn is a student at Las Lomas High School in Walnut Creek,
California. Dorn is the sports editor for the school paper,* The Page.
*In addition, he has been writing articles for SportsColumn.com, an
online sports forum, since 2005. Dorn is an avid sports fan who
plans to study journalism or creative writing in college. In "A Hero's
Last Ride," which was published on SportsColumn.com on July 29,
2005, Dorn points out that Lance Armstrong's unprecedented success
as a cyclist — winning seven consecutive Tour de France titles — is
not the only reason he is so greatly admired.*

"ULTIMATE SPORTS HERO MIX": MIXING INSTRUCTIONS   1

Step 1:   Fill pot with dedication and hard work, and turn up the desire until it is boiling.

Step 2:   Stir in the obstacles (the package containing France, cancer, and critics).

Step 3:   Now add the entire box of pressure and expectation, and supervise for seven years as it dissolves.

Step 4:   Add as much courage as you can find to the pot, stir for ten minutes, and then top it off by adding a touch of champagne and a yellow jersey to the mix and letting it sit in its glory for the rest of its life.

So what do you get with this strange concoction? If you fol-   2
low these directions, you receive the best, most inspirational athlete of this era. He overcame enormous odds to return to his sport; he cleared so many hurdles on his way back. He had to swim the English Channel while his opponents took a lap in a pool. He had to climb Mt. Everest; they took a stroll in the foothills. Lance Armstrong is not only riding away from his sport on top, but he is leaving as the best there ever was.

Everyone knows his story, what he accomplished, how he did   3
it. Lance Armstrong is a household name, and not just because of his yellow bracelets. So when he announced that 2005 would be his last Tour de France, was there really any doubt that he would capture that unprecedented seventh straight title?

He had already defeated so many demons on the way there,   4
what was going to stop him from winning again? Absolutely nothing. If the critics couldn't get to him, if he didn't crack under the pressure and expectations of an entire nation, why would a silly little race beat him? Cancer? He took it down. The almighty French? No problem. There is nothing he couldn't do and he left the same way he came in, by winning the Tour de France yet again.

How do the other riders compete with someone who has   5
made it through so much? They all know about the tragic event that could have taken his life, and that derailed his career for two years. He was ranked as the number one cyclist in the world going into 1996, when something his doctor told him put a quick stop to his certain stardom. He was diagnosed with advanced testicular cancer that had spread to his lungs and brain. He had less than a 50 percent chance of recovering. But, always determined, Lance began on a rigorous chemotherapy schedule and amazed everyone in 1999 when he was able to get back on his bike and ride in the Tour de France.

Though he was scarred from his fight with cancer, just lin-   6
ing up at the start of the race was a victory in itself for Lance.

When he actually came out and beat all the other world-class cyclists in that Tour, who could have known it would be the start to the most famous and inspirational record-setting career in cycling history? Not only did that first win shock the world, but it opened the eyes of American citizens to the man representing their country on foreign soil and winning the most demanding physical event in sports.

Lance went on to win again in 2000 and 2001. Then he won . . . again . . . and again . . . and again. By 2004 he had won six consecutive Tour de France races, breaking a record and infuriating the French. Why was this American so dominant in their race? There were talks of steroids involved, illegal substances, cheating on Armstrong's part. But he had done it all legitimately, and nothing could change that. He had no fear, knowing that he had already stared death in the face and survived. No rider could compete with someone with so much motivation.   7

Coming into 2005, the Tour de France committee even attempted to "Lance proof" the course to give other riders a chance at winning. Nothing they did would work, and the Tour de Lance continued; Armstrong's Discovery Team rode into Paris at the end of the last stage, with Armstrong maintaining his four-minute and forty-second lead over the second-place finisher. It had gotten to a point where if someone asked you who you thought would win the Tour de France, it was a natural response, a no-brainer to say: "Lance! Duh!" Lance Armstrong has provided us with seven years of excitement, and now he is leaving just the way he should: with that one last title.   8

He has done so much for the sport, gotten it recognition everywhere, and he is an amazing, inspiring role model to athletes everywhere. Even with his departure, cycling will become more and more popular because of the presence he had. He is a walking example of the phrase "nothing is impossible."   9

As Lance rides off into the sunset toward the rest of his life, let us wish him luck in whatever comes his way. Thank you, Lance Armstrong, for all you've done for athletes everywhere and how much hope you've given to anyone who didn't believe they could succeed. Your legacy will live on forever in the minds and memories of everyone who knows your name. Now go enjoy the rest of your life. You deserve nothing less.   10

READING ACTIVITY 11: Build Your Vocabulary

Determine the meanings of the following words from the context of Jeremy Dorn's essay. Then check their meanings by looking up the words in a dictionary: concoction (2), unprecedented (3), derailed (5), rigorous (5), consecutive (7), legacy (10).

READING ACTIVITY 12: Read to Improve Your Writing

Discuss the following questions about "A Hero's Last Ride" with your classmates.

1. List at least three groups for whom Lance Armstrong is a hero. Why, according to the author, is this one man a hero to so many different kinds of people?

2. How does Dorn's use of examples help you understand Armstrong's accomplishments?

3. What do you consider Armstrong's greatest accomplishment?

4. Jeremy Dorn introduces his subject with a mock recipe for the "ultimate sports hero." Does this use of process explanation create an effective introduction? Why or why not?

5. In your own words, what is the author's thesis? Does he provide a thesis statement, or is his main point implied?

Investigating a Workplace

6

Using Classification and Definition

In this chapter, you will write about an occupation that interests you, a style of workplace communication, or a job-related problem. As you follow the steps of the writing process, you will

- Gather ideas by freewriting, brainstorming, and consulting with others.

- Develop your ideas using classification and definition.

- Practice using researched material in your writing.

- Combine sentences with subordinate conjunctions.

- Learn to correct comma splices.

- Submit your essay to a newsletter.

One of the first questions most people ask when they meet someone new is, "What do you do?" This question shows the importance that people place on work. Most people want their occupations to be satisfying and rewarding. After all, we're likely to spend at least forty hours a week in the workplace. It's better to look forward to those hours than to dread them.

Finding the right occupation is not an easy task, however. Most people will hold many different jobs and change career fields a few times during their lives. Look at the résumés of just a few of America's presidents, for instance: Harry S Truman owned a clothing store, Jimmy Carter farmed peanuts, George W. Bush drilled for oil. You might already have had several jobs yourself, and if you're like most college students, you're probably preparing for a better future.

When you consider a particular occupation, you'll need to determine how well the job matches your interests and abilities. To succeed, you'll also need to understand the culture of a profession — how people think, dress, behave, and communicate. Finally, it helps to learn how people in an occupation go about solving the problems that they encounter.

In this chapter, you'll have the chance to learn more about a job that interests you. You'll also examine the communication styles in a given occupation, as well as look for ways to solve a problem you may have encountered in the workplace. Because your investigations will uncover information that will be helpful to your peers, you will share what you learn with other students who have similar career interests.

GROUP ACTIVITY 1: Think about Workplaces

With several classmates, examine the photograph on page 180. What kind of work appears to be going on? Would this type of work and workplace appeal to you? Why or why not? With your classmates, brainstorm a list of unusual occupations that might interest you.

READING ESSAYS ABOUT WORK

A good starting point for learning more about any occupation is to read about it. You can find information about a particular field in reference books and on Web sites, for example, as well as in personal essays and memoirs that describe people's experiences in the workplace. Successful businesspeople and professionals often publish books and magazine articles filled with advice for overcoming problems and achieving your career goals. To get a feel for this kind of writing, read the following short essays that describe an occupation, analyze communication in the workplace, and suggest ways to solve problems on the job. As you read, pay close attention to how the writers use definition and classification to explain their ideas.

An Occupation

THE EDITORS OF WETFEET.COM

Career Profile: Science

Because of the popularity of television shows featuring forensic detectives, many people have become interested in that field. However, the work of actual forensic detectives is very different from the way it's depicted on crime shows. Before committing yourself to a certain occupation, find out what it's really like to do that kind of work. The following article, "Career Profile: Science," describes what it's like to be a scientist. This article is taken from WetFeet.com, a Web site that publishes career guides and sponsors job searches.

So you like science — the test tubes, the cool high-tech equipment, the absolute certainty of knowledge — but you don't want to spend the rest of your life rambling around the marble hallways of a university. Those who've studied the pure sciences, such as physics, chemistry, and biology, can find lucrative and intellectually challenging careers in the private sector. 1

Scientists who work in the private sector are involved with applied research and development. While their work deals with the same concepts as scientists employed at universities, private sector scientists generally cope with a more stringent time frame and are more attuned to the bottom line. Scientists are in business to turn their ideas and hypotheses into products their companies can sell. 2

Of course, engineers also apply scientific principles to create products. But unlike engineers, applied scientists usually work on more fundamental research and are removed from the production lines. If you want to think of it in terms of a continuum, research scientists at universities deal with abstract principles of science. 3

Applied scientists use the same principles but shape them into more specific ideas, materials, and equipment. Engineers then use such equipment to make products within a budget, on a timetable. 4

That doesn't mean the lines between science and engineering don't occasionally get blurred. As one industry insider with a PhD in physics put it, "When I first started in industry, I was hired to build a lot of equipment. At the time, I felt a lot more like a cross between a plumber and an electrician than a physicist. But after 5 a while, I started to analyze the data and began feeling like a scientist again."

Scientists apply their skills to develop materials, products, equipment, and production methods in a variety of ways. Physicists, for instance, might be hired by biotechnology firms to design the equipment needed to work on materials at the molecular level; by semiconductor manufacturers to apply their knowledge of solid-state quantum mechanics (the study of crystalline solids such as silicon) to create computer chips that will run faster at lower temperatures; or by computer software firms to write and develop computer programs used to model complex processes, such as the blood flowing through a heart or money through a stock exchange. 6

Chemists work at such businesses as the Dow Chemical Co., of course, as well as at petroleum refining plants, pharmaceutical companies, paint manufacturers, and food-processing plants. 7

Many biological scientists work in the biomedical field and are known as medical scientists. They research infectious diseases (such as the common cold and AIDS) and develop vaccines, new drugs, and treatments. They may be employed by government agencies, such as the U.S. Centers for Disease Control and Prevention, or work for large drug companies such as GlaxoSmithKline. 8

Applied scientists need to be analytical thinkers and comfortable with math. There's a reason why scientists are often portrayed as people who speak in technical jargon impenetrable to the common ear: All fields of science require mastery of a host of precise terminology and complicated theories that have been piling up since the dawn of the Enlightenment. 9

Of course, that's not to downplay the role of solid communication skills. In today's business climate, scientists typically work in teams and need to be able to communicate efficiently what they've been doing and why it's important, especially if they're looking for a bigger budget. 10

To be sure, getting a well-rounded education is becoming especially important, because many scientists, both fresh out of school and those with experience, often decide they want a break, and find careers outside of laboratories. But getting a solid background in the sciences is rarely a waste of time. Increasingly, employers are realizing that the analytical skills and computer experience picked up learning science can be put to use in a host of other professions, such as technical writing, sales, marketing, and business consulting. 11

Of course, you can always teach high school or go back to academia to research or try to land a job as a professor. As one industry insider put it, "People are beginning to realize that someone who has mastered quantum physics usually treats something like analyzing the stock market or a complex business problem as an enjoyable break. Your options are really wide open." 12

READING ACTIVITY 1: Build Your Vocabulary

Determine the meanings of the following words from the context of the essay by the editors of WetFeet.com. Then check their meanings by looking up the words in a dictionary: private sector (1), hypotheses (2), infectious (8), jargon (9), analytical (9), impenetrable (9), academia (12).

READING ACTIVITY 2: Read to Improve Your Writing

Discuss the following questions about "Career Profile: Science" with your classmates.

1. In your own words, describe what an applied scientist does, and list the skills that an applied scientist needs.

2. This essay divides scientific work into several categories. Create a table that shows how the editors of WetFeet.com classify different kinds of science, and explain how this organization helps readers think about employment in the sciences.

3. In paragraphs 6, 7, and 8, the authors give examples of the types of work that applied scientists do. Give at least two reasons why they include these examples.

4. Based on this essay, do you have the characteristics and skills to be a scientist? Why or why not?

Workplace Communication

PERRI KLASS

She's Your Basic L.O.L. in N.A.D.

Often a doctor's work is hard for people to understand because it involves technical skills and terms. Because she's both a pediatrician and writer, Perri Klass has helped her readers better understand her profession. In "She's Your Basic L.O.L. in N.A.D.," Klass explains her introduction to the language of medicine. Klass focuses on what the language means and also on why doctors use it.

"Mrs. Tolstoy is your basic L.O.L. in N.A.D., admitted for a soft rule-out M.I.," the intern announces. I scribble that on my patient list. In other words Mrs. Tolstoy is a Little Old Lady in No Apparent Distress who is in the hospital to make sure she hasn't had a heart attack (rule out a myocardial infarction). And we think it's unlikely that she has had a heart attack (a *soft* rule-out).

1

If I learned nothing else during my first three months of   2
working in the hospital as a medical student, I learned endless
jargon and abbreviations. I started out in a state of primeval
innocence, in which I didn't even know that "s̄ C.P., S.O.B., N/V"
meant "without chest pain, shortness of breath, or nausea and
vomiting." By the end I took the abbreviations so for granted
that I would complain to my mother the English professor,
"And can you believe I had to put down *three* NG tubes last
night?"

"You'll have to tell me what an NG tube is if you want me to   3
sympathize properly," my mother said. NG, nasogastric — isn't
it obvious?

I picked up not only the specific expressions but also the   4
patterns of speech and the grammatical conventions; for
example, you never say that a patient's blood pressure fell or
that his cardiac enzymes rose. Instead, the patient is always the
subject of the verb: "He dropped his pressure." "He bumped his
enzymes." This sort of construction probably reflects that profound irritation of the intern when the nurses come in the
middle of the night to say that Mr. Dickinson has disturbingly
low blood pressure. "Oh, he's gonna hurt me bad tonight," the
intern may say, inevitably angry at Mr. Dickinson for dropping
his pressure and creating a problem.

When chemotherapy fails to cure Mrs. Bacon's cancer, what   5
we say is, "Mrs. Bacon failed chemotherapy."

"Well, we've already had one hit today, and we're up next,   6
but at least we've got mostly stable players on our team." This
means that our team (group of doctors and medical students)
has already gotten one new admission today, and it is our turn
again, so we'll get whoever is next admitted in emergency, but at
least most of the patients we already have are fairly stable —
that is, unlikely to drop their pressures or in any other way get
suddenly sicker and hurt us bad. Baseball metaphor is perva-
sive: a no-hitter is a night without any new admissions. A player
is always a patient — a nitrate player is a patient on nitrates, a
unit player is a patient in the intensive-care unit and so on, until
you reach the terminal player.

It is interesting to consider what it means to be winning, or   7
doing well, in this perennial baseball game. When the intern
hangs up the phone and announces, "I got a hit," that is not
cause for congratulations. The team is not scoring points;
rather, it is getting hit, being bombarded with new patients. The
object of the game from the point of view of the doctors, considering the players for whom they are already responsible, is to
get as few new hits as possible.

These special languages contribute to a sense of closeness   8
and professional spirit among people who are under a great
deal of stress. As a medical student, it was exciting for me to
discover that I'd finally cracked the code, that I could under-

stand what doctors said and wrote and could use the same for-
mulations myself. Some people seem to become enamored of
the jargon for its own sake, perhaps because they are so deeply
thrilled with the idea of medicine, with the idea of themselves
as doctors.

I knew a medical student who was referred to by the interns   9
on the team as Mr. Eponym because he was so infatuated with
eponymous terminology, the more obscure the better. He never
said "capillary pulsation" if he could say "Quincke's pulses."
He would lovingly tell over the multinamed syndromes — Wolff-
Parkinson-White, Lown-Ganong-Levine, Henoch-Schonlein —
until the temptation to suggest Schleswig-Holstein or Stevenson-
Kefauver or Baskin-Robbins became irresistible to his less reverent
colleagues.

And there is the jargon that you don't ever want to hear   10
yourself using. You know that your training is changing you,
but there are certain changes you think would be going a little
too far.

The resident was describing a man with devastating termi-   11
nal pancreatic cancer. "Basically he's C.T.D.," the resident concluded. I reminded myself that I had resolved not to be shy
about asking when I didn't understand things. "C.T.D.?" I asked
timidly.

The resident smirked at me. "Circling the Drain."   12

The images are vivid and terrible. "What happened to Mrs.   13
Melville?"

"Oh, she boxed last night." To box is to die, of course.   14

Then there are the more pompous locutions that can make   15
the beginning medical student nervous about the effects of
medical training. A friend of mine was told by his resident, "A
pregnant woman with sickle-cell represents a failure of genetic
counseling."

Mr. Eponym, who tried hard to talk like the doctors, once   16
explained to me, "An infant is basically a brainstem preparation." A brainstem preparation, as used in neurological research,
is an animal whose higher brain functions have been destroyed
so that only the most primitive reflexes remain, like the sucking
reflex, the startle reflex, and the rooting reflex.

The more extreme forms aside, one most important func-   17
tion of medical jargon is to help doctors maintain some distance from their patients. By reformulating a patient's pain and
problems into a language that the patient doesn't even speak, I
suppose we are in some sense taking those pains and problems
under our jurisdiction and also reducing their emotional impact.
This linguistic separation between doctors and patients allows
conversations to go on at the bedside that are unintelligible to
the patient. "Naturally, we're worried about adeno-C.A.," the
intern can say to the medical student, and lung cancer need
never be mentioned.

I learned a new language this past summer. At times it   18
thrills me to hear myself using it. It enables me to understand
my colleagues, to communicate effectively in the hospital. Yet I
am uncomfortably aware that I will never again notice the peculiarities and even atrocities of medical language as keenly as I
did this summer. There may be specific expressions I manage to
avoid, but even as I remark them, promising myself I will never
use them, I find that this language is becoming my professional
speech. It no longer sounds strange in my ears — or coming
from my mouth. And I am afraid that as with any new language,
to use it properly you must absorb not only the vocabulary but
also the structure, the logic, the attitudes. At first you may
notice these new alien assumptions every time you put together
a sentence, but with time and increased fluency you stop being
aware of them at all. And as you lose that awareness, for better
or for worse, you move closer and closer to being a doctor
instead of just talking like one.

READING ACTIVITY 3: Build Your Vocabulary

Determine the meanings of the following words from the context of
Perri Klass's essay. Then check their meanings by looking up the
words in a dictionary: primeval (2), inevitably (4), metaphor (6),
perennial (7), enamored (8), eponymous (9), locutions (15), jurisdiction (17), atrocities (18).

READING ACTIVITY 4: Read to Improve Your Writing

Discuss the following questions about "She's Your Basic L.O.L. in
N.A.D." with your classmates.

1. According to Klass, what are some examples of the jargon that
   health professionals use?
2. Why do medical practitioners use jargon in the workplace? For
   example, why do the interns say "He dropped his [blood] pressure"
   instead of "His [blood] pressure dropped"?
3. Explain the significance of the last sentence of the essay: "And as
   you lose that awareness, for better or for worse, you move closer
   and closer to being a doctor instead of just talking like one."
4. Have you ever heard medical professionals use terminology you
   couldn't understand? If so, describe what this experience was like.

A Job-Related Problem

DONALD TRUMP

You're Hired!

How do you get ahead in your job? In "You're Hired," Donald Trump — real estate tycoon, author, and reality TV star — suggests ways to solve workplace problems and get ahead. Trump has made a fortune in business, but most people know him more for the blunt, confident style that he's displayed on television — a style that he recommends to others.

I think it's funny that the phrase so closely associated with me these days is my line from *The Apprentice — You're fired*. The truth is, although I've had to fire employees from time to time, I much prefer keeping loyal and hard-working people around. At The Trump Organization, which has some 20,000 members at this point, Helen Rakotz has worked for me since I first moved to Manhattan, and she still puts in long hours. She's in her 80s. There's also a wonderful woman in her 90s, Amy Luerssen, who worked for my father, Fred, and still reports to work every day. Unless your boss is a total sadist, he or she doesn't want to fire you or cause hardship to your family. If you think you're in danger of losing your job, take control of the situation and ask for a meeting. Tell your boss you want to make sure you're communicating and doing your job to everyone's satisfaction.   1

Of course, if your boss *is* a sadist — or just a lousy communicator — you've got a problem. In that case, fire your boss and get a better job. There's no sense trying to cope with a bad situation that will never improve.   2

I never try to dissuade people from quitting. If they don't want to be here, I don't want them here either. People see how it works at The Trump Organization, and if it doesn't suit them, they move on. An experienced receptionist once worked here for a grand total of six hours. She realized right away that the pace just wasn't right for her, and she told us so and left. I appreciated her quick thinking and her ability to make a decision. She'll have a successful career somewhere else.   3

Fine-Tune Your Timing. When it comes to your career, certain moves shouldn't be made without careful consideration of the old and very apt saying "Timing is everything."   4

Jason Greenblatt, a brilliant young lawyer who works for me, is terrific at everything he does, but one time, I swear, he must have been wearing a blindfold — and earplugs. I was having an especially tough, vicious, terrible day that seemed never-ending   5 to me and everyone around me. It was a grand-slam rotten day. Late in the afternoon, I heard a polite knock on my door. I yelled out, *"What?"* Nonchalantly Jason entered my office and proceeded to ask me for a raise.

I could not believe a lawyer as smart as Jason could make   6
such a dumb move. I use his real name because Jason knows how much I like and respect him, despite this incredible faux pas. But I have to tell you, I was ready to kill him. Was he joking? It's amazing, but he wasn't. Did he get a raise? Not that day. He almost got fired for his stupidity. I told him that although he might be brilliant, his timing on certain things needed work — and that maybe he ought to pay more attention to what was going on around him.

Jason is still with me, and he gets lots of raises because he's   7
great at what he does. But now he waits for sunny days and blue skies before approaching me. I told you he was smart.

The best way to ask for a raise is to wait for the right time.   8
It indicates that you have a certain amount of discernment and appreciation for what your boss might be going through. If you knew your company was scheduled to give a major client presentation at 3 p.m., would you approach your boss at 2:45 to ask for a raise? Money, like comedy, is all about timing.

Toot Your Own Horn. I was originally going to call Trump   9
Tower by another name — Tiffany Tower, for the famous jewelry store next door. I asked a friend, "Do you think it should be Trump Tower or Tiffany Tower?" He told me, "When you change your name to Tiffany, call it Tiffany Tower."

We've all seen the power of a brand name, especially quality   10
brand names. Coco Chanel became world famous some 80 years ago by naming her perfume Chanel No. 5, and it's still going strong in a competitive market. Her fragrance, as well as her name, has become timeless. She proved the right ingredients can create a legend.

I've worked hard for decades to accomplish the same thing   11
in my business. My buildings are among the finest in the world, and that's not just bragging. Last year, an article by *Chicago Tribune* columnist Mary Umberger attributed the sales for Trump International Hotel and Tower in Chicago to "the Trump factor." She reported: "The sales velocity surprises even experienced real-estate players, who told me at the sales inaugural that they doubted Trump would gain enough momentum, because Chicago's luxury market was — and is — in a lull." And in an article by Herbert Muschamp, architecture critic for the *New York Times*, the Trump World Tower was described as "a handsome hunk of a glass tower." I was honored.

If you're devoting your life to creating something, and you   12
believe in what you do, and what you do is excellent, then you'd better damn well tell people you think so. Subtlety and modesty

are appropriate for nuns and therapists, but if you're in business, you'd better learn to speak up and announce your contributions to the world. Nobody else will.

Go with Your Gut. To be a success at anything, you have to trust   13
yourself. You may have superb academic credentials, but without instincts you'll have a hard time reaching — and staying at — the top. This is one of those gray areas that remain an enigma even to those who have finely honed business instincts. There are inexplicable signs that can guide you to or away from certain deals and certain people.

For example, within a few seconds of meeting Mark Burnett,   14
the creator of *The Apprentice*, I knew he was 100 percent solid, both as a person and a professional, which is a remarkable accomplishment in the entertainment industry. On the other hand, I've met people I have an aversion to, and while I try not to be judgmental, I have reason by now to trust my instincts.

Keep Critics in Perspective. In any job, you'll be criticized at   15
some point. While nobody wants criticism, there is a smart way to assess it. First, consider the source. Should this person's opinion matter to you? If it does, take a few minutes to consider if you can learn anything helpful from the criticism. Others can often see things that you've overlooked. Use their observations to your advantage if you can.

Second, remember that critics serve their purpose. *American*   16
Idol judge Simon Cowell can be critical of the performers on the program, but he's fair and he's honest, and I don't think the show would work without him.

Third, understand everyone has an opinion. In most cases,   17
it's not worth the paper it's written on. But if it is, and if it's in a paper people are buying and reading, then realize that if people didn't find you interesting enough, they wouldn't be taking the time to criticize you in the first place.

Practice Straight Talk. If you equivocate, it's an indication that   18
you're unsure of yourself and what you're doing. It's also what politicians do all the time, and I find it inappropriate, insulting and condescending.

I try not to do it. Fortunately, I don't have to try too hard at   19
this one, because I've been known to be on the blunt (and fast) side, which is good.

When I need to know something about my Atlantic City   20
casinos and hotels, I can call Mark Brown, my CEO, and get a fast, informed answer. If I call Laura Cordovano at Trump Park Avenue and ask about sales, she'll give it to me exactly as it is. Allen Weisselberg, my CEO, will tell me what I need in 20 words or less. My senior counsel and *Apprentice* advisor, George Ross, can do it in 10 words or less.

Once I asked an executive with my organization to give me   21
a synopsis of a new development we were considering. He'd
been to the city in question, spent time there, done careful
investigation. He described the pros and cons of the site in great
detail. He must've talked for ten minutes straight. There seemed
to be as many reasons to drop the project as there were reasons
to jump in and get going.

I asked more questions, and we ended up exactly where we   22
were before. This guy had a good track record, so finally I asked
him to tell me what he really thought — in ten words or less. "It
stinks," he said. He had eight words left, but he didn't need them.

All Ideas Are Welcome. If you're going to be bold enough to pre-   23
sent an idea, make it as clear as possible and don't take it casu-
ally. Think of it as a presentation that could cost your company
money if you were to lose the client. Your boss's time is important; you won't win points by wasting it.

Also, remember this: The boss has the big picture; you   24
don't. If your idea doesn't meet with hurrahs, it could be that a
similar idea is already in development, or your idea is not in
step with plans that have already been made. This shouldn't discourage you, because your initiative will always be noticed.

I like people who don't give up. But being merely a pest is   25
detrimental to everyone. Know when to ease up. Keep your eyes
open for another idea and a more appropriate opportunity.

There was one former employee I liked a lot, but he   26
reminded me of a jumping bean. He couldn't keep still for more
than three seconds. Riding in the car with him became an
ordeal, because being in an enclosed space seemed to warm
him up even more. I finally learned to avoid him, and that's too
bad, because he was a great guy. But enough is enough. Going
on and on will cause people to tune you out — or wish that you
would move to another state. Last I heard, the jumping bean
was living in Montana. I only hope they have enough space
there to contain him, and every time I hear about UFO sightings
in Montana, I have to laugh. I know just who it is.

One more thing: No one ignores a terrific idea. If your boss   27
says no to an idea of yours, it might not be the *right* terrific idea
for the company you're with. Maybe you're meant to go off on
your own as an entrepreneur. Let that be an indication to you. It
could be the beginning of your career, rather than the end of it.

READING ACTIVITY 5: Build Your Vocabulary

Determine the meanings of the following words from the context of
Donald Trump's essay. Then check their meanings by looking up the
words in a dictionary: sadist (1), dissuade (3), apt (4), nonchalantly
(5), faux pas (6), discernment (8), velocity (11), inaugural (11), enigma
(13), aversion (14), equivocate (18), synopsis (21), detrimental (25).

READING ACTIVITY 6: Read to Improve Your Writing

Discuss the following questions about "You're Hired!" with your classmates.

1. List at least four workplace problems that Trump identifies, and summarize his solutions in your own words.
2. Reread paragraphs 4 to 8. How does Trump use a story from his past to define what good timing is?
3. In paragraph 11, the author includes quotations from two newspaper articles. How do these quotations support his advice for succeeding in the corporate world?
4. What have you learned about doing well at work that you could share with readers?

Writing Assignment

Whether you are working toward a specific career goal or are considering several possibilities, it's always a good idea to investigate your options. For this assignment, you'll help yourself and other students plan for the future by writing about a career field that interests you or that you have experience with. You (or your instructor) may decide to approach this assignment in one of several ways:

- Examine an occupation that interests you.

  OR

- Analyze the ways people communicate in a place where you work now or have worked in the past.

  OR

- Suggest how to solve a workplace problem.

Follow the guidance and activities in this chapter to discover, develop, and polish your knowledge into a finished essay that readers will find interesting and informative.

STEP 1. EXPLORE YOUR CHOICES

What kind of occupation would you like to have? You may have a specific career in mind already, or perhaps you haven't decided yet. Either way, success takes effort. This chapter's writing assignment will help you to think about the possibilities and learn ways to achieve your goals. Before you choose an occupation, specialized language, or workplace problem to write about, you will think about who your readers are and what you want them to learn. Then you will experiment with three techniques for gathering ideas as you apply one to each of the assignment's topic choices. Gathering ideas before you start to write will give you a wealth of material to work with.

Analyzing Your Audience and Purpose

Before you begin gathering ideas about your topic, think about who will read your essay and what they might expect.

You are writing an essay that investigates the workplace for people who are interested in the same kind of work that appeals to you. Your readers, then, might be students in your major, members of a club or volunteer group that you belong to, or coworkers at your current place of employment. Before you begin writing for this audience, give some thought to their experiences and hopes, and ask yourself what will interest them. What can you tell them that they don't already know? How will they benefit from reading your essay?

Consider, also, what you want to accomplish by writing about the workplace. For example, is your purpose to share your feelings about an occupation, to inform your readers about something you have learned, or to persuade them to do something? Knowing your purpose will make it easier for you to write an essay that both you and your readers will value.

For more on audience and purpose, see pp. 8–12.

WRITING ACTIVITY 1: Analyze Your Audience and Purpose

Your responses to the following questions will help you decide how to approach this chapter's writing assignment.

1. Does this assignment call for primarily expressive, informative, or persuasive writing?
2. Who will read your essay? Will you share it with students in your major, members of a club or volunteer group, coworkers, or someone else?
3. What types of jobs have these readers had in the past?
4. What types of jobs do your readers want to have?
5. How do your job interests resemble or differ from those of your readers?
6. How can you interest your readers in an essay that deals with the workplace?

Gathering Ideas

Several techniques can help you find good ideas to write about, as you learned in Chapter 1. For this chapter's assignment, you will practice using three of these methods — freewriting, brainstorming, and consulting with others — as you explore your thoughts about workplace topics. Feel free, however, to gather additional ideas using any other methods that work for you. Your goal at this stage is to collect as many ideas and details as you can to help you determine what you want to write about.

For more on gathering ideas, see pp. 12–16.

Freewriting about an Occupation

Many of us decide to pursue a particular occupation without thinking it through. For instance, being an actor appears to be glamorous until you realize that most actors are unemployed in their chosen profession. Or you might daydream of flying until you learn that pilots are away from their families for days at a time. Before deciding on a particular career, you need to consider whether the job matches your interests, needs, and personality.

One useful way to investigate an occupation that appeals to you is to freewrite about it. To freewrite, you write for a set period of time without worrying about what you have to say or how you say it. You simply put all of your thoughts down as they come to you. If your mind wanders, let it. The point of freewriting is to discover ideas you didn't know you had.

If you don't know where to start or if you get stuck, the following questions can help to stimulate your thoughts:

- When did you first become interested in pursuing this occupation?
- If you're already in this occupation, in what way do you want to change (such as to obtain a higher position or go into another specialty)?
- List three things that interest you about this occupation.
- What aspects of your personality do you think will make you successful in this occupation?
- What don't you like about this occupation?
- List at least two things you want to learn about this occupation.

One student, Kathy Chu, freewrote about her desire to become a pediatrician.

I've wanted to become a pediatrician ever since I was a little girl. The doctor seemed so nice and knew so much. Then when my brother had to spend a week in the hospital, I got to see other pediatricians helping the sick children. My family is so grateful to the pediatricians who helped my brother get better. I know that being a pediatrician is hard. First you have to go through years of school. I guess I could handle that. But I'm not sure I could handle dealing with sick children all the time. It takes patience and dedication.

WRITING ACTIVITY 2: Freewrite about an Occupation

Gather ideas about an occupation you're interested in pursuing by freewriting about it for ten minutes. Follow your ideas without pausing, and do not stop, go back, or try to correct your writing. Just write.

Brainstorming about Workplace Communication

Put aside your writing about an occupation for a while so that you can gather ideas about another aspect of work.

Coworkers in every workplace develop their own way of communicating with each other, often by using specialized language known only to their peers. For instance, police officers use special terminology when referring to crimes, telemarketers label incoming and outgoing calls according to numerical codes, and attorneys write contracts that are difficult for nonspecialists to understand. One of the first things a person entering a profession needs to learn is its jargon.

Wherever you work now or may have worked in the past, you probably speak more jargon than you realize. To gather ideas for an essay that explains this language to others, try brainstorming a list of terms used in your chosen field. Write your general topic at the top of a page, and then list all of the words and phrases that come into your head. Jot down a brief definition for each term. Don't worry about whether your examples are good ones or not; just write down everything you think of.

One student, Javier, brainstormed about the jargon used by the teachers in the elementary school where he was a teacher's aide:

> TAAS test — the standardized test that the students have to take every year
> ADD — attention deficit disorder
> Hyper — a child with ADD
> SW — the "student of the week" award, also known as the "sweetheart" award
> Sub — substitute teacher
> Meeting with the Pal — a meeting with the principal
> Sight words — common words, like *dog* or *the*, that students should know
> Portfolio — a collection of student work
> In-service training — educational sessions to update experienced teachers
> Eager Beaver — a new teacher who thinks he or she knows everything

WRITING ACTIVITY 3: Brainstorm about Communication in the Workplace

Pick a job you're familiar with. It can be a job you've had or a job held by a friend or family member. Brainstorm about the jargon that you've encountered by listing words and their definitions. Alternatively, you may list examples of another aspect of communication that interests you, such as levels of formality, uses of humor, spoken versus written communication, or body language.

Consulting Others about a Job-Related Problem

Put aside the writing you've done on jargon for a while so that you can consider one last aspect of the workplace.

No matter how much you like your job, you're always going to encounter difficulties. Perhaps your boss is hard to talk to or one of your coworkers likes to gossip too much. Your hours might be long, or you might object to a recent change in policy. To be successful, you need to be able to find solutions to problems such as these.

An excellent way to find solutions is to ask other people what they think about your situation and what solutions they suggest. You might consult with an expert or two (as Donald Trump describes in "You're Hired!"), you might ask others who have had similar experiences what they have done, or you may simply wish to share your problem out loud and get reactions from people who can offer you a fresh perspective.

Student writer Alfredo was interested in writing about a problem he had been having at his job in a restaurant. He decided to describe the issue out loud to his classmates and ask for their suggestions. Here is what he told them:

> "Whenever I'm on the night shift at the restaurant where I work, I see other workers steal food. We're allowed to eat one meal after a shift, but what these people are doing goes way beyond that. They carry out bags of food! The owner is never there when we close up so I don't think she knows what's happening. If I tell on the workers they might hate me, but if I keep quiet my conscience bugs me. What should I do?"

Alfredo's classmates had these suggestions:

BRENDA: I think you should tell the owner. Who cares what the workers think? What they're doing is wrong.

JOE: But what if the other workers deny it? What if the owner doesn't believe Alfredo?

BRENDA: It's a chance Alfredo will have to take. It's the right thing to do.

ALFREDO: I make good tips at this job. I really don't want to lose it.

JOE: Maybe you could talk to the people who are stealing? Tell them they should knock it off.

RUDY: Can you change shifts? That way you won't see it being done.

KIM: But it will still be happening. Do you know why they're stealing food? Maybe they don't think they're paid enough. Or would it be thrown out if they didn't take it home?

Alfredo used his classmate's comments to gather more ideas about his topic. Kim's questions, for example, made him realize that his coworkers might not think they were doing anything wrong. He decided to investigate how other area restaurants handled the problem of employee theft before talking to his boss.

WRITING ACTIVITY 4: Consult with Others about Your Topic

Identify a problem or an issue related to your current job, a job you've held, or a job you'd like to have. For instance, you might have a problem with a work schedule, the attitudes of coworkers, or difficult customers. Describe the problem to your classmates, and ask them for suggestions. Alternatively, you might choose to interview an expert on the subject and ask how he or she would solve the problem. Take notes on the responses.

STEP 2. WRITE YOUR DISCOVERY DRAFT

For more on drafting, see pp. 16–21.

You have now gathered ideas about an occupation, workplace jargon, and a job-related problem. The next step is to write a discovery draft that explains something you have learned about working.

It's okay if your ideas and your writing are rough at this stage. The discovery draft is just your first try at putting your thoughts in essay form. You'll have plenty of time later to develop your ideas, add supporting information, and fix any mistakes.

Choosing a Topic

You have collected rich materials for writing, but you need to decide how to proceed. Keeping in mind that you are writing to share something you know with other students who may be interested in a particular occupational field, you need to pick a topic for your essay. Look over the ideas you have gathered, and try to identify a topic that will enable you to give your readers useful information.

Remember that you have three general choices to work with: examining a specific occupation, analyzing workplace communication, or solving a job-related problem. You may select one of the topics you have already explored, you might choose to gather ideas on a new topic, or you might decide to combine related topics. For example, while freewriting about an occupation you may have discovered that you have some concerns about it. Rather than decide the job is no good for you, you could consult with some people and write about ways to solve those problems. Whatever you do, be sure you select a topic that matters to you, that you have considered carefully, and that your readers will want to learn about.

WRITING ACTIVITY 5: Choose Your Topic

Review your freewriting, brainstorming, and consultation notes, and choose or create a topic that will be interesting for you and your readers. If you're not confident that you have something to say about your topic, you may go back and freewrite, brainstorm, or consult some more on the topic of your choice.

Sharing Your Ideas

When you sit down to write your discovery draft, first write a preliminary thesis statement that says what your topic is and what you think your main point will be. You can always revise your thesis statement if your writing takes you in an unexpected direction, but having a general plan in mind will help get you started.

Keep your audience and purpose in mind as you draft, but remember that your main goal at this stage is to find out what you have to say. Focus on writing, and don't worry about every supporting detail or how you express yourself. You'll have a chance later on to expand, revise, and edit your discovery draft.

Use E-mail or Networked Discussion

E-mail your discovery draft to your fellow students or coworkers for feedback. Alternatively, if you have access to a networked computer lab, discuss your draft online with other students in the class, on your campus, or even at different colleges. Whether you e-mail or discuss the draft online, ask your readers (1) what interested them the most about your draft and (2) what they want to know more about. Use their responses to help you decide where to add supporting details.

Here's a discovery draft written by Kathy Chu, the student whose freewriting about her desire to be a pediatrician you read earlier in this chapter. Notice that her preliminary thesis statement expresses her main idea and maps out a few of the reasons she is interested in pursuing a career in medicine. (Like most discovery drafts, this one includes errors; Kathy will fix them later.)

Preliminary Thesis Statement: I want to be a pediatrician so I can help children, make a good living, and have an interesting job.

Ever since I was a child, I wanted to be a pediatrician, which is a doctor who specializes in children. I hated going to the pediatrician when I was a child, but I was also fascinated by the woman in the white jacket who seemed to have all the answers. I want to be a pediatrician so I can help children, make a good living, and have an interesting job.

Ever since I can remember, I've wanted to take care of children. My little brother used to get earaches. I'd pretend I was the doctor and hold a cup to his chest so I could hear his heartbeat. In high school I volunteered at Providence Hospital in the children's wing. Seeing a sick child made me sad. I felt better when I'd play with them and cheer them up.

As a pediatrician, I can make a good living. Making a good living is important to me. My parents have had to cope with many financial difficulties. I want to be able to provide for my parents when they get old. I want to take care of my own family, too.

Pediatricians work long hours. This might be a problem for some people, but not for me. Right now I help take care of my family, carry a full class load at college, and work about 30 hours a week. I wouldn't know what to do with myself if I had free time!

I think pediatricians have exciting jobs. You never know what might be making a child sick. They might have a runny nose or something more serious. It's your job to make sure they get the right treatment so they can get well. The job might make me tired or stressed, but never bored.

For me, nothing beats helping a child get well.

WRITING ACTIVITY 6: Write Your Discovery Draft

Write at least three to five paragraphs that state why you are interested in an occupation, that analyze workplace communication, or that suggest ways to solve a job-related problem. Prepare a preliminary thesis statement, and use your prewriting materials to get started, but feel free to write anything that occurs to you while you're drafting. If you're not sure what to write about, that's fine. You may write drafts on several topics to see which one will be most productive for you.

STEP 3. REVISE YOUR DRAFT

Now that you have completed your discovery draft, it's time to make it better. Start by looking for anything you can improve by using the skills you have learned in other chapters of this book. For example, you can probably clarify and support your main ideas by improving your thesis statement and topic sentences (Chapter 4), making your ideas flow more smoothly by adding transitions (Chapter 5), organizing your paragraphs (Chapter 2), and strengthening your introduction and conclusion (Chapter 5).

As you revise your essay about the workplace, you will learn how to develop your ideas using classification and definition, and you will practice adding support with information from books, articles, and the Web. Keep your audience and purpose in mind as you revise by reviewing the analysis you completed in Writing Activity 1 (p. 194). What information do your readers need to know to understand your topic? How can you keep them interested as they read your paper?

For more on thesis statements, see pp. 19–20.

Developing Your Ideas

Because you are writing to teach other students something about the workplace, it's important that you explain your points clearly. Two methods of development — classification and definition — are especially useful when you want to help people unfamiliar with a topic understand what you have to tell them.

Classification

Classification shows the relationship between different people, things, or ideas by organizing them into logical categories. A single *principle,* or *theme,* links those categories together as a group. For

For more on classification, see pp. 68–69.

instance, college students can be classified according to the principle of demographics: age, place of birth, marital status, income. Or they can be classified by participation in groups: fraternities or sororities, athletic teams, clubs, and so on. Because classification breaks a large concept into parts, it makes a topic easier to understand.

Classification is used in all three of the essays that open this chapter. The writers of "Career Profile: Science" classify scientists according to where they might work — biotechnology firms, pharmaceutical companies, and so on. Perri Klass, in "She's Your Basic L.O.L. in N.A.D," classifies medical jargon according to how it helps health care professionals communicate. In "You're Hired!," Donald Trump classifies different kinds of strategies for succeeding in the workplace — such as "fine-tune your timing" and "toot your own horn" — and gives each category a heading to help readers follow his points. By using classification, these authors order their ideas logically and clearly.

When you classify, be sure to explain your principle of classification and to discuss each category separately. Although you occasionally might write one paragraph to classify the parts of your topic, you usually will need a full paragraph to identify and explain each category. (You may need to write two or three paragraphs to explain the most important category.)

HOW TO   Use Classification

- Decide on what basis you'll classify the topic. For example, the topic of "workplace stress" can be classified into "causes of workplace stress."

- Break the topic down into parts. "Causes of workplace stress" can be grouped into "stress from coworkers," "stress from supervisors," and "stress from customers."

- Discuss one category at a time.

- Give examples to support the classification.

Student writer Kathy Chu reviewed her discovery draft and noticed that she had several specific reasons for wanting to be a pediatrician: to help children, to earn a good living, and to be challenged on a daily basis. For her revised draft, she thought of some additional reasons for her interest in pediatrics and decided to use classification to explain each of those reasons in detail.

WRITING ACTIVITY 7: Use Classification to Develop Your Ideas

With several classmates, brainstorm ways you could use classification to make your essay easier to understand. For instance, if you wrote a discovery draft about dealing with a difficult supervisor, you might classify difficult supervisors into categories (those who yell, those who expect too much, those who give confusing instructions, and so on). If appropriate, use your classmates' suggestions to organize your topic into categories for your revision.

Definition

To *define* something is to explain what it means. *Definition* is a helpful strategy to use when developing your essay because it can help you clarify important points. When you define a term, first place it in a general category. Then explain how it fits within that category according to what sets it apart — its distinguishing features. For example, in the introduction of her discovery draft, Kathy Chu defines *pediatrician* by placing it in a general category — doctors. She then explains the characteristics of this type of doctor (they work with children), which highlights the occupation's distinguishing features.

For more on definition, see pp. 69–70.

Although a simple one-sentence definition is always useful, writers often develop whole paragraphs to define complex terms or concepts. In "Career Profile: Science," for example, the editors of WetFeet.com use a full paragraph to explain what medical scientists do. First, they place medical science in the general category of biology. They then explain what sets medical scientists apart from other biologists: they research disease; they develop vaccines, drugs, and treatments; they might work for the government or for drug companies; and so on.

HOW TO Use Definition

- Introduce the word, phrase, or concept to be defined.

- Place the word, phrase, or concept in a general category, and explain what sets it apart from others in that category.

- Provide details (such as description, narration, examples, process, or comparison and contrast) to explain your term.

- Organize the details so that a reader will easily understand your definition.

WRITING ACTIVITY 8: Use Definition to Develop Your Ideas

Exchange your discovery draft with a classmate. Underline any words, phrases, or concepts in your partner's draft that you don't understand or that could be made clearer with a sentence or paragraph of definition. Your classmate should do the same for your paper. Use your partner's suggestions to add definitions to your own draft as necessary.

Building Your Essay

In addition to developing your own ideas fully, you need to make sure that you have provided enough information to keep your audience interested and informed. Because you may be writing about a topic that is new to you or unfamiliar to your readers, consider doing a little research to gather additional information that will help you explain something about the workplace. Used carefully, a handful of facts and opinions from reliable sources can make your ideas more convincing.

Find Information to Strengthen Your Support

To learn more about any aspect of a workplace occupation, jargon, or problem, start by consulting a general reference — such as an encyclopedia, dictionary, or handbook — for basic facts. For instance, if you wrote your discovery draft about an occupation that interests you, you can look it up in the *Occupational Outlook Handbook*, updated every other year by the U.S. Department of Labor and available online at www.bls.gov/oco. The *Handbook* contains detailed information — such as job descriptions, educational requirements, and average salaries — about a wide variety of occupations. Some other useful references are listed on page 413 of this book; your school librarian will be happy to suggest additional resources if you ask.

Also helpful are newspaper, magazine, and Web articles written by people with related experience in the workplace. Consider Donald Trump's essay "You're Hired!," which you read earlier in this chapter. Even though Trump is highly respected by his readers, he includes information from two newspaper articles to support his claim that his "buildings are among the finest in the world." Like Trump, you can include the opinion of another writer to make one of your own points more convincing.

For more on library databases and keywords, see pp. 414–15.

To find additional information for your draft, search a library database or the World Wide Web for information about your topic. Use *keywords*, or words that pertain to your topic, to find useful articles. Keep in mind that you won't be able to use every source you find. As you read, look for facts, ideas, or opinions that can help you back up one of your points or explain one of your ideas.

Searching a Database or the Internet

For tutorials on how to use a library database or the Internet to conduct research, go to **bedfordstmartins.com/rewriting** and click on "The Bedford Research Room."

WRITING ACTIVITY 9: Locate Additional Information for Your Essay

Reread your discovery draft, and look for any ideas that could be better explained or made more convincing. Look for information to support these ideas by checking a reference work and reading some articles on your topic. Photocopy or print out any useful material that you find; you will refer to it in the next stage of revising your draft.

Outline Your Plan

Once you find facts, ideas, and opinions that can help you explain your topic to your readers, pay special attention to where you will include this information in your essay.

Review your discovery draft and your research notes, and make a rough outline of your major points. Indicate where you could add information from a book, an article, or a Web site to make your points clearer. Your outline should include the ideas you've already drafted and any additional support from your research that you plan to provide in each paragraph. Follow the outline format that works best for you. If you're unsure of how to make an outline, just create a simple list.

Student writer Kathy Chu, for example, found some good information about pediatrics in the online version of the *Occupational Outlook Handbook* and a *Time* magazine article about the future of the profession. Here is the rough outline she put together to plan her revised draft. (Note that *P* in this outline stands for *paragraph*. The research information she plans to add is underlined.)

P1:   Introduce topic. Define *pediatrician*. Thesis:
       Pediatricians help children, make a good living,
       work hard, and enjoy challenges.

P2:   My desire to help sick children. Experiences I've had
       with my brother and at the hospital.

P3:   Pediatricians get to make decisions about treatment.

P4:   Pediatricians make a good living. Why this is
       important to me. Information about salaries from the
       Occupational Outlook Handbook.

P5:   Pediatricians work long hours. This doesn't bother
       me. Information about number of hours per week and

education requirements from the *Occupational Outlook Handbook* and article from *Time*.

P6:   Pediatricians face many challenges. This will keep me from getting bored. Quote from *Time* magazine from pediatrician about challenges.

P7:   Conclusion. Go back to thesis. It's the job for me.

Remember that your outline, like Kathy's, is *tentative* — in other words, it is subject to change. As you revise, you might think of new ideas or a better way to order your points. Don't hesitate to rework your plan as needed.

Use the Outline View

To help you organize your outline, use the Outline View function found on many word-processing programs. This function will give you the option of outlining your ideas for the whole essay or for individual paragraphs. The Help function of your program will lead you through the appropriate steps.

WRITING ACTIVITY 10: Outline Your Revision Plan

Outline your ideas for your revised draft. Use the format in Kathy's outline or a format of your own. List the major ideas that you will keep from your discovery draft, and note where you'll add new ideas and information from your research.

Correctly Use Research Material

As you revise your draft, remember that you are writing to express your own ideas about the workplace and not to give a report on what other people have said. Although it can be tempting to include several long chunks of research in your essay, select only the most pertinent ideas to support your points. Do not let the research take over your paper. As a rule of thumb, limit information from outside sources (articles, books, Web sites) to no more than 10 to 20 percent of your essay.

Keep the following three principles in mind when you add information from research to your own writing.

For more information on quoting and paraphrasing information, see pp. 425–28.

Put Information in Your Own Words. Summarize or paraphrase — don't quote — facts or statistics from an article about your topic. You can select the key ideas that will support your point without having to repeat the whole of your source.

A *summary* is a short version of a piece of text that is written in your own words. To summarize, you explain the most important idea from a source while omitting the details. Suppose, for example, that you were writing an essay about your desire to be a biologist. To back up your claim that you have many options to choose from, you could summarize information from the article "Career Profile: Science," which you read earlier in this chapter:

> As the editors of WetFeet.com explain, the business world offers many opportunities for research scientists. Applied scientists think of new ideas, conduct research, and use their discoveries to develop products and techniques for government and industry. Science students with good analytical and communication skills can find a successful career in many different fields.

When you *paraphrase*, you also put information from a source into your own words, but you use about the same number of words as the original source uses, as Kathy does in this example:

ORIGINAL | Over one-third of full-time physicians and surgeons worked 60 hours or more a week in 2004. (*Occupational Outlook Handbook*, page 1)

PARAPHRASE | According to the *Occupational Outlook Handbook*, more than 30 percent of all doctors work over 60 hours a week (1).

Quote Sparingly. A well-placed quotation can help you express an idea in a distinct way, but you should use another writer's exact words only to emphasize or explain an important point. One or two quotations are sufficient for a three-page essay.

When you do include a direct quotation, weave it smoothly into your sentences. Use an introductory phrase, and put quotation marks around your source's words, as Kathy does in her revised draft:

> *According to one pediatrician,* "I never know what I'll encounter with every patient I see. One child might just have a cold or flu. But the next child could have a bruise that won't heal. This could be a symptom of cancer" (Turner 53).

Document Your Sources. Whether you summarize, paraphrase, or quote material from a source, you must always inform your readers

For more on documenting sources, see pp. 430–35.

that the ideas or words are not your own. Indicate where you obtained information by citing the source in the text of your essay and in a list of works cited at the end:

- In most cases, introduce a summary, paraphrase, or quotation by identifying the author or title of the book, article, or Web site in which you found the information.

- At the end of a quotation, paraphrase, or summary, provide author's last name and the page number where you found the information in parentheses. (Exclude the author's name if you gave it when you introduced the material.)

- At the end of the essay, include a Works Cited list that gives publication information for each source you used.

Use Color for Research Material

Use the color feature on your word-processing program to highlight quotations in your draft. Use another color to highlight paraphrased and summarized material. This technique will help you monitor how much research material you have in your draft. For instance, if more than 10 to 20 percent of the draft is in color, you know that the research is taking over your own ideas. (Be sure to return the typeface to black before printing the final draft.)

MLA Electronic Documentation

For the most recent information on documenting information from electronic sources, go to **bedfordstmartins.com/resdoc** and click on "Humanities."

HOW TO Use Research Material in an Essay

- Limit the amount of research material to no more than 10 to 20 percent of your essay.

- Use brief quotations only to emphasize or explain an important point.

- Summarize or paraphrase — put into your own words — information such as facts or statistics.

- Introduce most source material with a phrase such as *According to* or *In the words of.*

- Indicate where you obtained any quoted, summarized, or paraphrased information in the text of the essay and at the end of the essay.

GROUP ACTIVITY 2: Quote, Paraphrase, and Document Information

The following is a paragraph from a student essay about working while attending college.

Quoting, paraphrasing, and documenting information are essential. Otherwise, you can be accused of plagiarism. For more help, see pp. 418–19.

Working your way through college has many advantages. Unlike students who depend on large checks from their parents, working students learn to be self-reliant and independent. Because they pay their own bills every month, they realize the value of a college education in getting a well-paid job. They learn how to manage time well, an important skill in the working world. They also gain excellent work experience for their résumés after they graduate. While they might be tempted to grumble about lack of free time or the old car they drive, working students have many advantages over students who don't work.

Here's a quotation from a magazine article on the same topic:

I believe the fact that my husband and I are happy and financially stable is a direct result of our learning how to manage time and money in college.
— "Pay Your Own Way! (Then Thank Mom)," by Audrey Rock-Richardson, page 12 in *Newsweek* on Sept. 11, 2000.

Working in groups of two or three students, first rewrite the paragraph by inserting the quotation into it. Be sure to introduce the quotation and correctly document the source in parentheses.

Then rewrite the paragraph again. Rather than inserting the quotation into the paragraph, paraphrase the information by putting it into your own words. Don't forget to document the source in the paragraph.

Using Research Material
For more help in using research material in your essay, go to **bedfordstmartins.com/rewriting** and click on "The Bedford Research Room."

WRITING ACTIVITY 11: Add Researched Information
to Your Draft

Using the outline you prepared for Writing Activity 10 as a guide, add two or three summaries, paraphrases, or quotations to your draft. Be careful that you use this researched information to support your own points: don't expect it to speak for you. Also, make sure you correctly cite your sources in the body of your essay and in a Works Cited list.

A Student's Revised Draft

After writing a discovery draft about her desire to become a pediatrician, student writer Kathy Chu realized she needed more details to describe why she wants to be a doctor who works with children, so she did a little research to get more information. Before you read her revised draft, reread her discovery draft (p. 200). Notice how she has used classification to organize her ideas and added information from the *Occupational Outlook Handbook* and a magazine article to support her points. (You will also notice some errors in the revised draft; these will be corrected when Kathy edits her essay later.)

Helping Children Heal

Kathy Chu

This Introduction is more interesting.

When I was a child, going to the doctor was both frightening and exciting. I hated getting shots and seeing the crying babies. At the same time, the friendly doctor in the white jacket who seemed to have all the answers fascinated me. As an adult, I still admire the doctor from my childhood. Now I know that she was a pediatrician, which is a doctor who specializes in the health needs of children. I entered college and started to think of my future occupation. I thought more and

Her thesis is clearer.

more about becoming this kind of doctor. As a pediatrician, I can help children get well, make a good living, work hard, and enjoy challenges.

Ever since I can remember, I've wanted to take care of children. My little brother used to get earaches. I'd pretend I was the doctor and hold a cup to his chest so I could hear his heartbeat. In high school, I

An example is added.

volunteered at Providence Hospital in the children's wing. Seeing a sick child made me sad. I always felt better after playing with them and cheering them up.

A reason is added to her classification categories.

Being even a small part of a team that helped children heal, it made me feel worthwhile.

While volunteering at Providence Hospital, I observed many pediatric nurses give children shots, examine their progress, and cheer up their patients. Pediatric nurses work one-on-one with children. Pediatricians spend less time alone with the patients. However, being a pediatrician appeals to me more than being a nurse because pediatricians diagnose children and decide on a treatment plan. Nurses have to carry out the decisions of doctors. I prefer to be the one who makes the decisions in the first place.

As a pediatrician, I can make a good living. This is important to me. My parents have had to cope with many financial difficulties. I remember bill collectors calling us and my mother's car being repossessed. A pediatrician doesn't have trouble finding a job, and their median salary is $133,000 a year (U.S. Dept. of Labor 6). This job security will let me provide for my parents when they get old, as well as take care of my own family.

Summarized information from a Web site is added.

A source is cited in the body of the essay.

Pediatricians work long hours. According to the *Occupational Outlook Handbook,* published by the U.S. Department of Labor, more than 30 percent of all doctors work over 60 hours a week (1). In addition, a pediatrician, like all doctors, must complete four years of college, four years of medical school, and then three to eight years of further training in a hospital (Turner 54). It takes a high grade point average and being especially good in science. Fortunately, I like to work hard.

Paraphrased information from a Web site and an article is included.

Sources are cited in the body of the essay.

A reason is added to classification categories.

Finally, as a pediatrician I would encounter challenges every day. According to one pediatrician, "I never know what I'll encounter with every patient I see. One child might just have a cold or flu. But the next child could have a bruise that won't heal. This could be a symptom of cancer" (Turner 53). I look forward to helping children heal whether they have a runny nose or something more serious. The job might make me tired or stressed but never bored.

A quotation is used to support point.

A source is cited in the body of the essay.

While a pediatrician's job can be difficult, I think it's the job for me. Getting into medical school is tough, but I like to aim high. For me, nothing would be more satisfying than helping a child get well.

The conclusion is extended.

Works Cited

A Works Cited list is added.

United States. Dept. of Labor. Bureau of Labor Statistics.
    "Physicians and Surgeons." *Occupational Outlook
    Handbook, 2006–07 Edition.* Bureau of Labor
    Statistics, 2006. Web. 29 Mar. 2006.
Turner, Angela. "Pediatricians: An Endangered
    Species?" *Time* 7 Apr. 1999: 53–54. Print.

GROUP ACTIVITY 3: Analyze Kathy's Revised Draft

Use the following questions to discuss with your classmates how Kathy revised her draft.

1. How well has Kathy hooked the reader, given background information, and stated her thesis in her introduction?
2. What is Kathy's thesis statement? How much better is it than the thesis in her discovery draft? How can it be improved even more?
3. How has Kathy used classification and definition to develop her points? Are these revisions effective? Explain.
4. What kind of research did Kathy conduct on her topic?
5. How well has Kathy used research in her essay? Is the research connected to the ideas before and after it? Are quotations introduced? Is the research documented in her essay and in her Works Cited list?
6. In your view, what point or points are best supported with facts, examples, and statistics? Is there any idea that needs more support?
7. How could Kathy's draft benefit from more revision?

WRITING ACTIVITY 12: Peer Review

Form a group with two or three other students, and exchange copies of your current drafts. Read your draft aloud while your classmates follow along. Take notes on your classmates' responses to the following questions about your draft.

1. What did you like best about my essay?
2. How interesting is my introduction? Did you want to continue reading the paper? Why or why not?
3. What is my thesis statement? Do I need to make the essay's thesis clearer?
4. How well have I supported my points? Do I need to add facts, examples, or statistics to extend what I say?
5. How can classification or definition improve my supporting points?
6. How well have I used summaries, paraphrases, and quotations from my research? Have I given the correct information about my sources in the text of my essay and in the Works Cited list?

7. Where in the essay did my writing confuse you? How can I clarify my thoughts?

8. How effective is my ending? Do I end in such a way that you know it's the end?

Use Online Peer Review

If your class has a Web site, see whether the peer review questions are available on the site. If they are, you may be able to respond to your classmates' drafts online.

WRITING ACTIVITY 13: Revise Your Draft

Using the plan you outlined in Writing Activity 10 and the research you added in Writing Activity 11 as a starting point, take your classmates' peer review suggestions into consideration, and revise your essay. Use researched information only to support your most important points, and summarize, paraphrase, and quote properly. Finally, document your sources — both in the text of your essay and in a Works Cited list at the end.

STEP 4. EDIT YOUR SENTENCES

At this point, you have worked hard to investigate an occupation, analyze workplace jargon, or solve a workplace problem. Now that you have finished developing and supporting your ideas, you're ready to focus on your words and sentences. Remember that the fewer errors you make, the more your readers will pay attention to what you have to say. In this section, you'll concentrate on two editing tasks — combining sentences using subordinating conjunctions and correcting pronoun reference and agreement.

Combining Sentences Using Subordinating Conjunctions

By combining short, closely related sentences in your draft, you can eliminate unnecessary words, clarify connections between your sentences, and improve sentence variety. For now, you'll focus on combining sentences using subordinating conjunctions.

For more on subordination, see pp. 526–31.

Often, one sentence in a paragraph is *subordinate* to — less important than — another, closely related sentence. Combining sentences with a subordinating conjunction tells the reader that one idea is less important than another. Here are some of the most frequently used subordinating conjunctions:

SUBORDINATING CONJUNCTIONS

after	if	until	wherever
although	since	when	whether
because	though	whenever	while
before	unless	where	

The subordinating conjunction comes at the beginning of the less important sentence, which is called a *subordinate clause.*

Student writer Kathy Chu's revised draft has several short, closely related sentences that can be combined with subordinating conjunctions. In the following examples, the less important sentence, or subordinate clause, is italicized:

ORIGINAL   *My little brother used to get earaches.* I'd pretend I was the doctor and hold a cup to his chest so I could hear his heartbeat.

REVISED   *When my little brother used to get earaches,* I'd pretend I was the doctor and hold a cup to his chest so I could hear his heart beat.

ORIGINAL   Making a good living is important to me. *My parents have had to cope with many financial difficulties.*

REVISED   Making a good living is important to me *because my parents have had to cope with many financial difficulties.*

As these examples illustrate, the subordinate clause can appear at the beginning or end of the sentence. When the subordinate clause comes at the beginning of the sentence, a comma divides it from the rest of the sentence. When the subordinate clause comes at the end of the sentence, no comma is used.

HOW TO Combine Sentences Using Subordinating Conjunctions

- Combine sentences that are short and closely related in meaning.

- Decide which sentence is subordinate to, or less important than, the other.

- Turn the less important sentence into a subordinate clause by beginning it with an appropriate subordinating conjunction.

- When the subordinate clause begins the sentence, use a comma to divide it from the main clause.

- Don't use a comma when the subordinate clause is at the end of the sentence.

EDITING ACTIVITY 1: Combine Sentences Using Subordinating Conjunctions

Combine the following pairs of sentences. First, decide which sentence is less important in conveying the message; this sentence will become the subordinate clause. Then select an appropriate subordinating conjunction to begin the subordinate clause. Finally, combine the two sentences. You may need to eliminate unnecessary words or move some words around.

EXAMPLE   For many people, it's hard to decide on a career. ~~There~~ are
          because there
          so many careers to choose from.

1. I'm studying to become a photojournalist. I like both photography and journalism.

2. I've always wanted to be a photojournalist. I remember wanting to be a photojournalist when I was a child.

3. A photojournalist takes photographs of current events. These photographs are published in magazines and newspapers.

4. Often people read a magazine just for the photographs. This is why photojournalists are important to magazine editors.

5. Photojournalists have exciting jobs. They get to travel and take pictures of important people.

Exercise Central

For additional practice with combining sentences with subordinating conjunctions, go to **bedfordstmartins.com/choices** and click on "Exercise Central."

WRITING ACTIVITY 14: Combine Your Sentences

Examine your revised draft for short, closely related sentences. Where it makes sense to do so, combine them with subordinating conjunctions.

Correcting Pronoun Reference and Agreement

A *pronoun* usually refers to or takes the place of a specific noun in a sentence. If a pronoun does not clearly refer to a specific noun or agree in number with the noun it replaces, your readers will be confused.

Here are some of the most common English pronouns:

I, me, mine, we, us, our, ours
you, your, yours
he, him, his, she, her, hers
it, its
they, them, their, theirs
this, these, that, those
who, whom, whose, which, that, what
any, anyone, anybody, each, everybody, everyone, everything
someone, something

For more on pronoun reference, see pp. 515–16.

Pronoun Reference.   When you use a pronoun to refer to a noun, make sure the reference is clear, not vague. Here are two ways to correct vague pronoun reference:

- Replace the pronoun with the noun it refers to.
- Rewrite the sentence so that the pronoun is no longer needed.

VAGUE   In the article "Dealing with a Difficult Boss," *it* said that good communication between boss and employee is essential. [What does *it* refer to?]

CLEAR   In the article "Dealing with a Difficult Boss," *the author* said that good communication between boss and employee is essential.

VAGUE   Ms. Ortiz told Rachel *she* was going to be late. [Does *she* refer to Ms. Ortiz or to Rachel?]

CLEAR   Ms. Ortiz said, "I'm going to be late."

VAGUE   In the art world, *they're* used to unusual behavior and clothing. [Whom does *they* refer to?]

CLEAR   People in the art world are used to unusual behavior and clothing.

VAGUE   Raymond loved traveling with his band and recording a CD last summer. *It* made him decide to make music a career. [Does *it* refer to traveling with the band, recording a CD, or both?]

CLEAR   Because Raymond loved traveling with his band and recording a CD over the summer, *he* decided to make music a career.

For more on pronoun agreement, see pp. 516–18.

Pronoun Agreement.   Every pronoun must agree in number with the noun it takes the place of. That is, use a singular pronoun to replace a singular noun and a plural pronoun to replace a plural noun. Indefinite pronouns — such as *any, anyone, anybody, each, everybody,* *everyone, everything, someone,* and *something* — are singular. Here are two ways to correct pronoun agreement:

- Make the pronoun and noun agree in number.
- Rewrite the sentence to eliminate the problem.

INCORRECT	A successful job applicant will prepare for *their* job interview.
REVISED	A successful job applicant will prepare for *his or her* job interview.
REVISED	Successful job applicants will prepare for *their* job interviews.
INCORRECT	To get a good job, *everyone* should try to get the best education *they* can afford.
REVISED	To get a good job, *everyone* should try to get the best education *he or she* can afford.
REVISED	To get a good job, *young people* should try to get the best education they can afford.

As these examples illustrate, you may wish to use a plural noun (such as *young people*) to avoid saying *he or she* or *his or her* throughout an essay.

HOW TO Correct Pronoun Reference and Agreement

- Identify the pronouns in each sentence of your draft.
- Identify the noun that each pronoun replaces. Make sure the noun is easy to identify and is close to the pronoun.
- Check to see that the noun and pronoun agree in number.
- Remember that indefinite pronouns (*any, anyone, anybody, each, everybody, everyone, everything, someone,* and *something*) are singular. Use singular nouns with them.

EDITING ACTIVITY 2: Correct Pronoun Reference and Agreement

Correct the problems with pronoun reference and agreement in the following paragraph.

Whenever I tell anyone my college major is food science, they

get a puzzled look on their face. Most people haven't heard of it. I first read about food science in a magazine article about the invention of different varieties of corn for undeveloped countries. They said that scientists spend years in the laboratory and in greenhouses trying to get plants to grow in extreme climates or different types of soils. They take years to develop. Last semester in my Introduction to Food Science course they had us experiment with making a type of yogurt that doesn't need refrigeration. It isn't available to consumers in poor countries. It didn't taste very good, but it was interesting to make. My ultimate goal is to contribute to the elimination of starvation throughout the world.

Exercise Central

For additional practice with correcting pronoun reference and agreement, go to **bedfordstmartins.com/choices** and click on "Exercise Central."

WRITING ACTIVITY 15: Edit Your Sentences

Read your essay word for word, looking for errors in spelling, punctuation, and grammar. Also ask a friend or classmate to help you spot errors you might have overlooked. Pay particular attention to vague pronoun reference and faulty pronoun agreement. Use a dictionary and the Handbook in Part Four of this book to help you correct the errors you find. Finally, record those errors in your editing log.

A Student's Edited Essay

This essay shows how to give information about your sources in the body of the essay and in the Works Cited list. You can find another sample essay on pp. 437–41.

You may have noticed that Kathy's revised draft contained some choppy sentences as well as errors in spelling, punctuation, and grammar. Kathy fixed these problems in her edited essay. Her corrections are underlined.

Kathy Chu
Professor Mangelsdorf
English 0311
4 Apr. 2006

The correct MLA format is used.

Helping Children Heal

When I was a child, going to the doctor was both
frightening and exciting. I hated getting shots and
seeing the crying babies. At the same time, the
friendly doctor in the white jacket who seemed to
have all the answers fascinated me. As an adult, I
still admire the doctor from my childhood. Now I know
that she was a pediatrician, which is a doctor who
specializes in the health needs of children. <u>When I
entered college and started to think of my future
occupation, I thought more and more about becoming
this kind of doctor.</u> As a pediatrician, I can help
children get well, make a good living, work hard, and
enjoy challenges.

Sentences are combined.

Ever since I can remember, I've wanted to take care
of children. <u>When my little brother used to get
earaches, I'd pretend I was the doctor and hold a cup
to his chest so I could hear his heartbeat.</u> In high
school, I volunteered at Providence Hospital in the
children's wing. <u>Seeing sick children made me sad,
but I always felt better after playing with them and
cheering them up. Being even a small part of a team
that helped children heal made me feel worthwhile.</u>

Sentences are combined.

Sentences are combined.

A vague pronoun reference is eliminated.

While volunteering at Providence Hospital, I
observed many pediatric nurses give children shots,
examine their progress, and cheer up their patients.
<u>Pediatric nurses work one-on-one with children, while
pediatricians spend less time alone with the
patients.</u> However, being a pediatrician appeals to me
more than being a nurse because pediatricians
diagnose children and decide on a treatment plan.
Nurses have to carry out the decisions of doctors. I
prefer to be the one who makes the decisions in the
first place.

Sentences are combined.

As a pediatrician, I can make a good living. <u>This
is important to me because my parents have had to
cope with many financial difficulties.</u> I remember bill

Sentences are combined.

A pronoun-agreement problem is fixed.

collectors calling us and my mother's car being repossessed. Pediatricians don't have trouble finding jobs, and their median salary is $133,000 a year (U.S. Dept. of Labor). This job security will let me provide for my parents when they get old, as well as take care of my own family.

Pediatricians work long hours. According to the *Occupational Outlook Handbook,* published by the U.S. Department of Labor, more than 30 percent of all doctors work over 60 hours a week (1). In addition, a pediatrician, like all doctors, must complete four years of college, four years of medical school, and then three to eight years of further training in a hospital (Turner 54). People who want to be accepted to medical school must have a high grade point average and be especially good in science. Fortunately, I like to work hard.

A vague pronoun reference is eliminated.

Finally, as a pediatrician I would encounter challenges every day. According to one pediatrician, "I never know what I'll encounter with every patient I see. One child might just have a cold or flu. But the next child could have a bruise that won't heal. This could be a symptom of cancer" (Turner 53). I look forward to helping children heal whether they have a runny nose or something more serious. The job might make me tired or stressed but never bored.

While a pediatrician's job can be difficult, I think it's the job for me. Getting into medical school is tough, but I like to aim high. For me, nothing would be more satisfying than helping a child get well.

Works Cited

United States. Dept. of Labor. Bureau of Labor Statistics. "Physicians and Surgeons." *Occupational Outlook Handbook, 2006–07 Edition.* Bureau of Labor Statistics, 2006. Web. 29 Mar. 2006.

Turner, Angela. "Pediatricians: An Endangered Species?" *Time* 7 Apr. 1999: 53–54. Print.

STEP 5. SHARE YOUR ESSAY

You've worked hard to write an essay that will be useful to people who share your interest in a particular occupation, so give them a chance to read it. Many organizations distribute periodic newsletters that include articles of interest to their members. For example, your school might mail a few pages of news and career ideas to students every term, your volunteer group might have a quarterly newsletter, or your employer might share monthly updates on staff activities. Whether these newsletters are printed, posted to the Web, or e-mailed to a listserv, the people who distribute them are almost always looking for reader submissions. Find out who edits one of the newsletters you receive, and send your essay to him or her. The other members of your group will thank you!

CHAPTER CHECKLIST

❑ I gathered ideas on a workplace occupation, workplace jargon, and a workplace problem by freewriting, brainstorming, and consulting with others.

❑ I developed ideas using classification and definition.

❑ I located sources on my topic to help support my ideas.

❑ I wrote an outline before I revised.

❑ I correctly used summaries, paraphrases, and quotations in my draft.

❑ I documented source materials in the body and at the end of my essay in a Works Cited list.

❑ I combined short, closely related sentences using subordinate conjunctions.

❑ I corrected errors in pronoun reference and agreement.

❑ I submitted my essay to a newsletter.

REFLECTING ON YOUR WRITING

To help you reflect on the writing you did in this chapter, answer the following questions:

1. What did you learn from writing on your topic?
2. If you used research in your essay, what part of the research process was hardest? What was easiest?

3. Compare and contrast writing this essay with writing previous essays.

4. If you had more time, what further revisions would you make to improve your essay? Why would you make these revisions?

Using your answers to these questions, complete a Writing Process Report for this chapter (you can download a report form at **bedford stmartins.com/choices**). Once you complete this report, freewrite about what you learned in this chapter.

An Occupation

TAMERA HELMS

Lessons in Shrimping

What's the first thing that comes to mind when you think of fishing? Many people think of lazily drifting in a boat waiting for the fish to bite. Commercial fishing, however, is very different. In the following reading, "Lessons in Shrimping," Tamera Helms describes an occupation that is a mystery to many people: being a shrimper. Helms wrote this essay while attending college.

"It's stupid to throw fish to those gulls," the captain said for the dozenth time. 1

"But Daddy, they're hungry," I cried. 2

"All right, Sis, but you're gonna regret it." 3

Two fish later, I learned what he'd meant when a big white sea gull returned with a fish, like the ones I'd so generously thrown to him, only in a smellier and more liquid form. This was one of the many lessons I learned during the summers I worked on my father's shrimp boat. Shrimping, I was soon to learn, was much more complicated and interesting than just pulling up a net full of shrimp. 4

A shrimper's day starts long before sunrise, usually between 3:30 and 5 a.m., depending on how far out the boat's headed that day. There are even times when a captain will keep the boat out overnight to have first crack at the prior day's hot spots. In Texas, where I learned about shrimping, the first "drag" (as pulling the net underwater is called) can't be started until the sun has fully crossed the horizon, but in the light before full sunrise the captain or a deckhand puts the net into the water to be rinsed and soaked. The net ranges in length from twenty to forty feet on an average-sized boat, which is itself forty to fifty feet long. At this hour, many shrimpers use a miniature net to look for the best spot to begin the first drag. This mini net, called a "try net," gives shrimpers some idea of what they'll catch without having to waste much time or fuel. 5

As soon as the sun is up and the captain has chosen a spot, they "put over the big rig." Having already put the net in the water, they need only to put in the huge wooden "doors" (which resemble the doors on an ancient castle) to spread open the mouth of the net and hold it underwater. It is, however, a sizeable task, since the doors may weigh in excess of 150 pounds. A winch 6 is used to lift the doors up off the deck. Then the captain must swing the doors out over the water by revving the engine and causing the boat to jump quickly forward. At that exact moment, he must release the winch brake, dropping the heavy doors into the water. If he fails to get the doors out over the water, they could very easily put a hole in the deck or be damaged themselves. Next, he must adjust the length of cable let out. If he doesn't let out enough, the net will catch only fish; if he lets out too much, the net may bog down in mud or, worse, hit an old wreck and maybe destroy the net. Each time shrimpers put the rig over, they are risking two or three thousand dollars of equipment.

It would seem that the next hour or two would be just a wait-   7
ing period, but instead the captain must monitor the cables and depth finder closely. Many shrimpers also monitor their catch with a try net to avoid pulling for shrimp that aren't there. After an hour or two, the captain usually picks up the net, although three-hour drags are not uncommon. Using the winch again, he pulls the doors to the top of the water and, using a method similar to the one for dropping the doors, places them back in their rack. Then, using a rope tied to the bag of the net, he pulls the net up beside the boat. Using another rope and the winch again, he lifts the bag of the net up over the deck and unties the end, letting all the con- tents spill out. At this point, the captain decides, from looking at the catch, whether to put it back over or to look for a better place.

Once the first catch of the day is pulled up, the real work   8
starts. "Culling," as most people refer to it, is the art of separat- ing the shrimp from the myriad ocean creatures pulled out of the water. The majority of these creatures are harmless: croak- ers, spots, blow fish, baby flounder, trout, and whiting. Others, however, pose dangers to the culler. Crabs, sting rays, eels, jelly fish, hard heads, and sea leeches must be avoided and thus slow the culler down.

The most dangerous of them is the hard head. Hard heads   9
are saltwater catfish, usually from two inches to a full foot in length, all equally threatening. What makes these fish so dan- gerous is the poisonous barbs around their head. These very sharp barbs can cut skin badly, shooting a poisonous venom into the cut. This poison causes the wound to swell enormously and painfully. Some people even become sick to their stomach and may run a slight fever. When struck by a hard head, the experienced culler will immediately try to force the wound to bleed and thus push out the poison.

There is, of course, more to culling than just avoiding hard   10
heads. Depending on the ratio of fish to shrimp and the size of the shrimp, there are three different culling procedures. Each begins, however, with the clearing out of the crabs. The pile of shrimp and fish and other creatures is turned over again and again with a shovel to free any crabs that might be lurking underneath. Then the majority of them are pushed out the scupper holes in the side

of the railing. Next the deckhand decides whether to cull from the deck of the boat or on a table (which usually doubles as an ice box). If the shrimp are big and easy to see and grab, culling is usually done on the deck by picking up the shrimp and raking the "trash fish" overboard. If the shrimp are small and there are not too many of them, the deckhand shovels loads of the mix onto the table top, picks the fish out of the shrimp, and throws them over the side. He then rakes the remaining shrimp into baskets at his feet. The last method and the most ingenious is for a load that has just as many fish as shrimp in it. The deckhand uses an invention called a "salt barrel" to separate the fish from the shrimp. A salt barrel is a tub of seawater with a large amount of extra salt dissolved in it. The excess salt causes the fish to float to the top of the water, where they can be scooped out and thrown back into the bay. Then, using the net, the deckhand dips deep into the barrel and pulls out the remaining shrimp. Any fish that are left are picked out and thrown over. When the culling is finished, the shrimp are iced down, and the deck is cleaned of all remaining ocean creatures.

Then, depending on the speed of the deckhand, there may 11 be time to rest a few minutes before the next load is brought up. And so the work continues until sundown, at which time the captain pulls up the last drag of the day and turns the boat toward the port to sell the day's catch.

At the dock, they unload the catch into metal tubs with 12 holes at the bottom. The shrimp are washed to melt any ice that might add weight to the scales and are then weighed and counted. The "count" indicates the size of the shrimp and is determined by counting the number of shrimp to a pound.

It is at this time that shrimpers find out if they've made any 13 money for the day or if they've just broken even with the boat's overhead expenses. Despite what people may believe, shrimpers don't make a very prosperous living. It could cause one to wonder why they continue to work under these conditions. Some are trapped into it due to lack of a formal education. They know shrimping, and so that's what they do. Others, such as my father, do it because they love nature. They are addicted to the salt air, the freedom of being on the water, the beautiful sunrises and sunsets. These shrimpers pass their respect and love for nature on to their children. Often this is as simple as warning them to watch for bird bombs. Whatever their reasons for shrimping, they each deserve respect and admiration. The work they do is much harder than most of us will ever know.

READING ACTIVITY 7: Build Your Vocabulary

Determine the meanings of the following words from the context of Tamera Helms's essay. Then check their meanings by looking up the words in a dictionary: winch (6), culling (8), hard heads (9), barbs (9), lurking (10), scupper (10), ingenious (10), overhead (13).

READING ACTIVITY 8: Read to Improve Your Writing

Discuss the following questions about "Lessons in Shrimping" with your classmates.

1. Give three reasons why shrimping is a difficult profession.
2. Why do people remain in such a difficult job?
3. Explain the title of the essay.
4. Why does Helms explain the process of shrimping in such detail? In your view, is this level of detail effective or ineffective? Explain your answer.

Workplace Communication

RITA WARREN HESS

American Workplace Slang and Jargon

Slang and jargon help people in the workplace communicate quickly and effectively. Until people understand this language, however, they are at a disadvantage. "American Workplace Slang and Jargon" was originally published on the immigration resources Web site www .New2USA.com. In this essay, Rita Warren Hess helps people who are new to the United States understand some of the odd-sounding language used in the American business world.

Have you mastered the English language? Good! Can you also comfortably speak business-ese, the sometimes-unusual words and phrases like those in the following fictional American workplace? 1

Mega Music is a **brick and mortar** business (a traditional company with an actual building or store location, rather than an e-commerce business). Mega struggles to compete with online retailers, sometimes called **click and mortar** businesses. To remain financially sound, Mega Music used **headhunters**, paid recruiters who match hiring companies with employees or executives, to find a new CEO. The headhunter found a young energetic **Yankee** (a person from the northeastern region of the United States) named Bill Black. 2

Mega hired Bill because he possessed excellent **soft skills** (people skills). He interacted well with the public, was an excellent motivator and a good conversationalist. Soft skills are sometimes more important than **hard skills** (hands-on abilities) like programming or building cars. 3

The headhunter also located a **bean counter** to handle the 4
company's funds (beans). People often refer to *accountants* as
bean counters. The bean counter suggested Mega managers do
some **number crunching** (performing complex calculations) to
see if they could save the company money by lowering budget
estimates or postponing planned projects. Mega's new accoun-
tant further recommended **across the board** budget cuts
(reductions that applied to everyone equally). Slashing budgets
by 10% across the board meant *every* department received a
10% budget cut.

When budget projections still did not align with income esti- 5
mates, Mega Music **downsized** (went from one size to a smaller
size by reducing the number of employees through terminations
or retirements). Downsizing forced department managers to
make difficult decisions. Janet had to reduce her engineering
staff of four people by one. Each person was an excellent worker
and played an important role in the group. Deciding which one
to fire was hard for Janet.

All department managers were uncomfortable knowing cer- 6
tain employees would receive a **pink slip** (termination notice). A
person being fired (also known as *getting the axe*) does not actually receive a pink slip terminating his/her employment. This
term is one of many unusual phrases adopted by businesses.

One Mega employee reacted unfavorably to termination and 7
charged the company with age discrimination. This was expected
since the company had **deep pockets**, meaning they were a large
and reasonably successful business. People contemplating **litiga-
tion** (legal charges) often target companies with deep pockets
because they anticipate a large financial settlement.

Other employees welcomed the termination. They were tired 8
of the **rat race** — methodically getting up, going to work, performing job duties, going home, sleeping, and repeating the
process over again. They never felt refreshed, although they escaped the rat race on weekends by catching up on **R and R** (rest
and relaxation).

What else did Mega Music do to prevent **going under** (going 9
out of business)?

Bill, the new CEO, believed saving the company meant identi- 10
fying previous mistakes. He invited all managers to a **Monday
morning quarterback** session. This phrase originated after weekend football games, when fans discussed what the **quarterback**
(an important player on a football team) *should* have done or
could have done differently to change the game's outcome. Bill
felt that by evaluating past failures, they could avoid the same
mistake(s) in the future.

Following Bill's Monday morning quarterback session, his 11
staff presented a list of ideas for improvement.

First, they found their method of valuing and managing 12
warehouse products was a disaster. They switched to **FIFO**, an

inventory term meaning "first-in-first-out" and placing a value on items sold by using the cost of the oldest items first. FIFO was chosen over another inventory valuation method called **LIFO** (last-in-first-out).

Bill and his team also decided to decrease their inventory by using a process called **JIT** (just-in-time), in which they would stock little, if any, surplus goods or materials. Instead, buyers ordered items from suppliers to arrive just in time, or just before needed. 13

An internal investigation revealed that Mary, the warehouse manager, was receiving **kickbacks** (illegal payments made between two parties to give one person an unfair advantage over competitors). Mary routinely sent bid packages to obtain quotes on CD cases. John Jones, an employee at a plastics company that manufactures CD cases, paid Mary $500 cash each time she arranged it so that his company got the contract to supply the cases. 14

Besides firing Mary, Mega Music **outsourced** purchasing, meaning they hired an independent firm to provide the service rather than using employees on the company payroll. Financially, it benefited the company to outsource the function rather than having it done **in-house** (done by employees on the company payroll). 15

Bill's team also found that filling product orders was very **labor-intensive**, meaning labor costs were disproportionately high. They devised a plan to ship inventory twice as fast with fewer employees by **working smarter** (getting the work done more efficiently). Working smarter is different from working harder. For example, if your job is to move bricks from Pile A to Pile B all day, you could work harder and move more bricks. But if you load them in a wheelbarrow, push them across the yard, then go back for another load, you are working smarter. 16

Finally, Mega Music changed their advertising strategy by studying the **benchmark**, the best in their industry. Their largest competitor, Today's Tunes, had the ultimate advertising campaign for reaching young male audiences. Today's Tunes set the benchmark (the standard), so Mega used a similar format to devise a halftime Super Bowl Sunday commercial. 17

Mega encountered obstacles during the **eleventh (11th) hour**, the timeframe just before a deadline but not necessarily the *hour* before. After spending six months preparing the new commercial, they made several changes during the last three weeks (their 11th hour) before the spot aired. 18

Mega's CEO wondered if the company's efforts would be in vain. If the Super Bowl advertisement did not bring the anticipated returns, the company would **take a bath** (an unfavorable way of describing a person or group of people who did not fare well in some undertaking) and might face bankruptcy. Bill worried needlessly. Millions of viewers watched Mega Music's halftime commercial and the company telephones rang non-stop on Monday morning with new orders. 19

READING ACTIVITY 9: Build Your Vocabulary

Determine the meanings of the following words from the context of Rita Warren Hess's essay. Then check their meanings by looking up the words in a dictionary: business-ese (1), retailers (2), projections (5), align (5), termination (6), inventory (12), surplus (13), disproportionately (16).

READING ACTIVITY 10: Read to Improve Your Writing

Discuss the following questions about "American Workplace Slang and Jargon" with your classmates.

1. What is Hess's purpose in this essay? Is this purpose stated directly? If it is stated directly, where does it appear? If it's not stated directly, why not?

2. Describe the audience that the author is writing for. How does her understanding of her readers affect the way the author explains slang and jargon? Do you disagree with any of her definitions? Select at least one and research its origin.

3. Why did the author decide to write a fictional story — rather than a standard essay — to explain specialized language in the business world?

4. Among the business terms defined in this article are *pink slip, deep pockets,* and *rat race.* How do you suppose these terms came to be? Select at least one other jargon phrase not used in this essay, and guess (or research) its origin.

A Job-Related Problem

ELLEN GOODMAN

The Company Man

Ellen Goodman is a Pulitzer Prize–winning columnist for the **Boston Globe,** *which syndicates her column to more than 450 newspapers. With common sense and humor, Goodman writes about topics close to home. She focuses on families, parents, women in the workplace, and the poor. In the essay that follows, Goodman provides a vivid definition of "the company man."*

He worked himself to death, finally and precisely, at 3:00 a.m. Sunday morning.

The obituary didn't say that, of course. It said that he died of a coronary thrombosis — I think that was it — but everyone among his friends and acquaintances knew it instantly. He was a perfect Type A, a workaholic, a classic, they said to each other and shook their heads — and thought for five or ten minutes about the way they lived.

This man who worked himself to death finally and precisely 3 at 3:00 a.m. Sunday morning — on his day off — was fifty-one years old and a vice-president. He was, however, one of six vice-presidents, and one of three who might conceivably — if the president died or retired soon enough — have moved to the top spot. Phil knew that.

He worked six days a week, five of them until eight or nine 4 at night, during a time when his own company had begun the four-day week for everyone but the executives. He worked like the Important People. He had no outside "extracurricular interests," unless, of course, you think about a monthly golf game that way. To Phil, it was work. He always ate egg salad sandwiches at his desk. He was, of course, overweight, by twenty or twenty-five pounds. He thought it was okay, though, because he didn't smoke.

On Saturdays, Phil wore a sports jacket to the office instead 5 of a suit, because it was the weekend.

He had a lot of people working for him, maybe sixty, and most 6 of them liked him most of the time. Three of them will be seriously considered for his job. The obituary didn't mention that.

But it did list his "survivors" quite accurately. He is survived 7 by his wife, Helen, forty-eight years old, a good woman of no particular marketable skills, who worked in an office before marrying and mothering. She had, according to their daughter, given up trying to compete with his work years ago, when the children were small. A company friend said, "I know how much you will miss him." And she answered, "I already have."

"Missing him all these years," she must have given up part 8 of herself which had cared too much for the man. She would be "well taken care of."

His "dearly beloved" eldest of the "dearly beloved" children 9 is a hard-working executive in a manufacturing firm down South. In the day and a half before the funeral, he went around the neighborhood researching his father, asking the neighbors what he was like. They were embarrassed.

His second child is a girl, who is twenty-four and newly 10 married. She lives near her mother and they are close, but whenever she was alone with her father, in a car driving somewhere, they had nothing to say to each other.

The youngest is twenty, a boy, a high-school graduate who 11 has spent the last couple of years, like a lot of his friends, doing enough odd jobs to stay in grass and food. He was the one who tried to grab at his father, and tried to mean enough to him to keep the man at home. He was his father's favorite. Over the last two years, Phil stayed up nights worrying about the boy.

The boy once said, "My father and I only board here."   12

At the funeral, the sixty-year-old company president told the   13
forty-eight-year-old widow that the fifty-one-year-old deceased
had meant much to the company and would be missed and
would be hard to replace. The widow didn't look him in the eye.
She was afraid he would read her bitterness and, after all, she
would need him to straighten out the finances — the stock
options and all that.

Phil was overweight and nervous and worked too hard. If he   14
wasn't at the office, he was worried about it. Phil was a Type A,
a heart-attack natural. You could have picked him out in a
minute from a lineup.

So when he finally worked himself to death, at precisely   15
3:00 a.m. Sunday morning, no one was really surprised.

By 5:00 p.m. the afternoon of the funeral, the company   16
president had begun, discreetly of course, with care and taste,
to make inquiries about his replacement. One of three men. He
asked around: "Who's been working the hardest?"

READING ACTIVITY 11: Build Your Vocabulary

Determine the meanings of the following words from the context of
Ellen Goodman's essay. Then check their meanings by looking up the
words in a dictionary: obituary (2), extracurricular (4), board (12),
deceased (13), discreetly (16).

READING ACTIVITY 12: Read to Improve Your Writing

Discuss the following questions about "The Company Man" with
your classmates.

1. What details about Phil make him the definition of "the company man"?

2. What point is Goodman trying to make by ending her piece with
   the line: "He [the president] asked around: 'Who's been working
   the hardest?'"?

3. What about her style helps Goodman convince readers that Phil
   was a true "company man"?

4. In your view, does this essay accurately depict the modern workplace? Why or why not?

Evaluating a Subject

Using Comparison and Contrast

In this chapter, you will use evaluation to share your opinion of a product, a performance, or a place. As you follow the steps of the writing process, you will

- Gather ideas by brainstorming, asking questions, and freewriting.

- Develop your ideas using comparison and contrast.

- Practice expressing a judgment, using criteria, providing evidence, and keeping a balanced perspective.

- Combine sentences with relative clauses.

- Learn how to correct comma splices.

- Post your evaluation to a consumer-driven Web site.

Evaluation is something you do every day, often without even thinking about it. In the morning, you may decide that a new brand of breakfast cereal tastes better than your old brand. During the school day, you may realize that this semester's chemistry instructor explains experiments more carefully than a previous instructor did. In the evening, you may channel surf to find a television show that is worth watching.

When you *evaluate* something, you judge its value, worthiness, or merit. An evaluation is based on *standards*, or criteria: a breakfast cereal should taste good and be good for you, a chemistry instructor should know his subject and communicate it clearly, and a television show should entertain or inform you. When you evaluate, you apply standards like these to your subject. You taste the cereal and examine the nutritional label on the box. You listen to determine how well your chemistry instructor explains an experiment. You examine television shows for amusing plots or interesting settings. After applying the appropriate standards to your subject, you make a decision about its value, worthiness, or merit.

Everyday evaluations are usually simple, but you can apply standards to make decisions about less routine subjects — such as whether to buy a new computer game, to see a movie that looks interesting, or to eat at a particular restaurant. When you have limited personal knowledge of a subject, you probably seek out other people's opinions and experiences to help form a judgment about it. You might ask friends or family members what they think, look for expert reviews in newspapers and magazines, or search the Web for comments.

Just as you seek out people's evaluations when you need to make a choice, other people are interested in knowing your opinions. The readings and activities in this chapter will show you how to draw on your experience and knowledge to evaluate a product, a performance, or a place. Once you have evaluated your subject, you can write a convincing essay that shares what you have decided with others and helps them make their own choices.

GROUP ACTIVITY 1: Think about Subjects

The man holding a baby in the photograph on page 232 appears to be evaluating a piece of abstract art. What is your reaction to the art? The photograph itself can also be considered a piece of art. With your classmates, discuss what makes this an interesting photograph. Share ideas for other products, performances, or places to evaluate.

READING ESSAYS THAT EVALUATE

Evaluation essays, often called *reviews*, are popular with both readers and writers. Readers like them because they offer practical information; writers like them because they provide an opportunity to influence what other people think and do. Because they're so popular, formal reviews are a regular feature of newspapers, magazines, radio and television broadcasts, and Web sites. Although reviewers might not agree with each other and readers might have their own opinions, disagreement is part of the fun.

The following three essays are typical examples of evaluation. As you read them, try to identify some of the methods, such as comparison and contrast, that these writers use to explain their judgments and to persuade their readers to agree with them. Pay attention, also, to how you respond to the writers' arguments. Do they surprise you? Make you angry? Raise more questions? Jot down your reactions as they occur to you.

Evaluation of a Product

LEANDER KAHNEY

The Joy of iPod:
iCandy for the Ears

Leander Kahney lives and works in San Francisco, California, where he is an editor at Wired, *a magazine and Web site devoted to technology, pop culture, and current events. Kahney often writes about Apple computers and products. His books* The Cult of Mac *(2004) and* The Cult of iPod *(2005) are about the Mac community and its devotion to the Apple brand. His blog* Cult of Mac *(available at www.cultofmac.com) features articles about new Apple products and their influence on pop culture. In this review, which is an excerpt from* The Cult of iPod, *Kahney explains what makes the iPod the "most personal of personal devices."*

Fire, the wheel, and the iPod. In the history of invention, gadgets don't come more iconic than Apple's digital music player. The iPod is to the 21st century what the big band was to the '20s, the radio to the '40s, or the jukebox to the '50s — the signature technology that defines the musical culture of the era. And what a marvelous technology the iPod is. Inside Apple's little white box is magic, pure magic, in the guise of music. 1

Like a cell phone or a laptop, the iPod is kept close and carried everywhere. It's used every day, but not for work or to enslave you by persistent contact. The iPod is used to invoke euphoria. People are in love with music. The sparkling genius of the iPod is that it gives it to you in huge doses. The iPod can store an entire lifetime's worth of music. And so it becomes the most personal of personal devices. More than a computer, a car, or a fancy pair of shoes, it's part of your makeup, your personality. 2

What's on it — the music — tells who you are. Music is deep in your heart and soul.

I'm a music junkie from England, a nation of music junkies. Since late childhood, music has been a passion, sometimes an obsession, that often took precedence over all other interests — food, love, even cigarettes. Like a lot of people, I had a giant collection of vinyl LPs and CDs that grew over the years into an unmanageable archive weighing hundreds of pounds. Too heavy for shelves, the records sat on the floor, spilling into the room. But for the most part, the collection was merely for other people to gawk at. I didn't play most of the records, and except for a few disks at the front of the pile, I forgot and neglected most of them.

Fast forward, and now the entire collection can fit inside a small white box the size and weight of a pack of cards. This to me is a miracle. A crowning achievement of technology. That unwieldy pile of vinyl and cardboard has been freed from the living room and is available anywhere and everywhere I go: from the earliest, regrettable singles to my latest obsession.

Inside the iPod, a music collection comes alive. There's delight in loading up a ton of stuff from all genres, eras, and styles and seeing what the machine comes up with. Select Random Shuffle, and the iPod dredges up tunes you might never consciously choose to play. But chosen for you, they're a delight. This mode of play also allows you to discover gems in a collection that previously sat unplayed on a shelf of CDs. Songs previously neglected can become top favorites. And then there are all those tunes you never knew you had. Random Shuffle can create great surprises, selecting just the right song at just the right time. Or it can throw together unexpected combinations: Burning Spear followed by Ludacris. It doesn't always work, but when it does, you're in pop heaven.

The iPod has changed forever my listening habits. No longer do I want to hear an album all the way through (with rare exceptions). What I want is a playlist of my favorites. Listening to the iPod makes a cinematic adventure of a trip to the supermarket or a boring car drive. It adds a sense of otherworldliness to walking down the most familiar street. There's nothing better for exercise — pounding beats and breaks to get you energized to mount the summit of a hill. I like listening to the iPod while riding my bike (yeah, I know it's dangerous and probably illegal). High as a kite off the exercise, the music transports me to nirvana. Sometimes, when the right tune pops up, I'm truly in heaven.

READING ACTIVITY 1: Build Your Vocabulary

Determine the meanings of the following words from the context of Leander Kahney's essay. Then check their meanings by looking up the words in a dictionary: iconic (1), signature (1), guise (1), persistent (2), invoke (2), euphoria (2), precedence (3), cinematic (6), otherworldliness (6), summit (6), nirvana (6).

READING ACTIVITY 2: Read to Improve Your Writing

Discuss the following questions about "The Joy of iPod: iCandy for the Ears" with your classmates.

1. What is Kahney's opinion of the iPod? Where in the evaluation does he state this opinion?
2. List at least three of the reasons that the author provides to explain his opinion of the iPod.
3. Do you trust the author's evaluation of the iPod? Why or why not?
4. Why does Kahney compare the iPod to his collection of records and compact disks?
5. How does Kahney attempt to keep his audience interested in his topic?

Evaluation of a Performance

DIANE HEIMAN AND PHYLLIS BOOKSPAN

Sesame Street: *Brought to You by the Letters M-A-L-E*

Diane Heiman is an attorney and public policy consultant, and Phyllis Bookspan is a law professor at Widener University School of Law in Wilmington, Delaware. Both Heiman and Bookspan are mothers, and when they wrote this article for the Seattle Times *in 1994, their children were very young. In this evaluation of* Sesame Street, *Heiman and Bookspan explain how the popular children's television show could be more girl-friendly.*

A recent report released by the American Association of University Women, "How Schools Shortchange Women," finds that teachers, textbooks, and tests are, whether intentionally or unintentionally, giving preferential treatment to elementary-school boys. As a result, girls who enter school with equal or better academic potential than their male counterparts lose confidence and do not perform as well.

An earlier study about law students, published in the *Journal of Legal Education,* found a similar disparity. "Gender Bias in the Classroom" found that male law students are called upon in class more frequently than females, speak for longer periods of time, and are given more positive feedback by law professors.

The article raised some disturbing questions about whether   3
women and men receive truly equal education in American law schools.

Unfortunately, this insidious gender bias appears long before   4
our children enter school and pervades even the television show *Sesame Street*. Yes, *Sesame Street* is sexist! But, just as in the story of the emperor and his new clothes, many of us do not notice the obvious.

The puppet stars of the show, Bert and Ernie, and all the   5
other major *Sesame Street* animal characters — Big Bird, Cookie Monster, Grover, Oscar the Grouch, Kermit the Frog, and Mr. Snuffleupagus — are male. Among the secondary characters, including Elmo, Herry Monster, Count VonCount, Telemonster, Prairie Dawn, and Betty Lou, only a very few are girls.

The female Muppets always play children, while the males   6
play adult parts in various scenes. In a recently aired skit "Squeal of Fortune," this disparity is evident when the host of the show introduces the two contestants. Of Count VonCount of Transylvania the host asks, "What do you do for a living?" to which the count responds authoritatively, "I count!" Of Prairie Dawn, he inquires, "And how do you spend your day?" Sure, it would be silly to ask a schoolgirl what she does for a living. But none of the female Muppets on *Sesame Street* are even old enough to earn a living.

Further, almost all the baby puppet characters on *Sesame*   7
Street are girls. For example, Snuffie's sibling is Baby Alice; in books, Grover's baby cousin is a girl, and when Herry Monster's mother brings home the new baby — it's a girl. Since babies are totally dependent and fairly passive, the older (male) relatives take care of them and provide leadership.

Also, the female Muppets almost never interact with each   8
other. In sharp contrast, consequential and caring friendships have been fully developed between male Muppets: Ernie and Bert; Big Bird and Snuffie; even Oscar the Grouch and his (male) worm, Squirmy.

Any parent of toddlers or preschoolers can testify that the   9
"girls" on *Sesame Street* are not very popular. Children ask their parents for Bert and Ernie dolls not Baby Alice. Is this just because the girls are not marketed via books, tapes, placemats and toy dolls the same way the boys are? Or is it that the *Sesame Street* writers simply have not developed the girls into the same types of lovable, adorable personalities that belong to the main characters?

Interestingly and peculiarly, the minor "girls" look more   10
human than most of the well-loved animal roles. They are not physically cuddly, colorful or bizarre, as are the more important male characters. Prairie Dawn has ordinary blonde hair and

brown eyes — nothing even remotely similar to Big Bird's soft yellow feathers or Cookie Monster's wild, bright blue, mane.

Yes, we believe that *Sesame Street* is one of the best shows on 11 television for small children. Our children — boys and girls — are regular viewers. In addition to its educational value, lack of violence and emphasis on cooperation, the adult characters on the show are admirably balanced in terms of avoiding sexual stereotypes.

But even the best of the bunch has room for improvement. 12 Just as elementary through professional school educators must learn to be more sensitive to subtle and unintentional gender bias, so too should the folks at Children's Television Network. We can stop sexism from seeping into our children's first "formal" educational experience.

The message was brought to you by the letter F: fairness for 13 females.

READING ACTIVITY 3: Build Your Vocabulary

Try to determine the meanings of the following words from the context of Diane Heiman and Phyllis Bookspan's essay. Then check their meanings by looking up the words in a dictionary: disparity (2), insidious (4), authoritatively (6), inquires (6), consequential (8), peculiarly (10).

READING ACTIVITY 4: Read to Improve Your Writing

Discuss the following questions about "*Sesame Street:* Brought to You by the Letters M-A-L-E" with your classmates.

1. What is the authors' opinion of *Sesame Street*? Do they express this opinion in a single sentence? If so, indicate what sentence this is.
2. What elements of a children's television program are important to Heiman and Bookspan? How well does *Sesame Street* meet their expectations of a good children's show?
3. Throughout the essay, the authors compare and contrast male and female characters on *Sesame Street*. Do they use point-by-point or subject-by-subject order (or both) to organize their ideas? How effective is this organization?
4. How do Heiman and Bookspan support their argument that *Sesame Street* is sexist? Is their evidence convincing? Why or why not?

Evaluation of a Place

JOHN GARVEY

Christo's Gates:
An Unexpected Pleasure

John Garvey is a writer, a priest in the Orthodox Church in America, and a columnist for Commonweal, *a magazine about religion, politics, and culture. His books include* Prematurely Saved and Other Varieties of the Religions Experience *(1986),* Orthodoxy for the Non-Orthodox: A Brief Introduction to Orthodox Christianity *(2002), and* Death and the Rest of Our Life *(2005). In this review from* Commonweal, *Garvey writes about a work of public art called* The Gates *that was installed in New York's Central Park in the winter of 2005.*

It may seem pointless, and in a lovely way it is, to install a series of frames containing large hanging saffron rectangles over twenty-three miles of Central Park pathways. But after years of trying, in February the artists Christo and Jeanne-Claude managed to bring it off. Called *The Gates*, the project involved the installation of 7,532 frames, and the fabric was hung so high that the tallest people could walk along the paths easily. The money was raised by the artists, and much of it went to pay those who installed the work, and to pay monitors who directed people to interesting routes and also used poles to unfurl banners tangled by the wind.

A gate is an entrance point, and in the Christo/Jeanne-Claude installation one gate is the entrance to another, and another, all leading eventually to divergent points — do you go up this hill, down that one, or straight ahead? The light changes as you walk, shining through some panels, shadowed in others, and the winds change the vista. All is transitory, and by the time you read this, *The Gates* will be gone.

What you notice entering Central Park (we started at the south end, where the horse and carriage rides can be hired and even on a cold winter day the scent of horse manure perfumes the air) is how many people are smiling. They are uncommonly polite — maybe because so many are visitors and not New Yorkers — and a lot of them are taking pictures. I've never seen Central Park so crowded. The only negative note was a mad ranter who stood on one hill and shouted his message that everything about the world was lousy, but he may have been hired by the project to remind the international visitors that this is, after all, New York.

One of the most pleasant aspects of *The Gates* is that no one sponsored it. It really was free to the public, and not "brought

Smile all who enter here.

to you by [fill in the corporation]." It sold nothing but the artists and their art. It was free to all, and given the quietly festive atmosphere, it plainly delighted most of the participants, all of those who walked beneath the bright hanging saffron.

It was also, I am sure, a delight to the owners of the Central Park Boathouse, which, according to a friend who frequents it, is often nearly empty in February. We went there for a drink and found it packed. We left the park by walking down the path where telescopes have been set up to follow the storied falcons, Pale Male and Lola. They were expelled from their nest near the top of a tony Fifth Avenue co-op, but the outcry that followed led the co-op to construct a new nest. The falcons have in fact returned and are doing well.

Some of those who dislike *The Gates* object that it doesn't mean anything. Neither does good music, or good abstract art. But I have noticed — listening, for example, to John Cage — that his music can teach an acute and refreshed listening. When leaving the Museum of Modern Art after a couple of hours of the attention you have to bring to art, I have found myself seeing the colors and forms of the city outside with new eyes. It is this reawakening of the senses that makes many forms of art important, not any message. No good art is ever propaganda, even for the most noble cause.

The Gates reminded me of a Tibetan Buddhist tradition: monks construct a beautiful mandala in a frame with colored

sands, an elaborate, intricately patterned work of art that symbolizes the fullness of the universe. When it is finished, the
frame is taken to the edge of a river and the sands poured into
the flowing water. The point is, in part, the passing nature of
everything, as well as the fact that those things that pass are
wonderful and can be sources of joy and enlightenment in the
present. There is a Western echo in Yeats: "Man is in love and
loves what vanishes, / What more is there to say?"

As far as I know, no Buddhist connection has been claimed   8
by the artists. A couple of people have pointed out the resemblance to paths at the Fushimi-Inari Shrine in Kyoto, where
post and beam frames, colored saffron, have been placed over
paths. Christo and Jeanne-Claude say no lessons or points
should be drawn from their always temporary works, and I
know what they mean. But I think of the mandala, and *The
Gates*, which likewise were there for awhile and then, deliber-
ately, not there, and I'm grateful.

READING ACTIVITY 5: Build Your Vocabulary

Determine the meanings of the following words from the context of
John Garvey's essay. Then check their meanings by looking up the
words in a dictionary: saffron (1), unfurl (1), divergent (2), vista (2),
transitory (2), storied (5), tony (5), acute (6), propaganda (6), mandala (7).

READING ACTIVITY 6: Read to Improve Your Writing

Discuss the following questions about "Christo's *Gates:* An Unexpected
Pleasure" with your classmates.

1. In what ways are Christo's and Jeanne-Claude's art installment *The
   Gates* also a place?
2. What does Garvey like about *The Gates*?
3. How does the writer respond to people who didn't like the installation of orange banners at Central Park?
4. Why does Garvey compare *The Gates* to Buddhist temples and a
   Japanese shrine? How does this comparison help you picture the
   exhibit?

Writing Assignment

You make judgments and share your opinions all the time. For
example, you may have complained to a friend that your expensive new athletic shoes don't provide enough arch support,

argued with a coworker about the results of *American Idol,* or tried to persuade your spouse that Disneyworld would be a good honeymoon destination. Your task in this chapter is to share your opinion with a wider audience by writing an essay that evaluates something you feel strongly about. You (or your instructor) may decide to approach this assignment in one of several ways:

- Evaluate a product you are familiar with.

  OR

- Evaluate a performance you have seen.

  OR

- Evaluate a place you have been to.

Follow the guidance and activities in this chapter to discover, develop, and polish your ideas into a finished essay. After you complete your essay, you'll share it with others who are interested in your topic by posting it to a Web site that publishes consumer reviews.

STEP 1. EXPLORE YOUR CHOICES

You can write an evaluation essay about almost anything that you have an opinion about, from topics as narrow as the latest flash drive or whole-grain snack to those as broad as the full run of a television series or the National Park System. So how should you begin? The first two things to consider are who might read your essay and why you're writing it for them. Even more so than other kinds of writing, reviews are written to inform and persuade people who are curious about a particular subject. As you gather ideas for possible topics, choose something that you have personal experience with, that you have a strong opinion about, and that others are interested in.

Analyzing Your Audience and Purpose

Your audience will include people who have sought your opinion of a product, performance, or place because they are directly affected by your topic. Your readers might include consumers deciding whether they should purchase a product or employees of the company that makes the product. They might include people who are considering

For more on audience and purpose, see pp. 8–12.

seeing a play, movie, or television show as well as those who have already seen it. And your audience might include people interested in visiting a shopping mall, museum, or tourist attraction and possibly some of the managers or tour guides who are responsible for that site. Whatever your topic, your readers probably know something about it, but they are seeking other people's opinions to help themselves form a judgment or make improvements.

Knowing who your audience is will help you identify your purpose. What do you want your readers to do as a result of reading your essay? Do you want to encourage or discourage them from purchasing, watching, or visiting something? If your readers are in some way responsible for your subject, do you want to persuade them to change something about it?

WRITING ACTIVITY 1: Analyze Your Audience and Purpose

Your responses to the following questions will help you select possible topics for your evaluation. Be sure to come back to these questions after you have chosen a topic to write about.

1. Does this assignment call for primarily expressive, informative, or persuasive writing?
2. Are you writing for an audience of consumers or for the people who make or manage something?
3. Have you recently purchased any consumer products that your audience might be interested in reading about?
4. What movies, television shows, music groups, or books might your readers be curious about?
5. What places — restaurants, shopping malls, museums, amusement parks — have you visited recently? Why would readers be interested in them?
6. How interested will your readers be in an essay that evaluates a product, performance, or place? How can you make sure you keep your readers' interest as they read your essay?

Gathering Ideas

For more on gathering ideas, see pp. 12–16.

Before you settle on a product, performance, or place to evaluate, explore your choices by gathering ideas for at least one subject in each of these three categories. Even if you already have a specific subject in mind for your essay, you may be surprised by where your explorations lead you.

To gather ideas for your evaluation, you may use any of the techniques you learned in Chapter 2 and applied in previous assignments. The student writers in this chapter will use brainstorming, questioning, and freewriting.

Brainstorming about a Product

As a consumer, you evaluate products before purchasing them. If the product is inexpensive, such as a can of soup, your preliminary evaluation might be as simple as reading the label. If the product is a major purchase, such as a computer or a car, you might consult friends, check the reviews on a Web site like edmunds.com or epinions.com, read a magazine such as *Consumer Reports,* and comparison shop. Even after you purchase the product, you probably continue to evaluate it to confirm that you made a good choice.

To identify a product worth evaluating in your essay, try brainstorming a list of items you use every day or have recently purchased. Don't worry yet about whether they would be good essay topics. Just write down as many products as you can think of.

Student writer Ellie, for example, brainstormed the following list of products by looking around her apartment:

DVD player
electric pencil sharpener
Mary Kay hand-smoothing system
coffee maker
scanner/printer/fax machine
new laptop
dead laptop
George Foreman grill
foam pillow
iPod Shuffle
running shoes
fake butter spray
picture phone
Red Bull
tennis racquet

Once you have a list of products in hand, check off the items that you have strong feelings about. Think of your audience as people who are interested in purchasing the product. Your evaluation will affect their decision to purchase (or not to purchase) the item. Select one item, and brainstorm a list of what you like and don't like about the product. Student writer Ellie, for example, reviewed her list and realized that she had been telling friends how much she loved her new coffee maker, which she received as a gift. Here is her brainstorming on the Cuisinart Automatic Grind and Brew:

> I love this thing!
> wanted it for ages
> ridiculously expensive: $120
> couldn't bring myself to spend the money on it
> has the coffee grinder built right in
> and a timer
> fresh ground coffee tastes so much better
> grinder makes a lot of noise
> scares the cat every time
> wakes me up better than my alarm clock
> automatic shut-off
> can't figure out how to measure the beans for less than a full pot
> a lot of parts
> have to dismantle the pieces and wash them by hand every day
> sometimes the parts jam from the wet coffee grounds
> if you don't close the basket right, coffee pours all over the counter
> more maintenance than my old coffee maker
> it's worth it
> a luxury, but I don't think I could do without it now

WRITING ACTIVITY 2: Brainstorm about a Product

Brainstorm a list of products that you use every day or have recently obtained. Select one item from your list, and brainstorm again, this time writing down what you like and don't like about the product. You may brainstorm about as many products as you like, but focus on one at a time.

Asking Questions about a Performance

Put aside your writing about a product for now so that you can gather ideas for another type of evaluation — a performance.

As you probably know, newspapers, magazines, and Web sites carry reviews of all sorts of performances, including movies, concerts, art shows, dance recitals, television programs, and sporting events. Readers often rely on these reviews to help them decide whether a performance is worth seeing or not. Before investing your hard-earned money in a movie ticket, for example, you may decide to read a few reviews at RottenTomatoes.com or the Internet Movie Database (imdb.com). If the reviews are positive, you're more likely to see the film.

Because many professional critics are trained as reporters, they often use the journalist's questions as a starting point to gather ideas for their reviews:

- *Who* is (or was) involved in this performance? Include relevant producers, directors, and talent (such as actors, singers, dancers, and announcers).
- *What* is the show about?
- *Where* is (or was) the performance held or broadcast?
- *When* is (or was) the show performed or broadcast?
- *How* effective is (or was) the show?
- *Why* is (or was) this performance worth seeing or not worth seeing?

By using these questions as prompts, critics can be sure that their essays cover the basics that readers expect to find in a review. The questions also help writers gather details to explain what they liked or didn't like about a performance.

Here's how one student, Rob, used the journalist's questions to gather ideas about the cable television program *Mythbusters*. Here's a sample:

<u>Who</u> is involved?	Peter Rees, producer (Australian documentary filmmaker)
	Adam Savage, cohost (artist and model builder)
	Jamie Hyneman, cohost (Hollywood special-effects expert with a degree in Russian literature)
	Buster, subject of experiments (crash test dummy)
	Kari Byron, experimenter (sculptor, painter, actor)
	Grant Imahara, experimenter (electronics expert)
	Tory Belleci, experimenter (model builder)
	Scottie Chapman, experimenter (welder)
<u>What</u> is it about?	Cast members conduct science experiments to see if urban legends are true.
<u>Where</u> is it?	Discovery Channel
<u>When</u> is it?	Wednesdays at 9:00 p.m.
<u>How</u> effective is it?	I like that they use real science to bust the myths. The tests are really involved and over the top. Lots of surprises: sometimes the urban legends are actually true! The experiments are creative and always very

thorough, but sometimes they get carried away with themselves and forget the point. They'll redo an experiment if viewers write in and question their methods.

<u>Why</u> is it worth seeing?   Generally very informative, always entertaining. They manage to make science cool.

WRITING ACTIVITY 3: Ask Questions about a Performance

Select a performance that you might want to evaluate. The performance may be live (such as a concert, comedy show, sporting event, dance recital, or play) or recorded (such as a movie or television show). You may choose a past performance that you remember well or select a current performance and attend it in person. (If you select a movie or television show, you have the advantage of being able to watch a recording more than once.) Answer each of the reporter's questions — *who, what, where, when, why, how* — about the performance to gather ideas for an evaluation essay.

Freewriting about a Place

Put aside your ideas about a performance for now so that you can gather ideas for one more type of evaluation.

A new shopping mall opens near your town, and you spend an afternoon visiting the stores, examining the layout, and sampling products from the food court. Afterward, you decide that you like the mall but wish it had a parking garage: you have just evaluated a place. Other places you might evaluate include a museum, park, college or office building, classroom, theater, store, library, restaurant, or city. Almost any place you've been to and that other people might want to visit can be a good candidate for an evaluation essay.

Although a quick judgment of a place can be useful, a formal evaluation needs plenty of details to be convincing and useful for readers. To gather information to support a full essay that evaluates a place, consider freewriting (the practice of writing nonstop about a topic without trying to decide if your ideas are any good). Tell yourself that you will write for a certain amount of time or a certain number of pages, and keep writing. Don't pause to think, don't make corrections, and don't try to organize your thoughts. If you get stuck, write something like "I don't have anything to say" or "stuck! stuck! stuck!" until a new thought comes to you. Just keep writing, and see what you have to say.

One student, Jody, thought she might want to evaluate her dorm. Here is part of her freewriting:

Dryden Hall is such a rip-off, I can't believe it. My
room looks like a hospital room — no carpet, plain
furniture, a small window that looks out at a brick
wall. My roommate and I are squished together like
rats. There aren't any social activities, and every
time you turn on your computer or hair dryer, you
never know if there's going to be a blackout. If this
place were cheap, it might be okay, but it's one of
the most expensive dorms on campus! I wish I could
live in Johnson Hall, which looks a lot nicer, has a
lot of activities, and is cheaper.

WRITING ACTIVITY 4: Freewrite about a Place

Choose a place that is important to you and that others might want
to know about, such as a new restaurant close to campus or an entertainment park that recently opened. Freewrite about this place for at
least ten minutes. Follow your ideas without pausing, and do not
stop, go back, or try to correct your writing. Just write.

STEP 2. WRITE YOUR DISCOVERY DRAFT

At this point, you have explored at least three possible topics for
your evaluation essay. It's time now to choose a topic and prepare a
rough draft.

Don't be concerned if you're not sure how you're going to evaluate
a product, a performance, or a place. The purpose of writing a discovery draft is to discover what you have to say. For now, you'll focus on
organizing what you already know and try to put it into words. As you
draft, keep in mind that anything you write at this stage can (and
should) be revised later.

*For more on drafting, see
pp. 16–21.*

Choosing a Topic

Now that you have gathered ideas for three different subjects you
might evaluate, it's time to decide how you want to proceed.

When you choose a topic for an evaluation essay, it's crucial to
remember your audience and your purpose. Gather your notes from
brainstorming, questioning, and freewriting, and look again at your
responses to Writing Activity 1 on page 244. Of the topics you have considered for your essay, which one do you feel most strongly about? Even
more important, which one would be most interesting and informative

for your readers? After all, you don't want to put a lot of effort into evaluating something that nobody else cares about.

Because you will write a persuasive essay in which you make an evaluation, be sure to select a topic that you can judge. As you contemplate your choices, remember that you may combine closely related topics and may gather additional ideas on any topic that interests you. For example, in reviewing your notes about a movie, you might realize that you had a strong positive reaction to the new stadium-style seating at the local multiplex. If you decide to evaluate the theater rather than the movie, you could use brainstorming, questioning, or freewriting (or any other methods that work for you) to explore your thoughts.

WRITING ACTIVITY 5: Choose Your Topic

Review your responses to Writing Activities 1 to 4, and decide which of the topics you explored (a product, performance, or place) would be most useful for your readers. Be careful to select a topic that you can judge. If you're not confident that you can turn any of your working ideas into a well-supported evaluation, use your favorite techniques to gather ideas on additional topic possibilities until you find one that will interest both you and your readers.

Sharing Your Ideas

For more on thesis statements, see pp. 19–20.

Before you begin writing your discovery draft, narrow your topic and write a preliminary thesis statement that identifies your subject and expresses your judgment of it. You can always change your thesis later, but starting with a judgment in mind will help you to focus and stay on track.

As you write your draft, keep in mind that most readers expect an evaluation essay to address the following questions:

- What experiences have you had with the product, performance, or place you are writing about?
- What is your overall opinion of this product, performance, or place?
- Why do you have this opinion?
- What is good about your subject?
- What is bad about your subject?
- Compare your subject with other similar subjects: How is it better? How is it worse?

Answering each of these questions in order is one way to create your draft, but don't hesitate to follow your train of thought as you write — even if it means revising your thesis statement later on. Keep your audience and purpose in mind, and remember that your main goal at the drafting stage is to get your ideas down on paper. You'll have time later to revise and edit your discovery draft.

Gather Ideas during Drafting

If you run out of ideas while drafting, press your computer's Enter key a couple of times, and begin to use freewriting or brainstorming to gather ideas. When you think of something you can use in your evaluations, cut and paste it into the draft.

Here's the discovery draft written by a student, Jody Albert, whose freewriting you read earlier. In this draft, Jody evaluates her college dorm for an audience of students who are considering choosing it for their own residence. After reading the draft, discuss with your class-mates what Jody might do to revise it. (Note that the example includes the types of errors that typically appear in a first draft.)

```
             Avoid Dryden Hall

    I was away from home for the first time, eager
to move into my home away from home--Dryden Hall. I
excitedly opened the door to my new dorm room. What
I saw disappointed me. It was a little room with no
carpeting and a window with a view of a brick wall.
This was only the first of many disappointing things
about this dorm.
    Dryden Hall is one of the most expensive dorms on
campus, but you'd never know it by looking at it.
Repainting is needed. The colors are drab, and the
walls are chipped. The furniture in the lobby looks
like it came from a flea market. The rooms look like
hospital rooms, with plain cupboards and sterile
white tiles. Dryden Hall is unattractive. It has
shabby furniture and a stained carpet.
    Dryden Hall also needs to be renovated because so
many students now use computers to get into the
library's resources and to talk to each other on
e-mail. Right now, the dorm isn't plugged into the
campus computer system, so you can't do any of these
things. The dorm also has an out-of-date intercom
```

phone system. The intercom is useless because most residents have telephones. Sometimes the electricity goes out because the electrical wiring can't take all of our microwaves, televisions, and DVD players.

Socially, Dryden Hall is bad. It is a disaster. When I came here, I didn't know anyone. I thought that living in a dorm would help me make friends. Not in Dryden Hall! Yes, I have gotten to know my roommate and a few of the other girls on my floor. The social events are completely inadequate. These are the social events that are planned in advance. The monthly pizza party only lasts about fifteen minutes, we run out of food and drinks quickly. The other regular social activity is a Sunday morning breakfast from 8-10 a.m. Most of us sleep later than that.

If I could do it all over again, I'd choose Johnson Hall. Choosing Dryden Hall was definitely a mistake.

WRITING ACTIVITY 6: Write Your Discovery Draft

Using your preliminary thesis statement and the questions on page 250 as a guide, write a discovery draft that evaluates a product, performance, or place. For now, focus on getting your ideas in writing; you'll have a chance to clarify and support your ideas when you revise. If you're not sure that the topic you've selected is a good one, remember that you may write separate drafts on two or three other topics to see which one gives you the best results.

STEP 3. REVISE YOUR DRAFT

For more on revising, see pp. 21–23.

Most writers find that the discovery draft of an evaluation needs additional information to make it interesting and informative. Because reviews attempt to persuade readers, you'll also need to make sure that your ideas are clearly stated and well supported — from your audience's point of view.

How will you develop your ideas so that you communicate effectively with your readers? Start by applying the skills you acquired in earlier chapters: organize your paragraphs (Chapter 2), strengthen your focus (Chapter 4), outline your plan (Chapter 6), and write an effective introduction and conclusion (Chapter 5). As you build your essay, you will learn how to use comparison and contrast to help your readers understand your points. You will then focus on expressing your judgment clearly while explaining your criteria, providing convincing evidence, and keeping a balanced perspective.

Developing Your Ideas with Comparison and Contrast

One good way to support an evaluation is to compare and contrast your subject with other subjects. Your audience may not know very much about the product, performance, or place that you are reviewing, but they probably have some knowledge of similar products, performances, or places. By relating what your readers know to what they don't know, you can support your judgment while helping your readers better understand your subject.

When you compare two things, you point out similarities; when you contrast two things, you focus on differences. These two approaches are often combined. Consider, for example, how Leander Kahney compares and contrasts his new iPod with his old records and compact discs:

> Like a lot of people, I had a giant collection of vinyl LPs and CDs that grew over the years into an unmanageable archive weighing hundreds of pounds. Too heavy for shelves, the records sat on the floor, spilling into the room. But for the most part, the collection was merely for other people to gawk at. I didn't play most of the records, and except for a few disks at the front of the pile, I forgot and neglected most of them.
>
> Fast forward, and now the entire collection can fit inside a small white box the size and weight of a pack of cards. This to me is a miracle. A crowning achievement of technology. That unwieldy pile of vinyl and cardboard has been freed from the living room and is available anywhere and everywhere I go: from the earliest, regrettable singles to my latest obsession.

Even readers who don't have iPods probably have (or have seen) a collection of CDs like the one Kahney describes. By showing in detail how the iPod makes the music on those CDs easier to enjoy, Kahney helps his audience understand why the iPod's small size and large capacity are important features.

When making comparisons, be sure that you focus on similar subjects and that you explain the basis of your comparison. In evaluating the new campus recreation center, for example, you would not compare it to the college library (unless you are comparing the architecture of the buildings). Instead, you might contrast the new center with the old center to highlight the improvements that have been made. Once you have established the points of your comparison, provide several detailed examples to support each of those points, as Leander Kahney does.

HOW TO Use Comparison and Contrast

- Use comparison to explain similarities, and use contrast to explain differences.
- Decide on what basis you will compare and contrast. For instance, you can compare and contrast energy drinks on the basis of ingredients, flavor, and effectiveness.
- Support the comparison and contrast with examples.

Use Color to Compare and Contrast

Use the color feature on your word-processing program when you compare and contrast. When you write about the first thing you're comparing, use one color, and when you write about the second thing you're comparing, use another color. This technique makes it easier for you to examine how well you support your points. (Remember to return the typeface to black·before printing your final draft.)

WRITING ACTIVITY 7: Draft Comparisons for Your Essay

For your topic, list several similar subjects. (If you're evaluating a product, list similar products; if your topic is a performance, list similar performances; if your essay is about a place, list similar places.) Choose one of these subjects, and write one or two paragraphs that compare or contrast it with the subject of your essay. Remember that the point of using comparison and contrast is to support your judgment and to help your readers understand your subject better.

Building Your Essay

When you revise an evaluation essay, you need to make sure that you have stated your opinion clearly and have provided enough information to persuade your readers that your opinion is reasonable. To do this, you'll first revise your thesis statement to ensure that it expresses a judgment. Next, make sure that readers understand the reasons for your opinion, and double-check that you have included enough evidence to support your points. Finally, reexamine your evaluation from your readers' perspective to ensure that your audience will accept your judgment as fair and carefully considered — even if they don't agree with it.

Express Your Judgment

As you may recall, the thesis statement does three things — announces the topic of your essay; shows, explains, or argues a particular point about the topic; and gives readers a sense of what the essay will be about. For an evaluation essay, the thesis statement argues a particular point. Specifically, it expresses your judgment of the product, performance, or place that you are reviewing. Let's look in more detail at how to write an effective thesis statement for an evaluation.

For more on thesis statements, see pp. 19–20.

State an Opinion. A judgment is an opinion about the value or merit of something. It's not a fact. Notice the difference between fact and judgment in these statements:

FACT The Ford Mustang was among the most popular cars of the 1960s.

JUDGMENT The Ford Mustang was one of the best cars made in the 1960s.

The first statement is factual because it can be verified by statistics about the best-selling cars in the 1960s. The second statement expresses an opinion about the worthiness of the car. Some but not all people will agree with this statement.

Focus on the Subject. A judgment focuses on the subject being evaluated, not on the writer.

FOCUS ON THE WRITER I really like the new thirty-minute circuit program at the local health club.

FOCUS ON THE SUBJECT The new thirty-minute circuit program at the local health club is surprisingly effective.

In the first example, the first-person *I* emphasizes the writer. In the second example, the reference to the writer has been removed, shifting readers' focus to the product being evaluated — the new thirty-minute circuit program.

Be Moderate, Not Extreme. A good thesis statement for an evaluation essay gives a sensible opinion about the subject. A sensible opinion is moderate rather than extreme:

EXTREME   Central College's library is the best library in the state.

MODERATE   Central College's library has the most useful collection of business journals in Essex County.

The extreme statement cannot be proven without visiting every library in the state, whereas the moderate version is much easier to support.

Be Clear and Specific. A good thesis statement for an evaluation essay expresses a judgment that is immediately understandable. If your readers can't understand your thesis statement, they won't understand the rest of your evaluation either. To make your thesis statement clear, use standard written English, and tell readers why you have reached your judgment:

UNCLEAR   The new Student Union is gross.

CLEAR   The design of the new Student Union is disappointing because of its plain exterior and cold, gray cinderblock interior.

The nonstandard (in this context) *gross* has been replaced with *disappointing,* which is a more precise word. Details that explain the judgment have also been added to help readers better understand the writer's opinion about the topic.

HOW TO Write a Thesis Statement for an Evaluation Essay

- Express an opinion about the value or merit of something.
- Focus on the subject, not yourself.
- Use a moderate tone.
- Be clear and specific.

GROUP ACTIVITY 2: Express Judgments

Review the characteristics of a good thesis statement for an evaluation essay. Then, working with your peer response group, determine the fault in each of the following thesis statements. Revise the thesis statements to eliminate the faults.

1. The worst jeans ever made are manufactured by Salisbury, Inc.
2. Julia Roberts is an OK actor.
3. The Super Bowl is seen by millions of people around the world.

4. The National Air and Space Museum is my favorite museum.

5. The Bradley running shoe is one of the newest shoes on the market.

WRITING ACTIVITY 8: Express Your Judgment

Revise the thesis statement for your essay so that it meets the requirements for an evaluation essay. It needs to express an opinion about the value or merit of your subject, focus on the subject, be moderate and not extreme, and be clear and specific.

Give Criteria

To support your thesis statement in an evaluation essay, you must inform your readers of the *criteria,* or standards, on which you based your judgment. For example, John Garvey, in "Christo's *Gates:* An Unexpected Pleasure," uses sponsorship as one criterion. For him to evaluate a public art exhibit highly, it must be free of advertising messages. Remember, you should include enough criteria to inform your reader, your criteria should suit the topic, and if your criteria are not obvious, you should explain them.

Include Enough Criteria. An effective evaluation is based on having enough criteria. In most cases, a good evaluation essay will discuss three to five criteria. Judging a subject on the basis of only one or two criteria will usually not be enough to persuade your readers to accept your judgment. Imagine, for instance, if John Garvey had evaluated *The Gates* only on its lack of corporate sponsorship. As readers, we would have been left with unanswered questions about the exhibit's appearance, meaning, and overall effect.

Highlight Your Criteria

Use your computer's color function to highlight your criteria in your draft. The highlighting will show you how many criteria you have and help you decide if you need more.

Use Suitable Criteria. The criteria on which your judgment is based should be suitable for your subject. Leander Kahney, in "The Joy of iPod: iCandy for the Ears," does not claim that the iPod is a good technology because he likes the colorful cases he can buy for it. Rather, the criteria Kahney uses — capacity, size, weight, and ease of use — are appropriate because most music fans are concerned about such features in an MP3 player.

Suppose, however, that Kahney was writing his review for an audience of business students. In this case, the possibilities for increased profits from iPod accessories — including designer cases, arm bands, docking stations, speakers, and so on — would be suitable criteria. In other words, the criteria that are "suitable" depend on the characteristics or interests of your intended readers.

HOW TO Select Criteria

- Fill in the blanks: "I think that _____ is good/bad because _____."

- Identify between three to five reasons for your opinion.

- Review your reasons to make sure they're suitable for the topic and your audience.

Explain Your Criteria. If your readers might not understand your criteria, you'll need to explain them. For example, in an evaluation of a computer, you would probably need to explain the importance of memory capacity and processor speed. Similarly, in evaluating a fashion show, you would explain why music is essential to the show's success.

Not all criteria require explanation. In evaluating *Sesame Street*, for example, Diane Heiman and Phyllis Bookspan don't explain why the show's educational value is an important criterion. They are, however, careful to explain why a children's show should avoid gender stereotypes. Only when you think readers may have questions about a particular criterion should you explain it.

HOW TO Explain Criteria

- Will your readers automatically see why your criteria are suitable to your subject? If not, you need to explain the criteria.

- For readers familiar with your subject, include a brief explanation of the criteria (such as, "A pair of jeans needs to be comfortable because they're worn frequently").

- For readers unfamiliar with your subject, include a detailed explanation of the criteria (such as, "All the seats in a sports arena should give spectators good visibility. You shouldn't have to sit behind a post that partially obstructs your view").

GROUP ACTIVITY 3: Determine Criteria

Following is a list of subjects and audiences. Working with your classmates, determine the criteria to use for an evaluation essay for each subject and audience. Make sure that you provide enough criteria to evaluate the subjects and that the criteria are appropriate for the audiences.

EXAMPLE Subject: sports car

Audience: readers of *Consumer Reports*

Criteria: _____ handling, horsepower, style, price _____

1. Subject: grocery store chain

   Audience: readers of *Ladies' Home Journal*

   Criteria: _____

2. Subject: apartment

   Audience: readers of the classified ads in your local newspaper

   Criteria: _____

3. Subject: amusement park

   Audience: readers of *Parents* magazine

   Criteria: _____

4. Subject: the new Student Union at your college

   Audience: readers of the alumni magazine

   Criteria: _____

5. Subject: a television situation comedy

   Audience: potential advertisers

   Criteria: _____

WRITING ACTIVITY 9: Revise the Criteria in Your Essay

Examine the criteria in your discovery draft. Keeping your audience in mind, determine if you have enough criteria and whether your criteria are suitable. Then identify any criteria that need to be explained for your readers. Make any necessary changes, and add any necessary explanations.

Provide Evidence

An evaluation essay consists largely of evidence that supports a judgment. By presenting *evidence* — including examples, facts, and expert testimony — writers explain how a subject measures up to their criteria.

Write on Two Screens
Use a separate window when gathering evidence. Then use your computer's Cut-and-Paste function to move your evidence to the main screen that contains your draft.

Examples. Using *examples* to support your judgment makes your essay more interesting to a reader as well as more convincing. In "*Sesame Street:* Brought to You by the Letters M-A-L-E," Diane Heiman and Phyllis Bookspan give many examples to illustrate their points. For instance, they give examples to support their claim that the program portrays female characters as helpless:

> Further, almost all of the baby puppet characters on *Sesame Street* are girls. For example, Snuffie's sibling is Baby Alice; in books, Grover's baby cousin is a girl, and when Herry Monster's mother brings home the new baby — it's a girl. Since babies are totally dependent and fairly passive, the older (male) relatives take care of them and provide leadership.

Facts. *Facts* are a highly persuasive kind of evidence, primarily because they can be verified by readers. And because facts demonstrate your knowledge of the topic, including them makes readers more likely to trust your judgment. In "Christo's *Gates:* An Unexpected Pleasure," for example, John Garvey proves that he knows enough about his subject to form a reliable opinion of it. He begins with a series of facts about the installation in Central Park:

> Called *The Gates*, the project involved the installation of 7,532 frames, and the fabric was hung so high that the tallest people could walk along the paths easily. The money was raised by the artists, and much of it went to pay those who installed the work, and to pay monitors who directed people to interesting routes and also used poles to unfurl banners tangled by the wind.

Expert testimony. *Expert testimony* — the opinion of people knowledgeable about a subject — can be used as evidence to confirm the significance of a topic or to support a writer's own judgment. Diane Heiman and Phyllis Bookspan, for example, cite two published research studies to convince their readers that gender bias in *Sesame Street* should be taken seriously:

> A recent report released by the American Association of University Women, "How Schools Shortchange Women," finds that teachers, textbooks, and tests are, whether intentionally or unintentionally, giving preferential treatment to elementary-school boys. As a result, girls who enter school with equal or better academic potential than their male counterparts lose confidence and do not perform as well.
>
> An earlier study about law students, published in the *Journal of Legal Education,* found a similar disparity. "Gender Bias in the Classroom" found that male law students are called upon in class more frequently than females, speak for longer periods of time, and are given more positive feedback by law professors.

As you revise your evaluation essay, consider looking for expert testimony that can help to back up your judgment of a subject. In evaluating a product, you might refer to *Consumer Reports'* rating of the product. In evaluating a performance or a place, you could check a magazine or newspaper to see whether your subject has been evaluated by others. Awards can be considered a form of expert testimony because they're given by experts in a particular field. If a movie wins an Academy Award for best director, for example, it means that a team of successful movie directors thought highly of the film's director.

HOW TO Generate Evidence

- List examples that support your criteria.

- Identify facts that support your criteria by observing the subject carefully.

- Refer to expert testimony. Look in a library database and on the World Wide Web for articles on the subject you're evaluating.

Chart Your Criteria and Evidence
Use the Tables feature of your word-processing program to help you visualize the connections between your criteria and your evidence. First, write your thesis statement at the top of the page (to remind you of your judgment). Then create two columns. In the left column, list the criteria that you will use to make your judgment. In the right column, list the evidence that supports each criterion. Review your chart to check that you have enough evidence to support your judgment.

WRITING ACTIVITY 10: Provide Evidence for Your Judgment

Examine the evidence that you used in your discovery draft. Is your judgment supported by sufficient examples, facts, and expert testimony? Where can you include additional evidence to support your criteria and make your points more convincing? Add evidence where needed.

Keep a Balanced Perspective

Readers know that few subjects are all good or all bad. Acknowledging both the negative and the positive aspects of your subject shows readers that your judgment is fair, reasonable, and believable.

You may recall from the review of *Sesame Street* by Diane Heiman and Phyllis Bookspan that the authors remind us of the show's good qualities:

> Yes, we believe that *Sesame Street* is one of the best shows on television for small children. Our children — boys and girls — are regular viewers. In addition to its educational value, lack of violence and emphasis on cooperation, the adult characters on the show are admirably balanced in terms of avoiding sexual stereotypes.

By sharing this information with readers, Heiman and Bookspan maintain a balanced perspective and thereby strengthen the believability of their argument that *Sesame Street* is sexist.

You don't have to give equal space in an evaluation essay to the strengths and weaknesses of your subject. If your judgment about the subject is negative, briefly describe the positive aspects, as Heiman and Bookspan do in their essay. If your judgment about the subject is positive, briefly describe the negative aspects.

Student writer Jody Albert, for example, decided to add a paragraph about what's good at Dryden Hall to balance her criticism of the dormitory:

> It is true that Dryden Hall is a good place to study. Each floor has several study rooms (all of them in need of repainting, of course). Tutors are available in most of these study rooms in the evenings. Because there's not much socializing, the dorm is usually quiet, so it's easy to study whenever necessary.

WRITING ACTIVITY 11: Chart the Positive and Negative
                          Aspects of Your Subject

Gather ideas about the positive and negative aspects of your subject
in a two-column chart. Label the columns "Positive Aspects" and
"Negative Aspects." Then list the positive and negative features of
your subject. Number the items in each column in the order that you
plan to use them in your essay. As you revise your draft, use this chart
to maintain a balanced perspective in your evaluation essay.

A Student's Revised Draft

After charting her criteria and evidence, student writer Jody Albert
decided that she needed to give more details to help her readers understand why they shouldn't choose Dryden Hall as their residence. Before
you read Jody's revised draft, reread her discovery draft (pp. 251–52).
Notice, in particular, how Jody has expressed her judgment more ex-
plicitly, explained her criteria, and added evidence and comparison to
improve her evaluation. (You will also notice some errors in the revised
draft; these will be corrected when Jody edits her essay.)

Avoid Dryden Hall

    I walked down the long, gray hall, looking for room   *The introduction is more*
315 -- my room for the school year. My arms ached from   *interesting.*
carrying my two heavy suitcases. I put the key in the
lock, turned it, and opened the door. I couldn't
believe my eyes, the room looked like it belonged in
a hospital. The vinyl floor was scuffed and dull, the
window had a view of a brick wall, and the walls were
painted a drab green. This was only the first of many
disappointments I've had with my dorm. Dryden Hall is
an overpriced dorm that lacks many of the amenities
found in less expensive dorms. The inside of the   *The judgment is more specific.*
building is unattractive, the wiring is outdated, and
the social events are unsuccessful.
    Where a person lives is important to their
well-being. Since so many students live in dorms, the
college should try to make them attractive. The rooms
should be clean, the walls painted an uplifting
color, and the furniture fairly new. A dorm should
also have updated facilities so that students can
plug into the college computer system in their own
rooms. How else can students examine the library

The criteria are explained.

records or talk to their instructors on e-mail? Many students are away from home for the first time, a dorm should also offer opportunities for students to meet other people. Finally, a dorm should be a good place to study.

Unattractive from the first floor to the top floor, Dryden Hall has shabby furniture and a stained carpet. One of the couches even has its stuffing hanging out. The halls are painted a dark gray that makes them seem like tunnels, walls in most of the rooms are chipped or need cleaning. The walls in my room, for example, are filled with holes from where former occupants have hung pictures. The kitchen on the top floor has rusty cupboards and an ancient sink.

Examples and facts are added.

Dryden Hall also needs to be modernized. Part of our fee pays for an out-of-date intercom phone system. The intercom is useless because most residents have their own telephones. Sometimes the electricity goes out because the wiring can't take all of our microwaves, televisions, and DVD players. Most important, Dryden Hall isn't plugged into the campus computer system. Unlike students in other dorms, I can't use my computer to search the library records or communicate with instructors or students on e-mail. This is a major inconvenience when I'm working late at night on an assignment.

Additional facts are added.

Socially, as well, Dryden Hall is a disaster. When I came here, I didn't know anyone. I thought that living in a dorm would help me make friends. Not in Dryden Hall! The social events are completely inadequate. These are the social events that are planned in advance. For example, the main event here is a monthly pizza party. Unfortunately, the organizers run out of pizza after about fifteen minutes, so no one stays around to meet anyone else. The dorm also serves donuts and coffee in the lobby every Sunday from 8 to 10 a.m. This is way too early for me and many others. Surely some of the money we pay to stay in Dryden Hall could be used for more, and better, social events.

Facts support the judgment.

A balanced perspective is given.

It is true that Dryden Hall is a good place to study. Each floor has several study rooms (all of them in need of repainting, of course). Tutors are available in most of these study rooms in the evenings. Because there's not much socializing, the dorm is usually quiet, so it's easy to study whenever necessary.

If I could do it all over again, I'd choose Johnson Hall. Johnson Hall is older than Dryden Hall but it has been recently renovated inside and out. It has attractive rooms, new furniture, and modern wiring. Johnson Hall also has alot of good social activities, and it is less expensive compared to Dryden Hall.

The comparison strengthens the judgment.

As I sit in my dorm room, staring at the cracked ceiling and the brick wall outside my window, I'm reminded of the mistake I made when I moved into Dryden Hall. I only hope that the word gets out about Dryden Hall so that other students don't make the same mistake.

The conclusion restates the judgment.

GROUP ACTIVITY 4: Analyze Jody's Revised Draft

Use the following questions to discuss with your classmates how Jody has improved her discovery draft.

1. How has Jody improved her introduction?
2. Why is her thesis more effective now?
3. What criteria does Jody use to evaluate Dryden Hall? Does she use enough suitable criteria? Are they obvious, or do they need explanation?
4. How well does Jody support her judgment with examples, facts, and expert testimony?
5. Does the comparison with Johnson Hall further support Jody's judgment? Why or why not?
6. Does Jody maintain a balanced perspective? Explain.
7. How could Jody's revised draft benefit from further revision?

WRITING ACTIVITY 12: Peer Review

Form a group with two or three other students, and exchange copies of your revised drafts. Read your draft aloud while your classmates follow along. Then take notes on your classmates' responses to the following questions about your draft.

1. What did you like best about this essay?
2. How interesting is my introduction? Do you want to continue reading the paper? Why or why not?

3. What is my thesis statement? Is it effective? Does it express a judgment about the value or merit of my subject? Is it focused on the subject? Is it moderate rather than extreme? Is it clear and specific?

4. What are my criteria? Are there enough of them, and are they suitable? Are they obvious, or do I need to explain them?

5. How well do I support my judgment with examples, facts, and expert testimony?

6. Do I maintain a balanced perspective? Why or why not?

7. Do I make effective comparisons? Explain.

8. How effective is my ending? Do I conclude in such a way that you know it's the end?

Use Online Peer Review

If your class has a Web site, see whether the peer review questions listed in Writing Activity 12 are available on the site. If they are, you may be able to respond to your classmates' drafts electronically.

WRITING ACTIVITY 13: Revise Your Draft

Building on the work you have completed for Writing Activities 7 to 11, refer to your classmates' peer review suggestions as you finish revising your discovery draft. Focus on improving your thesis statement, criteria, and evidence. Add comparisons where they might be helpful, and ensure that your essay maintains a balanced perspective. You may decide to omit unnecessary material or to rearrange parts of your essay more effectively as well.

Comment on Your Draft

Use the Comment function of your word-processing program to insert suggestions for revision in your draft. This function highlights the suggestions for revision (or comments) in your text, similar to your instructor's or classmates' handwritten comments.

STEP 4. EDIT YOUR SENTENCES

At this point, you have worked hard to write a convincing evaluation of a product, performance, or place. But before you can share your essay with your audience, you must edit it for readability and correctness. Remember, an important part of the writing process is to revise your words and sentences to be clearer, more interesting, and free of distracting errors.

As always, consult a handbook, a dictionary, and your editing log to check that your words are the right ones and that your sentences are structured correctly. As you edit your evaluation, you will practice combining sentences with relative clauses. You will also learn how to correct comma splices.

Combining Sentences Using Relative Clauses

Although short sentences can be powerful, using too many of them in a row can force you to repeat yourself. To eliminate unnecessary repetition and help your readers know which of your ideas are most important, consider using *relative clauses* to combine sentences.

You can turn a short sentence into a relative clause by beginning it with a relative pronoun (*who, whose, which,* or *that*). A relative clause contains a subject and a verb but cannot stand alone as a sentence.

Here's how student writer Jody Albert combined two pairs of short sentences in her revised draft by using relative clauses:

ORIGINAL	The social events are completely inadequate. These are the social events that are planned in advance.
REVISED	The social events *that are planned in advance* are completely inadequate.
ORIGINAL	Part of our fee pays for an out-of-date intercom phone system. The intercom is useless because most residents have their own telephones.
REVISED	Part of our fee pays for an out-of-date intercom phone system, *which is useless because most residents have their own telephones.*

For more on combining sentences, see Ch. 17.

By combining these sentences, Jody eliminated unnecessary words and communicated her thoughts more clearly.

Notice that a relative clause can appear either in the middle or at the end of a combined sentence and that the revised sentence may or may not include commas. How do you know when to use commas?

- Use commas when the relative clause gives information that's *not* essential to understanding the sentence, as in the following example:

The book, *which is on the table,* is by one of my favorite authors.

Commas are used in this example because the relative clause — *which is on the table* — is simply adding information. The sentence makes sense without it: *The book is by one of my favorite authors.*

- Don't use commas when a relative clause identifies who or what it is referring to, as in the following example:

The book *that is on the table* belongs to Wilbur.

No commas are used before or after the relative clause because it's a necessary part of the sentence: it tells which book — the one on the table — is the one that belongs to Wilbur.

- Avoid using commas with relative clauses that begin with the word *that:*

The bicycle *that has been sitting in the garage* is too small for my children to ride.

HOW TO Combine Sentences Using Relative Clauses

- Turn the less important sentence into a relative clause by starting it with a relative pronoun: *who, whose, which,* and *that.*
- Check that the relative clause contains a subject and verb and cannot stand on its own.
- Add the relative clause to the middle or end of a complete sentence.
- Use a comma or commas when the relative clause adds information not necessary to the meaning of the sentence.
- Don't use commas when a relative clause identifies the word that it's referring to.
- Don't use commas when the relative clause begins with the word *that.*

EDITING ACTIVITY 1: Combining Sentences Using Relative Clauses

Combine the following pairs of sentences using relative clauses. You may need to eliminate unnecessary words or move words around. Use a comma or commas when the relative clause is unnecessary for the sentence to be understood.

EXAMPLE   *North by Northwest* is one of my favorite movies. ~~It was~~
, which Alfred Hitchcock directed in 1959,
~~directed by Alfred Hitchcock. It was made in 1959.~~

1. Cary Grant plays an advertising executive. His name is Roger Thornhill.

2. Cary Grant is framed for killing a U.N. diplomat. He is mistaken for a man named George Kaplan.

3. James Mason plays a foreign spy. The spy's name is Phillip Vandamm. James Mason was a British actor.

4. Eva Marie Saint plays a beautiful blonde woman. The woman's name is Eve Kendall. Eve Kendall is actually Phillip Vandamm's lover.

5. *North by Northwest* is typical of many Hitchcock movies. It has mistaken identities, a cool blonde woman, and a man. The man is chased by people he doesn't know.

Exercise Central
For additional practice with using relative clauses to combine sentences, go to **bedfordstmartins.com/choices** and click on "Exercise Central."

WRITING ACTIVITY 14: Combine Your Sentences

Search your revised draft for short, closely related sentences that cause unnecessary repetition. Where it makes sense to do so, combine them with relative clauses.

Correcting Comma Splices

A *comma splice* is a common error that occurs when two complete sentences are combined *only* with a comma. (Remember that a complete sentence contains both a subject and a verb and expresses a complete thought.)

For more on comma splices, see pp. 551–55.

COMMA SPLICE   The plot was full of twists, the ending of the movie was predictable.

There are three ways to correct a comma splice.

- Replace the comma with a period to make two sentences:

  The plot was full of twists. The ending of the movie was predictable.

- Add a coordinating conjunction after the comma:

  The plot was full of twists, *but* the ending of the movie was predictable.

- Replace the comma with a semicolon:

  The plot was full of twists; the ending of the movie was predictable.

When using a semicolon, many writers include a conjunctive adverb such as *in addition, although, nevertheless, however, moreover, in fact,* and *for example.* The conjunctive adverb will tell your readers how the two parts of the sentence connect together. The conjunctive adverb comes after the semicolon and is followed by a comma:

  The plot was full of twists; nevertheless, the ending of the movie was predictable.

Here is an example of a comma splice from Jody Albert's draft, followed by three different ways she could correct it:

COMMA SPLICE	I couldn't believe my eyes, the room looked like it belonged in a hospital.
CORRECT	I couldn't believe my eyes. The room looked like it belonged in a hospital.
CORRECT	I couldn't believe my eyes, as the room looked like it belonged in a hospital.
CORRECT	I couldn't believe my eyes; the room looked like it belonged in a hospital.

HOW TO Correct Comma Splices

- Break the comma splice up into two sentences.

  OR

- Use a comma and a coordinating conjunction (*for, and, nor, but, or, yet, so*).

  OR

- Use a semicolon instead of a comma. If you wish, you may follow the semicolon with a conjunctive adverb and a comma.

EDITING ACTIVITY 2: Correct Comma Splices

Correct each of the following comma splices.

EXAMPLE   My next-door neighbor is a great singer, ~~she's~~ always

. She's

entertaining my kids.

1. The chocolates are crunchy on the outside, they are soft on the inside.

2. Paris was wonderful, it was also expensive.

3. Some people think hybrid cars are sluggish, they're actually pretty quick.

4. When I was in Rome, I saw the pope say Mass, it was inspiring.

5. Some people find the movie *Grandma's Boy* offensive, I think it's funny.

Exercise Central
For additional practice with correcting comma splices, go to **bedfordstmartins.com/choices** and click on "Exercise Central."

WRITING ACTIVITY 15: Edit Your Essay

Using the Handbook in Part Four of this book as a guide, edit your revised essay for errors in grammar, spelling, and punctuation. In particular, look for comma splices and correct them using any of the three techniques listed on page 270. Your classmates can help you locate and correct errors you might have overlooked. Add the errors you find and their corrections to your editing log.

Create an Error File
Create a file in which you list the types of errors you tend to make. Review this file when you edit your essay.

A Student's Edited Essay

You might have noticed that Jody's revised draft contained some repetitive sentences and a few errors in grammar, spelling, and punctuation. Jody fixed these problems in her edited essay. Her corrections are underlined here.

*The correct MLA format
is used.*

Jody Albert
Professor Rowley
English 0311
19 March 2007

Avoid Dryden Hall

A comma splice is corrected.

I walked down the long, gray hall, looking for room 315 -- my room for the school year. My arms ached from carrying my two heavy suitcases. I put the key in the lock, turned it, and opened the door. <u>I couldn't believe my eyes. The room looked like it belonged in a hospital.</u> The vinyl floor was scuffed and dull, the window had a view of a brick wall, and the walls were painted a drab green. This was only the first of many disappointments I've had with my dorm. Dryden Hall is an overpriced dorm that lacks many of the amenities found in less expensive dorms. The inside of the building is unattractive, the wiring is outdated, and the social events are unsuccessful.

*Faulty pronoun-antecedent
agreement is corrected.*

Where a person lives is important to <u>his or her</u> well-being. Since so many students live in dorms, the college should try to make them attractive. The rooms should be clean, the walls painted an uplifting color, and the furniture fairly new. A dorm should also have updated facilities so that students can plug into the college computer system in their own rooms. How else can students examine the library records or talk to their instructors on e-mail? <u>Many students are away from home for the first time, so a dorm should also offer opportunities for students to meet other people.</u> Finally, a dorm should be a good place to study.

A comma splice is corrected.

A comma splice is corrected.

Unattractive from the first floor to the top floor, Dryden Hall has shabby furniture and a stained carpet. One of the couches even has its stuffing hanging out. <u>The halls are painted a dark gray that makes them seem like tunnels, and walls in most of the rooms are chipped or need cleaning.</u> The walls in my room, for example, are filled with holes from where former occupants have hung pictures. The kitchen on the top floor has rusty cupboards and an ancient sink.

Dryden Hall also needs to be modernized. <u>Part of our fees pays for an out-of-date telephone intercom system, which is useless because most residents have their own telephones.</u> Sometimes the electricity goes out because the wiring can't take all of our microwaves, televisions, and VCRs. Most important, Dryden Hall isn't plugged into the campus computer system. Unlike students in other dorms, I can't use my computer to search the library records or communicate with instructors or students on e-mail. This is a major inconvenience when I'm working late at night on an assignment.

Sentences are combined.

Socially as well, Dryden Hall is a disaster. When I came here, I didn't know anyone. I thought that living in a dorm would help me make friends. <u>I was wrong.</u> <u>The social events that are planned in advance are completely inadequate.</u> For example, the main social event here is a monthly pizza party. Unfortunately, the organizers run out of pizza after about fifteen minutes, so no one stays around to meet anyone else. <u>The dorm also serves donuts and coffee in the lobby every Sunday from 8 to 10 a.m., which is way too early for me and many others.</u> Surely some of the money we pay to stay in Dryden Hall could be used for more, and better, social events.

A sentence fragment is corrected.

Sentences are combined.

Sentences are combined.

It is true that Dryden Hall is a good place to study. Each floor has several study rooms (all of them in need of repainting, of course). Tutors are available in most of these study rooms in the evenings. Because there's not much socializing, the dorm is usually quiet, so it's easy to study whenever necessary.

If I could do it all over again, I'd choose Johnson Hall. Johnson Hall is older than Dryden Hall but it has been recently renovated inside and out. It has attractive rooms, new furniture, and modern wiring. Johnson Hall also has <u>a lot</u> of good social activities and is less expensive compared to Dryden Hall.

Spelling is corrected.

As I sit in my dorm room, staring at the cracked ceiling and the brick wall outside my window, I'm reminded of the mistake I made when I moved into

Dryden Hall. I only hope that the word gets out about
Dryden Hall so that other students don't make the
same mistake.

STEP 5. SHARE YOUR ESSAY

You're ready to share your evaluation with your audience — your instructor, your classmates, and others interested in your topic. For instance, if you evaluated a product, people who are deciding whether to purchase that product will want to know your opinion of it. If you evaluated a movie, other moviegoers will be curious to read your review, whether they've already seen the film or are trying to decide what to see over the weekend. If you evaluated a place, you could share your essay with someone who is interested in going to that place.

An excellent way to share your evaluation with people interested in your subject is to post your review to the Internet. As you probably know, many Web sites provide a forum for consumer reviews of products, performances, and places. Sites such as Epinions (www.epinions.com), Rating Bar (www.ratingbar.com), and Trip Advisor (www.tripadvisor .com) consist entirely of user comments. Others, such as the Internet Movie Database (www.imdb.com) and Amazon (www.amazon.com), encourage visitors to add their own reviews to the site's professional content. Choose an appropriate Web site, and add your essay to it. Be sure to check back for comments from other site visitors about how useful your review was for them.

You might also send your essay to someone who can take action on the issues related to your topic. Student writer Jody Albert, for example, sent a copy of her evaluation of Dryden Hall to the person in charge of maintaining the residence halls on campus. A few months later, the dorm's common areas were repainted.

 Consumer Reviews on the Web
Many Web sites make it easy to publish your review online. For links to sites where you can post your evaluation essay, go to **bedfordstmartins.com/choices** and click on "Annotated Web Links."

CHAPTER CHECKLIST

- ❏ I gathered ideas for evaluating a product, performance, and place.
- ❏ I compared my subject with other similar subjects to support a judgment.
- ❏ I revised my thesis statement to express an opinion or a judgment about the value or merit of the subject, to focus on the subject and not the writer, to be moderate and not extreme, and to be clear and specific.
- ❏ I gave the criteria on which the judgment is based, used enough suitable criteria, and explained those criteria that weren't obvious.
- ❏ I provided evidence — examples, facts, and expert testimony — to support each criterion.
- ❏ I gave both the positive and negative aspects of my subject to maintain a balanced perspective.
- ❏ I combined short, closely related sentences with relative clauses.
- ❏ I edited to eliminate comma splices and other errors in grammar, punctuation, and spelling.

REFLECTING ON YOUR WRITING

To help you reflect on the writing you did in this chapter, answer the following questions:

1. Compare your experience writing an evaluation with writing an expressive or informative essay. What did you find easiest and most difficult about these assignments?
2. What did you learn from writing this essay?
3. How will your audience benefit from reading your essay?
4. If you had more time, what more would you do to improve your essay before sharing it with readers?

Using your answers to these questions, complete a Writing Process Report for this chapter (you can download a report form at **bedford stmartins.com/choices**). Once you complete this report, freewrite about what you learned in this chapter.

ADDITIONAL READINGS

Evaluation of a Product

ANN HODGMAN

No Wonder They Call Me a Bitch

Ann Hodgman is a freelance writer whose articles have appeared in various print and online publications, including Good Housekeeping, Spy, Smithsonian, The New Yorker, *and* Slate.com. *She is also the author of cookbooks, humor books, and more than forty children's books. In "No Wonder They Call Me a Bitch," Hodgman evaluates dog food with a humorous twist: she tastes it herself.*

I've always wondered about dog food. Is a Gaines-burger really like a hamburger? Can you fry it? Does dog food "cheese" taste like real cheese? Does Gravy Train actually make gravy in the dog's bowl, or is that brown liquid just dissolved crumbs? And exactly what *are* by-products? 1

Having spent the better part of a week eating dog food, I'm sorry to say that I now know the answers to these questions. While my dachshund, Shortie, watched in agonies of yearning, I gagged my way through can after can of stinky, white-flecked mush and bag after bag of stinky, fat-drenched nuggets. And now I understand exactly why Shortie's breath is so bad. 2

Of course, Gaines-burgers are neither mush nor nuggets. They are, rather, a miracle of beauty and packaging — or at least that's what I thought when I was little. I used to beg my mother to get them for our dogs, but she always said they were too expensive. When I finally bought a box of cheese-flavored Gaines-burgers — after 20 years of longing — I felt deliciously wicked. 3

"Dogs love real beef," the back of the box proclaimed proudly. "That's why Gaines-burgers is the only beef burger for dogs with real beef and no meat by-products!" The copy was accurate: meat by-products did not appear in the list of ingredients. Poultry by-products did, though — right there next to preserved animal fat. 4

One Purina spokesman told me that poultry by-products consist of necks, intestines, undeveloped eggs and other "carcass remnants," but not feathers, heads or feet. When I told him I'd been eating dog food, he said, "Oh, you're kidding! Oh no!" (I came to share his alarm when, weeks later, a second Purina spokesman said that Gaines-burgers *do* contain poultry heads and feet — but *not* undeveloped eggs.) 5

Up close my Gaines-burger didn't much resemble chopped   6
beef. Rather, it looked — and felt — like a single long, extruded
piece of redness that had been chopped into segments and
formed into a patty. You could make one at home if you had a
Play-Doh Fun Factory.

I turned on the skillet. While I waited for it to heat up I pulled   7
out a shred of cheese-colored material and palpated it. Again, like
Play-Doh, it was quite malleable. I made a little cheese bird out of
it; then I counted to three and ate the bird.

There was a horrifying rush of cheddar taste, followed   8
immediately by the dull tang of soybean flour — the main ingredient in Gaines-burgers. Next I tried a piece of red extrusion.
The main difference between the meat-flavored and cheese-
flavored extrusions is one of texture. The "cheese" chews like
fresh Play-Doh, whereas the "meat" chews like Play-Doh that's
been sitting out on a rug for a couple of hours.

Frying only turned the Gaines-burger black. There was no   9
melting, no sizzling, no warm meat smells. A cherished childhood illusion was gone. I flipped the patty into the sink, where
it immediately began leaking rivulets of red dye.

As alarming as the Gaines-burgers were, their soy meal began   10
to seem like an old friend when the time came to try some
canned dog foods. I decided to try the Cycle foods first. When I
opened them, I thought about how rarely I use can openers
these days, and I was suddenly visited by a long-forgotten sen-
sation of can-opener distaste. *This* is the kind of unsavory place
can openers spend their time when you're not watching! Every
time you open a can of, say, Italian plum tomatoes, you infect
them with invisible particles of by-product.

I had been expecting to see the usual homogeneous   11
scrapple inside, but each can of Cycle was packed with smooth,
round, oily nuggets. As if someone at Gaines had been tipped
off that a human would be tasting the stuff, the four Cycles
really were different from one another. Cycle-1, for puppies, is
wet and soyish. Cycle-2, for adults, glistens nastily with fat, but
it's passably edible — a lot like some canned Swedish meatballs
I once got in a care package at college. Cycle-3, the "lite" one,
for fatties, had no specific flavor; it just tasted like dog food. But
at least it didn't make me fat.

Cycle-4, for senior dogs, had the smallest nuggets. Maybe old   12
dogs can't open their mouths as wide. This kind was far sweeter
than the other three Cycles — almost like baked beans. It was
also the only one to contain "dried beef digest," a mysterious
substance that the Purina spokesman defined as "enzymes" and
my dictionary defined as "the products of digestion."

Next on the menu was a can of Kal-Kan Pedigree with   13
Chunky Chicken. Chunky chicken? There were chunks in the
can, certainly — big, purplish-brown chunks. I forked one chunk
out (by now I was becoming more callous) and found that while

it had no discernible chicken flavor, it wasn't bad except for its texture — like meat loaf with ground-up chicken bones.

In the world of canned dog food, a smooth consistency is a sign of low quality — lots of cereal. A lumpy, frightening, bloody, stringy horror is a sign of high quality — lots of meat. Nowhere in the world of wet dog foods was this demonstrated better than in the fanciest I tried — Kal Kan's Pedigree Select Dinners. These came not in a can but in a tiny foil packet with a picture of an imperious Yorkie. When I pulled open the container, juice spurted all over my hand, and the first chunk I speared was trailing a long gray vein. I shrieked and went instead for a plain chunk, which I was able to swallow only after taking a break to read some suddenly fascinating office equipment catalogs. Once again, though, it tasted no more alarming than, say, canned hash.

Still, how pleasant it was to turn to *dry* dog food! Gravy Train was the first I tried, and I'm happy to report that it really does make a "thick, rich, real beef gravy" when you mix it with water. Thick and rich, anyway. Except for a lingering rancid-fat flavor, the gravy wasn't beefy, but since it tasted primarily like tap water, it wasn't nauseating either.

My poor dachshund just gets plain old Purina Dog Chow, but Purina also makes a dry food called Butcher's Blend that comes in Beef, Bacon, and Chicken flavor. Here we see dog food's arcane semiotics at its best: a red triangle with a *T* stamped into it is supposed to suggest beef; a tan curl, chicken; and a brown *S*, a piece of bacon. Only dogs understand these messages. But Butcher's Blend does have an endearing slogan: "Great Meaty Tastes — without bothering the Butcher!" *You know, I wanted to buy some meat, but I just couldn't bring myself to bother the butcher. . . .*

Purina O.N.E. ("Optimum Nutritional Effectiveness") is targeted at people who are unlikely ever to worry about bothering a tradesperson. "We chose chicken as a primary ingredient in Purina O.N.E. for several reasonings," the long, long essay on the back of the bag announces. Chief among these reasonings, I'd guess, is the fact that chicken appeals to people who are — you know — *like us.* Although our dogs do nothing but spend 18-hour days alone in the apartment, we still want them to be *premium* dogs. We want them to cut down on red meat, too. We also want dog food that comes in a bag with an attractive design, a subtle typeface and no kitschy pictures of slobbering golden retrievers.

Besides that, we want a list of the Nutritional Benefits of our dog food — and we get it on O.N.E. One thing I especially like about this list is its constant references to a dog's "hair coat," as in "Beef tallow is good for the dog's skin and hair coat." (On the other hand, beef tallow merely provides palatability, while the dried beef digest in Cycle provides palatability *enhancement.*)

I hate to say it, but O.N.E. was pretty palatable. Maybe that's because it has about 100 percent more fat than, say,

Butcher's Blend. Or maybe I'd been duped by the packaging; that's been known to happen before.

As with people food, dog snacks taste much better than dog meals. They're better-looking too. Take Milk-Bone Flavor Snacks. The loving-hands-at-home prose describing each flavor is colorful; the writers practically choke on their own exuberance. Of bacon they say, "It's so good, your dog will think it's hot off the frying pan." Of liver: "The only taste your dog wants more than liver — is even more liver!" Of poultry: "All those farm fresh flavors deliciously mixed in one biscuit. Your dog will bark with delight!" And of vegetable: "Gardens of taste! Specially blended to give your dog that vegetable flavor he wants — but can rarely get!" 20

Well, I may be a sucker, but advertising *this* emphatic just doesn't convince me. I lined up all seven flavors of Milk-Bone Flavor Snacks on the floor. Unless my dog's palate is a lot more sensitive than mine — and considering that she steals dirty diapers out of the trash and eats them, I'm loath to think it is — she doesn't detect any more difference in the seven flavors than I did when I tried them. 21

I much preferred Bonz, the hard-baked, bone-shaped snack stuffed with simulated marrow. I liked the bone part, that is; it tasted almost exactly like the cornmeal it was made of. The mock-marrow inside was a bit more problematic: in addition to looking like the sludge that collects in the treads of my running shoes, it was bursting with tiny hairs. 22

I'm sure you have a few dog food questions of your own. To save us time, I've answered them in advance. 23

Q. *Are those little cans of Mighty Dog actually branded with the sizzling word* BEEF, *the way they show in the commercials?* 24

A. You should know by now that that kind of thing never happens. 25

Q. *Does chicken-flavored dog food taste like chicken-flavored cat food?* 26

A. To my surprise, chicken cat food was actually a little better — more chickeny. It tasted like inferior canned pâté. 27

Q. *Was there any dog food that you just couldn't bring yourself to try?* 28

A. Alas, it was a can of Mighty Dog called Prime Entree with Bone Marrow. The meat was dark, dark brown, and it was surrounded by gelatin that was almost black. I knew I would die if I tasted it, so I put it outside for the raccoons. 29

READING ACTIVITY 7: Build Your Vocabulary

Determine the meanings of the following words from the context of Ann Hodgman's essay. Then check their meanings by looking up the words in a dictionary: palpated (7), malleable (7), rivulets (9), unsavory (10), homogeneous (11), scrapple (11), callous (13), imperious (14), arcane (16), semiotics (16), tallow (18), palatability (18), loath (21).

READING ACTIVITY 8: Read to Improve Your Writing

Discuss the following questions about "No Wonder They Call Me a Bitch" with your classmates.

1. What criteria does Hodgman use to evaluate different types of dog food?
2. How does the author show that she's knowledgeable about the topic?
3. List three of Hodgman's facts or examples that you think are effective in supporting her evaluation. Explain why you think they're effective.
4. Did this essay make you want to taste dog food or cat food yourself? Why or why not?

Evaluation of a Performance

ANTHONY BEAL

Let the Good Times Roll

Anthony Beal was born in the Bronx, New York. He is a columnist for American Chronicle *magazine, a poet, and a writer of short horror fiction. In this* American Chronicle *review, Beal describes how the city of New Orleans and the festival of Mardi Gras have endured in spite of the devastating effects of Hurricane Katrina, which ruined much of the city in August 2005.*

One could almost forget that mere months ago, its streets had lain ruined by toppled trees and shattered windowpanes. 1

In testament to the kind of courage in the face of uncertain times that has long defined it, New Orleans saw its first major Mardi Gras parades roll on Saturday, February 18 beneath cloudy skies that brooded in fashion reminiscent of the August 29th storm that decimated it six months ago, claiming over 1,300 lives. 2

The crowds, though lesser in number than previous years, appeared no less celebratory where they congregated along the solitary parade route to clamor for colored bead necklaces and other assorted treats. Colorful floats rolled onward in five consecutive parades, their riders cheerfully tossing coveted swag to crowds notably reduced in size considering that more than half the city's residents remain displaced throughout our nation by Hurricane Katrina. And so parade processions that ordinarily would have filled the entire day traveling several routes around town were completed along one major artery in just under two hours, but no one seemed to mind. 3

Confining parade processions to a singular route in order to alleviate the financial demands of widespread police and sanita- 4 tion resources was a decision reached by New Orleans officials determined not to cancel this one hundred-fiftieth Mardi Gras celebration. Their agreed-upon alternative, a downsizing and consolidation of the usual scale of festivities leading up to Fat Tuesday on February 28th, continues to meet mixed reactions.

Some tourists and locals uphold Mardi Gras celebration as   5
the soul of Orleans parish, as epitomizing defiance of death and adversity in a city determined to escape ghosts of the devastation laid by Hurricane Katrina. Others however, including many locals who have yet to recover any semblance of the lives they used to know, are less embracing of the festive mood pervading their city. That the city should spend 2.7 million dollars to cover the cost of the celebration — soldiering on despite city officials' failure to secure more than one corporate sponsor — rather than using those resources to rebuild homes and finance rebuilding seems extravagant and reckless. To those still sleeping on cots or bunking with friends and family in another state because their homes fell within the 80 percent of the town that was flooded when Lake Pontchartrain's levees crumbled, it seems downright inexcusable. Writing this article from the warm comfort and familiar surroundings of my home, I can't in good conscience suggest that they are wrong.

But the fat lady hasn't sung yet.   6

Like the city itself, Mardi Gras has shown us that it will   7
endure no matter what. As a person who numbered among those stranded during Hurricane Katrina's aftermath, I can attest to New Orleans' resilience. Lesser crowds, fewer tourists, and higher monetary costs notwithstanding, Mardi Gras carries more meaning this year than ever for the sheer, defiant intimacy of it in a city that will not bow to the decimation wrought against it six months ago. No, it is apparent that neither New Orleans nor Mardi Gras will go quietly into Hurricane Katrina's night. One can only hope that for all its symbolic tenacity, the end results of letting the good times roll as always will justify the financial cost.

READING ACTIVITY 9: Build Your Vocabulary

Determine the meanings of the following words from the context of Anthony Beal's essay. Then check their meanings by looking up the words in a dictionary: reminiscent (2), decimated (2), clamor (3), swag (3), alleviate (4), epitomizing (5), semblance (5), pervading (5), resilience (7), wrought (7), tenacity (7).

READING ACTIVITY 10: Read to Improve Your Writing

Discuss the following questions about "Let the Good Times Roll" with your classmates.

1. What criteria does the author use to support his evaluation of the first Mardi Gras after Hurricane Katrina?

2. List at least three facts or examples that the author uses to support his evaluation. Explain how effective you found this evidence.

3. Explain the significance of the sentence "But the fat lady hasn't sung yet" as applied to Mardi Gras.

4. Do you agree with the author's evaluation of the 2006 Mardi Gras celebration? Why or why not?

Evaluation of a Place

NICHOLAS JENNINGS

A Palace of Rock

Nicholas Jennings lives and works in Toronto, Canada, where he writes about music and pop culture. His books include Before the Gold Rush: Flashbacks to the Dawn of the Canadian Sound *(1998) and* Fifty Years of Music: The Story of EMI Music Canada *(2000). He is also a music critic for* Maclean's, *a Canadian magazine. In "A Palace of Rock," written soon after the Rock and Roll Hall of Fame and Museum opened in 1995 in Cleveland, Ohio, Jennings evaluates the museum's exhibits about rock and roll from its birth in the 1950s to the present.*

As museum pieces, they are the most humble of artifacts: a few report cards, a black leather jacket, a pair of government-issue eye glasses. Yet for many, the three objects are priceless. Once the property of John Lennon, those treasures are now on display at the recently opened Rock and Roll Hall of Fame and Museum in Cleveland, Ohio, where they are already among its most popular exhibits. Looking at the articles, it is easy to see why: each of them brings the viewer closer to the real Lennon. His elementary school report card reveals that one of his teachers found rock's future genius "hopeless," while the well-worn, sloppy jacket somehow perfectly captures the musician's irreverent charm. And Lennon's wire-rimmed spectacles trigger a flood of emotions because they are so evocative of the artist, who was fatally shot by a crazed fan in December, 1980. "Rock music has a power that makes you want to be a part of it," says museum director Dennis Barrie. "Hopefully, we represent some of that."

Judging by the scores of fans who flooded into the facility during its Labor Day weekend opening — an estimated 8,000 on the first day — Barrie need not worry: despite a once-shaky history, the Rock and Roll Hall of Fame and Museum is now a resounding success. Visitors can feast on more than 3,500 items, ranging from posters, album jackets and handwritten lyric sheets to movies and interactive exhibits that play requested songs and videos. Among the most memorable displays: a replica of the old Sun Studios in Memphis, Tenn., where Elvis Presley made his first records; a piece of Otis Redding's private airplane, which crashed in 1967; and the 1945 Magnavox tape recorder that pioneering musicologist Alan Lomax used to record blues legends such as Lead Belly and Muddy Waters. And Hall of Fame inductees Neil Young and The Band are reminders that rock has also thrived in Canada.

Meanwhile, hundreds of photographs, instruments and costumes — including Michael Jackson's famed sequinned glove and Madonna's gold bustier — are also housed in the museum's impressive, seven-level structure, a $123-million geometric shrine designed by New York City–based architect I. M. Pei, whose other accomplishments include the additions to the National Gallery of Art in Washington and the Louvre in Paris. From the air, the lakefront building resembles a record player with turntable, tonearm and a stack of 45s. But from the ground level, the elaborate structure is a cheeky mix of pyramid-like facades, rectangular towers and trapezoidal extensions that boldly jut out over Lake Erie. 3

The contents of the museum, like the all-star concert that launched it on Sept. 2 — the roster of performers included Chuck Berry, James Brown, The Kinks, Creedence Clearwater Revival, Robbie Robertson and Bruce Springsteen — reflect rock in all of its ragged glory. For some, the very idea of chronicling the history of rock 'n' roll in a serious, curated institution is offensive. They argue that, like caging a wild beast, it runs counter to the laws of nature, as though rock music should always be allowed to roam free of commerce and academia. "Absolute nonsense," scoffs Rob Bowman, a professor of rock at Toronto's York University. "Rock has been institutionalized for at least the last 40 years, by record companies, radio stations and other media. Anyone who doesn't understand that is a hopeless romantic." Still, it is difficult to ignore some of the contradictions raised by the museum. Thirty years ago, The Who's Pete Townshend was smashing his guitar in a display of anarchic frenzy, yet the museum has one of his instruments respectfully encased in a glass cabinet. The irony is not lost on Ron House of the Columbus, Ohio–based band Thomas Jefferson Slave Apartments. The musician has written a punk protest song called "RnR Hall of Fame" that angrily tackles the subject. "I don't want to see Eric Clapton's stuffed baby / I don't want to see the shotgun of Kurt Cobain," sings House. "I don't want to see the liver of David Crosby / Blow it up before Johnny Rotten gets in." 4

Although Rotten's Sex Pistols have yet to be inducted by the Hall of Fame Foundation (artists become eligible 25 years after their first recording), the British punk band is part of the museum's "Blank Generation" exhibit, which examines punk's birth in London and New York City between 1975 and 1980. Included is an 11-inch Sid Vicious doll, complete with chains, ripped T-shirt and swastika, that was used as a prop in the 1980 5 documentary, *The Great Rock 'n' Roll Swindle,* made a year after his death from a heroin overdose.

In fact, the museum strives mightily to keep up to date with   6
rock's more recent developments, charting the rise of rap music and Seattle's grunge scene. According to chief curator James Henke, a former editor at *Rolling Stone,* the museum's collection will be in constant flux. That is partly due to the fact that most display items are on loan, partly due to the nature of its subject matter. Says Henke: "Like the music, it'll always be evolving."

However, the collection is shamelessly skewed to the past.   7
Above the entrance to the main exhibition area is a neon sign quoting Chuck Berry: "Roll Over Beethoven." Berry and other such pioneers as Little Richard and Presley are well represented in a noisy, arcade-like space that includes small cinemas, record booths and computer screens. Amateur musicologists can trace the 500 songs that the museum has deemed to have shaped the history of rock 'n' roll. Among the oldest entries: Woody Guthrie's 1956 folk anthem "This Land Is Your Land" and Louis Jordan's jump-blues classic "Caldonia," written in 1945. But the most revealing exhibit is The Beat Goes On, which traces musical family trees. Touch-screen computers allow museum-goers to click on images of musicians and discover their influences through video clips and songs. In some cases, the technology bridges generations. Lucy Schlopy, an 82-year-old visitor from Bradford, Pa., found that her favorite artist, Roy Orbison, had in turn influenced one of her great-niece's musical heroes, Bruce Springsteen. "I'm learning all kinds of things," said Schlopy.

Responses like that, says director Barrie, who previously   8
worked at the Smithsonian Institution in Washington and Cincinnati's Contemporary Arts Center, prove that the museum is a success. "People are actually reading, taking in the content of the exhibits," he beamed. "They're not just looking at the glittery costumes, which is very gratifying." At the same time, the costumed mannequins throughout the museum are proving to be among the biggest draws. Especially popular are Presley's leather stage outfit from his 1968 comeback TV special, Lennon's lime-green Sgt. Pepper's uniform and the "butterfly dresses" of Motown's The Supremes. For the kids, rock's schlock meister Alice Cooper, standing next to a guillotine and a bloody, severed head, is an awesome, cartoonish highlight.

By contrast, the actual Hall of Fame, housed on the top   9
floor, is a model of decorum. To get there, visitors climb a long, spiral staircase to reach a darkened room honoring the inductees (123 so far). Images of such legends as Buddy Holly and Bob Marley dissolve on tiny video screens like ghosts, while their signatures, etched on backlit glass plaques, seem to float in the ether. After the musical cacophony and video chaos downstairs, the Hall of Fame is a welcome sanctuary.

For the Hall of Fame's creators, the museum was a pipe   10
dream that almost never materialized. Founders Jann Wenner,

editor of *Rolling Stone,* and Ahmet Ertegun, president of Atlantic Records, steered the project through three directors and one site change before the groundbreaking two years ago. Cleveland was chosen over Memphis and New York after residents collected 600,000 signatures and local businesses raised $87 million. But the city had already earned a place in rock history: Alan Freed, its famous deejay, popularized the term rock 'n' roll in the 1950s.

At the museum's ribbon-cutting ceremony, Jimi Hendrix's version of "The Star Spangled Banner" played over the loud-speakers. The guitarist's rendition, conceived as an anti-Vietnam statement at Woodstock in 1969, is full of feedback and guitar distortions designed to simulate war sounds. But suddenly, Hendrix's tortured notes were punctuated by the real-life sounds of two Marine Corps Harrier jets flying overhead. The irony was not lost on some in the crowd, including Wenner, who later addressed the issue of how rock has now joined the establishment. The hall, said Wenner, standing next to Lennon's widow Yoko Ono, was built to remind people of the "power of innocence, rebellion and youth," but also the value of "maturity and growth and perspective." Rock 'n' roll, once scruffy and rebellious, is all grown up. Although it will strike some as contradictory, a hall of fame and museum is simply a natural step in its evolution. 11

READING ACTIVITY 11: Build Your Vocabulary

Determine the meanings of the following words from the context of Nicholas Jennings's essay. Then check their meanings by looking up the words in a dictionary: artifacts (1), irreverent (1), replica (2), roster (4), contradictions (4), anarchic (4), inducted (5), skewed (7), sanctuary (9), scruffy (11).

READING ACTIVITY 12: Read to Improve Your Writing

Discuss the following questions about "A Palace of Rock" with your classmates.

1. What is the author's evaluation of the Rock and Roll Hall of Fame and Museum? Where in the essay is this evaluation expressed?

2. What criteria does Jennings use to support his evaluation?

3. Explain in your own words what Jennings means when he writes in paragraph 4 that "it is difficult to ignore some of the contradictions raised by the museum." What are these contradictions? Give an example.

4. Rock and roll artists can be inducted into the museum twenty-five years after their first recording. In your opinion, what current rock and roll groups or performers will be inducted into the Hall of Fame when they become eligible?

Considering the Media

8

Using Cause and Effect

In this chapter, you will write an essay that argues your position on a controversial issue about the media. As you follow the steps of the writing process, you will

■ Gather ideas by freewriting, brainstorming, and consulting others.

■ Develop your ideas using cause-and-effect analysis.

■ Practice making an argument claim, generating pro and con points to support your ideas, and ordering your points effectively.

■ Combine sentences using introductory phrases.

■ Learn to correct subject-verb agreement.

■ Submit your finished essay to a campus or city newspaper.

The media — which include newspapers, books, magazines, radio, television, and the Internet — profoundly influence the ways people live and think. When television was new, people watched a small screen in a large cabinet. They saw black-and-white images of actual events happening hundreds of miles away. Watching live newscasts, variety shows, sports, dramas, and comedies was an exciting novelty in the 1950s, but it also brought controversy. Critics worried, for example, that children would see too much violence and that viewers would be tricked by commercials. Even the comedian Groucho Marx, who later hosted a popular game show called *You Bet Your Life*, criticized television when it first became popular, saying, "I find television very educational. Every time someone switches it on, I go into another room and read a good book."

More than half a century after the first concerns were raised about television's effects on people's lives, media options have expanded to include e-mail, Web sites, online shopping, blogs, Internet-ready camera phones, chat groups, instant messaging, TiVo, M3P players, and podcasts. This interactive technology — often called *new media* — allows us to alter what we watch, listen, or read to suit our own tastes or to communicate with others. Instead of being vulnerable to the trickery of commercials, for instance, we can skip through them. We can create our own song playlists, shows, and videos and send them to people we've never met.

But do we really control the media, or do the media control us? Critics and consumers argue about many aspects of the media, such as the benefits and dangers of censorship, the ways that people are portrayed, and the media's effect on people's lifestyles. Which is more important: freedom of speech or national security? How are viewers and performers affected when the media portray people in particular ways? Are new forms of communication helpful or harmful to the people who use them?

In this chapter, you'll read and analyze argument essays on these issues. Then you will join the debate by writing an essay that tries to persuade newspaper readers to share your viewpoint on a controversial aspect of the media that interests you.

GROUP ACTIVITY 1: Think about the Media

The young woman in the photograph on page 286 is using two kinds of media at the same time — television and the Internet. List the types of media that you typically use in one day, and compare your list with those of your classmates. Do you think these kinds of media have mostly positive or mostly negative effects on your lives? Why?

READING ESSAYS ABOUT THE MEDIA

Debates about the media have become intense, as the following three readings show. The authors of these essays each take a position on a controversial issue associated with censorship, representation, or lifestyles. As you read, notice how they use cause-and-effect analysis to develop their points. Also note how these authors try to persuade their audience. What arguments do they make to support their points? How do they try to win over readers who disagree with them? How do they order their ideas? Consider, too, how you react to their arguments. To what degree do these authors change your mind on these topics?

A Censorship Issue

MICHAEL CROWLEY

Let's Shut Them Down

Freedom of expression is a fundamental right in the United States. In fact, the First Amendment to the U.S. Constitution states that "Congress shall make no law . . . abridging the freedom of speech, or of the press." But can freedom of speech be taken too far? Michael Crowley, a columnist for Reader's Digest, *believes that it can. In "Let's Shut Them Down," he argues that because Web technology can endanger national security, some forms of expression should be forbidden.*

In the weeks before New York City hosted the Republican National Convention last August, security officials spent millions securing the area around Madison Square Garden against a possible terrorist attack. They set up barricades, installed extra cameras on buildings, and assigned extra police to the streets. John Young, a 69-year-old New Yorker, was also surveying the neighborhoods. He spent hours wandering around midtown Manhattan, snapping photos of unprotected local streets and other vulnerable areas near the convention site. He even snapped the location of a major pipeline that carries highly explosive natural gas into Manhattan.

Young was not working for the NYPD or the FBI. Nor was he part of a terrorist plot. A self-employed architect, he claims to be just a concerned citizen, someone who thinks we're all safer if there are no government secrets.

So what did he do with all that sensitive information? He posted it on the popular website he runs, which typically gets 50,000 visitors in a day. Young featured dozens of maps and pictures, as well as observations about ways terrorists might attack the convention. Just trying to help, Young says.

Security officials didn't see it that way. The company that   4
owned the gas main took down a sign, photographed by Young, to make the line harder to spot. Young has been visited by FBI agents in the past, who made it clear they expect him to report suspicious inquiries to the Bureau.

Young may well have put lives at risk, but he doesn't regret   5
it. "The more information you have, the better protected you are," he argues. Young has no shortage of information on his website: maps, aerial photographs and security details about everything from the nation's Strategic Petroleum Reserve to a chemical weapons depot in Alabama to nuclear-weapons storage sites in Georgia and New Mexico.

You'd think that websites like Young's would be illegal,   6
especially since the Internet is one of the most critical battlegrounds in our war against radical Islamists. Terrorists not only use encrypted online messages to communicate, but they scan the Web for intelligence. "We shouldn't kid ourselves. Our adversaries are all reading the Internet," says Roger Cressey, a former White House national security official. "So those preaching freedom of information need to be very careful."

Yet there's little anyone can do to stop people like Young.   7
"You're protected by the First Amendment guarantee of free speech. It's hard to prosecute someone who uses public sources to pull together information — even when that information clearly shouldn't be revealed," says Steward Baker, a technology lawyer and former general counsel for the National Security Agency. "If the material is leaked to you, you can probably publish that too. Unfortunately, it's not illegal to be a jerk."

Recently I surfed the Web and checked out Young's site.   8
Among other items, I found detailed maps showing how to reach a secret government bunker that's reportedly one of Vice President Dick Cheney's emergency hideouts. There were also photos of the front entrance. Young isn't the only one using cyberspace in a grossly irresponsible way. Another website gave me personal information about government officials and police officers, including their home addresses.

To understand what nuts and zealots can do with this sort of   9
information, recall what happened in the early 1990s when three abortion doctors were killed after pro-life extremists created "wanted" posters displaying the physicians' names and photographs. A few years later, a website showed pictures of other abortion doctors, and listed the murdered ones with their names crossed out. Eventually the site's Web server shut it down.

No wonder police officers are unnerved by the growing num-   10
ber of anti-cop websites. One of them includes photographs of people at a demonstration who are identified as plainclothes cops.

At another site are the home addresses and phone numbers   11 of hundreds of officials around the country, from federal judges to mayors to attorneys general. You can bet this isn't about sending people birthday cards. Who else but crackpots or cold-blooded terrorists would want maps and aerial photos of the homes of CIA officials like director Porter Goss — as John Young cheerfully provides?

How frustrating that politicians who want to stand up to these websites find themselves stymied. When Anthony Weiner, a Democratic member of Congress from New York, discovered that a website was revealing the home addresses of undercover officers, he proposed a bill that would make such disclosers illegal. "Free speech does not include the ability to terrorize officers," Representative Weiner said in a press release.   12

Well, maybe it does. When others have pressed for similar legislation on the state level, they've found that it's extremely difficult to clamp down on a site unless it publishes a clear and open threat or calls for a terror attack on a specific target.   13

That may leave Weiner and every other concerned citizen hoping that Web-hosting providers will shut down dangerous websites voluntarily. But don't count on it.   14

Perhaps if more of us complain, that could change. One thing's for certain: We can't persuade the people who get a thrill exposing dangerous facts to sober up. When I asked John Young if there was anything he wouldn't reveal on his site — a fault in the President's Secret Service detail, for instance — he said, "Well, I'm actually looking for that information right now." Wonderful.   15

READING ACTIVITY 1: Build Your Vocabulary

Determine the meanings of the following words from the context of Michael Crowley's essay. Then check their meanings by looking up the words in a dictionary: aerial (5), encrypted (6), adversaries (6), cyberspace (8), zealots (9), stymied (12).

READING ACTIVITY 2: Read to Improve Your Writing

Discuss the following questions about "Let's Shut Them Down" with your classmates.

1. What is Crowley's main point in this essay? If there is a sentence or passage where he states this main point, point it out.
2. According to the author, what are some of the possible effects on the United States from the Web sites that he discusses?
3. What are two reasons for not shutting down these Web sites?
4. How does Crowley attempt to get his readers' attention?
5. What is your opinion about this topic?

A Representation Issue

SAMUEL L. JACKSON

In Character

Actor Samuel L. Jackson is a graduate of Morehouse College and has appeared in more than eighty films, including Do the Right Thing *(1989),* Jungle Fever *(1991),* Pulp Fiction *(1994),* Star Wars *(Episodes I–III; 1999, 2002, 2005),* Coach Carter *(2005), and* Snakes on a Plane *(2006). In the following essay, Jackson considers the issue of racism in Hollywood and argues that although roles for minority actors have improved over the last few decades, there's more work to be done.*

I think it's significant for the growth of the [movie] business that a black actor like me is being cast in race-neutral parts when 20 years ago I wouldn't have been. It's significant for young actors who have aspirations to be things other than criminals and drug dealers and victims and whatever rap artist they have to be to get into a film. The things I've done and Morgan's done and Denzel's done, that Fish has done, that Wesley's[1] done, everybody's done, have allowed us to achieve a level of success as other kinds of people. We've been successful in roles as doctors, lawyers, teachers, policemen, detectives, spies, monsters — anything that we have been able to portray on-screen in a very realistic way that made audiences say, I believe that, and that brought them into the theaters to see us do it. This has allowed young black actors the opportunity to become different kinds of characters in the cinematic milieu we're a part of.

Before, I used to pick up scripts and I was criminal number two and I looked to see what page I died on. We've now demonstrated a level of expertise, in terms of the care we give to our characters and in terms of our professionalism — showing up to work on time, knowing our lines, and bringing something to the job beyond the lines and basic characterizations. Through our accomplishments and the expertise we have shown, studios know there is a talent pool out there that wants to be like us, and hopefully, these young actors will take care to do the things we did.

As the fabric of our society changes in certain ways, the fabric of the cinematic world changes in the same ways. For a very long time, the people that were in power were white men. They tended to hire other white men, and when they saw a story, the

---

[1] Jackson is referring to African American actors Morgan Freeman, Denzel Washington, Laurence Fishburne, and Wesley Snipes.

people in those stories were white men or specific kinds of white women. As we get younger producers and younger people in the studios, we have a generation, or several generations, of people who have lived in a society where they have black friends. They have Asian friends. They have Hispanic friends who do a wide variety of jobs, who went into a wide variety of vocations. When the studio heads look at a script now, they can see their friend Juan or they can see their friend Kwong or they can see their friend Rashan. So all of a sudden you see a different look in the movies, as they reflect the way this younger generation of producers and studio executives live their lives. And consequently, through the worldwide network of cinema, you meet other top-quality actors from other cultures. The world of cinema brings us all together. And we've started to cast films in a whole other way that reflects the way we live and the pattern of our society. Outside of *Spider-Man,* all the big action heroes now seem to be ethnic. The new Arnold Schwarzenegger is The Rock, and the new Bruce Willis is about to be Vin Diesel. So we're doing something right. But it's difficult to do a film that's of a serious nature and that does not have guns, sex, and explosions in it if it's ethnic.

There are many ways to answer the question whether Holly-   4 wood is racist. The direct and honest answer, I guess, is yes, only because Hollywood is anti anything that's not green. If something doesn't make money, they don't want to be bothered with it. Therefore, it's still difficult to get a movie about Hispanics made; it's difficult to get a movie about blacks made that doesn't have to do with hip-hop, drugs, and sex. You can get a black comedy made. Eddie Murphy's funny, Will Smith is funny, Martin Lawrence is funny. We have huge black comics. But getting a film like *Eve's Bayou* made is practically impossible. For five years, nobody knew what that movie was. Like, what is it? It's a family drama. Yeah, but how do we market that? Nobody wanted to be bothered with it. Or *Caveman's Valentine.* What is it? It's a mystery, a murder mystery. But it's a black murder mystery. No, there's white people in it; it just happens that a black person is the lead. So Hollywood is racist in its ideas about what can make money and what won't make money. They'll make Asian movies about people who jump across buildings and use swords and swing in trees, like *Crouching Tiger,* but we can't sell an Asian family drama. What do we do with that? Or if we're going to have Asian people in the film, they've got to be like the tong, or they're selling drugs and they got some guns and it's young gang members. It's got to be that. And Hollywood is sexist in its ideals about which women are appealing and which women aren't. It's a young woman's game. Women have got to be either real old or real young to be successful. If they're in the middle, it's like, what do we do with her? Put her in kids' movies, you know, with some kids.

Hollywood can be perceived as racist and sexist, because 5 that's what audiences have said to them they will pay their money to come see. It's difficult to break that cycle, because it's a moneymaking business and it costs money to make films. Hollywood tends to copy things that make lots of money. The first thing they want to know is how many car chases are there and what's blowing up. They're over the how-many-people-die thing, because of 9/11. Now it's like, how many people can we kill and get away with it? We can't blow up anything right now unless it's in the right context. We can blow something up over there, and the bad guy can be a guy with a turban. So there's all kinds of things that go into what people say about Hollywood being racist. There have been times I had to go in a room and convince people I'm the right person for their script and the fact that I'm black will not impact on the script in a negative way. I've had to explain that my being black won't change the dynamics of the interaction; it won't change the dynamics of the story in terms of my character's interaction with the other characters. I'll just happen to be a black guy who's in that story doing those things.

We [African Americans] need to produce our own films. We 6 need to own our own theaters in addition to producing our own films. The more theaters we own, the sooner we can have our own distribution chain. It's a matter of us having that kind of network [as major Hollywood studios do], so when we do make small films that we want to distribute to a specific group of people or to a wider audience, we're able to do it.

I want to be able to produce films for friends of mine who 7 haven't had the opportunity to be seen in the way I've been seen. They're good at what they do, and they deserve an opportunity to be seen by a greater public.

READING ACTIVITY 3: Build Your Vocabulary

Determine the meanings of the following words from the context of Samuel L. Jackson's essay. Then check their meanings by looking up the words in a dictionary: milieu (1), cinematic (3), vocations (3), tong (4), dynamics (5).

READING ACTIVITY 4: Read to Improve Your Writing

Discuss the following questions about "In Character" with your classmates.

1. According to Jackson, is Hollywood racist?
2. Name at least three reasons that Jackson gives to support his opinion.

3. Assume that you disagree with Jackson. What two reasons can you give to explain your disagreement?

4. In Jackson's view, how does the desire to make money affect the way movies portray minority characters?

5. What are your views on this topic?

A Lifestyle Issue

BRENT STAPLES

What Adolescents Miss When We Let Them Grow Up in Cyberspace

Just as the introduction of television brought with it concerns about its effects on people's lives, so has the accessibility of the Internet raised questions, particularly about the impact of new technology on children and teenagers. In "What Adolescents Miss When We Let Them Grow Up in Cyberspace," Brent Staples, a columnist for the New York Times *and author of* Parallel Time: Growing Up in Black and White *(1995), voices his reservations about how the Internet has changed the ways some teenagers interact with other people.*

My 10th-grade heartthrob was the daughter of a fearsome 1 steelworker who struck terror into the hearts of 15-year-old boys. He made it his business to answer the telephone — and so always knew who was calling — and grumbled in the background when the conversation went on too long. Unable to make time by phone, the boy either gave up or appeared at the front door. This meant submitting to the intense scrutiny that the girl's father soon became known for.

He greeted me with a crushing handshake, then leaned in 2 close in a transparent attempt to find out whether I was one of those bad boys who smoked. He retired to the den during the visit, but cruised by the living room now and then to let me know he was watching. He let up after some weeks, but only after getting across what he expected of a boy who spent time with his daughter and how upset he'd be if I disappointed him.

This was my first sustained encounter with an adult outside 3 my family who needed to be convinced of my worth as a person. This, of course, is a crucial part of growing up. Faced with the same challenge today, however, I would probably pass on meeting the girl's father — and outflank him on the Internet.

Thanks to e-mail, online chat rooms and instant messages — 4 which permit private, real-time conversations — adolescents have at last succeeded in shielding their social lives from adult scrutiny. But this comes at a cost: teenagers nowadays are both more connected to the world at large than ever, and more cut off from the social encounters that have historically prepared young people for the move into adulthood.

The Internet was billed as a revolutionary way to enrich our   5 social lives and expand our civic connections. This seems to have worked well for elderly people and others who were isolated before they got access to the World Wide Web. But a growing body of research is showing that heavy use of the Net can actually isolate younger socially connected people who unwittingly allow time online to replace face-to-face interactions with their families and friends.

Online shopping, checking e-mail and Web surfing — mainly   6 solitary activities — have turned out to be more isolating than watching television, which friends and family often do in groups. Researchers have found that the time spent in direct contact with family members drops by as much as half for every hour we use the Net at home.

This should come as no surprise to the two-career couples   7 who have seen their domestic lives taken over by e-mail and wireless tethers that keep people working around the clock. But a startling body of research from the Human-Computer Interaction Institute at Carnegie Mellon has shown that heavy Internet use can have a stunting effect outside the home as well.

Studies show that gregarious, well-connected people actu-   8 ally lost friends, and experienced symptoms of loneliness and depression, after joining discussion groups and other activities. People who communicated with disembodied strangers online found the experience empty and emotionally frustrating but were nonetheless seduced by the novelty of the new medium. As Prof. Robert Kraut, a Carnegie Mellon researcher, told me recently, such people allowed low-quality relationships developed in virtual reality to replace higher-quality relationships in the real world.

No group has embraced this socially impoverishing trade-   9 off more enthusiastically than adolescents, many of whom spend most of their free hours cruising the Net in sunless rooms. This hermetic existence has left many of these teenagers with nonexistent social skills — a point widely noted in stories about the computer geeks who rose to prominence in the early days of Silicon Valley.

Adolescents are drawn to cyberspace for different reasons   10 than adults. As the writer Michael Lewis observed in his book *Next: The Future Just Happened,* children see the Net as a transformational device that lets them discard quotidian identities for more glamorous ones. Mr. Lewis illustrated the point with Marcus Arnold, who, as a 15-year-old, adopted a pseudonym a few years ago and posed as a 25-year-old legal expert for an Internet information service. Marcus did not feel the least bit guilty, and wasn't deterred when real-world lawyers discovered his secret and accused him of being a fraud. When asked whether he had actually read the law, Marcus responded that he found books "boring," leaving us to conclude that he had learned all he needed to know from his family's big-screen TV.

Marcus is a child of the Net, where everyone has a pseudo-   11
nym, telling a story makes it true, and adolescents create older, cooler, more socially powerful selves any time they wish. The ability to slip easily into a new, false self is tailor-made for emotionally fragile adolescents, who can consider a bout of acne or a few excess pounds an unbearable tragedy.

But teenagers who spend much of their lives hunched over   12
computer screens miss the socializing, the real-world experience that would allow them to leave adolescence behind and grow into adulthood. These vital experiences, like much else, are simply not available in a virtual form.

READING ACTIVITY 5: Build Your Vocabulary

Determine the meanings of the following words from the context of Brent Staples's essay. Then check their meanings by looking up the words in a dictionary: outflank (3), unwittingly (5), tethers (7), gregarious (8), disembodied (8), hermetic (9), quotidian (10), pseudonym (10).

READING ACTIVITY 6: Read to Improve Your Writing

Discuss the following questions about "What Adolescents Miss When We Let Them Grow Up in Cyberspace" with your classmates.

1. According to Staples, when adolescents spend time on the Internet, what happens to them? Summarize these effects in a sentence or two.

2. What reasons and evidence does the author give to support his main point?

3. What are some positive effects for adolescents of spending time on the Internet?

4. What is your opinion on this topic?

5. What might be two reasons that Staples began this essay with a story about meeting his tenth-grade girlfriend's father?

Writing Assignment

Types of media are all around you. Even this textbook is a medium of communication. While you read this book, for example, you might have a television on while your MP3 player pipes music into your ears and a text message appears on your camera phone. These technologies can have a strong influence on us. In this chapter, you'll write a persuasive essay that takes a position on a controversial aspect of the media that interests you. You (or your instructor) may approach this assignment in one of several ways:

- Argue for or against some type of censorship.

  OR

- Argue a point about how a group of people is represented in the media.

  OR

- Argue about how a particular communication medium has changed our lifestyles for good or bad.

Follow the guidance and activities in this chapter to discover, develop, and polish your ideas into a finished essay. After you complete your essay, you'll submit it to your campus or city newspaper so that others can understand and perhaps be convinced by your perspective.

STEP 1. EXPLORE YOUR CHOICES

For more on audience and purpose, see pp. 8–12.

Because the media encompass everything from "old" one-way media (newspapers, magazines, television, and radio) to "new" interactive media (computers, MP3 players, and text messaging), you have many possible topics to choose from for your essay. Remember that most writers do their best work when they really care about the topic. At the same time, the topic that you select needs to keep your readers engaged and willing to listen to what you have to say. Before you think about possible topics, take some time to think about who your readers are and what they care about. Consider also what you want them to believe or do after they read your essay.

Analyzing Your Audience and Purpose

Keep your readers in mind from the very beginning. For this assignment, you'll be writing to readers of your campus or city newspaper. The readers of your campus newspaper will be mostly students, while the readers of your local newspaper will be of various ages and have many kinds of occupations. The type of newspaper you select will affect the way that you write your essay.

Also, consider your purpose for writing this essay. You may need to inform your readers about something they know little about, and you may want to express your feelings about your topic, but the primary purpose of an essay that argues a position is persuasive. Are you trying to persuade your readers to change their minds about some aspect of the media or to do something about it? What do you want them to think? To do? Knowing your purpose will help you stay focused and make it more likely that your essay will succeed.

WRITING ACTIVITY 1: Analyze Your Audience and Purpose

Your responses to the following questions will help you decide how to approach your topic.

1. Consider the readers of your campus newspaper. How old do they tend to be? Approximately how many are male, and how many are female? Outside of being students, what are their occupations and interests?

2. Consider the readers of your city newspaper. How old do they tend to be? Approximately how many readers are male, and how many are female? Give some examples of occupations and interests they might have.

3. What types of media do the readers of your campus newspaper typically use? Are these types of media the same or different from the kinds that the readers of your city newspaper might use?

4. What, if anything, do you know about your readers' political views? Would most readers have conservative, moderate, or liberal views? Give examples.

5. How interested would your readers be in an essay on the media? Explain your answer.

Gathering Ideas

To make sure that you choose a topic that works for you, take the time to gather ideas on each of the three possible topics for this essay — censorship, representation, and lifestyles. Even if you already have an

For more on gathering ideas, see pp. 12–16.

idea for a topic, it's good to experiment with other ideas so that you don't miss an even better one. The activities and examples in this chapter will focus on using freewriting, brainstorming, and consulting others, but you may also use any additional techniques for gathering ideas that work for you.

Freewriting about a Censorship Issue

Even though the U.S. Constitution guarantees freedom of expression, restrictions on the media have always existed. For example, the Federal Communications Commission (FCC) has always regulated the content of radio, film, and television. It applied morals codes to movies in the 1930s and recently fined television stations for indecency. School boards often remove controversial books (including *Huckleberry Finn* and *The Catcher in the Rye*) from library shelves and reading lists, and churches sometimes discourage their members from reading or watching certain books or movies. Most Internet providers offer to block sites (often of a sexual or violent nature) that might upset their customers, and parents can prevent their children from viewing materials they find objectionable or inappropriate.

What is your opinion about these kinds of restrictions? You may have strong feelings about censorship, or you may not be sure what you think. Freewriting can be a productive way to explore your thoughts and get a better sense of where you stand on the issue. As you know, to freewrite you simply write for five or ten minutes without trying to make sense of your thoughts. By letting your mind wander on the page, you can discover ideas you didn't know you had.

If you've had a personal experience with some kind of censorship, try writing about that for a few minutes and see where it leads you. If you're stuck for ideas, you might explore your reactions to any of the following questions:

- Should the government attempt to regulate material on the Internet? Why or why not?
- How effective are the rating systems used for movies and the warning labels on television shows and CDs? What change, if any, do you suggest?
- Should commercials aimed at young children be restricted? Explain your position.
- Should magazines that glorify certain body types (such as extreme thinness) be restricted so that young people can develop healthy self-images? If so, who or what should restrict them?

One student, Reginald, was interested in a controversy that erupted over an unpopular ad that ran in his college newspaper. Here is his freewriting on the issue:

A school newspaper ad states that blacks should not receive reparations (a method of making up for past injustices) for slavery. There
were ten reasons given for why blacks aren't entitled to damages
for the effects of slavery. As you can imagine, a lot of people were
really worked up about this ad and wanted the paper to apologize.
But the editor of the paper said that he wouldn't, stating freedom
of speech as his reason. Well, I don't agree with the ad, either, but
I agree with the editor that the paper doesn't have to apologize.

WRITING ACTIVITY 2: Freewrite about a Censorship Issue

Select a recent controversy about media censorship that interests
you, and freewrite about it for at least ten minutes. If nothing comes
to mind, you may use one or more of the questions on page 300 to
stimulate your thinking.

Brainstorming about a Representation Issue

Mass entertainment — music, gossip magazines, radio programs,
movies, television shows, video games, and the like — has always represented people in ways that at least some audience members have
considered unfair or unrealistic. In the early days of television, for
example, the typical American family was represented as a white
mother, father, and children who lived in a large house in a safe suburb.
Today, television families are depicted in a variety of ways. For another
example, consider shows and movies that feature college students.
Typically, the students are portrayed as being young and having a lot of
spare time on their hands. In fact, many college students are older and
are busy balancing work and family with school. What effect do inac-
curate portrayals, such as this one, have on viewers?

How are other groups of people portrayed by different kinds of
media? As a starting point, think about the following questions:

- Do you believe that song lyrics that are hostile to women or gay people
  affect the way that these people are treated in the real world?

- Do you agree with Samuel L. Jackson that today's movies portray
  minorities more realistically than earlier movies did?

- How do video games typically represent people? Can gamers
  develop a distorted view of the world as a result of how characters
  are depicted?

- What do you think of the ways that contestants are represented on
  reality television shows?

To explore ideas about media representations, pick one type of
media, and consider how it portrays different types of people. Then
brainstorm a list of thoughts and questions that occur to you. One

student, for example, was concerned about the ways that women were depicted in fashion magazines. Hillary brainstormed the following list of ideas:

Skinny, skinny
Girls with different ethnicities
Still very skinny
Plastic surgery
Models look unhappy
Some look like druggies
Girls try to be like the models
Clothes are beautiful
Very expensive
I know it's fantasy, but girls still try to copy
Can't do anything about it
I'm always on a diet
I'm affected by it even though I know better

WRITING ACTIVITY 3: Brainstorm about a Representation Issue

Pick a form of media that you enjoy (such as a particular TV show, movie, or Web site), and think about how people are represented on it. Brainstorm your thoughts about this issue.

Consulting Others about a Lifestyle Issue

As new media emerge and become popular, they often change how we live our lives from childhood to adulthood. On long car trips, for example, many parents now use portable movie systems to keep their children occupied. College students can take classes on the Web and never see their instructors or classmates in person. Online dating profiles allow people to search databases for possible partners with specific character traits — and to reject undesirable dates without ever speaking to them. Satellite radio services and podcasting have let busy audiences choose exactly what kinds of music, news, or commentary they want to hear and when they will listen to it.

To what extent are such changes beneficial? And to what extent are they damaging? You don't need to rely on only your own experiences to decide. To understand how such changes have affected other people, it makes sense to ask them some questions.

To consult with others, first decide what you want to know more about. For instance, if you're interested in knowing how much time college students spend instant messaging each other, you might want to survey your classmates, perhaps on your class listserv or Web site. If you're curious about the effect that advertising in schools has on children, you could interview an elementary school teacher. Prepare a few questions before you talk to this person, and keep careful notes of the discussion.

Student writer Marshall was concerned that using television to keep small children occupied might stunt their intellectual growth. To gather ideas on this topic, Marshall consulted with a friend, Miguel, who was studying for a master's degree in child development. In an e-mail message, Marshall asked Miguel what experts thought about children who watch a lot of television. Here is Miguel's response:

> Most child development experts think that many children are being exposed to too much media. Some researchers have shown that more and more children have TV sets and video games in their bedrooms, and 53 percent of children ages 8 to 18 report that their parents don't restrict their TV watching. Children whose parents don't limit TV viewing report that they read less than children whose parents restrict their viewing. They're also more likely to be overweight, and they have fewer friends. In general, in households with parents who monitor children's TV viewing, the children are better off.

WRITING ACTIVITY 4: Consult with Others about a Lifestyle Issue

After choosing a topic on the media and lifestyles that interests you, consult with at least two people who are knowledgeable about the topic. Ask your consultants to give their opinions and describe their experiences with the topic.

STEP 2. WRITE YOUR DISCOVERY DRAFT

At this point, you've gathered ideas for three possible media-related topics for your persuasive essay: censorship, representation, and lifestyles. You'll now choose one of these topics and write a discovery draft.

For more on drafting, see pp. 16–21.

Choosing a Topic

You have explored three different topics, but which one should you pick for your discovery draft? When deciding on a topic to write about, keep these three points in mind:

- Choose a topic that you're interested in and that you know something about. Your knowledge can come from your personal experiences, the experiences of others, your reflections and observations, and your reading on the topic.

- Choose a topic that is controversial and about which you have a strong opinion. Keep in mind that your primary purpose is to persuade your readers.

- Choose a topic that you think would interest your audience — readers of your campus or city newspaper.

If one of the topics you've already explored meets all three of these criteria, you're in a good position to start drafting. But if you're not completely happy with any of your ideas, consider gathering some more ideas, trying a new topic, or combining relating topics for your essay.

For more on thesis statements, see pp. 19–20.

Your topic should be narrow enough to be well developed in a short essay. For instance, if you want to write about lifestyle changes, you couldn't cover all the ways that the media have affected how we live. Instead, select just one medium and just one change.

WRITING ACTIVITY 5: Choose Your Topic

Review your responses to Writing Activities 1 to 4 and the three criteria for a good topic listed above. Then choose or create a topic for your essay, and narrow it as necessary. If you wish, you may gather additional ideas before you start drafting.

Sharing Your Ideas

Before writing your discovery draft, write a preliminary thesis statement that identifies the issue you are writing about and expresses your position on it.

As you write, follow your train of thought, even if it means that you'll need to revise your thesis statement later on. Keep your audience and purpose in mind, but remember that your main goal at the drafting stage is to get your ideas down on paper. You'll have time later on to revise and edit your draft.

Add First, Then Delete
During the drafting stage of your writing process, focus on adding ideas. Later on, during revision, use the Delete function to omit irrelevant material.

Here's a discovery draft written by a student, Reginald Jones, on the issue of censorship in his college newspaper. After reading the draft, discuss with your classmates what Reginald might do to revise it. (Note that the example includes the types of errors that typically appear in a first draft.)

An advertisement ran in last weeks school newspaper that shocked a number of students and faculty. The title was "Ten Reasons Why Reparations for Blacks Is a Bad Idea for Blacks--and Racist." The ad stated a number of reasons why blacks should not receive any damages for the effects of slavery. Some of the reasons given were that not all blacks have suffered because of slavery and that welfare and affirmative action has served as reparations. Boy, did this ad rile everyone! Some people wanted to burn all of the newspapers, some wanted an apology from the editor, and some said the paper should never have planned to run this ad in the first place. I don't like the ad and don't agree with what it says, but I do believe in freedom of speech. For this reason, I defend the right of the school newspaper to run this ad.

The constitution of the United States provides for freedom of expression. If we value our Constitution, then we must protect it even if it means protecting "hate speech."

Universities are supposed to be a place where ideas are debated. If we eliminate every piece of writing that someone finds offensive, we will no longer have a free exchange of ideas. There are many examples of books that people would like to ban. If colleges had to remove from the library shelves every book that was offensive to someone, there would be few books left!

Burning the newspapers would be a crime just as burning books is. There are better ways to protest. Students could run an ad themselves or write to the author of the ad.

Rather than burning newspapers or demanding an apology, they should discuss the ideas expressed in the ad and not just refuse to run it. We must attack these ideas with better ideas of our own.

> ## WRITING ACTIVITY 6: Write Your Discovery Draft
>
> Using your preliminary thesis statement and the ideas you've gathered on your topic, write a discovery draft. Keep in mind that your purpose is to express and support your opinion. If you're unsure about your topic, consider writing two or three discovery drafts on different topics to see which topic will work best for you.

STEP 3. REVISE YOUR DRAFT

For more on revising, see pp. 21–23.

When you revise your draft, use the skills you acquired in the preceding chapters: organize your paragraphs (Chapter 2), strengthen your focus (Chapter 4), outline your plan (Chapter 6), and write an effective introduction and conclusion (Chapter 5). Also, consider conducting primary or secondary research to gather more information about your topic (Chapter 6).

In this chapter, you'll focus on writing a persuasive argument. You'll learn how to develop your ideas with cause-and-effect analysis, make an argument claim, develop support for that claim, respond to opposing arguments, and organize your points.

Developing Your Ideas with Cause-and-Effect Analysis

For more on cause and effect, see p. 72.

When you use cause-and-effect analysis, you explain the reason that something happened (the cause) or the result of something that happened (the effect). For more on cause and effect, see p. 132. You use cause-and-effect analysis often in your daily life. You might notice that when your tires aren't correctly inflated (cause) your car gets worse gas mileage (effect). After starting to drink high-calorie smoothies every day for breakfast (cause), you discover you've gained a few pounds (effect). With cause-and-effect analysis, you can show your readers a logical connection between two or more events.

The writers of the three essays at the beginning of this chapter all use cause-and-effect analysis to develop their arguments. In "Let's Shut Them Down," Michael Crowley claims that one of the causes of criminal activity is the easy access of information on the Internet. Samuel L. Jackson suggests in "In Character" that the movies have become more ethnically diverse because filmmakers have grown more comfortable with multiculturalism in their own lives. Brent Staples, in "What Adolescents Miss When We Let Them Grow Up in Cyberspace," writes that too much time online causes teenagers to become socially isolated and unprepared for adulthood.

When you use cause-and-effect analysis to develop your argument, remember that there is a difference between cause and coincidence. To prove that there is a true relationship between events, give evidence — in the form of examples, statistics, or facts — to show how they are related. Draw on your personal experiences and knowledge and on the experiences and knowledge of people you know. You might also want to include expert testimony to support your points. Consider, for example, how Brent Staples uses facts and expert testimony to support his point in this paragraph from his essay:

> Online shopping, checking e-mail and Web surfing — mainly solitary activities — have turned out to be more isolating than watching television, which friends and family often do in groups. Researchers have found that the time spent in direct contact with family members drops by as much as half for every hour we use the Net at home.

These facts (the solitary activities) and the expert testimony (the findings of researchers) support Staples's claim that too much time in cyberspace stunts teenagers' emotional development.

HOW TO Use Cause-and-Effect Analysis

- Use cause and effect to show why something happened or what the result was when something happened.

- Show a logical connection between the cause and the effect.

- Use examples, fact, and expert testimony to support your analysis.

WRITING ACTIVITY 7: Draft Sentences Containing Cause-and-Effect Analysis for Your Essay

Write several sentences that contain cause-and-effect analysis for your essay. Refer to these sentences when you revise your draft.

Building Your Essay

To be persuasive, your essay must be well developed. In other words, it must contain supporting details that convince your readers that your position is valid. First, though, you need to make an effective claim.

Make a Claim

A *claim* is a statement asserting that something is true. In persuasive writing, a claim is a type of thesis statement. As you may recall from Chapter 1, the *thesis statement* announces the topic of your essay; shows, explains, or argues a particular point about the topic; and gives readers a sense of what you will discuss in your essay. For an argumentative essay, you announce your topic and the point that you will argue. Let's look at each of the qualities of an effective claim in more detail.

Express an Opinion. An effective claim expresses an opinion, not a fact. An *opinion* is an idea that some but not all people share. In contrast, a *fact* is something that can be verified as true by an objective observer.

FACT   There is a great deal of spam on the Internet.

OPINION   Because spam wastes people's time and money, it should be better regulated by the government.

The first statement can be verified by turning on a computer. There's no need to prove that it's true. The second statement, however, is a claim because some people will disagree with it. Notice that the claim includes the word *should.* Similar words used in claims include *needs to, ought,* and *must.*

Relate to Your Readers. An effective claim also seeks to persuade readers by pointing out how the topic relates to their lives. A claim that conveys only your personal interests, tastes, or experiences is not likely to persuade or interest readers. Rather, connect the claim to some aspect of your readers' lives.

PERSONAL   Drivers should be able to use cell phones when they drive because I've never been in danger when this has happened.

PERSUASIVE Drivers should be able to use cell phones when they drive because researchers have shown that this practice is no more dangerous than any other distraction, such as changing the channel on the radio.

The first statement focuses on the writer. But the second statement relates the topic — drivers' use of cell phones — to a concept relevant to readers' lives.

Narrow the Focus. An effective claim focuses the topic so that it can be fully developed and supported. If your claim isn't sufficiently focused, you won't be able to discuss it in detail in your essay.

UNFOCUSED	There's too much violence on television.
FOCUSED	The excessive use of guns on *Cops and Gangs* glamorizes a deadly use of force.

To support the claim made in the first example, you would have to cover all types of violence on all types of television shows — a large topic that would be better suited for a book than an essay. The second claim requires only that you focus on one type of violence (the use of guns) on one television show (*Cops and Gangs*). Because it's narrowly focused, this claim could be fully supported in an essay.

In addition, a focused claim does not leave readers with unanswered questions.

UNFOCUSED	Pornography should be banned.
FOCUSED	To prevent the sexual abuse of children, Congress should pass a law banning child pornography on the Internet.

In the first example, readers might ask: "What type of pornography? How should it be banned? Why should it be banned?" In the second, readers are told the type of pornography, how it could be banned (through federal legislation), and why it should be banned.

HOW TO Make a Claim

- Express an opinion.
- Be persuasive by relating the claim to readers' lives.
- Keep the claim narrowly focused.

WRITING ACTIVITY 8: Revise Your Claim

Revise the claim for your essay so that it expresses an opinion, relates to your readers' lives, and is sufficiently focused.

Provide Pro Points

Once you have an effective claim, you need to concentrate on developing support for that claim — your reasons or pro points (*pro* means "in favor of"). *Pro points* tell readers why you believe your claim is true or valid. Keep in mind that pro points should always be supported with details (such as examples, facts, and statistics) and that the best supporting material is up-to-date, relevant, and easily understood by readers.

Pro and con points are usually stated in topic sentences. For more on topic sentences, see pp. 38–42.

HOW TO Support Pro Points

- **Use recent material.** Because you're probably writing about a current issue, be sure to use supporting material that is up-to-date. By using recent material, you show your readers you're knowledgeable about your topic.

- **Use relevant material.** If your information isn't directly related to your topic, your readers will dismiss or ignore it. For example, if your topic is the portrayal of smoking in recent movies, don't use examples from 1950s television shows as support.

- **Use understandable material.** You probably know more about your topic than your readers do. You may need to explain the plot of a book, the meaning of a term, or the lyrics of a song to readers who are not familiar with the subject.

A brief argumentative essay will usually need between three and five pro points. You can generate and develop pro points from your experiences, observations, and research.

Experience. When trying to persuade others, we often look first to our own experiences with the topic. This is what Brent Staples does when he begins his essay by describing his encounter with his teenage girlfriend's father. Suppose, for example, that you're writing about obscene lyrics in rock music and that you believe the lyrics are harmless because listeners tend to focus on the music, not the words. Thus, you have one pro point:

```
Because most listeners focus on the music and not
the words, obscene lyrics in rock music don't harm
listeners.
```

How would you support this pro point? You could detail your own experiences with music. For instance, you could point out that you don't know the lyrics to your favorite song. However, keep in mind that what might be true for you may not be true for others.

Observation. Personal experiences alone are not enough to support an argument convincingly. Your observations of how the issue has affected others can also lead to pro points. In the essay "In Character," part of Samuel L. Jackson's argument is based on his observations of obstacles that other ethnic actors and producers encounter in the movie business. Imagine, for instance, that you're arguing against censoring literature in high schools. Books weren't censored in your high school, but your cousin attended a school that banned several classics, including John Steinbeck's *Of Mice and Men* and George Orwell's *1984*. Because your cousin was unable to study these books in school, she was poorly prepared for her college entrance exams. From observing your cousin's experiences, you generate this pro point:

```
Censoring important works of literature can limit
students' opportunities in higher education.
```

You can support this point by describing your cousin's experience with censorship. However, what happened to your cousin might not happen to everyone, and unless your cousin is still in high school, her example might not be up-to-date. Thus, to strengthen your case, you could interview other students about their experiences with censorship or conduct research to collect facts and statistics that support your position.

Research. As we have seen, you will usually want to conduct some research on your topic to strengthen points gathered from your own experiences and observations. To argue for more regulation of Web sites, for example, Michael Crowley interviewed a national security expert and a private citizen who posted controversial material on the Internet. Perhaps you're arguing that cable television companies should fund community-access television because it provides a necessary forum for groups that are misrepresented or ignored by the mainstream media. You could interview producers, question viewers, or look for information about the kinds of programming that are available only on community-access TV. From your research, you might generate the following pro point:

```
Because commercial television news programs present
few positive portrayals of immigrant neighborhoods,
cable TV providers should use some of their profits to
give community groups access to production equipment
and free air time.
```

To support this pro point, you could provide information about the cable company's budget or describe a cable-access show that focuses on a community rarely seen in network news.

Use a Newsgroup

Consider joining a *newsgroup,* or Internet bulletin board, that focuses on issues related to your topic. For a list of newsgroups on various topics, refer to http://groups.google.com. Before using information from these sources, be sure that it is reliable.

GROUP ACTIVITY 2: Evaluate Supporting Material

Working in a group, examine the following claim. Determine whether the supporting material given for it is up-to-date, relevant, and easily understandable.

> CLAIM   The current rating system for movies needs to be improved.

1. More and more television shows are showing scenes of graphic violence.
2. Owners of movie theaters are reluctant to enforce the current rating system.
3. In 1995, half of all profitable movies contained sexually oriented material.
4. The profit margin for R-rated movies is almost 21 percent of all movies when aggregated.
5. When I sold movie tickets, I almost never checked people's IDs.
6. Movie producers avoid the R rating by making two versions of the same movie: a mild version for movie theaters and an explicit version for video stores.

WRITING ACTIVITY 9: List and Support Your Pro Points

Review the pro points in your discovery draft. Are they sufficient? Are they effectively developed? Draw on your experiences, observations, and research to add additional pro points if you need them, and make sure that each point is supported by recent, relevant, and understandable information.

Generate Pro Points

If you have a class listserv or Internet discussion group, you can post your claim and ask fellow students to suggest pro points in support of it. Refer to your classmates' ideas when revising your essay.

Respond to Con Points

An argument essay is most persuasive when you anticipate readers' objections and argue against them. Therefore, in addition to presenting pro points, you need to argue against the *con points* (*con* means "against"). To do this, put yourself in the place of the readers who might not agree with your pro points. Con points tell readers why someone might object to your claim, how these objections might be stated, and how you would respond to them.

List Con Points. First, you need to identify the most important con points against your claim. To do this, imagine that you disagree with your claim, and then think of reasons you might disagree with it. Suppose that this is your claim:

```
Companies that send unwanted spam e-mails and pop-up
advertisements should be heavily taxed and regulated
so they'll go out of business.
```

Now imagine that you disagree with this claim — that you think the government should leave these companies alone. Here are two reasons:

```
Although these companies are annoying, they still have a
right to exist.
If the government starts regulating these companies, it
can start regulating other companies as well, which
isn't right in a free-market economy.
```

These are your con points — the points that someone might make against the claim that you are making. List just the most important con points. Depending on your topic, you might end up with two or three con points.

Refute Con Points. Examine your list of con points, and consider how you would respond to readers' objections. You want to *refute,* or argue against, the con points so that you can persuade readers to accept your claim. First, acknowledge what, if anything, is true about the con point, and then explain what you think is not true about it.

Let's continue the example about spam and pop-up advertisements on the Internet. Here's your first con point:

```
Although these companies are annoying, they still
have a right to exist.
```

Here's what you can say to *refute,* or argue against, this point:

```
At times, annoyances can't be avoided. This is not
one of those times. Because the spam and pop-ups are
so numerous, individuals and companies have to spend
a lot of money and time to get rid of them, which
hurts productivity and the economy.
```

Here's your second con point:

```
If the government starts regulating these companies,
it can start regulating other companies as well,
which isn't right in a free-market economy.
```

Here's one way to refute this con point:

> Even a free-market economy needs some regulation to
> protect consumers. By taxing and regulating spam and
> pop-ups, we can protect consumers, just as we already
> protect consumers by outlawing false advertisements
> and regulating drugs.

As these examples show, when you refute your con points, you're actually arguing in support of your pro points.

WRITING ACTIVITY 10: List and Refute Your Con Points

Read your claim aloud to the students in your group. Ask them to disagree with your claim and to explain their reasons. List their responses, and use them as the con points for your claim. Refute each con point in writing (you will use them when you revise your draft).

Debate on a Computer
If your class has access to a computer terminal as a group, try holding a debate onscreen. Identify your claim and one pro point. Leave the screen on. Ask other students to read what you have posted and to respond to your claim by adding a pro point, adding a con point, or refuting a con point.

If you're in a class where students are online simultaneously, participate in an online debate. This online exchange can give you the opportunity to think about your pro and con points before you include them in your essay.

Organize Pro and Con Points

Now that you've developed the ideas in your draft, you're ready to begin organizing those ideas. If you order your pro and con points in a logical way, your readers will become more convinced of your claim as they read your essay.

Order Pro Points. Some of your pro points will be more persuasive than others. Save your most convincing pro point for last so that you leave readers thinking about it. You might begin a paper with the least convincing pro point and build up to the most convincing one. Or you might begin with the second most convincing point, place the less convincing points in the middle, and end with the most convincing one.

Arrange Con Points. Where should you put the con points? You have several options. You may put con points at different spots in an essay, particularly when certain con points are closely connected to certain pro points. This pattern can help make the pro and con points flow smoothly in an essay. You may also begin an essay with the con points. After refuting them, give your pro points. Finally, you may save your con points until the end of the essay but only when you can refute those points well. You don't want readers to finish your essay agreeing with the opposition.

HOW TO Organize Pro and Con Points

Pro points

- Save your most convincing pro point for last.

  OR

- Begin your essay with the least convincing pro point, and build up to the most convincing point.

  OR

- Begin with a fairly strong point, put the weaker points in the middle, and end with the strongest point.

Con points

- Connect each con point to the related pro point.

  OR

- Begin with con points, and then refute them with pro points.

  OR

- Save con points for near the end of the essay, and refute them all at one time.

GROUP ACTIVITY 3: Order Pro and Con Points

Review Reginald's discovery draft on page 305. Working in a group, list his pro points, and then create several con points. Put these pro and con points in the order that you think is the most effective. Finally, compare your group's ordering of the pro and con points with the order that Reginald uses in his revised draft (pp. 316–18). Notice how Reginald improved his pro and con points in the revised draft.

Move Your Pro and Con Points
Use the Cut-and-Paste function of your word processor to create several different lists of your pro and con points. Compare the various lists to determine the most effective ordering of the points for your revised draft.

WRITING ACTIVITY 11: Order Your Pro and Con Points

Think about the pro and con points for your essay about the media. List your pro points in the order in which they should appear in your revised draft. Then decide where you can include your con points, and add them to your list.

A Student's Revised Draft

Student writer Reginald Jones was relatively happy with his discovery draft about censorship in his campus newspaper, but his classmates weren't as persuaded by his argument as he thought they'd be. With their help, he added support for his pro points and identified con points that he needed to address. Before you read Reginald's revised draft, reread his discovery draft (p. 305). Notice how his argument is stronger in the revision. (You will also notice some errors in the revised draft; these will be corrected when Reginald edits his essay later on.)

Newspaper Ad Sparks Controversy

The introduction is more interesting.

An advertisement, "Ten Reasons Why Reparations for Blacks Is a Bad Idea for Blacks--and Racist" ran in last weeks school newspaper. A reparation is a repayment for damage done in the past. This ad stated a number of reasons why blacks should not receive repayments from the United States government because of the damages done by slavery. Some of the reasons given were that not all blacks have suffered because of slavery and that welfare and affirmative action has served as reparations. This ad, which some call a "hate" ad, upset a number of students and faculty. Some people wanted to burn all of the newspapers, some wanted a formal apology from the editor, and some said the paper should never have planned to run the ad in the first place. As a supporter of freedom of speech, I defend the right of the school newspaper to run this ad whether I agree with it or not.

The claim is more specific.

The editor of the school newspaper doesn't have to apologize for this ad. Because the Constitution of the United States provides for freedom of expression. The First Amendment to the Constitution states, "Congress shall make no law respecting an establishment of religion, or prohibiting the free exercise thereof; or abridging the freedom of speech, or of the press; or the right of the people peaceably to assemble, and to petition the Government for a redress of grievances." Linda Chavez, a writer for Creators Syndicate, says that "the reparations debate has the potential of replacing affirmative action as the most volatile race issue in America, with Americans deeply divided on the topic" (6A). If we value our Constitution, then we must protect it even if that means using our campus newspapers as the showcase for both sides of an issue.

A strong pro point comes first.

A pro point is supported with expert testimony.

Universities are supposed to be a place where ideas are debated. However, when David Horowitz, the founder of the Center for the Study of Popular Culture, requested ad space in 71 campus newspapers, only 21 would run the ad (Chavez 6A). This is unfortunate, if we eliminate every piece of writing that someone finds offensive, we will no longer have a free exchange of ideas. There are many examples of books that people would like to ban. Most recently, some people have called for the banning of the Harry Potter series of books because of their focus on wizardry and witchcraft. Some computer labs attempt to block students from visiting pornographic Web sites. If colleges remove every book and Web site that someone finds offensive, the free exchange of ideas would become nonexistent.

A second pro point is supported by facts and observations.

Cause and effect are used.

To those students who propose burning the newspapers, I remind them that this would be a crime. We don't want to encourage people to commit crimes just to ban material that make them uncomfortable. There are better ways to protest. Students could run an ad themselves explaining their views on the topic of reparations for blacks, or they could write to the author of the ad to protest his views. The topic has been debated as part of Black History Month activities. This has happened on our campus. We have set up debates and had students present both sides of the reparation argument.

A con point is refuted.

A third pro point is supported by observation.

A fourth pro point is supported by expert testimony.

Rather than burning newspapers or demanding an apology, they should discuss the ideas expressed in the ad and not just refuse to run it. We must attack these ideas with ideas that are even stronger. Joan Bertin of the National Coalition against Censorship says, "While student protests are an appropriate way to explore controversy, when students take it upon themselves to suppress ideas that they find objectionable they fail to meet the challenge of a free society--to counter offensive ideas with more persuasive arguments of their own" (par. 4). We

A con point is refuted.

recently had a campus debate. We concluded that reparations are not likely to occur and that the discussion of them only divides Americans.

The conclusion restates the claim.

As students and teachers, we must protect freedom of expression even if it means permitting some advertisements that we don't like to appear in our school newspapers. Instead of attempting to ban these advertisements, we must come up with constructive ways to encourage debate on the content of the ads themselves.

Works Cited

Bertin, Joan. "Free Speech Groups Express Concern
    over Student Reaction to Controversial Ad."
    NCAC. National Coalition against Censorship,
    1 Mar. 2002. Web. 3 Mar. 2002.
Chavez, Linda. "Reparations Issue Could Be Divisive."
    El Paso Times 3 Mar. 2002: 6A. Print.

GROUP ACTIVITY 4: Analyze Reginald's Revised Draft

Use the following questions to discuss with your classmates how Reginald has improved his draft.

1. Is Reginald's claim more effective now? Why or why not?
2. How has Reginald improved his pro points?
3. How well has he refuted his con points?
4. In your view, how well does he organize his pro and con points?
5. How could Reginald's draft benefit from further revision?

WRITING ACTIVITY 12: Peer Review

Form a group with two or three other students, and exchange copies of your drafts. Read your draft aloud while your classmates follow along. Take notes on your classmates' responses to the following questions about your draft.

1. What do you like best about my essay?
2. How interesting is my introduction? Do you want to continue reading the essay? Why or why not?
3. How effective is my claim? Suggest an improvement.
4. How well do I support my pro points? Is my supporting material recent, relevant, and easily understood?
5. How well do I refute the con points?
6. Are my pro and con points effectively organized? Can you suggest a better way to order them?
7. Where in the draft does my writing confuse you? How can I clarify my thoughts?
8. How clear is the purpose of my essay?

Use Online Peer Review
If your class has a Web site with peer review questions listed, you may be able to respond to your classmates' drafts electronically.

WRITING ACTIVITY 13: Revise Your Draft

Taking your classmates' suggestions for revision into consideration, revise your essay. Focus on using cause-and-effect analysis, making your claim more specific, supporting your pro points, refuting your con points, and organizing these points.

STEP 4. EDIT YOUR SENTENCES

At this point, you have worked hard to improve your essay's claim, development, and organization. Before it's ready to be sent to your campus or city newspaper, you need to edit it to polish the language and eliminate distracting errors. In this section, you'll focus on combining sentences with introductory phrases and on correcting subject-verb agreement errors.

Combining Sentences Using Introductory Phrases

As you know from previous chapters, sentence combining is a good way to connect closely related, short sentences. Sentence combining can make your writing clearer and more interesting.

One way to combine short, closely related sentences is to turn one of those sentences into an introductory phrase for the other. A *phrase* is a group of words that lacks a subject, a verb, or both. It cannot stand alone as a sentence. When you combine sentences with an introductory phrase, follow the phrase with a comma.

In Reginald's discovery draft, for example, he wrote two sentences to describe his opinion of the ad:

```
I don't like the ad and don't agree with what it
says, but I do believe in freedom of speech. For this
reason, I defend the right of the school newspaper to
run this ad.
```

In his revised draft, he combined these two sentences by using an introductory phrase and eliminating unnecessary words to create a stronger thesis statement:

```
As a supporter of freedom of speech, I defend the
right of the school newspaper to run this ad whether
I agree with it or not.
```

HOW TO Combine Sentences Using Introductory Phrases

- Combine two short, closely related sentences by turning the sentence with the least important information into a phrase (a group of words that lacks a subject, verb, or both).

- Place the phrase at the beginning of the remaining sentence.

- Use a comma after the introductory phrase.

EDITING ACTIVITY 1: Combine Sentences Using Introductory Phrases

Use an introductory phrase to combine the following pairs or groups of sentences. You may need to eliminate unnecessary words, change words, or move words around.

EXAMPLE   Started in 2001,
Wikipedia is an online, interactive encyclopedia. It was

started in 2001.

1. Its founder was Jimmy Wales. He wanted to create an encyclopedia that everyone on the planet could access for free.

2. Anyone can create an entry or edit an entry that already exists. Wikipedia uses software called wiki.

3. Hundreds of thousands of people contribute to Wikipedia. These contributors come from a variety of backgrounds.

4. Some people prefer to correct or change information that is already posted to the site. They don't actually add information.

5. Some researchers have studied the entries in Wikipedia. They have found that it contains more errors than traditional encyclopedias such as *Britannica*. Some of these errors are major.

Exercise Central
For additional practice with combining sentences, go to **bedfordstmartins.com/choices** and click on "Exercise Central."

WRITING ACTIVITY 14: Combine Your Sentences

Examine your revised draft for short, closely related sentences. Where it makes sense to do so, combine them with introductory phrases. You may also use any of the other sentence-combining techniques you have learned (coordinating conjunctions, conjunctive adverbs, subordinating conjunctions, or relative clauses) if you wish.

Correcting Subject-Verb Agreement Problems

You may recall that a complete sentence contains a subject and a verb. The subject tells who or what is doing the action, and the verb tells the action or links the subject to the rest of the sentence. The subject and the verb must *agree* in number. In other words, a *singular subject* must have a *singular verb*, and a *plural subject* must have a *plural verb*.

To make sure that your subjects and verbs agree in number, you need to identify the subject of your sentence and know whether it is singular or plural. Problems in subject-verb agreement often happen when the subject and verb of the sentence are not obvious.

INCORRECT	*Harry don't* care for my podcasts.
CORRECT	*Harry doesn't* care for my podcasts.
INCORRECT	Talk show *hosts* on the radio *is* meaner than they were a decade ago.
CORRECT	Talk show *hosts* on the radio *are* meaner than they were a decade ago.

The following pronouns are all singular. When using any of them as the subject of a sentence, use a singular verb.

anybody	everything	somebody
anyone	nobody	someone
anything	no one	something
everybody	everyone	nothing

INCORRECT	*Anybody write* better than I do.
CORRECT	*Anybody writes* better than I do.
INCORRECT	*Someone need* to take care of this.
CORRECT	*Someone needs* to take care of this.

EDITING ACTIVITY 2: Correct Subject-Verb Agreement Problems

Circle the correct form of the verb in the following sentences.

EXAMPLE   Everybody (needs, need) to be considerate of others in public places.

1. The movie I wanted to rent (has, have) been checked out.
2. Nobody (feel, feels) the way I do about WiFi hotspots.
3. Of all the bands I listen to, my favorite one (is, are) Red House Painters.
4. Everyone I talk to (agrees, agree) with me on this.
5. The Chicago Bears (doesn't, don't) excite me.

Exercise Central

For additional practice correcting subject-verb agreement problems, go to **bedfordstmartins.com/choices** and click on "Exercise Central."

WRITING ACTIVITY 15: Edit Your Essay

Using the Handbook in Part Four of this book as a guide, edit your revised draft for errors in grammar, spelling, and punctuation. Your classmates can help you locate and correct errors you might have overlooked.

Switch Terminals to Edit

If your class has access to a computer terminal as a group, ask several classmates to read your essay on the computer terminal and to boldface the errors they find. The more student readers you enlist to help you spot errors in your draft, the more error-free it will be. If necessary, consult your instructor, a tutor, or the Handbook in Part Four of this book to verify the errors and help you correct them.

A Student's Edited Essay

You may have noticed that Reginald's revised draft contained errors in grammar, spelling, and punctuation. Reginald corrected these errors in his edited essay. His corrections are underlined here.

Reginald Jones
Professor Heller
English 1301
4 Mar. 2006

The correct MLA format is used.

Newspaper Ad Sparks Controversy

An advertisement, "Ten Reasons Why Reparations for Blacks Is a Bad Idea for Blacks--and Racist" ran in last <u>week's</u> school newspaper. A reparation is a repayment for damage done in the past. This ad stated a number of reasons why blacks should not receive repayments from the United States government because of the damages done by slavery. Some of the reasons given were that not all blacks have suffered because of slavery and that welfare and affirmative action <u>have</u> served as reparations. This ad, which some call a "hate" ad, upset a number of students and faculty. Some people wanted to burn all of the newspapers, some wanted a formal apology from the editor, and

An apostrophe is corrected.

A subject-verb agreement problem is corrected.

some said the paper should never have run the ad in the first place. Linda Chavez, a writer for Creators Syndicate, says that "the reparations debate has the potential of replacing affirmative action as the most volatile race issue in America, with Americans deeply divided on the topic" (6A). If we value our Constitution, then we must protect it even if that means using our campus newspapers as the showcase for both sides of an issue. As a supporter of freedom of speech, I defend the right of the school newspaper to run this ad whether I agree with it or not.

A sentence fragment is corrected.

Because the Constitution of the United States provides for freedom of expression, the editor of the school newspaper doesn't have to apologize for this ad. The First Amendment to the Constitution states, "Congress shall make no law respecting an establishment of religion, or prohibiting the free exercise thereof; or abridging the freedom of speech, or of the press; or the right of the people peaceably to assemble, and to petition the Government for a redress of grievances."

A comma splice is corrected.

Universities are supposed to be a place where ideas are debated. However, when David Horowitz, the founder of the Center for the Study of Popular Culture, requested ad space in 71 campus newspapers, only 21 would run the ad (Chavez 6A). This is unfortunate. If we eliminate every piece of writing that someone finds offensive, we will no longer have a free exchange of ideas. There are many examples of books that people would like to ban. Most recently, some people have called for the banning of the Harry Potter series of books because of their focus on wizardry and witchcraft. Some computer labs attempt to block students from visiting pornographic Web sites. If colleges remove every book and Web site that someone finds offensive, the free exchange of ideas would become nonexistent.

A subject-verb agreement problem is corrected.

To those students who propose burning the newspapers, I remind them that this would be a crime. We don't want to encourage people to commit crimes just to ban material that makes them uncomfortable. There are better ways to protest. Students could run an ad themselves explaining their views on the topic of reparations for blacks, or they could write to the author of the ad to protest his views. <u>On our campus, the topic has been debated as part of Black History Month activities.</u> We have set up debates and had students present both sides of the reparation argument.

A sentence is combined.

Rather than burning newspapers or demanding an apology, <u>students</u> should discuss the ideas expressed in the ad and not just refuse to run it. We must attack these ideas with ideas that are even stronger. Joan Bertin of the National Coalition against Censorship says, "While student protests are an appropriate way to explore controversy, when students take it upon themselves to suppress ideas that they find objectionable they fail to meet the challenge of a free society--to counter offensive ideas with more persuasive arguments of their own" (par. 4). <u>At our most recent campus debate, we concluded that reparations are not likely to occur and that the discussion of them only divides Americans.</u>

A vague pronoun reference is corrected.

A sentence is combined.

As students and teachers, we must protect freedom of expression even if it means permitting some advertisements that we don't like to appear in our school newspapers. Instead of attempting to ban these advertisements, we must come up with constructive ways to encourage debate on the content of the ads themselves.

Works Cited

Bertin, Joan. "Free Speech Groups Express Concern over Student Reaction to Controversial Ad." *NCAC*. National Coalition against Censorship, 1 Mar. 2002. Web. 3 Mar. 2002.

Chavez, Linda. "Reparations Issue Could Be Divisive." *El Paso Times* 3 Mar. 2002: 6A. Print.

STEP 5. SHARE YOUR ESSAY

Now that you have gathered ideas on your topic and drafted, revised, and edited your essay, you're ready to share your essay. In addition to sharing it with your instructor and classmates, submit it to your campus or local newspaper. If your essay is about something that most college students are familiar with, such as downloading music or using cell phones in classrooms, your campus newspaper might be most appropriate. If your topic is about something with a broader appeal, such as censoring Web sites, your city newspaper might be best. By submitting your essay for publication, you can reach a wide audience and influence more people.

Submit Your Essay Online
Most newspapers have Web sites that allow you to submit essays online. Be sure to follow the site's directions so that the editor receives your writing.

CHAPTER CHECKLIST

- ❑ I used cause-and-effect analysis, as well as other methods of development, to support my ideas.
- ❑ I wrote an effective claim that expresses an opinion, relates to my readers' lives, and is focused.
- ❑ I used pro points — which came from experiences, observations, and research — to support my claim.
- ❑ I supported pro points with material that is recent, relevant, and easily understood.
- ❑ I refuted or argued against con points, or objections, to a claim.
- ❑ I arranged pro and con points so that readers become more convinced of my claim as they read through my essay.
- ❑ I combined short, closely related sentences using introductory phrases or other techniques to improve my flow of ideas.
- ❑ I edited my draft to correct errors, including problems with subject-verb agreement.

REFLECTING ON YOUR WRITING

To help you reflect on the writing you did in this chapter, answer the following questions:

1. How did you decide on your topic for this essay?
2. Which pro point do you think is your strongest?

3. How persuasive do you think your essay would be to someone who strongly disagrees with your claim?

4. How did you feel submitting your essay to your campus or city newspaper?

5. If you had more time, what more would you do to improve your essay before sharing it with readers?

Using your answers to these questions, complete a Writing Process Report for this chapter (you can download a report form at **bedford stmartins.com/choices**). Once you complete this report, freewrite about what you learned in this chapter.

ADDITIONAL READINGS

A Censorship Issue

JUDY BLUME

Is Harry Potter Evil?

In the following essay, Judy Blume, author of dozens of classic chil-
dren's books, presents her position on a controversy surrounding the
Harry Potter series. Blume is familiar with censorship because several
of her own books were censored when they were first published. In addi-
tion to selling millions of books for children and adults, Blume sits on
the board of directors for the National Coalition Against Censorship.

I happened to be in London last summer on the very day 1
Harry Potter and the Prisoner of Azkaban, the third book in the
wildly popular series by J. K. Rowling, was published. I couldn't
believe my good fortune. I rushed to the bookstore to buy a
copy, knowing this simple act would put me up there with the
best grandmas in the world. The book was still months away
from publication in the United States, and I have an 8-year-old
grandson who is a big Harry Potter fan.

It's a good thing when children enjoy books, isn't it? Most of 2
us think so. But like many children's books these days, the
Harry Potter series has recently come under fire. In Minnesota,
Michigan, New York, California and South Carolina, parents
who feel the books promote interest in the occult have called
for their removal from classrooms and school libraries.

I knew this was coming. The only surprise is that it took so 3
long — as long as it took for the zealots who claim they're protecting children from evil (and evil can be found lurking everywhere
these days) to discover that children actually like these books. If
children are excited about a book, it must be suspect.

I'm not exactly unfamiliar with this line of thinking, having 4
had various books of mine banned from schools over the last 20
years. In my books, it's reality that's seen as corrupting. With
Harry Potter, the perceived danger is fantasy. After all, Harry
and his classmates attend the celebrated Hogwarts School of
Witchcraft and Wizardry. According to certain adults, these stories teach witchcraft, sorcery and satanism. But hey, if it's not
one "ism," it's another. I mean Madeleine L'Engle's *A Wrinkle in*
Time has been targeted by censors for promoting New Ageism,
and Mark Twain's *Adventures of Huckleberry Finn* for promoting racism. Gee, where does that leave the kids?

The real danger is not in the books, but in laughing off ⁵ those who would ban them. The protests against Harry Potter follow a tradition that has been growing since the early 1980's and often leaves school principals trembling with fear that is then passed down to teachers and librarians.

What began with the religious right has spread to the politi- ⁶ cally correct. (Remember the uproar in Brooklyn last year when a teacher was criticized for reading a book entitled *Nappy Hair* to her class?) And now the gate is open so wide that some parents believe they have the right to demand immediate removal of any book for any reason from school or classroom libraries. The list of gifted teachers and librarians who find their jobs in jeopardy for defending their students' right to read, to imagine, to question, grows every year.

My grandson was bewildered when I tried to explain why ⁷ some adults don't want their children reading about Harry Potter. "But that doesn't make any sense!" he said. J. K. Rowling is on a book tour in America right now. She's probably befuddled by the brouhaha, too. After all, she was just trying to tell a good story.

My husband and I like to reminisce about how, when we ⁸ were 9, we read straight through L. Frank Baum's *Oz* series, books filled with wizards and witches. And you know what those subversive tales taught us? That we loved to read! In those days I used to dream of flying. I may have been small and powerless in real life, but in my imagination I was able to soar.

At the rate we're going, I can imagine next year's headline: ⁹ "*Goodnight Moon* Banned for Encouraging Children to Communicate with Furniture." And we all know where that can lead, don't we?

READING ACTIVITY 7: Build Your Vocabulary

Determine the meanings of the following words from the context of Judy Blume's essay. Then check their meanings by looking up the words in a dictionary: occult (2), zealots (3), suspect (3), sorcery (4), bewildered (7), befuddled (7), brouhaha (7), subversive (8).

READING ACTIVITY 8: Read to Improve Your Writing

Discuss the following questions about "Is Harry Potter Evil?" with your classmates.

1. What is Blume's claim or position on banning Harry Potter books from school libraries?
2. Blume states, "I knew this was coming" (par. 3). How did she know?
3. What does Blume identify as the real danger? Do you agree or disagree with her point?
4. How effective is Blume's argument? How could she improve it?

A Representation Issue

MARK ANDREJEVIC

"Reality" Camera Goes from Candid to Cruel

Candid Camera, *a popular television show that aired from 1960 to 1966 and that can still be seen in reruns today, was one of the first reality TV shows. In this show, unsuspecting people were filmed while a practical joke was played on them. The relative harmlessness of* Candid Camera, *however, has given way to a much harsher treatment of some reality-show participants, as Mark Andrejevic, a professor at the University of Iowa, explains in "'Reality' Camera Goes from Candid to Cruel."*

Reality TV is becoming more and more like reality itself on a bad day — almost impossible to escape and increasingly cruel. From the Sci-Fi Channel's *Scare Tactics* to MTV's *Punk'd,* the latest round of shows has turned to a time-tested strategy for breaking through the façade: the ambush. 1

One of the oldest reality formats around, *Candid Camera,* was a pioneer in the use of comparatively tame practical jokes played on unwitting victims. More recently, investigative journalism has demonstrated the importance of the ambush in getting at the truth. 2

But in a world in which undercover reporting has been replaced by a fascination with what's going on under the covers, we are no longer titillated by the spectacle of Mike Wallace ambushing wrongdoers. 3

Instead, we're tickled by a snide Shannen Doherty or a snickering Ashton Kutcher preying on hapless innocents (at least in part — Kutcher mercifully targets celebrities, who, in a way, asked for it). The current spate of prank shows exhibits a palpably vicious edge, summed up by the attitude of *Crank Yankers,* a Comedy Central show in which puppets act out crank phone calls. The goal is not to delight in the humorous foibles of people who don't realize they're being watched but to instill true terror and then burst in at the last moment with a laugh to let the victims know that they should be delighted because, after all, they're going to be on TV. 4

In one skit on Doherty's show, *Scare Tactics,* an unsuspecting man is lured into a fake biohazard zone and ambushed by men in hazmat suits warning that he has been exposed to dangerous materials and needs to strip to his underwear so he can be sprayed with foam. In another, a man watches as his friend, who is in on the gag, succumbs, bloodily, to a fatal parasite and 5 is taken away by paramedics. The victim is informed that he has likely been exposed to the same parasite, and the camera zooms in as he starts to look ill while the paramedic tells him that the symptoms are setting in.

We know that the agony of the victims is real because these people, unlike the buff and bronzed cast of CBS's *Survivor,* didn't even ask to be on TV. Indeed, if they knew what they were going to have to go through, they might well have passed on their 15 minutes. Such is the case of Thea Robinson, an out-of-work California woman who is suing the WB Network's *The Jamie Kennedy Experiment* after a trip to a restaurant for a job interview from hell.   6

Plenty of reality shows, including NBC's *Fear Factor,* thrive on sadistic challenges as a means of extracting authentic emotion from cast members. But even real people may be trying to play a part when they're in front of the camera. It's a different story when they gag on roasted rat or vomit or bleed. They're not just acting anymore. They're providing a bit of unscripted reality.   7

Ambush shows have the additional twist of showing up their innocent victims as dupes — and then forcing them to have a sense of humor about it. This is the strongest element of their appeal to a terminally hip audience.   8

The constant struggle is to retain one's savviness in the face of relentless media hype, political propaganda, and the metastasis of marketing and advertising appeals. The appeal of the real appears against the background of an increasingly mediated world — one in which we constantly have to be on guard to avoid the fate of the fool.   9

Ambush shows invite us, the viewers, to side with the manipulators and to see the real dupe as the poor sap dancing around in his underwear to get the ostensibly contaminated clothes away from his skin. In on the joke from the start, the viewer is placed, ever so briefly, in the privileged position of the insider — an increasingly inaccessible one in the real world (if not in reality TV), where power and wealth are becoming concentrated in the hands of a shrinking few.   10

At the same time, the "gotcha" scene, at the climax of every segment when the pranksters reveal themselves, provides a moment of release from a threatening reality. In an era of multiplying anxieties, it's nice to imagine a world in which, at the very moment when things seem to have gone terribly awry, a well-known face might just step out from behind the scenes to tell us that it was all just a big joke.   11

And as long as we get it, we're no longer the dupes, are we?   12

READING ACTIVITY 9: Build Your Vocabulary

Determine the meanings of the following words from the context of Mark Andrejevic's essay. Then check their meanings by looking up the words in a dictionary: façade (1), ambush (1), unwitting (2), titillated (3), hapless (4), foibles (4), sadistic (7), savviness (9), relentless (9), metastasis (9), mediated (9), awry (11).

READING ACTIVITY 10: Read to Improve Your Writing

Discuss the following questions about "'Reality' Camera Goes from Candid to Cruel" with your classmates.

1. What is Andrejevic's main point in this essay? State this in your own words.
2. List several of the author's pro points.
3. Where in the essay does Andrejevic use cause-and-effect analysis?
4. Explain in your own words the last sentence of the essay: "And as long as we get it, we're no longer the dupes, are we?"
5. What is your own opinion about this topic?

A Lifestyle Issue

JANNA MALAMUD SMITH

Online but Not Antisocial

New technology is often controversial, and the Internet is no exception. Brent Staples, in "What Adolescents Miss When We Let Them Grow Up in Cyberspace" (pp. 295–97), writes about what he perceives to be the dangers of cyberspace. In contrast, Janna Malamud Smith, a psychotherapist and writer, sees more positive aspects to spending time online. In "Online but Not Antisocial," she responds to critics such as Staples by arguing that sometimes being online instead of being with people can be a good thing.

The Internet is a member of our family. According to my   1
monthly bill, each of us spent about 5.4 hours a week online, which makes us pretty much average American Net users. I can't speak for the rest of my family, but I relish my online time. A new study tells me that I should feel bad about that. Bourbon, red meat, whole milk and the Internet, too?

According to the study, by Norman Nie, a political scientist   2
at Stanford University, the Web makes us even lonelier and more isolated than we already are. "The more hours people use the Internet, the less time they spend with real human beings," Professor Nie said. There is a danger, he claimed, of worsening social isolation and creating a deadened and atomized world without human emotion.

Could that be possible? Or are we perhaps confusing the 3
bandage with the wound? For starters, it seems that Professor
Nie is assuming that hours with real human beings are an
unqualified good thing. Call me a curmudgeon, but I often find
them to be something of a mixed bag.

Did I miss fighting the shopping mall crowds this Christmas 4
to buy one of my sons a hat he had really wanted? Not at all.
Spending 15 minutes online as opposed to two hours (mini-
mum) searching for parking, then trudging from store to store
to have indifferent teenage clerks shrug their shoulders and
mutter, "No problem," is not a human contact I crave.

The days when a trip to the milliner's meant a nice exchange 5
with a friendly proprietor you've known for years are long gone
in my neighborhood. On the other hand, thanks to Net shopping I was able to buy my husband a beautiful bow tie made by
hand by a woman in Maine.

Online in the last couple of weeks, I've kept in touch with 6
busy friends, some of whom live halfway around the world, and
tracked temperatures in Seville, Spain, which we are visiting
next month. I've easily located and purchased out-of-print
books from small secondhand dealers and looked up some useful exercises for a knee I had hurt.

Each of these little solitary outings made me shamefully 7
happy. In fact, learning that it was 65 degrees in Seville when
it was 10 above zero and icy in Massachusetts was the single most
mood-elevating discovery made in the first two weeks of February.

Driving to work this week, I listened to callers on a radio 8
talk show discuss a novel about transsexuals. Several callers
who identified themselves as transsexuals talked about how
much comfort and communion they felt from visiting certain
Web sites just for them. You can't tell me that this is worse than
spending endless hours interacting with the real people around
them who may think they are nuts. While "atomizing" culture
can be a problem, it can also allow more diverse stories to
emerge and so reduce the silent suffering of the tellers.

When I came home tonight, my 14-year-old son was ecstatic 9
because he had finally gotten access to the chat room his school
friends visit. Rather than sitting in front of the television to
unwind after his homework was done, he happily chatted with
his buddies. Yes, it would be better if all his friends lived on the
same block so they could all hang out together in person. But
connecting online may be the best alternative.

People already spend a lot of time alone, even when they are 10
with their families. I've heard many parents with multiple televisions in their homes talk about how everyone scatters after
supper to watch a separate program.

According to the Stanford report, of the people in the study 11
who are online five or more hours a week (about 20 percent of
those surveyed), 59 percent are spending less time watching

television. Is that making life worse? Online, some of the conversations are two-way.

I grant that there are concerns. My husband, who teaches at a boarding school, told me about an interesting faculty discussion about the pros and cons of wiring each dormitory room for Internet access. Would it help the students, or pull them away from their studies and their friends? 12

I recently told my 14-year-old that he couldn't put his computer in his bedroom, and had to keep it in the family room. I didn't explain that I had made that decision because I wanted to keep an eye on what he was downloading, nag him when he has spent too much time online and pat his head occasionally, but I think he guessed. Yes, we all need to monitor this powerful tool. 13

When people gain more money and more choices, it seems they often choose to move farther apart. Out of the one-room tenement, out of the bed shared with siblings, off the subway. 14

Why? Part of the answer is that privacy and solitude are very attractive and often emotionally salubrious states. People enjoy being unobserved and left in peace — some of the time. And I think "some of the time" is the vital point that's being lost. Privacy and solitude, even anonymity, feel wonderful when they are chosen. When they're imposed, they tend to feel awful. Then they mutate into isolation, loneliness, depression and anomie, and Prozac sales skyrocket. 15

But the problem isn't the Internet. The suburbs and the long automobile commutes to our workplaces have fragmented our lives and perhaps left us too far apart. And, yes, some people are too isolated and lonely. (Though I hold that in the past, many people were made equally miserable by too much forced contact.) So I suggest that we turn some attention to helping people find pleasurable ways to get back together. And helping them make time to do it. Even Ralph Waldo Emerson recommended "Society and Solitude." 16

To prosper emotionally, people need to feel wanted, needed and valued. Our failure to offer this prospect to many citizens long precedes the World Wide Web. And making sensational and premature proclamations about the Internet's harm simply distracts us from addressing those social conditions that drive us apart. Let's not go for the virtual damage when the real thing is before us. 17

READING ACTIVITY 11: Build Your Vocabulary

Determine the meanings of the following words from Janna Malamud Smith's essay. Then check their meanings by looking up the words in a dictionary: atomized (2), curmudgeon (3), milliner's (5), proprietor (5), transsexuals (8), ecstatic (9), salubrious (15), anonymity (15), imposed (15), anomie (15), virtual (17).

READING ACTIVITY 12: Read to Improve Your Writing

Discuss the following questions about "Online but Not Antisocial" with your classmates.

1. What is Smith's thesis? State this in your own words.
2. What are the author's pro points?
3. What are the arguments against the author's thesis (the con points)? How does she refute these?
4. Explain the last sentence of Smith's essay: "Let's not go for the virtual damage when the real thing is before us." What is "the real thing"?
5. Do you think the time that you have spent online has been mostly beneficial or mostly harmful? Explain your answer.

Making a Difference

9

Using Argument

In this chapter, you will identify a health, education, or environmental problem that is important to you and propose a solution for it. As you follow the steps of the writing process, you will

- Gather ideas by relating aloud, freewriting, and reading.

- Develop your ideas using argument.

- Learn how to persuade your readers, avoid faulty logic, and keep a reasonable tone.

- Combine sentences using appositives.

- Practice correcting shifts in person.

- Send your essay to someone with the authority to act on your proposal.

Think about some of the arguments you have been involved in. Did you ever become so angry that you couldn't discuss the issue at hand? Did you yell, stomp your feet, and leave the room, slamming the door behind you? Sometimes when we're angry, we don't think clearly, and afterward we realize that we said something we wish we could take back or forgot to say something important. Seldom is anything accomplished as a result of a heated argument, but an argument doesn't have to be a fight.

At the center of any argument is an *issue* — something on which people disagree. Because some issues — such as those involving health, education, or the environment — affect many people, we often read or hear about them in the media. What kind of diet will help us lose weight? Are the sun's rays good or harmful? Will school vouchers improve the educational system or undermine public schools? Should student financial aid be increased or decreased? How much money should be allocated to protect endangered species? Should we drill for oil in Alaska's Arctic National Wildlife Refuge? Politicians, columnists, and talk-show hosts argue with each other and their audiences about problems and solutions such as these every day.

People argue about important issues because they want to make a difference. Writing is an especially effective way to accomplish this goal. You can help to solve a problem by writing an essay that states your position on an issue, provides evidence that a problem exists, and proposes a solution to that problem. This chapter will show you how to write an argument that can convince your readers to take action on something that is important to you.

You might ask, "But who will listen to me?" Despite many college students' assumptions that they can't change "the system," most college administrators and state and federal representatives are eager to listen to students. After all, you're their constituents. However, they must be aware of problems, and more important, they must find solutions. As a student writer, you can play an important role in helping them perform these functions.

GROUP ACTIVITY 1: Think about Problems and Solutions

The young women in the photograph on page 336 are protesting cuts in children's benefits and social programs in Austin, Texas. The sign they carry says "Put Your Passion into Action." What health, education, or environmental issues concern you most? Can you think of any solutions to these problems? How might you put your own passion about this issue into action?

READING ESSAYS ABOUT PROBLEMS AND SOLUTIONS

Writing an argument that identifies an issue and proposes a solution requires all of your writing skills. You must identify a problem, use evidence to illustrate the problem, investigate what has worked and not worked to solve the problem, propose a solution, and then convince your readers that your proposal will work.

As you read the following three argument essays, jot down the evidence that the authors present to convince you that the problems exist. Do these authors convince you that their solutions are workable? Can you provide other possible solutions?

A Health Problem

GREG CRITSER

Don't Eat the Flan

Greg Critser is a freelance writer whose columns and essays have appeared in Harper's Magazine, USA Today, *the* Wall Street Journal, *and the* Los Angeles Times. *He often writes about addiction and health. In his book* Fat Land *(2004), he explores obesity in America; in* Generation RX *(2005), he explores overuse of prescription drugs in America. In "Don't Eat the Flan," which was published in* Forbes, *Critser argues that Americans are fat because they are never taught to avoid overeating.*

By now you have likely seen nearly every imaginable head- 1
line about obesity in America. You've seen the ominous statistical ones: "Nearly two-thirds of all Americans now overweight, study says." Or the sensational ones: "Two N.Y. teens sue McDonald's for making them fat." Or the medical ones: "Adult-onset diabetes now soars among children."

But one obesity headline you will not see is the one that deals 2
with morality. Specifically, it is the one that might read like this: "Sixth deadly sin at root of obesity epidemic, researchers say." This is because gluttony, perhaps alone among humanity's vices, has become the first media non-sin.

I first got a whiff of this transformation a few years ago while 3
working on a book about obesity. Looking for a book about food and morality, I asked a clerk in the religious bookstore at the Fuller Seminary in Pasadena where I might find one on gluttony.

"Hmm," he pondered. "Maybe you'd want to look under eat- 4
ing disorders."

"But I'm not looking for a medical book. I'm looking for 5
something about gluttony — you know, one of the seven deadly
sins." I was sure he'd point me to Aquinas, Dante or at least a
nice long shelf on sin. But he didn't.

"Oh, why didn't you say so?" the young man said, now quite 6
serious. "If we have anything like that, it'll be over in self-help."

I then made inquiries about interviewing a professor who 7
might be an expert on sin. I was told there was no one at this
conservative seminary who had anything to say on the subject.

What might be called the "therapization" of gluttony is 8
hardly limited to the sphere of conventional religion. Of much
greater import is the legitimizing of gluttony in medicine and
public health. For at least two decades any suggestion that
morality — or even parental admonition — be used to fight the
curse of overeating has been greeted like Ted Bundy at a Girl
Scout convention. Behind this lies the notion, widely propounded by parenting gurus, that food should never become a
dinner-table battle.

The operative notion here is simple: Telling people to not eat 9
too much food is counterproductive. Worse, it leads to "stigmatization," which can lead to eating disorders, low self-esteem, and
bad body image. Though the consequences of being overweight,
numerous and well documented, are dangerous, little if any evidence supports the notion that it is dangerous to stigmatize
unhealthy behavior. Nevertheless, suggest to an "obesity counselor" that people should be counseled against gluttony and
nine out of ten times you will be admonished as a veritable child
abuser.

That's too bad, because it eliminates a fundamental — and 10
proven — public health tactic. In the campaigns against unsafe
sex and smoking, stigmatizing unhealthy behaviors proved
highly effective in reducing risk.

Worse, this absence of moral authority in the realm of food 11
leaves children — everyone, really — vulnerable to the one force in
American life that has no problem making absolute claims: food
advertisers, who spend billions teaching kids how to bug their parents into feeding them high-fat, high-sugar foods. Combine that
with the lingering (albeit debunked) 1980s dogma — that "kids
know when kids are full" — and you get, as one nutritionist-parent
forcefully told me, the idea that "kids have the right to make bad
nutritional decisions."

You would have a hard time selling that to the one Western 12
nation that apparently avoided the obesity epidemic: France.
The French intentionally created a culture of dietary restraint in
the early 20th century, through a state-sponsored program known
as *puériculture*. Reacting to early cases of childhood obesity,
health activists wrote parenting manuals, conducted workshops
and published books. Their advice: Parents must control the dinner table; all portions should be moderate; desserts were for holidays. Eating too much food was a bad thing.

And therein lies at least part of the explanation for the leg-   13
endary leanness of the very confident French: They were taught
as children not to overeat. And they didn't even have to look in
the self-help section for the advice.

READING ACTIVITY 1: Build Your Vocabulary

Determine the meanings of the following words from the context of
Greg Critser's essay. Then check their meanings by looking up the
words in a dictionary: flan (title), ominous (1), gluttony (2), vices (2),
whiff (3), sphere (8), admonition (8), propounded (8), operative (9),
stigmatization (9), veritable (9), albeit (11), debunked (11).

READING ACTIVITY 2: Read to Improve Your Writing

Discuss the following questions about "Don't Eat the Flan" with your
classmates.

1. According to Critser, what is the problem? How does he convince
   you that the problem exists?
2. Why does the author refer to overeating as a "deadly sin" and
   "gluttony"? What is the tone of these words: angry, humorous,
   condescending?
3. What does Critser propose as a solution to the obesity problem? Is
   his proposal workable?
4. Can you identify another health issue facing Americans? What is
   your solution?

An Education Problem

LAURA D'ANDREA TYSON

Needed: Affirmative Action for the Poor

*Laura D'Andrea Tyson is dean of the Haas School of Business at the
University of California at Berkeley and a columnist for* Business
Week *magazine. She also taught at Princeton University and served
as President Clinton's National Economic Advisor. In "Needed:
Affirmative Action for the Poor," which was first published in*
Business Week, *Tyson argues that preferential admission to college
should be awarded on the basis of income, not race or ethnicity.*

In the Information Age, higher education is more and more   1
important as the ticket to economic success. Unfortunately,

access to this ticket depends on economic success itself. A young person's chance of getting a college or post-graduate education depends on family income. Children from low-income households are much less likely to graduate from college than children raised in high-income households. As family incomes become more unequal, there are signs that the relationship between income and college graduation is becoming stronger.

Children born into high-income households become part of a virtuous circle of success. Parents with university degrees tend to earn more, set higher educational goals for their children, and invest more time in the children's schooling than parents who have a high-school education or less. In addition, given local financing of K–12 public education and the segregation of most local communities by income, the children of high-income parents tend to attend better schools and receive better preparation for college.

A study on socioeconomic status and selective-college admissions by the Century Foundation provides stark evidence of the links between family background and higher education. The recent Supreme Court ruling that it was legal to give some preferential treatment to disadvantaged minorities speaks to this point.

Low-income students who graduate from high school with at least minimal qualifications for four-year institutions enroll at half the rate of their high-income peers. Only 78% of students from low-income families who rank as top achievers on tests of college readiness actually attend college. In contrast, nearly the same share of students from high-income families who rank at the bottom of such tests do so. The conventional view is that students from low-income families don't enroll or complete college because they are not academically qualified. But the New Century evidence paints a different and more hopeful picture. Despite the considerable obstacles they encounter as they grow up, many high school students from low-income, disadvantaged households are qualified but are choosing not to attend college or to attend colleges that are less selective than their qualifications justify.

What can be done to help such students get the ticket to college? Clearly, more generous financial aid is part of the answer. The financial barriers to college enrollment among students from low-income families are great — and growing. Since the early 1970s, the value of federal aid packages for low-income students has fallen precipitously as a percentage of college costs. In the same period, college costs as a portion of family income have remained unchanged for the top 40% of the family income distribution while increasing substantially for low-income families. Without a big increase in federal and state support for means-tested student aid programs, a growing number of qualified students from low-income households will find the door to higher education and upward mobility closed for them and their children.

The nation's colleges and universities should also do more to help children from low-income families. They should mount more aggressive efforts to identify and recruit students from low-income families with strong academic potential early in their high-school careers, providing them with better information about the course requirements and procedures for college admission. Colleges should also expand their financial aid programs for low-income students. Currently, more four-year colleges offer financial aid to athletes and students with "special nonacademic talents" than to disadvantaged students. Finally, more colleges should follow the lead of the Universities of California, Florida, and Washington and design admissions programs that evaluate the academic accomplishments of applicants in light of such obstacles as family income, parental education, and social environment. Doesn't an SAT total score of 1200 combined with an A average mean something different for an applicant raised in a low-income household and educated in a run-down public school than for an applicant from a high-income home and educated in an outstanding private school?

According to a recent survey, two-thirds of Americans support preferences in college admissions for equally qualified low-income students over high-income students. Century Foundation research demonstrates that such economic affirmative action policies would dramatically increase the share of students from the poorest half of the population in the total number of students admitted to the nation's top 146 colleges. Today, that share is just 10%, lower than it would be if admissions decisions were based on grades and test scores alone. Even the most selective colleges have preferential admissions programs for the offspring of their mostly affluent alumni. Surely there is scope for preferential admissions for qualified students who are poor.

READING ACTIVITY 3: Build Your Vocabulary

Determine the meanings of the following words from the context of Laura D'Andrea Tyson's essay. Then check their meanings by looking up the words in a dictionary: virtuous (2), socioeconomic (3), preferential (3), precipitously (5), affluent (7).

READING ACTIVITY 4: Read to Improve Your Writing

Discuss the following questions about "Needed: Affirmative Action for the Poor" with your classmates.

1. What educational problem does Tyson identify in her essay?
2. What is the author's proposed solution? What supporting details does she use to convince you that her solution will work?
3. What objections might you raise to Tyson's proposal?

4. Identify three educational problems, and propose a solution to one of them.

An Environmental Problem

PATRICK MOORE

Going Nuclear: A Green Makes the Case

Most readers would not expect environmentalist and Greenpeace cofounder Patrick Moore to suggest that nuclear technology is the solution to our energy problem. In this editorial, published in the Washington Post *on April 16, 2006, Moore argues that we have come a long way in our understanding of nuclear power and that we should embrace it as a way to improve the environment.*

In the early 1970s when I helped found Greenpeace, I believed that nuclear energy was synonymous with nuclear holocaust, as did most of my compatriots. That's the conviction that inspired Greenpeace's first voyage up the spectacular rocky northwest coast to protest the testing of U.S. hydrogen bombs in Alaska's Aleutian Islands. Thirty years on, my views have changed, and the rest of the environmental movement needs to update its views, too, because nuclear energy may just be the energy source that can save our planet from another possible disaster: catastrophic climate change.

Look at it this way: More than 600 coal-fired electric plants in the United States produce 36 percent of U.S. emissions — or nearly 10 percent of global emissions — of CO_2, the primary greenhouse gas responsible for climate change. Nuclear energy is the only large-scale, cost-effective energy source that can reduce these emissions while continuing to satisfy a growing demand for power. And these days it can do so safely.

I say that guardedly, of course, just days after Iranian President Mahmoud Ahmadinejad announced that his country had enriched uranium. "The nuclear technology is only for the purpose of peace and nothing else," he said. But there is widespread speculation that, even though the process is ostensibly dedicated to producing electricity, it is in fact a cover for building nuclear weapons.

And although I don't want to underestimate the very real dangers of nuclear technology in the hands of rogue states, we cannot simply ban every technology that is dangerous. That was the all-or-nothing mentality at the height of the Cold War, when anything nuclear seemed to spell doom for humanity and the environment. In 1979, Jane Fonda and Jack Lemmon produced a frisson of fear with their starring roles in *The China Syndrome,* a fictional evocation of nuclear disaster in which a reactor melt-down threatens a city's survival. Less than two weeks after the blockbuster film opened, a reactor core meltdown at Pennsylvania's Three Mile Island nuclear power plant sent shivers of very real anguish throughout the country.

What nobody noticed at the time, though, was that Three Mile Island was in fact a success story: The concrete contain-ment structure did just what it was designed to do — prevent radiation from escaping into the environment. And although the reactor itself was crippled, there was no injury or death among nuclear workers or nearby residents. Three Mile Island was the only serious accident in the history of nuclear energy generation in the United States, but it was enough to scare us away from further developing the technology: There hasn't been a nuclear plant ordered up since then.

Today, there are 103 nuclear reactors quietly delivering just 20 percent of America's electricity. Eighty percent of the people living within 10 miles of these plants approve of them (that's not including the nuclear workers). Although I don't live near a nuclear plant, I am now squarely in their camp.

And I am not alone among seasoned environmental activists in changing my mind on this subject. British atmospheric scientist James Lovelock, father of the Gaia theory, believes that nuclear energy is the only way to avoid catastrophic climate change. Stewart Brand, founder of the *Whole Earth Catalog,* says the envi-ronmental movement must embrace nuclear energy to wean our-selves from fossil fuels. On occasion, such opinions have been met with excommunication from the anti-nuclear priesthood: The late British Bishop Hugh Montefiore, founder and director of Friends of the Earth, was forced to resign from the group's board after he wrote a pro-nuclear article in a church newsletter.

There are signs of a new willingness to listen, though, even among the staunchest anti-nuclear campaigners. When I attended the Kyoto climate meeting in Montreal last December, I spoke to a packed house on the question of a sustainable energy future. I argued that the only way to reduce fossil fuel emissions from electrical production is through an aggressive program of renew-able energy sources (hydroelectric, geothermal heat pumps, wind, etc.) plus nuclear. The Greenpeace spokesperson was first at the mike for the question period, and I expected a tongue-lashing. Instead, he began by saying he agreed with much of what I said — not the nuclear bit, of course, but there was a clear feeling that all options must be explored.

Here's why: Wind and solar power have their place, but be-cause they are intermittent and unpredictable they simply can't replace big baseload plants such as coal, nuclear and hydroelec-tric. Natural gas, a fossil fuel, is too expensive already, and its price is too volatile to risk building big baseload plants. Given that hydroelectric resources are built pretty much to capacity, nuclear is, by elimination, the only viable substitute for coal. It's that simple.

That's not to say that there aren't real problems — as well as various myths — associated with nuclear energy. Each concern deserves careful consideration: 10

- *Nuclear energy is expensive.* It is in fact one of the least expensive energy sources. In 2004, the average cost of producing nuclear energy in the United States was less than two cents per kilowatt-hour, comparable with coal and hydroelectric. Advances in technology will bring the cost down further in the future. 11

- *Nuclear plants are not safe.* Although Three Mile Island was a success story, the accident at Chernobyl, 20 years ago this month, was not. But Chernobyl was an accident waiting to happen. This early model of Soviet reactor had no containment vessel, was an inherently bad design and its operators literally blew it up. The multi-agency U.N. Chernobyl Forum reported last year that 56 deaths could be directly attributed to the accident, most of those from radiation or burns suffered while fighting the fire. Tragic as those deaths were, they pale in comparison to the more than 5,000 coal-mining deaths that occur worldwide every year. No one has died of a radiation-related accident in the history of the U.S. civilian nuclear reactor program. (And although hundreds of uranium mine workers did die from radiation exposure underground in the early years of that industry, that problem was long ago corrected.) 12

- *Nuclear waste will be dangerous for thousands of years.* Within 40 years, used fuel has less than one-thousandth of the radioactivity it had when it was removed from the reactor. And it is incorrect to call it waste, because 95 percent of the potential energy is still contained in the used fuel after the first cycle. Now that the United States has removed the ban on recycling used fuel, it will be possible to use that energy and to greatly reduce the amount of waste that needs treatment and disposal. Last month, Japan joined France, Britain and Russia in the nuclear-fuel-recycling business. The United States will not be far behind. 13

- *Nuclear reactors are vulnerable to terrorist attack.* The six-feet-thick reinforced concrete containment vessel protects the contents from the outside as well as the inside. And even if a jumbo jet did crash into a reactor and breach the containment, the reactor would not explode. There are many types of facilities that are far more vulnerable, including liquid nat- 14 ural gas plants, chemical plants and numerous political targets. Nuclear fuel can be diverted to make nuclear weapons. This is the most serious issue associated with nuclear energy and the most difficult to address, as the example of Iran shows. But just because nuclear technology can be put to evil purposes is not an argument to ban its use.

Over the past 20 years, one of the simplest tools — the machete — has been used to kill more than a million people in Africa, far more than were killed in the Hiroshima and Nagasaki nuclear bombings combined. What are car bombs made of? Diesel oil, fertilizer and cars. If we banned everything that can be used to kill people, we would never have harnessed fire. 15

The only practical approach to the issue of nuclear weapons proliferation is to put it higher on the international agenda and to use diplomacy and, where necessary, force to prevent countries or terrorists from using nuclear materials for destructive ends. And new technologies such as the reprocessing system recently introduced in Japan (in which the plutonium is never separated from the uranium) can make it much more difficult for terrorists or rogue states to use civilian materials to manufacture weapons. 16

The 600-plus coal-fired plants emit nearly 2 billion tons of CO_2 annually — the equivalent of the exhaust from about 300 million automobiles. In addition, the Clean Air Council reports that coal plants are responsible for 64 percent of sulfur dioxide emissions, 26 percent of nitrous oxides and 33 percent of mercury emissions. These pollutants are eroding the health of our environment, producing acid rain, smog, respiratory illness and mercury contamination. 17

Meanwhile, the 103 nuclear plants operating in the United States effectively avoid the release of 700 million tons of CO_2 emissions annually — the equivalent of the exhaust from more than 100 million automobiles. Imagine if the ratio of coal to nuclear were reversed so that only 20 percent of our electricity was generated from coal and 60 percent from nuclear. This would go a long way toward cleaning the air and reducing greenhouse gas emissions. Every responsible environmentalist should support a move in that direction. 18

READING ACTIVITY 5: Build Your Vocabulary

Determine the meanings of the following words from the context of Patrick Moore's essay. Then check their meanings by looking up the words in a dictionary: synonymous (1), holocaust (1), compatriots (1), ostensibly (3), frisson (4), evocation (4), staunchest (8), volatile (9), proliferation (16).

READING ACTIVITY 6: Read to Improve Your Writing

Discuss the following questions about "Going Nuclear" with your classmates.

1. What problem does Moore identify?
2. What evidence does he provide that the problem exists?
3. What solution does the author propose? What, if anything, is unrealistic about his proposed solution?
4. Why is this argument more powerful because of Moore's stand on other environmental issues?
5. What environmental issues are important to you? List solutions to the issues you identify.

Writing Assignment

Think about the issues of health, education, and the environment. What problem do you complain about most often? Now is your chance to do something about it. By writing about a problem and suggesting a possible solution, you may help resolve an issue for yourself and others. In this chapter, you will select a problem, give your position on it, provide evidence that the problem exists, and propose a workable solution. You (or your instructor) may decide to do this assignment in one of several ways:

- Write about a health issue of importance to you.

  OR

- Write about an education issue that affects you or someone close to you.

  OR

- Write about an environmental issue that you know something about.

The activities in this chapter will walk you through the steps of writing an effective problem-and-solution argument. After you complete your essay, you will share it with someone in authority who can act on your proposal.

STEP 1. EXPLORE YOUR CHOICES

The radical civil rights activist Eldridge Cleaver once said, "You're either part of the solution, or you're part of the problem." You can, in fact, be part of the solution by writing a persuasive essay about an issue that is important to you.

To do that, start by identifying a problem and gathering evidence that supports a workable solution. If you want your essay to make a difference, you must be careful to choose a position that you can argue with some authority, either by drawing on your own knowledge or by reading to learn more about it. But if you think you don't know enough about any problems to write an effective essay, don't worry. You will evaluate your audience, your purpose, and at least three potential topics before you settle on a problem and a solution to write about.

Analyzing Your Audience and Purpose

If you take the time to write about an important issue, you want someone to read your essay and do something about the problem you identify. For example, if you choose a health issue, such as the need for a student health center on your campus, your audience might include a dean or the school's president. Similarly, for an education issue, such as the federal government's proposed cuts in financial aid benefits to students, your audience could include your congressional representative and possibly the U.S. president. For an environmental issue, such as the need to stop a local factory from polluting the air, your audience might include the factory owner, local government officials, or the state governor.

For more on audience and purpose, see pp. 8–12.

Because you're trying to convince at least one of your readers to act on your suggestions, you'll want to appear well-informed, respectful, and fairly formal. You'll also need to consider how they might disagree with you and what information might convince them to change their minds.

WRITING ACTIVITY 1: Analyze Your Audience and Purpose

Your responses to the following questions will help you decide how to approach this chapter's assignment. Be sure to come back to these questions after you have chosen a topic.

1. Does this assignment call for primarily expressive, informative, or persuasive writing?

2. What is the average age of your audience?

3. What is your readers' average educational level? Ethnic background? Economic level? Political orientation: conservative, moderate, or liberal?

4. How might your responses to the previous three questions affect how you write your essay?

Gathering Ideas

For more on gathering ideas, see pp. 12–16.

Before you decide which issue you want to write about, explore your choices by gathering ideas for at least one subject in three categories: health, education, and the environment. Even if you think you already know which issue you would like to write about, it's always a good idea to explore a few topics to be sure that you have chosen the best one. To gather possible topics, you may use any of the techniques you learned in Chapter 1. The student writers in this chapter gather ideas by using relating aloud, freewriting, and reading.

Relating Aloud about a Health Problem

Relating aloud means discussing your subject with others who might be able to give you additional insights into the problem or provide alternative solutions for you to consider. As you talk with others about your subject, you'll discover new ideas and gather additional evidence. Based on their responses, you'll also be able to determine if others are interested in this problem and if they think that your solution is workable.

Here's how one student, Bruce, related his ideas about a health problem to his peer response group:

```
    My biggest concern is how the health-care system
seems to ignore unwed mothers. Did you know that if a
teenage girl becomes pregnant, she can't receive
health care for her baby unless she moves out of her
parents' home? Because of this law, teenage girls
from poor families are forced to leave home and try
to make it on their own. They not only have a rough
time making it alone, but they also lose the
emotional support of their family at a time
they need it most. I would like to see this law
changed.
```

Bruce's topic idea prompted several reactions from his classmates. One student, for example, said she had never heard of this law and couldn't believe that it was true. Another student argued that free health care is available from private charities and asked why taxpayers should have to pay for it. A third student wondered if the law was intended to discourage teenage girls from becoming pregnant. In response to his group members' questions about his topic, Bruce admitted that he didn't know the answers and that he needed to do some additional research on his issue:

```
    I don't think we want to encourage unwed mothers
to have babies, but if they do, I think they should
be able to remain with their families and still
receive health benefits. I'll need to find more about
why the health-care system is set up this way and how
it could be changed without costing taxpayers more
money. I'm sure the idea is to save money, but I'm
not sure how this works. I think I'll call my
congressional representative and see if she has
any information. Then I'll rethink my position.
```

WRITING ACTIVITY 2: Relate Aloud about a Health Problem

Relate your ideas about a health issue aloud to the members of your peer response group. One member should take notes (or tape-record) on group members' responses to your description of the problem and your proposed solution. Respond to questions about your topic as best you can. Then use the group's suggestions to gather additional ideas about your topic.

Freewriting about an Education Problem

Think about some of the problems affecting students on your campus or in your community. What could be done to improve education or campus life? Perhaps you would like to see more courses offered in photography or more school spirit among students. Maybe you want the state to fund a new medical research lab at your university or the federal government to increase financial aid benefits.

Even if you have a problem in mind, you may not yet be sure what kinds of solutions are possible. To unearth ideas you may not even know you have, try freewriting. As you know, *freewriting* involves writing for a set number of pages or a limited period of time without trying to make sense of your thoughts. By exploring a topic without trying to get it right, you may discover solutions that wouldn't otherwise occur to you.

If you find yourself staring at a blank page without any ideas, you can use the following questions to stimulate your thinking:

1. What is the problem or issue you are interested in?
2. What do you already know about it?
3. What more do you need to know about the issue?
4. What do you think should be done?
5. Who has the power to act on your proposed solution?

Li Chiang, a student writer concerned about the computer lab on his campus, did some freewriting in response to these questions. Here's what he wrote:

> I am concerned about the computer lab on campus. It does not serve the needs of students. Even though we pay a $150 user fee each semester, we don't get good service. I spend most of my spare time at the lab. I don't own a computer and must use the lab to complete assignments. I really hate the computer lab it's so frustrating. The hardware is outdated. The software selection is inadequate. There's only one computer connected to the Internet! It's so dark in there. And it's always crowded. Long lines of people waiting for their turn. And most of the terminals are out of order! The students who work there are not very helpful. They ignore you and spend all their time on their own homework. Nice job if you can get it! I wonder if other students are as annoyed as I am. Why hasn't the college administration made any attempt to improve the computer lab? How expensive can decent equipment be? Shouldn't part of the fee we pay each semester be used to update the computer lab on a regular basis? What does the fee pay for anyway? The vice president for academic affairs is the person in charge of this matter. Why hasn't he done anything about it? Maybe he doesn't think it's a problem? Or maybe he doesn't think it's important?

WRITING ACTIVITY 3: Freewrite about an Education Problem

Choose an education problem that concerns and interests you. It might be a problem specific to your school, an issue that affects college students all over the country, or perhaps a problem that involves grade school children or high school students. Set aside ten or fifteen minutes, and freewrite on your topic. You may use the questions on this page as a starting point, but remember that the goal of freewriting is to go where your mind takes you. Don't try to organize your thoughts, make sense of your topic, or correct your writing, just write.

Reading about an Environmental Problem

Put aside your writing about an education issue for now so that you can gather ideas about an environmental problem.

Radio, newspapers, magazines, and television all carry pieces on environmental issues such as local recycling programs, low-emission vehicles, and the destruction of the rain forests. You have probably noticed other problems as well. Perhaps your neighbors insist on burning their leaves every fall. Maybe a local factory's wastewater leaks into the river, or nearby cities are taking water needed to irrigate farms in your county.

Sometimes writers think they know the solution to an environmental issue but can't provide evidence that the problem exists or that a solution is workable. Doing even a little reading on the issue can provide a lot of valuable information for an essay.

To gather ideas for an essay about an environmental issue, read some articles on your topic. You can find magazine and newspaper articles on any environmental issue in the reference section of your library or on the World Wide Web.

For more on conducting research, see Chapter 12.

Use these questions to evaluate the sources you find:

1. Do most of the articles support or oppose your position on the issue?
2. What supporting details do the authors use to convince readers of their views?
3. Can you add additional details to these arguments?
4. Do the authors propose any worthwhile solutions?

One student, Joy, was interested in writing about the air pollution near her home. She hoped to persuade her state's governor to share her view that something should be done to improve the air quality. To learn more about the issue, Joy read several articles about air pollution. Here is her statement of her topic and her answers to the questions listed above:

```
As a resident of this state, I am concerned about the
increasing air pollution in our cities and what can
be done about it.

1. Newspaper accounts on air pollution appear
   regularly. According to some articles I've read,
   investment in alternative fuels is one way to
   improve air quality.
```

2. Most authors use statistics to support the view that air quality is worsening. Since 1973, air pollution has more than doubled.

3. In support of those statistics, I can cite several recent examples of air pollution in my area.

4. The authors propose various solutions, including alternative fuels.

WRITING ACTIVITY 4: Read about an Environmental Issue

Identify an environmental problem that you might want to write about. Locate at least three newspaper or magazine articles on your topic, and read them carefully for ideas and supporting evidence. Use the questions on page 353 to evaluate the articles.

STEP 2. WRITE YOUR DISCOVERY DRAFT

For more on drafting, see pp. 16–21.

You have explored at least three possible topics for your argument essay. It's time now to choose one health, education, or environmental issue and prepare a discovery draft that explains a problem and proposes your solution. The purpose of this draft is to discover what you have to say, so focus on organizing what you already know by trying to put it on paper. Remember that you will have the opportunity to revise later.

Choosing a Topic

As you get ready to write your discovery draft, choose a topic that concerns you, that you know something about, and that your readers can take action on if you convince them to accept your position. Start by reviewing your materials from the gathering-ideas step. Which topic — health, education, or the environment — generated the most ideas for you? If you find that you feel strongly about one of the topics, it's probably a good pick for your discovery draft. On the other hand, if you're not excited about any of the topics you've explored so far, go back and try your favorite idea-gathering technique to try out some other possibilities.

Once you have a topic that interests you, make sure it is narrow enough to handle in a short essay. You would not be able to address AIDS, the cost of a college education, or global warming thoroughly in one essay, but you could focus on one specific aspect of the problem. To write about the cost of college, for example, you could narrow the topic to a proposed tuition hike at your school and explain why and how the administration might avoid the increase.

WRITING ACTIVITY 5: Choose Your Topic

Review your responses to Writing Activities 1 to 4, and decide which of the three issues you explored (health, education, or environment) is most important to you and would be most interesting to your readers. Be careful to select a problem for which you can propose a solution. If necessary, narrow your topic to something that can be fully addressed in the assigned length of your essay.

Sharing Your Ideas

Before you begin drafting, write a preliminary thesis statement that identifies a problem and proposes a solution. A working thesis statement will help keep you focused as you draft, but remember that you might change your mind about your topic as you write about it. You can always revise your thesis statement later on.

For more on thesis statements, see pp. 19–20.

Feel free to use material you've already gathered as part of your discovery draft. If you related your issue aloud to your classmates, for example, you might want to refer to your notes as you write. Parts of your freewriting will probably be useful. Similarly, if you read some articles about your topic during the gathering ideas step, you might want to include information from your research as you draft. Keep your audience and purpose in mind as you write, but remember that your main goal at this stage is to get your ideas down on paper.

Here's a discovery draft written by Li Chiang, the student whose freewriting about the campus computer lab you read earlier. (Note that Li's writing includes the types of errors that typically appear in a first draft.)

I am one of thousands of students who must use the campus computer lab. Due to the poor condition of this facility, I have been forced to go elsewhere to use a computer. The equipment is outdated, it breaks down often, and the lab staff doesn't seem very helpful. What really makes me angry is that students pay a $150 user fee as part of their tuition each semester. You would think that this fee would entitle students to first-rate computer facilities.

Instead, we have to use old IBM or Macintosh computers. These computers aren't even powerful enough to run the software that provides students access to the Internet. There is only one Macintosh G4.

It is fast enough and powerful enough for students to access the World Wide Web on the Internet. What's more, on any given day, one-third of the two hundred computers have Out of Order signs on them. What gives? With thousands of students needing these computers, they should all be kept in working order.

Also, the staff isn't very helpful. Who trains these clowns anyway? They often sit around doing their homework instead of offering to help students learn how to use the computers and the software programs. We need more software, too.

The college needs to upgrade the campus computer lab or quit charging students to use campus computing facilities. We questioned Dr. Bruhn. He is the vice president for instructional technology. He responded that the majority of the funds collected through the computer use fee were being used to create a computerized telephone registration system.

We're being ripped off! The way it is now, we pay a toll, but can't even get on the information superhighway.

WRITING ACTIVITY 6: Write Your Discovery Draft

Using your notes from the gathering-ideas step, write a preliminary thesis statement and a discovery draft to identify a problem and propose a solution on a health, education, or environmental issue of your choosing. For now, focus on putting your ideas into words, and try not to worry about the details. If you wish, you may write drafts on two or three topics to see which one you prefer to continue working on.

STEP 3. REVISE YOUR DRAFT

For more on revising, see pp. 21–23.

Because convincing others to act on your proposed solution to an issue can be a challenge, you must ensure that your essay provides evidence of the problem and offers a workable solution. Refer back to the audience analysis you completed in Writing Activity 1. What does your audience need to know to understand the problem? How can you propose your solution so that your readers will act on it?

As you review your discovery draft, use the skills you acquired in earlier chapters of this book: support and clarify your main ideas

(Chapter 5), organize your paragraphs (Chapter 7), make your ideas flow smoothly (Chapter 6), and write an effective introduction and conclusion (Chapter 6). In the pages that follow, you will learn how to further strengthen your draft by using argumentation, appealing to your readers, avoiding faulty logic, and improving your tone.

Developing Your Ideas with Argument

Now that you have recorded some of your ideas in a discovery draft, you have probably noticed that you need to further develop what you have to say. For example, you may need to present evidence that illustrates the seriousness of the problem, and you may need to investigate any solutions that have already been tried. You may also need to explain how your solution will resolve the issue.

To do all of this, use the techniques of argument, or a *logical appeal*. First, revise your thesis statement to be sure that it states a problem and your position on it. Next, check that you have provided evidence that the problem exists. Finally, check that you have proposed a workable solution. Let's see how these techniques of argumentation are put into action.

State the Problem

As you may recall from Chapter 2, the thesis statement announces your topic; shows, explains, or argues a particular point about the topic; and gives readers a sense of what the essay will be about. An effective thesis statement for a problem-and-solution essay also

- Describes a specific problem or issue.
- Conveys your position on the issue.

Underline Your Problem and Position
To ensure that you have described a specific problem and stated your position, underline the problem, and boldface your position. Is your position specific to the problem you underlined?

Here are some examples of vague and specific thesis statements:

VAGUE   Something should be done about students' health.

SPECIFIC   Our college should develop a wellness program to encourage students to take care of their health.

VAGUE   Students need financial aid.

SPECIFIC   Congress should reject proposed cuts to the Stafford Loan program because thousands of college students rely on it to finance their educations.

VAGUE   Cement factories pollute the water.

SPECIFIC   The local cement factory should be shut down because it is polluting Jacob's Creek.

GROUP ACTIVITY 2: Analyze Thesis Statements

Working in small groups, rewrite each of the following thesis statements to define the specific problem or issue at hand and to state a clear position on the issue.

1. Students shouldn't have to pay for vaccinations.
2. The cost of health care for illegal immigrants is an important issue.
3. The spotted owls in our area need protection.
4. Cigarette taxes should be raised.
5. Standardized testing is a bad idea.

WRITING ACTIVITY 7: Revise Your Thesis Statement

Evaluate the preliminary thesis statement you wrote for your essay about a health, education, or environmental issue. Does it identify a specific problem and clearly state your position? Revise your thesis accordingly.

Provide Evidence

When writing a persuasive essay, simply stating the problem isn't enough. You need to convince readers that the problem is serious enough to require a solution. *Evidence* — such as examples, facts, and expert testimony — can help you do this. You may also include a brief history of the problem, its causes, and the consequences of leaving it unsolved.

Let's look at an overview of Greg Critser's essay to see how he uses evidence to develop his argument that the sixth deadly sin, gluttony, is at the root of the American obesity epidemic. Note the evidence he provides to convince his reader that gluttony is a serious problem requiring a solution:

PROBLEM (PARS. 1–2)

- You have seen the headlines about the American obesity epidemic.
- You haven't seen the headline that says that overeating is the sin of gluttony.
- The media portrays gluttony as a "non-sin."

EVIDENCE OF THE PROBLEM (PARS. 3–6)

- Critser tried to find a book on food and morality at the Fuller Seminary.
- The bookstore clerk referred him to self-help books.
- No professors at the seminary were willing to talk about the topic of food and morality.

ADDITIONAL EVIDENCE (PARS. 8–9)

- Gluttony has also been legitimized in medicine and public health.
- Parents believe that the topic of food should not be a battle at the dinner table.
- Counselors do not advise against overeating for fear of stigmatizing their clients.

RESULTS OF THE PROBLEM (PARS. 10–11)

- All of us, especially children, are vulnerable to food advertisers.
- As a result, we all make poor food choices.

SOLUTION (PARS. 12–13)

- We should emulate the French by creating a culture of dietary restraint.
- Health activists should promote healthy eating.
- Parents should monitor what their children eat and teach them that eating too much is a bad thing.

 E-mail Your Supporting Details

Collect supporting details by asking your classmates for their suggestions. Send e-mails to your group members, or use a class chat room to share your thesis statement and a list of your supporting details.

WRITING ACTIVITY 8: Examine Your Evidence

Share discovery drafts with two or three other students in your class, and examine the types of evidence each draft uses to support its problem statement. Does each draft provide enough supporting details to convince readers that the problem is serious and in need of a solution? Ask your group members to suggest how you can revise to make your evidence more persuasive, and do the same for them.

Propose a Solution

After you state the problem and provide evidence of it, you're ready to propose a solution. A good *solution* recommends specific and workable actions for correcting the problem or addressing the issue.

Let's look again at the solutions proposed in this chapter's readings. Notice that in each case, the writer identifies a specific and workable resolution to the problem:

CRITSER'S PROBLEM	The sixth deadly sin, gluttony, is at the root of the American obesity epidemic.
CRITSER'S SOLUTION	Americans, especially children, should be taught that overeating is wrong.
TYSON'S PROBLEM	Students from low-income homes are less likely to go to college than those from high-income homes.
TYSON'S SOLUTION	Colleges should aggressively recruit students from low-income homes, consider economic background in admissions decisions, and work with the federal government to provide more financial aid.
MOORE'S PROBLEM	Coal-based energy is polluting the planet.
MOORE'S SOLUTION	The environmental community must update its views on the use of nuclear energy.

Critser suggests that one way to cut down on obesity is to convince people that overeating is a sin. Tyson's solution has been successfully implemented in some states. Moore makes his solution workable by telling us about its success in other countries. Your solution should be specific and workable, too.

HOW TO Propose a Solution

- Identify a problem.

- Provide evidence of the problem.

- Provide a specific solution.

- Make sure that the solution is workable.

WRITING ACTIVITY 9: Revise Your Solution

Working with your peer response group, use the following questions to discuss the solution you proposed in your discovery draft about a health, education, or environmental problem.

1. Is the proposed solution to the problem specific? Why or why not?
2. Is the proposed solution workable? Why or why not?
3. How would you implement your solution?

Use your classmates' feedback to revise your solution accordingly.

Building Your Essay

When you revise an argument essay, it's important to consider whether you have done all you can to persuade your readers. To do this, first make sure that your logical appeal makes sense. In addition, your argument will be more convincing if you appeal to your readers' emotions and trust and also use a reasonable tone.

Avoid Faulty Logic

Earlier in this chapter, you learned how to use argument to develop your ideas. The process of identifying a problem, providing evidence that the problem exists, and proposing a solution is often called *using a logical appeal.* By providing logical, believable evidence, you convince your readers that you know your topic well and that your solution has merit.

For a logical appeal to be effective, however, the logic must make sense. If all or part of an essay is based on faulty logic or flawed reasoning, the argument is usually not persuasive. Let's look at three common forms of faulty logic.

Hasty Generalization. A *hasty generalization* is a conclusion drawn from too little evidence. Suppose, for example, that you once had a bad experience with a nurse during a visit to the emergency room at a local hospital. Based on that single experience, you conclude that all nurses are rude. Your conclusion, based on insufficient evidence (your one experience), would be a hasty generalization. Just because one nurse was rude doesn't mean that all others are rude. One instance can't prove a point.

Here's another example: you argue that advertising in public schools has no harmful effects because it didn't harm you as a child. Your conclusion is based on insufficient evidence (only one example). More convincing evidence would include studies conducted to determine the effects of advertising on schoolchildren or surveys of children and teachers.

Either-Or Reasoning. *Either-or reasoning* proposes only two possible alternatives even though more than two options actually exist. For instance, you would use faulty either-or reasoning if you said, "Either

I lose ten pounds, or I won't get a date." The reasoning is faulty because more than these two alternatives exist. You might get a date without losing any weight. Or you might lose ten pounds and still not get a date. Or you could lose five pounds and get several dates.

A writer who argues "Either we regulate cigarette advertisements, or more and more people will die from lung cancer" is using faulty logic because other alternatives also exist, such as efforts to decrease smoking through public-service announcements and educational programs. Because of these efforts, fewer people might get lung cancer, whether or not cigarette advertising is regulated.

Faulty Cause-and-Effect Reasoning. *Faulty cause-and-effect reasoning* attributes an event to an unrelated cause. Superstitions are based on faulty cause-and-effect reasoning, such as when we blame a bad day on the black cat that crossed our path, the salt we spilled, or the mirror we broke. Logically, these events couldn't have caused the bad day because they were unrelated to what we experienced. Thus, we cannot assume that one event was caused by another event simply because one took place before the other.

Political candidates often use faulty cause-and-effect reasoning: "Since my opponent has been in the Senate, your taxes have increased." However, just because taxes went up after the senator was elected doesn't mean that the senator raised the taxes. Perhaps they were increased by the previous Congress. Similarly, an essay writer who argues, "Ever since certain types of music have become popular, teenage suicide rates have risen," fails to acknowledge other possible causes for the rise in teenage suicides. Unless the writer provides evidence to support this point, the argument is based on faulty cause-and-effect reasoning.

WRITING ACTIVITY 10: Eliminate Faulty Logic in Your Draft

Exchange your draft with a partner. Ask your partner to point out any hasty generalizations, either-or reasoning, or faulty cause-and-effect reasoning in your draft. (You should do the same for your partner.) Correct any logical errors that your partner identifies.

Persuade Your Readers

In identifying a problem or an issue and proposing a solution, you want your readers to understand the problem, accept your proposed solution, and perhaps take action on the issue. In addition to making a logical argument, two other types of appeals — emotional and ethical — can help you be persuasive.

Emotional Appeals. Sometimes even the tightest logic is not enough to spur readers to action. In this case, an *emotional appeal* may be more effective; it aims to make readers feel strongly about a problem or issue — compassionate, proud, sad, angry, or intolerant, for example. But be careful when using an appeal to emotion. Readers dismiss appeals that are overly emotional because they assume that the writer is too close to the problem to propose an objective solution. Remember, too, that emotional appeals should be made in addition to a logical argument. You must always include logical evidence to support your thesis statement.

Laura D'Andrea Tyson uses several emotional appeals in "Needed: Affirmative Action for the Poor." Even the title of her essay suggests Tyson's strong feelings about her topic. Tyson also points out that unless something is done to help students from low-income households attend college, "the door to higher education and upward mobility will be closed for them and their children." With such an appeal to emotion, Tyson hopes to foster a renewed conscience that will spur action.

Ethical Appeals.   With an *ethical appeal,* you aim to gain your readers' trust by demonstrating your genuine concern about the problem or issue, your commitment to the truth, and your respect for others' differing opinions. You acknowledge that reasonable people might disagree with your proposal. Finally, you support your position with verifiable evidence (such as examples that provide facts, statistics, and expert testimony), and you ask readers to make a fair judgment based on that evidence.

Earlier in the chapter, you saw how several writers use ethical appeals in this way. Each demonstrates a genuine concern for the problem identified: Critser for Americans' obesity, Tyson for low-income students, and Moore for the effects of global warming. These writers also provide verifiable evidence to demonstrate their commitment to the truth and show respect for their readers' opinions. In return, they ask us, as open-minded readers, to evaluate their arguments fairly.

HOW TO Use Logical, Emotional, and Ethical Appeals

- Use logical appeals to provide believable evidence for your position.

- Use emotional appeals to help readers feel strongly about your problem.

- Use ethical appeals to demonstrate your respect for your readers and your genuine concern about the problem.

WRITING ACTIVITY 11: Strengthen Your Appeals

Evaluate your draft to determine where an appeal to emotion or an appeal to ethics would make your logical argument more persuasive. Where in your essay might you appeal to your readers' compassion, pride, anger, or some other emotion to spur them to action? Do you demonstrate genuine concern about the issue, your commitment to the truth, and your respect for others' opinions? Add or revise your appeals as appropriate, and eliminate any details that are exaggerated or not factual.

Use a Reasonable Tone

Writers create *tone* through their choices of words and the structure of their sentences. You'll always want to strive for a reasonable tone, especially if you're proposing a solution. Readers rarely respond well to anger, sarcasm, accusation, hostility, or negativity. Calm, rational, and respectful language is always more effective.

Earlier you saw several examples of an angry and snide tone in Li Chiang's discovery draft, "Tollroad on the Information Superhighway":

ANGRY TONE   "What really makes me angry is that. . . ." "What gives?"

SNIDE TONE   "Who trains these clowns anyway?" "We're being ripped off!"

Venting your anger in writing has the same effect as raising your voice, stomping your feet, or slamming the door in an argument. Remember, your goal is to persuade your readers to acknowledge the problem and to accept your solution. A harsh, negative tone won't accomplish this because it makes the writer look immature and puts readers on the defensive. To be persuasive, you must show respect for your readers' opinions by maintaining a reasonable tone.

Help Others Improve Tone
Ask your peer response group to send their essays to you electronically. Read for angry or snide statements. Boldface any statements that you think could be revised to improve the tone, and then send the essay back to the author.

WRITING ACTIVITY 12: Improve Your Tone

Reread your draft, looking for remarks that come across as angry or that show a lack of respect for others' opinions. Revise as needed to create a reasonable tone.

A Student's Revised Draft

After considering the appeals he used and the tone of his essay, student Li Chiang decided that he could strengthen his appeals and moderate his tone. Before you read Li's revised draft, reread his discovery draft (pp. 355–56). Notice how Li has improved his tone and added evidence in the revision. (You will also notice some errors in the revised draft; these will be corrected when Li edits his essay later on.)

Tollroad on the Information Superhighway

Thousands of students on our campus must rely on the campus computer lab for their computing needs. We pay a $150 user fee each semester for access to this lab. The college administration should be congratulated for providing these computing services and for keeping the fee reasonable. However, the computer hardware, software, and student assistance provided in the campus computer lab are inadequate to meet students' needs. They should be improved, or the fee should be abolished.

Evidence is added to show that the problem exists.

An ethical appeal
The tone is adjusted.

The revised thesis states the problem and proposes a solution.

The computer hardware is outdated and is often not working, my roommate, for instance, has been forced to go off campus to find a computer powerful enough to run the statistical program required in his Introduction to Statistics class. Only one computer is fast enough and powerful enough for students to access the World Wide Web on the Internet. It is a Macintosh G4. As the director of the computer lab states, "This lab was founded in 2002, and we are still using the same computers we did on the day we opened.

Evidence is added.

As if outdated equipment weren't bad enough, some of the existing hardware doesn't even work. A quick survey of the equipment one day this week revealed that of the 150 machines available in the computer lab, 48 of them had Out of Order or Off the Network signs on them. Meanwhile, hundreds of fee-paying students must either wait in line for the remaining machines or make other arrangements to use a computer.

An emotional appeal

Evidence is added.

The tone is adjusted.

The software offered in this lab is also inadequate. Yes, you can do word processing, if a machine is available, but what if you want to add graphics, charts, or diagrams? You're out of luck, because there are no desktop publishing, database, or spreadsheet

Evidence is added.

Questions: emotional appeal

Evidence is added.

programs available. What's more, with only one computer connected to the Internet, access to the information superhighway is severely limited. One student claims, "I have waited in line up to three hours to get on the Internet. On the day before Thanksgiving, the computer lab director actually had to call in campus security to maintain order because several students started fighting over this one computer."

An emotional appeal

In addition, the students hired to work in this lab are not friendly or helpful. On three separate occasions, I observed lab tutors doing homework even though they were waiting for help with the software program Microsoft Word. According to a survey reported in last Friday's campus newspaper, 60 percent of the students who use the computer lab are dissatisfied with the service offered. Most would prefer more assistance with computer hardware and software and would like to see this assistance offered twenty-four hours a day.

Evidence is added.

Evidence is added.

We questioned Dr. Bruhn. He is the vice president for instructional technology. He responsed that the majority of funds collected through the computer use fee were being used to create a computerized telephone registration system. Once this system is in place, the computer lab will be upgraded and services improved. When asked, he acknowledged that students had no input into the decision on how these computer use fees are spent. Meanwhile, students on campus make do with woefully inadequate computing facilities.

A solution is proposed.

The tone is adjusted.

An ethical appeal

This situation is obviously unfair. Students are paying a fee for computing services that they are not receiving. This college needs to upgrade the campus computer lab or quit charging students for inadequate campus computing facilities. If students are going to pay the toll, at least give them access to the information superhighway.

GROUP ACTIVITY 3: Analyze Li's Revised Draft

Use the following questions to discuss with your classmates how Li improved his draft.

1. What is Li's thesis statement? Is it effective?
2. What kinds of evidence does Li provide to show a problem exists?

3. Does his solution seem workable?
4. How does Li appeal to his readers logically, emotionally, and ethically?
5. How has Li adjusted his tone to make it more reasonable than in his discovery draft?
6. How could Li's revised draft benefit from further revision?

WRITING ACTIVITY 13: Peer Review

Read your draft aloud to the members of your peer response group. Take notes on your classmates' responses to the following questions about your draft.

1. What do you like best about this essay?
2. How effective is my thesis statement? Do I clearly state the problem?
3. Do I provide adequate evidence of the problem?
4. Do I propose a workable solution to the problem?
5. How could I improve my logical, emotional, and ethical appeals?
6. Where in my essay do I need to adjust my tone?
7. How clear is the purpose of my essay?

 Use Online Peer Review
If your class has a Web site, see whether the peer review questions are available on the site. If they are, you may be able to respond to your classmates' drafts electronically.

WRITING ACTIVITY 14: Revise Your Draft

Using the work you have completed for Writing Activities 7 to 12 and taking your classmates' suggestions for revision into consideration, finish revising your discovery draft. Focus on improving your thesis, evidence, and solution. Also evaluate your use of emotional and ethical appeals, and adjust your tone as needed.

STEP 4. EDIT YOUR SENTENCES

At this point, you have worked hard to communicate your position on a health, education, or environmental issue. Now that you're satisfied with the content of your revised draft, you're ready to edit it for correctness.

For more on editing, see pp. 23–25.

Editing is important because it removes errors that distract readers from focusing on the writer's ideas. Errors create the impression that a careless writer is untrustworthy. A clean, error-free essay, in contrast, suggests that a writer is careful and probably genuinely concerned about the topic. Therefore, edit your essay carefully before sharing it with your readers.

Combining Sentences Using Appositives

For more on combining sentences, see Ch. 17.

As you have learned, combining sentences can turn short, weak sentences into longer, stronger ones. Thus far, you have used several techniques for combining sentences. Another way to combine sentences is by using appositives. An *appositive* is a word or group of words that is set off by commas and that defines or renames a person or thing in the sentence.

HOW TO Combine Sentences Using Appositives

- Eliminate the subject and verb in one sentence.
- Add the remaining phrase that describes the noun to the other sentence.
- Set off the phrase with commas.

Here's how Li used appositives to combine some short sentences when he edited his revised draft:

ORIGINAL   Only one computer is fast enough and powerful enough for students to access the World Wide Web on the Internet. It is a Macintosh G4.

REVISED   Only one computer, *a Macintosh G4*, is fast enough and powerful enough for students to access the World Wide Web on the Internet.

ORIGINAL   We questioned Dr. Bruhn. He is the vice president for instructional technology. He responsed that the majority of funds collected through the computer use fee were being used to create a computerized telephone registration system.

REVISED   When questioned about campus computing services, *Dr. Bruhn, the vice president for instructional technology,* responded that the majority of the funds collected through the computer use fee were being used to create a computerized telephone registration system.

EDITING ACTIVITY 1: Combine Sentences Using Appositives

Combine the following pairs of sentences using appositives.

EXAMPLE Jane ~~is my sister. She~~ has Type II diabetes.
, my sister,

1. The new campus plan is an improvement. It is called Student Access.

2. My biology book isn't difficult to understand. The title is *Life Science for Dummies*.

3. This holiday is important for the environment. It's called Arbor Day.

4. Jerry asked that the campus cafeteria serve more fresh vegetables. He is short and heavyset.

5. Don't even ask my girlfriend to go with you to the student council session. Luisa isn't interested in the college's problems.

Exercise Central
For additional practice with combining sentences, go to **bedfordstmartins.com/choices** and click on "Exercise Central."

WRITING ACTIVITY 15: Combine Your Sentences

Reread your discovery draft looking for short, closely related sentences. Where it makes sense to do so, combine them using appositives.

Correcting Shifts in Person

Authors write in one of three persons: first *(I, we)*, second *(you)*, or third *(he, she, they)*. Here is a complete list of singular and plural pronouns in first, second, and third person:

SINGULAR

First Person	Second Person	Third Person
I, you	he, she	it, one
me	you	him, her, it
my, mine	your, yours	his, her, hers, its

PLURAL

First Person	Second Person	Third Person
we	you	they
us	you	them
our	your, yours	their, theirs

As a general rule, avoid shifting from one pronoun to another because it confuses the readers:

CONFUSING   *I* never wanted to complain about the food served at the campus cafeteria. *You* know that it can be unhealthy. *I* finally wrote to the school newspaper to express *our* views. *We* believed something needed to be done about this situation, and so *I* took action.

REVISED   *I* never wanted to complain about the food served at the campus cafeteria even though *I* know that it can be unhealthy. *I* finally wrote to the school newspaper to express *my* views. *I* believed something needed to be done about this situation, and so *I* took action.

EDITING ACTIVITY 2: Correct Shifts in Person

Revise the following paragraph to correct unnecessary shifts in person.

My favorite pastime is writing letters to the editor. I always have something to say about what's going on in our city. And there is plenty for you to write about: poor water quality, smog, and trash everywhere. They are always saying how much we need to improve the environment. You can never take a beautiful city for granted. I know I will continue to let people know how we feel about changing things around here.

Exercise Central
For additional practice with correcting unnecessary shifts in person, go to **bedfordstmartins.com/choices** and click on "Exercise Central."

WRITING ACTIVITY 16: Edit Your Essay

Edit your revised draft, looking for errors in grammar, spelling, and punctuation. Focus on finding and correcting any unnecessary shifts in person. If you know you often make a particular type of error, read the essay one time while you look only for that error. Ask a friend, family member, or classmate to help you spot errors you may have overlooked. Then use a dictionary and the Handbook in Part Four of this book to help you correct the errors you find.

A Student's Edited Essay

You probably noticed that Li's revised draft contained errors in grammar, spelling, and punctuation. Li corrected these errors in his edited essay. His corrections are underlined here.

Li Chiang
Professor Bledsoe
English 101
7 April 2006

Li uses the correct MLA format.

Tollroad on the Information Superhighway

Thousands of students on our campus must rely on the campus computer lab for their computing needs. <u>Every student pays</u> a $150 user fee each semester for access to this lab. The college administration should be congratulated for providing these computing services and for keeping the fee reasonable. However, the computer hardware, software, and student assistance provided in the campus computer lab are inadequate to meet students' needs. They should be improved or the fee should be abolished.

An unnecessary shift in person is corrected.

<u>The computer hardware is outdated and is often not</u> working. My roommate, <u>for instance,</u> has been forced to go off campus to find a computer powerful enough to run the statistical program required in his Introduction to Statistics course. <u>Only one computer,</u> a Macintosh G4, is fast enough and powerful enough for students to access the World Wide Web on the Internet. As the director of the computer lab states, "This lab was founded in 2002, and we are still using the same computers we did on the day we opened. I

A comma splice is corrected.

Sentences are combined.

A citation is added.

would love to be able to serve our students better, but there just isn't money to upgrade the equipment" (Fagel).

As if outdated equipment weren't bad enough, some of the existing hardware doesn't even work. A quick survey of the equipment one day this week revealed that of the 150 machines available in the computer lab, 48 of them had Out of Order or Off the Network signs on them. Meanwhile, hundreds of fee-paying students must either wait in line for the remaining machines or make other arrangements to use a computer.

An unnecessary shift in person is corrected.

The software offered in this lab is also inadequate. <u>Yes, students can do word processing, if a machine is available, but what if they want to add graphics, charts, or diagrams? They're out of luck, because there are no desktop publishing, database, or spreadsheet programs available.</u> What's more, with only one computer connected to the Internet, access to the information superhighway is severely limited. One student claims, "I have waited in line up to three hours to get on the Internet. On the day before Thanksgiving, the computer lab director actually had to call in campus security to maintain order because several students started fighting over this one computer" ("Computing Facilities").

A citation is added.

An unclear pronoun reference is corrected.

In addition, the students hired to work in this lab are not friendly or helpful. <u>On three separate occasions, I observed lab tutors doing homework even though students were waiting for help with the software program *Microsoft Word*.</u> According to an editorial in last Friday's campus newspaper, 60 percent of the students who use the computer lab are dissatisfied with the service offered. Most would prefer more assistance with computer hardware and software and would like to see this assistance offered twenty-four hours a day.

Sentences are combined.

<u>When questioned about campus computing services, Dr. Bruhn, the vice president for instructional technology, responded that the majority of the funds collected through the computer use fee were being used to create a computerized telephone registration system.</u> Once this system is in place, the computer

lab will be upgraded and services improved. When
asked, he acknowledged that students had no input
into the decision on how these computer use fees are
spent. Meanwhile, students on campus make do with
woefully inadequate computing facilities.

Spelling is corrected.

   This situation is obviously unfair. Students are
paying a fee for computing services that they are not
receiving. This college needs to upgrade the campus
computer lab or quit charging students for inadequate
campus computing facilities. If students are going to
pay the toll, at least give them access to the
information superhighway.

                    Works Cited

A Works Cited list is added.

Bruhn, John. Personal interview. 1 Apr. 2006.
"Computing Facilities Need Upgrade." Editorial. *The
     Centennial* 15 Feb. 2006: B7. Print.
Fagel, Jerry. Personal interview. 2 Apr. 2006.

STEP 5. SHARE YOUR ESSAY

   You're ready to share your solution to a health, education, or environmental problem with your audience. In addition to submitting your
essay to your instructor and sharing it with your classmates, mail a
copy of it to someone with the authority to act on your proposal.
According to an ancient Chinese proverb, "A journey of a thousand
miles begins with a single step." Perhaps your essay will be the first step
in bringing about a needed change in health, education, or the environment. You may be surprised by the power of your writing. If you receive
a reply, share it with your instructor and classmates. Student writer Li
Chiang sent his essay to Dr. Bruhn, who then requested a review of the
student technology fee. As a result, Dr. Bruhn allocated additional funds
to the computer lab for new computers and software and required that
all tutors participate in a training program.

CHAPTER CHECKLIST

❑ I analyzed my audience and purpose.

❑ I gathered ideas by relating aloud, freewriting, and reading.

❑ I stated a specific problem and position in a thesis statement.

❑ I gave evidence to persuade my readers that the problem exists and merits their attention.

❑ I proposed a workable solution to the problem.

❑ I avoided faulty logic.

❑ I used emotional and ethical appeals to persuade my readers to accept my position on the issue.

❑ I used a reasonable tone.

❑ I combined short sentences by using appositives.

❑ I corrected shifts in person.

❑ I edited to eliminate errors in grammar, punctuation, and spelling.

REFLECTING ON YOUR WRITING

To help you reflect on the writing you did in this chapter, answer the following questions:

1. Why did you choose the issue you did?

2. How did you determine the audience for your essay?

3. Which supporting details in your essay do you think provide the strongest evidence for your position? Why?

4. Which type of appeal — logical, emotional, or ethical — do you think you use most effectively in your essay? Why?

5. If you had more time, what more would you do to improve your essay before sharing it with readers?

Using your answers to these questions, complete a Writing Process Report for this chapter (you can download a report form at **bedford stmartins.com/choices**). Once you complete this report, freewrite about what you learned in this chapter.

A Health Problem

ELIZABETH M. WHELAN

Perils of Prohibition

Solutions to health problems often require imaginative ideas. In "Perils of Prohibition," Elizabeth M. Whelan, president of the American Council on Science and Health, identifies a problem: the legal drinking age of twenty-one encourages irresponsible drinking. She then proposes a surprising solution: lower the drinking age to eighteen, and educate teens about alcohol abuse.

My colleagues at the Harvard School of Public Health, where I studied preventive medicine, deserve high praise for their recent study on teenage drinking. What they found in their survey of college students was that they drink "early and . . . often," frequently to the point of getting ill. 1

As a public-health scientist with a daughter, Christine, heading to college this fall, I have professional and personal concerns about teen binge drinking. It is imperative that we explore why so many young people abuse alcohol. From my own study of the effects of alcohol restrictions and my observations of Christine and her friends' predicament about drinking, I believe that today's laws are unrealistic. Prohibiting the sale of liquor to responsible young adults creates an atmosphere where binge drinking and alcohol abuse have become a problem. American teens, unlike their European peers, don't learn how to drink gradually, safely and in moderation. 2

Alcohol is widely accepted and enjoyed in our culture. Studies show that moderate drinking can be good for you. But we legally proscribe alcohol until the age of 21 (why not 30 or 45?). Christine and her classmates can drive cars, fly planes, marry, vote, pay taxes, take out loans and risk their lives as members of the U.S. armed forces. But laws in all 50 states say that no alcoholic beverages may be sold to anyone until that magic 21st birthday. 3

We didn't always have a national "21" rule. When I was in college, in the mid-'60s, the drinking age varied from state to state. This posed its own risks, with underage students crossing state lines to get a legal drink. In parts of the Western world, moderate drinking by teenagers and even children under their parents' supervision is a given. Though the per capita consumption of 4 alcohol in France, Spain and Portugal is higher than in the United States, the rate of alcoholism and alcohol abuse is lower. A glass of wine at dinner is normal practice. Kids learn to regard moderate drinking as an enjoyable family activity rather than as something they have to sneak away to do. Banning drinking by young people makes it a badge of adulthood — a tantalizing forbidden fruit.

Christine and her teenage friends like to go out with a group to a club, comedy show or sports bar to watch the game. But teens today have to go on the sly with fake IDs and the fear of getting caught. Otherwise, they're denied admittance to most places and left to hang out on the street. That's hardly a safer alternative. Christine and her classmates now find themselves in a legal no man's land. At 18, they're considered adults. Yet when they want to enjoy a drink like other adults, they are, as they put it, "disenfranchised."   5

Comparing my daughter's dilemma with my own as an "underage" college student, I see a difference — and one that I think has exacerbated the current dilemma. Today's teens are far more sophisticated than we were. They're treated less like children and have more responsibilities than we did. This makes the 21 restriction seem anachronistic. For the past few years, my husband and I have been preparing Christine for college life and the inevitable partying — read keg of beer — that goes with it. Last year, a young friend with no drinking experience was violently ill for days after he was introduced to "clear liquids in small glasses" during freshman orientation. We want our daughter to learn how to drink sensibly and avoid this pitfall. Starting at the age of 14, we invited her to join us for a glass of champagne with dinner. She'd tried it once before, thought it was "yucky" and declined. A year later, she enjoyed sampling wine at family meals. When, at 16, she asked for a Mudslide (a bottled chocolate-milk-and-rum concoction), we used the opportunity to discuss it with her. We explained the alcohol content, told her the alcohol level is lower when the drink is blended with ice and compared it with a glass of wine. Since the drink of choice on campus is beer, we contrasted its potency with wine and hard liquor and stressed the importance of not drinking on an empty stomach.   6

Our purpose was to encourage her to know the alcohol content of what she is served. We want her to experience the effects of liquor in her own home, not on the highway and not for the first time during a college orientation week with free-flowing suds. Although Christine doesn't drive yet, we regularly reinforce the concept of choosing a designated driver. Happily, that already seems a widely accepted practice among our daughter's friends who drink.   7

We recently visited the Ivy League school Christine will attend in the fall. While we were there, we read a story in the   8 college paper about a student who was nearly electrocuted when, in a drunken state, he climbed on top of a moving train at a railroad station near the campus. The student survived, but three of his limbs were later amputated. This incident reminded me of a tragic death on another campus. An intoxicated student maneuvered himself into a chimney. He was found three days later when frat brothers tried to light a fire in the fireplace. By then he was dead.

These tragedies are just two examples of our failure to 9
teach young people how to use alcohol prudently. If 18-year-olds don't have legal access to even a beer at a public place, they have no experience handling liquor on their own. They feel "liberated" when they arrive on campus. With no parents to stop them, they have a "let's make up for lost time" attitude. The result: binge drinking.

We should make access to alcohol legal at 18. At the same 10
time, we should come down much harder on alcohol abusers and drunk drivers of all ages. We should intensify our efforts at alcohol education for adolescents. We want them to understand that it is perfectly OK not to drink. But if they do, alcohol should be consumed in moderation.

After all, we choose to teach our children about safe sex, 11
including the benefits of teen abstinence. Why, then, can't we — schools and parents alike — teach them about safe drinking?

READING ACTIVITY 7: Build Your Vocabulary

Determine the meanings of the following words from the context of Elizabeth Whelan's essay. Then check their meanings by looking up the words in a dictionary: imperative (2), predicament (2), binge (2), proscribe (3), per capita (4), tantalizing (4), disenfranchised (5), dilemma (6), exacerbated (6), anachronistic (6), prudently (9).

READING ACTIVITY 8: Read to Improve Your Writing

Discuss the following questions about "Perils of Prohibition" with your classmates.

1. Why does Whelan believe the current legal drinking age is a problem?
2. What is the author's position on the issue?
3. What supporting details does she use to convince her readers that the problem exists?
4. What is her proposed solution to the problem?
5. Does Whelan persuade you that the problem exists? Why or why not?
6. Do you think Whelan's solution is workable? Why or why not?

An Education Problem

MARY SHERRY

In Praise of the F Word

In the following essay, "In Praise of the F Word," first published in Newsweek, *Mary Sherry identifies the problem of high school graduates who are poorly prepared for work or higher education. Sherry, who teaches in adult literacy programs, suggests that the threat of failure can be a valuable way to teach students that they must take responsibility for their own learning.*

Tens of thousands of 18-year-olds will graduate this year and be handed meaningless diplomas. These diplomas won't look any different from those awarded their luckier classmates. Their validity will be questioned only when their employers discover that these graduates are semiliterate.

Eventually a fortunate few will find their way into educational-repair shops — adult-literacy programs, such as the one where I teach basic grammar and writing. There, high-school graduates and high-school dropouts pursuing graduate-equivalency certificates will learn the skills they should have learned in school. They will also discover they have been cheated by our educational system.

As I teach, I learn a lot about our schools. Early in each session I ask my students to write about an unpleasant experience they had in school. No writers' block here! "I wish someone would have made me stop doing drugs and made me study." "I liked to party and no one seemed to care." "I was a good kid and didn't cause any trouble, so they just passed me along even though I didn't read well and couldn't write." And so on.

I am your basic do-gooder, and prior to teaching this class I blamed the poor academic skills our kids have today on drugs, divorce, and other impediments to concentration necessary for doing well in school. But, as I rediscover each time I walk into the classroom, before a teacher can expect students to concentrate, he has to get their attention, no matter what distractions may be at hand. There are many ways to do this, and they have much to do with teaching style. However, if style alone won't do it, there is another way to show who holds the winning hand in the classroom. That is to reveal the trump card of failure.

I will never forget a teacher who played that card to get the attention of one of my children. Our youngest, a world-class charmer, did little to develop his intellectual talents but always got by. Until Mrs. Stifter.

Our son was a high-school senior when he had her for

English. "He sits in the back of the room talking to his friends," she told me. "Why don't you move him to the front row?" I urged, believing the embarrassment would get him to settle down. Mrs. Stifter looked at me steely-eyed over her glasses. "I don't move seniors," she said. "I flunk them." I was flustered. Our son's academic life flashed before my eyes. No teacher had ever threatened him with that before. I regained my composure and managed to say that I thought she was right. By the time I got home I was feeling pretty good about this. It was a radical approach for these times, but, well, why not? "She's going to flunk you," I told my son. I did not discuss it any further. Suddenly English became a priority in his life. He finished out the semester with an A.

7   I know one example doesn't make a case, but at night I see a parade of students who are angry and resentful for having been passed along until they could no longer even pretend to keep up. Of average intelligence or better, they eventually quit school, concluding they were too dumb to finish. "I should have been held back" is a comment I hear frequently. Even sadder are those students who are high-school graduates who say to me after a few weeks of class, "I don't know how I ever got a high-school diploma."

8   Passing students who have not mastered the work cheats them and the employers who expect graduates to have basic skills. We excuse this dishonest behavior by saying kids can't learn if they come from terrible environments. No one seems to stop to think that — no matter what environments they come from — most kids don't put school first on their list unless they perceive something is at stake. They'd rather be sailing.

9   Many students I see at night could give expert testimony on unemployment, chemical dependency, abusive relationships. In spite of these difficulties, they have decided to make education a priority. They are motivated by the desire for a better job or the need to hang on to the one they've got. They have a healthy fear of failure.

10   People of all ages can rise above their problems, but they need to have a reason to do so. Young people generally don't have the maturity to value education in the same way my adult students value it. But fear of failure, whether economic or academic, can motivate both.

11   Flunking as a regular policy has just as much merit today as it did two generations ago. We must review the threat of flunking and see it as it really is — a positive teaching tool. It is an expression of confidence by both teachers and parents that the students have the ability to learn the material presented to them. However, making it work again would take a dedicated, caring conspiracy between teachers and parents. It would mean facing the tough reality that passing kids who haven't learned the material — while it might save them grief for the short

term — dooms them to long-term illiteracy. It would mean that teachers would have to follow through on their threats, and parents would have to stand behind them, knowing their children's best interests are indeed at stake. This means no more doing Scott's assignments for him because he might fail. No more passing Jodi because she's such a nice kid.

This is a policy that worked in the past and can work today. 12 A wise teacher, with the support of his parents, gave our son the opportunity to succeed — or fail. It's time we return this choice to all students.

READING ACTIVITY 9: Build Your Vocabulary

Determine the meanings of the following words from the context of Mary Sherry's essay. Then check their meanings by looking up the words in a dictionary: validity (1), impediments (4), flustered (6).

READING ACTIVITY 10: Read to Improve Your Writing

Discuss the following questions about "In Praise of the F Word" with your classmates.

1. What problem does Sherry identify?
2. What evidence of the problem does the author provide? She uses the words "cheats" and "excuses." Do you think that these words set a reasonable tone?
3. What is Sherry's proposed solution?
4. Is the solution specific and reasonable?

An Environmental Problem

MARK HERTSGAARD

A Global Green Deal

Mark Hertsgaard has written "A Global Green Deal" to encourage governments to develop incentives for businesses and consumers to use environmentally friendly technologies. Hertsgaard, a journalist who has written numerous other articles and five books, also teaches nonfiction writing at Johns Hopkins University.

The bad news is that we have to change our ways — and fast. 1 Here's the good news: it could be a hugely profitable enterprise.

So what do we do? Everyone knows the planet is in bad shape, 2 but most people are resigned to passivity. Changing course, they reason, would require economic sacrifice and provoke stiff resistance from corporations and consumers alike, so why bother? It's easier to ignore the gathering storm clouds and hope the problem magically takes care of itself.

Such fatalism is not only dangerous but mistaken. For much of the 1990s I traveled the world to write a book about our environmental predicament. I returned home sobered by the extent of the damage we are causing and by the speed at which it is occurring. But there is nothing inevitable about our self-destructive behavior. Not only could we dramatically reduce our burden on the air, water and other natural systems, we could make money doing so. If we're smart, we could make restoring the environment the biggest economic enterprise of our time, a huge source of jobs, profits and poverty alleviation.

What we need is a Global Green Deal: a program to renovate our civilization environmentally from top to bottom in rich and poor countries alike. Making use of both market incentives and government leadership, a twenty-first-century Global Green Deal would do for environmental technologies what government and industry have recently done so well for computer and Internet technologies: launch their commercial takeoff.

Getting it done will take work, and before we begin we need to understand three facts about the reality facing us. First, we have no time to lose. While we've made progress in certain areas — air pollution is down in the U.S. — big environmental problems like climate change, water scarcity and species extinction are getting worse, and faster than ever. Thus we have to change our ways profoundly — and very soon.

Second, poverty is central to the problem. Four billion of the planet's 6 billion people face deprivation inconceivable to the wealthiest 1 billion. To paraphrase Thomas Jefferson, nothing is more certainly written in the book of fate than that the bottom two-thirds of humanity will strive to improve their lot. As they demand adequate heat and food, not to mention cars and CD players, humanity's environmental footprint will grow. Our challenge is to accommodate this mass ascent from poverty without wrecking the natural systems that make life possible.

Third, some good news: we have in hand most of the technologies needed to chart a new course. We know how to use oil, wood, water and other resources much more efficiently than we do now. Increased efficiency — doing more with less — will enable us to use fewer resources and produce less pollution per capita, buying us the time to bring solar power, hydrogen fuel cells and other futuristic technologies on line.

Efficiency may not sound like a rallying cry for environmental revolution, but it packs a financial punch. As Joseph J. Romm reports in his book *Cool Companies*, Xerox, Compaq and 3M are among many firms that have recognized they can cut their greenhouse-gas emissions in half — and enjoy 50 percent and higher returns on investment through improved efficiency, better lighting and insulation and smarter motors and building design. The rest of us (small businesses, homeowners, city governments, schools) can reap the same benefits.

Super-refrigerators use 87% less electricity than older, standard models while costing the same (assuming mass production) and performing better, as Paul Hawken and Amory and L. Hunter Lovins explain in their book *Natural Capitalism.* In Amsterdam the headquarters of ING Bank, one of Holland's largest banks, uses one-fifth as much energy per square meter as a nearby bank, even though the buildings cost the same to construct. The ING center boasts efficient windows and insulation and a design that enables solar energy to provide much of the building's needs, even in cloudy Northern Europe.

Examples like these lead even such mainstream voices as AT&T and Japan's energy planning agency, NEDO, to predict that environmental restoration could be a source of virtually limitless profit. The idea is to retrofit our farms, factories, shops, houses, offices and everything inside them. The economic activity generated would be enormous. Better yet, it would be labor intensive; investments in energy efficiency yield two to 10 times more jobs than investments in fossil fuel and nuclear power. In a world where 1 billion people lack gainful employment, creating jobs is essential to fighting the poverty that retards environmental progress.

But this transition will not happen by itself — too many entrenched interests stand in the way. Automakers often talk green but make only token efforts to develop green cars because gas-guzzling sport-utility vehicles are hugely profitable. But every year the U.S. government buys 56,000 new vehicles for official use from Detroit. Under the Global Green Deal, Washington would tell Detroit that from now on the cars have to be hybrid-electric or hydrogen-fuel-cell cars. Detroit might scream and holler, but if Washington stood firm, carmakers soon would be climbing the learning curve and offering the competitively priced green cars that consumers say they want.

We know such government pump-priming works; it's why so many of us have computers today. America's computer companies began learning to produce today's affordable systems during the 1960s while benefiting from subsidies and guaranteed markets under contracts with the Pentagon and the space program. And the cyberboom has fueled the biggest economic expansion in history.

The Global Green Deal must not be solely an American project, however. China and India, with their gigantic populations and ambitious development plans, could by themselves doom everyone else to severe global warming. Already, China is the world's second largest producer of greenhouse gases (after the U.S.). But China would use 50% less coal if it simply installed today's energy-efficient technologies. Under the Global Green Deal, Europe, America and Japan would help China buy these technologies, not only because that would reduce global warming but also because it would create jobs and profits for workers and companies back home.

Governments would not have to spend more money, only shift 14 existing subsidies away from environmentally dead-end technologies like coal and nuclear power. If even half the $500 billion to $900 billion in environmentally destructive subsidies now offered by the world's governments were redirected, the Global Green Deal would be off to a roaring start. Governments need to establish "rules of the road" so that market prices reflect the real social costs of clearcut forests and other environmental abominations. Again, such a shift could be revenue neutral. Higher taxes on, say, coal burning would be offset by cuts in payroll and profits taxes, thus encouraging jobs and investment while discouraging pollution. A portion of the revenues should be set aside to assure a just transition for workers and companies now engaged in inherently anti-environmental activities like coal mining.

All this sounds easy enough on paper, but in the real world 15 it is not so simple. Beneficiaries of the current system — be they U.S. corporate-welfare recipients, redundant German coal miners, or cutthroat Asian logging interests — will resist. Which is why progress is unlikely absent a broader agenda of change, including real democracy: assuring the human rights of environmental activists, and neutralizing the power of Big Money through campaign-finance reform.

The Global Green Deal is no silver bullet. It can, however, 16 buy us time to make the more deep-seated changes — in our often excessive appetites, in our curious belief that humans are the center of the universe, in our sheer numbers — that will be necessary to repair our relationship with our environment.

None of this will happen without an aroused citizenry. But a 17 Global Green Deal is in the common interest, and it is a slogan easily grasped by the media and the public. Moreover, it should appeal across political, class and national boundaries, for it would stimulate both jobs and business throughout the world in the name of a universal value: leaving our children a livable planet. The history of environmentalism is largely the story of ordinary people pushing for change while governments, corporations and other established interests reluctantly follow behind. It's time to repeat that history on behalf of a Global Green Deal.

READING ACTIVITY 11: Build Your Vocabulary

Determine the meanings of the following words from the context of Mark Hertsgaard's essay. Then check their meanings by looking up the words in a dictionary: passivity (2), fatalism (3), profoundly (5), deprivation (6), retrofit (10), entrenched (11), abominations (14).

READING ACTIVITY 12: Read to Improve Your Writing

Discuss the following questions about "A Global Green Deal" with your classmates.

1. What problem does Hertsgaard identify?
2. What evidence of the problem does the author provide? How does he use logical, emotional, and ethical appeals?
3. What is the proposed solution? Is the solution specific and reasonable?
4. What environmental problem would you like to see eliminated?

Writing for Different Situations

10. Keeping Journals

11. Writing Summaries

12. Conducting Primary, Library, and Internet Research

13. Taking Timed Writing Tests

14. Writing Résumés and Cover Letters

Whether writing for personal enjoyment, for class, or for the workplace, you can use specialized writing strategies to help you do an even better job. In Part Three, you'll practice some of these writing strategies. You'll learn to keep journals as a way to gather ideas and practice your writing. You'll learn to write summaries to present information concisely. You'll learn how to conduct research to help you support what you have to say with interesting and informative details. You'll discover tips for doing your best on timed essay exams and standardized writing tests. And you'll learn how to write résumés and cover letters that will help you land that important job.

10

Keeping Journals

In this chapter, you will begin your own journal. As you work on your journal, you will

- **Discover why writers keep journals.**

- **Learn how to keep a journal.**

- **Practice keeping three types of journals.**

Imagine that you want to become a great musician or athlete. How would you go about it? First, knowing that achieving this goal takes hard work and a long time, you would have to be motivated to achieve your goal. Then you would seek out a teacher or coach to work with you. Finally, you would do what great musicians and athletes do — practice: musicians rehearse, and athletes work out. The same is true if you want to be a writer. But you might think, "I don't want to become a great writer — another Shakespeare. I just want to write well enough to get better grades on my term papers or a promotion at work." The path is still the same, whether you're aiming for the major leagues, the minors, or a spot on your neighborhood sandlot team. You'll need to make a commitment to study and practice.

You have demonstrated your motivation to improve your writing by enrolling in a writing course. In class, you'll have the opportunity to learn what you need to do to become a better writer. But to become a truly effective writer, you'll also need to practice what you have learned. Just as the musician practices scales and the athlete lifts weights, writers practice by writing. Often, writers do this in a *journal*, a notebook in which they express their thoughts and ideas.

You may ask, "Aren't some people just born musicians, athletes, or writers? Why should I bother to learn and practice if I wasn't born with this talent?" Some people may have more natural skill, but that doesn't mean the rest of us can't become better if we set our minds to it. Even people with natural talent must be willing to learn and practice to realize their potential. Musicians don't reach the concert hall, athletes don't reach the big time, and writers don't have their work published unless they are committed and are willing to study and practice.

Writing Assignment

Begin to keep a journal. You can either use a computer or write in a notebook. If you choose a notebook, be sure to use one that has at least one hundred pages so you can write in it daily.

You may choose to keep one or more of three types of journals: a personal journal, a dialogue journal, or a learning log. If a journal is required for one of your classes, your instructor may ask you to keep a particular type of journal. Once you decide which type you will keep, set aside some time each day to write in your journal.

WHY WRITERS KEEP JOURNALS

Let's think more about practice. Would a musician wait until the night before a concert to practice the music? Would a basketball player wait until the day before the big game to practice slam dunks? Of course not. The same is true with writing. If you want to write well, you must start practicing now. As a writer, your equivalent to the musician's instrument or the athlete's equipment is a journal — a notebook for jotting down your ideas, opinions, feelings, and memories. The more time you spend writing in your journal, the more practice you'll get as a writer.

LUCY CALKINS

From The Art of Teaching Writing

Lucy Calkins is a professor of English education at Teachers College, Columbia University, where she specializes in the teaching of reading and writing. She is the author of several books on teaching and education, including Lessons from a Child *(1983) and* The Art of Teaching Reading *(2000). In the following excerpt from* The Art of Teaching Writing *(1994), Calkins describes how she uses her notebook journal as a place to try out ideas.*

1   I write to hold what I find in my life in my hands and to declare it a treasure. I'm not very good at doing this. When I sit down at my desk, I'm like my students. "Nothing happens in my life," I say. I feel empty-handed. I want to get up and rush around, looking for something Big and Significant to put on the page.

2   And yet, as a writer I have come to know that significance cannot be found, it must be grown. Looking back in my notebook I find a brief entry about how my son Miles uses one of my cotton T-shirts as his "pretend blanket," replacing the original blanket, which has disintegrated. My inclination is to dismiss the entry as trivial, or something only a mother could care about, but then I remember the writer Vicki Vinton saying, "It is an illusion that writers live more significant lives than non-writers; the truth is, writers are just more in the habit of finding the significance that is there in their lives."

3   Vicki's words hang over my desk, as do the words of the poet Theodore Roethke, who said, "If our lives don't feel significant, sometimes it's not our lives, but our response to our lives, which needs to be richer." It's not only these quotations that nudge me to believe I can find significance in my son's "pretend blanket." I'm also instructed by memories of times when I've

begun with something small, and seen significance emerge on my page. From my experiences as a writer and from the experiences of other authors, I have developed a small repertoire of strategies to draw on when I want to take a seed idea and grow it into a speech, a story, a book. This, for me, is what the writing process is all about.

Use your journal as a place to plant seeds of ideas, experiment with different ways of writing, and write without the pressure of being evaluated. Journal writing can help you find topics for writing. It can also help you clarify and organize your ideas. But most important, writing in a journal helps you become an active thinker, rather than being a passive reader or listener. This, in turn, will help you write better papers in college and get that promotion at work.

Use a Blog to Journal
A *blog*, or Web log, is an online journal where writers can post entries and readers can post comments. Blog Web sites such as **blogger.com**, **livejournal.com**, **myspace.com**, and **typepad.com** allow users to set up free accounts and post unlimited entries online. If you would like to keep a journal online, consider setting up a blog. Keep in mind, however, that anyone with access to the Internet will be able to read and comment on your blog.

PERSONAL JOURNALS

A *personal journal* is a collection of your thoughts and feelings. You write simply to express yourself. You need not be concerned about grammar, spelling, or punctuation, and you need not write in complete sentences. Just as the musician practices scales and the sprinter runs laps to loosen up, you develop fluency and the ability to express yourself smoothly and easily by writing in a personal journal. In addition to written entries, you may include lists, pictures, drawings, newspaper clippings — anything that gives you ideas for writing.

Because you do not share a personal journal, you can write without worrying about others' reactions to your writing. You can relax and write in your own style, using language that is natural to you.

Here are some sample entries from student writer Alyssa's personal journal:

```
April 4

    Here I am on a cloudy day headed to my house. My mom is
driving at thirty-five miles per hour. She has always been a
```

cautious driver. Every other car seems to be passing us. Some of the drivers turn, maybe wondering why my mother is driving so slow. Now we're passing the old factory. Sometimes it looks nice, especially at night. But today it looks really ugly. All the smoke is more noticeable because it is cloudy, too. I get sick just thinking about how many chemicals we breathe every day.

As I look around, I notice that this town is desperately in need of some trees. All I can see are poles, billboards, and dirt.

April 5

I called to see if I can get my old job back again. It's not exciting, but the pay's good and the people are nice. Maybe there'll be more part-timers around my age now. I hope I hear soon because otherwise I've got to get to work on finding something else.

April 7

I wrote this poem while I was waiting for the bus . . .

Wheels go, people go
Turning, turning, turning
Places to see and things to do
Waiting, waiting, waiting
Impatiently I check my watch
I have no book to pass the time
Just my journal

April 8

Heard from APCO. Got my summer job. Wow! That takes a load off of my mind.

GROUP ACTIVITY 1: Start a Personal Journal

To help you brainstorm ideas for starting a personal journal, form a group with several classmates, and answer the following questions. After the group has discussed the questions, have each member freewrite about his or her answer to one of the questions. Use this freewriting as the first entry in your new personal journal.

1. What are two things I would rather be doing right now?
2. Am I well organized? How often must I search for something that I have misplaced?
3. If I could change anything about the way I have been raised, what would it be?
4. If I could take a one-month trip anywhere in the world (and if money were not a consideration), where would I go and what would I do?
5. What do I most strive for in life: accomplishment, security, love, power, excitement, knowledge, or something else?
6. Is there something I have dreamed of doing for a long time? Why haven't I done it?
7. Do I have long-term goals? What is one such goal, and how do I plan to reach it?
8. What is the greatest accomplishment of my life?
9. What is my most treasured memory?
10. What do I see myself doing in ten years' time?

Keep a Personal Journal on Computer
You may prefer to keep your personal journal on disk. Set up a file called "journal," and then add entries to it each day, just as you would to a notebook. Enter text as quickly as you can, concentrating on your ideas and resisting the urge to backspace, delete, or correct your writing.

DIALOGUE JOURNALS

The *dialogue journal* is a written conversation — or dialogue — between you and another person. As in a personal journal, your primary concern in a dialogue journal is expressing your thoughts. Unlike a personal journal, however, what you write in a dialogue journal will be read by someone else. You need not be overly concerned with grammar, spelling, and punctuation, but your thoughts and ideas should be complete enough for your reader to understand them. You may exchange your dialogue journal with one or more friends or classmates. You also may focus on one topic or change topics each time you exchange journals.

One advantage of a dialogue journal is that it allows you to clarify your understanding of an idea or issue by explaining it to someone else. Another advantage is that it allows you to determine how clearly you communicate your thoughts to someone else. You may even ask your reader specific questions.

In the following sample entry from a student's dialogue journal, Kirk writes about a school issue that concerns him. Because he is writing to get his thoughts down on paper, Kirk makes some errors in grammar and punctuation.

> One incident that really upset me this past week was the fact that on tests people are always cheating. It makes me mad that people expect others to always do their work for them. This might have been okay in high school but this is college and that means everyone has to make it on their own. We don't go to college expecting to "just pass." Well maybe some people do and those who do feel that way have no business in college.
>
> However what do my friends say. "Oh what a small classroom. Great for cheating. Come sit by me and let me see your paper, okay." What kind of people are they. They are wasting their parents money because it is obvious they don't plan to study or have a career.

Here's how Kirk's student reader, Michelle, responded to his journal entry:

> Kirk, rather than thinking so much about other people's cheating, concentrate on your own goals. In the long run, the cheaters will be the ones who lose out for not doing their own work. Just don't let them cheat off of you. Concentrate on not cheating yourself. Be honest to your own work, your own future.

And here's what Kirk's writing instructor had to say after reading the same journal entry:

> Kirk, I can see that you have strong feelings about cheating. You may want to write a persuasive letter to the editor of the campus newspaper about the problem of cheating on campus. Why do you suppose students cheat? Why do you say that cheating might have been okay in high school? Is cheating acceptable at some times but not at other times? How would you solve this problem? What do you think should happen to students who are caught cheating?

GROUP ACTIVITY 2: Start a Dialogue Journal

Ask a classmate to exchange journals with you for a few days. Write about anything of interest to you. If you need help getting started, try answering a few of the following questions.

1. What do I value most in a relationship?
2. Do I judge others by higher or lower standards than I use to judge myself?

3. When did I last yell at someone? Why? Did I later regret it?

4. Do I find it hard to say no to family and friends? Why or why not?

5. Who is the most important person in my life? Why?

6. Are there people whose lives I envy enough to want to trade places with them? Who are they?

7. Have I ever disliked someone? If so, why and for how long?

8. What do I most regret not having told someone? Why haven't I told that person yet?

9. What is my best advice for getting along with others?

10. How important is family life to me? Do I think of family as including only those people related to me by birth? Or do I include close friends and neighbors as well?

Keep a Dialogue Journal Online

Dialogue online by posting your entries on a personal or class blog or listserv. Alternatively, dialogue by sending e-mails back and forth to your classmates or instructor.

LEARNING LOGS

A *learning log* is a journal that focuses on your responses to course content. In it, you summarize, synthesize, or react to a class lecture, discussion, or assigned reading. You may restate the objectives of each class or try to pinpoint what confuses you about a particular topic. By keeping a learning log, you'll improve not only your understanding of the subject but also your attitude toward the course in general. Asking questions and voicing your concerns in your log will help you become an active learner and contribute in class discussions. You'll also find yourself making connections between new ideas and previous knowledge.

Get into the habit of placing the letter *T* (for *Topic*) in the margin next to learning-log entries that you think might make good essay topics. What makes a good topic? A good topic is one that you're interested in and that others might also want to learn about. Consider, too, how much you already know about the topic and whether you can find additional information about it.

Student writer Tom's learning-log entry is about his first-year college composition class. By writing about his own writing, Tom gains insight into how to become a better writer.

I am glad to hear that I am not expected to write excellently from the beginning. I now understand that everyone can improve their writing. I like the idea that we will be sharing our work with our classmates. I always thought that in college we would not have an opportunity to share.

Today we learned about freewriting, which means to write off the top of your head as fast as you can. We did freewriting in my English class. I liked it because it lets ideas flow out freely without worrying about grammar or punctuation. I'm glad we will be freewriting this semester.

The essays we have to do seem hard. I already feel the pressure of my first paper. Maybe freewriting will help me.

Tom keeps his learning log in a traditional full-page format. Some students, however, prefer to integrate their logs with their class notes in a double-column format. To do this, simply divide each page down the middle, with one column labeled *Notes* and the other *Thoughts*. In the Notes column, record key concepts, important details, and examples from class lectures and outside reading. In the Thoughts column, reflect on what you're learning: What does it mean to you? How do you feel about it? How will you use this information in the future? You may also summarize, keep a list of new vocabulary words, and jot down notes on upcoming assignments.

Keeping a two-column learning log helps you integrate what you're studying in college into the fabric of your own thinking and past experiences. Personal examples help you understand the course material and the ways it relates to your life. Whichever type of learning log you choose to keep, responding to your class notes will help you recall information when you need it for a class discussion or an exam.

Here's an entry from the two-column learning log that student writer Tammy kept for her psychology class:

Notes	Thoughts

Memory —
 Where information is held.
   3 types
   sensory
   short-term
   long-term
 sensory — all info that enters the senses
 short-term — where all conscious thought takes place
 long-term — representation of all that is known
	I never realized there were three kinds of memory. I'm not surprised that we forget so much sensory info: there's so much of it. Short-term memory is what I am thinking now, drawing on what is happening around me. I think of long-term memory kind of like a book in the library. If I want to retrieve it, I hope that it is there.

HOW TO   Keep a Learning Log

- During class or as you read, take notes on the left-hand side of the paper.

- On the right-hand side, summarize, define words, connect to your own experiences, or jot down ideas about upcoming assignments.

- After class, write two or three paragraphs about what you learned using a full-page format (either with pen or in a computer file).

GROUP ACTIVITY 3:   Start a Learning Log

During class, take notes as you always do. Afterward, along with a class-mate, reflect in your logs by asking yourselves the following questions.

1. How can I summarize what I learned in class today?
2. What parts did I not understand?
3. How might I clarify this information?
4. What new vocabulary words do I need to look up?
5. What key points are likely to appear on an exam?
6. Which ideas would make good future paper topics?
7. Do I agree or disagree with what I have learned today?
8. How can I apply what I learned to other classes?
9. How can I apply what I learned to my work?
10. How will I use this information in the future?

Keep a Learning Log on Computer
Using the Format command in your word-processing program, you can easily create a two-column learning log. Consider using a different font for summaries. Boldface new vocabulary words and concepts you don't understand so that you can look them up later.

HOW TO   Select the Right Journal for You

- Keep a personal journal if you want to explore your own thoughts and feelings.

- Keep a dialogue journal if you want to exchange ideas with others.

- Keep a learning log if you want to increase what you learn in your college classes.

CHAPTER CHECKLIST

❑ Use a journal to jot down ideas, opinions, feelings, and insights.

❑ A journal can be kept in a notebook or on a computer.

❑ There are three types of journals:

   ❑ The personal journal.

   ❑ The dialogue journal.

   ❑ The learning log.

❑ The personal journal is for its writer's eyes only and contains personal thoughts and feelings.

❑ The dialogue journal is shared with someone who reads and responds to it.

❑ The learning log is kept for a particular course and contains class notes, reading notes, and its writer's own thoughts, sometimes in a two-column format.

REFLECTING ON YOUR WRITING

You have practiced writing three types of journals: a personal journal, a dialogue journal, and a learning log. To help you decide which one you want to continue to keep throughout this semester, answer the following questions.

1. Do any of my instructors require a journal? If so, which type of journal is required?

2. How will keeping a personal journal be worthwhile to me as a student?

3. If I keep a dialogue journal, who will I ask to read and respond to it?

4. For which course would I keep a learning log?

5. How will keeping a journal help me discover topics for future papers?

6. How will journal writing give me practice as a writer?

Using your answers to these questions, complete a Writing Process Report for this chapter (you can download a report form at **bedford stmartins.com/choices**). Once you complete this report, begin your journal by writing on what you learned in this chapter about journals and what you still hope to learn. Continue to add entries daily.

Writing Summaries

In this chapter, you will write a summary of a favorite reading in this textbook. As you work on your summary, you will

- Learn about the parts of a summary.

- Practice using your own words to write a summary.

A *summary* is a condensed version of a piece of writing. Many of us have summarized the plot of a favorite book for a friend, and some of us have written summaries on the job and in college classes.

Instructors may ask you to summarize books, articles, essays, plays, television shows, movies, or speeches. These summaries help you condense important source information, reflect on what you have learned, and demonstrate your knowledge to others. You may also choose to write summaries of a reading assignment, a lecture, or other classroom materials for yourself as a way to learn and recall information for class discussions, reports, or exams.

A summary includes the main ideas and important supporting points from the original, and it leaves out overly specific details and examples. A summary is written in your own words but does not include your judgment or opinion. To summarize well, you must be able to analyze and evaluate the source information and then condense it, using your own words. Doing this can help you develop your writing, reading, listening, and thinking skills. Summaries test your understanding of the original information as well as your ability to communicate effectively what you have learned.

Writing Assignment

Your instructor is revising the syllabus for this course for next year and is asking students to give feedback about the essays in this book. Your instructor wants to know which readings interest students, which essays they understand fully, and which ones they do not understand. To help determine which essays students like best and how clearly students understand them, your instructor would like you and your classmates to select a favorite essay from any of the chapters in Part Two of this textbook. Write a summary of your favorite essay, and share it with your instructor.

WRITING A SUMMARY

As with other skills, writing a good summary takes practice. If you are writing an e-mail to a friend or family member in which you describe the movie you saw last night, you would draft quickly and hit the Send button. Other times — especially if you are summarizing a document for an employer or a textbook reading assignment for an instructor — you may need to use the writing process to gather ideas, write and revise several drafts, and edit your final summary to eliminate errors. A number of strategies will help you consistently write better summaries.

Reread the Original Text

As soon as you are assigned a summary or decide to write one for yourself, go back and reread the original material. A summary allows you to condense a long piece of writing into one or a few paragraphs. This can be important when your reader doesn't have the time to read the original. When you summarize, you filter out unnecessary details and focus on main points only.

1. Preview the reading.
   - Think about the title and what it means to you.
   - Note the author's name.
2. Read the text.
   - Read carefully, underlining the most important points.
   - Circle and look up the meanings of words you don't know.
3. Write to comprehend and remember.
   - List the most important points.
   - Note the page numbers of the original text.

Write the Summary

A summary helps you and your reader figure out what you do and don't know. You can write a good summary only if you fully understand the original text. A sure way for you and your reader to test whether you know a certain piece of material is to see whether you can summarize it accurately. Your summary will include these parts:

Main Idea

In the first sentence, identify the title, the author's name, and the main idea of the original source in your own words. This is the sentence that tells your readers the source of the original text and its main topic. Remember, even when you use your own words, you must let the reader know that you borrowed the information from another source.

EXAMPLE

In the essay "Prison Studies," Malcom X describes how he learned to love reading while serving time in prison.

Important Supporting Points

Learning to summarize helps you streamline the process of reading and recording information. Because you can't quote everything you read, you select and include only the most important points. Summaries also provide you with a version that you can reread later as you prepare for a class discussion, a report, or an exam.

Decide which pieces of information you need to include to get the main idea across quickly. Write these down in your own words. Try to stay true to the meaning the original author intended. Use direct quotes sparingly — no more than one or two.

For more on using direct quotations, see pp. 602–3.

EXAMPLE

Malcolm X was impressed with one of his fellow inmate's knowledge, but he lacked the reading skills to effectively state his own opinions. To develop his vocabulary, he began copying the pages of a dictionary and then memorizing the meanings of the words. Once he learned some words, he began to read more and more books, often reading into the night after lights out. He states: "I knew right there in prison that reading had changed forever the course of my life."

Conclusion

Write a conclusion that restates the main idea or the author's opinion or recommendations. The conclusion helps bring the summary to a close and helps your reader understand what you consider to be important.

EXAMPLE

After Malcolm X was released from prison, he continued to read everything he could get his hands on and used what he learned to help his community. These prison studies helped him become an educated man (pages 86–89).

GROUP ACTIVITY 1: Identify the Parts of a Summary

With several classmates, reread the essay "Don't Eat the Flan" on pages 339–41, and then read the summary below. In the spaces provided, identify each element of the summary. Write *M* for the main point of the summary. Number each of the supporting points. Write *C* for the concluding sentence. Discuss how this summary condenses the original essay.

Summary Paragraph for Greg Critser's "Don't Eat the Flan"

_____ In the essay "Don't Eat the Flan," author Greg Critser argues that obesity is not only a health issue but also a morality issue. _____ He begins by discussing his interest in food and morality. _____ He continues by describing the "'therapaziation' of gluttony." _____ According to Critser, society is afraid to tell obese people to eat less or exercise more because of a fear of hurting obese people's feelings. _____ Critser states that using shame to stigmatize unhealthy behaviors such as smoking and unsafe sex has worked to reduce those activities and should be used to discourage overeating and physical inactivity. _____ He also feels that children have taken away parents' authority over the dinner table and should not be able to choose what foods they will and will not eat. _____ Critser strongly disagrees with idea that "'kids have the right to make bad nutritional choices.'" _____ Critser believes that the way to combat obesity is to help parents take control of their children's diets and to view overeating as a sin, just as the French do (pages 339–41).

HOW TO Write a Summary

- Reread the material to be summarized, underlining the important points.

> - Write a sentence that states the title, the author's name, and the main point of the original text.
>
> - In your own words, write the important supporting points.
>
> - Leave out overly specific details and examples.
>
> - Write a conclusion that restates the main point and includes the page numbers of the original text.

GROUP ACTIVITY 2: Write a Summary

Imagine that your class will be tested on the information in Diane Helman and Phyllis Bookspan's essay "Sesame Street: Brought to You by the Letters *M-A-L-E*" on pages 237–239. Write a summary that will help you remember this information. Share your summary with several classmates. Discuss ways to improve each summary.

CHAPTER CHECKLIST

❑   A summary is a condensed version of a piece of writing.
❑   A summary has three sections:
   ❑   Main idea.
   ❑   Supporting points.
   ❑   Conclusion.
❑   Use your own words to summarize someone else's writing.
❑   Give credit to the author of the original text.

REFLECTING ON YOUR WRITING

To help you continue to improve your summary writing, answer the following questions about the assignment.

1. Other than for this class, when have you been asked to write summaries?

2. Have you found writing summaries a useful way to study? Why or why not?

3. What elements of writing a summary do you need practice with? Why?

Using your answers to these questions, complete a Writing Process Report for this chapter (you can download a report form at **bedford stmartins.com/choices**). Once you complete this report, freewrite about what you learned in this chapter about summary writing and what you still hope to learn.

CHAPTER

12

Conducting Primary, Library, and Internet Research

In this chapter, you will write a brief researched essay. As you work on your essay, you will

- **Prepare to research a topic.**

- **Make observations, survey others, and conduct interviews.**

- **Locate sources of information in the library and on the Internet.**

- **Evaluate sources of information.**

- **Learn what plagiarism is and how to avoid it.**

- **Learn note-taking strategies.**

- **Quote, paraphrase, and summarize information.**

- **Document sources correctly.**

Imagine that you received the following writing assignments in your college courses:

- Describe the life cycle of the diamondback rattlesnake.
- Analyze Cesar Chavez's leadership of migrant farmworkers.
- Explain the origin of the Internet in the late 1970s.

How do you find information on these topics? Of course, you head to the library or the Internet. But then what?

If you had looked for this information in a library thirty years ago, you would have headed to the card catalog to find the name of a book on your topic and to see where it was located. You also might have examined a large book that listed magazine articles on your subject. Today, however, computers contain this information — and much more. Because of computer technology, libraries can now access information from around the world in seconds. How do you sort through this information to decide what is most useful and valid? How do you use this material in an essay? This chapter will give you strategies for conducting research and using information in your own essays. You will also learn to find information by becoming a researcher yourself.

Writing Assignment

The International Students Office on your campus is holding a public meeting to help students from other countries adjust to their new surroundings. Your psychology instructor has volunteered your class to participate in this forum. To prepare for the forum, your instructor has broken the class into teams. Each team is to write an essay with ideas on helping international students adjust to a new country and university. You and your classmates will present these essays at the forum at the end of the term.

PREPARING TO CONDUCT RESEARCH

To conduct research, you need to know what information you're seeking. Otherwise, you might spend a great deal of time finding information that doesn't pertain to your topic.

Narrow Your Topic

Before beginning your research, narrow your topic so that your ideas can be well developed. For the International Students Office forum, you could explain aspects of American culture that are important for international students to understand. You could also suggest how international students can increase their enjoyment of their new culture. Another choice would be to focus on the stress that people suffer when they encounter a new culture or setting — in other words, culture shock. Narrowing your topic to just one of these ideas will allow you to give sufficient detail in your report. It will also help you know exactly what information you need to find to support your points.

Write Research Questions

After you narrow your topic, think of questions that you want to answer. These *research questions* will guide you in conducting your research. For instance, if you are writing about culture shock, you might ask these questions:

- What is the definition of *culture shock*?
- Who gets culture shock?
- What are the emotional and physical effects of culture shock?
- How can culture shock be prevented?

As you research your topic, refer to your research questions to help you stay focused on the information you need.

HOW TO Plan a Research Project

- Choose a topic that interests you.
- Review your purpose and audience.
- Narrow your topic.
- State the following questions: Who? What? When? Where? Why? How?
- Select a few of these questions to explore.
- Establish a timeline for conducting research to answer these questions and for completing the project. Allow plenty of time to work on each part of the project.

PRIMARY RESEARCH

Research that you do on your own, rather than read about, is called *primary research*. Thus, when you conduct an experiment in science, you're doing primary research. When you ask friends to suggest a good movie, you're essentially taking a survey, another form of primary research.

Three common types of primary research involve making observations, surveying others, and conducting interviews. These types of primary research are used for different purposes:

- When you want to explain how something works or how something is done, consider making observations.
- When you want to explain your topic's importance in people's lives, consider conducting a survey.
- When you require specialized information or information known only to experts, consider conducting an interview.

Making Observations

To *observe* something is to watch it closely. Observations enable you to explain your points clearly to your readers. For example, if you're explaining cell mitosis, you can observe cell division under a microscope. In your essay, you can describe what you saw to make the process come alive for your readers. Similarly, in an essay about the Internet, you might describe your observations of some online conversations and include a quotation that illustrates a key point.

HOW TO Make Observations

- Obtain permission (if necessary) to observe an event relevant to your topic.
- Remain visible, but do not participate in the event.
- Decide what to focus on when you observe.
- Take detailed notes as you observe the event.
- Ask questions about what you observe but may not understand.

Surveying Others

A *survey* contains information collected from many people about a certain topic. Newspapers often conduct surveys to find out how citizens plan to vote in an upcoming election. Manufacturers hire market-research companies to survey users of their products and thereby learn how to improve the products. In writing, a survey can help you point out people's opinions or knowledge about an issue. For example, if your topic for the International Students Office forum is culture shock, you could survey people to determine how many of them know the definition of *culture shock*. Your research findings might support the point that many people experience culture shock but few know what it is or how it can be alleviated.

HOW TO Conduct Surveys

- Decide how you will conduct the survey — with an *oral survey* or a *written survey*. In an oral survey, respondents reply immediately but do not have much time to think about the questions. A written survey generates detailed responses, but many people may not have the time to fill out a questionnaire.

- Decide where you will conduct the survey. You want to find a place where many people come and go, such as the entrance of the college library or Student Union.

- Create five to ten survey questions. Make them brief and easy to understand. Also use various types of questions, such as questions that can be answered with yes or no mixed with questions that require short answers. Test questions on classmates for suggestions to improve.

- Decide whom you will survey. For instance, do you want to survey both men and women from various age groups? Avoid surveying only people you know.

- Decide how many people you will survey. The more people you include in a survey, the more reliable your results will be. But you need to consider your time limitations as well.

- If you conduct an oral survey, write out your questions ahead of time, and take careful notes.

Conducting a Survey Online
A survey can be sent to people in writing via e-mail or posted online for people to fill in electronically. Be sure to include a deadline for responding. Consider sharing the results of the survey for those who participated in it. If you want the opinions of people who may not have access to the Internet, though, a printed survey is a better choice.

Conducting Interviews

In addition to making observations and surveying others, you can conduct an *interview* to learn more about a research topic. By interviewing a knowledgeable person, you can collect information and gain an expert's perspective on your topic. If you're writing an essay on water quality in your region, you could interview an environmental engineer who has studied this subject. For the topic of culture shock, you could interview international students who can describe what it's like to experience culture shock.

HOW TO Conduct Interviews

- Choose a knowledgeable person to interview. To determine whether someone is an expert on your topic, check his or her credentials (such as academic degrees, professional activities, and published works). In some situations, a person's personal experience with your topic is more relevant than formal credentials.

- Contact the person in advance to set up an appointment.

- Prepare your interview questions.

- If you conduct the interview in person, dress appropriately, and arrive on time.

- Keep the conversation focused on your questions. Be considerate of your interviewee's limited time.

- Listen carefully, and take good notes. Put quotation marks around the person's actual words. You may tape-record the conversation only if you obtain the interviewee's permission beforehand.

- Ask the interviewee to clarify anything you do not understand.

- Send a thank-you note to the person soon after the interview. Here's one more tip: if you're reluctant to contact a stranger for an interview, remember that most people enjoy talking about what they know and sharing their knowledge with interested students.

Interviewing others is a great way to gather information. For a review of how to consult with others, see pp. 15–16.

GROUP ACTIVITY 1: Conduct Primary Research

Discuss your writing topics with students in other groups. Determine the type of primary research that will best suit each group's topic. Then use the appropriate set of questions to discuss how members of each group can go about making observations, surveying others, or conducting interviews.

QUESTIONS ABOUT MAKING OBSERVATIONS

1. What information do you need to obtain from your observations?

2. Where will you make the observations?

3. Do you need permission to observe? If so, from whom?

4. What questions do you have about the event you want to observe?

QUESTIONS ABOUT SURVEYING OTHERS

1. What information do you want the survey to provide?

2. Do you want your respondents to answer orally or in writing? Why?

3. Who will your respondents be, and how many people will you survey?

4. Where will you conduct the survey?

5. What questions will you ask in the survey?

QUESTIONS ABOUT CONDUCTING AN INTERVIEW

1. What information do you hope to obtain from the interview?

2. Who could give you this information?

3. What questions will you ask?

SECONDARY RESEARCH

Secondary research involves reading what others have written about your topic. To conduct secondary research, you need to know how to locate relevant sources of information; how to evaluate sources; how to avoid plagiarism; how to take notes; how to quote, paraphrase, and summarize sources of information; and how to document the sources you cite in your research paper.

Locating Sources of Information

Traditionally, sources of information in libraries have been in print form, such as books or newspapers. Magazines, which are written by journalists for a general audience, and journals, which contain articles by experts for a more specialized audience, are other print sources. However, many materials that used to appear only in print now also appear in electronic form. To do secondary research, you need to know how to access both print and electronic sources.

Print Sources.   To begin your search for information, consult an encyclopedia. You're probably familiar with such general encyclopedias as *Encyclopaedia Britannica*, but specialized encyclopedias are a better source of in-depth information because they cover specific fields. Some specialized encyclopedias are the *Encyclopedia of Computer Science and Technology*, *Encyclopedia of Psychology*, *Encyclopedia of*

Biological Sciences, and *Harvard Guide to American History*. You can locate specialized encyclopedias by checking the library catalog or consulting a reference librarian.

After consulting an encyclopedia, you can find further information by checking an *index*, which lists magazine, journal, or newspaper articles by subject or author. After finding the title of a useful article in an index, you will need to locate it in your college's library using a *call number*, the number the library assigns to each item in its collection. Most libraries gather magazine and journal articles into volumes, which are then placed on the library shelves (called *stacks*). You can find books on your topic by consulting your college library's subject catalog; the books will be shelved in the stacks by call number.

Electronic Sources.   In addition to the print versions, many encyclopedias, magazines, journals, and newspapers are available online. Indexes, or databases, contain titles of articles from thousands of magazines, journals, and newspapers. Some databases, such as *Periodical Abstracts* and *Readers' Guide Abstracts*, list magazine and journal articles, whereas others, such as *InfoTrac Newspapers*, include only newspaper articles. A reference librarian can help you choose the databases that are most useful for your topic. Compared with print sources, computer databases are generally more current because they can be more easily updated. You may even be able to access your library's computer databases from your home or another campus computer. Many databases are also available on the World Wide Web.

When consulting a database, use *keywords*, or words that pertain to your topic, to locate articles. The wrong keywords can give you either too many or too few items from the database. For her report on culture shock, one student, Leslie Lozano, searched the database *Academic Search Premier* using the keywords "culture shock." She received a list of 138 articles — too many for her to review. To narrow

---

HOW TO   Use Keywords to Search

- Narrow your search by connecting keywords with the word *AND*, as in "culture shock AND education."

- You can also narrow your search by using the word *NOT*, as in "culture shock NOT immigration."

- If your keywords don't result in enough items for you to examine, broaden your search by using the word *OR*, as in "culture shock OR cultural studies."

- If you still can't find the right keywords, ask a reference librarian. He or she can then check the subject headings in the database for you.

her search, she used the keywords "culture shock AND international students." These keywords produced no items for her to examine. On the advice of a librarian, she used "culture shock AND education." This produced seven items for her to examine — a more manageable number than the initial 138.

A database often gives you an *abstract*, or brief summary, of each article it contains. This abstract will help you determine whether the article is likely to answer one of your research questions. Leslie Lozano checked the abstract of the first article the database had given her, "Culture Club." Based on the abstract, she decided she might be able to use it in her report on culture shock. She was in luck. The full article was included in the database, saving her the time of retrieving it from the periodical section of the library. After reading the article, she printed it out so she could take notes on it at a later time.

Leslie's Search Results

Another electronic source of information is the World Wide Web, which is a system of linked computer files on the Internet. Because topics are linked together, the Web allows you to jump from one topic to another quickly and easily. Computer programs such as *Microsoft Internet Explorer, Mozilla Firefox*, and *Netscape Navigator*, known as *browsers*, allow access to the Web. As with databases, use keywords to locate material on your topic.

HOW TO Find Electronic Resources

- Identify a database, such as *LexisNexis*, on which to search for information. A list of databases is available at your campus library.
- Enter keywords on your topic to access information.
- Read the abstract or summary to determine whether an article sounds useful.
- If the article seems useful, print or take notes on the information.
- Record the publication information for your Works Cited page.

Other Sources of Information.   Secondary research need not be limited to library sources. Check television listings for relevant documentaries or news shows. *All Things Considered*, broadcast daily on National Public Radio, is another excellent source of current news.

GROUP ACTIVITY 2: Conduct Library Research

Team up with a classmate to do some library research on your topic. First, explain to your partner the type of information you need to find. Then visit the campus library, and working together, locate specialized encyclopedias, magazine and newspaper articles, and books on your topics. Don't hesitate to ask a librarian for assistance if you can't find the sources you need. Finally, record the titles and authors of the various sources you find on your topic.

1. Specialized encyclopedia (Give the title.)
2. Magazine article (Give the title of the article, the title of the magazine, and the author's name.)
3. Newspaper article (Give the title of the article, the title of the newspaper, and the author's name.)
4. Book (Give the title and the author's name.)

Using Search Engines
When you explore the World Wide Web for information on your topic, use a *search engine*, which is a Web site that indexes other Web sites. Some common search engines are Yahoo! (**yahoo.com**), Google (**google.com**), Dogpile (**dogpile.com**), and Ask (**ask.com**). You will need to use keywords to access Web sites on a search engine. Read the Help screens for the search engine. They will help you to focus your keywords so that you will get a manageable number of sites.

Annotated Web Links

For a list of online sources of information for a researched essay, go to **bedfordstmartins.com/choices** and click on "Annotated Web Links."

Evaluating Sources of Information

The credibility of the sources you consult is an important concern. A report isn't necessarily objective simply because it appears in print or on television. Many magazines have a political bias. *The National Review*, for instance, has a conservative slant, whereas *The Nation* is considered liberal. Recent sources (that is, those published within the last five years) are more up-to-date than older ones. If you gather information from television sources, be especially skeptical about what you watch. Many television news discussion programs also have a political bias, and some news-entertainment shows may exaggerate facts to make their stories more interesting to their audience. Avoid using material from a talk show unless you are certain it's not hearsay or gossip.

Evaluating sources you find on the World Wide Web is especially important. For the most part, no independent person or agency screens material before it is put on the Web. Therefore, *you* need to screen the material. When accessing information on culture shock, for instance,

---

HOW TO Evaluate Web Resources

- Determine who put the information on that Web site. Does this person have credentials, such as college degrees or university affiliations? If no author is named or if the author's credentials aren't given, find another source of information.

- Is the Web site trying to sell you something? If so, it might not contain objective information.

- Be cautious when accessing Web sites with *com* in their addresses, as in **elvispresley.com**. *Com* is an abbreviation for "commercial"; most of these Web sites are connected to commercial companies that are trying to sell you something.

- Web sites with *edu* in their addresses, as in **lib.iastate.edu**, are usually maintained by a college or university, and Web sites with *gov* in their addresses, as in **lcweb.loc.gov**, are sponsored by a governmental agency. Information provided on such sites is likely to be reliable, although you still need to determine the author of the site and its purpose.

you might find Web pages advertising a therapist's treatment for culture shock, a site dedicated to a rock band named "Culture Shock," or a high school student's research paper on this topic.

GROUP ACTIVITY 3: Evaluate Web Sites

With a few of your classmates, evaluate several Web sites that deal in some way with culture shock. (To access these Web sites, use a search engine such as Google, Yahoo!, Dogpile, or Ask, and type in the keywords "culture shock.") Which sites would be appropriate for an essay on culture shock? How did you determine their appropriateness?

Using Favorites and Bookmarks
Use the Bookmark feature in your browser to help you quickly access Web sites you plan to examine more than once. A bookmark allows you to link directly to a site rather than typing in the entire URL address. You can return to the site by choosing it from your list of favorites or bookmarks.

Avoiding Plagiarism

A very serious offense, *plagiarism* is the use of another writer's ideas or words without giving credit to that writer as the source. Handing in someone else's work with your name on it is an obvious act of plagiarism. But using another writer's words or ideas in your paper without indicating where they came from, even if you do so unintentionally, is also an act of plagiarism.

Therefore, you must be careful to avoid plagiarism. Always identify your sources when you borrow ideas, information, or quotations so that your readers can clearly distinguish between what has been borrowed and what is your own.

HOW TO Avoid Plagiarism

- When you reproduce a writer's exact words, use quotation marks to enclose the quote. Be sure to name your source.

- When you restate an author's words in your own words, omit the quotation marks, but you must still name your source.

- List all of the sources named in your paper on the Works Cited page.

The following sections on taking notes and on quoting, paraphrasing, summarizing, and documenting sources will also help you avoid plagiarism.

GROUP ACTIVITY 4: Talk about Plagiarism

Plagiarism can come in many forms. Discuss the following situations with your classmates.

1. Because of her busy work schedule, Anne puts off writing a research paper until the night before the deadline. As a result, she doesn't take the time to identify the sources of borrowed words and ideas in her paper. A week later, her instructor calls her into his office and tells her that she has plagiarized.

   - Why is this plagiarism?
   - How should Anne respond?
   - How should Anne be penalized?

2. Joanne belongs to a sorority that keeps a file of term papers written by its members. Looking in that file, she finds a paper on the same topic as an English paper she's writing. She copies several paragraphs from the paper, word for word, without indicating where they came from. Later, Joanne's instructor asks her why part of her paper sounds as if someone else wrote it.

   - Why is this plagiarism?
   - Should Joanne offer to rewrite the paper?
   - How should Joanne be penalized?

3. Coworkers Sam and Eloise are asked by their supervisor to write a report on the company's recent sales figures. Eloise volunteers to draft the report, and Sam agrees to revise, edit, and submit it to the supervisor. The report that Sam submits, however, has only his name on it.

   - Why is this plagiarism?
   - What should Eloise do?
   - How should Sam be penalized?

4. Frank and Joe are roommates. Frank is enrolled in the same history course that Joe took last semester. Frank comes across one of Joe's old notebooks, and in it is the history paper that Joe wrote for last semester's course. Frank retypes the paper and submits it as his own.

   - Why is this plagiarism?
   - Do you think Frank's plagiarism of Joe's paper will be discovered?
   - If it is discovered, how should Frank be penalized? If it isn't, how might Frank's experience influence his behavior in the future?
   - What advice would you give Frank if you could?

Avoiding Plagiarism Tutorial
For more help with understanding what plagiarism is and how to avoid it, go to **bedfordstmartins.com/plagiarismtutorial**.

Taking Notes

Once you locate a book, an article, or another source on your topic, skim it to see if it answers any of your research questions. To *skim* a source, simply read the introduction, the headings and subheadings, and the conclusion. If the source answers any of your research questions, take notes. You can also photocopy the relevant pages and highlight the important ideas. However, highlighting shouldn't replace taking careful notes. Note-taking forces you to select only what is useful from a source, to restate the information in your own words, and thereby to reflect on its meaning.

Consider using index cards for your notes. Because they're small, index cards help you focus on the information you need. Also, you can arrange the cards in various ways, which can be helpful in organizing your ideas during revision. Take notes for only one source per notecard.

Take Notes on Computer
If possible, use a computer to take notes. This will make writing your essay easier because you won't have to retype your notes when you write your paper. To take notes on a computer, you can create a directory or folder for your essay and then use separate files within the directory or folder for your notes. For example, the directory or folder can be called "Culture Shock," and the files can be called "Effects of Culture Shock" or "How to Prevent Culture Shock."

For each source you use, be sure to record the author's name, the title, and the publication information you will need for your Works Cited page at the end of your essay. This information varies depending on the type of source you consult. For magazine, journal, and newspaper articles, encyclopedia entries, books, and Web sites, you must record the following information for each source you use:

MAGAZINE OR NEWSPAPER ARTICLE

- Author (if given)
- Title of article

- Name of magazine or newspaper
- Date of publication
- Page numbers of the whole article or printout
- Page numbers for the information you use

If you accessed the article on a database from your library, also write the following:

- Name of the database (such as *ProQuest*)
- Name of your library and where it is located
- Date that you accessed the article
- The electronic address (URL) of the database

Journal Article

- Author
- Title of article
- Name of journal
- Number of volume and issue
- Date of publication (month and year)
- Page numbers of the whole article or printout
- Page numbers for the information you used

If you accessed the article on a database from your library, write the following:

- Name of the database
- Name of your library and where it is located
- Electronic address (URL) of the database

Encyclopedia Article or Entry

- Author (if given, it usually appears at the end of the entry)
- Title
- Name of the encyclopedia
- Year and place of publication
- Volume and page number (if the encyclopedia is not arranged alphabetically)

Book

- Author
- Title
- City and name of publisher

- Year of publication
- Page numbers

WEB SITE

- Author
- Title
- Name of any institution or organization associated with the site
- Date of publication
- Date of access
- Electronic address (URL) of the database

Following is an example of a notecard Leslie Lozano wrote based on Yleana Martinez's article "Culture Club." This article helped Leslie answer her research question, "What can students do to help them cope with culture shock?"

Side one of notecard

The information Leslie will need for her Works Cited page →

This information helps answer one of Leslie's research questions. →

Author's exact words in quotation marks →

para. = paragraph numbers

An interesting fact Leslie learned from the article →

> *Yleana Martinez. "Culture Club" Hispanic. Vol. 11, Issue 4, April 1998. P. 42. Academic Search Premier database. UTEP library, El Paso, TX. 5 April 2002. <http://0-web.ebscohost.com.lib.utep.edu>.*
>
> *At Harvard's Kennedy School of Government, Latino students formed the Latino Caucus to help Latino students cope with the "inevitable culture shock." (para. 2)*
>
> *The Latino Caucus also is an "advocacy group" and fights for causes like bilingual education. (para. 2)*
>
> *Out of 700 students at the Kennedy School, only about 20 are Latino! (par. 2)*

Leslie's Notes on "Culture Club"

HOW TO Take Notes

- Refer frequently to your research questions to keep you focused on your topic.

- Don't just copy information from sources. Add your own thoughts. You might note, for instance, where you could use the information in your essay.

- Use quotation marks to indicate where you record an author's exact words. Write the rest of your notes completely in your own words.

- When you change a source's words and sentence structure into your own words, you are *paraphrasing* the source. Most of your notes should be paraphrased.

GROUP ACTIVITY 5: Practice Taking Notes

Imagine that you're writing an essay on culture shock and that one of your research questions is "What can be done to help people cope with culture shock?" To answer this question, take notes on an index card on the following essay. Compare your notecard with several classmates' notecards. Did you answer the research question without giving unnecessary information? Did you put quotation marks around the authors' exact words? Did you record the necessary publication information for the source?

PHILIP ZIMBARDO AND ANNE WEBER

Cross-Cultural Perspective: Culture Shock

Philip Zimbardo is a professor of psychology at Stanford University and a former president of the American Psychological Association, the world's largest association of psychologists. Anne Weber is a professor of psychology at the University of North Carolina, Asheville. In the following excerpt from Zimbardo and Weber's college textbook Psychology, *the authors discuss the causes and psychological effects of the experience known as culture shock.*

Many people can point to a part of their culture that they 1 consider *home*. Their feelings of "home" include positive emotions, familiarity, knowledge about ways to satisfy everyday needs, and attachment to others who demonstrate acceptance and affection. Feelings that people have about home often are associated with the length of time they spend in one place. Because time spent in one place is connected to feelings of home, some people may not react positively to the concept of "home." For example, the children of migrant workers or the children of military families may never have lived in one place long enough to consider it home.

For those people who do have strong emotional ties to a 2 home, moves from their familiar surroundings can cause stress. Consider a time in your own life when you were away from home and felt discomfort because of your move. This may have occurred when you first went away to college. It could have occurred in years past when your family relocated due to a job transfer by one of your parents, or when you left home in the summer to attend summer camp or visit distant relatives. What were your feelings? Did you feel lonely, out-of-step with others, frustrated at your inability to satisfy everyday needs, or clumsy because you did not know how to behave in acceptable ways? With these thoughts in mind, consider the following situations.

1. An 18-year-old Navajo female from rural Arizona, who had won awards as a high-school basketball player, begins studies at one of the large state universities on an athletic scholarship.
2. An African-American businessman accepts a vice-presidential position in a large company where 95 percent of the upper-level executives are male Caucasians.
3. A student participates in a study-abroad program in Europe.
4. An American businesswoman travels to Japan to establish joint trade agreements for the marketing of computer hardware and software.

What do these experiences (including your own) have in common? All of these experiences involve moves away from familiar surroundings and the need to adjust to many new social situations. All of the individuals involved moved on their own, without others who had long shared their respective support groups. When faced with everyday demands such as finding food, housing, and local transportation, these people had only their own resources to help them cope. Often, such individuals feel overwhelmed in their new surroundings and experience high levels of stress (Barna, 1991). *Culture shock* is the term commonly used to describe the stress experienced by people who move to unfamiliar surroundings. 3

The term *culture shock* was originally coined to explain the intense experiences of people who found themselves on overseas assignments in roles such as diplomats, international students, technical assistance advisers, or businesspeople (Oberg, 1960). 4

Over the last thirty years, the term has expanded to include other types of experiences people have when they move across cultural boundaries *within any one country.* Occasionally, culture shock is used to explain reactions to the new and the unfamiliar. Examples include going away to college, getting married, or being forced to go on welfare after years of productive employment. 5

The complaints people have when experiencing culture shock are very similar, whether they are international students, overseas businesspeople, or members of an underrepresented ethnic group (Furnham & Bochner, 1986). Such individuals 6 experience a sense of frustration and helplessness at their inability to meet their everyday needs. They feel lonely and find it hard to meet people and to develop good interpersonal relationships. Victims of culture shock often become suspicious of others and come to believe that others are "out to get them." People also report a predictable set of physical symptoms. They complain of stomachaches, inability to sleep, diarrhea, headaches, lack of sex drive, general feelings of tiredness, mild depression, and a lack of enthusiasm for life.

Many organizations now sponsor programs to help prepare   7
people for life's transitions. Most commonly called *cross-cultural training programs* (Brislin, 1993), one of the goals of such curricula is to introduce people to the various experiences they are likely to encounter. During the programs, participants are commonly told that the experiences associated with "culture shock" are normal and are to be expected. Knowledge of what culture shock is, how frequently it is experienced, and effective coping strategies can aid in reducing people's stress.

Quoting Information

As a general rule, use quotations sparingly. But when an author uses an especially memorable phrase, you might want to quote it directly in your paper. You also might use quoted material to emphasize a point or sum up an idea. These should be brief quotations of one or two sentences.

You should include an introductory phrase to tell your readers the source of each quotation. After the quoted information, put the page number of the source in parentheses. Here are some examples:

Refer to pp. 602–3 for guidelines about punctuating quotations.

```
According to psychologists Philip Zimbardo and Anne
Weber, "Knowledge of what culture shock is, how
frequently it is experienced, and effective coping
strategies can aid in reducing people's stress" (425).
```

```
Psychologists Philip Zimbardo and Anne Weber write,
"Knowledge of what culture shock is, how frequently
it is experienced, and effective coping strategies
can aid in reducing people's stress" (425).
```

```
"Knowledge of what culture shock is, how frequently
it is experienced, and effective coping strategies
can aid in reducing people's stress," write
psychologists Philip Zimbardo and Anne Weber (425).
```

Also notice in the examples how the quotations are punctuated.

When you use a quotation, you can't just drop it into a paragraph. You need to explain its relevance to your topic or point. In the following paragraph from a student essay on culture shock, for example, the writer quotes a phrase from the Zimbardo and Weber essay and then explains its relevance to his point:

> When you think of people who experience culture shock, you might picture immigrants moving to a new land or students studying in foreign countries. Not everyone who experiences culture shock, though, is in a foreign country. According to psychologists Philip Zimbardo and Anne Weber, "Over the last thirty years, the term has expanded to include other types of experiences people have when they move across cultural boundaries *within any one country*" (424). Therefore, people may experience culture shock when they leave home to go to college, lose their jobs, or move to a much bigger or smaller city.

For more information about using the TIE method of paragraph organization, refer to p. 44.

Note, too, as this paragraph demonstrates, that the topic-illustration-explanation (TIE) pattern of organization is often used in paragraphs containing quotations.

HOW TO Quote Information

- Use quoted information to repeat memorable phrases, to emphasize a point, or to sum up.
- Include a phrase that provides the source of the information.
- Add quotation marks at the beginning and end of the quoted material.
- Explain why the quotation is relevant to your topic.

GROUP ACTIVITY 6: Quote Sources

Working with several other students, write a paragraph about one of the main ideas in "Cross-Cultural Perspective: Culture Shock." Use a quotation from the essay to help you develop the paragraph. Then create an introductory phrase for the quotation, and consider using the topic-illustration-explanation pattern of paragraph organization. Compare your group's paragraph with those written by the other groups in the class.

Paraphrasing Information

To *paraphrase* is to restate a source in your own words. By paraphrasing information, you simplify complicated information and use your own writing style.

A paraphrase should be about the same length as the original passage and express the same ideas. Although when paraphrasing you might be tempted simply to substitute keywords with synonyms (words that have the same meaning), this can lead to plagiarism. Use your own writing style instead. This might mean changing the sentence structure or word order. Here's an example of an original passage, a poor paraphrase, and a good paraphrase. In the poor paraphrase, words from the original are in **boldface type**:

ORIGINAL
"Over the last thirty years, the term has expanded to include other types of experiences people have when they move across cultural boundaries *within any one country*" (Zimbardo and Weber 424).

POOR PARAPHRASE
Over the last thirty years, the concept has broadened to **include other** kinds **of experiences people have when they** cross **cultural boundaries *within any one country*** (Zimbardo and Weber 424).

GOOD PARAPHRASE
The meaning of this concept has broadened during the last three decades. Now it encompasses what happens to people crossing cultural borders *within a single country* (Zimbardo and Weber 424).

When paraphrasing, you don't need to use quotation marks because the words are your own. You must, however, indicate the source of the idea or information.

Here is the same student paragraph on culture shock you saw on page 426, except here the quotation is replaced with a paraphrase (in boldface type):

```
When you think of people who experience culture
shock, you might picture immigrants moving to a new
land or students studying in foreign countries. Not
everyone who experiences culture shock, though, is in
a foreign country. The meaning of this concept has
broadened during the last three decades. Now it
encompasses what happens to people crossing cultural
borders within a single country (Zimbardo and
```

```
Weber 424). Therefore, people may experience culture
shock when they leave home to go to college, lose
their jobs, or move to a much bigger or smaller city.
```

For more information about using the TIE method of paragraph organization, refer to p. 44.

Notice, too, that the TIE (topic-illustration-explanation) method of paragraph organization is used with the paraphrased information.

HOW TO   Paraphrase Information

- Read the material you want to paraphrase. Then put it away. Write down the information or idea on a notecard, using your own words and writing style.

- After the paraphrase, write the name of the author whose ideas you have borrowed (if you haven't already given the author's name) and the page number of the source.

- Reread the original passage to make sure you have accurately captured the author's information or ideas without plagiarizing.

GROUP ACTIVITY 7: Paraphrase Sources

Working with a group of students, paraphrase one or two paragraphs from "Cross-Cultural Perspective: Culture Shock." Compare your group's paraphrases with those of the other groups in your class.

Summarizing Information

A *summary* is a condensed version of a piece of text that contains that text's key ideas. A summary is always much shorter than the original because it omits most details. Summary writing is one of the most common types of writing used in college and the workplace. On the job, you might write a summary of sales over the past six months. In college courses, you might be asked to write summaries of lectures, lab experiments, or journal articles. In an essay, information summarized from primary or secondary research can provide good supporting examples, observations, definitions, facts, statistics, and expert testimony.

For more on summarizing, see Chapter 11.

Depending on your purpose for writing, a summary may be as short as a sentence or as long as a paragraph. Here's a one-sentence summary of "Cross-Cultural Perspective: Culture Shock."

```
In "Cross-Cultural Perspective: Culture Shock,"
Philip Zimbardo and Anne Weber explain what culture
shock is, who experiences it, how it affects people
```

emotionally and physically, and what people can do to cope with it.

Here's a longer summary of the same article:

> In "Cross-Cultural Perspective: Culture Shock," Philip Zimbardo and Anne Weber define *culture shock* as "the stress experienced by people who move to unfamiliar surroundings" (424). According to the authors, people may experience culture shock when they move to a new country or to a new place within their own country. A sudden life change, such as the loss of a job, can also create culture shock. This condition produces a variety of emotional problems, such as depression, loneliness, and unreasonable suspicions of other people. Culture shock can also cause physical problems, including stomach disorders and insomnia. Many programs now exist to help people about to undergo a life change that could result in culture shock.

When you summarize information in your essay, remember that your ideas come first. Summarized information should be used only to support your own points.

HOW TO Summarize Information

- Reread the source, and write down the main ideas. These ideas are usually expressed in the thesis statement, the topic sentences, and, at times, the conclusion. If the source has headings and subheadings, they may express main ideas as well.

- Focus on the main points only, and omit the details.

- At the beginning of your summary, give the title and author of the source.

- Write the summary in your own words. Use a quotation only to emphasize an important point that cannot be conveyed as powerfully in your own words.

GROUP ACTIVITY 8: Analyze Summaries

Read the following two summaries of "Cross-Cultural Perspective: Culture Shock." With your group, discuss how these summaries could be improved.

1. In "Cross-Cultural Perspective: Culture Shock," Philip Zimbardo and Anne Weber explain that culture shock is "the stress experienced by people who move to unfamiliar surroundings." People who might have culture shock are a Navajo student who moves to a large university, an African American businessman who takes a job in a company where the workers are 95 percent Caucasians, a student who travels to Europe to study, and an American businesswoman who travels to Japan for her job.

2. According to Philip Zimbardo and Anne Weber in "Cross-Cultural Perspective: Culture Shock," many people feel attached to a place that they call "home." When they leave this comfortable place, they often experience stress, which is called *culture shock*. They have problems doing ordinary things such as shopping or finding a place to live. When the term *culture shock* was coined, it referred to the stress felt by people who lived abroad.

Documenting Sources

Documentation of sources is an important aspect of the research paper. To *document* is to refer your reader to your primary and secondary research sources. Proper documentation allows readers to locate and verify your sources for their own future research. It also keeps you from inadvertently plagiarizing others' words or ideas. You document sources both in the essay itself (where you identify the author and page number for quotations, paraphrases, and summaries) and in a list of sources at the end of the paper (called a Works Cited page).

In-Text Documentation.   You need to document whenever you quote, paraphrase, or summarize a secondary research source in the text of the paper itself. For each source you refer to, you will write a citation. Follow these guidelines for writing citations:

- Identify the author in an introductory phrase, and give the page number in parentheses.

  As psychologist Liu Chang has noted, "Students experiencing culture shock will benefit from participating in support groups" (107).

- If you don't give the author's name in an introductory phrase, include the author's last name along with the page number in parentheses.

  It is also true that "students experiencing culture shock will benefit from participating in support groups" (Chang 107).

- If the source has two or three authors, include all of the last names in the citation.

  According to Johnson and Hall, "Culture shock is an
  inevitable result of traveling to a new place" (189).

  Psychologists now understand that "culture shock is
  an inevitable result of traveling to a new place"
  (Johnson and Hall 189).

- If the source has four or more authors, either give the names of all the authors, or give the name of the first author followed by *et al.*, which is an abbreviation for "and others."

  As Gibson et al. have noted, "Culture shock can
  ultimately become a beneficial experience" (233).

  Experts point out that "Culture shock can ultimately
  become a beneficial experience" (Gibson, Emerson, Chang,
  and Zimmerman 233).

- If no author is given for a source, give the title in an introductory phrase or a shortened version of the title in parentheses.

  According to "Tips for Success for New Students,"
  a brochure produced by the International Students'
  Office, culture shock will not "derail students'
  dreams of academic success" as long as they learn
  about this condition (3).

  Culture shock will not "derail students' dreams of
  academic success" as long as they learn about this
  condition ("Tips for Success" 3).

- If you're using an article reprinted from an electronic database, no page numbers will be given. In this case, use the paragraph number if it is given.

  Professor Caroline Edmunds has indicated that
  "even students who move away from home to attend a
  university only an hour away" can still experience
  culture shock (par. 5).

  In fact, "even students who move away from home to
  attend a university only an hour away" can still
  experience culture shock (Edmunds, par. 5).

- Remember that you need to include in-text documentation for paraphrased or summarized information, in addition to quoted information.

```
In fact, students can experience culture shock even
if they enroll in a university that's only sixty
minutes from their homes (Edmunds, par. 5).
```

- Use transitions or keywords to connect the documented material to the point being made. Some keywords and transitions used in the above examples are "It is also true that," "psychologists now understand," and "in fact."
- Finally, study the format of the above examples. Notice that only the number of the page is given (don't use *page* or *p.*). Also, put the period after the parentheses.

Works Cited Page.   The *Works Cited page* is a list of sources that appears at the end of your paper. Every source you mention in your essay should be included in the Works Cited list.

Different fields of study use different formats and titles for the Works Cited list. The following discussion and sample entries are based on the format established by the Modern Language Association (MLA).

HOW TO Use MLA Format

- Put the Works Cited list on a separate page at the end of your paper.
- Arrange the source entries alphabetically by the authors' last names or by title if the author is not named.
- Double-space the entries.
- The first line of each entry should line up with the left-hand margin. The other lines of each entry should be indented five spaces or one-half inch.
- Italicize the titles of books, journals, magazines, and newspapers.
- Put the titles of magazine and newspaper articles in quotation marks.

MLA format also requires that you present the information about your sources in a specific way. Books, magazines, journals, and newspapers require different formats. Encyclopedias are different still, and there is a particular way to list an interview. Also, the form varies slightly when a source has more than one author. Here are some sample MLA-style entries.

BOOK WITH ONE AUTHOR

Pedersen, Paul. *The Five Stages of Culture Shock.*
      Westport: Greenwood, 1995. Print.

BOOK WITH MORE THAN ONE AUTHOR

Furnham, Adrian, and Stephen Bochner. *Culture*
      Shock: Psychological Reactions to Unfamiliar
      Environments. New York: Methuen, 1986. Print.

CHAPTER OR ARTICLE FROM AN EDITED BOOK

Burton, Robert S. "Talking across Cultures."
      Understanding Others: Cultural and Cross-
      Cultural Studies and the Teaching of Literature.
      Ed. Joseph Trimmer and Tilly Warnock. Urbana:
      NCTE, 1992. 115-213. Print.

MAGAZINE ARTICLE (PRINT SOURCE)

Plagens, Peter. "These Days, It's the 'Old
      of the Shock.'" *Newsweek* 29 Dec. 1997: 89.
      Print.

JOURNAL ARTICLE (PRINT SOURCE)

After the author and title of the article, follow with the journal title, volume and issue numbers (if given), and the date.

Schwarz, Adam. "Culture Shock." *Far Eastern Economic*
      Review 34 (1997): 63-68. Print.

In this example, "34" refers to the volume number.

Meyer, Lisa. "Academic Acculturation for Foreign
      Graduate Students: Meeting New Concepts of
      Research and Writing." *College ESL* 5.2 (1995):
      83-91. Print.

In this example, "5.2" refers to volume 5, issue 2.

Newspaper Article (Print Source)

> Newman, Bruce. "From the Land of Private Freeways
>   Comes Car Culture Shock." *New York Times* 16 Oct.
>   1997: G8. Print.

If the article appears on more than one page, and the pages are not consecutive, add a plus sign after the number of the first page: *C4+*.

Encyclopedia Article (Print Source)

> "The Characteristics of Culture." *Encyclopaedia
>   Americana*. 1998 ed. Print.

Personal Interview

> Wucinich, Sophia. Personal interview. 10 Jan. 2006.

Telephone Interview

> Schroeder, Niels. Telephone interview. 14 Apr. 2006.

Article from an Online Database

To cite a source you obtained from an online database, give the same information you would give if you had used a print format. Additionally, give the name of the database, italicized; the medium (*Web*); and the date of access.

> Bulik, Beth Snyder. "Culture Shock." *Advertising Age*
>   8 Jan. 2001: 1-11. *Academic Search Premier*. Web.
>   8 Apr. 2002.

Work from a Web Site

If you used information from a Web site, give the author's name (if included), the title of the document, and the title of the site (italicized); follow with the name of any institution or organization sponsoring the site (use *N. p.*, if none is given), the date of publication, the medium (*Web*), and the date you accessed the site.

> Do, Thi Thuan. *Asian American Students' Culture
>   Shock*. U of California, Irvine, 1 Nov. 2001.
>   Web. 6 Nov. 2001.

For more information on how to document sources, consult the *MLA Handbook for Writers of Research Papers*, seventh edition (2009). This should be available in the reference section of your library.

Online Help for Documenting Sources

For help using MLA citation format and creating a Works Cited list, go to **bedfordstmartins.com/resdoc** and click on "Diana Hacker's Research and Documentation Online." You also can go to **bedfordstmartins.com/bibliographer** and click on "Bedford Bibliographer."

GROUP ACTIVITY 9: Create a Works Cited Page

With several classmates, write up a Works Cited page in the MLA format for the following five sources. All necessary information is given (as well as unnecessary information you need not use).

1. *The Art of Crossing Cultures* by Craig Storti. Page 89. 1990. International Press, located in Yarmouth, Maine.

   _____

   _____

   _____

2. Interview by telephone with Helen Mar, who is Chinese, about her experiences as an international student. Boise, Idaho. June 30, 2002.

   _____

   _____

   _____

3. "Culture Shock" by Toni Mack, p. 188. Published in *Forbes* magazine in May 1997 on pp. 188–190.

   _____

   _____

   _____

4. Janice C. Simpson's article, called "Chronicler of Culture Shock," which appeared in *Time* on May 8, 2006 on p. 156. Obtained online from the Academic Search Premier database on Feb. 9, 2007.

   _____

   _____

   _____

5. "Going to Teach in Prisons: Culture Shock" by Randall Wright. Published in a journal called *Journal of Correctional Education*, volume 56, issue 1, in March 2005 on pp. 19–38. Appeared online in the database Academic Search Premier on December 15, 2006.

_____

_____

_____

_____

SAMPLE RESEARCH PAPER

The following essay was written by student writer Leslie Lozano for the international students' forum on her campus. She used the writing process — exploring choices, drafting, revising, and editing — before presenting this paper to the audience at the forum. (We have reproduced the essay in a narrower format than you will have on a standard eight-and-a-half-by-eleven-inch sheet of paper so that we could annotate it.)

½"

Lozano 1

1"

Leslie Lozano

Professor Lee

Psychology 101

1 May 2002

Culture Shock

    People who have the opportunity to live and

1" study in a new country usually are eager to master a 1"

new language, taste different foods, and see new

sights. But after a while they might begin to feel

lonely and confused. They don't understand others,

and others don't understand them. Nothing tastes

right. They get lost easily. They have trouble doing

even simple things such as shopping or taking a bus.

They realize that the way they speak, act, and

perceive things is different from other people in

their new environment. They are experiencing

culture shock.

    People do not have to travel to another country

to experience culture shock. At one point or another,

everyone becomes uncomfortable in an unfamiliar

environment or in the presence of people different

from themselves. However, international students, in

particular, are likely to experience culture shock

because their culture and the host culture can be so

different. Because culture shock can affect students'

academic success, it is important for them to

understand the four stages of culture shock: the

honeymoon stage, the crisis stage, the recovery

stage, and the adjustment stage. These stages were

Note proper heading.

Note double-spacing throughout.

The introduction tries to attract the reader's attention. It also defines culture shock.

Thesis is given.

Lozano 2

first described by anthropologist Kalvervo Oberg in 1960 (Thomas and Althen 213).

This citation shows where Leslie learned this information.

The honeymoon stage takes place when people first arrive in their country. They feel excited about the new and different environment. After a few weeks, though, they become more aware of how different the new country is compared to their home country. They also begin to feel homesick. This is when the crisis stage begins. During this stage, students feel confused because they are confronting new behaviors and lifestyles (Thomas and Althen 221). Sometimes students disapprove of the values and beliefs of the new country. According to psychologists Philip R. Harris and Robert T. Moran, "Traditions provide people with a 'mindset' and have a powerful influence on their moral system for evaluating what is right or wrong, good or bad, desirable or not" (135). Because of their negative evaluations of the new culture, students can feel alienated from their surroundings. Other symptoms of the crisis stage include depression, boredom, lack of focus, and inability to sleep ("Culture Shock," par. 4).

Source is paraphrased and cited.

Last name of authors and page number are given in parentheses.

Quote is introduced.

Quotation is used to support the concept of negative evaluations.

Page number follows quotation.

Source is paraphrased, and cited.

Paragraph number is cited for an electronic source without page numbers.

How can students help themselves during the crisis stage? They can begin by making friends with other international students at events organized by the International Students Office. They could even create an organization for international students experiencing culture shock. This is what Latino students at Harvard did when they formed the Latino Caucus, which helps Latino students overcome

Note that most of the essay consists of Leslie's ideas rather than information from the research.

Lozano 3

loneliness and homesickness as well as serving as an advocate for other Latino students (Martinez). Sharing feelings with others in groups such as these can reduce loneliness. Also, students can always go to the campus counseling center for one-on-one help from a counselor.

Although getting together with other international students is helpful, it doesn't mean that the new culture should be ignored. In fact, students will get over culture shock faster if they learn as much as they can about the new culture. Christina Bernal, a Mexican student advisor from the Office of International Programs, suggests that international students "should be like a sponge and absorb as much information as possible." Students suffering from culture shock should read local newspapers, watch television, and listen to the radio to learn about customs and habits that are foreign to them. They can also take advantage of opportunities to get to know people from the new culture. For instance, this university sponsors a host family program in which international students are paired up with families who get together with them regularly. This type of program allows the international students to educate members of the new culture about where they are from, which encourages mutual understanding and tolerance.

After a month or so, international students' anxieties begin to lower and they enter the recovery stage. During this stage, they still experience the

Source is paraphrased.

No page number is given because the article was retrieved from an electronic database.

Quote is introduced.

These ideas are Leslie's, so no citations are needed.

Lozano 4

This information is summarized from the article by Thomas and Althen.

symptoms of culture shock but not as intensely. The final stage of culture shock is the adjustment stage, when students begin to relax and enjoy being in the new culture, though they still can experience confusion and worries every once in a while (Thomas and Althen 221). By the time people reach the adjustment stage, they are usually more flexible and open-minded about cultural differences than they were before entering the new culture.

This is an important idea, so Leslie uses a quotation for emphasis.

Although culture shock can feel overwhelming at times, students need to remember that it "usually passes if a person stays in a new culture long enough to understand it and get used to its ways" (Kottak). In the long run, the benefits of living in a different culture--such as being fluent in a second language, understanding a new value system, and getting around in a totally different environment--far outweigh the hardships.

1"

½"

Lozano 5

Works Cited

1" Bernal, Christina L. Personal interview. 25 Mar. 2002. 1"

"Culture Shock." *Loyola U*. International Students

Office of Loyola U, 14 Jan. 1998. Web. 2 Apr.

1999.

Harris, Philip R., and Robert T. Moran. *Managing*

Cultural Differences. 4th ed. Houston: Gulf,

1996. Print.

Kottak, Conrad Phillip. "Culture." *The World Book*

Encyclopedia. 1996 ed. Print.

Martinez, Yleana. "Culture Club." *Hispanic* 11.4

(1998): 42. *Academic Search Premier*. Web.

5 Apr. 2002.

Thomas, Kay, and Gary Althen. "Counseling Foreign

Students." *Counseling across Cultures*. 3rd ed.

Ed. Paul B. Pedersen, Juris G. Draguns, Walter

J. Lonner, and Joseph E. Trimble. Honolulu: U of

Hawaii P, 1989. 205-41. Print.

Source from an interview

Note double-spacing throughout.

Web site source

Source from a book with 2 authors

Encyclopedia source: no page number is needed.

Source from an article that came from a database Web.

Source from an edited book

CHAPTER CHECKLIST

❑ Narrow your topic before beginning research.

❑ Write research questions to help keep the research process focused.

❑ Conduct primary research by observing, surveying, and interviewing.

❑ Conduct secondary research by reading what others have written about your topic in books, magazines, journals (or specialized magazines), newspapers, encyclopedias, and other sources.

❑ Use a computer to access magazine, journal, and newspaper articles electronically.

❑ Avoid plagiarism by documenting sources.

❑ Note-taking is an effective research tool.

❑ Use quotation marks to indicate an author's exact words.

❑ Use your own words to paraphrase an author's ideas.

❑ Summarize main idea to condense a lengthy passage.

❑ Document sources properly by identifying them in the essay and listing them on a Works Cited page at the end of the essay.

❑ Include a Works Cited entry with full publication information for every source cited in your essay. Format these entries correctly.

REFLECTING ON YOUR WRITING

To help you continue to improve as a writer, answer the following questions about the writing assignment for this chapter.

1. What was the easiest part of doing research?

2. What was the hardest part of doing research?

3. Compare writing a researched essay with writing an essay that doesn't contain research.

4. What information about your topic did you learn from conducting research?

5. If you could do the research for your essay over again, what would you do differently?

Using your answers to these questions, complete a Writing Process Report for this chapter (you can download a report form at **bedford stmartins.com/choices**). Once you complete this report, freewrite about what you learned in this chapter about conducting research and writing a researched essay and what you still hope to learn.

Taking Timed Writing Tests

13

In this chapter, you will write a brief essay in which you describe your feelings about taking exams. As you work on your essay, you will

- Learn how to prepare for and take essay exams.

- Learn how to prepare for and take in-class timed writings about readings.

- Learn how to prepare for and take multiple-choice writing tests.

It's getting close to midterm, and you're feeling confident about your classes. Everything seems to be going well. As you read your syllabi, though, you begin to panic because in the next week you have three tests. Two of them include essay-exam questions, and the third is an in-class timed writing assignment about a reading you haven't even seen yet. You might have the same reaction as student writer Sherman, who wrote the following in his journal:

> Three tests in a week. Help! I've done all of the work (most of the reading), but I don't write well under pressure. How will I ever survive? I'm stressed out just thinking about all of these tests.

The most common type of timed writing you will do in college is the essay exam. But you may also be asked to do an in-class timed writing about a reading or to take a multiple-choice exam on sentence structure, grammar, and punctuation.

The good news is that you can use everything you have already learned about writing to help you do well on these timed writing tests. For example, you can use the process of gathering ideas, drafting, revising, and editing when answering essay-exam questions or when writing in response to a reading. And you can use everything you have learned about grammar, spelling, and punctuation to help you do well on multiple-choice writing tests.

Writing Assignment

For this assignment, write an essay for your instructor and classmates in which you describe how you feel about taking exams. How do you reduce test anxiety, and what do you do during the test to ensure that you do your best? Share your responses with your classmates as a way to begin a discussion about how best to prepare for and take timed writing tests.

To review the writing process, see Chapter 1.

THE ESSAY EXAM

An essay exam includes questions to which you must respond in writing. Your responses must be written in sentences and paragraphs and should reflect your thoughts in an organized, clear way. The main difference between writing an essay outside of class and an in-class essay exam is that you must work through the first four stages of the writing process (gathering ideas, drafting, revising, and editing) in the time allowed for the exam.

Preparing for an Essay Exam

Learn about the Test.   You will do your best on an essay exam if you know what to expect when you walk into class on exam day. If possible, find out what type of essay questions will be on the test, how long you will have to complete the test, and how it will be graded. You can find out about the test by reading your syllabus, asking your instructor, and talking with former students. If your instructor permits, obtain copies of old essay-test questions, or ask your instructor to provide sample test items.

Online Exam Questions
Ask your instructor if there is a class Web site or other online source of sample essay-test questions and student responses. If yes, access this source to learn as much as you can about the instructor's essay exams.

Anticipate the Questions.   Whether or not you can look over copies of old essay-test questions, anticipate the questions for your upcoming exam. Remember, your instructor will probably ask only a few essay questions, so they will most likely be on the most important topics in the course. If your instructor provides a review session or gives you a study guide, check these for possible essay questions. Most instructors take test items directly from these reviews or study guides. Reread your class notes, and mark the topics that your instructor spent the most time on in class. For example, if your history instructor discussed the Bill of Rights for an entire week, you could anticipate an essay question on this topic. If this same instructor defined the First Amendment to the Constitution and then gave you a list of First Amendment rights, you could expect an essay question on this topic.

Sherman, the student who wrote the journal entry on page 446, knew that one of his upcoming exams was in psychology. His instructor had spent a week lecturing on the topic of Abraham Maslow's hierarchy of needs. The textbook assignment also contained several pages on this topic. Because of the amount of class time devoted to this topic, Sherman predicted that there would be an essay question on it. He was right. The instructor included this essay question on the test:

> Define Maslow's hierarchy of needs, classify these needs, and briefly describe each.

Develop a Study Routine.   If you manage your study time wisely, you should have no difficulty studying for essay exams. You can manage your time wisely by setting aside two to three hours of study time a week for each hour that you are in class. During this time, review your lecture notes, read your textbooks, and complete any other assignments.

You might also consider forming a study group. Research suggests that studying in groups can increase your knowledge of course material because you and your classmates share the information you have learned. To form a study group, ask a few of your classmates to meet with you a week or two before a major exam. Share your class notes, and discuss the textbook readings.

As a group, discuss and write down what you expect the essay-exam questions to be. Then write your individual responses to these possible essay questions. Discuss the strengths and weaknesses of each response so that each group member leaves the study session with a better idea of how to respond to possible essay questions.

GROUP ACTIVITY 1: Prepare for an Essay Exam

With several classmates, take a moment to reflect and freewrite on how you have prepared for an essay exam in the past. As a group, discuss each member's study strengths and weaknesses. How could you improve? If you were to form a study group, how could you best help others? How could they best help you?

Taking the Essay Exam

Analyze the Questions.   Most students have had the experience of writing an excellent answer that received no credit because it didn't answer the question asked. To prevent this from happening to you, use the following strategies to help you analyze the questions.

Quickly read over the exam. Notice the kinds of questions asked and the point value of each, and estimate the amount of time you will need to complete each response. With this information in mind, plan your answers, allowing the most time for questions with the most points.

As you read each essay question, be sure that you understand what is expected of you. One way to be sure that you understand the question is to mark it. Marking the question forces you to concentrate on what you need to do — reducing the chances that you will forget to answer part of the question or, even worse, will write a response that doesn't answer the question at all. To mark the question, underline the keywords that indicate what the essay should be about, and then circle the words that explain how you should organize and develop your response. Here is how Sherman marked the psychology question on Maslow's hierarchy of needs:

(Define) Maslow's hierarchy of needs, (classify) these needs, and

briefly (describe) each.

You probably noticed that the words *define, classify,* and *describe* used in this essay question are all words you recognize as patterns of development. Just as you develop and organize essays using description, narration, exemplification, process explanation, classification, definition, comparison and contrast, cause and effect, and argument, you can develop and organize your essay-exam responses using these same patterns.

Here are some words you might see in essay-exam questions. Notice how each points to which pattern of development to use.

See Chapter 3 for additional information on the patterns of development.

Description

    Describe the following . . .

    Explain . . .

    Illustrate . . .

    Give details of . . .

    Discuss . . .

Narration

    Relate the events . . .

    Tell what happened . . .

    Tell what a character said . . .

    Describe the conversation between . . .

Exemplification

    Give examples of . . .

    Support with evidence of . . .

    Provide support for . . .

    Explain . . .

    Describe what the author says . . .

Process explanation

    Provide the steps for . . .

    Outline the sequence of events in . . .

    Give the procedure . . .

    Analyze the following stages in . . .

Classification

    List the types of . . .

    Analyze the parts of . . .

    List the kinds of . . .

Definition

    Define . . .

    Give the meaning of . . .

    Identify . . .

Comparison and contrast

Compare and contrast . . .

Discuss the similarities . . .

Discuss the differences . . .

Cause and effect

Give the reasons for . . .

Discuss the causes of . . .

Describe the consequences of . . .

Discuss the effects of . . .

Explain why . . .

Argument

Argue for . . .

Justify your opinion . . .

Take a position . . .

To review how to brainstorm and cluster, see pp. 12–14.

Gather Ideas.   Once you have analyzed the essay question, you might be tempted to begin writing your response right away. If you look at students around you, some of them may have already started writing. Resist the urge to begin writing before you gather ideas. Taking the time to gather ideas first will help you write an organized essay. Set aside five minutes to brainstorm a list of the points you want to make or to create a cluster of your main ideas and supporting details. Once you have a list or cluster, number the key points in the order that you would like to write about them.

Here is an example of the list that Sherman brainstormed as he prepared to respond to the psychology question:

I <u>need</u> to do well on this test!
Abraham Maslow — 1970 I think
Described needs as part of a hierarchy
A hierarchy is something arranged in ranks or stages
Maslow's hierarchy
    Hunger, thirst
    Need to feel safe and secure
    Need to feel loved
    Need for recognition
    Need to be all you can be!
But what are the stages? Help!
    Physiological (sp?)
    Safety
    Belongingness
    Esteem
    Self-actualization

How would I define these needs?
Priorities to be met.

Write Your Response.   Now that you have taken five minutes to brainstorm or cluster your ideas, you'll want to draft quickly but carefully. Organize your essay response just as you would an essay that you write outside of class. Begin with a brief introduction that includes a thesis statement that directly answers the exam question. Write your essay using complete sentences and paragraphs. Each paragraph should include a topic sentence or main idea, and each paragraph should include at least one or two specific details to support the topic sentence. Write a brief conclusion or concluding statement to sum up your essay.

More information on organizing an essay can be found on pp. 20–21.

Revise and Edit Your Response.   When you have completed your essay exam, you may want to turn it in right away. However, you should allow five to ten minutes to reread the questions and your responses to be sure that you have answered the questions completely. If you wish to add content, write it neatly in the margin or at the bottom of the page, and draw an arrow to the place where it belongs. For deletions or corrections, draw a line through the material to be deleted or corrected, and write the correction above the text. Where appropriate, you may wish to add transitions such as *then, however, moreover,* or *in conclusion* to help your instructor follow your train of thought.

As you reread your response, also proofread for errors in grammar, spelling, and punctuation. Remember, your responses are judged not only for content but also for how clearly they are written. Too many errors may make it difficult for your instructor to understand what you have written, resulting in a lower test grade. One more thing: be sure your name is on your exam before you turn it in.

HOW TO Write an Essay Exam

- Read the exam. Divide your time according to the point value of each question.

- Mark up the question. Underline keywords that tell you what your essay should be about. Circle words (such as *classify*) that indicate how your essay should be developed.

- Take a few minutes to gather and organize ideas in a rough outline form.

- Write the essay. Include a brief introduction with a thesis statement that directly answers the exam question, body paragraphs with supporting details, and a short conclusion.

> ■ After you finish writing, take a few minutes to read over the exam and make quick corrections.
>
> ■ Keep track of the time.

Sample Essay Question and Student Response

Remember the psychology essay-exam question: "Define Maslow's hierarchy of needs, classify these needs, and briefly describe each." Here's how Sherman responded to this question. Notice that he made additions, deletions, and corrections neatly.

Abraham Maslow described five needs that each person has and ranked them in order of importance. This order is a hierarchy because a person must fulfill each need in order beginning with the most basic one. These needs are hunger and thirst, ~~love, safety,~~ safety, love, self-esteem, and the need to reach full potential.

The most basic need is hunger and thirst. What this means is that a person who is hungry or thirsty can't think of anything else. This was demonstrated during World War II when a researcher, Keys, fed 36 volunteers just enough food to maintain their weight and then cut their food in half. The effects showed that Maslow was correct. The men became obsessed with food and lost all interest in social activities.

The second need is for safety. A person who doesn't feel safe can't worry about the higher needs of love, ~~love,~~ self-esteem, and reaching full potential. People must feel they can predict what will happen and that they have some control over it.

The third need is love. Humans form relationships with other people and like to hang on to those relationships. That is why when we meet people at school or on vacation we always promise to keep in touch. Most people like to be with other people. If they are deprived of this need, they often become depressed.

The fourth ~~next~~ need is self-esteem. A person needs to feel capable of achieving something in life and needs the respect

of other people. Motivation is what causes a person to
work to earn
~~fear~~ other people's respect. Intrinsic motivation is

when a person does something just for the challenge of it.
                    motivation
Extrinsic is when a person does something to be rewarded or

out of fear of punishment.

    Maslow called the fifth need self-act͟alization. When

Maslow studied people who had very successful lives, he

discovered that they were open and loving and didn't worry

about what other people think. They usually had a mission in

life and had a few very good relationships instead of a lot

of not so meaningful ones.

    Maslow's hope was that developing this ~~heirarchy~~
                                          hierarchy
would help others think about how to motivate people to

do their best.

GROUP ACTIVITY 2: Take an Essay Exam

Read and mark the following essay-exam questions. With several
classmates, select one, and brainstorm or cluster to gather ideas for a
response. Then draft, revise, and edit your response. Share your
response with the other groups in your class. What suggestions do
they have for improving your response?

1. Explain the stages of the writing process as described in *Choices: A
   Basic Writing Guide with Readings.* Describe how you have used
   this process to improve your writing.
2. Compare and contrast an informative essay and a persuasive
   essay.
3. List the three types of journals. Give the advantages and disadvantages of each type.
4. Describe the process of preparing for and taking an essay exam.

IN-CLASS TIMED WRITING
ABOUT A READING

    Instructors occasionally ask students to read a short article or
essay just before or during class and to respond to a question or questions about this reading during class. This type of timed writing
assignment requires that you read and write well under pressure.

Preparing for In-Class Timed Writing about a Reading

Develop a Reading Routine. You will be most successful writing about a reading if you are already an active reader. Active readers think as they read. They ask questions, challenge the author, and look for the author's next point. They also know why they're reading (either for entertainment or for information) and stay focused on that purpose. Often, active readers write notes in the margins summarizing or commenting on what they have read.

Working with a study group can also help you become a more active reader. Ask study-group members to help you summarize readings, discuss difficult passages, and define unknown vocabulary words. Reviewing your reading assignments as a group will help each of you better understand the content.

Keep a Reading Journal. Keeping a reading journal is yet another way to become an active reader. Writing in a journal helps you explore your ideas more extensively than if you just think or talk about a text. By writing down your ideas, you can understand the reading more thoroughly. Reading journals also provide a place to reflect on what you have read. Writing in a reading journal helps you formulate questions and clarify ideas. Your journal is a place to collect and arrange your thoughts, draw conclusions, and evaluate what you have learned.

For more information on learning logs, see pp. 394–96.

To begin keeping a reading journal, find a notebook that is comfortable to write in. One of the most effective types of reading journals is the two-column learning log. You write down the main points of the reading selection in one column and your thoughts about it in another column. The advantage of the two-column learning log is that the two columns make it easier both to summarize and to think about the reading.

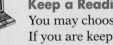

Keep a Reading Journal on Computer

You may choose to keep a reading journal in a computer file. If you are keeping a two-column learning log, use the word-processing feature that sets up columns. When it's time to review for an in-class timed writing, you may want to print out your file.

Keep a Vocabulary List. The larger your vocabulary, the greater your chances of understanding even the most difficult reading. As you read a text, circle unfamiliar words. Then look them up in a dictionary, or ask someone in your study group to tell you the meaning. Keep a list of these words, and review the list once a week. In addition to writing the definition of the word, use the word in a phrase or a sentence to help you remember it.

GROUP ACTIVITY 3: Prepare for In-Class Writing

With several classmates, take a moment to reflect and freewrite on how you have read in the past. What are your strengths as a reader? What are your weaknesses? How could you improve your reading to ensure that you would do your best on an in-class timed writing in response to a reading?

Performing In-Class Timed Writing about a Reading

Although active readers already have an advantage when assigned to write in class, all students can benefit from following these steps.

Read Carefully.   Not all good readers read faster than others or fully understand what they read the first time through, but they have ways to improve their understanding. Important reading strategies include previewing, distinguishing between main and supporting ideas, annotating the text, and learning how to read confusing passages.

To fully understand a piece, you should preview it first. Quickly scan the entire reading selection for clues about the author's main ideas. Previewing helps you begin to think about the most important ideas even before you begin to read carefully. To preview,

1. Examine the title to determine what it suggests about the topic.
2. Look at the author's name. Do you know anything about this author?
3. Read the headnote at the beginning of the reading. What does it suggest about the topic?
4. Examine the headings and any illustrations. These are clues to what the author considers important.
5. Read the first paragraph.
6. Look at the first sentence of each remaining paragraph. This is where the author most often puts the topic sentence (the main point of the paragraph).
7. Read the conclusion. Authors often restate their main points in their conclusions.

Once you have previewed the reading selection, read it carefully to distinguish main ideas from supporting details. The main ideas are the

To review main ideas and supporting details, see Chapter 2.

writer's general points, and the supporting details are the specific points that explain or justify the main ideas. For example, one of the main ideas of this section is that you can use specific strategies to improve your understanding of a reading; a supporting detail is that previewing is one of these strategies. Once you can distinguish between main ideas and supporting details, you can respond more effectively to a reading selection.

Another strategy is to annotate the text. Just as you read and mark essay-exam questions, you can read and mark the article or essay you are reading for a timed in-class writing. As you read, underline the main ideas. Once you have read the article, look back at what you have underlined. Which is the author's thesis statement? Which are the main ideas and supporting details that help explain or justify the thesis statement? In the margin, you may also wish to write brief phrases that restate key ideas, note unfamiliar words to look up in the dictionary, and express your own thoughts about the reading.

One of the most difficult things to learn is how to read a confusing passage. You might be tempted to skip over it, or you might panic and stop reading altogether. Instead, use these strategies to help you.

- Reread the confusing section again, sentence by sentence. Also, reread the paragraph just before and the one just after to provide you with a context.
- Underline words and phrases that seem significant.
- If permitted, use a dictionary to look up words that you don't know.
- If possible, ask your instructor for clarification of the confusing passage.

Write Your Response.   Now that you have actively read the essay or article your instructor has assigned, you are ready to write a response to the question or questions that accompany the reading. Follow the same steps that you use when answering essay-exam questions.

1. Analyze the question by marking it.
2. Gather ideas by brainstorming or clustering.
3. Write your response in an essay format.
4. Revise and edit it by making additions and deletions neatly.

Sample In-Class Writing Question and Student Response

Ofelia read the following essay titled "Freedom from Choice" as part of an in-class writing assignment.

BRIAN A. COURTNEY

Freedom from Choice

Brian A. Courtney graduated from the University of Tennessee at Nashville in 1995 with a degree in journalism. He is currently vice president of communications for the Nashville Area Chamber of Commerce, where he manages the organization's community, media, and public relations. In the following essay, Courtney recounts his struggle as a biracial college student trying to find an identity that was neither black nor white.

As my friend Denise and I trudged across the University of Tennessee campus to our 9:05 a.m. class, we delivered countless head nods, "Heys" and "How ya' doin's" to other African Americans we passed along the way. We spoke to people we knew as well as people we didn't know because it's an unwritten rule that black people speak to one another when they pass. But when I stopped to greet and hug one of my female friends who happens to be white, Denise seemed a little bothered. We continued our walk to class, and Denise expressed concern that I might be coming down with a "fever." "I don't feel sick," I told her. As it turns out, she was referring to "jungle fever," the condition where a black man or woman is attracted to someone of the opposite race.

This encounter has not been an uncommon experience for me. That's why the first twenty-one years of my life have felt like a never-ending tug of war. And quite honestly, I'm not looking forward to being dragged through the mud for the rest of my life. My white friends want me to act one way — white. My African American friends want me to act another — black. Pleasing them both is nearly impossible and leaves little room to be just me.

The politically correct term for someone with my racial background is *biracial* or *multiracial*. My mother is fair-skinned with blond hair and blue eyes. My father is dark-complexioned with prominent African American features and a head of woolly hair. When you combine the genetic makeup of the two, you get me — golden-brown skin, semi-coarse hair, and a whole mess of freckles.

Someone once told me I was lucky to be biracial because I have the best of both worlds. In some ways this is true. I have a huge family that's filled with diversity and is as colorful as a box of Crayolas. My family is more open to whomever I choose to date, whether that person is black, white, biracial, Asian, or whatever. But looking at the big picture, American society makes being biracial feel less like a blessing than a curse.

One reason is the American obsession with labeling. We feel the need to label everyone and everything and group them into neatly defined categories. Are you a Republican, a Democrat or an Independent? Are you pro-life or pro-choice? Are you African American, Caucasian, or Native American? Not everyone fits into such classifications. This presents a problem for me and the many biracial people living in the United States. The rest of the population seems more comfortable when we choose to identify with one group. And it pressures us to do so, forcing us to deny half of who we are.

Growing up in the small, predominantly white town of Maryville, Tennessee, I attended William Blount High School. I was one of a handful of minority students — a raisin in a box of cornflakes, so to speak. Almost all of my peers, many of whom I've known since grade school, were white. Over the years, they've commented on how different I am from other black people they know. The implication was that I'm better because I'm only *half* black. Acceptance into their world has meant talking as they talk, dressing as they dress, and appreciating the same music. To reduce tension and make everyone feel comfortable, I've reacted by ignoring half of my identity and downplaying my ethnicity.

My experience at UT has been very similar. This time it's my African American peers exerting pressure to choose. Some African Americans on campus say I "talk too white." I dress like the boys in white fraternities. I have too many white friends. In other words, I'm not black enough. I'm a white "wanna-be." The other day, an African American acquaintance told me I dress "bourgie." This means I dress very white — a pastel-colored polo, a pair of navy chinos, and hiking boots. Before I came to terms with this kind of remark, a comment like this would have angered me, and I must admit that I was a little offended. But instead of showing my frustration, I let it ride, and I simply said, "Thank you." Surprised by this response, she said in disbelief, "You mean you agree?"

On more occasions than I dare to count, black friends have made sweeping derogatory statements about the white race in general: "White people do this, or white people do that." Every time I hear them, I cringe. These comments refer not just to my white friends but to my mother and maternal grandmother as well. Why should I have to shun or hide my white heritage to enhance my ethnicity? Doesn't the fact that I have suffered the same prejudices as every other African American — and then some — count for something?

I do not blame my African American or white friends for the problems faced by biracial people in America. I blame society for not acknowledging us as a separate race. I am speaking not only for people who, like myself, are half black and half white but also for those who are half white and half Asian, half white and half Hispanic, or half white and half whatever. Until American society recognizes us as a distinct group, we will continue to be pressured to choose one side of our heritage over the other.

Job applications, survey forms, college-entrance exams, and the like ask individuals to check only *one* box for race. For most of my life, I have marked BLACK because my skin color is the first thing people notice. However, I could just as honestly have marked WHITE. Somehow when I fill out these forms, I think the employers, administrators, researchers, teachers, or whoever sees them will have a problem looking at my face and then accepting a big X by the word WHITE. In any case, checking BLACK or WHITE does not truly represent me. Only in recent years have some private universities added the category of BIRACIAL or MULTIRACIAL to their applications. I've heard that a few states now include these categories on government forms.   10

One of the greatest things parents of biracial children can do is expose them to *both* of their cultures. But what good does this do when in the end society makes us choose? Having a separate category marked BIRACIAL will not magically put an end to the pressure to choose, but it will help people to stop judging us as just black or just white and see us for what we really are — both.   11

Ofelia then responded to the following essay question: "What is the main point of Brian A. Courtney's essay? Provide examples of the evidence he uses to support his main point. Do you agree or disagree with him? Explain your answer." Here's Ofelia's response.

```
Brian A. Courtney's main point is that American
society forces us to identify ourselves as members
of one race. Having to choose keeps many people from
identifying themselves as biracial or multiracial.

     Courtney uses many examples as evidence. For
example, he describes his friend Denise's reaction
to his hugging a white girl. Denise accuses him of
having "jungle fever." His black friends say he is
too white because he dresses in chinos and hiking
boots. He also points out that he must choose one
race when he fills out job applications, college
entrance exams, and surveys.

     I agree with Courtney that Americans place too
much emphasis on race and ethnicity. As he says, this
comes from Americans' obsession with pigeonholing
each person. I am a Mexican American, but I could
refer to myself as a Cholo, a Latino, a Chicano, a
```

Hispanic, a Mexican, or an American. But the point is I am constantly pressured to choose.

    If each of us refused to be pigeonholed, then we could take the first step toward ending the obsession with labeling. And once we quit labeling, maybe some of the problems Courtney and I have experienced will begin to disappear.

HOW TO Take a Writing Test about a Reading

- Preview the reading for clues about the main ideas. Examine the title, headings, first paragraph, topic sentences, and conclusions.

- Read the text, distinguishing between main and supporting ideas.

- Annotate the text by taking notes in the margins about the main ideas. Look up unfamiliar words, and reread confusing passages.

- Before writing your response, analyze the question, gather ideas, and outline your answer.

- Use an essay format.

- After you write, take a few minutes to make corrections.

- Keep track of the time.

GROUP ACTIVITY 4: Respond to a Reading

Actively reread the essay "Freedom from Choice." Respond in writing to this question: "Do you agree or disagree with Brian A. Courtney's idea of including *biracial* or *multiracial* on forms that ask for ethnicity? Why or why not?" Share your response with members of your peer response or study group. What suggestions do they have for improving your response?

MULTIPLE-CHOICE WRITING TESTS

Some colleges require that students take multiple-choice writing tests to be placed in suitable classes or to advance to higher-level courses. Some writing instructors also administer multiple-choice writing tests as a way to determine each student's need for additional help with writing skills. For such tests, you may be asked to read a short passage and then determine the author's purpose and audience, to recognize main ideas and supporting details, and to recognize effective organization. A test on sentence structure may require that you identify sentence fragments, run-on sentences, incorrect subject-verb agreement, and incorrect word choice. You may also have to identify sentences that are poorly constructed because of too many words, misplaced words, or too few words. A test of grammar and punctuation skills requires that you identify standard sentence structure and standard punctuation.

Just as there are strategies for taking an essay exam and a timed in-class writing in response to a reading, there are strategies for doing your best on multiple-choice writing tests.

Preparing for a Multiple-Choice Writing Test

Learn about the Test.   Review the skills that will be tested. For example, if you are not sure what the parts of speech are or what the phrases *standard sentence* and *standard punctuation* mean, you should review these. One way to review is to find out if there is a study guide for the test. Check with your college bookstore, tutoring center, or instructor. If a guide is available, review it before taking the test. Identify other resources, such as textbooks (including the Handbook in this book), workbooks, and worksheets that may be available to help you practice. Find out if you will be able to use any aids such as a dictionary or thesaurus during the test.

Online Study Guides

If the test is standardized, there may be a computerized study guide available that tests and scores your present skills and tutors you on those skills you need to practice. Check on the World Wide Web for the study guide you need.

Anticipate the Questions.   Answer any sample test questions provided in study guides or provided by your instructor. Then score yourself on these sample questions. If you answer a question incorrectly, review the study materials to determine how you should have answered it. Using your overall score as a guide, assess your strengths and weaknesses, and plan a strategy for overcoming them.

Develop a Study Routine.   Consider the amount of time you have before the exam, the resources you have on hand, and the availability of instructors and tutors to help you. Then develop a study plan. To prepare for an essay exam, you focus on a few general topics, but to prepare for a multiple-choice writing exam, you must review everything that will be on the exam. Consequently, you may need to schedule several review sessions.

GROUP ACTIVITY 5: Prepare for a Multiple-Choice Writing Test

With several classmates, take a moment to reflect on and freewrite about how you have prepared for multiple-choice writing tests in the past. What were your study strengths? What were your weaknesses? How could you improve?

Taking a Multiple-Choice Writing Test

Analyze the Questions.   When taking a multiple-choice writing test, read the instructions carefully. Often there are both general instructions for taking the test and specific instructions for completing each part. Read each set carefully. If you don't understand any of these instructions, ask for clarification.

Read over the test items. Notice the kinds of questions asked and the point value of each. Estimate the amount of time you will need to complete each part of the test. With this in mind, plan your strategy, allowing the most time for the questions with the greatest point value.

Choose Your Responses.   Once you begin the test, glance at your watch occasionally to ensure that you are working at a steady pace. Read each question carefully, and select the best answer to the question. To best manage your time, skip questions you can't answer right away. If there is a separate answer sheet, be sure that the number of the question on the test and the number on the answer sheet match.

When you have answered all the questions you know, return to the questions you skipped. If you are not penalized for guessing, choose the one that seems most reasonable. Reading and answering all the other questions may provide clues to the answers to the questions you skipped. If time still remains, double-check all your answers.

HOW TO Take a Multiple-Choice Writing Test

- Use study guides to learn about the types of questions that will be asked.

- Study for the test by reviewing what will be on it.

- When taking the test, read and follow the directions carefully.

- Save the most time for the questions with the highest point value.

- Skip questions you don't know, and return to them later.

- Keep track of the time.

GROUP ACTIVITY 6: Take a Multiple-Choice Writing Test

With several classmates, read the following three passages. Then read the questions that follow each passage, and as a group, choose the one best answer. (Note that the questions refer to the numbered sentences or word groups in the passages.)

[1]Archeologists are probably best known for discovering buried relics and ruins of ancient civilizations in faraway lands. [2]Many archeologists work right here in the United States, however. [3]Scholars have learned much about human history from studying the remains of past societies, not only the origins of modern humans but also the origins of our own country. [4]Even though the original colonies and settlements that became the United States are young when compared to the centuries-old Mayan and Egyptian civilizations, there are still many questions left to be answered about what life in colonial America was like. [5]By investigating questions and researching evidence found at the sites of old European settlements, archeologists and historians alike hope to find enough evidence to answer their many questions.

[6]Among the questions to be answered is the nature of the relationship between the European settlers and the Native Americans. [7]Some people believe that the relationship between these two groups was usually hostile, while others believe it was often peaceful. [8]Building foundations, fragments of pottery, and bits of trash is the pieces of evidence archeologists are using to help learn more about how colonists and Native Americans got along. [9]Evidence discovered at the site of Jamestown Colony in Virginia suggests that the relations between the settlers and Native Americans were at times peaceful and at other times hostile.

[10]Although written records from colonial settlements have survived, these documents alone cannot tell the entire story.

1. Which of the following versions of sentence 5 eliminates the unnecessary repetition in the original?

   A. By investigating questions and researching evidence found at the sites of old European settlements, archeologists hope to find evidence to answer their many questions.

   B. Archeologists and historians, by investigating and researching evidence found at the sites of old European settlements, hope to find enough evidence to answer their many questions.

   C. By investigating and researching artifacts found at the sites of old European settlements, archeologists and historians alike hope to answer many questions about the settlements.

D. Archeologists and historians alike hope to find evidence at the sites of old European settlements to answer their many questions.

2. Which of the following corrections should be made in the second paragraph?

A. Sentence 6: Change "European" to "european."

B. Sentence 7: Change "usually" to "usual."

C. Sentence 8: Change "is" to "are."

D. Sentence 9: Change "discovered" to "discovering."

3. Which of the following sentences is the best choice to use as a conclusion for the third paragraph?

A. To find evidence, historians must always dig things up.

B. Sometimes, three-hundred-year-old garbage can be just as instructive as what has been written down.

C. Nobody can trust the written word at all because the person writing it is always biased.

D. Archeologists have a difficult and valuable job to perform.

Read the passage below, which has been taken from a student's essay, and answer the questions that follow.

¹Aldo Leopold (1887–1948) was a well-known ecologist who believed that all life benefits when humans live in balance with nature and respect the environment. ²His *Sand County Almanac*, a book of essays, is one of the most important books on ecology and conservation. ³Observing the environment, the interconnected relationships among the animals, and the disruptions to the web of life caused by humans. ⁴Leopold reached a number of important conclusions.

⁵After receiving a master's degree in forestry from Yale University, Leopold began his career by working for the Forest Service in the Southwest. ⁶While there, he helped to establish the first protected wilderness area, the Gila National Forest in New Mexico. ⁷He was also interested in landscape processes, such as fire and erosion, and the role of predators such as wolves in the wild. ⁸Both interests helped shape his view of the natural world as an interconnected system, "a foundation of energy flowing through a circuit of soils, plants, and animals."

⁹Several years later, he bought and restored an abandoned farm where he worked on the land and studied nature. ¹⁰He also pioneered an effort to re-create Wisconsin's prairie-savanna ecosystem.

¹¹In 1948, as Leopold set out from his farm to help a neighbor put out a fire, he suffered a heart attack and died at sixty-one.

4. Which of the word groups from the first paragraph is not a complete sentence?

    A. Word group 1

    B. Word group 2.

    C. Word group 3

    D. Word group 4

5. Which of the underlined words in the third paragraph should be replaced by more precise or appropriate words?

    A. "Several years later"

    B. "an abandoned farm"

    C. "pioneered an effort"

    D. "prairie-savanna ecosystem"

6. Which of the following sentences would best fit after sentence 11, as a conclusion for this passage?

    A. He had a wife and five children.

    B. His influence is greater than ever, though, and his book has sold over 1.5 million copies since its publication in 1949.

    C. The chicken coop on Leopold's farm, where he lived and worked, still exists.

    D. Leopold was born in Iowa in 1887.

Read the following passage, which is written in the style of a science textbook. Then answer the questions that follow.

[1]Alzheimer's disease, an illness that slowly deprives people of their memory, reasoning, judgment, and language skills, causes the gradual destruction of a person's brain cells. [2]For over ten years, scientists have known that this disease starts with the action of an enzyme. [3]This enzyme, beta secretase, divides a protein that sticks out from brain cells in two. [4]Then gamma-secretase, another enzyme, further divides the resulting protein fragments. [5]This action creates the toxic A beta protein. [6]Theoretically, scientists could stop the production of A beta by blocking either enzyme, both enzymes have been difficult to block. [7]Recently, however, researchers have found the gene that causes cells to make beta-secretase. [8]Using a process of elimination, they started with a pool of one hundred genes and narrowed it down to one. [9]Having found this, scientists hope to be able to prevent Alzheimer's or slow its progress with medicine that can block beta-secretase. [10]Unfortunately, this next step may still be years away.

7. Which sentence is a comma splice?

   A. sentence 2

   B. sentence 4

   C. sentence 5

   D. sentence 6

8. Which of the following changes is needed in this paragraph?

   A. Change "causes" to "caused" in sentence 1.
   B. Change "then" to "also" in sentence 4.
   C. Change "Having found this" with "With this finding" in sentence 9.
   D. Change "slow" to "slowing" in sentence 9.

CHAPTER CHECKLIST

❑ Prepare for an essay exam by learning about the test, anticipating the questions, and developing a study routine.

❑ When taking an essay exam, analyze the question, gather and outline ideas, use an essay format, and make corrections.

❑ Prepare for an essay exam in response to a reading by developing a reading routine, keeping a reading journal, and making a vocabulary list.

❑ Write an essay exam in response to a reading by previewing the essay, taking notes on the main ideas, and using the writing process.

❑ Prepare for a multiple-choice writing test by learning about the test, anticipating the questions, and developing a study routine.

❑ Take a multiple-choice writing test by following the directions, reading the questions carefully, and selecting the best responses.

❑ For all tests, spend the most amount of time on items with the highest point value, and always keep track of the time.

REFLECTING ON YOUR WRITING

To help you reflect on your test-taking skills, answer the following questions.

1. Which type of timed writing test do you prefer to take? Why?

2. Does your college require such a test for placement?

3. Do any of your instructors give timed writing tests? If so, what do you know about the tests?

4. How will you study for each of these tests?

5. What strategies will you use during the test?

Using your answers to these questions, complete a Writing Process Report for this chapter (you can download a report form at **bedford stmartins.com/choices**). Once you complete this report, freewrite about what you learned in this chapter about taking timed writing tests and what you still hope to learn.

Writing Résumés and Cover Letters

In this chapter, you will write a résumé and a cover letter. As you work on your résumé and cover letter, you will

- **Learn about the sections of a résumé.**

- **Learn how to write a cover letter.**

- **Read a student's résumé and cover letter.**

What was your first job? You probably were hired because someone knew you personally — a neighbor who asked you to babysit, for instance. To get other types of jobs — such as delivering pizzas, waiting tables, or packing groceries — you might have filled out an application and had a brief interview. More professional jobs, however, require that you submit a résumé and cover letter. The word *résumé* derives from the Old French word for "to summarize." A *résumé* is a short account of your qualifications for a particular job. When you submit a résumé, you often include a cover letter that explains why you are the best person for the job. Typically, employers read submitted résumés and cover letters to select a few people to interview. Based on these interviews, they will select the best applicant for the job.

Writing Assignment

Write a résumé and cover letter for a job you're qualified for. To find job listings, go to Web sites such as **hotjobs.com** or **monster.com**, look through classified ads in newspapers, or consult professional and trade publications. When you locate a job that interests you, learn more about the company or organization by going to its Web site. The more informed you are about a company, the more likely you are to get the job.

THE RÉSUMÉ

A résumé consists of several different sections intended to showcase your achievements. The most common type of résumé is called *chronological* because information is presented in time order, from most recent to least recent jobs and educational achievements. The required sections of a chronological résumé include your contact information, educational background, and work experience. Optional sections include career objective, skills, honors and awards, and references. Keep in mind that a résumé is a persuasive document because you are trying to persuade your reader to grant you an interview. Unless you have significant work experience, it is best to keep your résumé to one page.

Required Information

You should include your contact information, education, and work experience in the résumé. The contact information should appear at the top of the page. The next section can be education or work experience, whichever one you feel will impress your reader the most.

Contact Information. Your contact information allows a potential employer to reach you.

- Give your name, address, phone number, and e-mail address (if you have one).
- If you list more than one phone number, indicate whether it's a home, work, or cell number, and always include the area code: for example, (555) 123-4567 (cell).
- Be sure that your e-mail address sends a professional message. It should consist of some form of your name rather than a nickname. For example, it is more professional to list an e-mail address such as **j.rodriguez@yahoo.com** than **hollyweirdo@yahoo.com**.

Creating E-mail Accounts
You can create a free e-mail account through Yahoo! (**mail.yahoo.com**), Google (**gmail.com**), or HotMail (**hotmail.com**). You can access these e-mail accounts from any Internet-connected computer. Consider designating an e-mail address for professional correspondence so that you can keep your personal and business messages separate.

Education. Include your college studies in this section. If you have just started college, you can also include your high school, especially if you had a good grade point average.

- Begin the list with the most recent achievement.
- List your college or university, your degree and major, and your expected graduation date.
- Indicate if you are on the dean's list or belong to an honor society.
- List particular courses you've taken that relate to the job you are applying for.
- Include any certificates or special training credentials you have earned.

Work Experience. Even if your work experience doesn't directly relate to the job you're applying for, your skills from one job can transfer to another job.

- List your most recent job first.
- List your job title, the company, the location, and the date for each of the jobs you've held.
- Following each job listing, briefly describe your responsibilities. Give facts such as the number of employees you supervised, the

amount of money you dealt with, the number of customers you served, and so on. Use sentence fragments that begin with action verbs: for example, "worked with technicians to fix breakdowns" or "designed Web pages."

- Include volunteer jobs if they consisted of a significant number of hours.

Optional Sections

Include the following sections in your résumé if you think they will help you get the job.

Career Objective. This section shows a potential employer what you can achieve in the job.

- "To create memorable advertisements that will sell Carsten cars"
- "To become a dynamic, highly rated d.j. at KACL radio"
- "To break all sales records at Gale's Outdoor Wear"

HOW TO Write a Good Career Objective

- Begin with an infinitive form of a verb (*to sell, to make, to win*).
- Use strong verbs.
- Mention the name of the company or organization.
- Be concise.

Skills. This section highlights your special expertise.

- List computer skills ("Proficient with Word, Excel, and PowerPoint").
- Give languages you speak ("Fluent in spoken and written Spanish").
- Indicate other skills that relate to the job, such as typing speed, ability to lift heavy objects, or graphic design skills.

Honors and Awards. If you have won any academic awards, been voted employee of the month, or received other accolades, list them here.

References. Your references should be people such as supervisors and professors who can attest to your qualifications. Because they are biased, friends and family members are not considered good references. Due to space concerns, you may simply say "Available upon request" or omit this section altogether (the employer will contact you for a list of references). If you do list your references, give their names, titles, and contact information.

Format and Grammar

Your résumé represents you. Remember that any errors or sloppiness will send the message to the employer that you are careless and disorganized. Therefore, your résumé should be tidy, easy to read, and grammatically correct.

- Fill up the page.
- Use white space to make your résumé easy to read (but not so much white space that the résumé appears skimpy).
- Center your name in at least 14-point type. Use 12-point for headings and 11-point for the text.
- Edit carefully. Some employers will discard a résumé if it contains only one error.

Sample Résumé

One student, Rachel, applied for a job as a sales representative at a marketing company that sells restaurant supplies. As her résumé shows, she is a college student who is working her way through school.

Rachel Serrano

4115 Oakdale Avenue

El Paso, TX 79909

(555) 915-1544

rserrano@aim.net

OBJECTIVE

To become an outstanding sales representative for Restaurant Marketing

EDUCATION

9/04–present　University of Texas at El Paso
- B.A. expected in May 2006
- Major: Business Marketing
- GPA: 3.0 (on a 4-point scale)

9/02–5/04　El Paso Community College
- A.A., Business Administration, May 2004
- GPA: 3.1 (on a 4-point scale)

SKILLS

- Proficient in Microsoft Word, Excel, Access, and PowerPoint
- Fluent in spoken and written Spanish

WORK EXPERIENCE

10/01–present　Hostess/Cashier, Geppetto's Restaurant, El Paso, Texas
- Greet customers, answer phones, prepare carry-out orders
- Close and balance register at end of shift
- Train new personnel

6/99–9/99　Sales Associate, Western Cell Phones, El Paso, Texas
- Assisted customers select cell phones and service providers
- Trained new personnel

HONORS AND AWARDS

- Employee of the month, Geppetto's Restaurant, March 2003
- Top seller, Western Cell Phones, July 1999

REFERENCES

Available upon request

GROUP ACTIVITY 1: Write a Résumé

After carefully reading the job listing you've selected, draft a résumé for that job. Put the most impressive information early in the résumé. Ask classmates to make suggestions for revision. After revising the résumé, edit it carefully for format and grammar.

COVER LETTER

In your cover letter, make an argument about why you are the best person for the job. Rather than simply repeating information included in your résumé, add specific details that will make you stand out from other applicants.

A cover letter has an introduction, body, and conclusion.

- In your introduction, give the title of the job you're applying for, and explain where you found the listing. Then summarize your qualifications.
- In the body of the letter, explain why you can help the company meet its goals. Point to experiences such as managing people, dealing with difficult customers, or meeting deadlines. Demonstrate that you know important characteristics of the company, such as its sales records or community work. You usually can find this information on the company's Web site.
- In the conclusion restate your interest, give your contact information, and express appreciation for being considered.

As with any job-related document, be sure that the letter is correctly and clearly written. Use standard letter format, and limit the letter to one page. In addition, make sure your cover letter includes the specific information the job listing asks for, such as your salary requirements or your willingness to travel.

Sample Cover Letter

Rachel wrote this cover letter for the Restaurant Marketing job. Notice the letter format that she used, and follow this format when you write your own letter.

Rachel Serrano
4115 Oakdale Ave.
El Paso, TX 79909

September 15, 2005

Mr. Byron Millis
Restaurant Marketing
15313 Mesquite Ave.
Austin, TX 78734

Dear Mr. Millis:

Please consider this letter as an expression of my interest in the customer sales and service position for Restaurant Marketing that was posted on careerbuilder.com on September 13. As a marketing student, I am interested in this opportunity to use my skills in the sales and marketing industry. Through my experience working in the restaurant business as well as in sales, I have learned the skills necessary to communicate to customers the value of a product.

My experience in training personnel has taught me the value of teamwork, and I pride myself on being a team leader. I am goal oriented, strive to be the best, and enjoy motivating others to do the same. Because sales representatives for Restaurant Marketing deal individually with the customer, being able to communicate clearly is crucial. I am fluent in Spanish, which will be of great advantage to Restaurant Marketing because of its location in the Southwest. I am confident that I can contribute to your company's current $180 million dollars in sales.

I would appreciate the opportunity to meet with your company representatives to discuss your company needs and what I can do to benefit Restaurant Marketing. I can be reached by phone at (555) 915-1544 or by e-mail at rsserrano@aim.net. Thank you for your consideration.

Sincerely,

Rachel Serrano

Rachel Serrano

Enclosure: Résumé

GROUP ACTIVITY 2: Write a Cover Letter

Keeping in mind the job ad and your résumé, draft a cover letter. Make an argument, using information not included in the résumé, for why you're the best person for the job. Show the draft to your classmates for suggestions for revision. After revising the letter, edit it for format and grammar.

CHAPTER CHECKLIST

❑ Search for jobs for which you are qualified.

❑ A résumé includes your contact information, education, and work experience.

❑ Include other sections in your résumé when you think the extra information would help you land the job.

❑ Always draft, revise, and edit your résumés.

❑ A cover letter makes the argument for why you should be hired.

❑ In the cover letter, include information not given in your résumé, and organize it with an introduction, a body, and a conclusion.

❑ Always draft, revise, and edit your cover letters.

REFLECTING ON YOUR WRITING

To help you continue to improve as a writer, answer the following questions about the writing assignment for this chapter.

1. What was the easiest part about writing a résumé and cover letter? Explain.

2. What was the hardest part about writing a résumé and cover letter? Explain.

3. How are résumés and cover letters alike? How are they different?

4. How much did this assignment help prepare you for applying for a job?

Using your answers to these questions, complete a Writing Process Report for this chapter (you can download a report form at **bedford stmartins.com/choices**). Once you complete this report, freewrite about what you learned in this chapter about writing résumés and cover letters and what you still hope to learn.

PART FOUR

Handbook with Exercises

When we write, we want to communicate our ideas clearly to demonstrate our knowledge of our topic and to ensure that our readers understand what we mean. In this Handbook, you'll find opportunities to practice and improve your writing. For example, you'll learn to improve your sentences and to combine short sentences into longer, more interesting ones. You'll learn how to vary your word choice and to eliminate errors. If you are a multilingual writer, you'll find an entire section devoted to helping you write more effectively.

Plan to use this Handbook in several ways. Use it as a reference guide when you have a question about sentence structure, grammar, spelling, or punctuation. Complete certain practice exercises to help you target specific errors that occur in your writing. Consult it during the editing stage. And most important, use it to help eliminate errors from your writing.

Handbook Contents

Chapter 15: Writing Sentences   481
- A. Subjects   481
- B. Verbs   487
- C. Subject-Verb Agreement   497

Chapter 16: Expanding Sentences   505
- A. Phrases   505
- B. Clauses   508
- C. Pronouns   514
- D. Adjectives   518
- E. Adverbs   520

Chapter 17: Combining Sentences   522
- A. Coordination   522
- B. Subordination   526
- C. Sentence-Combining Exercises   531

Chapter 18: Improving Sentences   542
- A. Sentence Fragments   542
- B. Run-on Sentences   546
- C. Comma Splices   551
- D. Misplaced Modifiers   556
- E. Dangling Modifiers   558
- F. Active and Passive Voice   560
- G. Parallelism   562

Chapter 19: Improving Word Choice   565
- A. Vocabulary   565
- B. Unnecessary Repetition   568
- C. Wordiness   569

Chapter 20: Improving Spelling   571
- A. Spelling Rules   571
- B. Commonly Misspelled Words   576
- C. Commonly Confused Words   578

Chapter 21: Improving Punctuation   581
- A. Commas   581
- B. Semicolons   592
- C. Colons   594
- D. End Punctuation   595
- E. Apostrophes   597
- F. Quotation Marks   602

Chapter 22: Improving Mechanics   606
- A. Capital Letters   606
- B. Italics   610
- C. Abbreviations   611
- D. Numbers   612

Chapter 23: Guide for Multilingual Writers   614
- A. Articles   614
- B. Count and Noncount Nouns   616
- C. Prepositions   618
- D. Omitted or Repeated Subjects   621
- E. Word Order   624
- F. Verbs   627

CHAPTER 15

Writing Sentences

Every sentence needs to have a subject and a verb and to express a complete thought.

A. SUBJECTS

The subject tells *who* or *what* is doing something or being something. Usually, the subject is a noun — a person, place, or thing. But a subject can also be a pronoun — a word that takes the place of a noun:

Anita laughs.
She is in a good mood.

Compound Subjects

Sometimes a sentence has more than one subject. A subject with more than one part is called a *compound subject*:

John and Mary planned the party.
The dog and the cat ran across the street.

Tips for Multilingual Writers

Be careful not to leave out the subject in a sentence.

INCORRECT	My brother likes his geology course. Is his favorite class.
CORRECT	My brother likes his geology course. *It* is his favorite class.
INCORRECT	Calls her best friend every day.
CORRECT	*Kim* calls her best friend every day.

Remember not to include a pronoun that refers to the subject as part of the subject.

INCORRECT	Greg he went fishing.
CORRECT	Greg went fishing.
INCORRECT	Snow White she ate a poisoned apple.
INCORRECT	Snow White ate a poisoned apple.

ACTIVITY 1: Add Subjects

Complete each of the following sentences by adding a subject.

EXAMPLE   The ___puppy___ chases his tail all day long.

1. My _____ served in the marines for twenty-five years.

2. The _____ complained about the slow service.

3. _____ and _____ lived together after college.

4. Every _____ deserves a quality education.

5. _____ attended the concert last weekend.

6. The dark _____ made the room feel small.

7. The _____ is very hot and spicy at that restaurant.

8. Lola's _____ is due tomorrow morning.

9. _____ and _____ want to visit the Grand Canyon.

10. The _____ is often crowded in the afternoon.

Subject Pretenders

Sometimes the subject of a sentence is hard to identify because of a *subject pretender*. One type of subject pretender is a prepositional phrase, which begins with a preposition.

Prepositions

A *preposition* is a word that expresses how other words are related in time, space, or another sense.

COMMON PREPOSITIONS

about	despite	on
above	down	out
after	during	over
against	except	past

among	for	since
as	from	to
at	in	toward
before	inside	under
behind	into	until
below	like	up
beneath	near	upon
beside	next to	with
between	of	within
by	off	without

Tips for Multilingual Writers

Prepositions that show time — such as *for, during,* and *since* — may have differences in meaning.

For usually refers to an exact period of time that something lasts — one that has a beginning and an end:

I worked as a cook *for* two years.

We have been waiting *for* thirty minutes.

I've been a nonsmoker *for* one month.

During usually refers to an indefinite period of time in which something happens:

Several times *during* the week I thought of you.

I want to go home *during* the holidays.

It got hot *during* the night, but I don't know exactly when.

Since usually refers to a period of time that has passed between an earlier time and the present:

Since losing weight, I've been happy.

Mae has been happy *since* she got married.

Eddie has been more confident *since* winning the race.

ACTIVITY 2: Identify Prepositions

Underline the prepositions in the following paragraph.

EXAMPLE Bob and Trevor drove <u>to</u> the library.

They had many questions for the reference librarian because they had a research project due in their history class the following week. Bob left the assignment directions in his car, but Trevor carried an extra copy with him in his backpack. The librarian found several history reference books on the shelves behind her desk. She helped Bob and Trevor find newspaper and magazine articles by using the library databases and looking under the most useful subject headings. They sent copies of the best articles to their e-mail accounts. Then they copied entries from the reference books using the photocopier under the library stairs.

ACTIVITY 3: Add Prepositions

Complete each of the following sentences by writing a preposition in the space provided.

EXAMPLE I never travel __without__ my cell phone charger.

1. The swimmer dove _____ the pool.

2. The novel *The Color Purple* was written _____ Alice Walker.

3. Kendra has several tattoos _____ her back.

4. Evan found a pen pal _____ the Internet.

5. _____ her last class, Berta checks her e-mail.

6. Malcolm never goes to sleep _____ midnight.

7. Hiding your house key _____ the doormat is a bad idea.

8. Jessica had Dr. Millhauser _____ her biology professor.

9. Jo suspected everyone had been talking _____ her.

10. I walk _____ the playground every morning on my way to work.

Prepositional Phrases

A *prepositional phrase* consists of a preposition and its object. The object is a noun or pronoun, together with any words that describe or refer to the object. Here are some examples.

Preposition	+ Object	= Prepositional Phrase
into	the classroom	into the classroom
before	you	before you
on	a bright summer day	on a bright summer day

ACTIVITY 4: Write Prepositional Phrases

Complete each of the following sentences by adding a prepositional phrase.

EXAMPLE   The babysitter took the children _____*for a walk*_____ .

1. Isaac bought his iPod _____ .

2. My economics study group meets _____ .

3. Movies _____ are very popular.

4. I ate the meatloaf that I found _____ .

5. When Sal called, I was _____ .

6. _____ , Lucy practiced her violin.

7. _____ , the plumber fixed the leak.

8. Zaini caught the train _____ .

9. The seagulls flew _____ .

10. Jim and Ralph walked home _____ .

A prepositional phrase cannot be the subject of a sentence.

The children *in the bus* need to be brought inside.

In the sentence above, *in the bus* is a prepositional phrase. The subject of the sentence is *children*.

The dog *from across the street* chased my cat.

From across the street is a prepositional phrase. The subject of the sentence is *dog*.

Because you know that the subject of a sentence is never in a prepositional phrase, you can find the subject easily. First, cross out all the prepositional phrases. Then decide which of the other words is doing something or being something.

The man ~~in the photograph~~ looks ~~like my grandfather~~.

The subject of the sentence is *man*.

The phone ~~in Karen's office~~ rang three times.

The subject of the sentence is *phone*.

HOW TO Find the Subject of a Sentence

- Cross out all prepositional phrases.
- Decide which of the remaining words is doing something or being something.

ACTIVITY 5: Identify Prepositional Phrases and Sentence Subjects

In each of the following sentences, cross out the prepositional phrases and circle the subject.

EXAMPLE   The (box) ~~on the table~~ was open.

1. The neighbors down the hall are very loud.
2. Darryl bought a used computer for five hundred dollars.
3. The pumpkins in that garden need to be picked.
4. After the midterm, the sociology class became more difficult.
5. Inside those drawers, you will find my old sweaters.
6. The guests at the wedding loved the food.
7. Without his friends, Nicky felt somewhat shy.
8. The information in that article is not very reliable.
9. The questions on the test covered the whole semester.
10. Two of Kristina's brothers joined the military.

ACTIVITY 6: Identify Subject Pretenders

In the following paragraph, cross out the prepositional phrases and circle the subject of each sentence.

EXAMPLE   (I)entered the photographs ~~on that wall in the art show.~~

Everybody who participated in the student art show benefited from the experience. My friend Jill won a prize for one of her paintings. Consequently, three of her pieces now are on display in the student center. Although I did not win anything, I received lots of compliments on my photographs. A person who asked for my telephone number has purchased a photo from me. Around the campus green where the show took place were temporary walls made of plywood. Graffiti artists painted the walls with their best efforts. These walls were the most popular work of art at the show. They have been moved next to the art building and will remain on display.

Exercise Central
For additional practice with using subjects, go to **bedford stmartins.com/choices** and click on "Exercise Central."

B. VERBS

The *verb* in a sentence expresses action or links the subject to the rest of the sentence.

Action and Linking Verbs

Action Verbs

In the following sentences, the verb expresses action:

Mary Louise *owns* an antique quilt.
The dog *ate* my homework.
I *love* that band's music.

Linking Verbs

In these next sentences, the verb links the subject to the rest of the sentence. The most common linking verbs are forms of the verb *to be*: *am, are, is, was, were, be, been, being*:

I *am* short.
The children *were* grumpy.
Miriam *is* ready to perform.

Helping Verbs

Helping verbs include *am, are, is, was, were, be, have, has, had, do, does, did, may, might, must, can, could, shall, should, will, would*. A helping verb is used with another verb form, called the *main verb*, to form a phrase that acts as the verb of the sentence:

Moira *was helping* her brother prepare the meal.
Nancy *had studied* all morning.
You *must reply* this afternoon.

Compound Verbs

Sometimes a sentence has more than one verb. A verb with more than one part is called a *compound verb*:

Edgar Allan Poe *frightened* and *thrilled* readers.
The children *sat* and *waited* for their parents to get them.
I *can use* your help and *would be* grateful for it.

ACTIVITY 7: Identify Subjects and Verbs in Sentences

In each of the following sentences, circle the subject and underline the verb.

EXAMPLE   (I) enjoy performing in front of people.

1. My friends and I started a band a few years ago.

2. Currently, we are writing new songs.

3. We have enjoyed playing music together.

4. A neighbor helped us record our first demo.

5. She was happy to offer us advice.

6. We have played shows at a small club downtown.

7. The club owner has asked us to come more often.

8. Our bass player and our drummer are brothers.

9. They have written some of our best songs.

10. We have dreamed of stardom since we were kids.

ACTIVITY 8: Add Verbs

Complete each of the following sentences by adding a verb.

> EXAMPLE   A typical student ____desires____ many electronic devices,
>
> such as a computer, calculator, and personal CD player.

1. An anonymous donor _____ a million dollars to the scholarship fund.

2. Lisa _____ student body president.

3. A flock of seagulls _____ overhead.

4. The children _____ free swimming lessons.

5. Armando _____ a rabbit hide behind the fence.

6. Our biology class _____ DNA last week.

7. Frederick _____ a friend's house last night.

8. The soccer team _____ at the football field.

9. Police officers _____ the hillside for clues.

10. Many champion gymnasts _____ their training at a very young age.

Verb Pretenders

Verb pretenders (also called *verbals*) look like verbs but do not act as verbs in sentences. The most common verb pretenders are verb + *-ing* and *to* + verb combinations.

cooking	to cook
working	to work
studying	to study

Verb + -ing

When an *-ing* verb appears in a sentence without a helping verb, it does not act as the verb of the sentence. Instead, it modifies, or describes, other words in the sentence:

I took a picture of the boy *swimming* in the fountain. [*Swimming* describes the boy.]

Working hard, we completed the job in a day. [*Working* describes the subject of the sentence, *we*.]

The *laughing* partygoers kept me awake at night. [*Laughing* describes the partygoers.]

ACTIVITY 9: Identify *-ing* Verbs

In the space provided, indicate whether the *-ing* verb in each of the following sentences acts as a modifier or as part of a verb.

EXAMPLE   The panting dog needed to drink some water. ____modifier____

1. Claudia is hiking the Appalachian Trail. _____

2. Joanne sent her father a singing telegram for his birthday. _____

3. That diving board is too high. _____

4. I was weeding the garden when I scraped my knee. _____

5. The cookie recipe requires a tablespoon of baking powder. _____

6. Stomping on the floor, William showed his displeasure. _____

7. Susan is moving to Las Vegas the day after tomorrow. _____

8. Nina went to the mall for a new pair of knitting needles. _____

9. Because of her back problems, Kata felt better sleeping on the floor. _____

10. Jumping up and down, the children showed their excitement. _____

ACTIVITY 10: Use Verbs and Verb Pretenders

For each of the following *-ing* verbs, write two sentences. In the first sentence, use the word as a verb. (You'll need a helping verb, too.) In the second sentence, use the word as a modifier to describe another word.

EXAMPLE   drinking

Verb: _____I was drinking cranberry juice when you called._____

Modifier: _____Clean drinking water is harder and harder to find._____

1. viewing

Verb: _____

Modifier: _____

2. planting

Verb: _____

Modifier: _____

3. sleeping

Verb: _____

Modifier: _____

4. playing

Verb: _____

Modifier: _____

5. surfing

Verb: _____

Modifier: _____

To + Verb

The *to* + verb combination also looks like a verb but does not act as a verb in a sentence. Instead, it acts as either a noun or a modifier that describes something:

I can't wait to open my gifts. [Because *to* comes in front of *open, open* does not act as a verb. Instead, *to open* modifies *wait.*]

I always open my gifts before my birthday. [Here *open* acts as a verb.]

Susan had a plan to buy apples. [Because *to* comes in front of *buy, buy* does not act as a verb. Instead, *to buy* modifies *plan.*]

Susan buys apples from the farm. [Here *buys* acts as a verb.]

My goal is to study medicine. [Because *to* comes in front of *study, study* does not act as a verb. Instead, *to study* acts as a noun.]

Many Americans study medicine overseas. [Here *study* acts as a verb.]

HOW TO Find the Verb in a Sentence

- Locate the word or words that express the action or link the subject to the rest of the sentence.

- Check that the word is not a verb pretender.

- When a verb + *-ing* combination appears in a sentence without a helping verb, it's a verb pretender.

- When a *to* + verb combination appears, it's a verb pretender.

ACTIVITY 11: Use *to* + Verb Combinations

Complete each of the following sentences with a *to* + *verb* combination.

  EXAMPLE   Mauricio used a hammer _____*to crack the coconut*_____.

1. Rebecca waited _____.

2. _____ was the children's favorite thing to do.

3. Sunay promises _____.

4. Half the apartments in this building do not seem _____.

5. Before sitting down to breakfast, Erica's parents needed _____.

6. _____ is Kyle's only chore this morning.

7. Bryan likes _____.

8. After a day of skiing, Richard and Elizabeth want _____ _____.

9. Connie's old job was _____.

10. _____ may be Lon's greatest talent.

ACTIVITY 12: Find Subjects and Verbs

In each of the following sentences, circle the subject and underline the verb. Do not confuse verbs and verb pretenders.

  EXAMPLE   The smiling (woman) accepted the award.

1. Kim agreed to have the meeting at her house.

2. While taping the playoffs, Hugo watched a documentary.

3. Stepping carefully, Nizar tried to avoid the wet paint.

4. The hikers reached their campground by sunset.

5. Mosquitoes were annoying the hikers.

6. Adam washed his hands before kneading the bread dough.

7. The people on the street hoped to glimpse the famous actress.

8. Opening the newspaper, Maya began to read the classified ads.

9. After work, Tim and Linda lack the energy to cook dinner.

10. Slipping the diamond ring on Leticia's finger, Nahum asked her to marry him.

ACTIVITY 13: Identify Subjects and Verbs

In the following paragraph, circle the subjects and underline the verbs.

EXAMPLE (Ivor) decided to major in music.

Ivor needed to interview a local drummer for a term project. Before contacting the musician, he read about her career. Feeling nervous, he wrote her a letter to request an appointment. To his surprise, the drummer invited him to watch a rehearsal. Her band was playing a new song. Ivor took many notes while listening to them. He wanted to describe his first impressions completely. After the rehearsal, the band kept asking him questions about his assignment. Answering the musicians politely, he wondered how to change the subject. Finally, the drummer told the band to let Ivor begin his interview.

Verb Tense

The *tense* of a verb shows the time that the action or condition takes place. The three basic tenses in English are *present, past,* and *future.*

The *present tense* shows an action or condition taking place at the time the writer is writing. The present tense can also show an action that happens more than once:

Anthony *has* a big kitchen.
He *cooks* every evening.

The *past tense* shows something that began and ended in the past. To form the past tense of most verbs, use the *-ed* form of the verb:

Last week, Anthony *cooked* for his friends and family.

The *future* tense shows something that will take place or will probably take place. To form the future tense, use *will* or *be going to* and the present tense of the verb:

I *will learn* my lines by next week.

This extra credit assignment *is going to* make a difference in my grade.

As a general rule, stay with the tense you begin with at the start of a paragraph unless the time you are talking about changes. Avoid shifting from one tense to another for no reason because these shifts may confuse your readers.

ACTIVITY 14: Correct Awkward Shifts in Verb Tense

Edit the following paragraph to correct unnecessary shifts in verb tense. The first sentence in the paragraph is correct.

EXAMPLE   My stepson angered me, but I ~~try~~ tried to understand.

For a long time, my stepson, Jonathan, was unhappy to have me as part of his family. I try to get to know him better, but he will complain that I invade his privacy. As a newcomer, I understood that our relationship will require effort from both of us. It was not enough that I was friendly. Jonathan also has to want us to be friends. I am not happy with the two of us being strangers, but I can wait for him to feel more comfortable around me.

ACTIVITY 15: Correct Awkward Shifts in Verb Tense

Edit the following paragraph to correct unnecessary shifts in verb tense. The first sentence in the paragraph is correct.

EXAMPLE   Anne Marie finds bottles on old farmland, where she likes to explore.

Anne Marie collects antique bottles. She will buy bottles if she liked them, but she prefers to find them in the ground. She will find bottles everywhere. However, she has the best luck at construction sites on old farmland. Often, bottles appeared on the surface after a good rain. She will use special tools for excavating bottles, including a set of brushes. She did not want to break the bottles as she removed them from the ground. After finding a new bottle, Anne Marie will add it to her display case.

Regular Verbs

Regular verbs are verbs whose past tense and past participle end in -ed. Past participles are forms of a verb that are used with *has, have,* or *had,* as in the following examples:

I *have* studied Portuguese for three years.
Niko *had drunk* all of the free champagne.

COMMON REGULAR VERBS

Verb	Past Tense	Past Participle
cook	cooked	cooked
measure	measured	measured
study	studied	studied
walk	walked	walked

Irregular Verbs

Irregular verbs are verbs whose past tense and past participle do not end in -ed but are formed in a variety of other ways. As a result, they are often misused or misspelled. Review the forms of irregular verbs so you won't make errors.

COMMON IRREGULAR VERBS

Verb	Past Tense	Past Participle
be	was, were	been
begin	began	begun
catch	caught	caught
choose	chose	chosen
come	came	come
do	did	done
drink	drank	drunk
eat	ate	eaten
feel	felt	felt
fly	flew	flown
get	got	got, gotten
go	went	gone
leave	left	left
ride	rode	ridden
seen	saw	seen

ACTIVITY 16: Identify Regular and Irregular Verbs

In each of the following sentences, underline the verb and identify it as a regular or an irregular verb.

EXAMPLE   The letter carrier <u>knocked</u> on the door. _____ *regular*

1. Kate placed the grapes in the bowl. _____

2. Nathan knew Robin and Simon already. _____

3. Somebody stole my purse! _____

4. Dwayne read comic books at night. _____

5. Chen baked a cake for his family. _____

6. The moths flew around the lamp. _____

7. Alice drank a bottle of water. _____

8. Zafir caught a cold on the airplane. _____

9. The mechanic looked under the hood. _____

10. The telephone rang at midnight. _____

ACTIVITY 17: Use Regular and Irregular Verbs

In each of the following sentences, write the correct form of the verb in the space provided. If necessary, consult your dictionary for the correct form.

EXAMPLE   Richard _____*lost*_____ his train ticket last night. *(lose)*

1. When she was young, Jayne _____ her money under her bed. *(hide)*

2. Isabel has _____ with a gospel choir for five years. *(sing)*

3. Last semester, Meg _____ about her grades. *(worry)*

4. Yesterday morning, the actors _____ very convincing in their costumes. *(look)*

5. Patrick and Hugh have _____ music at every school in town. *(teach)*

6. Experts say that the ocean liner *Titanic* _____ because it was too big. *(sink)*

7. My grandmother _____ that picture when she was ten years old. *(draw)*

8. Who has _____ my car without my permission? *(drive)*

9. The cousins _____ for hours at the family reunion last July. *(talk)*

10. Sigrid has _____ Naomi for her dance partner. *(choose)*

Exercise Central

For additional practice with using verbs, go to **bedford stmartins.com/choices** and click on "Exercise Central."

C. SUBJECT-VERB AGREEMENT

A complete sentence contains a subject and a verb. The subject tells who or what is doing something or being something, and the verb expresses the action or links the subject to the rest of the sentence. To maintain *subject-verb agreement,* a singular subject must have a singular verb form, and a plural subject must have a plural verb form.

Singular and Plural Forms

A *singular* subject consists of one thing:

the student

A singular verb form in the present tense usually ends in -*s:*

The student studies for the test.

A plural subject consists of more than one thing:

the students

A plural verb form in the present tense generally does not end in -*s:*

The students study for the test.

To check for subject-verb agreement, you must first identify the subject of the sentence. Remember that prepositions and other words sometimes occur between the subject and verb. Once you identify the subject, you can add the correct verb form.

INCORRECT Elaine go to the recycling center. [singular subject, plural verb form]

CORRECT Elaine goes to the recycling center. [singular subject, singular verb form]

INCORRECT The cars swerves to avoid hitting the dog. [plural subject, singular verb form]

CORRECT The cars swerve to avoid hitting the dog. [plural subject, plural verb form]

ACTIVITY 18: Identify Subject-Verb Agreement

In each of the following sentences, underline the correct verb form.

> EXAMPLE   I (naps, <u>nap</u>) every afternoon.

1. This book (costs, cost) less online than at the store.
2. The swimmers (competes, compete) against one another every year.
3. The windows (sticks, stick) in humid weather.
4. The airlines (offers, offer) advice for children traveling alone.
5. Lester (works, work) as a computer help desk operator.
6. Strawberries (remains, remain) fresh for only a few days.
7. Dr. Perry (sees, see) new patients.
8. Phoebe (drives, drive) a vintage Ford truck.
9. Kathy and Karen (attends, attend) an accelerated Spanish program.
10. Dancing (is, are) a form of art, a form of exercise, and a form of recreation.

ACTIVITY 19: Add Verbs That Agree

Add a singular or plural verb form to each of the following sentences as needed to maintain subject-verb agreement.

> EXAMPLE   My mother-in-law ___*bakes*___ the best oatmeal raisin cookies.

1. At dusk, the city's skyline _____ especially beautiful.
2. I _____ your good grades.
3. This radio _____ only three AM stations.
4. Those magazines _____ the best information on fly fishing.
5. Katie _____ French and Spanish fluently.
6. Empanadas _____ best when served fresh from the oven.
7. Professor Boyers _____ his students to write two research papers.
8. Bruce _____ at a gym several times a week.
9. Tracy and Lincoln _____ together at the soup kitchen.
10. Listening to soothing music _____ an effective way to relax.

To determine correct subject-verb agreement, be sure that you have correctly identified the subject. Watch out for subject pretenders such as prepositional phrases.

Read about subject pretenders on pp. 482–87.

INCORRECT The cup of pencils *are* on the table. [The prepositional phrase *of pencils* is a subject pretender.]

CORRECT The cup of pencils *is* on the table. [*The cup* is the subject of the sentence.]

ACTIVITY 20: Use Correct Verbs

In each of the following sentences, underline the correct verb form.

EXAMPLE The books on those shelves (belongs, belong) to my

roommate.

1. To do one hundred sit ups a day (is, are) my goal.

2. The pieces of gum (sticks, stick) to the roof of my mouth.

3. The keys lost in bushes (needs, need) to be found.

4. The Halloween masks in the store (looks, look) scary.

5. The books that I like best (is, are) mysteries and thrillers.

6. One of the professors (has, have) a bad cold.

7. To beat my brother in checkers (is, are) my greatest wish in the world.

8. Oprah Winfrey's outfits (is, are) always in the news.

9. Movies of popular books often (becomes, become) very successful.

10. My pet ferrets, whose names are George and Laura, (eats, eat) more food than I do.

ACTIVITY 21: Maintain Subject-Verb Agreement

Add a singular or plural verb form to each of the following sentences as needed to maintain subject-verb agreement.

EXAMPLE The CDs in that box ____belong____ to Malcolm.

1. That television station always _____ reruns.

2. The vase of tulips _____ on the kitchen counter.

3. The applicants did not _____ a good first impression.

4. Those mushrooms around that tree _____ poisonous.

5. Our basement, filled with broken furniture and old toys, _____ to be cleaned out.

6. Professor Wu, joined by many of her students, _____ for animal rights.

7. The apples on that tree _____ ripe.

8. The nurses in the children's hospital _____ excellent care.

9. Poppy's collection of amusement park souvenirs _____ valuable.

10. A jar full of pennies _____ in the back of my closet.

ACTIVITY 22: Insert Correct Verbs

In the following paragraph, underline the correct verb forms.

> EXAMPLE   Many people (is, <u>are</u>) interested in football, but few
>
> people (is, <u>are</u>) as obsessed as my husband.

Paul, who (has been, have been) my husband for three years, (is, are) in love with the sport. Being married to a football fanatic (has, have) its drawbacks. During the football season, each and every Sunday (is, are) dedicated to the sport. Paul and his friends (gather, gathers) at our house before noon to begin watching the games. Fortunately, his friend Rico, who is one of the best cooks I've ever met, (bring, brings) the snacks and drinks. All day, I (hear, hears) cheers and boos coming from the living room. Paul and his friends (take, takes) the game so seriously they get depressed when their teams lose. Personally, I'd rather have a hobby that is less stressful.

Indefinite Pronouns

Sometimes the subject of a sentence is an *indefinite pronoun.* Here are some singular indefinite pronouns that take singular verb forms:

anybody	everyone	nothing
anyone	everything	somebody
anything	nobody	someone
each	no one	something
everybody		

INCORRECT   Each of us *need* to pay twenty dollars. [*Each* is singular and requires a singular verb form.]

CORRECT   Each of us *needs* to pay twenty dollars.

INCORRECT   Anyone *know* the answer. [singular pronoun, plural verb form]

CORRECT   Anyone *knows* the answer. [singular pronoun, singular verb form]

INCORRECT   Everybody *go* to the movies on Friday night. [singular pronoun, plural verb form]

CORRECT   Everybody *goes* to the movies on Friday night. [singular pronoun, singular verb form]

HOW TO Check for Subject-Verb Agreement

- Remember that singular subjects take singular verb forms and that plural subjects take plural verb forms.

- Be sure that you have correctly identified the subject.

- Watch out for subject pretenders, such as prepositional phrases.

- Indefinite pronouns — such as *everyone, anyone, something,* and *no one* — are singular and take singular verb forms.

ACTIVITY 23: Identify Subject-Verb Agreement

In each of the following sentences, underline the correct verb form.

EXAMPLE   Something about that story (<u>makes</u>, make) me uneasy.

1. Nothing about that movie (is, are) worthwhile.

2. Everybody with a special permit (parks, park) in the same lot.

3. Somebody living on my street (plays, play) bongos in the middle of the night.

4. No one in that laboratory (has, have) a degree in science.

5. Something inside the car (makes, make) a strange clunking noise.

6. Everyone in Carmela's family (speaks, speak) English and Italian.

7. Everything remaining on the floor (does, do) not belong there.

8. Nobody with a new computer (uses, use) version 2.0 of the software.

9. Someone wearing strong perfume (leaves, leave) a trail of scent behind her.

10. Anything made of wood that is exposed to rain (requires, require) a waterproof finish.

ACTIVITY 24: Add Singular Verbs

Add a singular verb form to each of the following sentences to maintain subject-verb agreement.

EXAMPLE   No one in the room ____*wants*____ to stand up.

1. Everyone on the roller coaster _____ a little queasy.

2. Someone in this class _____ the answers to the test.

3. Anything in that store _____ a dollar or less.

4. Somebody _____ to clean the dishes in the sink.

5. Nobody _____ Sunay to pass his driving test.

6. Something in this room _____ like oranges.

7. Nothing _____ wrong with your plan.

8. Everything in the storage unit _____ to Lorraine and Howie.

9. No one in my class _____ group projects.

10. Everybody _____ to return next year.

ACTIVITY 25: Write Sentences with Correct Subject-Verb Agreement

Complete each of the following sentences, making sure that the verb you add agrees with the subject that is provided.

EXAMPLE   Everybody ___*goes to the movies*___ after work on Friday.

1. These young couples _____.

2. This Web site _____.

3. Everyone on this list _____.

4. We _____.

5. I _____.

6. None of the telemarketers _____.

7. The little boy who should have a permission slip _____

_____.

8. The director of the church choir _____.

9. The presidents of both classes _____.

10. Nobody _____.

ACTIVITY 26: Select Subjects and Verbs That Agree

In the following paragraph, underline the correct verb forms.

EXAMPLE   Guo (<u>feel</u>, feels) proud of his Chinese heritage.

Guo (belongs, belong) to a troupe of lion dancers. Beginning
in October, Guo meets once a week with the other lion dancers
and (begins, begin) rehearsing for Chinese New Year. After being
in the troupe for three years, Guo now (dances, dance) as the
lion's head. He (shakes, shake) the mane and (pretends, pretend)
to roar. Being the lion's head (is, are) a great honor as well as hard
work. After Christmas, as Chinese New Year approaches, the
troupe members, who all attend the same university, (rehearses,
rehearse) every night. Everyone (looks, look) forward to the festivities. In addition to dancing in the New Year's parade, the group
of dancers (visits, visit) city schools to teach children about
Chinese culture. The children sitting closest to the lion (screams,
scream) when it approaches them. The dancing creature, with his
comical but threatening gestures, (delights, delight) and (frightens,
frighten) young spectators.

ACTIVITY 27: Correct Subject-Verb Agreement

Revise the following paragraph as needed to correct errors in subject-
verb agreement.

EXAMPLE   Tanya's job of managing a plumbing supply business
                              satisfies
                              ~~satisfy~~ her.
                              ^

Tanya manage her father's plumbing supply business. The first thing every morning, with the telephone already ringing, she turns on the computer and take the first orders of the day. The orders early in the morning is usually for emergency jobs and generates repeat business. Tanya's father, who has a good reputation among local plumbers, ask her to give these orders priority. No one, especially someone with clogged pipes, want to wait longer than necessary for repairs. Filling emergency orders are not Tanya's only job. She maintains the company budget and decide which bills to pay each day. Surrounded by boxes of hardware, Tanya admit that she had expected to work somewhere more glamorous after receiving her business degree. However, everybody who remembers the company before her improvements admire her work. Her decision to computerize office procedures have made the company more efficient and more profitable.

Exercise Central

For additional practice with subject-verb agreement, go to **bedfordstmartins.com/choices** and click on "Exercise Central."

CHAPTER 16

Expanding Sentences

In addition to containing subjects and verbs, sentences can be expanded to include phrases, clauses, pronouns, adjectives, and adverbs. These expansions give you the opportunity to express yourself effectively for a variety of audiences.

A. PHRASES

If a group of words lacks a subject or a verb or both, it's a *phrase*. A phrase is not a complete sentence. Notice the difference between phrases and sentences in these examples:

See pp. 481–87 and 487–97 for more information about subjects and verbs.

PHRASE   To get a good lock for my house.

SENTENCE To get a good lock for my house, I need to talk to a locksmith.

PHRASE   To come up with the right answer.

SENTENCE Mel was unable to come up with the right answer.

PHRASE   Making her a good dinner.

SENTENCE I want to please my girlfriend by making her a good dinner.

PHRASE   Such as a new backpack, a Barbie, a walkie-talkie, a stuffed lizard, and even a computer.

SENTENCE My daughter says she wants a lot of things for her birthday, such as a new backpack, a Barbie, a walkie-talkie, a stuffed lizard, and even a computer.

PHRASE   On the shelf.

SENTENCE I can't reach the box on the shelf.

ACTIVITY 1: Identify Phrases and Sentences

For each of the following items, write *S* next to the word groups that are sentences and *P* next to the word groups that are phrases.

EXAMPLE   Within the last fifteen years. _P_

1. To drive over the bridge at night. ___

2. Before sending the letter, she carefully reviewed it. ___

3. To find a new job, Frida updated her résumé. ___

4. On Friday my singing lesson. ___

5. The love letter turned out to be a joke. ___

6. For example, a pencil, a notebook, and an eraser. ___

7. Over there on the floor. ___

8. He slammed shut the closet door. ___

9. To study for Spanish, English, algebra, biology, and economics. ___

10. The fire in the national forest was caused by a careless smoker. ___

ACTIVITY 2: Turn Phrases into Sentences

Expand each of the following phrases into a complete sentence.

EXAMPLE   after the fire

After the fire, there was nothing left of the house.

1. talking with their parents

2. before the start of the semester

3. finished his oral report

4. due to the increase in gas prices

5. to maintain a good relationship

6. avoiding his old friends from high school

_____

7. a flight of creaky stairs

_____

8. the park in my family's neighborhood

_____

9. an unusual but attractive hairstyle

_____

10. saving her wages from her after-school job

_____

ACTIVITY 3: Connect Phrases to Sentences

Revise the following paragraph to connect the phrases to the sentences that come before or after them.

EXAMPLE   Families need to be flexible./In order to deal with hard

times.

   Ever since my early teen years. My parents have had an untraditional marriage. My mother held a full-time job while my father stayed at home. Taking care of us kids. Until I was thirteen, both my parents worked full-time. Then my dad lost his job. Mom earned enough to support the family as a buyer. For a large department store. She frequently had to travel. The whole family enjoyed her stories about the exciting places she visited. Including Beverly Hills, New York City, Paris, and Milan. It was comforting having Dad there. Caring for us when we were sick and congratulating us when we did well at school. Because of this unconventional arrangement. We kids learned that people sometimes have to be flexible to succeed.

Exercise Central
For additional practice with using phrases, go to **bedford stmartins.com/choices** and click on "Exercise Central."

B. CLAUSES

A *clause* can be a whole sentence or a part of a sentence. There are two kinds of clauses: independent and dependent.

Independent or Main Clauses

An *independent clause,* also called a *main clause,* is a group of words with a subject and a verb that can stand alone as a complete sentence. All sentences contain at least one independent clause, and some contain more than one:

Rita enjoyed her first piano lesson. [This sentence is an independent clause because it contains a subject and a verb and can stand alone as a sentence.]

She learned how to hold her hands, and she learned how to sit. [This sentence consists of two independent clauses.]

She decided to sign up for more lessons through the summer. [This sentence consists of one independent clause.]

HOW TO Identify an Independent Clause

- Check that the word group has a subject and a verb.
- Check that the word group can stand alone as a sentence.

ACTIVITY 4: Write Independent Clauses

Expand each of the following word groups into a sentence so that it contains an independent clause.

EXAMPLE   After my divorce, <u>I felt determined not to make the same</u>

<u>mistake again.</u>

1. The day my divorce became final _____

_____.

2. Although my wife and I were not getting along, _____
   _____.

3. Because I had sworn to be with her forever, _____
   _____.

4. _____ even though we tried
   so hard to stay together.

5. Because we had no children, _____.

6. When we saw each other for the last time, _____
   _____.

7. _____ because the bad memories
   are fading.

8. A year after the divorce, _____.

9. Although I haven't found someone else to love, _____
   _____.

10. Because I don't want to make the same mistake again, _____
    _____.

Dependent or Subordinate Clauses

Although a *dependent clause* contains a subject and a verb, it cannot stand alone as a sentence. To be part of a complete sentence, it needs to be attached to or part of an independent clause. Dependent clauses are also called *subordinate clauses* because they often begin with one of these words, called *subordinating conjunctions*:

after	if	until
although	since	when
as	that	where
because	though	while
before	unless	

Because my car broke down, I had to reschedule the dentist appointment. [The subordinate clause at the beginning of the sentence contains a subject and a verb, but it cannot stand alone as a sentence.]

Before my uncle retired, he was a welder. [This sentence also starts with a subordinate clause.]

I didn't fly in a plane *until I was seventeen years old.* [This subordinate clause comes at the end of the sentence.]

As these examples show, you use a comma after a subordinate clause that begins a sentence. You generally do not use a comma before a subordinate clause that ends a sentence.

HOW TO Identify a Subordinate Clause

■ Check that the word group has a subject and a verb.

■ Check that it begins with a subordinating conjunction (such as *because, until, before, after, although, when,* or *while*).

■ Check that it cannot stand alone as a sentence.

ACTIVITY 5: Identify Subordinate Clauses

In each of the following sentences, underline the subordinate clause. One sentence contains two subordinate clauses.

EXAMPLE   <u>Though I had a bad cold</u>, I still played in the championship game.

1. When the supervisor entered the office, Dean stopped playing his computer game.

2. On my street, the garbage is always collected before I wake up.

3. We toasted marshmallows and told ghost stories until the fire died.

4. If nobody has any questions, Ms. Skov will distribute the free samples.

5. Antonio wants to become a social worker because a social worker helped him through his long stay in the hospital.

6. While the turkey roasted in the oven, the family played touch football.

7. Unless you pay your parking fines, you will not be allowed to register for classes when the next semester begins.

8. Since Kerry began jogging, she has been having pain in her knees.

9. After he graduates, Conrad wants to tour Mexico.

10. I have hidden your birthday present where you will never find it.

ACTIVITY 6: Identify Subordinate Clauses

In the following paragraph, underline the subordinate clauses.

EXAMPLE <u>Before he moved into his own apartment</u>, Lewis lived with his parents.

This year Lewis moved into his own apartment. After he moved in, he began to clean house regularly. In fact, he enjoys doing housework. If he cleans a little every day, his place always looks presentable. Solutions to his problems pop into his head while he is scrubbing something. When he was cleaning his bathtub, he thought of a better way to budget his paycheck. Although Lewis is not a perfectionist, he takes pride in his apartment because it represents a new stage in his adult life.

Relative Clauses

A subordinate clause may also begin with one of these words, called *relative pronouns:*

that	who
what	whoever
whatever	whom
which	whomever
whichever	whose

A subordinate clause that begins with a relative pronoun is often called a *relative clause*:

Whoever cooked the food should be thanked. [This relative clause is the subject of the sentence.]

Any soldier *who passes the obstacle course* will be allowed to leave. [This relative clause describes the subject and is essential to the meaning of the sentence.]

Private Mejia, *who passed the obstacle course,* was allowed to leave. [Here the relative clause also describes the subject but is not essential to the meaning of the sentence.]

As the last example shows, sometimes commas are used to set off relative clauses from the rest of the sentence. If the relative clause interrupts the flow of the sentence and could be removed without changing the basic meaning of the sentence, use a comma before it, and use another comma after it unless it is at the end of the sentence. Do not use a comma before or after a relative clause that is essential to the meaning of the sentence, as in the first two examples.

HOW TO Identify a Relative Clause

- Check that the word group has a subject and a verb.
- Check that the word group begins with a relative pronoun (such as *that, who, what, which, whoever,* or *whichever*).
- Check that the word group cannot stand alone as a sentence.

ACTIVITY 7: Identify Relative Clauses

In each of the following sentences, underline the relative clause.

EXAMPLE   I will support whomever you nominate for club president.

1. Janice is the only student who talked to the professor on the first day of class.

2. Ogbert is one of those people who work at night and sleep all day.

3. I worry about students whose extracurricular activities interfere with their studies.

4. Whoever ate Asher's sandwich should fix him another one.

5. I recommend you buy the vehicle that has the least impact on the environment.

6. Jolene is the only student whose research paper received an A.

7. Whoever comes home last needs to let the cat out.

8. Frankie is the only boyfriend who ever gave me a bouquet of roses.

9. Miss Sweden is the only contestant who played the accordion in the talent contest.

10. I feel sorry for the people whose jobs were eliminated last year.

ACTIVITY 8: Turn Relative Clauses into Sentences

Add information to each of the following relative clauses to make it a complete sentence.

EXAMPLE   Who can sing, dance, and act

The play requires performers who can sing, dance, and act.

1. That tasted the best

2. Who do not smoke

3. Whoever sits at the head of the table

4. Whom Elena admires

5. Who just left for vacation.

6. That leaves at 11:15 tonight

7. Who does not mind a little hard work

8. That does not require batteries

9. Whose smile could light up a room

10. That the dog ate

ACTIVITY 9: Expand Sentences with Subordinate Clauses

Expand each of the following sentences by adding a subordinate clause.

EXAMPLE   Andrew is studying geology.

Andrew is studying geology because he likes exploring caves.

1. Carmen wanted a new job.

2. The day-care center is having a bake sale.

3. Derek rode a bicycle to work.

_____

4. The drugstore downtown is closed.

_____

5. The coffee will not taste any better.

_____

6. Cynthia collects old magazines.

_____

7. The roads have been undergoing repairs.

_____

8. The Johnsons hired a gardener.

_____

9. Monique wanted a laptop computer.

_____

10. You will not improve your physical condition.

_____

Exercise Central
For additional practice with using clauses, go to **bedford stmartins.com/choices** and click on "Exercise Central."

C. PRONOUNS

When you expand sentences, you'll be making grammatical choices about how you express your thoughts. One of these choices will concern the use of pronouns. A *pronoun* is a word that grammatically takes the place of a noun or another pronoun. Usually, it refers to a specific noun that appears earlier in the sentence or in a previous sentence. The following are common pronouns:

I, me, mine, we, our, ours
you, your, yours
he, him, his, she, her, hers
it, its
they, them, their, theirs
this, these, that, those

who, whom, whose, which, that, what
all, any, another, both, each, either, everyone
few, many, most, nobody, several, some, such
myself, yourself, himself, herself, itself
ourselves, themselves, yourselves

For more information about pronoun reference, see pp. 215–18.

Pronoun Reference

When you use a pronoun that refers to a noun, make sure that it's clear what the noun is. Don't use a pronoun that refers just to a vague idea or that could refer to more than one noun.

VAGUE	In my history class, *they* claimed that the Vietnam War protestors were unpatriotic. [Who are *they*?]
CLEAR	In my history class, *a group of students* claimed that the Vietnam War protestors were unpatriotic.
UNCLEAR	John told Martin *he* needed to study. [Who needed to study?]
CLEAR	John told Martin, "I need to study."
CLEAR	John told Martin, "You need to study."
CLEAR	John needed to study, as he told Martin.
CLEAR	John thought Martin needed to study and told him so.

HOW TO Identify and Correct Vague Pronoun Reference

■ Check that every pronoun clearly refers back to a noun.

■ If the reference isn't clear,

  ■ Replace the pronoun with a noun, or

  ■ Rewrite the sentence to delete the pronoun.

ACTIVITY 10: Correct Vague Pronoun Reference

In each of the following sentences, correct vague pronoun references.

EXAMPLE On that television show, ~~they~~ are always saying the dumb-
                          the characters
est things.

1. At that office, they prefer both male and female employees to

   wear suits.

2. The musicians played a waltz and a traditional ballad. It was beautiful.

3. Fabiola confessed to Leah that she left her class notes at the restaurant.

4. At my health club, they recommend that we warm up before we do aerobics.

5. Seth told Andrew that he needed to drink less on weekends.

6. There are too many scenes of violence and brutality. It should not have won the Academy Award.

7. In the documentary, it claimed that the mayor is corrupt.

8. While on vacation, I learned how to water ski and how to play croquet. It is not as easy as it looks.

9. In San Francisco, they have many landmarks of interest to tourists.

10. If Alicia tries to explain logarithms to Megan, she will become confused.

Learn more about pronoun agreement on pp. 215–18.

Pronoun Agreement

A pronoun should agree in number with the noun it refers to. To maintain pronoun agreement, use a singular pronoun to refer to a singular noun and a plural pronoun to refer to a plural noun. Remember that a singular noun also requires a singular verb form and a plural noun requires a plural verb form.

INCORRECT PRONOUN AGREEMENT	My *friend* is bringing *their* own food to the picnic. [*Friend* is singular, but *their* is plural.]
CORRECT PRONOUN AGREEMENT	My *friend* is bringing *her* own food to the picnic.
CORRECT PRONOUN AGREEMENT	My *friends* are bringing *their* own food to the picnic.

Remember also to use a singular pronoun to refer to a singular indefinite pronoun. Singular indefinite pronouns include *anybody, anyone, anything, everybody, everyone, everything, nobody, somebody, someone,* and *something.*

INCORRECT PRONOUN AGREEMENT	My professor told *everyone* to take *their* laptop off the counter. [*Everyone* is singular, but *their* is plural.]

| CORRECT PRONOUN AGREEMENT | My professor told the *students* to take their *laptops* off the counter. |
| CORRECT PRONOUN AGREEMENT | My professor told everyone to take *his or her* laptop off the counter. |

HOW TO Correct Errors in Pronoun-Antecedent Agreement

- Check that singular pronouns (such as *I, he, she, his or her*, or *it*) refer either to singular nouns or to singular indefinite pronouns (such as *anyone, everyone, everybody, somebody,* and *someone*).
- Check that plural pronouns (such as *we, us, them,* and *their*) refer to plural nouns.
- Correct errors in pronoun agreement by making pronouns and nouns agree in number.

ACTIVITY 11: Correct Errors in Pronoun Agreement

In each of the following sentences, correct the errors in pronoun agreement.

EXAMPLE ~~A plumber~~ Plumbers will have to charge you more if they find cracks in the pipes.

1. A student will find more errors in an essay if they wait a few hours after writing it before proofreading it.

2. I need to talk to someone who has put snow chains on their tires.

3. Everybody brought their donation to the main office.

4. The player shouts "Bingo!" as soon as they have a winning card.

5. A psychiatrist must not betray their patients' confidentiality.

6. A movie star saves their biggest smile for the camera.

7. Nobody admitted that they committed the vandalism.

8. Someone allows their dog to bark all day long.

9. Let me know when everyone has completed their questionnaires.

10. Every parent wants their children to be happy and successful.

ACTIVITY 12: Correct Pronoun Agreement

In the following paragraph, correct the errors in pronoun agreement.

EXAMPLE   The proudest day of a parent's life is when ~~their~~ children
                                                    ^his or her^
graduate from college.

The last meeting of my statistics study group was disastrous. We met at the studio apartment of one of the group members, and they did not have enough chairs. Everyone who came was worried about their grade, but not everyone had completed their section of the homework problems. One person had loaned their calculator to a friend and had to share mine. Someone else only wanted us to do their work for them. A third person had to have every little thing explained to them. Finally, somebody left angrily, saying they would save time by doing all the work themselves. This experience taught me something. The success of a study group requires every member to contribute as much as they can. Each person must still understand the basic concepts for themselves. The group then helps the individual refine what they already know.

Exercise Central
For additional practice with using pronouns, go to **bedford stmartins.com/choices** and click on "Exercise Central."

D. ADJECTIVES

One of the best ways to expand sentences is to use adjectives, which can add interest to your writing. *Adjectives* modify nouns or pronouns by describing or adding information about them:

My *beautiful* mother never goes outside without makeup.
The *green* meadow is always restful on the eyes.

Adjectives may also show comparisons between things. When comparing two things, add *-er* or *more* to the adjective. When comparing three or more things, add *-est* or *most*:

This car is *larger* than the one I owned before.
This car is the *largest* one I have ever owned.
This car is *more unusual* than my other one.
This car is the *most unusual* one on campus.

ACTIVITY 13: Identify Adjectives

In each of the following sentences, underline the adjectives. Some sentences have more than one adjective.

EXAMPLE   Senator Johnson is a <u>powerful</u> person.

1. Professor Michaels teaches a worthwhile class.
2. The overdue book is a biography.
3. Andrea likes to eat dark chocolate with a glass of cold milk.
4. Jerome is the tallest person in his family.
5. The blind student folded her collapsible cane and waited for the next train.
6. Rene wears a waterproof jacket in rainy weather.
7. Among the three friends, Didi is the best dancer.
8. Jamie owns a dented blue car.
9. I returned by the fastest route.
10. The defeated team ran off the muddy field.

ACTIVITY 14: Add Adjectives

Complete each of the following sentences by adding an adjective.

EXAMPLE   The __*green*__ coat fits you well.

1. The _____ cat sits in the window.
2. These cherries taste _____.
3. Alfredo took his _____ friend to the party.
4. Soraya has _____ brothers and sisters.
5. On _____ days we wear _____ clothing.

6. I think that the _____ carpet looks pretty with the _____ wallpaper.

7. His family needs to move to a _____ house.

8. That hospital serves _____ meals to its patients.

9. That _____ child never seems to get what he deserves.

10. Arzella is one of the _____ workers but one of the best students.

Exercise Central
For additional practice with using adjectives, go to **bedford stmartins.com/choices** and click on "Exercise Central."

E. ADVERBS

Adverbs are another useful way to expand sentences. *Adverbs* modify verbs, adjectives, or other adverbs by describing or adding information about them. Adverbs usually answer the questions *how, when, where, why,* or *how often*. Many adverbs end in *-ly*, such as *slowly, noisily,* and *loudly:*

My favorite music is *never* played on the radio. [The adverb answers the question *How often is the music played?*]

The children played *joyfully*. [The adverb answers the question *How did the children play?*]

My wife *heartily* ate the dinner I made. [The adverb answers the question *How did the wife eat the dinner?*]

ACTIVITY 15: Identify Adverbs

In each of the following sentences, underline the adverbs.

EXAMPLE   Doro <u>forcefully</u> threw the ball at the hitter.

1. The fans waited eagerly for concert tickets.

2. Is it true that crime never pays?

3. Traffic moved slowly on Van Ness Avenue.

4. The bored, complaining student soon dropped the class.

5. The pupils entered school reluctantly.

6. My aunts and uncles secretly planned a surprise party for my grandfather.

7. The instructor of my Introduction to Ceramics class is very interesting.

8. My study group often remains in the library until it closes.

9. The candidate campaigned well in the urban neighborhoods.

10. Klaus speaks persuasively in front of large groups.

ACTIVITY 16: Add Adverbs

Complete each of the following sentences by adding an adverb.

> EXAMPLE Guy practiced the saxophone ____daily____.

1. The customers _____ drank their iced tea.

2. You have _____ been to work on time.

3. Melina _____ eats at fast-food restaurants.

4. The punishment for plagiarism is _____ severe.

5. Darryl worked _____ on his English essay.

6. Winnie was talking _____ before she was interrupted.

7. On Sunday nights, my classmates _____ do their homework.

8. The football team _____ won the game.

9. Chong is _____ reliable.

10. Yolanda _____ sneaked up behind her boyfriend.

 Exercise Central
For additional practice with using adverbs, go to **bedford stmartins.com/choices** and click on "Exercise Central."

17

Combining Sentences

To express different kinds of ideas, you need to know how to write different kinds of sentences. One way to create different kinds of sentences is to combine them. In this chapter, you'll learn to combine sentences using sentence coordination and sentence subordination.

A. COORDINATION

When you have two or more short, closely related sentences in a row that are equally important, your ideas can seem choppy and unconnected. To avoid this problem, combine the sentences, making them *coordinate*, or equal. To join two equally important sentences, use a coordinating conjunction and a comma or conjunctive adverb and a semicolon.

Coordinating Conjunctions and Commas

One way to combine equally important sentences is to use one of the coordinating conjunctions, which are *for, and, nor, but, or, yet,* and *so.* To remember these conjunctions, imagine the word *FANBOYS.* Each letter in this word is the first letter of one of the coordinating conjunctions.

COORDINATING CONJUNCTIONS

Conjunction	Definition
F — for	because
A — and	in addition, also
N — nor	not, neither
B — but	however, unless
O — or	as another possibility
Y — yet	however, unless
S — so	as a result

When you use a coordinating conjunction to combine short, closely related sentences, put a comma before the conjunction. Be sure to select a conjunction that logically connects the sentences.

CHOPPY SENTENCES	The traffic jam delayed us. We arrived on time for the party.
SENTENCES COMBINED WITH *BUT*	The traffic jam delayed us, *but* we arrived on time for the party.
CHOPPY SENTENCES	I braided my niece's hair. I ironed her dress.
SENTENCES COMBINED WITH *AND*	I braided my niece's hair, *and* I ironed her dress.
CHOPPY SENTENCES	The guest of honor arrived. We yelled, "Surprise!"
SENTENCES COMBINED WITH *SO*	The guest of honor arrived, *so* we yelled, "Surprise!"

HOW TO Combine Sentences Using Coordinating Conjunctions

- Use one of the *FANBOYS* conjunctions (*for, and, nor, but, or, yet, so*).
- Put a comma before the conjunction.

ACTIVITY 1: Combine Sentences Using Coordinating Conjunctions and Commas

Combine each of the following pairs of sentences using a coordinating conjunction and a comma.

EXAMPLE   Jorge has a law degree. ~~He~~ has never practiced law.
, but he

1. Leigh was upset when she opened her cell phone bill. She owed more than four hundred dollars.

2. Rosa insisted on buying strawberry ice cream. I would have preferred chocolate chip.

3. I fell asleep in class. I missed next week's reading assignment.

4. Elizabeth carefully read the contract for the loan. She still couldn't understand it.

5. I went grocery shopping this morning. I did the laundry this afternoon.

6. Michael set his alarm clock for 7:30. He had an early class this morning.

7. Hetty forgot to return the library book. She received a fine.

8. Malik worked really hard on his résumé. He got the job he wanted.

9. You can buy the racy red sports car. You can buy the practical brown sedan.

10. Adrianna spent hours looking over travel brochures. She ended up going to the same beach she had visited for the past three years.

Conjunctive Adverbs and Semicolons

Another way to join equally important sentences is to use a *conjunctive adverb* and a *semicolon*. The conjunctive adverb (often called a *transition*) shows how the two sentences fit together. A semicolon is used before the conjunctive adverb, and a comma is used after it.

CONJUNCTIVE ADVERBS
Add an idea: *also, furthermore, in addition, moreover*
Show a different point: *however, instead, nevertheless, otherwise*
Show a similar point: *likewise, similarly*
Stress a key idea: *indeed, in fact, undoubtedly, certainly*
Show a consequence or result: *as a result, consequently, therefore, thus*
Point out a sequence: *first, second, next, finally*

CHOPPY SENTENCES	My daughter majored in psychology in college. She really wanted to be a writer.
SENTENCES COMBINED WITH *HOWEVER*	My daughter majored in psychology in college; *however,* she really wanted to be a writer.
CHOPPY SENTENCES	I traveled to Argentina as a child. I want to learn Spanish.
SENTENCES COMBINED WITH *AS A RESULT*	I traveled to Argentina as a child; *as a result,* I want to learn Spanish.
CHOPPY SENTENCES	The neighborhood grocery store is small. It's very expensive.
SENTENCES COMBINED WITH *MOREOVER*	The neighborhood grocery store is small; *moreover,* it's very expensive.

HOW TO Combine Sentences Using Conjunctive Adverbs

- Select a conjunctive adverb that shows the logical connection between the sentences.
- Use a semicolon before the conjunctive adverb.
- Use a comma after the conjunctive adverb.

ACTIVITY 2: Combine Sentences Using Conjunctive Adverbs and Commas

Combine each of the following pairs of sentences using a semicolon, a conjunctive adverb, and a comma.

EXAMPLE   My hours at work have been increased /I have more money to save.

; therefore,

1. Akio disliked the political ads during the last election. He decided to register as an Independent.

2. The children gathered roses, violets, and irises from their grandmother's garden. They ironed the flowers in waxed paper and labeled them with black ink.

3. Owners of small specialty stores find it hard to compete with large department stores. They need to advertise their products on television and the Internet.

4. Corinne was hired as a salesclerk. She got a better job the following week and quit.

5. Einstein had a reputation as an absentminded scientist. He could be very forgetful.

6. Landscape artists are more than just gardeners. They are both scientists and artists.

7. I stepped out into the foggy morning unable to see a thing. I heard something crunch beneath my feet.

8. This semester I'm working the graveyard shift at the food mart. I can barely stay awake in my 8:00 a.m. class.

9. Pacifists often demonstrate against warfare. They have been conscientious objectors during different wars.

10. Kurt Cobain revealed his personal problems in his songs. He talked about these problems in his journals.

 Exercise Central
For additional practice with using coordination, go to **bedford stmartins.com/choices** and click on "Exercise Central."

B. SUBORDINATION

Use *sentence subordination* to combine two sentences that aren't equally important. Subordinating conjunctions and relative pronouns help you express the logical connection between the sentences.

Subordinating Conjunctions

One way to combine two sentences using subordination is to use an appropriate *subordinating conjunction*.

SUBORDINATING CONJUNCTIONS

after	until
although	when
because	whenever
before	where
if	wherever
since	whether
though	while
unless	

The subordinating conjunction begins the part of the combined sentence that's less important to expressing your message.

CHOPPY SENTENCES	People are marrying later in life. The divorce rate hasn't decreased.
SENTENCES COMBINED WITH *ALTHOUGH*	*Although* people are marrying later in life, the divorce rate hasn't decreased.
CHOPPY SENTENCES	Greg made sure to save several thousand dollars. He did this before he quit his job.

SENTENCES COMBINED WITH *BEFORE*	Greg made sure to save several thousand dollars *before* he quit his job.
CHOPPY SENTENCES	You'll never understand the experience of being homeless. The only way to understand it is to live through it.
SENTENCES COMBINED WITH *UNLESS*	You'll never understand the experience of being homeless *unless* you live through it.

Sometimes you can just put the conjunction before the less important sentence of the original two, as in the first example. But often you'll also need to delete part of that sentence or change it in other ways, as in the second and third examples. Sometimes the conjunction you need will already be in the less important sentence, like *before* in the second example.

The word group that begins with a subordinating conjunction is called a *subordinate clause* or a dependent clause. Put a comma after a subordinate clause when it begins a sentence. In general, don't use a comma before a subordinate clause that ends a sentence.

COMMA	*After the children sat down,* the family began Thanksgiving dinner.
NO COMMA	The family began Thanksgiving dinner *after the children sat down.*

HOW TO Combine Sentences Using Subordinating Conjunctions

- Decide which sentence is less important.

- Choose an appropriate subordinating conjunction to express the way the ideas in the two sentences are connected.

- Combine the sentences by putting the subordinating conjunction before the less important part of the new sentence and then deleting or changing any other words as necessary.

- Use a comma after the subordinate clause when it begins the combined sentence.

- In general, don't use a comma before the subordinate clause when it ends the sentence.

ACTIVITY 3: Combine Sentences Using Subordinating Conjunctions

Combine each of the following pairs of sentences using a subordinating conjunction. Add or delete words as necessary.

> EXAMPLE   I aced my art history exam̸ I studied for three hours last
>   because
> night.

1. The number of arrests for drunk driving has increased. This has happened because there are stricter DUI laws.

2. The newspaper arrived late. I wasn't able to read about the big earthquake in Alaska.

3. I couldn't find the book at the library. Finally, I asked one of the librarians for help.

4. The friends were in the restaurant. They gossiped about their coworkers.

5. I have a hard time recycling my garbage. The recycling center is too far from my house.

6. You have to create a password. Then, you can start using the chat rooms.

7. I kept the music low. My roommate left.

8. The politician gave her speech and her followers cheered. I left the rally.

9. I would have stayed in class. The professor did not show up.

10. I didn't rent the apartment. The building was too far away from campus.

Relative Pronouns

Another way to combine choppy sentences is to use a *relative pronoun* to subordinate the information in the less important sentence.

RELATIVE PRONOUNS

that	who
whose	whom
whoever	which
what	whatever
whomever	whichever

As with a subordinating conjunction, the relative pronoun goes before a part of the combined sentence that is less important to the meaning. The word group that begins with a relative pronoun is called a *relative clause.*

CHOPPY SENTENCES	Athletes will stay in shape. They'll stay in shape if they work out regularly.
SENTENCES COMBINED WITH *WHO*	Athletes *who work out regularly* will stay in shape.
CHOPPY SENTENCES	Dorothea baked the cupcakes. They were moist and delicious.
SENTENCES COMBINED WITH *WHICH*	Dorothea baked the cupcakes, *which were moist and delicious.*
CHOPPY SENTENCES	One of my favorite songs is "Red, Red Wine." I mean the version Neil Diamond recorded.
SENTENCES COMBINED WITH *THAT*	One of my favorite songs is the version of "Red, Red Wine" *that* Neil Diamond recorded.

Don't use commas before or after a relative clause that is necessary to identify what it refers to, as in the following example:

The letter to the editor *that Anita wrote* was published in the local newspaper.

No commas are used before or after the relative clause because it's a necessary part of the sentence. It tells which letter — the letter that Anita wrote — was published in the newspaper.

In contrast, use commas when the relative clause gives information that's not essential to the sentence:

The letter, *which is on the topic of school funding,* is still in my backpack.

Commas are used in this example because the relative clause — *which is on the topic of school funding* — simply adds information about an essay that's already been mentioned. The meaning of the sentence is still clear without it: *The letter is still in my backpack.*

Don't use commas with relative clauses that begin with *that:*

The letter *that I wrote* was not published.

HOW TO Combine Sentences Using Relative Pronouns

- Decide which sentence is less important.

- Choose an appropriate relative pronoun to connect the information in the less important sentence to that in the other sentence.

- Use commas when the relative clause can be deleted and the sentence still includes all necessary information.

- Don't use commas when the relative clause is a necessary part of the sentence.

ACTIVITY 4: Combine Sentences Using Relative Pronouns

Combine each of the following pairs of sentences using a relative pronoun. Add or delete words as necessary.

EXAMPLE My dog ~~is my new best friend. She's~~ part beagle and part poodle. *, who's* *, is my new best friend.*

1. Jeans have changed a great deal over the years. Jeans are very popular.

2. Jeans were invented by Levi Strauss. They were first worn by miners in the 1850s.

3. The jeans never tore or fell apart. The jeans were worn by the miners.

4. In the 1950s, jeans became popular with teenagers. The teenagers thought that they were cool.

5. Jeans were a big part of the 1960s. Hippies started wearing them.

6. One popular style was bell-bottom jeans. This style was often decorated with flowers and peace signs.

7. I have a picture of my mother wearing jeans. The jeans have frayed hems and many holes.

8. Now just about everyone wears jeans. These jeans come in many styles.

9. One style is cut very low at the waist. This style is popular with young girls.

10. People wear jeans. These people live all over the world.

Exercise Central
For additional practice with using subordination, go to **bedford stmartins.com/choices** and click on "Exercise Central."

C. SENTENCE-COMBINING EXERCISES

The following sentence-combining exercises will give you practice using sentence coordination and subordination.

Specific Methods of Combining Sentences

Use the methods identified in the directions for combining sentences in the following activities.

ACTIVITY 5: Combine Sentences Using Coordination

Combine each of the following pairs of sentences using either a comma and a coordinating conjunction or a semicolon and a conjunctive adverb. Add or delete words as necessary.

EXAMPLE   In March 2002, *The Osbornes* debuted on MTV. The show

, and the

received the highest ratings of any MTV show up to that time.

1. The show was "reality based." Cameras followed the real-life adventures of rocker Ozzy Osborne and his family.

2. The producers filmed the Osbornes doing ordinary things. The show was anything but ordinary.

3. The family's Beverly Hills mansion featured Gothic décor. The Osbornes' clothing was equally unusual.

4. Ozzy had tattoos all over his body. His daughter Kelly's hair kept changing color.

5. The Osbornes' behavior at first seemed outrageous. They were a loving family.

6. Ozzy was befuddled and clumsy. He had used hard drugs for many years.

7. Kelly and Jack squabbled like typical teenagers. Sharon, the wife, held the family together.

8. Unlike typical teenagers, they weren't forced to go to school. As the show became popular, they began to sing and act professionally.

9. The show depicted the family dogs messing on the carpet. The family once threw a ham at their loud neighbors.

10. Despite the Osbornes' behavior, many people admired them. They clearly loved each other very much.

ACTIVITY 6: Combine Sentences Using Coordination

Combine each of the following pairs of sentences using either a comma and a coordinating conjunction or a semicolon and a conjunctive adverb. Add or delete words as necessary.

EXAMPLE   The station wagon used to be one of America's most pop-
           ; however, the
ular cars. ~~The~~ SUV (sports utility vehicle) has now replaced
           ^
the station wagon in popularity.

1. In recent years, SUVs have become popular with many American consumers. They have helped automobile companies make bigger profits.

2. At first, they were built for people to drive in extreme conditions and on dirt roads. Now, they are used mostly for city driving.

3. They are bought by parents who like the large size of the cars. They can fit their growing families into SUVs with ease.

4. Some buyers imagine themselves driving off-road in a rugged, beautiful area of the country. They would never actually do that.

5. Energy conservationists have criticized SUVs. SUVs remain very popular.

6. Americans prefer large cars. Europeans buy much smaller cars.

7. Gas in Europe is much more expensive than in the United States. European consumers have good reason to use as little as possible.

8. Japanese-made SUVs are becoming more and more popular with American consumers. The profits of American car companies are expected to decline.

9. In general, Japanese-made cars are still more popular than American cars. Their resale rates are higher.

10. Many Americans love their SUVs. It will be interesting to see how this love affair affects the American economy.

ACTIVITY 7: Combine Sentences Using Subordination

Combine each of the following pairs of sentences using a subordinating conjunction. Add or delete words as necessary.

EXAMPLE Scientists often use placebos in experiments. ~~They~~ want to test the effectiveness of a new treatment.
because they (inserted)

1. A placebo is a fake treatment for an illness. Sometimes a placebo works as well as real medicine.

2. Scientists use placebos when they test the effectiveness of a new medicine. They do this to make sure the new medicine will really help patients get well.

3. In an experiment, one group of patients will receive the medicine being tested. Another group of patients will receive the placebo.

4. Both the medicine being tested and the placebo can be given in the form of a pill. The placebo pill might be made up entirely of sugar or some other harmless substance.

5. The patients who receive the new medicine are called the *experimental group.* The patients who receive the placebo are called the *control group.*

6. The patients don't know which group they're in. This process is called a "blind" experiment.

7. The new medicine must be very successful in treating the patients in the experimental group. The power of suggestion is so strong.

8. Sometimes the patients who received placebos improved a great deal. The patients who received the actual medicine improved less.

9. Scientists speculate that placebos work for some people. These people believe strongly that the placebo will make them get better.

10. The placebo effect can be very powerful. Scientists are beginning to study it seriously.

ACTIVITY 8: Combine Sentences Using Subordination

Combine each of the following pairs of sentences using a subordinating conjunction. Add or delete words as necessary.

EXAMPLE   People who rush into marriage often end up divorced. because they
~~They~~ don't know their partner well enough.

1. The institution of marriage has changed greatly over the years. Most people still get married.

2. Most experts agree that people should take their time getting to know each other. They should do this before they get married.

3. The couple should know each other well. They have a better chance of not getting divorced.

4. Couples first come to understand the strengths and weaknesses of their potential partners. They do this when they are getting to know each other.

5. Couples find out if they have similar beliefs and interests. These similar beliefs and interests will help them have a happy marriage.

6. Couples should discuss each partner's religious beliefs. They need to do this to prevent conflicts in the marriage.

7. Couples might have problems. This could happen if one partner is a very conservative person and the other is very liberal.

8. Couples also need to find out how responsible their potential partners are. They need to do this to make sure they can rely on their partners.

9. Couples need to learn to communicate well. Good communication will help them get through difficult times together.

10. Marriage is rewarding but often very difficult. It is important for couples to know their partners well before the wedding day.

ACTIVITY 9: Combine Sentences Using Subordination

Combine each of the following pairs of sentences using a relative pronoun. Add or delete words when necessary.

EXAMPLE   Rocky Mountain National Park is located in one of the
          , which
          most beautiful areas in the country. ~~It~~ contains remote

          areas where you can find solitude.

1. Rocky Mountain National Park is in Colorado. It is one of America's favorite vacation spots.

2. This park is also one of America's most popular national parks. It is visited by 3 million people a year.

3. Several trails in the park are not well known. These trails are in remote locations.

4. The Tonahutu Creek trail follows the Continental Divide. The trail is 21 miles long.

5. The Never Summer Loop trail is well named. This trail has mountains that are almost 13,000 feet high.

6. Sometimes the snow never melts on this trail. The snow can be very deep.

7. Another trail people don't use very much is the Lost Lake trail. This trail is very steep.

8. The Lost Lake trail leads to Lost Lake. This lake is surrounded by breathtaking mountain scenery.

9. These three trails are great for backpacking. Not many people use these trails.

10. If you go backpacking, you can experience nature without crowds. Backpacking is strenuous and fun.

ACTIVITY 10: Combine Sentences Using Subordination

Combine each of the following pairs of sentences using a relative pronoun. Add or delete words when necessary.

who

EXAMPLE   Teenagers are part of the abstinence movement. ~~These~~ ^ ~~teenagers~~ don't have sex until they're married.

1. Abstinence is growing in popularity among young people. Abstinence consists of waiting until marriage to have sex.

2. Abstinence has been called a "sexual revolution." It is a sexual revolution very different from the sexual revolution of the 1960s.

3. The sexual revolution involved not waiting until marriage to have sex. The sexual revolution was the one that happened in the 1960s.

4. The current sexual revolution is a result of several factors. These factors include religion, family pressure, and health issues.

5. One reason for the interest in abstinence is that people are afraid of sexually transmitted diseases (STDs). STDs can cause illness and even death.

6. Other people remain abstinent until marriage because of religious beliefs. These beliefs discourage people from having sex outside of marriage.

7. Although abstinence is becoming more popular, most young people don't wait until marriage to have sex. These young people live in the United States.

8. Some people maintain that sex-education programs should promote only abstinence. These people are usually conservatives.

9. Other people say that sex-education programs should mention abstinence as only one possibility. These people are usually liberal.

10. The abstinence movement is an interesting social trend. This social trend might continue to grow in popularity.

Various Methods of Combining Sentences

Up to now, you have practiced combining sentences using just one or two methods at a time. Now you will be given more choices about the best method to join particular sentences:

1. A comma and a coordinating conjunction (*for, and, nor, but, or, yet, so*)
2. A semicolon and a conjunctive adverb (*however, in addition, moreover, in contrast, on the other hand, then, finally, indeed, in fact, instead, next, therefore, certainly*)
3. A subordinating conjunction (*after, before, although, because, even though, if, once, that, though, unless, until, when, where, while*)
4. A relative pronoun (*who, whom, which, that, what, whoever, whomever, whichever, whatever*)

ACTIVITY 11: Combine Sentences Using Different Methods

Combine each of the following pairs of sentences using an appropriate method from the preceding list. Add or delete words as necessary.

EXAMPLE   Rap music has always been controversial. ~~Rap music is~~ *, which is related to hip-hop,*

~~related to hip-hop.~~

1. Rap music is the subject of much debate. It often contains swear words and insults to women and gay people.

2. At the same time, rap music is popular with many young people. These young people say it has been treated unfairly in the media.

3. In December 2002, Eminem made his acting debut in *8 Mile*. Eminem is a controversial white rapper.

4. *8 Mile* tells the story of a rapper in Detroit. The rapper is very similar to Eminem.

5. The main character is Rabbit. He is a factory worker in Detroit.

6. Rabbit wants out of his working-class ghetto. He participates in rap contests.

7. He is good at these contests. He beats most of his black competitors.

8. In *8 Mile*, Rabbit is shown as angry. He is also responsible and gentle with his younger sister.

9. *8 Mile* made people more aware of Eminem's talents. He became more popular with people of all ages.

10. Eminem will remain in the spotlight for years to come. Some people may not like it.

ACTIVITY 12: Combine Sentences Using Different Methods

Combine each of the following sets of sentences using an appropriate method from the list on page 537. Add or delete words as necessary.

EXAMPLE   Movies about spring break have been popular for years. *, which often show college students partying on a beach,*

~~These movies often show college students partying on a~~

~~beach.~~

1. To many people, spring break is a time when college students go wild. Spring break is a weeklong break in March or April.

2. Spring break is notorious for misbehavior. Some college students drink excessively at this time.

3. Not all college students party over spring break. Many college students don't have time to party.

4. Last spring break, I worked overtime to save up money. I needed the money to go to summer school.

5. This spring break, I'll probably catch up on my classes. I'm taking six different courses. In three of these courses, I have to write research papers.

6. My friend Mike spent spring break taking care of his children. Mike is a single father. He has sole custody of the kids.

7. Some people think college students just goof off. Those people don't know what we go through.

8. Most college students have to work their way through college. They might have children to raise. They might have parents to support.

9. Nationwide, only a small percentage of college students are supported by their parents. Most college students pay their own way.

10. I wish spring break were a real break. It's really just a chance to do more work.

ACTIVITY 13: Combine Sentences Using Different Methods

Combine each of the following sets of sentences using an appropriate method from the list on page 537. Add or delete words as necessary.

EXAMPLE   Blindness can lead to lifestyle restrictions. ~~These restrictions will occur~~ unless help is available.

1. Dan Shaw's life was changed. His doctor diagnosed him with retinitis pigmentosa. This is an incurable eye disease. This happened when Dan Shaw was seventeen.

2. Slowly he lost his sight. His life became very limited.

3. He wanted to be more involved with the world. He checked out his options.

4. He didn't want a seeing-eye dog. He had had a dog. The dog died.

5. He heard about a program run by Janet and Don Burleson. They were training miniature horses as guides for the visually impaired.

6. Dan was interested in having a guide horse. Miniature horses live for thirty to forty years. He would not have to endure the death of the horse.

7. His guide horse leads him everywhere. His guide horse is named Cuddles.

8. Cuddles responds to more than twenty-five voice commands. She is housebroken. She can see in the dark.

9. People are often curious. This happens when they see Dan being guided by Cuddles. They ask Dan questions about Cuddles.

10. Dan is happy to talk to people about Cuddles. He wants others to know about guide horses.

ACTIVITY 14: Combine Sentences Using Different Methods

Combine each of the following sets of sentences using an appropriate method from the list on page 537. Add or delete words as necessary.

EXAMPLE   ~~People~~ If people have a healthy lifestyle. ~~Their~~ , their chances of getting diabetes will be reduced.

1. About 17 million people in the United States are believed to have diabetes. Nearly 6 million of these people don't know they have diabetes.

2. Diabetes has no cure. It can be controlled.

3. Diabetes can cause heart disease, blindness, kidney failure, and amputations. It is a very serious disease.

4. Most diabetes is Type II. It is associated with obesity. It is also associated with poor lifestyle habits.

5. Children now are fatter. Children exercise less. They eat unhealthy food.

6. Obese children will develop serious health problems. This will happen if they don't lose weight.

7. Children are our future. We need to help children be healthier. We need to help them live long lives.

8. Many schools are teaching children about diabetes. They have many other subjects to teach.

9. Parents should be good role models. They are very busy. Parents should eat well and exercise regularly.

10. Diabetes is a major health problem. It will continue to get worse. We need to stop the spread of this disease.

Exercise Central
For additional practice with combining sentences, go to **bedford stmartins.com/choices** and click on "Exercise Central."

18

Improving Sentences

To improve sentences, eliminate sentence fragments, run-on sentences, and comma splices. Also, correct misplaced and dangling modifiers, try to use the active voice as much as possible, and use parallel sentence structure for groups of words that are part of a pair or series.

A. SENTENCE FRAGMENTS

A sentence fragment is an incomplete sentence that is presented as if it were a complete sentence. Some sentence fragments are *phrases:* they lack a subject or a verb or both.

The grocery store next to the bank.

Built a play house in the backyard.

At the bus station.

Other sentence fragments are *subordinate clauses:* they have a subject and a verb, but they begin with a subordinating conjunction or a relative pronoun.

SUBORDINATING CONJUNCTIONS

after	until
although	when
because	whenever
before	where
if	wherever
since	whether
though	while
unless	

For more about subordinate clauses, turn to pp. 509–11.

Here are three sentence fragments that begin with subordinating conjunctions:

After the party is over.

Because it was raining outside.

When I come back from vacation.

RELATIVE PRONOUNS

that	who
whose	whom
whoever	which
what	whatever
whomever	whichever

Here are three fragments that begin with relative pronouns:

That they ate at the bakery.
Who left the rambling message.
Which caused him to cry.

ACTIVITY 1: Identify Sentence Fragments

In the space provided, indicate whether each of the following word groups is a sentence fragment or a complete sentence.

EXAMPLE   Since it will be rainy tomorrow. ____*fragment*____

1. My son plays soccer and basketball. _____

2. In Mimi's old backpack. _____

3. Which was the first house constructed of recycled materials.

   _____

4. May I charge that to your credit card? _____

5. Because these French fries are too salty. _____

6. The shoe salesman earned a large commission. _____

7. Speaking as softly as she could. _____

8. A perfect score on the pop quiz. _____

9. This vacuum cleaner is effective on both deep carpets and bare floors. _____

10. Vandalized mailboxes throughout the neighborhood. _____

How do you correct a sentence fragment? One way is to connect it to the sentence that comes before or after it.

FRAGMENT   *Although he had to get up early in the morning.* Ralph didn't get home until midnight.

SENTENCE   Although he had to get up early in the morning, Ralph didn't get home until midnight.

FRAGMENT   Her favorite gift was the silk scarf. *That her grand-mother had given her.*

SENTENCE   Her favorite gift was the silk scarf that her grand-mother had given her.

Another way to correct a sentence fragment is to turn it into a complete sentence. If the fragment is a phrase, add any missing subject or verb. If the fragment begins with a subordinating conjunction, delete the conjunction. If the fragment begins with a relative pronoun, change the pronoun to a noun.

FRAGMENT   Running down the hall.

SENTENCE   Matthew was running down the hall.

FRAGMENT   *Because* the plane was late getting into Austin.

SENTENCE   The plane was late getting into Austin.

FRAGMENT   *Which* violated the drug laws in Michigan.

SENTENCE   The prescription violated the drug laws in Michigan.

HOW TO Correct Sentence Fragments

- Connect it to the sentence that comes before or after it.

- Rewrite it as a complete sentence.

ACTIVITY 2: Correct Sentence Fragments

Make each of the following fragments a complete sentence.

EXAMPLE   *Trash from campers is polluting*
~~Polluting~~ our beautiful national parks.

1. After taking a month-long tour of Europe.

2. Because the batteries were low.

3. The load of sheets in the dryer.

4. The pencil sharpener next to the photocopier.

5. Who looked frightened enough to faint.

6. The car with a small scratch.

7. Although fried food is not very healthy.

8. While Victor was learning how to type.
9. If I knew these people better.
10. Surprised by the unexpected news.

ACTIVITY 3: Correct Sentence Fragments

Each of the following word groups contains one or more sentence fragments. Make each word group into a single complete sentence, either by connecting each fragment to a complete sentence or by rewriting each fragment as a complete sentence.

EXAMPLE Magda jogged every morning~~. Because~~ ^because^ she was preparing to run a marathon.

1. The concert that begins at 8:30 tonight.
2. Whomever Ryan picks as his wife. I'm prepared to like her.
3. That gave the children more freedom.
4. Alonzo cares for his sister's children on Wednesday and Thursday nights. Because he's free on these nights.
5. Let's try to go to the concert. If the tickets aren't too expensive and my car is working.
6. I'm jealous of Pilar. Who received an A on her report. Even though she didn't spend much time writing it.
7. I could clean my whole house. While the Web page loads.
8. His mother didn't like Jason's dyed blue hair. Said it was an embarrassment to the family.
9. I really liked my blind date. Until he lit up a cigarette.
10. Trying to keep my balance while standing on one foot, bending at the waist, and holding my arms in a graceful arc above my head.

ACTIVITY 4: Correct Sentence Fragments in a Paragraph

Edit the following paragraph to eliminate sentence fragments.

EXAMPLE   ~~Studying~~ to become an elementary schoolteacher.

I am studying

Because I want to teach my students to take care of themselves I have a special interest in physical education. During my student teaching I remembered my childhood experiences playing team sports like softball. Alone in left field. My classmates laughing at my mistakes. I should have been taught how to catch a fly ball. Without fear of being hit in the face. I never learned games like soccer and basketball. Which keep every player constantly involved in the game. I want P.E. to be better for my students. All children can learn to enjoy using their bodies. Though not everybody can become a professional athlete. I want my future students to enjoy a lifetime of fitness.

Exercise Central

For additional practice with eliminating sentence fragments, go to **bedfordstmartins.com/choices** and click on "Exercise Central."

B. RUN-ON SENTENCES

A *run-on sentence* occurs when two sentences (or sometimes more) are incorrectly presented as a single sentence, without any punctuation between them.

RUN-ON   The computer was old it needed to be given away.

CORRECT   The computer was old. It needed to be given away.

RUN-ON   I went to the store I forgot to get the flour.

CORRECT   I went to the store, but I forgot to get the flour.

ACTIVITY 5: Identify Run-on Sentences

In the space provided, indicate whether each of the following word groups is a run-on sentence or a correct sentence.

> EXAMPLE   Moby Grape was a rock band from the 1960s it was based
>
> in San Francisco. _____run-on_____

1. David is friendlier than he appears he only frowns to hide his nervousness. _____

2. With her fingers poised over the piano keys, Carmel waited for the conductor's baton to drop. _____

3. That yogurt is too high in carbohydrates for my diabetic diet I need to have the low-fat cottage cheese. _____

4. Hard hats are required in this area the roof is being replaced. _____

5. No one volunteered to supervise the dance until the principal offered to buy the chaperones dinner. _____

6. My wife likes pizza my son likes hamburgers I prefer sushi. _____

7. Ray and Serena put a green decal on their black suitcase so they could recognize it more easily at the airport. _____

8. Delia ran out the door in such a hurry that she left her coat draped over the sofa. _____

9. Kazuko welcomed the visitor into her office she asked her assistant to bring them both coffee. _____

10. Nigel was astonished when he received first prize he never thought that he would win an award. _____

One way to correct a run-on sentence is to turn it into two sentences, adding a period at the end of the first sentence and capitalizing the first word of the second sentence.

> RUN-ON   The concert was supposed to begin at 8:00 it actually began at 9:30.
>
> CORRECT   The concert was supposed to begin at 8:00. It actually began at 9:30.
>
> RUN-ON   The digital camera is too expensive it costs more than $300.

CORRECT   The digital camera is too expensive. It costs more than $300.

See Chapter 17 to find out more about these methods of combining sentences.

A run-on sentence can also be corrected by putting a comma and a coordinating conjunction (*for, and, nor, but, or, yet, so*) between the two sentences.

RUN-ON   The apartment is dirty the kitchen appliances are broken.

CORRECT   The apartment is dirty, and the kitchen appliances are broken.

RUN-ON   I registered for classes late I still got a good schedule.

CORRECT   I registered for classes late, but I still got a good schedule.

A third way to correct a run-on sentence is to put a semicolon between the two sentences. Often you can also use a conjunctive adverb such as *however, therefore, also, instead,* or *as a result* after the semicolon. If you use a conjunctive adverb, put a comma after it.

RUN-ON   I've been working out I still haven't lost any weight.

CORRECT   I've been working out; however, I still haven't lost any weight.

RUN-ON   Computer technology is improving computers are getting cheaper.

CORRECT   Computer technology is improving; computers are getting cheaper.

HOW TO Correct Run-on Sentences

- Separate it into two sentences, or

- Add a comma and a coordinating conjunction, or

- Add a semicolon and, if appropriate, a conjunctive adverb.

ACTIVITY 6: Correct Run-on Sentences

Correct each of the following run-on sentences using a period and a capital letter, a comma and a coordinating conjunction, or a semicolon and a conjunctive adverb.

EXAMPLE   While Fred was watching the news, the electricity went

, and

out it was two hours before it came back on again.

1. Solange posed for the picture, the feather on her antique hat framing her face she found the waist and collar of the dress a little confining.

2. Before Benjamin applied for a job at Datacorp, he researched the company at the library he wanted to be well-prepared for the interview.

3. Waiting for the tour bus, the family shivered on the windy corner they had expected warmer weather on their summer vacation.

4. Leland's motorcycle is his prized possession he had to sell it to pay his college tuition.

5. Because Olivia had never been surfing, she took lessons she felt ready to tackle the waves.

6. Paolo has thinning hair, glasses, and stooped shoulders everyone thinks that he is a librarian he is a meteorologist at an Antarctic research station.

7. Toni gives her son a generous allowance and does not expect any help around the house from him Toni's brother expects his children to do chores if they want spending money.

8. Dark clouds gather overhead while trees toss in the wind rain does not fall.

9. Eileen wanted to prove her trustworthiness to her parents she made it her responsibility to take her younger brother and sister to school.

10. Using a sharp jerk of his wrist, Simón flipped the pancake in the skillet his uncle taught him this trick when Simón was a child.

ACTIVITY 7: Correct Run-on Sentences

Correct each of the following run-on sentences using a period and a capital letter, a comma and a coordinating conjunction, or a semicolon and a conjunctive adverb.

> EXAMPLE Jake loved NASCAR races $\overset{; \text{ in fact,}}{\underset{\wedge}{\text{he}}}$ he had the autographs of several famous drivers.

1. Jasmine's parents made her return the prom dress they insisted that she find one that was less revealing.

2. Aunt Edna poured tea into everyone's cup we sipped politely although we would have preferred coffee.

3. I cannot sleep the shadows of the tree branches outside my window stretch across my bedroom wall like grasping fingers.

4. Damien put his ear to the door but heard nothing he wished that doors still had keyholes that he could look through.

5. The rain began as soon as Kenneth washed his car it always rained after he washed his car.

6. Hadley smiled at his bookshelf with pride it was his first one that was not made of boards and cinder blocks.

7. Not a single car at the dealership had been within Bob and Carol's budget they drove their old car home in disappointment.

8. With the trees trimmed back, Malik enjoyed a better view from his living room the lights of the city twinkled below.

9. I turned in someone else's essay as my own the professor never found out.

10. Alvin experimented with one hair color after another starting with burgundy, he then tried orange, blue, and purple none looked natural, but all looked funky.

ACTIVITY 8: Correct Run-on Sentences in a Paragraph

Edit the following paragraph to correct the run-on sentences.

> EXAMPLE Watching the natural world is soothing $\overset{; \text{ in fact,}}{\underset{\wedge}{\text{it}}}$ it is as good for the soul as meditating.

The sun burns bright and hot the world is shady and cool under the pine tree. Nestled within a deep hole in the thick needles underfoot, a turtle dozes. I look up a bird feeder is in my hand. The feeder weighs over four pounds I search for a strong, low branch. Two startled doves take flight their wings whistle as if to express their alarm. Three grackles hop from limb to limb, black and almost as big as crows. More grackles join the flock they scream their long, thick beaks gape menacingly. A tiny hummingbird darts between the large, black birds its bright patch of throat feathers flashes red in the flickering light. Several sparrows wait on a nearby telephone wire. Far from the trunk, I find a good branch and attach the feeder with sturdy twine. After I step back, a sparrow flies to the feeder another sparrow joins its companion. The grackles become quiet the doves return. I watch the birds gather on the branches around the feeder it is like a doorway to a world where I do not belong.

Exercise Central

For additional practice with eliminating run-on sentences, go to **bedfordstmartins.com/choices** and click on "Exercise Central."

C. COMMA SPLICES

A *comma splice* consists of two sentences incorrectly joined with only a comma.

COMMA SPLICE	Mary liked the aroma of coffee, she never liked the taste.
CORRECT	Mary liked the aroma of coffee, but she never liked the taste.
COMMA SPLICE	My daughter is based in Afghanistan, she'll be home for Thanksgiving.

> CORRECT   My daughter is based in Afghanistan. She'll be home for Thanksgiving.

> COMMA SPLICE   The domestic cat is a great pet, it's a ferocious hunter.

> CORRECT   The domestic cat is a great pet; furthermore, it's a ferocious hunter.

One way to correct a comma splice is to make the comma splice into two separate sentences by changing the comma to a period and capitalizing the first word of the second sentence.

> COMMA SPLICE   The Department of Homeland Security was created in 2002, it is responsible for the protection of the United States within its own borders.

> CORRECT   The Department of Homeland Security was created in 2002. It is responsible for the protection of the United States within its own borders.

Turn to pp. 522–26 for more information about these ways of combining sentences.

Another way to correct a comma splice is to add a coordinating conjunction (*for, and, nor, but, or, yet, so*) after the comma.

> COMMA SPLICE   Our car trip across country was exhausting, it was also exciting and educational.

> CORRECT   Our car trip across country was exhausting, but it was also exciting and educational.

A third way to correct a comma splice is to change the comma to a semicolon. You can also add a conjunctive adverb (such as *however, therefore, also, instead,* or *as a result*) after the semicolon. If you use a conjunctive adverb, put a comma after it.

> COMMA SPLICE   Antibiotics have been widely used, they aren't as effective as they used to be.

> CORRECT   Antibiotics have been widely used; as a result, they aren't as effective as they used to be.

HOW TO Correct Comma Splices

- Separate it into two sentences, or

- Add a coordinating conjunction after the comma, or

- Change the comma to a semicolon and, if appropriate, add a conjunctive adverb with a comma after it.

ACTIVITY 9: Correct Comma Splices

Correct each of the following comma splices by making two separate sentences, adding a coordinating conjunction after the comma, or changing the comma to a semicolon and adding a conjunctive adverb.

EXAMPLE   Graduating from college in four years is always good, don't worry if you can't do it.

(but inserted after the comma)

1. There were never two people more different than Arnulfo and Hadley, they have been best friends since the second grade.

2. The audience members jumped to their feet and would not stop applauding, I was very proud that I had started the Drama Club.

3. Frank set the tray of ice cream cones on the passenger seat to his right, the children would be delighted with his surprise.

4. Dora gave the old dog a pat on the head, he thumped his tail in greeting without opening his eyes.

5. When we returned home, all the clocks were blinking, the power had gone off and come back on while we were away.

6. Alex balanced her baby brother on her hip, almost three, he was becoming too big for her to carry.

7. Ceci inhaled the rich perfume of the cactus flower, the glowing white blossom would last less than a day.

8. Todd knew that there was a spare key hidden in the rock garden, he could not remember which rock concealed the key.

9. Eddie bought several folk paintings while sailing around the Caribbean islands, his friends appreciated these colorful souvenirs.

10. Waiting for class to begin, Abigail read her essay one last time, she found a few remaining errors.

ACTIVITY 10: Correct Comma Splices

Correct each of the following comma splices by making two separate sentences, adding a coordinating conjunction after the comma, or changing the comma to a semicolon and adding a conjunctive adverb.

EXAMPLE   The number of young people who vote is declining,⁄the

; however,

number of elderly people who vote is increasing.

1. Akio immersed the spinach in a basin of water, he separated the leaves from the stems.

2. Our sixth-grade class collected starfish, sea urchins, and periwinkles on our field trip to the tide pools, we kept the animals alive in a saltwater aquarium.

3. When Noel was in high school, his aunt gave him five hundred dollars to invest in the stock market, six months later, he had doubled his money.

4. After Corinne became a salesclerk, she realized that she had not always been a very nice customer, she resolved to be more patient when she went shopping.

5. I got my first paycheck, the government deducted a lot in taxes.

6. The war in Iraq disrupted Neil and Joanna's wedding plans, they decided to marry at the courthouse and have a reception after Neil returned home.

7. I heard a sickening crunch, I realized I had stepped on another snail.

8. Tim appreciated the rich, nutty aroma of fresh coffee, he did not like its taste nearly as much.

9. The firefighters shook their heads in disgust, another pedestrian had tossed a lit cigarette onto a restaurant awning.

10. Reaching the top of the steep, narrow trail, Bronwen admired the view, the beauty of the green river valley made her forget her fear of heights.

ACTIVITY 11: Correct Comma Splices in a Paragraph

Eliminate the comma splices from the following paragraph.

EXAMPLE   Single people always envy married people ⌃, and married people

always envy single people.

After Rachel became engaged, the first person she told was her sister, Bonnie. Rachel was hesitant to tell her parents because they wanted her to wait until after she graduated from college to get married, Bonnie would understand because she had married Kurt when she was Rachel's age. Rachel didn't want her parents to overhear her on the telephone, she went to the couple's apartment to talk. Rachel did not mind helping her sister carry dirty clothes down to the laundry room, she did not mind giving Bonnie change for the machines, ever since she got married, Bonnie never seemed to have any money. Although the laundry room was hot and stuffy, Bonnie said it was a good place for them to talk. Kurt was studying for a midterm, the apartment was so small that Rachel and Bonnie's conversation would have disturbed him. Bonnie admired her sister's new diamond ring, she was even more interested in the ski trip that the engaged couple had planned. Bonnie and Kurt used to take weekend trips together when they each lived with their parents. Folding Kurt's worn jeans, Bonnie said that she envied Rachel, being engaged, according to Bonnie, is much more romantic than being married.

Exercise Central
For additional practice with eliminating comma splices, go to **bedfordstmartins.com/choices** and click on "Exercise Central."

D. MISPLACED MODIFIERS

A *modifier* is a word or group of words that describes or adds information about another word. A modifier should appear as close as possible to the word it modifies:

Jane spent *almost* fifty dollars on her haircut. [The modifier appears next to the word it modifies, *fifty*.]

Spinach contains lutein, a vitamin *that strengthens the eyes*. [The modifier appears next to *vitamin*, which is the word it modifies.]

A modifier is *misplaced* when it appears in the wrong place in the sentence. Either it seems to modify a word other than the one the writer intended, or there's more than one word it could modify and the reader can't tell which one.

MISPLACED   The carpentry student nailed the plank to the floor *with red hair*. [Did the floor have red hair?]

CLEAR   The carpentry student *with red hair* nailed the plank to the floor.

MISPLACED   The restaurant *only* serves lunch on Sundays. [Is lunch the only meal served on Sundays, or are Sundays the only days that lunch is served?]

CLEAR   The restaurant serves *only* lunch on Sundays.

CLEAR   The restaurant serves lunch on Sundays *only*.

MISPLACED   Leo walked outside to smell the flowering rosemary plant *wearing his bathing suit*. [Is the plant wearing his bathing suit?]

CLEAR   *Wearing his bathing suit,* Leo walked outside to smell the flowering rosemary plant.

ACTIVITY 12: Identify Misplaced Modifiers

Underline the misplaced modifiers in each of the following sentences.

EXAMPLE   My supervisor said I needed to improve my attitude <u>in her office</u>.

1. The beer can almost hit my grandmother thrown out of the car window.
2. The new standards for graduation only required a low-level statistics class.

3. Boris found a pink and squirming nest of baby mice.

4. Leo borrowed a shirt from his brother with long sleeves.

5. The waiter brought a steak to the man covered with mushrooms.

To correct a misplaced modifier, place the modifier closer to the word it describes.

MISPLACED   The Italian visitors drove a rental car *leaving on vacation.* [It appears the rental car is leaving on vacation.]

CLEAR   *Leaving on vacation,* the Italian visitors drove a rental car. [The modifier is placed closer to the word it describes, *visitors.*]

HOW TO Correct Misplaced Modifiers

- Place them as close as possible to the word they modify.

ACTIVITY 13: Correct Misplaced Modifiers

Edit each of the following sentences to eliminate misplaced modifiers.

EXAMPLE   Wearing his expensive new suit,
Parker told the noisy employees to shape up ~~in his expensive new suit.~~

1. My husband and I volunteered at the school antique sale with the best of intentions.

2. The volunteers put out the hillside fire from the next county.

3. The kids I was babysitting from next door played video games for hours.

4. Liam greeted the unexpected guests in his old pajamas.

5. My learning group always arranged to meet in the Student Union at my previous college.

6. Rosie almost spent two weeks in Las Vegas and went on to Reno for another week.

7. Dean took the rabbit to the veterinarian that had the sore paw.

8. Taka polished the antique cabinet standing on a stepladder.

9. Annick only told her coach what the doctor had said, but the coach told her parents.

10. My leaky faucet dripped water all day that I need to replace.

Exercise Central

For additional practice with eliminating misplaced modifiers, go to **bedfordstmartins.com/choices** and click on "Exercise Central."

E. DANGLING MODIFIERS

A modifier is *dangling* when there's no word in the sentence that it can logically modify. Most dangling modifiers occur at the beginnings of sentences.

DANGLING   *Smiling broadly,* the award fulfilled Renee's dreams. [It appears that the award is smiling.]

CLEAR   *Smiling broadly,* Renee accepted the award that fulfilled her dreams.

DANGLING   *In running for the taxi,* my foot tripped on the crack in the sidewalk. [Is the foot running for the taxi?]

CLEAR   *As I was running for the taxi,* my foot tripped on the crack in the sidewalk.

ACTIVITY 14: Identify Dangling Modifiers

Underline the dangling modifiers in each of the following sentences.

EXAMPLE   <u>Deciding to join the team,</u> the coach enthusiastically shook Sara's hand.

1. After finishing all of the basic classes, college became easier.
2. Staring into the distance, dark skies approach.
3. No one realized the problem with the proposal, pleased by the low cost.
4. To control your anger, a psychologist may be necessary.
5. Tired from the long flight, the crowds in the parking lot were depressing.

To correct a dangling modifier, rewrite the sentence so the reader knows what is being modified. You can add this information either to the modifier or to the rest of the sentence.

DANGLING   *Waiting in line,* the wind began to blow. [The reader can't tell who is waiting in line.]

CLEAR   *While I was waiting in line,* the wind began to blow.

CLEAR   Waiting in line, *I* felt the wind begin to blow.

HOW TO Correct Dangling Modifiers

■ Add information about what or whom the modifier is describing.

ACTIVITY 15: Correct Dangling Modifiers

Edit each of the following sentences to eliminate dangling modifiers.

EXAMPLE   ~~Gusting~~ to forty-five miles an hour, the tree limb ~~loudly~~ hit the tin roof.
(The wind, gusting ... caused ... to ... loudly ...)

1. Shaking the principal's hand, Clarence's goal of earning a high school diploma became a reality.

2. Fed by hot winds and dry grass, the firefighters faced a difficult challenge.

3. Mom's jigsaw puzzle was complete, snapping the last piece into place.

4. Searching for a new way to treat diabetes, medical advances were made.

5. Seeing her grandson win a prize at the science fair, her heart was overwhelmed with pride.

6. Removing her foot from the accelerator, Diana's car came to a stop.

7. Having saved for years to buy a house, it was exciting that the Kangs' dream was coming true.

8. While window shopping at the mall, a sports watch caught my eye.

9. Deliriously happy, the newlyweds' limousine slowly drove to their hotel.

10. Water leaked into my boat while rowing as fast as possible.

 Exercise Central
For additional practice with eliminating dangling modifiers, go to **bedfordstmartins.com/choices** and click on "Exercise Central."

F. ACTIVE AND PASSIVE VOICE

In a sentence written in *active voice,* the subject performs the action; it does something. In a sentence written in *passive voice,* the subject receives the action; something is done to it. Readers prefer the active voice in most sentences because they normally expect the subject to be performing the action, so a sentence where the subject doesn't perform the action takes longer to understand. The active voice is also less wordy than the passive voice.

PASSIVE VOICE   The tail of the kite *was caught by* the boy.

ACTIVE VOICE   The boy *caught* the kite by the tail.

PASSIVE VOICE   The newspaper *is read by* my mother each morning.

ACTIVE VOICE   My mother *reads* the newspaper each morning.

HOW TO Use Active Voice

■ Decide who or what is performing the action in a sentence.

■ Make the performer of the action the subject of the sentence.

ACTIVITY 16: Use the Active Voice

Edit each of the following sentences to eliminate passive voice.

EXAMPLE   Tiger Woods ~~was given~~ the green jacket ~~by the tournament's sponsor.~~
_{The tournament's sponsors gave}

1. The runners were encouraged by the spectators.

2. The memos had been signed by the manager.

3. A doctoral degree in physics was earned by Professor Patel.

4. An educational play about AIDS was performed by the juniors.

5. The baby was taken to the park by his older brother.

6. The party was planned by Milo, but all the work was done by his family.

7. The assignment was given at the beginning of class by the teaching assistant.

8. A swimming pool was installed by the previous owners of the house.

9. The movie was made by the Coen brothers, and the hero was played by George Clooney.

10. Our pets were fed by a neighbor.

ACTIVITY 17: Correct Passive Voice in a Paragraph

Edit the following paragraph so that all sentences are in the active voice.

EXAMPLE   *A bus smashed the* ~~The~~ car that I used to get to school ~~was smashed by a bus.~~

A university education must be paid for. School and work are balanced differently by my friends and me. Monica had both a full-time and a part-time job for two years following high school. Now a job isn't needed during college. She earns high grades because she doesn't have to divide her energies between work and school. A full-time night job was chosen by Willy, and only nine credits are taken by him. He does data entry for the business office of a department store. An administrative position in the same office will be taken by him after graduation. Willy earns enough money by working at night to make payments on a new car. I don't need a car. However, money for college is needed. I chose to take out student loans to pay for my education. My friends and I live very different lives.

Exercise Central

For additional practice with using active and passive voice, go to **bedfordstmartins.com/choices** and click on "Exercise Central."

G. PARALLELISM

When two or more groups of words in a sentence are parts of a pair or series, these word groups should be *parallel*, or similar in their grammatical structure. The following sentences are written using parallel structure:

> Today, we drove to Philadelphia, visited the Liberty Bell, and ate at our favorite restaurants.

The underlined parts of this sentence are parallel because the group of words in each part follows the same grammatical structure: past-tense verb followed by words that modify the verb or complete its meaning.

> My girlfriend is smart in school, friendly to everyone, and fun to be with.

The underlined parts of this sentence are parallel because they follow the same sentence structure: adjective followed by words that modify the adjective.

Here are examples of sentences that do not have parallel structure, each followed by a revised sentence using parallel structure. Notice that the revised sentences are easier to read and understand.

NOT PARALLEL	I love going to the movies, reading, and to walk.
PARALLEL	I love going to the movies, reading, and walking.
NOT PARALLEL	He drove dangerously fast, missed the curve, and wrecks his car.
PARALLEL	He drove dangerously fast, missed the curve, and wrecked his car.
NOT PARALLEL	I don't like to fill out these financial aid forms that are difficult, long, and have too many words.
PARALLEL	I don't like to fill out these financial aid forms that are difficult, long, and wordy.

HOW TO   Write Using Parallel Sentence Structure

- Reread each sentence looking for pairs or series of word groups in a sentence.

- Check that each of the groups of words in the pair or series has a similar sentence structure.

- Rewrite any parts of the pair or series that are not parallel in structure.

ACTIVITY 18: Use Parallelism

Edit each of the following sentences for correct parallel structure.

EXAMPLE   My favorite activities include horseback riding, hiking, and ~~to play~~ soccer.
_{playing}

1. My mother was a hairdresser, taxi driver, and being a secretary.

2. In my University Studies class, I have learned how to study more effectively and preparing for an exam.

3. The bookstore has my favorite books: books about cooking, biographies, and novels.

4. I found the concert to be loud, expensive, and was not very entertaining.

5. Going to the dentist is worse than to go to the hospital.

6. The buffet included undercooked shrimp, limp lettuce, and the muffins were stale.

7. Ceci was filled with fear, anticipation, excited.

8. The squirrel peeked out, stole the nut, and then back to his home.

9. The Ferris wheel is my favorite carnival ride, but my sister prefers the haunted house and to ride the merry-go-round.

10. He thinks the world of her, and she thinks he is her world, too.

ACTIVITY 19: Correct Faulty Parallelism in a Paragraph

Edit the paragraph so that all sentences are parallel.

> EXAMPLE We need a visionary leader in each of our groups, but
> <u>we're knowing</u> ~~we know~~ this isn't likely.

A visionary leader is someone who is not afraid to lead and of taking the group to a place it would not be otherwise. A visionary leader isn't necessarily the most dynamic person in the group, but who is willing to listen to others. Such a leader constantly works hard to improve conditions for every member of the group, seeks to put the needs of the group members first, and a desire to see the group succeed as a whole. The visionary leader is not always the group member with the most imaginative ideas, but is the member who has the skills and energy to put these ideas into action. We could use more visionary leaders: they touch, inspire, and are changing the world we live in.

 Exercise Central
For additional practice with using parallelism, go to **bedford stmartins.com/choices** and click on "Exercise Central."

CHAPTER 19

Improving Word Choice

Speaking and writing are key ways to communicate your thoughts and feelings to others, and different situations require different word choices. Just as you wouldn't go to a job interview in a wedding dress or to a football game in a bathing suit, you wouldn't write to your boss in the same way that you write to a friend or daughter. You choose the best words for the person and the occasion. But how do you improve your word choice? Following are several strategies for expanding and improving the choice of words you use when you write.

A. VOCABULARY

One way to expand your word choice and to better understand what you read is to develop a broad vocabulary. How can you tell if your vocabulary needs improvement? Do you have difficulty finding the words to express what you want to say or write in class? At a party, do you hesitate to join a conversation because you can't follow what others are saying? Do you find yourself skipping a lot of words in newspapers, magazines, or your college textbooks because you don't know what they mean? If you have answered "yes" to any of these questions, you'll want to work to improve your vocabulary.

HOW TO Improve Your Vocabulary

- Read. The more you read, the more words you'll learn.

- Just ask. If you are with friends or classmates, don't hesitate to ask the meaning of words you don't understand.

- Play word games. Try Scrabble, crossword puzzles, a Word of the Day calendar, or a Web site that sends you a word each day.

- Keep vocabulary index cards. Write each unfamiliar word on one side of an index card. On the other side, write the definition and use the word in a sentence. Keep these index cards with you for easy study and reference.

ACTIVITY 1: Build Your Vocabulary

Using Chapters 15–18 of this Handbook, create vocabulary cards for unfamiliar grammar terms such as *linking verbs*. Write the word on one side of the index card. On the other side, write the definition and a sentence that provides an example.

✗ Meaning from Context

Reading is the most effective way to improve vocabulary. While reading, if you come across a word you don't know, see if you can determine the meaning of the word from the *context* — that is, from the other words in the sentence. For example, consider this sentence:

Although Bree is often *morose,* she seems happy today.

What does *morose* mean? Because you know that the word *although* shows contrast and that Bree seems happy today, then *morose* must be the opposite of *happy.* Bree must often be sad.

ACTIVITY 2: Determine Meaning from Context

Read the following passage from an article about figure skating. Try to determine the meanings of the underlined words from the words around them. Write the meanings next to the words in the spaces provided.

There are many athletic and artistic <u>elements</u> in figure skating. <u>Initial</u> skills include the all important basics — stroking forward, skating backward, and doing forward and backward crossovers. Jumps are so <u>predominant</u> in modern figure skating that we could say that this is the "jump era." In the six <u>preliminary</u> jumps, the skater <u>rotates</u> once in the air. Since their <u>inception</u> in the beginning of the twentieth century, these jumps have been doubled and now are commonly <u>trebled</u> by both men and women.

elements _____

initial _____

predominant _____

preliminary _____

rotates _____

inception _____

trebled _____

Learn Roots, Prefixes, and Suffixes

Another way to improve your vocabulary is to memorize the meanings of common word roots, prefixes, and suffixes. A *word root* is the main part of a word, a *prefix* is added to the beginning of a word or word root, and a *suffix* is added to the end of a word or word root. Here are the meanings of some common English word roots, prefixes, and suffixes.

ENGLISH WORD ROOTS

Root	Meaning	Examples
audi	to hear	audience, audio
bene	to help	benefit, benevolence
geo	earth	geography, geometry
logo	word or thought	logic, biology, geology
manu	hand	manufacture, manual
photo	light	photography, telephoto
tele	far away	telepathy, telegraph
vid, vis	to see	visit, vision, video

ENGLISH PREFIXES

Prefix	Meaning	Examples
ante-	before	antebellum, antedate
anti-	against	antisocial, antibody
bi-	two	bilateral, bipolar
de-	from	declaw, desensitize
hyper-	over, more	hypersensitive
mal-	bad	malpractice
post-	after	postwar, postscript
trans-	across	transport, transition
uni-	one	uniform, unicycle

ENGLISH SUFFIXES

Suffix	Meaning	Examples
-acy	state or quality	democracy, privacy
-dom	state of being	kingdom, freedom
-en	cause or become	cheapen, blacken

-ish	having the quality of	clownish
-less	lack of, without	childless, humorless
-ology	the study of	psychology
-ment	condition of	impediment, payment
-sion, -tion	state of being	confusion, transition

ACTIVITY 3: Learn Roots, Prefixes, and Suffixes

Create a vocabulary card for each root, prefix, and suffix in the first column above. Write the root, prefix, or suffix on one side of the index card. Write the meaning and an example on the other side. Review these cards regularly until you have memorized them.

B. UNNECESSARY REPETITION ✳

Repetition results from repeating the same idea in different words. Although repetition can help you emphasize and connect ideas as you write, too much repetition may lose your reader's attention. Sometimes, you may not even realize that you're repeating words or using words that mean the same thing. Notice the unnecessary words in the following sentences:

REPETITION   I wouldn't choose or select that blouse.

REVISED   I wouldn't choose that blouse.

REPETITION   We tried to forget the sad events of that day and put them out of our minds.

REVISED   We tried to forget the sad events of that day.

REPETITION   The positive benefits of this course of action were obvious and apparent.

REVISED   The benefits of this action were obvious.

HOW TO Avoid Unnecessary Repetition

Check that each word in a sentence

- Adds interest.

- Is specific.

- Does not restate what you have already said.

ACTIVITY 4: Avoid Unnecessary Repetition

Revise each of the following sentences to avoid unnecessary repetition.

EXAMPLE   I will never ever do anything like that again ~~in the future.~~

1. My very favorite song I like the most is "I Can't Make You Love Me."
2. Jerry wanted to get caught up and be up-to-date on what was going on in class.
3. Don't confuse me with the facts and data!
4. We never knew or realized how important this event would be.
5. Let's just wait and pass the time until she returns.

Exercise Central

For additional practice with eliminating unnecessary repetition, go to **bedfordstmartins.com/choices** and click on "Exercise Central."

C. WORDINESS

Eliminating wordiness is similar to avoiding unnecessary repetition. *Wordiness* results from using too many words to say something or using "filler" phrases that don't contribute to the meaning of a sentence. Notice the wordiness in the following sentences:

WORDY   I would really very much like to go to that game.

REVISED   I would like to go to that game.

WORDY   I get to make the choice of where I go.

REVISED   I get to choose where I go.

WORDY   I feel that we have a greater amount of freedom to choose these days.

REVISED   We have more freedom to choose today.

ACTIVITY 5: Eliminate Wordiness

Revise the following sentences to eliminate wordiness.

EXAMPLE ~~I believe that you~~ are wrong.

You (inserted above "I believe that you")

1. I would like to say that I agree with you.

2. I am of the opinion that anyone who writes on this topic as a subject for an essay is not thinking straight.

3. A large number of students in the near future will agree with us.

4. At an earlier point in time, this wouldn't have happened, or it would have been postponed until a later time.

5. I believe that this is true for the reason that students feel differently today than they did at an earlier point in time.

20

Improving Spelling

As you edit your writing, you'll want to be sure to check your spelling. Misspelled words will cause your reader to focus on your lack of spelling skills rather than on the meaning of what you have written. You can often tell if a word is misspelled just by looking at it, or you can use a computer spell-check to catch errors. Because the spell-check can't catch all errors, though, it's useful to improve your spelling.

A. SPELLING RULES

One way to improve your spelling is to learn spelling rules that can help you master the spelling of commonly misspelled words.

Rule 1. Use *i* before *e* except after *c* or when sounded like *ay* as in *neighbor* and *weigh*.

> believe, niece, piece, fierce
> receive, ceiling, conceive, deceive
> eight, freight, sleigh, weight

Exceptions: either, neither, leisure, height, seize, weird, science, counterfeit

ACTIVITY 1: Use *i* before *e* Except after *c*

In the space provided, correct each of the following misspelled words, or write "correct" if the word is spelled correctly.

EXAMPLE   hieght _____height_____

1. conceited _____

2. recieve _____

3. neighbor _____

4. weigh _____

5. cieling _____

6. decieve _____

7. seize _____

8. beleive _____

9. niether _____

10. neice _____

ACTIVITY 2: Correct *i* before *e* Except after *c* Errors

Underline each of the misspelled words in the following sentences. Then write the correct spelling of these words in the space provided. If a sentence has no spelling errors, write "correct."

EXAMPLE   Jerry has a <u>neice</u> and nephew. _____*niece*_____

1. Patrice asked Amando for a piece of paper. _____

2. It is important not to carry excess wieght when you are back-packing. _____

3. A good pair of shoes releived Kenia's backaches. _____

4. In his liesure time, Hal likes to go bow hunting. _____

5. Majel concieved of a way to pass the exam without reading the textbook. _____

6. Leonard was so concieted that people tried to avoid him. _____

7. On Christmas, Grandfather treated us to an old-fashioned sleigh ride. _____

8. My favorite beige jacket always looks dirty. _____

9. Tim decieved his teacher by forging his father's signature on his report card. _____

10. When we recieve your order, we will notify you by e-mail. _____

Rule 2.   When adding an ending that begins with a vowel (such as *-ed* or *-ing*) to a word that ends with a consonant, double the consonant if it (1) is preceded by a single vowel and (2) ends a one-syllable word or stressed syllable.

    bet, betting
    stop, stopped
    commit, committed
    occur, occurrence

Exception: Even if the consonant ends a stressed syllable, do not double it if the syllable is no longer stressed when the ending is added: *refer, reference.*

ACTIVITY 3: Double the Final Consonant

In the space provided, add the correct ending to each of the following words.

    EXAMPLE   get + ing _____ *getting* _____

1. travel + ed _____
2. dig + ing _____
3. omit + ed _____
4. control + ing _____
5. prefer + ence _____

6. scan + er _____
7. nag + ing _____
8. good + ness _____
9. defer + al _____
10. hop + ed _____

ACTIVITY 4: Correct Final Consonant Errors

Underline each of the misspelled words in the following sentences. Then write the correct spelling of these words in the space provided. If a sentence has no spelling errors, write "correct."

    EXAMPLE   The rabbit hoped to the side of the house. _____ *hopped* _____

1. Mary stoped kicking the bottom of Bill's chair only when he fell asleep. _____

2. They never succeeded at ridding their house of ants. _____

3. Felicia felt deep saddness when her friend moved away. _____

4. After tiping over his glass, Lewis apologized and left the room. _____

5. Ron and Leni held hands and planed their future. _____

6. Efren made a referrence to his former girlfriend. _____

7. Delphine repeatted her name three times before the clerk said it correctly. _____

8. The occurence of car theft in the parking lot has doubled in the last year. _____

9. Pegeen believed that Neville was betting on a losing team. _____

10. Stuart labored over his statistics homework for six hours. _____

Rule 3.   Drop a final silent *e* from a word when adding an ending that begins with a vowel. Keep the final *e* if the ending begins with a consonant.

> retire, retiring; age, aging; desire, desiring
> hate, hateful; state, statement; lone, lonely

Exceptions: ninth, truly, argument, judgment, courageous, manageable

ACTIVITY 5: Drop the Final Silent *e*

In the space provided, add the specified ending to each of the following words.

EXAMPLE   perspire + ing ___perspiring___

1. bite + ing _____   6. shine + ing _____

2. encourage + ment _____   7. true + ly _____

3. safe + ty _____   8. fade + ing _____

4. nine + th _____   9. use + able _____

5. care + ful _____   10. state + ment _____

ACTIVITY 6: Correct Final Silent *e* Errors

Underline each of the misspelled words in the following sentences. Then write the correct spelling of these words in the space provided. If a sentence has no spelling errors, write "correct."

EXAMPLE   He thought that he was <u>ageing</u> too quickly. ____*aging*____

1. Mira's greatest achievment was hiking the entire Appalachian Trail. _____

2. This coat has a removeable lining. _____

3. The lavish meal left us desireing nothing more. _____

4. Stan remained quiet to avoid an arguement with his friends in public. _____

5. The shoppers were hopeing to find bargains. _____

6. The audience made hatful remarks as the senator tried to speak.

   _____

7. Clarence did not use the best judgement in choosing a roommate. _____

8. The surest way to be fired from a job is not to show up.

   _____

9. Denise found her courses in managment more interesting than those in marketing. _____

10. Sheldon spent the rest of the afternoon writeing his résumé.

    _____

Rule 4.   When adding an ending other than -_ing_ to a word that ends in _y_, you sometimes need to change the _y_ to _i_. If the _y_ is preceded by a consonant, change it to _i;_ if you're adding _s_, also add an _e_ after the _i_. If you're adding -_ing_ or the _y_ is preceded by a vowel, don't change it to _i_.

> easy, easiest; duty, dutiful; reply, replies
>
> marry, married; monkey, monkeys; play, played
>
> apply, applying; dry, drying; stay, staying

ACTIVITY 7: Change _y_ to _i_

In the space provided, add the specified ending to each of the following words, and write the new word.

> EXAMPLE   carry + ed _____carried_____

1. pay + ing _____
2. turkey + s _____
3. say + ing _____
4. fry + ed _____
5. pretty + ily _____
6. plenty + ful _____
7. hurry + s _____
8. fly + ing _____
9. happy + ness _____
10. play + ful _____

ACTIVITY 8: Correct _y_ to _i_ Errors

Underline each of the misspelled words in the following sentences. Then write the correct spelling of these words in the space provided. If a sentence has no spelling errors, write "correct."

> EXAMPLE   The couple's happyness left us inspired. _____happiness_____

1. To find employment, he read the classified ads. _____

2. We were puzzled by the trickyness of the test question.

   _____

3. Lester has been studiing all day. _____

4. After several apologys, Wanda finally forgave her brother.

   _____

5. Rainer easyly jumped over the puddle. _____

6. It was difficult to say which sister was most beautyful.

   _____

7. In warm weather, the clothes dryed very quickly on the line.

   _____

8. The sounds of the children playing in the street carryed into my sixth-floor apartment. _____

9. The two attornies made an agreement to avoid going to court.

   _____

10. After staying at campgrounds, I found the motel luxurious.

    _____

 Exercise Central
For additional practice with spelling, go to **bedford stmartins.com/choices** and click on "Exercise Central."

B. COMMONLY MISSPELLED WORDS

The following are one hundred commonly misspelled words. Create spelling lists or cards to practice spelling them correctly.

absence	corroborate	February
accommodate	counterfeit	forty
all right	dealt	fulfill
analyze	definitely	government
anoint	despair	grammar
anonymous	dilemma	guarantee
benefit	disappoint	guard
boundary	ecstasy	height
business	eighth	hoarse
category	embarrass	holiday
committee	exceed	hygiene
conscience	existence	icicles
conscious	fascinate	imagine

indispensable	parallel	sheriff
innocent	peculiar	sophomore
irresistible	persistent	subtle
irritable	phenomenon	succeed
jealousy	perseverance	supersede
league	principal	surgeon
leisure	principle	tongue
license	privilege	tragedy
losing	procedure	truly
maneuver	pursue	tyranny
marriage	receipt	undoubtedly
meant	receive	until
minute	recommend	vacuum
misspelled	repetition	vengeance
necessary	rhythm	vicious
ninth	ridiculous	warrant
noticeable	roommate	weird
occurrence	schedule	wholly
often	seize	yacht
optimistic	separate	
pamphlet	sergeant	

ACTIVITY 9: Correct Sentences for Spelling

Underline the misspelled words in each of the following sentences. Then write the correct spelling of these words in the space provided. (There may be more than one error in each sentence.)

EXAMPLE   I always <u>recomended</u> <u>vacumming</u>, but I <u>definitly</u> see the

<u>benafit</u> of it now.

recommended, vacuuming, definitely, benefit
_____

1. When Rafa telephoned, Yoli was studing her chemistry, so he apologyzed for bothering her.

_____

2. After beging for three weeks to be given a better work schedule, Alvin stoped asking.

_____

3. Gino had been liveing in his apartment for fifteen years when he recieved the eviction notice.

_____

4. A counterfiet coin may wiegh less than a genuine one.

_____

5. Shelley was carful when she tryed to remove the splinter from the child's finger.

_____

6. You can easyly waste your liesure time on activities that you don't really enjoy.

_____

7. A student writeing a persuasive essay needs to construct a very strong arguement supporting his or her opinions.

_____

8. Krystle prefered ordering from a catalogue to shoping at the mall.

_____

9. Unfortunately, Vincent omited his social security number when he applyed for a scholarship.

_____

10. The dutys of the store manager never stoped at five o'clock.

_____

C. COMMONLY CONFUSED WORDS

Commonly confused words are words that sound similar but have different spellings and meanings.

accept: to agree to	I *accept* your offer.
except: excluding	Everyone *except* Joan was invited.
adapt: to adjust	He had to *adapt* to his new town.
adopt: to take on	He realized that he would have to *adopt* a new attitude.
advice: a suggestion	Please take my *advice*.
advise: to suggest	I *advise* you to slow down.
affect: to influence	Her partying did not *affect* her grades.
effect: a result	The *effect*, though, was that she was under stress.

all ready: prepared	We are *all ready* for the holidays.
already: previously	We have *already* bought all of the food we need.
cite: to refer to	Jerome is always careful to *cite* his sources.
sight: vision	The eye surgery improved her *sight*.
site: a location	This paper was about the *site* of the new museum.
complement: to go well with; something that goes well with something else	This tie does not *complement* your shirt.
compliment: to admire; an expression of admiration	I *compliment* you on your choice of pants.
conscience: moral principles	Josue's *conscience* wouldn't permit him to cheat.
conscious: aware	He was *conscious* of students cheating around him.
farther: a longer physical distance	My aunt lives *farther* away than my family can drive in one day.
further: additional; more	The committee agreed to *further* discussion of the issue.
loose: not tight or secure	Jerry's tooth was *loose*.
lose: to misplace	He didn't want to *lose* it if it fell out.
principal: head of a school; main or leading	The *principal* of my high school was one of the *principal* supporters of the new gym.
principle: a basic truth or belief	He believed in the *principle* of daily exercise.
to: toward	Abigail ran *to* the lake.
too: excessively; also	Her brother, Michael, was *too* slow to keep up and stopped along the way, *too*.
two: the number between one and three	The *two* of them arrived an hour apart.
weather: conditions such as sun, rain, and wind	The *weather* in Washington, D.C. was beautiful.
whether: a word indicating choice or possibility	I had to decide *whether* to leave or stay.

ACTIVITY 10: Correct a Paragraph for Spelling

Correct the misspelled words in the following paragraph by writing the correct spelling above each misspelled word.

EXAMPLE Ahmad loves computers because they ~~effect~~ *affect* the way he writes.

Ahmad feels the campus computer labs need improveing. Before geting his own computer, he relyed heavily on the labs. Although they were convient, they were to noisey and crowded. Often computers were unavailable because the maintance was so bad. When he found a free computer, he was distractted by the rowdyness of the other students. After recieving a computer from his father, Ahmad lookked foreward to his life being easyer. Unffortunatly, he still had problems when continueing projects that he had begun at home. Once, he used a Macintosh by mistake and accidently reformated his diskete, loosing all his data. Often, he had difficultys printing at the lab, discoverring pages of wierd symbols weather he wanted two or not. The technicians say that his home software isn't compattible with the software at the lab. Now, he's more conscience of mistakes than ever. Ahmad's father tells him that computers have all ready created new problems while solveing other ones.

CHAPTER 21

Improving Punctuation

You use punctuation to make it easier for your readers to follow your meaning. Just as your car's taillights communicate that you are planning to stop, turn right, or turn left, punctuation communicates to your readers what to expect next. Readers depend on punctuation to guide them through your text. For example, what does this sentence mean?

Don't let the snake eat Ryan.

Is the snake about to eat Ryan, or is Ryan supposed to prevent the snake from eating? Adding a comma to this sentence makes it clear.

Don't let the snake eat, Ryan.

The reader now understands that Ryan is supposed to prevent the snake from eating its food.

The following punctuation rules will help you make your meaning clear and communicate to your readers more effectively.

A. COMMAS

The *comma* (,) is used to separate parts of a sentence to make the meaning clear.

Rule 1.   Use a comma after an introductory word, phrase, or clause.

Actually, snakes like to eat rodents.
After feeding the snake, you can leave for the NASCAR race.
As Ryan explained, snakes eat a variety of foods.

ACTIVITY 1: Use Commas with Introductory
            Words, Phrases, or Clauses

Add a comma after the introductory word, phrase, or clause in each of the following sentences.

EXAMPLE   While I usually like the operaˏ I didn't like this one.

1. Smelling Janelle's perfume in the apartment Oscar knew that she was ready to go to the party.

2. First Corey fastened his seatbelt and put on his sunglasses.

3. Whether you agree or not I'm taking biology next semester.

4. In Wendy's opinion renting a large apartment is more convenient than owning a house.

5. While the children ate ice cream and cake and played games their parents became better acquainted.

ACTIVITY 2: Write Sentences Using Commas with Introductory Words, Phrases, or Clauses

In each of the following sentences, add an introductory word, phrase, or clause followed by a comma.

EXAMPLE   During the movie, Gil and Chet would not stop talking.

1. I heard the drone of a small airplane overhead.

2. She put on more lipstick and mascara.

3. Your parents were watching you through the kitchen window.

4. We keep reams of paper and extra cartridges for the printer.

5. Philip admitted that he was wrong.

Rule 2.   Use commas to separate three or more words, phrases, or clauses in a series. Do not use a comma before the first item in the series or after the last item.

Jane bought books, games, and CDs at the bookstore.

Before leaving, she talked to her roommate, turned off her computer, and locked her desk.

Jane forgot to feed the dog, she didn't make her bed, and she didn't clean the bathroom as she promised.

ACTIVITY 3: Use Commas in a Series

Add commas as needed to each of the following sentences to separate words, phrases, or clauses used in a series.

EXAMPLE   My favorite foods are salmon fried rice and chocolate cake.

1. All I had in the refrigerator was a pint of sour milk a block of moldy cheese and a jar of olives.

2. Eileen packed underwear jeans sweaters socks shoes and maps.

3. Vikram walked down the street past the supermarket and around the corner.

4. Jorge filled the sandbox Gunilla set up the swings Noah built the seesaws Calvin welded the slide and Mahela painted the benches.

5. Chewing gum pacing the floor and looking at the clock were the only things to do in the waiting room.

ACTIVITY 4: Write Sentences Using Commas with a Series

For each of the following lists of items, write a complete sentence using these items in a series.

EXAMPLE   hills, river beds, dusty trails

We hiked hills, river beds, and dusty trails.
_____

1. pens, pencils, notebooks, folders, erasers

_____

2. a pad of paper, a pair of scissors, a bottle of glue

_____

_____

3. on the dashboard, under the front seat, in the trunk

_____

_____

4. decorating the house, preparing a festive meal, spending time with family

_____

_____

5. sang songs, told funny stories, did magic tricks, made balloon animals

_____

_____

Rule 3.   Use a comma to separate two independent clauses joined by a coordinating conjunction.

> I wanted to go to the concert, and I wanted to study for my exam.
> I knew my test was important, but Shakira is my favorite singer.
> I studied all afternoon, so I was able to go to the concert after all.

ACTIVITY 5: Use Commas with Coordinating Conjunctions

Add a comma to each of the following sentences to separate the two independent clauses joined by a coordinating conjunction.

> EXAMPLE   I wanted to leave early‸ yet my husband wanted to leave at noon.

1. The wind howled and the snow fell more thickly.
2. Margarita stood on a stepladder but she could not reach the ceiling.
3. Julio drank a second bottle of water yet he still was thirsty.
4. Marcia couldn't sleep for tomorrow she started a new job.
5. I wanted to call you on your birthday but you were out all night.

ACTIVITY 6: Join Sentences with Commas and Coordinating Conjunctions

Use a comma and a coordinating conjunction to join each of the following pairs of sentences into a single sentence.

> EXAMPLE   My mother loves to travel. She's a little afraid of flying.
>   (, but she's)

1. Yusef sat in the driver's seat. His brothers pushed the car.
2. Aurelia found the strength to run even faster. She saw the banners at the finish line.
3. I realized that I had answered the essay question on my history midterm badly. I had only enough time to write a brief concluding paragraph.
4. The doctor gave Samia a pair of crutches. She could walk without further injuring her foot.

5. You could come to the dance with me. You could watch reruns on television.

Rule 4.   Use commas before and after a descriptive word, phrase, or clause or an appositive (a noun that renames the noun right before it) if the word, phrase, clause, or appositive interrupts the flow of the sentence or could be removed from the sentence without changing its meaning. If the word, phrase, clause, or appositive is at the end of the sentence, use a comma before it.

> My high school reunion, sadly, was missing the person I most wanted to see.
>
> Jessie, who was my high school sweetheart, doesn't live here anymore.
>
> The reunion, held over the Thanksgiving weekend, wasn't nearly as much fun as the last one.
>
> I would really like to see Jessie, my old flame.

ACTIVITY 7: Use Commas with Descriptive Words, Phrases, and Clauses and Appositives

Add commas to each of the following sentences to set off the descriptive word, phrase, or clause or the appositive.

EXAMPLE   Johnny, my closest friend, never has to study.

1. Mateo the youngest person in his family is the first to attend a university.

2. The driver of the car in front of us ignoring the stop sign sped through the intersection.

3. Ricky's new saxophone which had cost him his life savings enabled him to join his favorite swing band.

4. My date a massage therapist named Yolanda asked me in to meet her parents.

5. Janine's former roommate surprisingly was happy to see her.

ACTIVITY 8: Add Descriptive Words, Phrases, and Clauses with Commas and Appositives

Rewrite each of the following sentences by inserting the descriptive word, phrase, or clause or appositive provided. Include the required commas.

EXAMPLE Corky flew from his perch to my shoulder. (*my parakeet*)

Corky, my parakeet, flew from his porch to my shoulder.

1. Mr. Gardner ran unsuccessfully for state senator. (*my history teacher in junior high school*)

   _____

   _____

2. Hector's grandchildren ran into the kitchen. (*smelling the cookies in the oven*)

   _____

   _____

3. The library book gathered dust at the back of my closet. (*which I had never read*)

   _____

   _____

4. Gavin's wife has just published a magazine article about their trip to Bhutan. (*an agricultural advisor*)

   _____

   _____

5. Sally could not afford a new truck. (*unfortunately*)

   _____

   _____

Rule 5. Use commas to set off transitional words and phrases from the rest of the sentence.

It wasn't until I visited the museum, however, that I realized how much I liked art.

For example, I discovered I really enjoyed Remington's sculptures.

My friend, on the other hand, preferred Monet's paintings.

ACTIVITY 9: Use Commas to Set Off Transitional Words and Phrases

Add commas as needed to each of the following sentences to set off the transitional words and phrases.

EXAMPLE Surely my car will be ready soon.

1. Subsequently the rest of the family came down with the flu.
2. Fritz likewise saved copies of his work in his e-mail files.
3. Furthermore the larger company has superior benefits.
4. The two-lane road alongside the freeway nevertheless is very scenic.
5. Only when Belinda heard the applause however did she realize that her speech was convincing.

ACTIVITY 10:   Add Transitional Words and Phrases with Commas

Rewrite each of the following sentences by inserting the transitional word or phrase provided. Include the required commas.

EXAMPLE   Sandy wants to try out for the marching band. (*nonetheless*)

Sandy, nonetheless, wants to try out for the marching band.

1. Consuelo is allergic to feathers and animal fur. (*however*)

_____

_____

2. Farak prefers snorkeling to scuba diving. (*on the other hand*)

_____

_____

3. The people who arrived late waited in the lobby for the first intermission. (*meanwhile*)

_____

_____

4. Some members of the city council want to increase the budget for public parks. (*in addition*)

_____

_____

5. The tenants are pooling their money to buy the apartment building from the bank. (*as a result*)

_____

_____

Rule 6. Use a comma to separate the day of the month from the year. If the year is in the middle of a sentence, also use a comma after it.

> I will start graduate school on September 4, 2008.
>
> I was born on July 4, 1970, and immediately became the center of my grandmother's attention.
>
> My goal is to have my Master's degree by the time I turn forty on July 4, 2010.

ACTIVITY 11: Use Commas in Dates

Add commas as needed to each of the following sentences.

> EXAMPLE   My birthday is December 8 1977.

1. My father was born September 18 1956.

2. The automobile accident occurred October 30 1999.

3. February 29 2001 is a date that never existed.

4. I first filed an income tax return on April 15 1997.

5. November 8 1990 was the day that my aunt and uncle were married.

ACTIVITY 12: Write Sentences Using Commas in Dates

Complete each of the following sentences, giving the month, day, and year. Use commas as necessary.

> EXAMPLE   I received my degree on _____ May 5, 1999 _____.

1. Today's date is _____.

2. _____ is the date that I was born.

3. The date that I first attended class this semester was _____.

4. _____ is the date of the last holiday that I celebrated.

5. Next Saturday's date is _____.

Rule 7. Use commas in addresses and place names to separate the various parts, such as the street, city, county, state or province, and country. If the address or place name ends in the middle of a sentence, also use a comma after it.

> I have lived at 400 Elm Street, Chicago, Illinois, all of my life.
>
> My closest friend now lives at 402 Oak Avenue, Bexar County, Texas.

ACTIVITY 13: Use Commas in Addresses and Place Names

Add commas as needed to each of the following sentences.

EXAMPLE   Another friend lives at 632 Pecan Street, Toronto, Canada.

1. His office is located at 4100 Manchester Drive Albany New York.
2. I have some relatives who live in Atlanta Georgia and some who live in Tampa Florida.
3. There is a large medical center in Dane County Wisconsin.
4. Tamara celebrated New Year's Eve in Paris France.
5. I mailed the warranty card to 762 Wallingford Boulevard Fremont Virginia.

ACTIVITY 14: Write Sentences Using Commas in Addresses and Place Names

Complete each of the following sentences, providing the information indicated. Use commas as necessary.

EXAMPLE   My favorite relative lives at <u>13 Main, Phoenix, Arizona</u>.

(*street address • city • state*)

1. I know someone who lives at _____.
(*street address • city • state*)

2. I was born in _____.
(*county • state* or *city • country*)

3. A place that I have visited is _____.
(*city • state*)

4. My dream vacation would be in _____.
(*city • state*)

5. My address is _____.
(*street address • city • state*)

Rule 8.   Use commas to set off dialogue or a direct quotation from the rest of the sentence. Commas always go *before* quotation marks.

"Go ahead and start your engines," the announcer said.

According to my brother, "He didn't say it loud enough for all of the racers to hear."

"I said it loud enough," the announcer replied, "for all of the other racers to hear."

ACTIVITY 15: Use Commas with Dialogue and Direct Quotations

Add commas as needed to each of the following sentences.

EXAMPLE   My father always says "Don't judge a book by its cover."

1. "I think Douglas likes you" Charlene whispered to Amber.
2. Brian Wilson sang "I guess I just wasn't made for these times."
3. "Don't kill that spider" Alberto told his son.
4. "You don't need to insure your car" Yasmin joked "if you never drive it."
5. Professor Ambrosini reminds us "Even if it's not on the test, you still need to know it."

ACTIVITY 16: Write Sentences Using Commas with Dialogue and Direct Quotations

Complete each of the following sentences by providing a one-sentence piece of dialogue or quotation. Use commas as necessary.

EXAMPLE   I heard a singer on the radio repeat , "I'm a creep; I'm a weirdo."

1. My friend always tells people _____
2. I like to say _____
3. My favorite movie character says _____
4. _____ according to someone in my family.
5. One memorable teacher often said _____

ACTIVITY 17: Use Commas Correctly in Sentences

Using all of the comma rules you have learned in this chapter, add commas as necessary to each of the following sentences.

EXAMPLE   Since I had never been to that ski resort he explained that

it was in Jackson Hole Wyoming.

1. The oldest son Steven surprised his family by bringing home his new wife for they had not known that he had even been dating somebody special.

2. In high school Sofia amazingly decided to take a cooking class to learn how to read package labels how to select and store fresh vegetables and how to prepare quick meals from basic ingredients.

3. Because he knew that I was worried Alexei my oldest friend telephoned to announce "Jackie my new address is 1561 Kendall Avenue Minneapolis Minnesota."

4. Mastering new software therefore involves solving two important problems which are learning what the software can do and figuring out how to get the software to do it.

5. On July 20 1969 when Neil Armstrong stepped onto the surface of the moon he said "One small step for a man; one giant leap for mankind."

ACTIVITY 18: Use Commas Correctly in a Paragraph

Using all of the comma rules you have learned in this chapter, add commas as needed to the following paragraph.

EXAMPLE   The day that John F. Kennedy died, November 22, 1963,

remains important to older Americans.

One of them remarked "On that day everything changed." Many people began working to end war racism sexism and poverty. Violence increased and two other leaders were shot and killed: Martin Luther King Jr. and Robert Kennedy the president's brother. Finally public figures lost their privacy. In a famous photograph President Kennedy's son salutes the funeral procession. No situation should be more private than a boy saying goodbye to his father. However a child had to share this moment with millions of strangers.

Exercise Central
For additional practice with using commas, go to **bedford stmartins.com/choices** and click on "Exercise Central."

B. SEMICOLONS

The *semicolon* (;) is used to join independent clauses and to make meaning clear.

Rule 1. Use a semicolon to join two related independent clauses that could each stand alone as a sentence. Semicolons work especially well if the two independent clauses are short and closely related.

> I never liked science fiction; it just doesn't make sense to me.
>
> Stephen King is my favorite writer; he knows how to grab his reader's attention.
>
> I can't believe how many books King has written; *Carrie* is still my all-time favorite.

ACTIVITY 19: Write Sentences Using Semicolons to Join Independent Clauses

Add a semicolon and an independent clause to each of the following independent clauses.

EXAMPLE   Candace is an accomplished figure skater *; she studied* _____ *ballet to add grace to her routines.*

1. For me, the morning is the most frustrating time of day _____

   _____

2. My cousin is an excellent athlete _____

   _____

3. They have a beautiful view from their window _____

   _____

4. Every day, I put up with someone with an annoying habit _____

   _____

5. Next semester, I will have an ideal schedule _____

   _____

Rule 2. Use a semicolon to link two clauses that are joined by a transitional word.

> Some people think Stephen King is too gory; nevertheless, they read every one of his books.
>
> I wanted to send a copy of *Misery* to my cousin; however, my father wouldn't let me.
>
> I will buy every book King publishes; for example, I just bought *Dreamcatcher.*

Rule 3. Use a semicolon to separate items in a series that already includes commas.

> My favorite places to visit are Des Moines, Iowa; Orlando, Florida; and Denver, Colorado.

ACTIVITY 20: Use Semicolons Correctly

Use a semicolon to correctly punctuate each of the following sentences.

> EXAMPLE I always go to the movies on Friday night that's the night
>
> new movies open.

1. It would be difficult to work full-time while he had five classes however, Noe accepted the job.

2. In the heat of the afternoon, the flowers began to droop a single bee stirred the roses.

3. Next summer, Nadine will see Madrid, Spain Paris, France Rome, Italy and Athens, Greece.

4. Patrick did not have enough time to finish cooking dinner consequently, the stew is very watery.

5. We had to wait two hours to pose for the family photograph by that time, unfortunately, the children were no longer clean and neat.

Exercise Central

For additional practice with using semicolons, go to **bedford stmartins.com/choices** and click on "Exercise Central."

C. COLONS

The *colon* (:) is also useful for making meaning clear.

Use a colon to introduce a list or an explanation. However, use the colon only when the words before it are a complete sentence that could stand alone. Do not use a colon after expressions like *such as* or *for example*.

When you go to the movies, be sure to get the following snacks: popcorn, soda, and a dill pickle.

There is only one way to please Brandon at the movies: buy the foods he loves.

His friends know this about Brandon: the food is more important to him than the film.

ACTIVITY 21: Use Colons Correctly

Add colons as needed in each of the following sentences to introduce a list, clause, or phrase that explains the independent clause. If the sentence is correct without a colon, write "correct" in the space provided.

EXAMPLE   I went to the bookstore to buy supplies a ruler, graph

paper, and a calculator. _____

1. To make your own salsa, you need tomatoes, onions, chiles, cilantro, and salt. _____

2. I have to do many things to prepare for my guests clean the house, shop for groceries, buy concert tickets, and repair the brakes on my car. _____

3. Ian can play four different wind instruments flute, clarinet, oboe, and bassoon. _____

4. This afternoon, two-year-old Ryan was impossible he poured maple syrup on the floor, tore the pages out of a photo album, and flushed a doll down the toilet. _____

5. Vanessa's mother taught her many old popular dances, such as the twist, pony, swim, jerk, frug, and monkey. _____

ACTIVITY 22: Write Sentences Using Colons

To each of the following sentences, add a list or a clause or phrase of explanation. Introduce your list, clause, or phrase with a colon.

EXAMPLE   Many courses fulfill your science requirement <u>: *Crime and*</u>

<u>*Chemistry, Urban Geography, and Celestial Myths.*</u>

1. Vanessa has autographs from her favorite actors _____

   _____

2. There are many things we can do next Saturday _____

   _____

3. That couple broke up for some very good reasons _____

   _____

4. I have a lot of homework for tonight _____

   _____

5. In spite of its reasonable prices, that restaurant has its bad points

   _____

Exercise Central

For additional practice with using colons, go to **bedford stmartins.com/choices** and click on "Exercise Central."

D. END PUNCTUATION

The *period* (.), the *question mark* (?), and the *exclamation mark* (!) are the three types of punctuation used to end sentences.

Rule 1.   Use a period to end most sentences, including indirect questions and commands. An indirect question reports a question rather than asks one.

He never believed her lies.
He asked her where she had heard such things.
Never lie to me again.

Rule 2.   Use a question mark to end a direct question.

Why didn't he realize that she was telling the truth?
How could she make herself any clearer?

Rule 3.   Use an exclamation mark to give emphasis or show emotion.

Don't ever doubt my word again!

I will always tell you the truth!

ACTIVITY 23: Add End Punctuation to Sentences

Insert the correct end punctuation mark at the end of each of the following sentences.

EXAMPLE   Would you like to go to the store ?

1. Now that he is an adult, Rogelio relies on his parents' good advice more than ever

2. When Vera stepped into the cabin that had been in her family for years, she noticed its old, familiar smell

3. Caleb and Genevieve were happy to see that Mr. Siegel had not changed much over the years

4. What did people do with their evenings before the invention of television

5. How dare you behave that way with my friends

ACTIVITY 24: Revise for Correct End Punctuation

Revise each of the following sentences as needed for end punctuation. If the end punctuation does not need to be changed, write "correct" in the space provided.

EXAMPLE   Jessie likes me. __correct__

1. Ah, this is the life! _____

2. Does anyone know where the nearest police station is? _____

3. I wondered what my boss had planned for me? _____

4. This coat appears to be still in good condition! _____

5. Olga wanted to know whether a new director had already been chosen. _____

ACTIVITY 25: Add End Punctuation to a Paragraph

In the following paragraph, insert the correct end punctuation in the spaces provided.

EXAMPLE   Because of my cousin, Martin, our family just had the

best reunion ever _!_

After leaving the army, Martin decided to go to college ___ Did he study something normal, like history or psychology ___ You don't know Cousin Martin ___ He majored in recreation ___ We all used to ask ourselves if this was a real major ___ It is very real, for our reunion was his senior project ___ He organized everything: transportation, accommodations, catering, and even our matching T-shirts ___ Among the games he invented for us, my favorite was the scavenger hunt ___ The family has become so big that many of us had never met before, so instead of finding objects in our scavenger hunt, Martin made us become acquainted with our more distant relatives ___ For example, I had to find a rocket scientist, and to my surprise, Gwen Zawada, my second cousin, works for NASA ___ Even the newest family members were involved; I met the very young man who had just learned to stand up unassisted ___ Who was that ___ The answer is on the family reunion Web page that Martin constructed as part of his project ___ What grade did he receive ___ The professor gave him an A, of course ___

Exercise Central
For additional practice with using end punctuation, go to **bedfordstmartins.com/choices** and click on "Exercise Central."

E. APOSTROPHES

An *apostrophe* (') is used to show possession and to form contractions.

Rule 1.   Use an apostrophe to show that something belongs to someone. If the thing belongs to one person, use *'s* after the noun that refers to the person, even if the noun already ends in *-s*.

Jessica's nose ring is the topic of conversation in class.
Her friend's ear stud, however, does not generate much interest.
Classmates do not even know about Elvis's belly button ring.

Rule 2. If the thing belongs to more than one person and the noun that refers to these persons ends in *-s*, use only an apostrophe *after* the *-s*.

> All of the students' conversation is about Jessica.
>
> Her friends' body piercings never come up.
>
> The professors' reaction was especially interesting.

If the noun doesn't end in *-s*, use *'s* after it.

> The men's faces were painted with white streaks.
>
> The women's hair was braided with vines and flowers.

Rule 3. Do not use an apostrophe in the plural form of a name unless the word is also showing possession. In that case, use an apostrophe after the *-s* of the plural.

> We always enjoyed seeing the Kennedys.
>
> The Kennedys' house always seemed warm and welcoming.

Rule 4. Do not use an apostrophe in possessive forms of pronouns: *yours, his, hers, its, ours,* or *theirs.*

> The car was missing one of its rear hubcaps.
>
> Because our car was being repaired, our friends let us use theirs.

ACTIVITY 26: Use Apostrophes to Show Possession

In each of the following sentences, add any missing apostrophes. If the sentence is not missing any apostrophes, write "correct" in the space provided.

> EXAMPLE   The Smiths home is located in town. ____Smiths'____

1. Donalds clothes were always neatly pressed. _____

2. The three professors worksheets needed to be photocopied. _____

3. The womans umbrella refused to open, but the rain came down steadily. _____

4. This couch is ours. _____

5. Seth Wilsons motorcycle fell over while he was in the restaurant. _____

6. Javiers favorite movie is *New Jack City*. _____

7. The Smiths always spend holidays together. _____

8. The Georges favorite holiday is Labor Day. _____

9. Jennys wedding will be on Labor Day weekend. _____

10. The Varelas and Fraires will be at the wedding. _____

ACTIVITY 27: Write Sentences with Apostrophes That Show Possession

Each of the following words has an apostrophe that shows possession. Use each word correctly in a sentence of your own.

> EXAMPLE driver's
>
> The driver's windshield was covered with dust and squished bugs.

1. Doctor Rice's

_____

2. children's

_____

3. man's

_____

4. baseball players'

_____

5. Melissa's

_____

6. Today's

_____

7. girls'

_____

8. Brandon's

_____

9. Joneses'

_____

10. club's

_____

Rule 5. Use an apostrophe to form a contraction. A contraction is formed by combining two words into one and omitting one or more letters, with an apostrophe taking the place of the omitted letter or letters. Some college instructors prefer that you not use contractions in college writing.

It's [it is] always fun to go hunting.

I don't [do not] care if others think that my father and I shouldn't [should not] hunt.

We've [we have] always enjoyed it and wouldn't [would not] stop for anything.

ACTIVITY 28: Use Apostrophes in Contractions

In each of the following sentences, correct any contractions that have missing apostrophes.

EXAMPLE   I can't find my way home.

1. Perry doesnt think that its a good idea for his daughter to go swimming while shes getting over a cold.

2. When youre tired of shoveling snow, have some of the hot cocoa that I just made.

3. Well arrive at Yellowstone Park before sunset.

4. The Mitchells arent going to the restaurant tomorrow because they cant get a reservation for that night.

5. Because its breezy today, Ive decided to show you how to fly your new kite.

6. Dont even get me started on where theyre going.

7. Were never going to make it to the top of the hill.

8. Weve always wanted to try our hand at racquetball, but I couldnt find anyone who wanted to play.

9. She isnt my favorite, but shes my brother's favorite singer.

10. Hell never come around to your way of thinking.

ACTIVITY 29: Identify Possible Contractions

In each of the following sentences, underline the words that can be made into common contractions. Then write the contractions in the space provided.

EXAMPLE   It does not matter if he is ready to take the test. <u>doesn't, he's</u>

1. Although it is against the rules, we are going to allow you to photo-graph the science exhibit for your school newspaper. _____

2. Greg and Celine are not sure if the bridge is safe because they cannot see very far ahead through this thick mist. _____

3. The Hendersons hope that they will stay with us. _____

4. After you are finished with the weight bench, please wipe it down with the towel. _____

5. Sidra and Darrell do not realize that it is easier to replace the toner in the copy machine before it warms up. _____

6. There is never enough bread in your house. _____

7. Who is going to the movies with me? _____

8. I would rather not have to take the dog's toy away. _____

9. You should not recommend that restaurant to someone if you would not eat there yourself. _____

10. It is hard to talk with Dylan because he does not seem to listen to what I say. _____

ACTIVITY 30: Use Apostrophes Correctly

Each of the following sentences contains apostrophe errors. Add apostrophes where necessary to correct those errors.

EXAMPLE   I went with the Joneses to their summer cabin. They're

really lucky to have such a place.

1. If I could earn my employers trust, Id be able to do more to improve her business.

2. If hed accept that Jenny isnt interested in him, Isaac would notice the other attractive women in his life.

3. After were finished with the days chores, we can go to the beach.

4. Because Colin still had Raquels car, she wasnt able to join us at the club.

5. Misty couldnt admit to the professor that she hadnt written the research paper herself.

ACTIVITY 31: Use Apostrophes Correctly in a Paragraph

The following paragraph contains several apostrophe errors. Add apostrophes where necessary to correct those errors.

EXAMPLE   It isn̓t always pleasant for my son, Donnie, and me to visit my mother on Sundays.

Donnie doesnt like dressing up, and Mom wont let him accompany her to church unless he wears slacks, a long-sleeved shirt, and a tie. Long before the ministers sermon, hes squirming in the pew and pulling at his collar. His grandmothers stern glances certainly dont help the situation. After church, she ignores her grandsons request to go out for hamburgers. My moms idea of a perfect Sunday lunch is a nice plate of liver and onions, which even I cant eat without a lot of ketchup. Mom believes that its childrens duty to obey their elders. As Donnies father, I believe that its an adults responsibility to make obedience fun and easy.

 Exercise Central
For additional practice with using apostrophes, go to **bedford stmartins.com/choices** and click on "Exercise Central."

F. QUOTATION MARKS

Quotation marks (" ") are used to enclose the exact words of a speaker or writer and the titles of essays, articles, poems, songs, and other short works.

Rule 1.   Use quotation marks to set off a speaker's or a writer's exact words.

"I can't believe I said that!" Joshua exclaimed.
"I don't know what you were thinking," I replied, "when you said that."

According to my textbook author, "We often say things we don't mean when we're stressed."

As these examples show, a period or a comma always goes before closing quotation marks. A question mark or an exclamation mark, on the other hand, sometimes goes before the quotation marks and sometimes after them. It goes before the quotation marks if the quotation itself is a question or an exclamation, as in the first example on the bottom of the previous page. It goes after the quotation marks if your sentence is a question or an exclamation but the quotation itself isn't, as in the following example:

When did people begin to say "Have a nice day"?

Do not use quotation marks around an *indirect quotation* — one that doesn't use the speaker's or writer's exact words. An indirect quotation is usually introduced with *that:*

Henry said that he had always wanted to study medicine.

ACTIVITY 32: Use Quotation Marks to Show Exact Words

In the following sentences, place quotation marks around each occurrence of a speaker's or writer's exact words.

EXAMPLE "That was my favorite blouse," she said to her roommate.

1. How was the play? my professor asked the class.

2. You should get more exercise, the doctor said.

3. I'll take popcorn and a soda, I said to the clerk.

4. My aunt always says, A bird in the hand is worth two in the bush.

5. Guess what? she said. I'm pregnant.

6. Kim thought, You should have told me that the dog would bite!

7. Harold shouted, Let's play ball!

8. Even though I didn't want to go, my brother said, Give it a try; you'll have a great time.

9. The officer stated the obvious: Don't drink and drive.

10. How did you respond when he said, Forget about it?

Rule 2. Use quotation marks to enclose the titles of articles, essays, book chapters, speeches, poems, short stories, and songs.

I especially enjoy the newspaper column "Our Views."

My last essay was entitled "Dia de los Muertos."

Emily Dickinson wrote the poem "I Dwell in Possibilities."

Sandra Cisneros wrote my favorite short story: "House on Mango Street."

When we go caroling, we always sing "Deck the Halls."

Use italics or underlining, not quotation marks, for the titles of longer works such as books, newspapers, and magazines.

ACTIVITY 33: Use Quotation Marks to Enclose Titles

In the following sentences, place quotation marks around the title of each short work. Some sentences do not require any quotation marks.

EXAMPLE   Martin Luther King's "I Have a Dream" speech is often heard in history classes.

1. Her essay, Women in the Military, was a hit with the ROTC cadets.

2. Vivek's favorite column is My Turn.

3. I'm currently reading the novel *Best Friends* by Martha Moody.

4. I bought *People* magazine to read the article Jen and Ben Break Up.

5. Edgar Allan Poe's poem The Raven is usually assigned in American literature courses.

6. In this textbook, Bruce read the chapter titled Marketing Genius.

7. Shailendra never left home without reading her daily horoscope in *USA Today*.

8. Hugo wrote an essay titled Get the Most out of College While Jogging.

9. Eminem's Lose Yourself is an extremely popular song.

10. The short story Hills Like White Elephants is written almost entirely in dialogue.

ACTIVITY 34: Use Quotation Marks Correctly

In each of the following sentences, insert quotation marks as necessary.

EXAMPLE   My favorite essay this term was "Giving It My All."

1. Dencil said, Ms. Levin will be sorry that she missed you.

2. Yes, Aunt Lydia agreed, the autumn leaves were prettier last year.

3. Why do you always wear purple clothing? asked Josh.

4. Angela recited Walt Whitman's poem A Noiseless Patient Spider at her eighth-grade graduation ceremony.

5. After we read the essay Shooting an Elephant by George Orwell, our class had an interesting discussion.

ACTIVITY 35: Revise for Quotation Marks

In the following paragraph, insert quotation marks as necessary.

EXAMPLE   I recited John Gould Fletcher's poem "The Groundswell" for the challenge of mastering the difficult pronunciation.

     In my speech class last fall, we began the semester by reciting short creative works to practice using our voices well. Choose anything you like, Professor Keroes told us, but make it sound like natural speech. I enjoyed the variety presented by my classmates. Two students performed the husband and wife in the poem The Death of the Hired Man by Robert Frost. Three classmates took turns telling Shirley Jackson's short story The Lottery. Many students chose songs. Alan did a great job reciting Daysleeper by R.E.M. Professor Keroes seemed pleased. I wish I had a copy of everything to read for fun, he said.

Exercise Central

For additional practice with using quotation marks, go to **bedfordstmartins.com/choices** and click on "Exercise Central."

CHAPTER

22

Improving Mechanics

Just as with punctuation, the correct use of the mechanics of writing — elements like capital letters, italics, numbers, and abbreviations — helps your reader understand your meaning. This chapter focuses on the correct use of these elements.

A. CAPITAL LETTERS

Rule 1. Capitalize proper nouns: nouns that refer to a specific person, place, event, or thing. Do not capitalize common nouns: nouns that refer to a general category of persons, places, events, or things.

Proper Noun	*Common Noun*
Ball State University	a university
Costa Rica	a country
Thursday	a day
Dad (used as a name)	my dad
President Bush	a president
Professor Lee	a professor
God	a god
the North	north of the city
Bill of Rights	amendments
Political Science 102	a political science class

Rule 2. Capitalize the names of organizations, institutions, and trademarks.

My father belongs to the Order of the Elks.

I always vote for the Independent Party candidate.

My next computer will be a Dell.

ACTIVITY 1: Correct Errors in Capitalization

Correct the errors in capitalization in each of the following sentences.

EXAMPLE   Have you read the book *the four agreements*?
                                    T   F   A

1. Gabriel has wanted to be a green beret since he was a little boy.

2. Pearl dreams of owning a lexus.

3. Rita's family goes to extremes when they decorate their house for halloween.

4. Among the police officers who helped me after my backpack was stolen, officer franklin was the most sympathetic.

5. Avner's Uncle is a transit worker in new york city.

6. At one time, president's day was two separate holidays, lincoln's birthday and washington's birthday.

7. There are better things for you to do than sit around watching soap operas and eating doritos.

8. Alfredo's Mother wants us to join her at the opera.

9. I rode the elevator to the top of the empire state building, but I took the stairs back down.

10. Is Deanna from kansas city, kansas, or kansas city, missouri?

ACTIVITY 2: Use Correct Capitalization in a Paragraph

Correct the errors in capitalization in the following paragraph.

EXAMPLE On ͭhursday night after our ͭhanksgiving dinner, the family was sitting around.

aunt edna, who teaches geography at middlefield junior high school, proposed a contest. The losers would have to clean up. We divided into teams to see who could name the most states of the united states. My team included my youngest cousins and uncle raymond, who always falls asleep after a meal, so we only had thirty-two states. The best team, which had both grandpa and aunt edna, named only forty-five, and all the teams together couldn't name every one. While little tracy insisted that mexico

was a state, everyone forgot delaware. aunt edna said that we were
all losers and distributed reese's pieces as a consolation prize. Then
we all did the dishes together.

Rule 3.   Capitalize all words in titles except articles (*a, an, the*),
coordinating conjunctions (*for, and, nor, but, or, yet, so*), and prepositions (*of, on, in, at, with, for*), unless they are the first or last word in
the title. Do not capitalize *the* before the names of newspapers.

> *For Whom the Bell Tolls*
> *Law and Order*
> *The Art of Possibility*
> the *Washington Post*

ACTIVITY 3: Capitalize Titles

Correct the errors in capitalization in each of the following sentences.

EXAMPLE   Students from Westwood Community College sold Walnuts
and Pecans before Thanksgiving.

1. Because we have pets, my children enjoyed the movie *Cats
   And Dogs*.

2. Fran was surprised to learn that *Gone With The Wind* was a book
   before it was a film.

3. Because of the clever robotic toys that she invented, Meredith was interviewed by a reporter from the *Christian science
   monitor*.

4. At my high school, a history teacher and an English teacher both
   discussed *a tale of two cities* during the same two weeks.

5. When I was a child, my favorite album was *Peter And The Wolf*.

6. My favorite teacher recommended that I read *the House of the
   seven Gables* by Nathaniel Hawthorne.

7. Naturally, the only holiday song that my grumpy sister likes is
   Elvis's "blue Christmas."

8. Harlan dreams of winning a lot of money by appearing on *American idol.*

9. Chrissie always has the latest issue of *reader's digest* on her coffee table.

10. I had to reserve my niece's copy of *Harry Potter and the order of the Phoenix* before it arrived at the bookstore.

ACTIVITY 4: Capitalize Titles in a Paragraph

Correct the errors in capitalization in the following paragraph.

EXAMPLE   During $\overset{S}{\text{study}}$ $\overset{S}{\text{skills}}$ 101, $\overset{P}{\text{professor}}$ Weston used the materials we had with us to demonstrate how readers use different techniques.

My instructor compared the *Campus sun* and the *New York times* to show that not even two newspapers should be read the same way. *Portrait Of The Artist As A Young Man* is a difficult book that should be read slowly because the sound of the words helps the meaning. The textbook *physics* also should be read slowly; its vocabulary is difficult, but the sound of these words adds little to their meaning. Both *Applications in electrical engineering* and *Western Architecture* have diagrams, but for different reasons. A student is not expected to construct a church from the floor plan in a textbook!

Exercise Central

For additional practice with using capitalization, go to **bedfordstmartins.com/choices** and click on "Exercise Central."

B. ITALICS

Italicize (or underline in handwritten or typewritten copy) the titles of books, magazines, movies, television shows, newspapers, journals, computer software, and longer musical works, such as compact disks. Do not italicize (or capitalize) *the* before the title of a newspaper.

I read *The Scarlet Letter* in my American literature class.

People magazine is always interesting to read while you're waiting for the doctor.

Matrix Reloaded is exciting to watch.

I'm glad to see *Project Runway* doing so well in the ratings.

A copy of the *New York Times* is delivered to my door daily.

I have seen copies of the journal *College English* in my instructor's office.

Windows XP works well on Jerry's computer.

Tequila Sunrise by Santana is a departure from his past music.

ACTIVITY 5: Use Italics Correctly

Use underlining to indicate where italics are needed in each of the following sentences.

EXAMPLE   How to Lose a Guy in Ten Days was a funny movie.

1. The first novel that I ever read was Treasure Island by Robert Louis Stevenson.

2. When Uriel and Shayna got married, they received a subscription to National Geographic magazine.

3. Every spring the family gathers around the television to watch our favorite movie, The Wizard of Oz.

4. Brendan has every episode of the original Star Trek series on video.

5. Penny reads the Wall Street Journal and the New York Times every day.

ACTIVITY 6: Use Italics Correctly in a Paragraph

In the following paragraph, underline to indicate where italics should be used.

EXAMPLE   The reference librarians were happy to receive Professor
David's complete <u>Oxford English Dictionary</u>.

When Professor David retired, he donated much of his large
personal library to the university. For thirty years, he had sub-
scribed to the Classics Journal. His copies filled a gap in the library's
collection. He also donated extra copies of books that were important to his career, including the Iliad and the Odyssey, both trans-
lated by Richmond Lattimore. Friends of the professor say that his
collection of vinyl jazz records is equally impressive. His copy of the
album Kind of Blue, autographed by Miles Davis, is very valuable.

Exercise Central
For additional practice with using italics, go to **bedford
stmartins.com/choices** and click on "Exercise Central."

C. ABBREVIATIONS

An *abbreviation* is a shortened version of a word or phrase.

Rule 1.   Use standard abbreviations for titles before or after proper
names.

Dr. Charles Elerick
Ms. Nancy Chin
Peggy Sullivan, D.D.S.
William Smith Jr.

Rule 2.   Use abbreviations for the names of organizations, corporations, and societies. The first time you use the name in a piece of writing, spell out the name and give the abbreviation in parentheses after
it. If you mention the name again, you may use just the abbreviation.

National Broadcasting System (NBC)
International Business Machines (IBM)
Young Men's Christian Association (YMCA)

Rule 3.   Use abbreviations for specialized terms. If the term is unfamiliar to your readers, spell it out the first time you use it.

> videocassette recorder (VCR)
> random access memory (RAM)
> extrasensory perception (ESP)

ACTIVITY 7: Use Common Abbreviations

In each of the following sentences, underline the words that could be written as abbreviations. Write the abbreviation in the space provided.

EXAMPLE   My favorite news station is <u>Cable News Network</u>. _CNN_

1. Doctor Koster is always very busy late in the afternoon. _____

2. The headquarters of the United Nations is in New York City. _____

3. The stores sold out of U2's latest compact disk before noon. _____

4. Many people observe the birthday of Martin Luther King Junior by going to church. _____

5. Don't forget to program the videocassette recorder before we leave for the game. _____

Exercise Central
For additional practice with using abbreviations, go to **bedford stmartins.com/choices** and click on "Exercise Central."

D. NUMBERS

When to spell out numbers and when to use numerals can be confusing. In general, spell out numbers from one through ninety-nine, numbers expressed in two words (two hundred, three thousand), or numbers that begin a sentence. Use numerals for all other numbers, including decimals, percentages, page numbers, years, and time of day.

> Justin borrowed thirty-two diskettes from Casey.
> Casey had offered 150 from his personal supply.
> One hundred fifty diskettes seemed like a lot to keep on hand.

The diskettes measure 3.25 inches.

Justin needed diskettes for 50 percent of his classes.

His computer science professor asked the students to turn to page 48 in the text.

Justin's class was at 7:00 p.m.

ACTIVITY 8: Use Numbers Correctly

Using the preceding guidelines, underline the correct form in each of the following sentences.

EXAMPLE   Page (thirteen/<u>13</u>) contains all of the information you need.

1. (One hundred/100) winners were selected at random.

2. Students who are in the top (10 percent/ten percent) of their graduating class in high school are guaranteed a place at state universities.

3. (3 out of 4/Three out of four) people who take the motivational training say that they notice significant benefits.

4. Becky intends to have (6/six) children.

5. Roger bought a bottle of (50/fifty) aspirin for his desk drawer at work.

ACTIVITY 9: Decide How to Write Numbers

Complete each of the following sentences, spelling out a number or writing a numeral as necessary.

EXAMPLE   Bookings of international flights are down ____40____ percent.

1. There are approximately _____ people in my smallest class.

2. When I was a child, _____ people lived with me.

3. I own _____ pairs of shoes.

4. Where I live, the sales tax is _____ percent.

5. I plan to graduate in _____ semesters.

Exercise Central

For additional practice with using numbers, go to **bedford stmartins.com/choices** and click on "Exercise Central."

CHAPTER 23

Guide for Multilingual Writers

A. ARTICLES

English has three articles: *the, a,* and *an. The* is the *definite article; a* and *an* are *indefinite articles.*

All three of these articles appear before the noun they refer to. If the noun is preceded by one or more adjectives, the article comes before the adjectives.

- *The* is used with nouns that refer to one or more specific things.

  I love *the* beautiful Victorian house. [Here *the* is referring to a specific house.]

  I love beautiful Victorian houses. [No house in particular is being referred to.]

  The roses bloom in May. [Particular roses are indicated.]

  Roses bloom in May. [Roses in general bloom in May.]

- In many cases, *the* refers to a noun that has been mentioned before.

  In buying a *car,* Chon focused mainly on appearance.

  The car he purchased looked sleek and sporty.

- *A* and *an* are used with nouns that refer to things not specifically known to the reader, perhaps because they haven't been mentioned before.

  A bird swooped out of the sky. [The reader has no prior knowledge of the bird.]

  A factory can create both jobs and pollution. [No factory in particular is being mentioned.]

  A day in the sun would do me good. [This article refers to some day in the sun but not to a specific day.]

- *A* and *an* are used only with singular count nouns. Count nouns name things that can be counted, such as *book* or *cat.* They have plural as well as singular forms: *books, cats. The* is used with both singular and plural count nouns and also with noncount nouns. Noncount nouns name things that can't be counted, such as *information, homework,* or *advice.*

- *A* comes before words that begin with consonant sounds (such as *b, c, d, f, g*). Notice that even though the letter *u* is a vowel, *a* is used before some words beginning with *u,* in which the *u* is pronounced with a *y* sound before it.

  a book   a hat   a cat   a movie   a speech

  My husband said he will never wear *a* tie again.
  I plan to buy *a* uniform at the store.

- *An* comes before words that begin with vowel sounds (*a, e, i, o, u*) to make them easier to pronounce. Notice that even though the letter *h* is a consonant, *an* is used before some words beginning with *h,* in which the *h* is silent (not pronounced).

  an effort   an honor   an illness   an opera   an umbrella

  An elephant is an interesting animal to watch.
  An umbrella would have been useful today.

ACTIVITY 1: Add Missing Articles

In each of the following sentences, add the missing articles.

EXAMPLE ~~First~~ concert of the season is always held first week in
          The first   the
          September.

1. I found wallet and key chain; wallet was leather, and key chain was brass.

2. On plane flight to Chicago, Ramon met old friend.

3. Only way to succeed as writer is to write and learn from your mistakes.

4. When she tripped over rock, Penny tore jeans that she had bought yesterday.

5. When you finish with stationary bicycle, please let Howard use it.

6. Please come to our party on first Saturday of April.

7. Spices in bottles on shelf are too old to use.

8. Campground near beach is best place for us to spend night.

9. After hour, Yesenia decided to leave house and go to movie.

10. Sandor bought T-shirt and decal for his car at only bookstore on campus.

ACTIVITY 2: Add Missing Articles in a Paragraph

Revise the following paragraph to include the missing articles.

EXAMPLE   Cynthia completed her homework for *the* last day of class.

Beryl is specialist in textiles. She can tell difference between handmade and machine-made lace and knows names of different kinds of lace. Mostly she works with antique rugs, because purchase of rug is big investment. When investor wants to buy rug, he or she consults Beryl. Beryl will tell buyer if rug was made from natural or synthetic fibers. She also can tell whether dyes used in rug were natural or synthetic. These factors determine true value of rug. She has prevented many people from making big mistake.

Exercise Central
For additional practice with using articles, go to **bedford stmartins.com/choices** and click on "Exercise Central."

B. COUNT AND NONCOUNT NOUNS

As mentioned earlier, *count nouns* can be singular or plural: *computer* or *computers*. *Noncount* (or *mass*) nouns usually can only be singular, even though their meaning may be plural. Here are some noncount nouns:

advice	mail	information	homework
equipment	education	knowledge	evidence

furniture	vocabulary	justice	poverty
anger	honesty	courage	employment

- Don't use indefinite articles (*a* and *an*) with noncount nouns.

  INCORRECT   Her mother gave Molly an advice about her boyfriend.
  CORRECT   Her mother gave Molly advice about her boyfriend.

- Noncount nouns can't be made plural, so don't add *s* or *es* at the end.

  INCORRECT   I need to buy furnitures for my apartment.
  CORRECT   I need to buy furniture for my apartment.

- To express a quantity for a noncount noun, use *some, any,* or *more.*

  CORRECT   Her mother gave Molly some advice about her boyfriend.
  CORRECT   I need to buy more furniture for my apartment.

ACTIVITY 3: Use Count and Noncount Nouns Correctly

Revise each of the following sentences in which there is an error in the use of count and noncount nouns. If a sentence is correct, write "correct" in the space provided.

EXAMPLE   Cynthia completed her homeworks a few minutes before

class started. _____

1. All four of my grandparents experienced poverties when they were young. _____

2. Too much knowledges can be a dangerous thing. _____

3. My roommate showed more courage than I did by confronting the burglar in the kitchen. _____

4. I will buy furnitures after I move into my new apartment. _____

5. My mails arrived every day by 3:00. _____

6. I learned some vocabularies by keeping a list of words and their definitions. _____

7. My professor lets me use an equipment in the lab. _____

8. You will need more evidence to prove your hypothesis. _____

9. I gained so much informations just by reading the book about economics. _____

10. Martin Luther King Jr. fought for civil rights and a justice for African Americans. _____

Exercise Central
For additional practice with using count and noncount nouns, go to **bedfordstmartins.com/choices** and click on "Exercise Central."

C. PREPOSITIONS

To learn more about prepositions, turn to pp. 482–87.

Prepositions always begin a *prepositional phrase* — that is, a phrase that includes a preposition and its object.

at her dinner   in her office   on his folder

In English, the most common prepositions are *in, on,* and *at.*

- *In* indicates an enclosed area; a geographical area such as a city, state, or country; or a period of time, such as a month, a year, a season, or part of a day.

in a box	in the car	in the fall
in England	in the classroom	in 2002
in June	in the evening	in winter
in Chicago	in Texas	in the 1990s

In New Mexico, you can find Pueblo pottery in Santa Fe.
He wanted to get the book that was in the math lab.
In 2009, I will graduate from college.
I hoped to take a short trip in June.

- *On* indicates the top of something, a street or road, a day of the week, or a specific date.

You'll find the envelope on the table.
I prefer to live on a mountain.
Harriet lives on Memorial Drive.

Let's go to a movie on Friday night.

I'll start my new job on September 18.

- *At* indicates a specific address or location or a specific time.

    I live at 100 Main Street.

    You'll find the snowshoes at the Army-Navy Store.

    I'll meet you at your favorite restaurant.

    I'll see you at 7:30 p.m.

    At midnight, Cinderella turned into a pumpkin.

ACTIVITY 4: Use *in, on,* and *at* in Sentences

Fill in the blanks in each of the following sentences, using *in, on,* and *at* correctly.

> EXAMPLE   I arrived __at__ the party a few minutes early.

1. Calvin is always ready to leave the house _____ 7:15 a.m.

2. Professor Chen's office is _____ the Physical Sciences building.

3. Please don't leave your shopping bags _____ the floor.

4. There is a telephone _____ the kitchen.

5. We live _____ an apartment but are looking for a house to buy.

6. Elliot is paid _____ the first and fifteenth of the month.

7. Your lunch break is _____ 1:00.

8. The ice cream bars are _____ the freezer _____ the top shelf.

9. Geneva will leave for Padre Island _____ June 5.

10. Like Easter, Passover is celebrated _____ the spring.

ACTIVITY 5: Use *in, on,* and *at* in a Paragraph

Fill in the blanks in the following paragraph, using *in, on,* and *at* correctly.

> EXAMPLE   I first met Mireille __at__ the university.

Last summer, I visited my friend, Mireille, who lives _____

Québec City. She and I met _____ Toronto two years ago. I arrived

_____ Jean LeSage Airport _____ June 3 _____ 3:30 the afternoon.

That evening, she took me to dinner _____ a bistro _____ the Old City. The moonlight sparkled _____ the surface of the Saint Lawrence River. I stayed with Mireille for five days. While I was there, we made plans to see each other again _____ the fall. We plan to stay _____ a small hotel _____ Victoria.

Besides *in, on,* and *at,* the most common prepositions for showing time are *for, during,* and *since.*

- *For* usually refers to an exact period of time that something lasts, a period that has a beginning and an end.

  I went into the army for six years.
  It has been snowing for two hours.
  I've been jogging for three weeks.

- *During* usually refers to an indefinite period of time in which something happens.

  Several times during the hike, I stopped to catch my breath.
  I plan to climb Mount Everest sometime during the summer.
  It hailed during the night.

- *Since* usually refers to a period of time that has passed between an earlier time and the present.

  I've gained weight since the holidays.
  Since last spring, Nicola has been working at the zoo.
  Pete's been so happy since quitting smoking.

ACTIVITY 6: Use *for, during,* and *since* in Sentences

Fill in the blanks in each of the following sentences, using either *for, during,* or *since* correctly.

EXAMPLE   I visited my mother ___during___ spring break.

1. Madeline has been a vegetarian _____ thirteen years.

2. _____ he turned eighteen, Trent has been living on his own.

3. The telephone rang _____ dinner.

4. I haven't seen Benny _____ three weeks.

5. Advertisers make special commercials to show _____ the Super Bowl.

6. After taking the pills, you should not eat _____ two hours.

7. The air conditioner runs nonstop _____ the hottest weeks of summer.

8. Somebody in the audience started coughing _____ the performance.

9. Caronne has been feeling sick _____ last night.

10. Mr. Jensen will be out of town _____ five days.

ACTIVITY 7: Use *for, during,* and *since* in a Paragraph

Fill in the blanks in the following paragraph, using either *for, during,* or *since* correctly.

EXAMPLE   Karate has been popular in the United States __for__ many

years.

Anthony has been practicing karate _____ seven years,

_____ he was twelve years old. _____ the school year, he

trains three days a week, and _____ vacations, he trains nearly

every day. He intends to practice this martial art _____ the rest

of his life.

Exercise Central
For additional practice with using prepositions, go to **bedford stmartins.com/choices** and click on "Exercise Central."

D. OMITTED OR REPEATED SUBJECTS

In English, every sentence has a subject and a verb. The *subject* tells who or what is doing the action; the *verb* expresses an action or a state of being.

For more help with subjects, turn to pp. 481–87.

Omitted Subjects

The subject of a sentence must be stated, even when the meaning of the sentence is clear without its being stated.

INCORRECT	Want to get my degree in mechanical engineering.
CORRECT	*I* want to get my degree in mechanical engineering.
INCORRECT	My sister loves to read. Goes to the library twice a week.
CORRECT	My sister loves to read. *She* goes to the library twice a week.

A dependent clause is sometimes called a subordinate clause. *To learn more about subordinate clauses, turn to pp. 509–10.*

The subject of a dependent clause must also be stated. A *dependent clause* contains a subject and verb but can't stand alone as a sentence because it begins with a subordinating conjunction (such as *because* or *although*) or a relative pronoun (such as *who, that,* or *which*).

INCORRECT	I already knew that wanted to major in math.
CORRECT	I already knew that *I* wanted to major in math.
INCORRECT	I threw the package away because was empty.
CORRECT	I threw the package away because *it* was empty.

English sentences and dependent clauses often begin with the word *it* or *there* followed by a form of *be,* as in *it is, there is,* and *there were.* In such a sentence or clause, the *it* or *there* acts as a kind of subject and can't be omitted.

INCORRECT	Is too late to hand in the paper.
CORRECT	It is too late to hand in the paper.
INCORRECT	Are three bottles on the shelf.
CORRECT	There are three bottles on the shelf.

ACTIVITY 8: Add Missing Subjects to a Paragraph

Using the preceding guidelines, add a subject in each place where one is missing in the following paragraph.

EXAMPLE   There are
~~Are~~ several different kinds of friends.
       ^

Every Friday evening, a group of us meet at a café. Enjoy the time we spend together. Formerly, we went to bars. Then my friend Cassie developed a problem with alcohol because was going to bars too often. We decided to stop drinking as a group. Is still fun sometimes to go to clubs to dance and to meet new people. Is a strange connection between dancing and alcohol.

Repeated Subjects

Be careful not to repeat a subject that has already been stated earlier in the sentence.

INCORRECT   The lady in the store *she* was rude.

CORRECT   The lady in the store was rude. [The pronoun *she* repeats the subject *lady.*]

INCORRECT   Some people *they* like to go to parties.

CORRECT   Some people like to go to parties. [The pronoun *they* repeats the subject *people.*]

ACTIVITY 9: Identify Repeated Subjects

Draw a line through the repeated subjects in the following paragraph.

EXAMPLE   The people in the class ~~they~~ decided to postpone the test.

The members of my fraternity we decided to give holiday presents to children in local hospitals. Cliff and Rodney, who suggested the project in the first place, they contacted businesses for contributions. Andre, whose family owns a discount store, he was able to purchase toys at wholesale prices. Several members with trucks and vans they delivered the gifts to hospitals. All of us who worked on this charitable project we enjoyed watching the children open their presents.

Exercise Central

For additional practice with using subjects, go to **bedford stmartins.com/choices** and click on "Exercise Central."

E. WORD ORDER

In English, the basic word order of a sentence is *subject, verb, object*.

<small>S</small> <small>V</small> <small>O</small>
Jordan ironed the dress.

Adjectives and adverbs are placed close to the words they modify.

<small>S</small> <small>V</small> <small>O</small>
Jordan quickly ironed the blue dress.

Adjective Placement

In English, adjectives almost always come before the noun they modify.

See pp. 518–20 for more information about adjectives.

An *important* thing to remember is to stop at stop signs.

George prepared to take the *difficult* test.

Ulie bought the *red* motorcycle.

In addition, different kinds of adjectives appear in a particular order. Though exceptions exist, this order is usually followed:

Articles and pronouns: *a, an, the, my, your*
Words that evaluate: *ugly, handsome, honest, appealing, flavorful*
Words about size: *big, small, large*
Words about length or shape: *small, big, round, square, wide, narrow*
Words about age: *old, young, new*
Words about color: *red, blue, yellow*
Words about nationality: *Irish, Mexican, Canadian, Chinese*
Words about religion: *Muslim, Buddhist, Protestant, Jewish*
Words about the material of the noun: *wooden, glass, brick, adobe, stucco*
Nouns used as adjectives: *bathroom floor, track team*

Finally, the noun goes last: *book, car, movie, church, bench, computer.*

The handsome old house sat at the top of the hill.
My German Catholic grandmother died last year.
The square wooden jewelry box sat on the table.

HOW TO Determine Whether to Use Commas between Adjectives

How do you decide whether you need a comma between two or more adjectives? If you can place *and* between the adjectives and the sentence still makes sense, then you need the comma.

Suppose you want to write this:

The tall fragile rosebush was blooming.

A comma is needed between *tall* and *fragile* because "the tall *and* fragile rosebush" makes sense.

The tall, fragile rosebush was blooming.

ACTIVITY 10: Revise Sentences to Use Adjectives Correctly

Revise each of the following sentences so that the adjectives are placed correctly and commas are used between them where necessary.

EXAMPLE   Please hand me the brown ~~big~~ box.
          _{big}

1. We bought the leather sofa most comfortable.

2. Curtis promised to throw out his plaid old pajamas.

3. The dark Belgian delicious chocolates were a gift.

4. A spotted big snake crawled under the house.

5. The car little red fit in the parking space.

6. After the movie, Marisol remembered her assignment boring and difficult.

7. I gave the cheerful friendly child a cookie.

8. His leather black beautiful jacket was ruined.

9. We admired the aluminum elegant animal sculptures.

10. My grandmother recited a Jewish short prayer over the candles.

ACTIVITY 11: Add Adjectives Correctly

In each of the following sentences, add the number of adjectives indicated in parentheses in the space provided. Use commas as necessary.

EXAMPLE   A _____curved stone_____ path led to the house. (2)

1. I wanted a _____ car. (2)

2. Smoking is a _____ habit. (2)

3. The sight of the _____ tacos made my mouth water. (3)

4. Linda wanted to take one of the _____ puppies home with her. (2)

5. The _____ sweater fit Ivan perfectly. (2)

6. Whenever Kevin wanted to quit school, he remembered his _____ parents back home. (2)

7. To be accepted into the program, I had to pass a _____ exam. (2)

8. Eunice refused to climb the _____ steps. (3)

9. Last year, I dated a _____ student. (2)

10. Our assignment was to read a chapter in our _____ textbook. (3)

Adverb Placement

For more information about adverbs, turn to pp. 520–21.

Adverbs that modify verbs can appear at the beginning or end of a sentence, before or after the verb, or between a helping verb and the main verb. Most often, the adverb appears as close as possible to the verb.

Hurriedly, we escaped out the back door.
The dog scratched *frantically* against the window.
Abner *eagerly* wrote the letter.
My brother has *often* stayed out after midnight.

Do not put an adverb between a verb and its direct object. A direct object receives the action of the verb.

INCORRECT Li put quickly the package on the table.
CORRECT   Li quickly put the package on the table.

INCORRECT The hairdresser cut carefully my hair.
CORRECT   The hairdresser carefully cut my hair.

ACTIVITY 12: Place Adverbs Correctly

Revise the following paragraph, adding at least one adverb to each sentence.

EXAMPLE Many students <u>wait</u> in long lines during late registration.
_{impatiently}

Some students complain to the people around them about the lack of classes. Other students, who had to bring their children, make sure the kids don't run around the building screaming. A few students laugh with their friends. Many students check their watches and wonder how long they can wait. Everyone wishes the lines were shorter.

Exercise Central
For additional practice with using correct word order, go to **bedfordstmartins.com/choices** and click on "Exercise Central."

F. VERBS

A *verb* expresses an action (*smile, work, hit*) or a state of being (*be, seem, become*). Depending on your language background, verbs in English can be particularly challenging to master. This section will help you correctly use verb tenses, helping verbs, and verbs followed by gerunds and infinitives.

To learn more about verbs, turn to pp. 487–97.

Verb Tense

The *tense* of a verb indicates the time in which the action or condition that the verb expresses took place. The three basic tenses in English are the *simple present, simple past,* and *simple future.* These must be distinguished from the *present perfect, past perfect, future perfect, present progressive, past progressive,* and *future progressive* tenses.

Simple Present Tense. The *simple present tense* shows an action or a condition that is taking place at the time it is mentioned. The simple present can also show an action or a condition that occurs repeatedly or one scheduled to occur in the future. Except for *be* and *have,* the simple present uses the base form of the verb (*swim, work*), with an -*s* or -*es* added if the subject is a singular noun or *he, she,* or *it.*

Jamilla *seems* depressed recently.
Pierre *studies* at least five hours a day.

I *drive* my daughter to school every weekday morning.

The new store *opens* next week.

Simple Past Tense.

For a list of common irregular verbs and their past-tense forms, see pp. 495.

The *simple past tense* indicates an action or a condition that began and ended in the past. Except for irregular verbs like *go* or *teach,* the simple past consists of the base form of the verb with *-ed* added to the end.

Yesterday I *passed* my driver's test.

When he *was* a student, he *walked* wherever he *had* to go. (The action of walking happened more than once in the past, but it's not happening now.)

Future Tense.

The *future tense* shows an action or a condition that will take place or will probably take place. The future tense requires the use of *will* or *be going to* followed by the base form of the verb.

I *will spend* next summer in Kansas City.

These economic conditions *are going to continue* indefinitely.

Present Perfect Tense.

The perfect tenses show a completed action or condition. They are formed using the past participle of the verb and the appropriate form of *have.*

The *present perfect tense* shows an action or a condition that began in the past and that either is now finished or continues into the present. Unlike with the past tense, the specific time of the action or condition is not given. To form this tense, use *has* or *have* followed by the past participle. Except for irregular verbs, the past participle consists of the base form of the verb with *-ed* added to the end.

For a list of common irregular verbs and their past participles, see p. 495.

Alex *has cooked* the dinner.

The lawyers *have argued* their case.

When the present perfect expresses an action or condition that began in the past and continues into the present, it usually is used with an expression of time beginning with *since* or *for.*

Susan *has played* the trumpet since she was a child.

(Susan has played in the past and continues to play in the present.)

They *have been* in Seattle for three years.

(They went to Seattle in the past, and they are still there.)

Past Perfect Tense.

The *past perfect tense* indicates an action or a condition occurring in the past before another time in the past. To form this tense, use *had* and the past participle of the verb.

I *had learned* the formulas by the day of the test.

They *had smelled* smoke before they saw the fire.

Future Perfect Tense.
The *future perfect tense* indicates a future action or condition that will end by or before a specific future time. To form this tense, use *will have* and the past participle of the verb.

By next Tuesday, I *will have finished* all my classes for the semester.

Heather *will have left* the office before you get there.

Present Progressive Tense.
The progressive tenses show a continuing action or condition. They are formed using the present participle (the *-ing* form of the verb) and the appropriate form of *be*.

The *present progressive tense* indicates an action that is happening at the time it is mentioned or an action that is scheduled to happen in the future. To form this tense, use *am, is,* or *are* and the *-ing* form of the verb.

Eduardo *is helping* us move the furniture.

We *are leaving* for the beach tomorrow.

Past Progressive Tense.
The *past progressive tense* shows an action or a condition that continued for some time in the past and is now over. To form this tense, use *was* or *were* and the *-ing* form of the verb.

Over the summer I *was spending* my money mostly on food.

Last night the sick man's words *were becoming* very faint.

Future Progressive Tense.
The *future progressive tense* indicates a continuing action or condition in the future. To form this tense, use *will be* and the *-ing* form of the verb.

The judge *will be hearing* your case soon.

By next week you *will be feeling* better.

ACTIVITY 13: Identify Verb Tenses

Identify the verb tense in each of the following sentences.

EXAMPLE   The cake *will be* ready tonight. _____future_____

1. Julian *has completed* all the prerequisites. _____

2. You *have wasted* the whole semester. _____

3. Before getting married, Bill and Jenny *had decided* to move to Colorado. _____

4. Last week, I *was recovering* from surgery. _____

5. The tomatoes *will be ripening* next week. _____

6. They *work* at City Hall. _____

7. *Will* Marcie *compete* in the next essay contest? _____

8. They *have taken* all morning to buy groceries. _____

9. Wayne *drank* an entire pitcher of iced tea. _____

10. Dolores *is talking* to her doctor. _____

ACTIVITY 14: Use Verb Tenses Correctly

For each of the following sentences, write the required verb tense of the verb in parentheses.

> EXAMPLE You ___had been___ (be) doing very well in that class until now. *(past perfect)*

1. I _____ (do) my best to make you happy. *(present progressive)*

2. Lillian _____ (whisper) her secret to Josie. *(past)*

3. The children _____ (play) for an hour. *(present perfect)*

4. Hans _____ (be) here tomorrow. *(future)*

5. We _____ (hire) a DJ for the party. *(future)*

6. The sales associate _____ (consult) the manager before lowering the price. *(present)*

7. The procedure _____ (work) more effectively last year. *(past progressive)*

8. Before the concert, the advertisements _____ (say) the tickets would be thirty-five dollars apiece. *(past perfect)*

9. The senator _____ (decide) to run for reelection. *(present perfect)*

10. Fred _____ (take) the children to the circus. *(present perfect)*

Helping Verbs

See p. 488 for more information about helping verbs.

A *helping verb* is a verb that is used with another verb, called the *main verb,* to create a phrase that acts as a verb in a sentence. Sometimes, such a phrase includes two or even three helping verbs in addition to the main verb. Helping verbs are used for a number of different purposes, including to form the future, the perfect, and the progressive tenses and the passive voice; to ask questions and make negative statements; and to show that something is possible or required.

Micah *has* left the room. (*Has* is the helping verb; *left* is the main verb.)

You *must* wait for the train to leave the station. (*Must* is the helping verb; *wait* is the main verb.)

I *have been* sitting here for two hours. (*Have* and *been* are the helping verbs; *sitting* is the main verb.)

Modals. Some helping verbs, known as *modals*, are used only as helping verbs:

can	might	should
could	must	will
may	shall	would

When using a modal in a sentence, use the base form of the main verb after it unless the modal is followed by another helping verb.

Luisa *might travel* to Thailand.

My sister *would sing* if she could read music.

Rupert *can carry* the suitcase.

Carlos *could have been* a better candidate.

Our chorus *may be performing* in New York next year.

Unlike other helping verbs, a modal does not change form to agree in number with the subject, and neither does the main verb that follows it.

INCORRECT	He wills leave.
INCORRECT	He will leaves.
CORRECT	He will leave.

ACTIVITY 15: Identify Modals

Circle the modals in the following paragraph.

EXAMPLE Friends (should) help each other out.

Three of my best friends are leaving town next week. Frank is

going to Los Angeles, where he will begin his career as a movie

editor. He should be able to find a job quickly. Janice is moving to

Chicago to attend medical school. She might be able to afford her own apartment, should she be able to find one. Finally, Leroy is going to New York. Because he has little money saved up, he must find a job right away.

Do, Does, Did.   Like modals, the helping verbs *do, does,* and *did* are followed by the base form of the verb. These verbs are used

- To ask a question:
  Do you want to dance?
  Did my brother pick up his suit?

- To make a negative statement (when used with *not*):
  I did not request this car.
  Sammy does not eat broccoli.

- To emphasize a main verb:
  Once again, I do appreciate the gift.
  She does look beautiful.

Unlike modals, the helping verbs *do* and *does* change in number to agree with the subject of the sentence.

> INCORRECT   He do not enjoy watching football.
> CORRECT   He does not enjoy watching football.

Have, Has, Had.   The helping verbs *have, has,* and *had* are used to indicate the perfect tenses. *Have* and *has* change form to agree in number with the subject.

> INCORRECT   They has broken all the good plates.
> CORRECT   They have broken all the good plates.

Forms of Be.   Forms of the verb *be — be, am, is, are, was, were, been —* are used as helping verbs for two purposes. Together with the present participle of the main verb, they are used to indicate the progressive tenses.

> I am taking calculus this year.
> The birds were singing in the tree near my window.

For more information about the passive voice, turn to pp. 560–62.

Together with the past participle of the main verb, forms of *be* are used to indicate the passive voice, in which the subject doesn't perform the action of the verb but receives the action. Here are some examples:

Jonathan was hit by the flying glass.

The book was written by Tom Wolfe.

Parts of the city have been closed by the chief of police.

ACTIVITY 16: Use Helping Verbs

In each of the following sentences, fill in the blank with an appropriate helping verb followed by the correct form of the verb in parentheses.

> EXAMPLE   After our argument, my brother __did not speak__ (speak)
>
> to me for two years.

1. Nobody _____ (see) Caroline for the past few weeks.

2. Barney _____ (paint) the kitchen last Saturday.

3. Until Halloween, the weather _____ (be) pleasant.

4. With this excellent progress, you _____ (convince) me that you are motivated.

5. For three years, I _____ (accept) these strict rules.

6. Until she took organic chemistry, Aunt Lucy _____ (want) to be a doctor.

7. To my surprise, Angel _____ (win) a spelling bee when he was in the fifth grade.

8. Johnny Depp _____ (act) in many unusual roles.

9. To be independent in many rural areas, you _____ (own) your own car.

10. Shawna _____ (work) at McDonald's while she takes college classes.

ACTIVITY 17: Use Helping Verbs in a Paragraph

In the following paragraph, fill in each of the blanks with an appropriate helping verb followed by the correct form of the verb in parentheses.

> EXAMPLE   Elyse __should thank__ (thank) her family for their support.

Later today, at the graduation ceremony, Elyse _____

(receive) her diploma from the university. She began her studies

at the age of forty, after she _____ (work) for many

years. Since then, she _____ (struggle) to earn her degree. Many obstacles _____ (interrupt) her education, mostly health and financial difficulties. However, nothing _____ (stop) her from reaching her goal. Indeed, she _____ (graduate) with honors. Throughout these difficult and rewarding years, her family _____ (remain) her first priority. She _____ (celebrate) tonight among her loved ones.

Verbs Followed by Gerunds or Infinitives

A *gerund* is a form of a verb that ends in -*ing* and is used as a noun.

I enjoy *walking.*
Cooking is his favorite hobby.

In contrast, an *infinitive* is the base form of a verb with the word *to* in front of it.

I decided *to stop* my car.
I went home *to wash* my clothes.

The following verbs can be followed by either a gerund or an infinitive without changing the meaning of the sentence:

begin	like
stand	love
continue	start
hate	

I started *to like* him right away.
I started *liking* him right away.

With other verbs, the meaning changes depending on whether they're followed by a gerund or an infinitive.

She stopped *smoking* cigarettes. [She gave up the habit of smoking.]
She stopped *to smoke* a cigarette. [She paused so she could light up a cigarette.]

George remembered *to buy* the gift. [George had planned to buy the gift and did so.]

George remembered *buying* the gift. [George recalled the act of purchasing the gift.]

The following verbs may be followed by a gerund but not by an infinitive:

admit	escape	quit
appreciate	finish	recall
avoid	imagine	resist
deny	miss	risk
discuss	practice	suggest
enjoy	put off	tolerate

Jonah denied *witnessing* the car accident.

My father missed *opening* the presents.

These verbs may be followed by an infinitive but not by a gerund:

agree	expect	mean	promise
ask	have	need	wait
beg	hope	offer	want
decide	manage	plan	wish

She planned *to take* the 7 a.m. flight.

Fred asked *to leave* the room.

ACTIVITY 18: Use Verbs Plus Gerunds or Infinitives Correctly

Complete each of the following sentences with the gerund or infinitive form of the verb in parentheses, whichever is correct.

EXAMPLE   Lucy enjoyed _____*seeing*_____ (see) her parents.

1. We decided _____ (take) the scenic road to the lake rather than the freeway.

2. Theodore can't stand _____ (wait) for an elevator, so he always takes the stairs.

3. April decided _____ (attend) the community college before transferring to a university.

4. Ward denied _____ (be) my secret admirer.

5. Nora practiced _____ (drive) in a parking lot before she went on the road.

6. Chester started _____ (collect) fossils when he was in high school.

7. The teens expected _____ (receive) a reward for returning the lost wallet.

8. Dorcas imagined _____ (win) the lottery.

9. Students resist _____ (use) the university library.

10. My little sister continues _____ (bother) me when my friends visit.

ACTIVITY 19: Write Sentences Using Verbs Plus Gerunds or Infinitives Correctly

Complete each of the following sentences with a gerund or an infinitive, as well as other words if necessary.

EXAMPLE   Because of her age, my daughter avoided __taking the test__.

1. Tomorrow, Richie will finish _____.

2. Whenever possible, I avoid _____.

3. My children love _____.

4. You do not need to beg _____.

5. Sheila only pretended _____.

6. A busy student certainly appreciates _____.

7. I made a New Year's resolution to quit _____.

8. I never succeed when I try _____.

9. In one hour, Maurice will start _____.

10. My parents hope _____.

Two-Part Verbs

Many verbs in English consist of two words. Here are some of the most common ones:

ask out	clean up
break down	drop in
call up	get along

give up	pick up
help out	play around
keep up	put together
leave out	shut up
make up	wake up

Be careful not to leave out the second word of such verbs.

INCORRECT   Susan picked aspirin at the drugstore.

CORRECT   Susan picked up aspirin at the drugstore.

INCORRECT   When buying gifts, James left his cousin.

CORRECT   When buying gifts, James left out his cousin.

ACTIVITY 20: Use Two-Part Verbs Correctly

For each of the following sentences, complete the two-part verb.

EXAMPLE   Let me help you clean _____up_____ the kitchen.

1. Professor Zindell wants us to drop _____ for a visit whenever we wish.

2. Please pick _____ your dirty clothes before you go to sleep.

3. The cat and dog get _____ very well.

4. Whenever I make that fruit salad, I always leave _____ the bananas.

5. Children always want to help _____ in the kitchen when they are too young to be useful.

ACTIVITY 21: Add Two-Part Verbs

Use a two-part verb to complete each of the following sentences.

EXAMPLE   Roland __called up__ his girlfriend on his cell phone.

1. Mary Alice has _____ a professional wardrobe using a few basic garments.

2. I _____ my mess so well that nobody knew that I had made one.

3. Yesterday, Jim _____ a story to amuse the neighbor's children.

4. The truck always _____ in hot weather.

5. If you do these assignments, you will be able to _____ your classmates.

Participles Used as Adjectives

The present participle and past participle of verbs that refer to feelings or senses are often used as adjectives. Such verbs include the following:

interest	excite	fascinate	charm
disappoint	bore	tire	embarrass
disturb	encourage	frighten	confuse

When the adjective refers to a person or an animal *having* the feeling, use the past participle form, the one that ends in *-ed*.

The *frightened* cat jumped on the shelf.

The student was *bored.*

The *confused* child began to cry.

When the adjective refers to a thing or person *causing* the feeling, use the present participle form, the one that ends in *-ing.*

The *frightening* movie scared the children.

The book was *boring.*

The *confusing* message was not conveyed.

INCORRECT	I was interesting in the show.
CORRECT	I was interested in the show.
INCORRECT	The story was excited.
CORRECT	The story was exciting.

ACTIVITY 22: Use Participles as Adjectives

Complete each of the following sentences with the correct participle of the verb in parentheses.

EXAMPLE   I was _encouraged_ (encourage) by the positive reviews of

my show.

1. I was _____ (fascinate) by the butterfly collection.

2. The butterfly collection was _____ (fascinate).

3. Jane, who was _____ (embarrass) by all the attention, wanted to be left alone.

4. The children's play was _____ (charm).

5. I have never seen such a _____ (disturb) collection of art-work in my life.

6. The spectators enjoyed the _____ (excite) fireworks display.

7. Frankly, I found the speech rather _____ (tire).

8. The _____ (disappoint) viewers turned off the television.

9. I am _____ (charm) to meet you.

10. When will this _____ (embarrass) display of affection end?

Exercise Central

For additional practice with using verbs, go to **bedford stmartins.com/choices** and click on "Exercise Central."

Acknowledgments

Mark Andrejevic. "'Reality' Camera Goes from Candid to Cruel." From *Reality TV: The Work of Being Watched* by Mark Andrejevic. First published in *Newsday*, July 29, 2003, p. A30, titled: "Sadistic? Yes, But Ambush TV Is Also Fresh." Copyright © 2003 Mark Andrejevic. Reprinted by permission of the author. Mark-andrejevic@uiowa.edu.

Anthony Beal. "Let the Good Times Roll." From *American Chronicle*, February 20, 2006. Original title, "Laissez Les Bon Temps Roulez [sic]: New Orleans' Head Remains Bloody but Unbowed." Copyright © 2006 Anthony Beal. Reprinted with permission of the author.

Joshua Bell. "My Maestro." Copyright © 2004 by The Reader's Digest Assn., Inc. Reprinted with permission from the April 2004 Reader's Digest.

Judy Blume. "Is Harry Potter Evil?" National Coalition against Censorship News, Winter 1999–2000. Originally printed in *The New York Times*. Reprinted by permission of the author.

Lucy Calkins. Excerpt from *The Art of Teaching Writing* by Lucy Calkins. Copyright © 1994 by Lucy Calkins. Published by Heinemann, a division of Reed Elsevier, Inc., Portsmouth, NH. Reprinted with permission of the publisher. All rights reserved.

Greg Crister. "Don't Eat the Flan." First published in *Forbes*, February 3, 2003. Reprinted by permission. Copyright © 2005 Forbes, Inc. Reprinted by permission of Forbes Magazine.

Michael Crowley. "Let's Shut Them Down." Copyright © 2005 by *The Reader's Digest*. Reprinted with permission from the March 2005 *Reader's Digest*.

John Cullane. "Oprah Winfrey: How the Truth Changed Her Life." Copyright © 1989 by The Reader's Digest Assoc., Inc. Reprinted with permission from the February 1989 *Reader's Digest*.

James Dillard. "A Doctor's Dilemma." From *Newsweek*, June 12, 1995. Copyright © 1995 Newsweek Inc. Reprinted by permission of Newsweek, Inc. and the author. All rights reserved.

Jeremy Dorn. "A Hero's Last Ride." Posted on www.SportsColumn.com, July 29, 2005. Reprinted with permission of the author: jdwc@sbcglobal.net.

Thomas L. Friedman. "My Favorite Teacher" from *The New York Times*, January 9, 2001. Copyright © 2001 by The New York Times Company, Inc. Reprinted by permission.

John Garvey. "Christo's 'Gates': An Unexpected Pleasure." Copyright © 2005 Commonweal Foundation. Reprinted with permission. For subscriptions: www.commonwealmagazine.org.

Henry Louis Gates Jr. "Samuel L. Jackson: In Character." Edited text from *America Behind the Color Line* by Henry Louis Gates Jr. Copyright © 2004 Henry Louis Gates Jr. Reprinted by permission of Warner Books, Int.

Ellen Goodman. "The Company Man." From *Value Judgments* by Ellen Goodman. Copyright © 1993 by Ellen Goodman. Reprinted by permission of International Creative Management, Inc.

Gerald Hausman. "Feather" from *Turtle Island Alphabet* by Gerald Hausman. Copyright © 1992 by Gerald Hausman. Reprinted by permission of St. Martin's Press, LLC.

Diane Helman and Phyllis Bookspan. "*Sesame Street:* Brought to You by the Letters M-A-L-E." From *The Seattle Times*, July 28, 1992. Scripps Howard News Service. Reprinted with permission.

Tamera Helms. "Lessons in Shrimping" from *The Great American Bologna Festival and Other Student Essays* by Elizabeth Rankin. Copyright © 1991 Bedford/St. Martin's. Reprinted by permission of Bedford/St. Martin's.

Mark Hertsgaard. "A Global Green Deal." First published in *Time*, April/May 2000. Reprinted with permission of the author.

Rita Warren Hess. "American Workplace Slang and Jargon." From the Web site: www.coming2american.com. Reprinted by permission of the author. Author's Web site: www.enidprofessionalwriters.org.

Ann Hodgman. "No Wonder They Call Me a Bitch." From *Spy Magazine*, 1989. Copyright © 1989, Sussex Publishers. Reprinted with permission of the author.

Nicholas Jennings. "A Palace of Rock." First published in *Maclean's*, Volume 108, September 18, 1995. Copyright © 1995. Reprinted by permission of the author.

Leander Kahney. "The Joy of iPod." From *The Cult of iPod* by Leander Kahney. Copyright © 2005 Leander Kalney. Reprinted with the permission of No Starch Press.

Nora Okja Keller. "My Mother's Food." Copyright © 1997 by Nora Okja Keller. First published in *New Woman*, September 1997. Reprinted by permission of Susan Bergholz Literary Services, New York. All rights reserved.

Perri Klass. "She's Your Basic L.O.L. in N.A.D." Originally titled "Learning the Language" from *Not an Entirely Benign Procedure* by Perri Klass. Copyright © 1987 by Perri Klass. Used by permission of G.P. Putnam's Sons, a division of Penguin Putnam, Inc.

Kevin Kling. "Hook, Line, and Television." Originally published in the *Smithsonian*, February 2006. Reprinted with the permission of the author.

Malcolm X. "Prison Studies." From *The Autobiography of Malcolm X* by Malcolm X and Alex Haley. Copyright © 1994 by Alex Haley and Malcolm X. Copyright © 1965 by Alex Haley and Betty Shabazz. Used by permission of Random House, Inc.

Patrick Moore. "Going Nuclear: A Green Makes the Case." First published in the *Washington Post*, April 16, 2006; B01. Copyright © 2006 Patrick Moore. Reprinted by permission of the author.

Cheryl Peck. "Fat Girls and Lawn Chairs." From *Fat Girls and Lawn Chairs* by Cheryl Peck. Copyright © 2002, 2004 by Cheryl Peck. Reprinted by permission of Warner Books, Inc.

Anastacia Marx de Salcedo. "Pass the Pernil, Save Room for the Tarta." First published in *The Boston Globe*, February 12, 2006. Copyright © 2006 Anastacia Marx de Salcedo. Reprinted with permission of the author.

Mary Sherry. "In Praise of the F Word." Originally published in *Newsweek*, May 6, 1991. Copyright © 1991 by Mary Sherry. Reprinted with permission of the author.

Janna Malamud Smith. "Online but Not Antisocial." From the *New York Times*, February 17, 2004, p. A19. Copyright © 2004 by The New York Times Company. Reprinted with permission.

Brent Staples. "What Adolescents Miss When We Let Them Grow Up in Cyberspace." From *The New York Times*, May 29, 2004. Copyright © 2004 by The New York Times Company. Reprinted with permission. "Black Men and Public Space." First published in *Harper's*, December 1986. From *Parallel Time* by Brent Staples. Copyright © 1994 by Brent Staples. Reprinted with permission of the author.

Donald J. Trump and Meredith McIver. "You're Hired!" From *Trump: How to Get Rich* by Donald J. Trump and Meredith McIver. Copyright © 2004 by Donald J. Trump. Used by permission of Random House, Inc.

Laura D'Andrea Tyson. "Needed: Affirmative Action for the Poor." From *Business Week*, July 7, 2003. Copyright © 2003 by The McGraw-Hill Companies, Inc. Reprinted by special permission.

"Career Profile: Science" from The Editors of www.webfeet.com. Copyright © 2002 Wetfeet.com, Inc. Reprinted with permission.

Elizabeth Whelan. "Perils of Prohibition" from *Newsweek*, May 29, 1995, pp. 14–15. Copyright © 1995 Newsweek, Inc. Reprinted by permission. All rights reserved.

Philip Zimbardo and Ann L. Weber. "Cross-Culture Perspective: Culture Shock" from *Psychology* by Philip Zimbardo and Ann L. Weber. Copyright © 1997. Published by Allyn & Bacon, Boston, MA. Copyright © 1994 by Pearson Education. Reprinted by permission of the publisher.

Photo Credits
p. 2, © Garry Conner/PhotoEdit; **p. 36**, © Esbin-Anderson/The Image Works; **p. 60**, © David Kressler/Nonstock/Jupiter Images; **p. 78**, © Richard Lord/The Image Works; **p. 126**, © Kayte M. Deioma/PhotoEdit; **p. 180**, © David Frazier/PhotoEdit; **p. 232**, © UPPA/Topham/The Image Works; **p. 241**, © Tony Iannotti; **p. 286**, © Peter Byron/PhotoEdit; **p. 336**, © Bob Daemmrich/The Image Works; **p. 386**, © Corey Rich/Outdoor Collection/Aurora; **p. 398**, © Bonnie Kamin/PhotoEdit; **p. 406**, © Spencer Grant/PhotoEdit; **p. 415**, © Courtesy of Mozilla; Courtesy Ebsco Information Services; **p. 444**, © James Marshall/The Image Works; **p. 468**, © Wang Leng/Asia Images/IPN.

Index

a, an
   and noncount nouns, 616–17
   uses of, 614–15
abbreviations, 611–12
abstracts, 415
action verbs, 487
active and passive voice, 560–61
active reading, 6
addresses, commas in, 588–89
adjectives
   participles used as, 638–39
   use of, to expand sentences, 518–20
   and word order, 624–26
adverbs
   conjunctive, 163–65, 524–26
   use of, to expand sentences, 520–21
   and word order, 626–27
"Against the Great Divide" (Jarvis), 70
agreement
   pronoun-antecedent, 216–17, 516–18
   subject-verb, 321–22
Albert, Jody, "Avoid Dryden Hall"
   discovery draft, 251–52
   edited essay, 272–74
   freewriting, 249
   revised draft, 263–65
American Association of Retired Persons Bulletin, 12
"American Workplace Slang and Jargon" (Hess), 226–28

"America's Worst Drivers" (Ecenbarger), 49
Andrejevic, Mark, "'Reality' Camera Goes from Candid to Cruel," 330–31
And the Beat Goes On: A Survey of Pop Music in America (Boeckman), 160
anecdotes, 49, 154–55
apostrophes
   in contractions, 600–601
   to show possession, 597–99
appeals, 362–64
appositives
   combining sentences using, 368–69
   commas with, 585–86
argument, 72–73, 357–61
articles, 614–16
Art of Teaching Writing, The (Calkins), 389–90
asking questions, 15, 246–48
at, use of, 619
audience, analyzing, 8–9
   Chapter 4: Explaining a Personal Change, 91
   Chapter 5: Examining a Culture, 142
   Chapter 6: Investigating a Workplace, 194
   Chapter 7: Evaluating a Subject, 243–44
   Chapter 8: Considering the Media, 299

audience, analyzing (*continued*)
  Chapter 9: Making a Difference, 348
"Avoid Dryden Hall" (Albert)
  discovery draft, 251–52
  edited essay, 272–74
  freewriting, 249
  revised draft, 263–65
Awalt, L. Christopher, "Brother, Don't Spare a Dime," 45–46

Badinter, Robert, "Death Be Not Proud," 72–73
balanced perspective, keeping a, 262
"Baseball Memories" (Ramirez)
  brainstorming, 92–93
  discovery draft, 98–99
  edited essay, 114–15
  revised draft, 106–8
be, forms of, 632–33
Beal, Anthony, "Let the Good Times Roll," 280–81
Beijing Review, "Camera Collector Cheng Jianguo," 69
Bell, Joshua, "My Maestro," 81–83
"Black Children, Black Speech" (Seymour), 24
"Black Men and Public Space" (Staples), 122–25
"Blue Magic" (Keillor), 41, 42
Blume, Judy, "Is Harry Potter Evil?", 328–29
Boeckman, Charles, *And the Beat Goes On: A Survey of Pop Music in America*, 160
bold function, 159
Bookspan, Phyllis, "Sesame Street: *Brought to you by the Letters M-A-L-E*" (with Heiman), 237–39
Bragin, Irina Hremia, "What Heroes Teach Us," 48
brainstorming, 12–13
  about a product, 245–46
  about a representation issue, 301–2
  about a significant person, 92–93
  about workplace communication, 196–97
broadening focus, 52–53, 156

"Brother, Don't Spare a Dime" (Awalt), 45–46

Calkins, Lucy, *The Art of Teaching Writing*, 389–90
"Camera Collector Cheng Jianguo" (Beijing Review), 69
capitalization
  organizations, institutions, and trademarks, 606
  proper nouns, 606
  titles, 608–9
"Career Profile: Science" (WetFeet.com), 183–84
"Case of 'Severe Bias,' A" (Rayborn), 41–42
cause-and-effect analysis
  errors in, 362
  as pattern of development, 72, 306–7
Chiang, Li, "Tollroad on the Information Superhighway"
  discovery draft, 355–456
  edited essay, 371–73
  freewriting, 352
  revised draft, 365–66
choosing a topic, 17–18
  Chapter 4: Explaining a Personal Change, 97
  Chapter 5: Examining a Culture, 147–48
  Chapter 6: Investigating a Workplace, 198–99
  Chapter 7: Evaluating a Subject, 249–50
  Chapter 8: Considering the Media, 303–4
  Chapter 9: Making a Difference, 354–55
"Christo's *Gates*: An Unexpected Pleasure" (Garvey), 240–42
chronological order, 64–65
Chu, Kathy, "Helping Children Heal"
  discovery draft, 200
  edited essay, 219–20
  outline, 205–6
  revised draft, 210–12
claims, 308–9
Clark, Mary Higgins, *While My Pretty One Sleeps*, 6

classification
  in introductions, 50
  as pattern of development, 68–69,
    201–3
clauses
  commas with, 585–86
  dependent (subordinate):
    expanding sentences with,
    509–11; as sentence fragments,
    166–67, 542–43
  independent: expanding
    sentences with, 508–9;
    semicolons with, 592
  relative: combining sentences
    with, 267–69; expanding
    sentences with, 511–12
clustering, 14
  about a cultural symbol, 143–44
  about an important period,
    95–96
Collins, Scott, "*Idol's* Fifth-Season
    Opener Its Biggest Yet," 10
colons, 594–95
color feature, 104, 208
combining sentences
  using appositives, 368–69
  using coordination: conjunctive
    adverbs, 524–26; coordinating
    conjunctions, 522–24
  using introductory phrases,
    320–21
  using subordination: relative
    pronouns, 267–69, 528–30;
    subordinating conjunctions,
    213–15, 526–28
commas
  in addresses and place names,
    588–89
  with coordinating conjunctions,
    522–24, 584–85
  in dates, 588
  with descriptive words, phrases,
    and clauses and appositives,
    585–86
  with dialogue and direct
    quotations, 589–91
  with introductory words, phrases,
    clauses, 581–82
  in relative clauses, 267–68, 529
  in series, 582–83

  with transitional words and
    phrases, 586–87
comma splices, 269–71, 551–55
comment feature, 153
commonly confused words, 578–79
commonly misspelled words,
    576–77
common nouns, 606
"Company Man, The" (Goodman),
    229–31
comparison and contrast
  as opening strategy, 6
  as pattern of development, 70–71,
    253–54
compound subjects, 481–82
compound verbs, 488
computers, brainstorming or
    freewriting with, 14
Comtrad Industries Catalog, 11–12
conclusions, 52–54, 156–57
  in summaries, 402
conjunctions
  coordinating: combining
    sentences with, 110–12,
    522–24; commas with, 584–85
  subordinating: combining
    sentences with, 213–15,
    526–28; in sentence fragments,
    542
conjunctive adverbs, 163–65,
    524–26
connecting ideas
  keywords, 157–58
  transitions, 158–59
con points
  organizing, 315
  responding to, 312–14
Considering the Media (Chapter 8)
  chapter checklist, 326
  step 1: exploring choices:
    analyzing audience and
    purpose, 299; gathering ideas,
    299–303
  step 2: drafting: choosing a topic,
    303–4; sharing ideas, 304
  step 3: revising: cause-and-effect
    analysis, 306–7; making a
    claim, 308–9; organizing pro
    and con points, 314–15;
    providing pro points, 309–12;

Considering the Media (Chapter 8)
(*continued*)
responding to con points,
312–14
step 4: editing: introductory
phrases, 320–21; subject-verb
agreement, 321–22
step 5: sharing, 325–26
student writing: "Newspaper Ad
Sparks Controversy" (Jones):
discovery draft, 305; edited
essay, 323–25; freewriting,
300–301; revised draft, 316–18
writing assignment, 298
consonant doubling, 572–73
consulting others, 15
about a job-related problem,
197–98
about a lifestyle issue, 302–3
contractions, apostrophes in,
600–601
coordinating conjunctions
combining sentences with,
110–12, 522–24
commas with, 584–85
coordination
with conjunctive adverbs,
524–26
with coordinating conjunctions,
111–12, 522–24
Cordero, Sandra, "El Grito de
Dolores"
discovery draft, 148–49
edited essay, 168–69
reporters' questions, 145–46
revised draft, 161–62
corporations, names of, 611
count nouns
a and *an* with, 614–15
general uses, 616–18
Courtney, Brian A., "Freedom from
Choice"
essay, 457–59
student response, 459–60
cover letters, 475–77
criteria, evaluation, 234, 257–59
Critser, Greg, "Don't Eat the Flan,"
339–41
"Cross-Cultural Perspective: Culture
Shock" (Zimbardo and Weber),
423–25

Crowley, Michael, "Let's Shut Them
Down," 289–91
Culhane, John, "Oprah Winfrey:
How Truth Changed Her Life,"
136–40
"Cult of Ethnicity, Good and Bad,
The" (Schlesinger), 50–51,
53–54
culture, examining. *See* Examining
a Culture
"Culture Shock" (Lozano), 437–41
cut-and-paste function, 22

dangling modifiers, 558–60
databases, 414–15
dates, commas in, 588
"Death Be Not Proud" (Badinter),
72–73
definite article, 614
definition
in introductions, 50
as pattern of development, 69–70,
203–4
dependent clauses
expanding sentences with, 509–11
as sentence fragments, 166–67,
542–43
description
in introductions, 49, 153–54
as pattern of development, 63–64,
100–101
descriptive words, commas with,
585–86
dialects, 23–24
dialogue
commas with, 589–91
as narrative technique, 65–66
dialogue journals, 392–94
difference, making a. *See* Making a
Difference
Dillard, James, "A Doctor's
Dilemma," 83–86
directional order, 45
discovery drafts
choosing a topic, 17–18
defined, 16–17
revising: building the essay,
22–23; developing ideas, 21–22
sharing ideas: getting organized,
20–21; thesis statements, 19–20
do, does, did, 632

"Doctor's Dilemma, A" (Dillard), 83–86

documenting sources
  in-text documentation, 430–32
  requirements for, 207–8
  works cited page, 432–34

"Don't Eat the Flan" (Critser), 339–41

Dorn, Jeremy, "A Hero's Last Ride," 176–78

drafts, discovery. *See* discovery drafts

during, use of, 620–21

Ecenbarger, William, "America's Worst Drivers," 49

either-or reasoning, 361–62

electronic information sources
  documenting, 208
  identifying, 414–15

"El Grito de Dolores" (Cordero)
  discovery draft, 148–49
  edited essay, 168–69
  reporters' questions, 145–46
  revised draft, 161–62

emotional appeals, 362–63

encyclopedias, 413–14

end punctuation, 595–97

essay exams
  preparing for, 447–48
  sample, 452–53
  taking, 448–52

ethical appeals, 363

Evaluating a Subject (Chapter 7)
  chapter checklist, 275
  step 1: exploring choices: analyzing audience and purpose, 243–44; gathering ideas, 244–49
  step 2: drafting: choosing a topic, 249–50; sharing ideas, 250–51
  step 3: revising: expressing judgment, 255–57; giving criteria, 257–59; keeping a balanced perspective, 262–63; providing evidence, 260–62; using comparison and contrast, 253–54
  step 4: editing: relative clauses, 267–69
  step 5: sharing, 274

student writing: "Avoid Dryden Hall" (Albert): discovery draft, 251–52; edited essay, 272–74; freewriting, 249; revised draft, 263–65
  writing assignment, 242–43

evaluating sources of information, 417–18

events, 150

evidence, 260–62, 358–59

Examining a Culture (Chapter 5)
  chapter checklist, 170
  step 1: exploring choices: analyzing audience and purpose, 142; gathering ideas, 143–47
  step 2: drafting: choosing a topic, 147–48; sharing ideas, 148–49
  step 3: revising: conclusions, 156–57; connecting ideas, 157–60; developing ideas, 150–53; introductions, 153–55
  step 4: editing: conjunctive adverbs, 163–65; sentence fragments, 166–68
  step 5: sharing, 169–70
  student writing: "El Grito de Dolores" (Cordero): discovery draft, 148–49; edited essay, 168–69; reporters' questions, 145–46; revised draft, 161–62
  writing assignment, 141

examples
  as pattern of development, 66–67, 150–51
  as type of evidence, 160

exclamation marks, 595–97

experience, 310

expert testimony, 67, 260–61

Explaining a Personal Change (Chapter 4)
  chapter checklist, 116
  step 1: exploring choices: analyzing audience and purpose, 91; gathering ideas, 91–96
  step 2: drafting, 96–99
  step 3: revising: building the essay, 102–6; developing ideas, 100–102

Explaining a Personal Change (Chapter 4) (*continued*)
step 4: editing: coordinating conjunctions, 110–12; correcting run-on sentences, 112–13
student writing: "Baseball Memories" (Ramirez): brainstorming, 92–93; discovery draft, 98–99; edited essay, 114–15; revised draft, 106–8
expressive writing, 9–10

facts
in examples, 66–67, 150
in introductions, 49, 154
as type of evidence, 260
vs. opinions, 255, 308
"Fat Girls and Lawn Chairs" (Peck), 119–22
"Feather" (Hausman), 171–72
feedback, 23
finding information. *See* research
Fischer, Rosie, *Quilters: Women and Domestic Art, The,* 23–24
flashbacks, 65
focus
broadening, 52–53, 156
narrowing, 308–9
strengthening, 105–6
for, use of, 620–21
"Freedom from Choice" (Courtney)
essay, 457–59
student response, 459–60
freewriting, 13–14
about a censorship issue, 300–301
about a cultural hero, 146–47
about an education problem, 351–53
about an occupation, 195–96
about a place, 248–49
Friedman, Thomas L., "My Favorite Teacher," 117–19
"Frommer's *Australia*" (Hansen), 12
future perfect tense, 629
future progressive tense, 629
future tense, 628

Garvey, John, "Christo's *Gates:* An Unexpected Pleasure," 240–42

gathering ideas
asking questions, 15, 246–48
brainstorming, 12–13; about a product, 245–46; about a representation issue, 301–2; about a significant person, 92–93; about workplace communication, 196–97
clustering, 14; about a cultural symbol, 143–44; about an important period, 95–96
consulting others, 15; about a job-related problem, 197–98; about a lifestyle issue, 302–3
freewriting, 13–14; about a censorship issue, 300–301; about a cultural hero, 146–47; about an education problem, 351–53; about an occupation, 195–96; about a place, 248–49
reading, 15, 353–54
relating aloud, 16, 350–51
generalizations, hasty, 361
general-to-specific order, 43–44
gerunds, 634–36
Gibbs, Nancy, "The Magic of the Family Meal," 67
"Global Green Deal, A" (Hertsgaard), 380–83
"Going Nuclear: A Green Makes the Case" (Moore), 344–47
Goodman, Ellen, "The Company Man," 229–31
grammar-check function, 25
Griffith, Carolyn, "Sharing the Road," 49, 52

Hansen, Elizabeth, "Frommer's *Australia*", 12
Hausman, Gerald, "Feather," 171–72
have, has, had, 632
Heiman, Diane, "Sesame Street: *Brought to You by the Letters M-A-L-E*" (with Bookspan), 237–39
Helms, Tamera, "Lessons in Shrimping," 223–25
"Helping Children Heal" (Chu)
discovery draft, 200
edited essay, 219–20

outline, 205–6
revised draft, 210–12
helping verbs, 488, 630–34
"Hero's Last Ride, A" (Dorn), 176–78
Hertsgaard, Mark, "A Global Green Deal," 380–83
Hess, Rita Warren, "American Workplace Slang and Jargon," 226–28
Hiker's Guide to New Mexico, The (Parent), 68
Hodgman, Ann, "No Wonder They Call Me a Bitch," 276–79
"Honor Principle, The" (Houk), 51
"Hook, Line, and Television" (Kling), 133–35, 150–51
hooks, 48
Houk, Andrea L., "The Honor Principle," 51
"How to Catch Crabs" (Zeigler), 50

i before *e* rule, 571–72
"*Idol's* Fifth-Season Opener Its Biggest Yet" (Collins), 10
"I Have a Dream" (King), 10
in, use of, 618
"In Character" (Jackson), 292–94
indefinite articles
    general uses, 614–15
    and noncount nouns, 617
indefinite pronouns, 500–501
independent clauses
    expanding sentences with, 508–9
    semicolons with, 592
indexes, 414
infinitives, 634–36
informative writing, 10
-*ing* verbs, 489–90
"In Praise of the F Word" (Sherry), 378–80
instances (as type of example), 150
institutions, names of, 606
interviews, 411–12
in-text documentation, 430–32
introductions, 48–52, 153–55
introductory phrases, 320–21, 581–82
Investigating a Workplace (Chapter 6)
    chapter checklist, 221

step 1: exploring choices: audience and purpose, 194; gathering ideas, 195–98
step 2: drafting: choosing a topic, 198–99; sharing ideas, 199–201
step 3: revising: building the essay, 204–10; developing ideas, 201–4
step 4: editing: coordinating conjunctions, 213–15; pronoun reference and agreement, 215–18
step 5: sharing, 221
student writing, "Helping Children Heal" (Chu): discovery draft, 200; edited essay, 219–20; outline, 205–6; revised draft, 210–12
writing assignment, 193
irregular verbs, 495–96
"Is Harry Potter Evil?" (Blume), 328–29
italics, 610–11
italics function, 159

Jackson, Samuel L., "In Character," 292–94
Jarvis, Brian, "Against the Great Divide," 70
Jennings, Nicholas, "A Palace of Rock," 282–85
Jones, Reginald, "Newspaper Ad Sparks Controversy"
    discovery draft, 305
    edited essay, 323–25
    freewriting, 300–301
    revised draft, 316–18
journals
    dialogue journals, 392–94
    learning logs, 394–96
    personal journals, 390–92
"Joy of iPod, The" (Kahney), 235–36
judgments, 255–57

Kahney, Leander, "The Joy of iPod: iCandy for the Ears," 235–36
Keillor, Garrison, "Blue Magic," 41, 42
Keller, Nora Okja, "My Mother's Food," 129–33
keywords, 157–58, 414

King, Martin Luther, Jr., "I Have a Dream," 10

Klass, Perri, "She's Your Basic L.O.L. in N.A.D.", 185–88

Kling, Kevin, "Hook, Line, and Television," 133–35, 150–51

Krajick, Kevin, "One Toad over the Line," 5–6

Kramer, Karen, "The Little Drummer Boys," 50

"Lessons in Shrimping" (Helms), 223–25

"Let's Enforce Our Movie Ratings" (Poussaint), 49

"Let's Shut Them Down" (Crowley), 289–91

"Let the Good Times Roll" (Beal), 280–81

library research. *See* secondary research

linking verbs, 488

"Little Drummer Boys, The" (Kramer), 50

logic, faulty, 361–62

Lozano, Leslie, "Culture Shock," 437–41

Lu, Kwan, "Mediation, Not Lawsuits"
discovery draft, 27–29
edited essay, 32–34
revised draft, 29–32

"Magic of the Family Meal, The" (Gibbs), 67

main idea, identifying, 401–2

Making a Difference (Chapter 9)
chapter checklist, 374
step 1: exploring choices: analyzing audience and purpose, 349–50; gathering ideas, 350–54
step 2: drafting: choosing a topic, 354–55; sharing ideas, 355–56
step 3: revising: building the essay, 361–64; using argument, 357–61
step 4: editing: shifts in person, 369–70; using appositives, 368–69
step 5: sharing, 373

student writing: "Tollroad on the Information Superhighway" (Chiang): discovery draft, 355–456; edited essay, 371–73; freewriting, 352; revised draft, 365–66

writing assignment, 348

Malcolm X, "Prison Studies," 86–89

Marriage and Family Experience, The (Strong and DeVault), 67

Marx de Salcedo, Anastacia, "Pass the Pernil, Save Room for the Tarta," 173–76

mechanics
abbreviations, 611–12
capitalization: organizations, institutions, and trademarks, 606; proper nouns, 606; titles, 608–9
italics, 610–11
numbers, 612–13

media, considering. *See* Considering the Media

"Mediation, Not Lawsuits" (Lu)
discovery draft, 27–29
edited essay, 32–34
revised draft, 29–32

misplaced modifiers, 556–58

misspelled words, 576–77

MLA style
citation format, 432–34
electronic documentation, 208

modals, 631–32

modifiers
dangling, 558–60
misplaced, 556–58

Moore, Patrick, "Going Nuclear: A Green Makes the Case," 344–47

multilingual writers, guide for
articles, 614–16
count and noncount nouns, 616–18
omitted or repeated subjects, 621–23
prepositions, 618–21
verbs: with gerunds and infinitives, 634–36; helping verbs, 630–34; participles used as adjectives, 638–39; tense, 627–30; two-part, 636–38

word order: adjective placement, 624–26; adverb placement, 626–27
multiple-choice writing tests
  preparing for, 461–62
  sample, 463–66
  taking, 462
"My Favorite Teacher" (Friedman), 117–19
"My Maestro" (Bell), 81–83
"My Mother's Food" (Keller), 129–33

narration, 64–66, 101–2
narrowing a topic, 18
  in introduction, 50–51
  as research preparation, 408–9
narrowing focus, 308–9
"Needed: Affirmative Action for the Poor" (Tyson), 341–43
"Newspaper Ad Sparks Controversy" (Jones)
  discovery draft, 305
  edited essay, 323–25
  freewriting, 300–301
  revised draft, 316–18
noncount nouns, 616–18
notes, taking, 420–23
nouns
  count and noncount, 616–18
  proper and common, 606
"No Wonder They Call Me a Bitch" (Hodgman), 276–79
numbers, 612–13

observation, 310–11, 410
omitted subjects, 622–23
on, use of, 618–19
"One Toad over the Line" (Krajick), 5–6
One Writer's Beginnings (Welty), 12
"Online but Not Antisocial" (Smith), 332–34
online research, 414–15
opinions
  as type of example, 150
  vs. facts, 308
"Oprah Winfrey: How Truth Changed Her Life" (Culhane), 136–40
organization of drafts, 20–21

organization of paragraphs
  directional order, 45
  general-to-specific order, 43–44
  progressive order, 44–45
  question-and-answer order, 45–46
  specific-to-general order, 46
  topic-illustration-explanation (TIE) order, 44
organizations, names of
  abbreviations for, 611
  capitalization of, 606
outline view, 206
outlining, 205–6

"Palace of Rock, A" (Jennings), 282–85
paragraphs
  organization of: directional order, 45; general-to-specific order, 43–44; progressive order, 44–45; question-and-answer order, 45–46; specific-to-general order, 46; topic-illustration-explanation (TIE) order, 44
  special kinds of: conclusions, 52–54; introductions, 48–52
  student example: Step 1: prewriting, 55–56; Step 2: drafting, 56; Step 3: revising, 57; Step 5: sharing, 58
  topic sentences, 38–42
  unity, 42–43
parallelism, 562–64
paraphrasing, 206–7, 427–28
Parent, Laurence, The Hiker's Guide to New Mexico, 68
participles, 638–39
passive voice, 560–61
"Pass the Pernil, Save Room for the Tarta" (Marx de Salcedo), 173–76
past perfect tense, 628–29
past progressive tense, 629
patterns of development
  argument, 72–73, 357–61
  cause and effect, 72, 306–7
  classification, 68–69, 201–3
  comparison and contrast, 70–71, 253–54
  definition, 69–70, 203–4
  description, 63–64, 100–101

patterns of development (*continued*)
  examples, 66–67, 150–51
  narration, 64–66, 101–2
  process explanation, 68, 151–53
Peck, Cheryl, "Fat Girls and Lawn
    Chairs," 119–22
peer review, 162–63, 212–13
"Perils of Prohibition" (Whelan),
    375–77
periods, 595–97
person, shifts in, 369–70
personal change, explaining.
      See Explaining a Personal
      Change
personal journals, 390–92
persuasion, 10–11, 362–64
phrases, 166, 505–7
  commas with, 585–86
place names, commas in, 588–89
plagiarism, 418–20
plural and singular forms
  and pronoun-antecedent
    agreement, 516–18
  and subject-verb agreement,
    497–500
possession, using apostrophes to
    show, 597–99
Poussaint, Alvin, "Let's Enforce Our
    Movie Ratings," 49
prefixes, 567–68
prepositional phrases, 485–86
prepositions, 618–21
  as subject pretenders, 482–84
present perfect tense, 628
present progressive tense, 629
primary research
  interviews, 411–12
  observations, 410
  surveys, 410
print sources, 413–14
"Prison Studies" (Malcolm X),
    86–89
process explanation, 68, 151–53
progressive order, 44–45
pronoun-antecedent agreement,
    516–18
pronouns
  indefinite, 500–501
  reference, 215–18, 515–16
  relative, 511, 528–30
proper nouns, 606

pro points
  organizing, 314
  providing, 309–12
punctuation
  apostrophes: in contractions,
    600–601; to show possession,
    597–99
  colons, 594–95
  commas: in addresses and place
    names, 588–89; with
    coordinating conjunctions,
    584–85; in dates, 588; with
    descriptive words, phrases,
    and clauses and appositives,
    585–86; with dialogue and
    direct quotations, 589–91; with
    introductory words, phrases,
    clauses, 581–82; in series,
    582–83; with transitional words
    and phrases, 586–87
  end punctuation, 595–97
  quotation marks: to show exact
    words, 602–3; with titles, 603–4
  semicolons: with independent
    clauses, 592; in series, 593; with
    transitional words, 593
purpose, analyzing
  Chapter 4: Explaining a Personal
    Change, 91
  Chapter 5: Examining a Culture,
    142
  Chapter 6: Investigating a
    Workplace, 194
  Chapter 7: Evaluating a Subject,
    243–44
  Chapter 8: Considering the
    Media, 299
  Chapter 9: Making a Difference,
    349–50

question-and-answer order,
    45–46
question marks, 595–97
questions
  in introductions, 48, 155
  reporters', 145–46
*Quilters: Women and Domestic Art,
    The* (Fischer), 23–24
quotation marks
  to show exact words, 602–3
  with titles, 603–4

quotations
  commas with, 589–91
  in conclusions, 53
  incorporating, 207

radio, 416
Ramirez, Jesus, "Baseball
    Memories"
  brainstorming, 92–93
  discovery draft, 98–99
  edited essay, 114–15
  revised draft, 106–8
Rayborn, Patricia, "A Case of
    'Severe Bias'," 41–42
reading
  gathering ideas by, 15
  to improve writing, 5–7
"'Reality' Camera Goes from
    Candid to Cruel" (Andrejevic),
    330–31
reference, pronoun, 216, 515–16
regular verbs, 495–96
relating aloud, 16, 350–51
relating to readers, 308
relative clauses
  combining sentences with, 267–69
  expanding sentences with, 511–12
relative pronouns
  combining sentences with, 528–30
  in sentence fragments, 543
repeated subjects, 623
repetition, 568–69
reporters' questions, 145–46
rereading, 401
research, 204–5, 311
  checklist, 442
  preparing for, 408–9
  primary: interviews, 411–12;
    observations, 410; surveys,
    410–12
  secondary: documenting sources,
    430–34; electronic sources,
    414–15; evaluating sources of
    information, 417–18;
    paraphrasing, 427–28;
    plagiarism, 418–20; print
    sources, 413–14; quoting
    information, 425–26;
    summarizing information,
    428–30; taking notes, 420–23;
    television and radio, 416

research material, using, 206–9
research paper, sample, 436–41
research questions, 409
résumés
  checklist, 477
  format and grammar, 473
  optional sections, 472–73
  required information, 470–72
  sample, 474
revising
  developing ideas, 21–22
  student example (Kwan Lu),
    29–32
roots, word, 567–68
run-on sentences, 112–13, 546–51

Sadie Shapiro's Knitting Book
    (Smith), 24
Schlesinger, Arthur, Jr., "The Cult of
    Ethnicity, Good and Bad,"
    50–51, 53–54
search engines, 416
secondary research
  documenting sources: in-text
    documentation, 430–32; works
    cited page, 432–34
  electronic sources, 414–15
  evaluating sources of
    information, 417–18
  paraphrasing, 427–28
  plagiarism, 418–20
  print sources, 413–14
  quoting information, 425–26
  summarizing information,
    428–30
  taking notes, 420–23
  television and radio, 416
semicolons
  with conjunctive adverbs, 524–26
  with independent clauses, 592
  in series, 593
  with transitional words, 593
sentence fragments, 166–68
sentences
  active and passive voice, 560–61
  and adjectives, 518–20
  and adverbs, 520–21
  and clauses: dependent
    (subordinate), 509–11;
    independent, 508–9; relative,
    511–12

sentences (*continued*)
and comma splices, 551–55
complete, 166
and modifiers: dangling, 558–60; misplaced, 556–58
parallelism, 562–64
and phrases, 505–7
and pronouns: agreement, 516–18; reference, 515–16
run-on, 546–51
sentence fragments, 542–46
subjects: compound, 481–82; subject pretenders, 482–86
subject-verb agreement: indefinite pronouns, 500–501; singular and plural forms, 497–500
verbs: action and linking, 487–89; tense, 493–96; verb pretenders, 489–93. *See also* combining sentences
series
commas in, 582–83
semicolons in, 593
"Sesame Street: *Brought to You by the Letters M-A-L-E*" (Heiman and Bookspan), 237–39
Seymour, Dorothy Z., "Black Children, Black Speech," 24
"Sharing the Road" (Griffith), 49, 52
Sherry, Mary, "In Praise of the F Word," 378–80
"She's Your Basic L.O.L. in N.A.D." (Klass), 185–88
silent *e*, final, 574–75
simple past tense, 628
simple present tense, 627–28
"Simplicity" (Zinsser), 41
since, use of, 620–21
singular and plural forms
and pronoun-antecedent agreement, 516–18
and subject-verb agreement, 497–500
Smith, Janna Malamud, "Online but Not Antisocial," 332–34
Smith, Robert Kimmel, *Sadie Shapiro's Knitting Book*, 24
societies, names of, 611
solutions, proposing, 360
specialized terms, 612

specific-to-general order, 46
spell-check function, 25
spelling
commonly confused words, 578–79
commonly misspelled words, 576–77
rules: changing *y* to *i*, 575–76; consonant doubling, 572–73; final silent *e*, 574–75; *i* before *e*, 571–72
standards, evaluation, 234, 257–59
standard written English (SWE), 23–25
Staples, Brent
"Black Men and Public Space," 122–25
"What Adolescents Miss When We Let Them Grow Up in Cyberspace," 295–97
stating the problem, 357–58
stories, in introductions, 49, 154–55
Strong, Bryan and DeVault, Christine, *The Marriage and Family Experience*, 67
subject, evaluating a. *See* Evaluating a Subject
subject pretenders
prepositional phrases, 485–86
prepositions, 482–84
subjects
compound, 481–82
omitted or repeated, 621–23
subject pretenders: prepositional phrases, 485–86; prepositions, 482–84
subject-verb agreement, 321–22
indefinite pronouns, 500–501
singular and plural forms, 497–500
subordinate clauses
expanding sentences with, 509–11
as sentence fragments, 166–67, 542–43
subordinating conjunctions
combining sentences with, 213–15, 526–28
in sentence fragments, 542
subordination
with relative pronouns, 528–30
with subordinating conjunctions, 526–28

suffixes, 567–68
summaries
  in conclusions, 53
  and secondary research, 206–7,
    428–30
  writing, 400–405
supporting points, identifying, 402
surveys, 410
SWE (standard written English),
  23–25

television, 416
tense, verb, 627–30
tests, writing
  chapter checklist, 466
  essay exams: preparing for,
    447–48; sample, 452–53; taking,
    448–52
  multiple-choice: preparing for,
    461–62; sample, 463–66; taking,
    462
  timed writing assignments:
    performing, 455–56; preparing
    for, 454–55; sample, 456–60
the, 614
thesis statements, 19–20
  in introductions, 51
  repeating, in conclusion, 52–53,
    156
  revising, 102–3
  vague and specific, 357–58
TIE (topic-illustration-explanation)
  order, 44, 426
time, prepositions for showing,
  618–21
timed writing assignments
  performing, 455–56
  preparing for, 454–55
  sample, 456–60
titles (of persons), 611
titles (of works)
  capitalization of, 608–9
  italics with, 610–11
  quotation marks with, 603–4
"Tollroad on the Information
  Superhighway" (Chiang)
  discovery draft, 355–456
  edited essay, 371–73
  freewriting, 352
  revised draft, 365–66
tone, 364

topic, choosing a. *See* choosing a
  topic
topic-illustration-explanation (TIE)
  order, 44, 426
topic sentences, 6, 38–42, 103–4
to + verb combination, 491
trademarks, capitalization of, 606
transitional words and phrases
  commas with, 586–87
  connecting ideas with, 158–59
  semicolons with, 593
Trump, Donald, "You're Hired!",
  189–92
two-part verbs, 636–38
Tyson, Laura D'Andrea, "Needed:
  Affirmative Action for the
  Poor," 341–43

unity of paragraphs, 42–43

verb pretenders, 489–93
verbs
  action and linking, 487–89
  active and passive voice, 560–61
  with gerunds and infinitives,
    634–36
  helping verbs, 630–34
  participles used as adjectives,
    638–39
  tense, 493–96, 627–30
  two-part, 636–38
  verb pretenders, 489–93. *See also*
    subject-verb agreement
vocabulary, 565–66
  meaning from context, 566–67
  roots, prefixes, and suffixes,
    567–68
voice (active and passive), 560–61

Weber, Anne, "Cross-Cultural
  Perspective: Culture Shock"
  (with Zimbardo), 423–25
Welty, Eudora, *One Writer's
  Beginnings*, 12
WetFeet.com, "Career Profile:
  Science," 183–84
"What Adolescents Miss When We
  Let Them Grow Up in
  Cyberspace" (Staples), 295–97
"What Heroes Teach Us" (Bragin),
  48

Whelan, Elizabeth M., "Perils of Prohibition," 375–77
word choice
  repetition, 568–69
  vocabulary, 565–66; meaning from context, 566–67; roots, prefixes, and suffixes, 567–68
  wordiness, 569–70
word order
  adjective placement, 624–26
  adverb placement, 626–27
word-processing functions
  boldface, 159
  color, 104, 208
  comment, 153
  cut and paste, 22
  italics, 159
  spell check and grammar check, 25
workplace, investigating a. *See* Investigating a Workplace
works cited page, 432–34
World Wide Web, 415, 417
writing assignments
  Chapter 1: The Writing Process, 4–5
  Chapter 2: Crafting Paragraphs, 38
  Chapter 3: The Patterns of Development, 62
  Chapter 4: Explaining a Personal Change, 90
  Chapter 5: Examining a Culture, 141
  Chapter 6: Investigating a Workplace, 193
  Chapter 7: Evaluating a Subject, 242–43
  Chapter 8: Considering the Media, 298
  Chapter 9: Making a Difference, 348
  Chapter 10: Keeping Journals, 388
Writing Process, The (Chapter 1)
  chapter checklist, 34–35
  reading to improve writing, 5–7
  step 1: exploring choices: analyzing audience and purpose, 8–12; gathering ideas, 12–16
  step 2: drafting: choosing a topic, 17–18; sharing ideas, 19–21
  step 3: revising: building the essay, 22–23; developing ideas, 21–22
  step 4: editing: correcting errors, 25; using standard written English, 23–25
  step 5: sharing, 25–26
  student writing: "Mediation, Not Lawsuits" (Lu): step 1: exploring choices, 27; step 2: drafting, 27–29; step 3: revising, 29–32; step 4: editing, 32–34; step 5: sharing, 34
  writing assignment, 4–5

X, Malcolm, "Prison Studies," 86–89

"You're Hired!" (Trump), 189–92
y to *i* rule, 575–76

Zeigler, Mary, "How to Catch Crabs," 50
Zimbardo, Philip, "Cross-Cultural Perspective: Culture Shock" (with Weber), 423–25
Zinsser, William, "Simplicity," 41

A QUICK REFERENCE TO EDITING SYMBOLS

adj	adjective error	518, 624
adv	adverb error	520, 626
awk	awkward wording	
cap	capital letter needed	606
coord	correct coordination in sentence	110, 163, 522
cs	comma splice	269, 551
dm	dangling modifier	558
frag	sentence fragment	166, 542
jar	avoid jargon	
lc	use lowercase letter	606
mm	misplaced modifier	556
no cap	no capital	606
pass	avoid passive voice	560
prep	preposition error	482, 618
pr agr	pronoun agreement error	215, 514
ref	error in pronoun reference	215, 515
rep	repetitious	568
r-o	run-on sentence	112, 546
-s	*s* needed at the end of word	
sp	spelling error	571, 576
sub	correct subordination in sentence	213, 267, 509
s-v agr	error in subject-verb agreement	321, 497
trans	transition needed	158, 163
v or vb	verb error	487, 627
vt	shift in verb tense	493
w	too wordy	569
ww	wrong word	578
¶	begin new paragraph	38
?	meaning unclear	
√	good idea or expression	
x	error marked or crossed out	
^	insert	
℘	delete	